THE NEW
BOOK OF KNOWLEDGE

Q·R
volume
16

THE NEW
BOOK OF
KNOWLEDGE

GROLIER
INCORPORATED
DANBURY, CONN.

ISBN 0–7172–0514–2
Library of Congress Catalog Card Number: 82–48428

The publishers with to thank the following for permission to use copyrighted material:
Houghton Mifflin Company and Marie Rodell for excerpt from *Johnny Tremain* by Esther Forbes.
Random House, Inc. for excerpt from *Robin Hood: The Outlaw of Sherwood Forest* by Orville Prescott,
copyright 1959 by Orville Prescott.

Trademark
THE BOOK OF KNOWLEDGE
registered in U.S. Patent Office

Q q 2 q

Q, the 17th letter in the English alphabet, was the 19th letter in the ancient Hebrew, Phoenician, and early Greek alphabets. The Hebrews and Phoenicians called it *qoph*. The Greeks called it *koppa*.

The Phoenician letter names were also used by the Phoenicians as words. Many were names of animals or objects. Some language scholars believe that the Phoenician word *qoph* meant "monkey" and that the letter represented a monkey. One version of the letter *qoph* looked like this:

The Greeks based their alphabet on that of the Phoenicians. But by the 5th century B.C. *koppa,* the Greek Q, had disappeared from the main eastern branch of the Greek alphabet and existed only in the western branch. The western version of the letter looked like this:

The Athenians, who were eastern Greeks, kept the letter form as a symbol for the number 90.

The Greek alphabet that the Romans learned from the Etruscans still had the letter Q in it. The Romans gave the letter the shape it has in English today.

The Romans used their letter Q for the K sound in "ku." There were really three letters the Romans used for this sound: C, K, and Q. C was used most often. K was rarely used. Q was used only before a W sound, which in those days was written with the letter V. Later the letter V was sometimes written U. Thus the Roman QV combination became QU, as in "quick."

In English, Q is used almost exclusively in the QU combination, whether it appears at the beginning of a word, as in "quince"; in the middle of a word, as in "equal"; or as a final consonant, as in "grotesque." The English custom of using the QU combination did not become firmly established until the end of the 13th century. Before that, as we can see from early manuscripts of the Middle Ages, the CW combination was used instead.

Today the letter Q appears in English without a U following it only in a few words borrowed from Middle Eastern languages. An example of one of these words is the name of the country Iraq, in which the Q is pronounced like the K in "ku."

The letter Q is used in many abbreviations. In the army QM stands for quartermaster, or supply officer, and HQ means headquarters. A slang expression for doing something secretly or on the quiet is to do it "on the q.t." The abbreviation q. stands for query or question.

Reviewed by MARIO PEI
Author, *The Story of Language*

See also ALPHABET.

Qatar is a small Arab country in the part of the world known as the Middle East. It is located on a desert peninsula on the eastern—or Persian Gulf—side of the Arabian Peninsula. To the south, Qatar is bordered by Saudi Arabia and the United Arab Emirates.

Like its neighbors, Qatar has rich oil deposits. Since the production of oil began in the 1950's, Qatar has become a prosperous country. Its oil riches and its location on major oil routes have made it increasingly important in world affairs.

▶ **THE PEOPLE**

For centuries, the people of Qatar lived in small fishing villages along the coast or tended herds of camels in the dry inland areas. But oil has changed the lives of the people, giving them one of the highest per capita (per person) incomes in the world. Today the majority of the people live in the bustling capital city of Doha, which has been transformed by the oil boom.

Most of the people living in Qatar are Arabs. But only about half of them are native-born Qataris. The rest are immigrants who have been attracted by the economic growth that has taken place since oil production began. The immigrants come mainly from other Arab countries and from Iran and Pakistan. There are some Europeans and Americans, most of whom work in the oil industry. Arabic is the official language as well as the language of the majority of the people. English is also used, especially in business. The people are predominantly Muslims, and Islam is the official religion.

Qataris usually prefer the traditional dress of the Arab countries—long, loose, light-weight robes and head coverings, which give protection from the sun and windblown sand. But workers in the oil industry and in government and business offices in Doha often wear Western-style dress. In Doha, which is situated on the eastern coast of Qatar, many changes have been made in recent years. Doha has a new deepwater port, desalting plants to provide fresh water, wide streets crowded with traffic, modern air-conditioned shops, and gracefully designed public buildings. Other main centers of activity in Qatar are Dukhan, a town on the western coast surrounded by oil fields, and Umm Said, a port south of Doha. Umm Said's industries include a flour mill and a fertilizer plant.

Income from oil has made it possible for the government to provide a growing number of services for the people of Qatar. The system of free public schools is divided into three levels—six years of primary school, three years of preparatory school, and three years of secondary school. Students in the secondary schools may receive training in technical or commercial subjects to prepare them to work in various trades or in business or government. Teacher-training colleges were opened in 1973, and the government pays the expenses of qualified students who wish to study at universities in foreign countries. Other services include medical and hospital care and housing for low-income families.

▶ **THE LAND**

Most of the country consists of the Qatar peninsula, which juts northward into the Persian Gulf. It is about 160 kilometers (100 miles) long and less than half as wide.

FACTS AND FIGURES

STATE OF QATAR is the official name of the country.

CAPITAL: Doha.

LOCATION: Eastern coast of the Arabian Peninsula.

AREA: 11,000 km² (4,247 sq mi).

POPULATION: 200,000 (estimate).

LANGUAGE: Arabic.

GOVERNMENT: Emirate. **Head of state and government—** emir. **International co-operation—**United Nations, Arab League, Organization of Petroleum Exporting Countries (OPEC).

ECONOMY: Agricultural products—vegetables. **Industries and products—**oil, natural gas, fertilizer, cement, flour, fish. **Chief minerals—**oil, natural gas. **Chief exports—** crude oil. **Chief imports—**construction machinery, foodstuffs, motor vehicles, building materials, cloth and clothing, electrical goods, air-conditioning machinery, livestock, radio and television sets. **Monetary unit—** Qatar riyal.

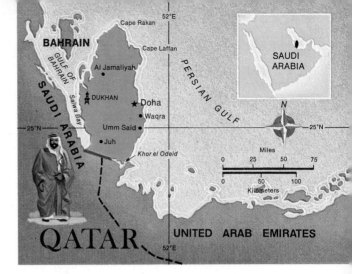

The state also includes some small islands. On the west Qatar is bordered by parts of the Persian Gulf called Salwa Bay and the Gulf of Bahrain. The State of Bahrain, an Arab country made up of islands, is situated in those waters northwest of Qatar.

Except for limestone ridges on the western coast, the land surface of Qatar is flat. Loose sand covers much of the southern half of the peninsula. Rainfall, which is very slight, comes only in the winter months of December through March. The summer months are hot and humid.

Natural vegetation is found around wells in the northern part of the country and in low places after rains. Elsewhere there are only small patches of a shrub called camel thorn and a few date palms. The main kinds of animal life are camels and birds such as flamingos and ospreys. The chief natural resource is oil, which is found both on the land and offshore. Other resources are natural gas, limestone, and clay.

▶ **ECONOMY**

Qatar's national income is obtained almost entirely from the production of oil. But the government is taking steps to establish a variety of industries so that the country will have other sources of income. Factories for packaging frozen fish and for producing fertilizer, flour, and cement were in operation by the early 1970's. Plans then were made for refining oil and making various products based on oil and natural gas. Although the development of agriculture is difficult in a desert country, the government provides free seeds and insecticides and helps the people find ways to manage the land so that some crops can be grown. As a result, Qatar produces enough vegetables for its own use and also exports some, especially tomatoes, to neighboring countries.

The development of transportation and communications networks and of electric power has been a great help to the economy. Doha's port can accommodate oceangoing ships, and jumbo jets can land at the Doha international airport. New roads connect the capital city with other parts of the country and with Saudi Arabia, and a system of pipelines has been built to carry oil and gas. A government-owned radio and television station broadcasts within Qatar and to other states on the gulf.

▶ **HISTORY AND GOVERNMENT**

For many years Qatar was governed by the rulers of neighboring Bahrain. In 1872, Qatar came under the domination of the Ottoman Turks, who then ruled much of the Middle East. The Turks controlled the peninsula until they were expelled by the British during World War I. In 1916, Britain signed a treaty with the Qataris. The treaty brought the territory under British protection and recognized a member of the al-Thani family as ruler of Qatar. A second treaty was signed between the two countries in 1934.

Oil was first discovered in Qatar in 1940. But large-scale oil exports did not begin until the early 1950's. The economic growth of the country began at this time. Britain voluntarily ended the treaty agreements, and Qatar gained full independence in 1971.

Qatar is an absolute monarchy ruled by an emir, who must be a member of the al-Thani family. A provisional constitution was adopted in 1970 and later revised. It provides for an appointed council of ministers and an advisory council to assist the emir.

The present emir, Sheikh Khalifa ibn Hamad al-Thani, came to power in 1972 after deposing his cousin. The government has gradually nationalized, or taken control of, the oil industry. Agreements with foreign oil companies were completed in 1977. In 1980, Qatar's oil supply routes were threatened when war broke out between Iran and Iraq.

Reviewed by Majid Khadduri
Johns Hopkins University

QUAKERS

The Quakers call themselves the Society of Friends. In 1650 the English justice Gervase Bennett gave this Christian group the name of Quakers. This was when George Fox (1624–91), the founder of the society, called upon Bennett to "tremble at the word of God." However, the early Quakers themselves often trembled or quaked with religious feeling in their meetings for worship, and the name soon became a popular one.

George Fox began preaching in England in 1647. Like thousands of other people living in England at that time, Fox did not like either the forms and ceremonies of the Church of England or the strict beliefs of the Puritan preachers. Fox led these people in a search for a new, more spiritual religion.

Fox preached of the "true light, which lighteth every man." Through it, he believed, God made his will known to men and women without the help of priests or ministers and without the rituals and sacraments used in most Christian churches.

For holding such extreme ideas, Quakers were severely punished. English judges jailed hundreds of them for their refusal to attend the established church. Quakers were also jailed for failure to pay church tithes (a tenth of one's income or possessions given for support of the church) and for refusing to take an oath when standing trial. Between 1659 and 1661, Massachusetts Puritans hanged three Quaker men and one woman who had insisted on coming into that colony.

In spite of cruel and unjust treatment, the early Quakers preached widely in Britain, Europe, and elsewhere. Many English settlers in the British West Indies and along the coast of North America became Quakers. By 1700 there were probably 50,000 Friends in Great Britain and almost that many in the New World, with small groups in Ireland, the Netherlands, and Germany. In Rhode Island, Maryland, and North Carolina they had considerable political power in the 17th century. By 1700 they had organized monthly meetings in all the colonies except South Carolina and Connecticut.

William Penn (1644–1718), a young English convert to Quakerism, helped establish the colony of New Jersey. He received Pennsylvania as a royal grant in 1681. Quakers ruled Pennsylvania as a "Holy Experiment" until 1756, 2 years after the outbreak of the French and Indian War. Their religious belief that violence was wrong made it almost impossible for them to carry out the military policies of the colonial government in its war with the French and the Indians.

Beliefs and Practices

From the basic Quaker idea of the light of God in the heart of every man came certain beliefs and practices that made Friends different from other Christians. It made for equality and democracy among men and women. Formerly "you" was a form of address reserved for persons of higher rank. The early Quakers, however, used the simple "thee" and "thou" to everyone, regardless of rank. They refused to take off their hats as a sign of special respect. They wore plain clothing without color or jewelry. They gave up music and art. Friends lived simply and honestly, as sober as the soberest of Puritans. They adopted no formal religious beliefs. Quiet meetings for worship were held in what they called meetinghouses, rather than in churches. There were no pastors, no set service of worship, and no hymns. Friends waited for God to speak through one of their members.

There was less persecution in the American colonies after the Toleration Act of 1689. The Quakers lived quietly, keeping very much to themselves. Their beliefs led them to pioneer in many social reforms. They attacked slavery, capital punishment, and many other practices they considered evil. They advocated prison reforms and improved care of the insane. They worked for women's rights, education for the poor, and peace with the Indians.

English law did not allow Quakers to enter politics and the universities, and by their own choice they stayed away from professions in the church, the armed forces, and the stage. They did enter agriculture, business, industry, science, and medicine. In these fields they often made excellent records.

The 19th Century

During the 19th century there was a movement in the Protestant churches that made Bible teachings and an exact interpretation of

At Quaker meetings women shared with men the right to speak in public worship.

the Bible more important than following a set form of service. This movement also affected the Quakers, particularly in America. In 1827 a series of Quaker "Separations" began. This resulted in the formation of several branches of the Society of Friends. Many branches began to have paid ministers and meetings with regular programs. They also had revival meetings, Sunday schools, and missionary societies. They even came to be called the Friends Church.

Quakers Today

Since 1900 the Quakers have moved toward greater unity among themselves and with other Christians. Some of the branches have united. Some Friends take part in the World Council of Churches. Friends served among the Protestant observers at the Roman Catholic Vatican Council in 1962 and 1963.

In 1917 all branches joined, under the leadership of Rufus M. Jones, in forming the American Friends Service Committee. This committee provided opportunities for service by Quakers and others whose religious beliefs made it impossible for them to serve in the armed forces. During and after World War I this committee did relief and reconstruction work in France and other war-torn countries of Europe. Millions of Russian and German children received "Quaker food" in times of shortages and famine during the postwar years. Friends set up volunteer work camps

for young people to help in depressed areas at home and abroad. During and after World War II they expanded their relief work. They also worked to promote international peace and understanding. In 1947 the American Friends Service Committee and the Friends Service Council of England together received the Nobel peace prize.

The Society of Friends has spread widely in the 20th century through the migration of Quakers and through their missionary work and their efforts for peace and reconstruction. There are over 200,000 Quakers throughout the world, divided roughly as follows: Africa, 38,000; Asia, 1,000; Australia, 1,000; Europe, 25,000 (24,000 in Great Britain and Ireland); Central and South America, 14,000; and North America, 123,000.

Quakers have schools open to children of all faiths, especially in England and the northeastern United States. Quakers founded Cornell University, Johns Hopkins University, Haverford and Swarthmore colleges near Philadelphia; Whittier College in Whittier, California; and Bryn Mawr College. Colleges founded and controlled by Quakers include Earlham College in Richmond, Indiana; and Guilford College near Greensboro, North Carolina.

THOMAS E. DRAKE
Haverford College

See also PENN, WILLIAM.

QUARANTINE. See PUBLIC HEALTH.

QUARRYING

Quarrying is the process by which rock materials are removed from the ground. Sandstone, limestone, marble, granite, and slate are some of the rocks that are quarried. Rocks may be quarried as solid blocks or slabs or as crushed and broken stone. Block or slab rock is most often used for buildings. Crushed rock is most often used for roadbeds.

▶ TYPES OF QUARRIES

In some quarries the rock is in huge, solid masses. Marble and granite usually occur in this form. In some other quarries, such as slate quarries, the rock forms layers of different thicknesses.

Pit Quarries. A pit quarry is a big hole in the ground. It may be a wide and shallow hole or a deep, narrow shaft. Workers must use ladders or stairs, or they must be lowered and raised by mechanical hoists.

Water is a problem in pit quarries. The quarry is like a big stone bowl, collecting and holding all the rainwater that pours into it. When this happens, the water has to be pumped out.

Shelf Quarries. Sometimes rock suitable for quarrying is found above the ground. This can be worked as a shelf quarry. A shelf quarry is much easier to operate than a pit quarry because machines can be moved right up to the face of the quarry. The rock can be hauled away directly. In a pit quarry the rock must be hoisted up carefully before it can be hauled away.

▶ HOW ARE QUARRIES OPERATED?

When people want to open a quarry, they have little choice of location. They must go where suitable layers of rock have formed. Geologists study the earth's surface and can advise people where a good grade of rock may be found. Then the rock must be tested.

Testing the Rock

In testing, a number of holes are drilled at various spots in the area. Special drills are used to cut out a core of rock about 5 centimeters (2 inches) in diameter. This core is brought up to the surface and analyzed. The test indicates whether there is enough good stone available to make quarrying profitable.

Some of the drills bring up cores from 880 meters (almost 2,900 feet) below the surface. But most quarries generally are less than about 100 meters (325 feet) deep.

Stripping the Rock

The process of removing the material over the rock is called **stripping**. The material itself is called **overburden**. Overburden may be made up of loam, clay, gravel, sand, boulders, and often a poor grade of the stone to be quarried.

Stripping can be done with a powerful stream of water that washes away the soil. However, this method is not practical unless the overburden is loose or crumbly.

Earth-moving machines also are used for stripping. The machines dig, lift, and carry the overburden away. Bulldozers scrape and pile up the dirt. Power shovels or clamshell buckets lift and move the material. Trucks haul it away.

Separating the Rock

Rock is not found in the earth in the shapes and sizes that people need. Instead, quarriers must cut out or blast off stone from a large mass. The chief methods of separating, or cutting off, a section of rock are drilling, channeling, wire sawing, and blasting. To separate a block of stone from the mass, both vertical cuts and horizontal crosscuts must be made. Cuts are planned so as to be made at the natural breaks, or cleavage lines, of a rock. Rock in quarries, like all rock, may be found tilted, or it may be vertical or flat. A quarrier usually follows the natural tilts and breaks of the rock when removing it.

Drilling. Drilling is used to make vertical cuts. Holes about 2 or 3 centimeters (1 inch) apart are drilled straight down the line of separation. The solid material left between the holes may then be removed by further drilling. Or it may be split by wedges.

Many kinds of drills are used in quarrying. Many of them are mounted on tractors and can be easily moved from place to place. The **diamond core drill** has black diamonds set into the edge of a rotating steel drum that cuts out a core of rock. The **shot drill** has a rotating head fed with steel shot that wears the rock away. The machine shoots thousands of pieces of steel onto the rock at the same time

A limestone quarry in Bermuda.

its spinning head grinds into the rock. A **rotary drill** works like a corkscrew. It chews its way through the rock. **Pneumatic hammer drills** use air pressure for their power. A hammer drill throws 2,000 violent blows against the rock every minute. Hand-operated hammer drills are employed for small drilling jobs and cleanup work.

Channeling. Channels through rocks are cut by either a **channeling machine** or the **jet piercing** method. A channeling machine has a strong chopper blade, something like a huge butcher's cleaver. The machine travels on a track. It chops a channel about 5 centimeters (2 inches) wide and a meter deep. In the jet piercing method of channeling, a very hot flame is directed at the stone, causing it to flake. As the flame nozzle is moved back and forth, a channel gradually forms.

Wire Saws. Another method of separating the rock from the mass is with wire saws. First, small holes are blasted in the rock and stakes are driven into the holes. Then a power-driven wire belt is strung between the stakes. The wire belt is fed with abrasive sand in a stream of water. As the wire belt moves, it eats its way through the stone. In this way, it cuts a channel that is about 6 millimeters (¼ inch) wide.

Blasting. When broken stone is wanted for use in highways, jetties, breakwaters, and fill, explosives are still used. However, explosives are not commonly used to quarry building stones because they waste the stone by breaking it up. Many jobs that once required blasting are now done better by machine.

Moving the Rock

Quarries have huge hoists for lifting the rough blocks to the quarry's rim. The blocks are often cut to be as large and heavy as the hoists can handle. At times, blocks weighing 50 tons or more have been lifted out.

From the quarry to the point where they are sawed or split into slabs, the blocks of rock are usually transported by truck or rail. After being processed, they are finished for use in buildings or are prepared for use as statues and monuments.

Reviewed by CHRISTINE E. WILLENBROCK
Building Stone Institute

See also STONE.

A natural quartz crystal.

QUARTZ

Quartz is the most common mineral on earth. It is a part of most rocks. Almost all sand is made up of quartz grains. Quartz has a crystalline structure, but perfect crystals are seldom found. Pure crystalline quartz is six-sided, has sharp pyramids at the ends, and is transparent. Quartz also appears in a form in which the crystals are so tiny they cannot be seen. This form is usually translucent or opaque. Some types of quartz are of great value in industry; other forms are valuable gemstones.

▶ INDUSTRIAL QUARTZ

Quartz is used in many industries. It has special properties that give it particular value. For example, quartz is a very hard substance—harder than a steel file. Most forms of quartz do not split easily. Also, quartz can transmit rays of ultraviolet light, something glass cannot do. Still another property of quartz is its ability to generate a small electric charge when put under pressure.

Because pure quartz transmits the short waves of ultraviolet light better than glass does, clear quartz crystals are melted to make special lenses and prisms and quartz-glass tubes for sunlamps. Less clear quartz crystals are used to make laboratory tubes and crucibles. The quartz crystals may be melted and then fused together to form a glass that is useful for making precise laboratory experiments. Since this glass has a high chemical resistance, it does not affect the chemicals used in experiments. It expands very little when it is hot, and it can be taken from a flame and cooled immediately without shattering. Sand that is rich in quartz is used for making ordinary types of glass.

Quartz sand has many other uses. Because crystals of quartz sand are very strong, large quantities of the sand are used in construction work and foundry molds and as a filter for some liquids. Broken grains of quartz crystals are very hard and sharp. They are used in sandpapers, whetstones, and scouring powders and in sandblasting.

When very clear quartz crystals are cut at a certain angle and placed under pressure, they generate electricity. This characteristic, called **piezoelectricity,** makes quartz useful in radio, television, and radar. Electrical parts using piezoelectric quartz crystals are able to turn vibrations into electrical signals or to do the opposite—turn electrical signals into vibrations. The crystals can be cut so that they vibrate at only one frequency. Thus they can control radio wavelengths. Because only a limited amount of quartz is suitable for this use, scientists have developed ways of growing pure quartz crystals in the laboratory. One of the chief uses of laboratory, or artificial, quartz is in quartz and digital watches. The key part in these watches is a tuning fork, which is made of artificial quartz.

Two building stones are made up almost entirely of quartz. **Sandstone** is a rock made up of quartz sand held together by a natural cement. **Quartzite** is a harder rock than sandstone. It is made up of quartz sand held together by a cement as strong as the quartz itself. **Granite**, the most important building stone, is about 30 percent quartz.

Flint, a very hard variety of quartz, was one of the materials used for prehistoric cutting tools. Flint chips easily, forming sharp cutting edges. American Indians made arrowheads of flint. When a piece of flint is struck against steel, sparks are given off. Flint was used with steel to produce sparks in flintlock guns, which were used in the 17th and 18th centuries.

▶ GEM QUARTZ

Quartz is the most common gem mineral known. It comes in many varieties. The gems are often very beautiful and relatively inexpensive. Gem quartz comes in crystalline and cryptocrystalline forms.

CRYSTALLINE GEM QUARTZ

Gem	Color
Amethyst	Violet or purple
Aventurine	Green, brown, yellow, or black with flakes of mica or hematites
Citrine	Yellow-brown
Rose quartz	Pale to deep rose-pink
Smoky quartz or cairngorm	Varies from smoky yellow to brown and black

CRYPTOCRYSTALLINE GEM QUARTZ

Gem	Color
Agate	Two or more tones of brownish-red with white bands, or shades of gray and white
Carnelian	Deep flesh-red or clear red
Chalcedony	Various colors
Chrysoprase	Apple green
Jasper	Tile-red, dark brownish-red, brown or brownish-yellow
Moss Agate	Green intertwined hairlike material appears in this type of quartz
Onyx	Usually black and white or brown and white
Sard	Orange-brown or reddish-brown
Sardonyx	Red and white bands

Crystalline quartz is the most common type of quartz. However, well-developed clear crystals are rare. Clear quartz crystals, called **rock crystal**, are sometimes found in limestone caves. When they are cut as gemstones, they may sparkle as brightly as diamonds.

The word "crystal" came from ancient Greece. There is a story that mountain climbers saw crystal gleaming in caves near Mount Olympus and called it *krystallos,* meaning "ice."

At one time in the Mediterranean countries rock crystal was used for barter in the same way as salt, gold, and silver. Crystal was mined in the Mediterranean region and the Orient. Now the best clear crystal is found in Brazil. Huge crystals have been found, some weighing well over 300 pounds.

FRANK TUFARO
Executive Secretary
Building Stone Institute

See also GEMSTONES.

QUASARS AND PULSARS

In recent years astronomers have made two important discoveries—quasars and pulsars. Quasars are starlike objects that are radio-emitting—they send out strong radio waves. Pulsars are a mysterious new source of radio waves whose signals "pulse," or repeat, at regular intervals.

▶ QUASARS

For hundreds of years astronomers have used optical telescopes to observe the stars. An optical telescope has a mirror or lens that gathers light. We can see the stars because they send out light. But stars also send out radio waves. Radio waves cannot be seen but they can be detected by a radio telescope. This is a special kind of radio receiver with a huge antenna. The radio telescope receives the radio waves from space. Then it amplifies (strengthens) them.

The stars we see at night, plus billions of others that can be seen only through telescopes, make up our galaxy. This galaxy, called the Milky Way, is shaped somewhat like a pancake. It is over 100,000 light-years in diameter. A light-year is the distance that light travels in one year. This distance is about 6,000,000,000,000 (trillion) miles.

In the early 1950's astronomers began to use radio telescopes to search the skies. They found several kinds of objects that emitted radio waves. A few of these objects were old supernovas. They are the remains of stars that have exploded. These lie within our galaxy.

But the astronomers were in for some surprises. They found, for example, that most of the radio waves came from vastly distant galaxies. These galaxies are so far away that hardly any of them can be detected with even the most powerful optical telescopes. The radio waves from these galaxies take several billion years to reach us, although radio waves travel just as fast as light.

Another surprise came with the discovery of some radio-emitting objects that could also be detected with optical telescopes. The photographs of these objects showed that they looked somewhat like stars, so they were named quasi-stellar radio sources. This means radio sources somewhat like stars. The name was soon shortened to "quasars."

Astronomers often use an instrument called a **spectroscope**. It is attached to the telescope. Light coming from a star, a galaxy, or some other object in space is separated by the spectroscope into a rainbow of colors, called a **spectrum**. A study of the spectrum can tell the scientists much about the composition and motion of the star or galaxy.

The radio astronomers were mystified by the spectra of the quasars. The quasars seemed to be among the most distant objects in the universe, and they were moving even farther away at tremendous speeds. Yet, even at these vast distances, their radio waves were very powerful. In fact, they were stronger than the waves that might be expected to come from the biggest, brightest galaxies. This was hard to understand, for quasars seemed to be no more than one ten-thousandth of the size of an average galaxy.

Some astronomers have begun to doubt that the quasars are really as far away as their spectra show. They offer theories to explain the mystery of the quasars.

One theory states that some galaxies go through a phase in which large numbers of their stars explode. Enormous amounts of light and radio energy are released at such a time. When this happens these galaxies are seen as quasars.

Another theory is offered by Fred Hoyle, an English astronomer. Many years before quasars were discovered Hoyle developed the "steady-state" theory. According to this theory, the matter that makes up the universe is constantly being created. Perhaps, says Hoyle, the quasars are the place where this creation takes place.

▶ **PULSARS**

In 1967 a group of radio astronomers at Cambridge, England, were searching for new quasars. They were astounded to find a strange kind of radio signal coming from certain places in the sky. The signals were short on-and-off bursts, or pulses, and they were repeated with amazing regularity. Each pulse lasted only a few hundredths of a second. Before long, all the large radio telescopes in the world were aimed at the mysterious pulsars, as they came to be called. By 1970, about 50 of these pulsars had been discovered.

The astronomers found that the pulsars are between 100 and several thousand light-years from the earth. To an astronomer, this is rather close. The pulsars lie within our galaxy, the Milky Way. In fact, they are nearer to us than most of the stars that make up the Milky Way. Pulsars appear to be rather small objects, perhaps no bigger than the earth.

Scientists cannot explain fully the strange on-and-off signals of the pulsars. But a big step toward solving the mystery came when astronomers in the United States were able to photograph the fastest-repeating pulsar through an optical telescope.

The location of this pulsar may be the key to the mystery. The pulsar lies right in the center of the Crab Nebula. This is a supernova, the remains of a star that exploded.

The light from the explosion was actually seen by Chinese astronomers in the year 1054. They described a starlike object in the sky so brilliant that it could be seen in the daytime. It may be that the pulsar in the Crab Nebula, and other pulsars as well, are the final result of the explosion of a star.

One theory that attempts to explain pulsars states that they are **neutron stars**. Matter is made up of atoms. The atoms contain several kinds of particles. Neutrons are among these. According to the theory, a star may collapse and explode when all its nuclear fuel has been used up. The explosion blows the outer material of the star far out into space. The resulting neutron star is only a tiny fraction of its former size, but it still contains an enormous amount of matter.

The star was rotating before it collapsed. It is much smaller than it was before, and it rotates at hundreds or thousands of times its former speed. Particles that surround the neutron star are dragged along by the rotation of the star. As they move faster and faster they give off waves of energy. These are the radio waves. Bunched together in a beam, the radio waves sweep through space like a beam of light from a rotating lighthouse beacon. Like the light, the radio waves go on and off with the rotation. The result is the strangely regular on-and-off signals picked up by the radio telescopes.

ANTONY HEWISH
Mullard Radio Astronomy Observatory
Cambridge University

QUEBEC

Quebec, Canada's largest province, lies in the eastern part of the country, touching the international boundary between Canada and the United States.

Quebec was first settled by the French. Scattered throughout the countryside are old stone houses, outdoor ovens, windmills, wayside shrines, and other reminders of the early settlement. A tall-steepled Roman Catholic church stands guard over almost every village. Farms laid out by **seigneurs** (early land-owners) and **habitants** (early settlers) still line the shores of the lower St. Lawrence River. In Quebec City, the capital of the province, horse-drawn carriages called *calèches* carry sightseers along the narrow cobblestone streets. Part of the old stone wall that once encircled the town is still standing.

In contrast to the gentle charm of rural Quebec and Quebec City, there is growing industrial activity in other parts of the province. Most of Quebec's industry is concentrated in and around Montreal and along the St. Lawrence and Ottawa rivers. Montreal is Canada's second largest city (after Toronto) and one of the world's most important ports.

▶ THE LAND

The province of Quebec covers one sixth of the total area of Canada. Three natural land-

---

FACTS AND FIGURES

LOCATION: Eastern Canada. **Latitude**—45° N to 62° 35′ N **Longitude**—57° 07′ W to 79° 33′ W.

JOINED CANADIAN CONFEDERATION: July 1, 1867, as one of the original provinces.

POPULATION: 6,438,403 (1981 census). **Rank among provinces**—2nd.

CAPITAL: Quebec City, pop. 166,474 (1981 census).

LARGEST CITY: Montreal, pop. (metropolitan area) 2,828,349 (1981 census).

PHYSICAL FEATURES: Area—1,540,700 km² (594,860 sq mi). **Rank among provinces**—1st. **Rivers**—St. Lawrence, Ottawa, Koksoak, Outardes, Fort George, Saguenay, Nottaway, St. Maurice, George, Bersimis, Manicouagan, Rupert. **Lakes**—Mistassini, Clearwater, Minto, St. John, Bienville, Payne, Abitibi, Allard, Timiskaming. **Highest mountain**—Mont Jacques-Cartier, 1,268 m (4,160 ft). **Bays**—Hudson, James, Ungava. **Offshore Islands**—Anticosti, Île d'Orléans, the Magdalen islands.

INDUSTRIES AND PRODUCTS: Pulp and paper, lumber, mining, agriculture, furs, commercial fisheries.

GOVERNMENT: Self-governing province. **Titular head of government**—lieutenant governor, appointed by the governor-general in council. **Actual head of government**—premier, elected by the people of the province. **Provincial representation in federal parliament**—24 appointed senators; 75 elected members of House of Commons. **Voting age for provincial elections**—18.

PROVINCIAL MOTTO: *Je me souviens* (I remember).

PROVINCIAL FLOWER: Madonna lily.

Coastal village on Gaspé Peninsula. Offshore is Percé Rock, a seabird sanctuary.

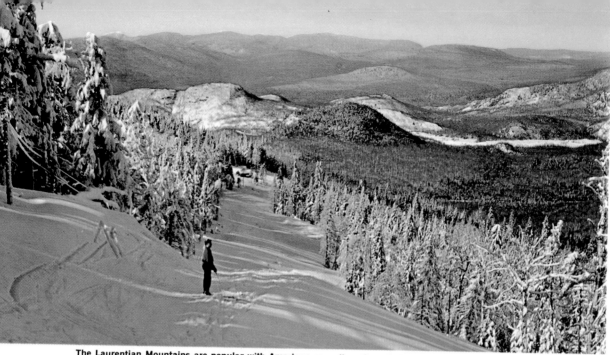

The Laurentian Mountains are popular with American as well as Canadian skiers.

A farm near Baie St. Paul in the St. Lawrence Lowland.

form regions lie within the boundaries of the huge province. They are the Canadian Shield, the St. Lawrence Lowland, and the Appalachian Highlands.

The Canadian Shield covers 95 percent of Quebec. This is an area of ancient rock, worn down through the ages to form a peneplain ("almost a plain"). Rivers have cut through the land and formed valleys divided by low, rounded hills. Such swift-flowing rivers as the St. Maurice, the Manicouagan, and the Saguenay are important sources of hydroelectric power. These rivers eventually empty into the St. Lawrence. Timber is obtained from the forests that cover much of the area. The Shield contains rich deposits of iron ore, copper, and gold.

Many thousands of years ago, during the Ice Age, all this part of Canada was covered with ice. When the ice melted, in some places it left behind a thin, irregular covering of clayey soil. In other places the melting ice took away all the soil, leaving only bare rock. Therefore the only places that are good for farming in the Shield are where the clayey soils were deposited. Agricultural production (usually dairy products and fodder crops) is limited mainly to the Lake St. John–Saguenay River lowland and to the Clay Belt near the Ontario border.

The St. Lawrence Lowland is a small region in the southeast of the province. It is a flat, low plain made up of clays and sands left by the waters that flooded the area after the ancient ice melted. Near Montreal the Monteregian Hills rise from the plain. Five of these eight hills are more than 300 meters (1,000 feet) high. The best known is Mount Royal, overlooking Montreal. The St. Lawrence River valley covers most of the lowland.

This is the most heavily industrialized and the most densely populated part of the province.

The Appalachian Highlands lie south of the St. Lawrence River and border the northeastern United States. The highlands cover three sections known as the Eastern Townships, the South Shore, and the Gaspé Peninsula. The largest deposits of asbestos in the world are located in the Eastern Townships. This section also contains many stock and dairy farms as well as apple orchards.

The South Shore is another fertile farming area, lying between the St. Lawrence River and the Notre Dame Mountains.

The Gaspé Peninsula extends east into the Gulf of St. Lawrence—between the St. Lawrence River and Chaleur Bay. A range of high hills called the Shickshock Mountains forms the backbone of the peninsula. Mont Jacques-Cartier is the tallest of the Shickshocks. It is also Quebec's highest peak.

Rivers, Lakes, and Coastline

Of all the Canadian provinces, Quebec contains the largest area of inland waters. The swiftly running rivers and countless lakes are abundant sources of waterpower, much of which has already been developed. The principal waterway is the St. Lawrence River and Seaway, which links the Great Lakes with the Atlantic Ocean. The Ottawa River is the chief tributary of the St. Lawrence. It forms part of the boundary between Quebec and Ontario. Other important tributaries are the St. Maurice, the Saguenay, the Richelieu, and the St. Francis. All the rivers of Quebec belong to two groups—those that flow into the Atlantic Ocean and those that flow into Hudson Bay. The largest lakes are Mistassini, Minto, Clearwater, and St. John.

Partly surrounded by the waters of Hudson, James, and Ungava bays, Hudson Strait, and the Gulf of St. Lawrence, Quebec has a coastline about 8,000 kilometers (5,000 miles) long.

Climate

Quebec's climate ranges from bitter cold northland (Arctic) in the northwest to continental—warm summers and cold winters—in the southeast. Between the heavy winter snowstorms, there are many cold but sunny days. The average annual snowfall in the Laurentian Mountains area is over 300 centimeters (120 inches). The average annual rainfall varies within the different landform regions—from about 350 millimeters (14 inches) in the far north to three times that amount in the south.

Natural Resources

Rich soils and an abundance of fresh water are among Quebec's greatest natural resources. In addition, vast forests cover about four fifths of the province. The Canadian Shield region is a storehouse of mineral resources, notably iron, copper, gold, and asbestos.

▶ THE PEOPLE AND THEIR WORK

Most of the people of Quebec live in the St. Lawrence lowland, the Lake St. John–Saguenay River lowland, the Clay Belt and mining regions near Abitibi and Noranda, and the Eastern Townships. The most heavily populated area is along the St. Lawrence River—in and between Montreal and Quebec City. Greater Montreal alone contains 45 percent of Quebec's population. About 90 percent of the province is almost uninhabited.

Quebec's population is the second largest in Canada, after Ontario's. About 80 percent of the people are of French origin. The French Canadians have retained the language, the Roman Catholic faith, the civil code of laws, and many traditions of their ancestors.

Many French-Canadian families still farm the same strips of land that have been handed down from parents to children since the colonization of New France. But more and more young people are leaving the farms to find jobs in Quebec's expanding industries.

By the time the French lost control of New France in 1759, the population had grown to about 65,000. By 1850 many Irish, Scottish, and English, as well as some American, colonists had settled in the Eastern Townships section of southern Quebec. Many French Canadians also moved to the Eastern Townships area.

Descendants of the Algonkin Indians still earn their living in the same way as their forebears—hunting and fur trapping. Others work in lumber or mining camping. Some present-day Iroquois Indians are farmers, while others work in factories or with construction companies.

Industries and Products

Love of the land has always been a characteristic of the French Canadians. But today it is manufacturing, rather than farming, that is Quebec's largest source of income.

Agriculture. At the turn of the century, 65 percent of Quebec's income was based on agricultural production. Today agriculture accounts for only 4 percent. But the productivity of the farms has increased. Quebec leads the provinces in dairy products. Also of major importance are the raising of poultry and hogs and the growing of corn and tobacco. Many truck farms and extensive apple orchards are located near Montreal and in the Monteregian Hills area. Nine tenths of Canada's maple sugar and syrup are produced in Quebec. This is a traditional industry of the province.

Forest Industries. Quebec's forests yield nearly one third of Canada's pulp and paper products. Quebec is the world's leading newsprint producer. The products of its forests form the province's largest export. The many rivers provide the hydroelectric power and transportation that are necessary to the expansion of the timber industry. Together with commercial fishing, timber is the economic mainstay of the Gaspé Peninsula.

Mining and Mineral Industries. Gold and copper are mined in the vicinity of Noranda and Val d'Or; copper, at Chibougamau; iron and titanium, at Allard Lake; and iron ore, along the Quebec-Labrador border. The town of Schefferville is the center of the Quebec-Labrador iron belt. The opening of the iron mines in this area has made Canada one of the world's leading producers of iron ore. Much of the ore is shipped by rail from Schefferville to Sept Îles for export to the eastern United States. More minerals are found in the Appalachian Highlands region. Murdochville, in the Gaspé Peninsula, produces large quantities of copper. The Eastern Townships region is the world's largest producer of asbestos.

Manufacturing. The St. Lawrence lowland region in Quebec and the adjoining Great Lakes lowland region in Ontario form the industrial heartland of Canada. Manufacturing accounts for 65 percent of the net value of goods produced in Quebec. The province is Canada's major producer of textiles, aluminum, petroleum products, and railway rolling stock. Quebec's forests, minerals, and hydroelectric power resources have played a large part in the development of manufacturing in the province. The leading industries include the processing and production of food, beverages, tobacco, timber, textiles, and clothing. Others include iron smelting, petroleum refining, and the manufacture of steel products. Most of the industries that turn out consumer products—foods and beverages, medical supplies, electrical appliances, and shoes and boots—are concentrated in the Montreal area.

Transportation and Communication

The St. Lawrence River is the most important feature of Quebec's transportation network. It brings oceangoing freighters 1,600 kilometers (1,000 miles) inland from the Atlantic Ocean to the great port of Montreal, which is now open about 360 days a year. From Montreal the St. Lawrence Seaway—the world's longest inland waterway—allows ships to continue on to the ports along the Great Lakes except in winter. The Seaway, which was opened in 1959, is vitally important to the transportation of iron ore, grain, and coal. During the winter, when shipping on the St. Lawrence is limited, Quebec's railway links with Boston, Saint John, and Halifax are equally important. The main railway lines in Quebec follow the St. Lawrence and Ottawa river valleys and connect the major cities. The air lanes between Montreal, Toronto, and New York City are among the most heavily traveled in North America. Airplanes are also used extensively in the exploration of northern Quebec and in prospecting for minerals.

Both French and English newspapers and periodicals are published in Quebec's major cities. *La Presse* and *Le Devoir,* which are published in Montreal, are major French-language newspapers. *The Gazette* of Montreal is the major English-language daily newspaper. Most radio and television broadcasts are in French. But there are many English-language programs as well. Most homes in the province have telephone, radio, and television.

▶ EDUCATION

In the past, the school system of Quebec was divided between Roman Catholic and non-Roman Catholic schools. Roman Catholic schools were predominant. But in 1977, the province enacted a law dividing Quebec

Grandes Bergeronnes is a typical Quebec village.

schools along lines of language instead of religion. Accordingly, the school system was reorganized into French-language schools and English-language schools. The law also requires that the children of most immigrants entering Quebec attend French-language schools.

Quebec has more private schools than any other province. Between high school and the three-year universities, students are now required to attend two-year institutes. These are similar to junior, or community, colleges.

Universities and Colleges. There are seven degree-granting institutions of higher learning in Quebec. Various colleges and institutes are affiliated with these universities. In addition, there are smaller independent colleges and technical and commercial institutions.

The Université de Montréal has long been the major French-language university in Quebec. Laval, in Quebec City, was founded as a seminary in 1663. The other French-language institutions of higher learning in the province are the Université de Sherbrooke, in the Eastern Townships, and the Université de Québec, which has campuses in Quebec City, Montreal, Trois Rivières, and Chicoutimi. McGill University and Concordia University, both English-language universities, are in Montreal. McGill is especially well known for its medical school. Bishop's University, in Lennoxville, is also English-language.

Cultural Institutions. There are many cultural institutions in Quebec. The first public library in Canada was built in Quebec City in 1779. Large and small art galleries are located in all the cities. The Place des Arts in Montreal is one of the largest centers in Canada for symphony concerts and choral performances.

▶ **PLACES OF INTEREST**

Quebec has a number of places of scenic and historic interest. Most of the historic places reflect the French heritage.

Chateau de Ramezay, in Montreal, was built in 1705 by the French governor, Claude de Ramezay, and served as his residence until 1724. It is one of the oldest buildings in Montreal. After the British conquest of Canada, the Chateau became the official residence in Montreal of the governor in chief of British North America (until 1849). In 1894 it became a museum. The Chateau now contains a large collection of Indian and early Canadian historical material.

The Citadel, in Quebec City, situated on Cape Diamond overlooking the city, was built between 1823 and 1832. It was here that Prime Minister Winston Churchill and President Franklin D. Roosevelt met in 1943 and 1944 to discuss World War II. Today it is the summer residence of Canada's governor-general. It contains a military museum.

Fort Chambly National Historic Park is on the Richelieu River, east of Montreal. The fort was originally built by the French in 1665.

The Parliament Building in Quebec City.

It was the scene of action during the American Revolution and the War of 1812. Colonel Charles de Salaberry, who defeated the Americans at Châteauguay in 1813, is buried in the Chambly cemetery.

Fort Lennox National Historic Park is located on an island, Île aux Noix, in the Richelieu River near St. Jean. The fort was built in the 18th century as Fort Île aux Noix. In 1775, during the American Revolution, the island was captured by American forces. The Americans later

Aerial view of Montreal's business district and a section of the harbor.

abandoned the fort, and the British rebuilt its fortifications and named it Fort Lennox. After the fort ceased to be used for military purposes in 1820, it served as a penitentiary. It became a national historic park in 1921. The park covers 85 hectares (210 acres) and includes a museum.

Île Ste. Hélène is an island park in the St. Lawrence River at Montreal. It was named by Champlain in 1611 in honor of his wife, Hélène Boulé. For many years it was used as a garrison for British troops in Canada. Barracks built in 1824 and a blockhouse erected in 1849 are points of interest that today house a museum. The island was the site of Expo 67.

Notre Dame Church, in Montreal, built between 1824 and 1829, was modeled on Notre Dame in Paris. It is one of the largest churches in North America and is noted for its great bell, which weighs about 11,300 kilograms (25,000 pounds). In addition, there is a museum attached to the church.

Notre Dame de Bonsecours, erected in 1657 and rebuilt in 1771, is the oldest church in Montreal. It overlooks Montreal's harbor.

Plains of Abraham, at Quebec City, was the scene of the 1759 battle between British and French forces during the Seven Years War. Statues commemorate the valor of the military leaders of the battle, generals Wolfe and Montcalm. The Provincial Museum is also located here.

Other places of interest in Quebec include the St. Lawrence Seaway, an outstanding engineering achievement (its Beauharnois complex includes two locks that lift ships from Lake St. Louis to Lake St. Francis); the asbestos mining area in the Eastern Townships; and the beautiful Gaspé Peninsula with its small French-Canadian villages dotting the coastline.

In addition to places of historic and scenic interest, Quebec offers various types of sports and recreation. These activities change with the seasons. Winter carnivals are held in many towns—Quebec City organizes the most spectacular one. An exciting event of the Quebec City carnival is the iceboat race across the frozen St. Lawrence River. In winter, both indoor and outdoor ice hockey are played. Skiing has become very popular, and ski runs are located close to almost all the major towns. Many ski enthusiasts from the United States travel north to enjoy Quebec's snowy slopes. Mont Tremblant, north of Montreal, provides excellent skiing.

In summer and fall all the typical European and North American sports are played. During these seasons, many people leave the cities for cottages on the shores of the Laurentian lakes, on the St. Lawrence River, in the Eastern Townships, and on the Gaspé.

CITIES

Besides the metropolitan regions of Montreal and Quebec City, there are four cities in the province of Quebec with populations of more than 50,000. These cities are Sherbrooke, Hull, Trois Rivières, and Chicoutimi-Jonquière.

Hull and **Trois Rivières** are major centers of pulp and paper manufacturing. **Sherbrooke** is the manufacturing and marketing center of the Eastern Townships. **Chicoutimi-Jonquière** and nearby Arvida form one of the major iron-ore refining centers in Canada.

Quebec City is the capital of Quebec and the seat of the provincial government. An article on this city appears in Volume Q.

Montreal is Canada's second largest city and its second major manufacturing center. An article on Montreal is to be found in Volume M.

GOVERNMENT

Like the other Canadian provinces, Quebec has a one-house legislature. It is called the National Assembly of Quebec and is made up of 108 members elected for 5-year terms. The province's chief executive officer, the premier, is chosen by the Assembly.

FAMOUS PEOPLE

The following are among the many persons who achieved distinction in the history and development of Quebec.

Brother André (Alfred Bessette) (1845–1937), founder of St. Joseph's Oratory, Montreal, was born at St. Grégoire d'Iberville, Quebec. He gained a reputation for performing miracles and in 1904 was given permission to erect a small chapel to his patron saint, St. Joseph, on Mt. Royal. In 1924 work was begun on the Oratory, one of the world's largest shrines.

Henri Bourassa (1868–1952), French-Canadian journalist and political leader, was born in Montreal. He was the founder (1910) and editor in chief of the Montreal Nationalist daily *Le Devoir,* a member of the House of Commons at different times (1896–1935), and a leader of the Nationalist Party (about 1900–30).

Sir Guy Carleton (1724–1808), 1st Baron Dorchester, a British army officer and colonial governor, was born in Strabane, Ireland. He served as lieutenant governor (1766–68) and governor of Quebec (1768–78), and promoted the passage of the Quebec Act (1774). He was governor in chief of British North America (1782–83, 1786–96).

Sir George Etienne Cartier (1814–73), Canadian political leader, was born in St. Antoine, Quebec. He was a member of the Canadian legislative assembly (1848–67) and the Canadian House of Commons (1867–73) and served as attorney general for Lower Canada (1856, 1864). He became joint prime minister (1858–62) with Sir John Macdonald and was noted for his role in the movement toward Confederation. Cartier was a minister (1867–73) in the first Cabinet of the Dominion of Canada.

Jean Drapeau (1916–), mayor of Montreal, was born in Montreal. He became active in slum clearance and the redevelopment of large areas of the city. Drapeau played a large part in bringing Expo 67 and the 1976 Olympics to Montreal.

Maurice Le Noblet Duplessis (1890–1959), Quebec politician, was born at Trois Rivières, Quebec. In 1927 he was elected to the Quebec legislature and in 1933 was chosen provincial Conservative Party leader. He founded the National Union Party (1936) and was premier and attorney general of Quebec (1936–39, 1944–59).

Sir Wilfrid Laurier (1841–1919), was Canada's first French-speaking prime minister. A biography of Laurier appears in Volume L.

René Lévesque (1922–), premier of Quebec and leader of the Parti Québécois (Quebec Party), was born in New Carlisle, Quebec. He studied law at Laval University in Quebec City. Lévesque distinguished himself as a journalist before entering politics in the 1960's as a member of the Liberal Party. He served in the Quebec legislature and held several cabinet posts. In 1967, Lévesque broke with the Liberal Party after it rejected his views favoring the separation of Quebec from Canada. He formed a separatist political movement, which became the Parti Québécois. In 1976, Lévesque became premier when his party won a majority of the seats in the provincial legislature.

Wilder G. Penfield (1891–1976), Canadian neurosurgeon, was born in Spokane, Washington. In 1928, he went to Canada to serve on the staff of McGill University. A recipient of many honors, Penfield is best known for his experiments with the brain's "memory bank."

Louis Stephen Saint Laurent (1882–1973), Canadian political leader, was born at Compton,

Quebec. He entered politics at 59 and was minister of justice and attorney general (1941–46) and secretary of state for external affairs (1946–48). He was a member of the Canadian delegation to the San Francisco Conference (1945) to organize the U.N. He succeeded William Lyon Mackenzie King as prime minister and Liberal Party leader (1948-57). He retired in 1958.

Pierre Elliott Trudeau (1919–), born in Montreal, became prime minister of Canada in 1968 and served for eleven years. After almost a year out of office, he became prime minister again in 1980. A biography of Trudeau appears in Volume T.

Georges Philias Vanier (1888–1967), Canadian army officer, diplomat, and governor-general, was born in Montreal. Aide-de-camp to the governor-general of Canada (1921–22, 1926–28), he later served as representative to the League of Nations. He was minister to France (1939–40), ambassador to France (1944–53), and delegate to the United Nations Conference in Paris (1948). He served as governor-general of Canada from 1959 until his death in 1967.

▶ **HISTORY**

Jacques Cartier was the first European to

INDEX TO QUEBEC MAP

Allard Lake	F4	Lake Timiskaming	B5
Anticosti Island	F4	La Tuque	C5
Arvida	D4	Lennoxville	D5
Baie Saint Paul	D5	Lévis	D5
Cap de la Madeleine	C5	Lower Seal Lakes	C2
Chaleur Bay	E5	Magdalen Island	F5
Chibougamau	C4	Manicouagan Lake	D4
Chicoutimi	D4	Matane	E4
Clearwater Lake	C2	Mattagami Lake	B4
Decelles Reservoir	B5	Montreal	C5
Drummondville	C5	Mount Jacques Cartier	E4
Fort Chimo	D2	Mount Tremblant	C5
Gaspé Passage	E4, F4	Murdochville	E4
Gaspé Peninsula	E4	Nitchequon	D3
Gouin Reservoir	C4	Noranda	B4
Granby	C5	Payne Lake	C2
Grand 'Mere	C5	Port Harrison	B2
Great Whale River	B3	Quebec	D5
Gulf of Saint Lawrence	F4	Rimouski	D4
Hudson Bay	A2, B2	Rivière du Loup	D5
Hudson Strait	C1, D1	Rouyn	B4
Hull	C5	Rupert House	B4
Île d'Orléans	D5	Saint Jérôme	C5
Ivugivik	B1	Schefferville	E3
Jacques Cartier	C5	Sept Îles	E4
Jacques Cartier Passage	F4	Shawinigan	C5
James Bay	A3	Sherbrooke	D5
Joliette	C5	Sorel	C5
Jonquière	D4	Strait of Belle Isle	G4
Lake Albanel	C4	Thetford Mines	D5
Lake Allard	F4	Timiskaming	B5
Lake Bienville	C3	Trois Rivières	C5
Lake Kaniapiskau	D3	Ungava Bay	E2
Lake Minto	C2	Ungava Peninsula	C1-2
Lake Mistassini	C4	Val d'Or	B4
Lake Saint John	C4	Valleyfield	C5

sail beyond Newfoundland into the Gulf of St. Lawrence. In 1534 he landed on the Gaspé Peninsula and claimed the land for France. The next year he traveled up the St. Lawrence to the site of Montreal. There he established friendly relations with the Iroquoian Indians.

Samuel de Champlain, the "founder of New France," explored the St. Lawrence River in the early 1600's. He established a trading post at the Indian village of Stadacona on the banks of the river. This trading post grew into the city of Quebec. After 1642, Montreal became the center of the fur trade. Champlain, the Sieur de La Salle, Louis Jolliet, and others continued to explore the interior of New France—the French name for Lower Canada. By 1750, France claimed all the land as far west as the mouth of the Mississippi River. But England also wanted control of these lands in North America, and soon war broke out. In 1759 the British defeated the French at a great battle on the Plains of Abraham outside the city of Quebec. A year later, Montreal was captured. Under the Treaty of Paris, signed in 1763, France ceded Canada to the British. For purposes of government, the British divided Canada into two prov-

---

IMPORTANT DATES

1534 Jacques Cartier landed on the Gaspé Peninsula and claimed the new land for France.

1535 Cartier sailed up the St. Lawrence River to the Indian villages of Stadacona and Hochelaga—the sites of Quebec City and Montreal.

1608 Samuel de Champlain established a settlement at the site of Quebec City.

1642 A permanent settlement was made at the site of Montreal under the leadership of Paul de Chomedey, Sieur de Maisonneuve.

1759 The French were defeated by the British on the Plains of Abraham outside Quebec.

1763 New France, including the region of Quebec, was ceded to Great Britain under the terms of the Treaty of Paris, which ended the Seven Years War.

1774 The Quebec Act was passed guaranteeing religious and linguistic freedom to Quebec.

1791 Canada was divided into two separate colonies— Lower Canada (Quebec) and Upper Canada (Ontario)—under the Constitutional Act.

1841 Upper and Lower Canada were re-united under the Union Act.

1867 British North America Act brought about Canadian Confederation of Quebec, Ontario, New Brunswick, and Nova Scotia.

1885 Canadian Pacific Railway was completed, linking Quebec with the West.

1912 Quebec area was enlarged to include part of the Northwest Territories.

1959 St. Lawrence Seaway was completed.

1967 Centennial of Confederation; opening of Expo 67 at Montreal.

1970 The provincial legislature passed the Health Insurance Act.

1974 French became the official language of Quebec.

1976 Summer Olympic Games held in Montreal; René Lévesque became premier of Quebec.

1979 First generators of massive James Bay hydroelectric power project began operation.

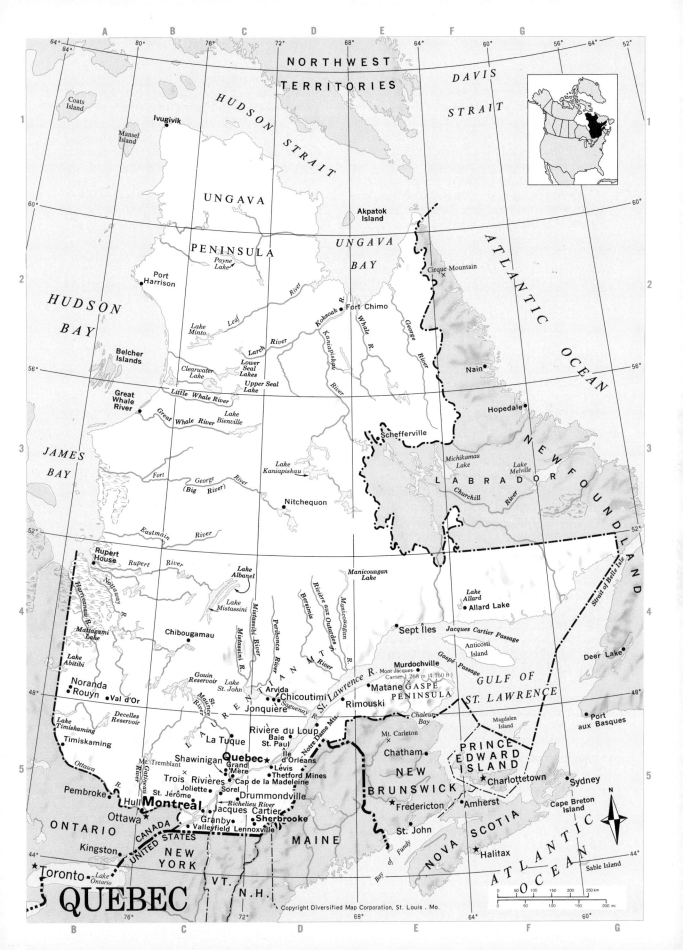

inces in 1791. The province west of the Ottawa River was called Upper Canada (now Ontario). The province east of the Ottawa was called Lower Canada (now Quebec). The two provinces each elected an assembly. These assemblies were the forerunners of the present provincial governments, but they had no real power. In 1837 the people of Lower Canada rebelled against their English-speaking governors. The rebellion was put down. But partly because of it, Upper and Lower Canada were re-united under the Act of Union of 1841.

The issues of political, economic, and language rights have always been of concern to the people of Quebec. From World War II until the mid-1960's, the Quiet Revolution in Quebec brought about many social, cultural, and economic changes. As a result of improvements in education, many French Canadians are entering professions once closed to them.

In the 1970's, a radical group of French-Canadian separatists drew attention to the grievances of French Canadians in a series of militant actions. In November, 1976, René Lévesque, president of the Parti Québécois, became premier of Quebec. A major goal of Lévesque's government was to separate Quebec from the rest of Canada. But the people of Quebec voted against separation in a referendum held on May 20, 1980.

THEO L. HILLS
McGill University

QUEBEC CITY

Quebec, one of Canada's oldest cities, is the capital of Quebec province. It is a city that combines the tempo of modern living with the traditions and memories of past centuries. It is also the heart of French Canada—95 percent of the more than 570,000 inhabitants of metropolitan Quebec speak French. It was at Quebec, on the Plains of Abraham, that one of the most famous battles in North American history was fought. In 1759 the British under General James Wolfe defeated the French general Louis de Montcalm. This battle was part of a global war in which France lost its North American empire.

Quebec is located on the northern bank of the St. Lawrence River, about 240 kilometers (150 miles) northeast of Montreal. The city is divided into two sections—the Upper Town and the Lower Town. The Upper Town is situated on Cape Diamond, a cliff that towers above the St. Lawrence River. High on Cape Diamond, outlined against the sky, is the Citadel. This huge stone fortress, composed of some 25 buildings, was built between 1823 and 1832. The heavy walls that still partly surround Upper Town were built during the same period. The Citadel serves as the summer residence of the governor-general of Canada.

Just below the Citadel towers the magnificent Château Frontenac. This beautiful old building, resembling a French castle, is one of the world's famous hotels. Other outstand-

ing buildings in Upper Town include the City Hall and the Basilica of Notre Dame. The Hôtel-Dieu du Précieux-Sang, founded in 1639, is one of the oldest hospitals in North America. The Legislative Buildings are noted for their French Renaissance architecture, their tiled corridors, and the imposing chambers of the National Assembly.

Below Cape Diamond, on a narrow plain level with the river, lies the Lower Town. This is the financial and commercial section of the city and many of Quebec's leading industries are located on this strip of land.

In the older sections of both the Lower Town and the Upper Town there are narrow, winding cobblestone streets and old stone houses. These sections have the look and feel of a medieval French town. Most of the streets have French names. One of them, Sous le Cap in the Lower Town, is claimed to

The Château Frontenac (*left*) overlooks Quebec City's harbor and part of Lower Town.

be the narrowest street in North America. It is only 2.4 meters (8 feet) wide.

Elsewhere in the city, modern office buildings, factories, supermarkets, and tall apartment houses line wide streets and boulevards. These are the outward signs of expanding, industrial Quebec.

Industry and Transportation

Quebec is a vital transportation center—two railroads have their terminals in the city. Major airlines use the large, busy airport located at Ancienne Lorette, a suburb of Quebec. The city is some 970 kilometers (600 miles) from the Atlanitc Ocean, but it is a busy port, handling a great volume of transatlantic trade. The large, well-equipped harbor has more than 16 kilometers (10 miles) of wharves. Huge grain elevators are among the buildings on the waterfront.

Quebec's industries include newsprint milling, metalworking, tanning, shipbuilding, textiles, clothing, bricks, soap, tobacco products, and electrical and electronic equipment.

Culture and Recreation

Quebec has many first-class art galleries, libraries, and theaters. In the theaters of this historic city, some plays are presented in French and others in English. Two outstanding musical organizations are the Quebec Symphony Orchestra and the orchestra of the Provincial Conservatory of Music.

Of the several fine institutions of higher learning in the city the most noted is Laval University. Founded as a seminary in 1663 by the famous bishop François Laval (1623–1708), it is the oldest university in Canada.

History

The site of what is now the city of Quebec was visited by Jacques Cartier in 1535. But the first permanent settlement was made by Samuel de Champlain in 1608. In 1663 Quebec became the capital of New France.

In 1864 a historic conference was held in the city to lay plans for the confederation that created the Dominion of Canada in 1867. During World War II the famous Quebec Conferences between Prime Minister Winston Churchill and President Franklin D. Roosevelt were held in the Citadel.

Reviewed by RAYMOND MARTIN
Information Officer
Communauté Urbaine de Québec

QUEZON, MANUEL (1878–1944)

Manuel Luis Quezon, crusader for Philippine independence, was born on August 19, 1878, in the village of Baler on Luzon Island. His father and mother, both teachers, tutored young Manuel. In 1893 he graduated from the Colegio de San Juan. He then went on to study law in Manila.

During the Spanish-American War (1898) the United States won control of the Philippines. As a young man, Quezon took part in an uprising against Spanish, and later United States, rule. He was imprisoned for 6 months for his actions. After his release he took an oath of loyalty to the United States.

Quezon became a lawyer in Baler. In 1906 he was elected governor of Tabayas province, but resigned to run for the Philippine Assembly. He became the Assembly's floor leader.

From 1909 to 1916 Quezon served in the United States Congress as resident commissioner for the Philippines. During his stay in Washington the Jones Act was passed. This act provided for the abolition of the United States Commission to the Philippines and gave the Filipinos a greater degree of self-rule. When Quezon returned to the islands he was hailed as a hero. For the next two decades he served as president of the Philippine Senate. In 1934 the United States Senate passed a bill providing for a commonwealth government to serve until 1946, when the islands would become completely independent. In 1935 Quezon became the first president of the new commonwealth. He was re-elected in 1941.

In 1942, during World War II, the Japanese invaded the Philippines. Quezon set up a government-in-exile in Australia. Later he transferred his operations to Washington, D.C.

In 1944, at Saranac Lake, New York, Quezon died of tuberculosis. His death came 2 years before the realization of complete independence for the Philippines. Quezon City, the former capital, was named in his honor.

QUICKSAND

You've probably read about quicksand in adventure stories. Perhaps you've seen a movie in which somebody was trapped in quicksand and sank from sight. The whole idea of quicksand seems terrifying, and people were terrified by it for centuries. They believed quicksand had some strange kind of suction that pulled victims under. They believed there was little hope of getting out alive if you ever fell in.

But all this was before scientists studied quicksand and found out what it really is. Despite those movies and adventure tales, the truth is that quicksand can't hurt you if you know something about it and know how to handle yourself in it.

Quicksand isn't always made of sand. It can be any kind of loose soil—pebbly mud, mixtures of mud and sand. The thing that makes it "quick" is that water is flowing upward through it.

The sand you walk on at a beach isn't quick no matter how wet it gets—even when it's underwater. You can't sink in it. This is because water is just lying on top of it or soaking downward through it. But when water wells up through sand or loose soil, as from an underground spring, it makes the whole sand mass swell. The sand is no longer packed, like beach sand. Each grain rests partly on a cushion of upwelling water. If you step in this, you sink.

But don't believe those old adventure stories. You won't sink out of sight. The depth to which you'll sink in any liquid depends on the weight of the liquid. The heavier the liquid, the higher you'll float. Since quicksand is heavier than water, you'll float higher in it than you do in water.

Quicksand is found most often in valleys, bogs, and river or stream beds. You can't always recognize it by looking at it, for it may be covered by dead leaves or water, or grass may grow on top of it. If you ever find you've stepped into quicksand, here's what to do:

(1) Try to run. Some quicksands are just firm enough for this.

(2) If you sink too fast to run, drop anything heavy you're carrying. If you're wearing a pack, unbuckle it and let it fall.

(3) Lie flat on your back. The quicksand will buoy you up.

(4) Shout for help. If you know help is nearby, just lie still.

(5) If no help comes, **slowly** roll yourself to firm ground. This may take you an hour or more, but don't panic. Remember, you can't sink.

(6) Whatever you do, make all your movements slow and deliberate. The quicksand must have time to flow around your arms and legs as you move them, and since it's thick, it flows slowly. If you give it time, it will behave just as water does when you're swimming. Otherwise you may pull yourself into an awkward position, and escape will be much more difficult.

MAX GUNTHER
Author, "Quicksand—Nature's
Terrifying Death Trap"

QUOTATIONS

Writers and speakers try to reach others through words, but sometimes the mind fails to come up with the words that will best express an idea. It is then that an apt quotation is likely to fill the need. Ralph Waldo Emerson, American poet and essayist of the 19th century, said, "Our best thoughts come from others."

Many people sprinkle their everyday conversation with quotations. These familiar sayings answer a special need of orators and statesmen, who search for quotations with which they can drive home a point or sum up their speeches. Often the fruit of many years' study is brought together into a single sentence, and nothing adorns a composition or speech better than a fitting quotation. It backs up one's own beliefs. At the same time it shows that those beliefs have been shared by other minds.

"I quote others only in order the better to express myself," wrote Michel de Montaigne, a French essayist who lived during the 16th century. This is another way of saying that, just as a picture sometimes tells more than a thousand words, a single quotation can do the work of many words. Care should be taken, however, not to quote others too often. To do so tends to make a person sound as if he has no thoughts of his own.

Quotations can be long or short, in verse or in prose. They come from countless sources. Writers and men in government service have contributed a large number of standard sayings. Lasting quotations have also come from athletes' offhand remarks or sailors' excited battle cries, from advertising slogans and from popular songs.

There are many collections of quotations. Two of the most popular books of quotations are Burton Stevenson's *Home Book of Quotations* and John Bartlett's *Familiar Quotations*. In the indexes of these collections, quotations are grouped according to subject matter. Typical headings are "anger," "beauty," "dog," and so on. If you are vaguely familiar with a quotation and want to look it up, pick out the key word of the quotation. For example, Keats's "A thing of beauty is a joy for ever" would be found among the listings under "beauty."

JACOB M. BRAUDE
Editor, *Speaker's Encyclopedia of Stories,
Quotations and Anecdotes*

A sampling of memorable quotations follows.

BACON, Francis (1561–1626)

Some books are to be tasted, others to be swallowed, and some few to be chewed and digested.　　　　　　　　　　　*Essays*

BIBLE

Am I my brother's keeper?
Genesis 4:9

Go to the ant, thou sluggard;
consider her ways, and be wise.
Proverbs 6:6

Beware of false prophets, which come to you in sheep's clothing, but inwardly they are ravening wolves.　　　　Matthew 7:15

A good name is rather to be chosen than great riches.　　　　Proverbs 22:1

For the love of money is the root of all evil.
I Timothy 6:10

Let us eat and drink; for to-morrow we die.
I Corinthians 15:32

BROWNING, Robert (1812–89)

God's in his heaven—
All's right with the world!
Pippa Passes, Part I

BURNS, Robert (1759–96)

O wad some Pow'r the giftie gie us
To see oursels as others see us!

"To a Louse"

CAESAR, Gaius Julius (100?–44 B.C.)

Iacta alea est ("The die is cast").
Suetonius, *Divus Julius Caesar* XXXII

CERVANTES SAAVEDRA, Miguel de (1547–1616)

A gift-horse should not be looked in the mouth.

Don Quixote, Part II, Chapter 62

COLERIDGE, Samuel Taylor (1772–1834)

Water, water, every where,
And all the boards did shrink;
Water, water, every where.
Nor any drop to drink.

The Rime of the Ancient Mariner, Part II

EDISON, Thomas Alva (1847–1931)

Genius is one per cent inspiration and ninety-nine per cent perspiration.

Newspaper Interview, quoted in *Life* (1932)

EMERSON, Ralph Waldo (1803–82)

Hitch your wagon to a star.

Society and Solitude

FRANKLIN, Benjamin (1706–90)

But in this world nothing is certain but death and taxes.

Letter to Jean Baptiste Le Roy
13 November, 1789.
Writings, Volume X

GRAY, Thomas (1716–71)

Where ignorance is bliss,
'Tis folly to be wise.

"Ode on a Distant Prospect of Eton College"

HENLEY, William Ernest (1849–1903)

I am the master of my fate;
I am the captain of my soul.

"Invictus"

HEYWOOD, John (1497?–1580)

Two heads are better than one.

Proverbs

JEFFERSON, Thomas (1743–1826)

That government is best which governs least.

Attributed

KENNEDY, John F. (1917–63)

And so, my fellow Americans: Ask not what your country can do for you—ask what you can do for your country.

My fellow citizens of the world: Ask not what America will do for you, but what together we can do for the freedom of man.

Inaugural Address (Jan. 20, 1961)

LINCOLN, Abraham (1809–65)

You can fool some of the people all of the time, and all of the people some of the time, but you cannot fool all of the people all the time.

Speech, Bloomington, Ill., May 29, 1856

LYLY, John (1554?–1606)

As busy as a bee.

Euphues and his England

PLAUTUS, Titus Maccius (254?–184 B.C.)

A word to the wise is sufficient.

Persa

POPE, Alexander (1688–1744)

A little learning is a dang'rous thing.

An Essay on Criticism

To err is human, to forgive, divine.

An Essay on Criticism

ROOSEVELT, Franklin D. (1882–1945)

This great nation will endure as it has endured, will revive and will prosper. So, first of all, let me assert my firm belief that the only thing we have to fear is fear itself—nameless, unreasoning, unjustified terror which paralyzes needed efforts to convert retreat into advance.

First Inaugural Address (Mar. 4, 1933)

SCOTT, Sir Walter (1771–1832)

Breathes there the man, with soul so dead,
Who never to himself hath said,
This is my own, my native land!

The Lay of the Last Minstrel, Canto VI, Stanza I

SHAKESPEARE, William (1564–1616)

The course of true love never did run smooth.

A Midsummer Night's Dream, Act I, scene 1

All the world's a stage,
And all the men and women merely players.

As You Like It, Act II, scene 7

Brevity is the soul of wit.

Hamlet, Act II, scene 2

The better part of valour is discretion.

King Henry IV, Part I, Act V, scene 4

This above all: to thine own self be true,
And it must follow, as the night the day,
Thou canst not then be false to any man.

Hamlet, Act I, scene 3

THOMAS A KEMPIS (1380–1471)

And when man is out of sight, quickly also is he out of mind. *Imitation of Christ*

TWAIN, Mark (1835–1910)

The report of my death was an exaggeration.

Cable from Europe to the Associated Press

WILDE, Oscar (1854–1900)

I can resist everything except temptation.

Lady Windemere's Fan, Act I

R, the 18th letter of the English alphabet, was the 20th letter in the ancient Hebrew and Phoenician alphabets and the 17th letter in the classical Greek alphabet. The Hebrews and Phoenicians called it *rosh*. The Greeks called it *rho*.

Phoenician letter names were also used as words. The word *rosh* meant "head." The form of the letter may have been a simplified picture of a head. The letter *rosh* looked like this:

The Greeks based their alphabet on that of the Phoenicians. The early Greeks, like the Hebrews and the Phoenicians, wrote from right to left. Later they wrote in ox-plow fashion, going from right to left, then from left to right. Eventually they wrote only from left to right. When they settled on this style of writing, many of their letters were reversed. The letter *rho* was one of the letters that changed direction:

The Etruscans, an ancient people who ruled in Rome in the 6th century B.C., had an alphabet that was based on that of the Greeks. They sometimes added a small stroke to their letter R, so that it would not be confused with their letter P. When the Romans learned the alphabet from the Etruscans, they decided to use only this form of the letter for the R sound. It is the Roman R that is used in English today.

In English, R is pronounced with the point of the tongue approaching the palate just behind the teeth. In many languages, such as Italian, the tongue is also vibrated in pronouncing the letter. An R pronounced this way is called a trilled or rolled R. A trilled R is almost never heard in the United States. It is sometimes used in Great Britain. In some parts of the United States the R is dropped at the end of many words and syllables. This is especially true in the South.

Throughout the history of English speech the letter R after a vowel has strongly influenced the way that vowel was pronounced. In the late Middle Ages, for example, the combination ER was usually pronounced like an AR. In some cases words with this combination eventually changed their spelling to fit the pronunciation: "sterve" became "starve," "derk" became "dark," "herte" became "heart." In other words the ER spelling has been kept despite an AR pronunciation, as in the word "sergeant."

People buying oysters often refer to the R months. These are the months September through April, all of which have the letter R in their name. During these months oysters are in season.

The letter R is used in many abbreviations. In chemistry, Rn is the symbol for radon and Ra is the symbol for radium. In the Navy the letters RA stand for rear admiral. R is an abbreviation for radius in mathematics and for resistance in electricity. The letters R.S.V.P. following an invitation stand for the French words *Répondez s'il vous plaît,* or "Reply, if you please."

Reviewed by MARIO PEI
Author, *The Story of Language*

See also ALPHABET.

RABBITS AND HARES

Nibbling clover at the edge of the lawn, a cottontail rabbit hears a dog barking. The dog wanders toward it, and the little rabbit freezes, as motionless as a statue. Perhaps the dog will not notice it. But in a few moments the dog comes too close for comfort. Suddenly the cottontail leaps forward in zigzag flight, its powder puff of a tail bobbing behind it. Barking furiously, the excited dog gives chase. With a mighty bound the cottontail disappears

into a thicket of tangled brambles, where the dog cannot follow. Again it has escaped from one of its many enemies.

In North America the cottontail is by far the most familiar member of the order Lagomorpha. These are the "hare-shaped" mammals. The various kinds of rabbits and hares are part of this order. So are their little-known relatives, the pikas. Members of the group are native to almost all areas except Australia. The European rabbit was introduced into Australia more than 100 years ago. Now it flourishes there too.

▶ CHARACTERISTICS OF RABBITS AND HARES

Rabbits, hares, and pikas were once considered rodents. They have two pairs of big gnawing teeth, or incisors, in the front of their jaws, as rodents do. But rabbits, hares, and pikas have a second pair of upper incisors. These are small teeth that are almost hidden by the larger gnawing teeth in front. Rodents do not have these smaller teeth. Because of this and other differences, rabbits, hares, and pikas are now placed in a separate order from rodents.

In general, rabbits and hares have big, long ears and stubby tails. They have short front legs and long, powerful hind legs. They are

Furry, wide-eyed, and active, a newborn hare contrasts sharply with the blind and helpless newborn rabbit.

NEWBORN HARE

NEWBORN RABBIT

expert runners and leapers. Some live in burrows, but others make open nests in hollows in the ground. All of them are vegetarians and eat grass, leaves, tender buds, and twigs.

WHAT IS THE DIFFERENCE BETWEEN A RABBIT AND A HARE?

In Europe the best-known member of the order is the European rabbit—the original for the famous Peter Rabbit. In North America there are the cottontail and its close relatives. There are also the varying hare, or snowshoe rabbit, and the western jackrabbits; all of these are really hares.

What is the difference between a rabbit and a hare? Rabbits are generally smaller than hares, and their ears are not so long. At birth the young of rabbits are blind, naked, and helpless. Newborn hares are wide-eyed and fully furred. They are able to hop about on the day of their birth. The European rabbit, a true rabbit, digs far-reaching burrows and bears its young in an underground nest. Hares, on the other hand, make their nests in ground hollows. (So does the cottontail. But in other ways it is a true rabbit.)

THE COTTONTAIL RABBIT

A full-grown eastern cottontail is about 40 centimeters (16 inches) long and weighs between 1 and 2 kilograms (2 to 4 pounds). The mother bears several litters of young every year. In early spring she makes a shallow nest in a small hollow, usually hidden in tall grass or underbrush. She lines it with grass and soft hair plucked from her belly. Here, about a month after mating, she bears her first litter of the season. There are four to six babies in it. When the mother goes away to eat, she covers the naked, helpless babies with fur and grass. This helps to keep them warm and to hide them from enemies. When they are a week or so old, their eyes open. Soon they are covered with thick, warm coats. Now they venture out of the nest and begin to nibble vegetation for themselves. Soon their mother may be nursing another litter.

Many different species of cottontails and their close relatives are found from southern Canada to South America and from coast to coast. They are prey for many animals, and they are the targets of more human hunters in the United States than all big game combined. But cottontails are fertile and resourceful. They hold their own against many enemies.

A cottontail rests among the leaves.

JACKRABBITS

Several different kinds of jackrabbits live in western North America. All of them are bigger than the typical cottontail. They have much longer ears and more powerful hind legs. The big white-tailed jackrabbit of the Northwest may measure close to 60 centimeters (2 feet) long and weigh around 4 kilograms (9 pounds). It can cover 6 meters (20 feet) with one leap and is able to speed along at close to 72 kilometers (45 miles) an hour. In the northern part of its range it grows a white winter coat, which blends with the snow.

The slightly smaller, black-tailed jackrabbit is the common species on the southwestern plains. Under favorable conditions it breeds very rapidly. Then the black-tailed jackrabbits multiply in such numbers that they sometimes do great damage to crops and range grasses.

The antelope jackrabbit lives in desert areas of Arizona and northwestern Mexico. It has more white on its sides than the other jackrabbits have.

VARYING AND ARCTIC HARES

The varying hare is a true hare, even though it is sometimes called the snowshoe rabbit. It

The varying hare, or snowshoe rabbit, in its summer coat (*left*) and in its white winter coat (*right*). The broad hind feet act as snowshoes to help the hare move in snow.

ranges across Alaska, Canada, and the northern United States. In summer it looks very much like an overgrown cottontail with big hind feet. It may weigh up to 2.5 kilograms (5 pounds). In winter it has a coat of white fur, which helps conceal it against the snowy background. Its broad, thickly furred feet act as snowshoes during the winter months.

The Arctic hare is an even larger hare that lives in northern Alaska, Canada, and Greenland. It sometimes measures as much as 70 centimeters (28 inches) long and weighs up to 5.5 kilograms (12 pounds). Usually brownish or grayish in summer, the Arctic hare becomes snow-white in winter, except for the black tips of its ears. In far northern areas it may be white the year round.

▶ THE PIKAS

The strange little pika looks more like a hamster or a guinea pig than like a rabbit. Its ears are short and rounded. Its hind legs are only a little longer than its front legs. It is 15 to 20 centimeters (6 to 8 inches) long. The pika ranges through mountain areas of western North America, eastern Europe, and Asia. Pikas usually inhabit rock areas,

A pika gathers grass in summer and stores it for winter food.

where they live in colonies and build their nests under sheltering stones or ledges.

One interesting activity of the pika is its habit of gathering grass and drying it in the sun. The cured hay is then piled into a haystack near the den and used as food during the winter. The pika has a variety of common names. It is also known as the rock rabbit, coney, whistling hare, or haymaker.

▶ THE EUROPEAN RABBIT

Domestic rabbits of the United States are descended from the common rabbit native to Europe and North Africa. This species looks very much like the American cottontail, but some of its habits are different. Unlike the cottontail, the European rabbit digs far-reaching burrows. Hundreds of individuals may live in one area where trails and underground burrows are linked. Such a maze of trails and burrows is called a rabbit warren.

More than 100 years ago about two dozen European rabbits were taken to Australia, where they multiplied very fast. Soon there were millions of them. They overran much of the country, stripping vegetation from huge areas. The meat industry was in danger because livestock needed grassy places to graze. The Australians had to set traps and infect the rabbits with a deadly disease to control their spread.

ROBERT M. McCLUNG
Author, science books for children

See also RODENTS.

RABIES. See INSECTS AND ANIMALS HARMFUL TO PEOPLE.

RACCOONS AND THEIR RELATIVES

Raccoons are small animals with long bushy tails and front paws that they use like hands. Raccoons often search for food along stream banks. Busily scratching and digging, they feel about in sand and mud for crayfish and other small animals. Sometimes they pause in their hunting to splash and play in the water.

Raccoons are members of a family of animals, the Procyonidae, that contains two distinct groups. The American branch of the family includes the raccoons and their close relatives—ringtails, coatis, and kinkajous. The pandas—the bearlike giant panda and the lesser (smaller) panda—are the other branch of the family. The pandas live only in Asia.

The animals in both these groups are alike in several ways. All have sharp teeth, and most are meat-eaters, although their diet may include plants as well. Like bears, they walk on the soles of their feet. All have feet that end in five clawed toes, and many have fur on the soles of their feet. Most of the animals are small, with pointed faces, short ears, and circles or other markings around the eyes. Most of them also have long tails ringed by several dark bands. The only large member of the family is the giant panda. It has a stubby tail and looks like a black-and-white bear.

In general, these animals are good climbers and make their homes in hollow trees. However, they may also live in caves or among rocks. Most sleep during the day, coming out at night to hunt for food.

▶ RACCOONS

The word "raccoon" probably comes from an American Indian word meaning "feeler" or "hand scratcher." The raccoon has sensitive fingers. With its handlike front feet a raccoon feels for insects in hollow logs or for fish in water. Raccoons seem to enjoy playing with pebbles or stones, rolling them about in their hands.

Brownish gray in color, a raccoon has a long bushy tail with several dark bands. Its face is pointed. The coloring of the fur around the eyes makes the raccoon look as if it were wearing a mask.

Raccoons live in wooded areas, usually near water. They eat a variety of foods: fish and insects as well as fruits and berries.

Raccoons are often found very close to where people live. In some areas they are considered pests, for they may raid farms to feed on young corn. Every now and then they steal chickens. They may remove lids from garbage cans to get at the scraps inside.

In the wild, raccoons plunge their front paws into water to grasp for food. Raccoons in captivity will still follow this instinct by placing food such as fish in water and handling it before eating. But most scientists agree that raccoons do not "wash" their food, as was once thought.

Although they are usually gentle, raccoons are fierce fighters when cornered. Furiously clawing and biting, a raccoon can beat a dog

A litter of ringtails. These members of the raccoon family sleep during the day and hunt for food at night.

twice its size. However, the animal is no match for an enemy such as the fisher.

Raccoons are good climbers and make their family homes in hollows high up in trees. In colder climates raccoons sleep away the worst winter days, coming out only when it is warm or sunny.

A mother raccoon bears three to six young. Usually the mother raises the cubs by herself. The mother and her cubs live together in the hollow until the cubs can take care of themselves.

There are many kinds of raccoons. Although they may differ slightly in body structure, all have very similar habits. The most common raccoon is found in southern Canada and throughout the United States. Another type—the crab-eating raccoon—lives in Central and South America. It has shorter fur and longer legs than most other types of raccoons. Its favorite food is said to be crabs. But its diet, like that of all raccoons, includes a wide variety of plants and animals.

▶ RINGTAILS, OR CACOMISTLES

Ringtails look somewhat like raccoons but are smaller and more slender-bodied. The bushy ringed tail is proportionately much longer than the raccoon's tail, measuring more than half the total length of the ringtail's body.

The ringtail is brownish, often with lighter underparts. It has a small head with large eyes and ears. Its feet have short, straight claws.

Ringtails are found chiefly in Mexico and the southwestern United States, although they range as far north as southwestern Oregon and Colorado. They live in rocky country broken by clumps of trees. Usually their homes are holes in trees, although sometimes they live in caves or rock shelters. Young ringtails, usually three or four to a litter, are born in the den, where they are raised by the mother. In about 5 months the young are nearly as big as their parents.

Ringtails usually sleep during the day. Sometimes they sunbathe on a branch of a tree. They are active at night and hunt in the trees as well as on the ground. They dart about, catching mice, birds, and insects. Ringtails are good hunters, and early settlers sometimes kept them as pets to rid their homes of mice and rats.

▶ COATIS

Unlike the ringtail, the coati is often seen during the day. Coatis have slender bodies and long hind legs. Their fur is usually tawny with darker markings. But many color varieties, even bright red-orange, are known. A coati can move its upturned snout as though it were a trunk. When it runs, the coati tilts

A coati uses its long, upturned snout, as well as its sharp claws, to hunt for food.

The kinkajou has a long tail that it can wrap around the branch of a tree. Its paws are then free to hold the fruit it has picked.

and rolls from side to side, holding its long, thin tail high in the air.

Although males and older coatis may move about alone, females and young coatis usually travel in groups. Good climbers, coatis hunt through the trees for various kinds of fruits. They also hunt on the ground. They are fond of insects, which they dig out of the ground with their sharp claws. Sometimes coatis poke their long snouts into insect nests to feed on the insects inside.

▶ KINKAJOUS

Kinkajous are tree-dwelling animals that live deep in the forests of Central and South America. Their soft fur is yellow-brown in color and blends well with the forest. Kinkajous have slender bodies with short legs and sharp-clawed feet. They move quickly and quietly through the trees.

Like the coati, the kinkajou has a very long tail. A kinkajou can use its tail as an extra paw to grasp branches or other objects. The tail helps the kinkajou as it travels through the trees. A kinkajou is firmly anchored when it wraps its tail around a branch.

One or two kinkajous are born in the spring or summer. The young develop quickly, and within a few weeks they can hang by their tails.

During the day, kinkajous sleep in their tree homes. They hunt at night, sometimes in groups. Their chief food is fruit. They have very long tongues, which they use to remove the pulp from fruits. Kinkajous also eat insects and sometimes birds' eggs. Kinkajous are very fond of honey. Because of this, they are sometimes called honey bears, although they are not closely related to bears.

Olingos

Another animal of Central and South America is sometimes called a kinkajou, but it is really a different animal. Its correct name is olingo. An olingo is more slender-bodied than a kinkajou. Its tail is covered with longer hair and cannot be used for grasping, as the kinkajou's can.

Giant pandas, like this one, make their homes in the bamboo forests of remote mountain areas in western China. They often sit upright while eating.

LESSER PANDAS

Lesser pandas are fairly small animals, measuring a little over 1 meter long. They are gentle animals. They use their sharp claws for climbing—generally not as weapons. They move about slowly and deliberately.

Lesser pandas live in the hill forests of the southeastern Himalayas. Their bodies are covered with long, thick fur that is glossy red on the back, shading to black below and on the legs. Their faces are mostly white.

Usually, lesser pandas live in tree holes. Here one or two young are born. They are raised by the mother, and they remain with her for about a year. Lesser pandas move about in pairs or small family groups. Their chief food is bamboo, but they also eat fruits, roots, and insects.

GIANT PANDAS

Like lesser pandas, giant pandas are mountain dwellers. They live in western China, usually making their homes at elevations of more than 1,500 meters (5,000 feet). Pandas live in such remote areas that very few people have seen them in the wild. In fact, it was not until 1936 that the first live panda was captured.

Giant pandas sometimes weigh more than 135 kilograms (about 300 pounds). They look much like bears and have long, sharp claws and short tails. Much of the giant panda's fur is white, but it also has large areas of black. Giant pandas have black ears, black legs, and black "spectacles" around the eyes. A black band runs across the shoulders.

Bamboo is the chief food of the giant panda. In the summer giant pandas eat young bamboo shoots. In the winter they feed on stalks and leaves. Giant pandas grasp food with their front paws.

There is usually one panda to a litter. Pandas are playful animals and are great favorites at zoos, but they are hard to acquire. A pair of giant pandas donated by the People's Republic of China can be seen at the National Zoological Park in Washington, D. C.

Reviewed by ROBERT M. McCLUNG
Author, science books for children

RACES, HUMAN

Humankind, like all living species, is made up of a number of natural populations, commonly called races. Such races occupy the major continents and the Pacific island chains. These geographical races developed where groups of people were separated from one another for long periods of time—10,000 years or more. They often experienced very different climates and were subject to different diseases. Therefore, geographical races developed many differences. Yet all humanity has a common origin. People are more alike than they are different. They are all part of the same species, which scientists call *Homo sapiens*.

▶ HOW DIFFERENCES ARE DETERMINED

For a long time, geographical human races were described on the basis of the most obvious differences. These were the color of the hair, the form of the hair, and the amount of brown pigment in the skin. But many differences can be seen in the skeleton as well. Anthropologists (scientists who study people) can tell the difference between an American Indian skeleton and that of a European settler. Anthropologists compare the shape of the teeth, the form of the skull, and the shape of the bones of the face. Classes of fingerprints also differ from one geographical race to the next. So do the amount of hair on the face, the extent to which men become bald, and the thickness of the bones of the arms and legs.

As might be expected, geographical races that live closer together tend to be more similar. The people of India somewhat resemble the people of Europe. They probably have been separated for only a few thousand years. American Indians resemble the people of Asia in many ways. Some Indians may have come from Asia less than 10,000 years ago. From the study of blood groups it is clear that the people of Africa and the people of Europe also had common origins before they became separated on different continents.

Blood Groups. The blood group, or blood "types," that are important in making blood transfusions have been very helpful in the study of races. Most American Indians are of blood group M, but Australian aborigines are usually of blood group N. Probably these two groups have been separated for the longest time—30,000 years or more. Europeans, Asians, and Africans have both blood group M and blood group N. There is another set of blood groups that anthropologists use in the study of races. This is the A-B-O blood group system. American Indians almost never have blood group B. Thirty percent of Asians and 15 to 20 percent of Europeans have blood group B. So it is thought that American Indians came from Asia before blood group B was common there. There are many other blood factors that are helpful in comparing races. Scientists know exactly how blood factors are inherited. Therefore, blood groups are more useful than skin color or height in comparing races. Skin color can be affected by the sun. Growth can be affected by the food eaten in childhood.

Local Differences. In each geographical human race, there are many local differences. The Bushmen of South Africa are smaller and have lighter skin than the famous Masai warriors. The Indians who live on the highlands of Central America are clearly different from the Penobscot Indians of Maine. The people of Sweden, Norway, and Denmark are lighter in skin and hair than the Europeans who live along the Mediterranean Sea. Such local groups are what anthropologists call local races. They show to a lesser degree the differences that come from separation and time. Some day a rocketload of men and women may leave for a distant planet. Separated from people on earth, they may eventually form a local race of their own. Time and separation are responsible for race differences.

▶ CHANGES IN RACES

Over the years all races change. Some small local races have become extinct within recent times. For example, the last Tasmanian died in 1876. Some local races have become greatly reduced in number. Before 1800 there were about 25,000 Aleuts in the Aleutian Islands off the coast of Alaska. Today there are scarcely one tenth as many. Other local races have remained about the same size for thousands of years. This is true for the short Bushmen of South Africa and for

FRENCHMAN

AUSTRIAN

EAST INDIAN

BURMESE

CHINESE

MAYA INDIAN

JAPANESE

ESKIMO

ETHIOPIAN

ZULU

DYAK (BORNEO)

POLYNESIAN

the aborigines of the central Australian desert. Still other local races have grown tremendously in numbers. Such growth was particularly true of the people of northwestern Europe, who colonized much of North America, Australia, and New Zealand. Important new foods brought from the Americas, particularly corn and potatoes, have been responsible for the increase in the number of people in other parts of the world.

New Races. Some new races have come into being. One is a blend of West African and northwestern European ancestry that has developed in the United States over the last 150 years. A new race is in the process of formation in Hawaii. Much of Central and South America is now made up of a new race, which began at the time of Columbus' voyages. New races continue to form, some small local races die out, other local races mix and lose their separate nature. As races continually change, the human species changes. Such change is a part of evolution (continuing change in all living things).

▶**THE PROPER MEANING OF RACE**

When scientists use the word "race," they mean the natural populations that make up the species as a whole. Together they form the human species and not the human "race," as it is sometimes incorrectly called. When scientists use the word "race," they mean natural populations, not nations or religions or groups that use the same language. Language, nationality, and religion have only temporary boundaries that change rapidly in the course of a century or two.

In their homelands people of different races

GEOGRAPHICAL HUMAN RACES

African	Africa south of the Sahara.
American Indian	North and South America.
Asian	Mainland Asia, Japan, Malaysia, and Indonesia.
Australian	The island continent of Australia.
East Indian	The subcontinent of India, south of the Himalayas.
European	Europe, European Russia, the Middle East, and North Africa.
Melanesian	Oceania and New Guinea.
Micronesian	Micronesian islands of the western Pacific.
Polynesian	The Pacific islands from New Zealand to Easter Island.

▶**QUESTIONS THAT ANTHROPOLOGISTS ASK**

Scientists study races to find out where they came from. Through scientific detection work, anthropologists have learned that the Navajo Indians of New Mexico originally came from Canada. They know this from their language and their blood groups and their appearance. Anthropologists would like to know where the Pygmies of the African Congo came from and why they are short. The Ainu, who live in northern Japan, may be the last remnant of a local race that was there before the present-day Japanese came from the Asian mainland. Today expeditions are sent to far lands, and ancient skeletons are recovered by archeologists to solve just such problems. As human beings, we want to understand the history of our own species— from the very first people to the changing groupings of local natural populations that exist today.

STANLEY M. GARN
University of Michigan

obviously have different customs and different beliefs. When they move to new lands, they adopt new customs and new beliefs and new ways of behaving. There is nothing in the nature of race that determines how people behave, and there is nothing in the nature of race that prevents people from learning new rules of behavior.

RACINE, JEAN BAPTISTE (1639–1699)

The French dramatist Jean Baptiste Racine is famous for his ability to portray deep human emotions in a simple, classical style. Racine was born about December 21, 1639, at La Ferté-Milon. His parents died when he was a child, and he was brought up by his grandparents. When he was 10, he was sent to school in Beauvais. At 16 he began attending school at Port-Royal, a religious community. This school's strict form of Catholicism, known as Jansenism, influenced him strongly.

At Port-Royal, Racine read religious and philosophical works and gained a wide knowledge of Greek and Latin literature. Later, he studied philosophy and theology. In 1660, a poem he wrote in honor of Louis XIV won him favor at court, as well as the friendship of other writers. But when he began to write for the theater, he met with the disapproval of his former masters at Port-Royal.

Racine's first play, *La Thébaïde (The Story of Thebes)* (1664), was produced by Molière. It was a momentary success, but it was *Andromaque* (1667) that made Racine famous. Over the next ten years, he wrote the great tragedies

Britannicus (1669), *Bérénice* (1670), *Bajazet* (1672), *Mithridate* (1673), *Iphigénie* (1674), and *Phèdre* (1677).

In 1677, Racine retired from writing for the stage, probably because of the renewed influence of Port-Royal and Jansenism. That same year, he married Catherine de Romanet and began to devote more time to his duties at court. As the king's official historian, he accompanied the king and his armies to the Netherlands and Belgium.

The only plays Racine wrote after *Phèdre* were biblical dramas to be performed by the schoolgirls of Saint-Cyr. *Phèdre* is generally considered Racine's greatest tragedy. Like some of his other plays, it is based on characters in Greek mythology. All his plays show the destructive force of human passions, and all obey the classical rules for unity of action, place, and time. His style was to be much imitated throughout the following century.

Racine died on April 21, 1699.

Reviewed by WILLIAM D. HOWARTH
Author, *French Literature from
1600 to the Present*

RACING

Racing is a contest of speed. There are many kinds of racing, involving almost every means of transportation and physical activity. There are races on foot, in vehicles of all kinds, and on horses. There are races between animals large and small—horses, dogs, turtles, and even frogs. Sometimes prizes are awarded for victory, but often the satisfaction of winning is enough reward.

Foot racing was a major sport at the ancient Greek Olympic Games. Winners were crowned with a laurel wreath and honored by the people. This sport was also popular at the Roman games. Foot racing is a sport in which endurance is often important. In short races contestants run the course as fast as they can. But in longer races they must save enough strength to end the race in a strong finish.

As various machines made for speed were developed, man raced them. He has raced boats, bicycles, motorcycles, automobiles, and airplanes.

Bicycle racing is an Olympic event and an internationally popular amateur sport. The tour races of France and Italy, held each year, cover more than 2,000 miles.

Animal racing has attracted great interest for centuries. Horse racing has been traced to the Olympic games of about 600 B.C. These were harness races, in which the horse pulled a cart and driver. Horseback racing did not become common for several centuries.

Dog racing was a spectator sport in ancient Egypt. Today it is particularly widespread in England. Greyhounds are the most common racing dogs. The main dog-racing event is the Waterloo Cup race at Liverpool, England. Originally the dogs raced after live game. Often rabbits were caged at the finish line. This kind of racing was known as coursing. It is illegal in the United States.

In modern dog racing the dogs chase a mechanical rabbit that circles the track on an electrified rail. This rabbit was invented by an American, Oliver P. Smith, in 1919. Today there are more than 30 legal dog tracks in the United States. They use Smith's mechanical rabbit.

Most races involve direct competition by the participants. They start at the same time from a starting line. The first to cross the finish line is the winner. However, mass starts are dangerous in some racing, such as skiing and bobsledding. In these events competitors run the course individually. The person or team to complete the course in the least time is the winner.

Relay races are team races. Each team member races the same distance. As the first man finishes, the second starts. This continues until each team member completes his part of the race. Victory is awarded to the team rather than to an individual.

See also AUTOMOBILE RACING; AVIATION; BICYCLING; BOATS AND BOATING; BOBSLEDDING; CANOEING; HORSE RACING; ICEBOATING; ICE-SKATING; ROLLER-SKATING; ROWING; SAILING; SOAP BOX DERBY; SWIMMING; TRACK AND FIELD.

RACKET SPORTS

Almost all racket (or racquet) sports come from a game that was invented in France in the Middle Ages. It was called **court tennis** because it was first played by monks in the monastery courtyards. Gradually, the game was adopted by kings and nobility. It was from court tennis that other racket and paddle games such as squash racquets, paddleball, racquetball, and platform tennis developed.

Millions of people all over the world play a wide variety of racket sports for fun, exercise, and competition. Racket sports can be played all through your lifetime. The governing bodies of the various racket sports organize tournaments. There are competitions for young people as well as national men's and women's championships.

▶ SQUASH RACQUETS

Squash was invented in England during the mid-19th century by students attending an exclusive school called Harrow, located outside of London.

They named the game squash because of the sound the ball made as it was hit against the walls. In addition, the ball was softer or "squashier" than the one used for another, more difficult game called **hard racquets**.

Squash arrived in the United States in 1882. The first court was built at St. Paul's School in Concord, New Hampshire. From there it spread to other schools, colleges, universities, and many private clubs.

Equipment

The wooden racket weighs between 227 grams (8 ounces) and 284 grams (10 ounces). It is 69 centimeters (27 inches) long. It has a hitting surface that is 17 centimeters (6¾ inches) in diameter and is strung with nylon or gut.

Squash racquets, singles or doubles, is a game of speed, power, and finesse.

The ball is hollow. Its diameter is 4.4 centimeters (1¾ inches). For years, the ball was made of hard, black rubber. It was a rather dead ball. But in 1976, the "70+" ball was introduced to bring liveliness to the sport. This ball is slightly smaller, lighter, bouncier, and more like the "English" or "International" ball that is used in every country except the United States, Mexico, and parts of Canada.

The Court

The official four-walled American singles court is 9.8 meters (32 feet) long, 5.6 meters (18½ feet) wide, and 4.9 meters (16 feet) high at the front wall. Running along the lower part of the front wall there is a sheet of metal

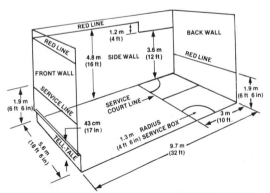

DIAGRAM OF A SQUASH RACQUETS COURT

43 centimeters (17 inches) high. This sheet of metal, called a tell-tale, clangs when hit with a ball. Hitting the tell-tale is the same as hitting into the net on a tennis court. You lose the point.

There is also a doubles court on which two teams of two players compete. This court is 7.6 meters (25 feet) wide by 13.7 meters (45 feet) long.

Rules and Play

The object of squash is to hit the ball against the front wall so that it rebounds to an area in the court where the opposing player cannot return it to the front wall. The opposing player must hit the ball before it bounces twice on the floor. The basic idea is the same in racquetball and paddleball. The ball can hit many walls and still be in play, as long as the player returns it to the front wall before it bounces on the floor a second time.

To win a match, you must win three out of five games. Fifteen points usually wins a game. But if the score is tied at 13-all or 14-all, the game may be extended up to a maximum of 18 points.

There are red lines on the floor and walls within which the ball must bounce to remain in play. If you hit outside these lines or into the tell-tale, you lose the point. If you interfere with your opponent's shot, a **let** is called, and the point has to be played over. If you get in the way of your opponent on purpose, you lose the point.

Points can be won whether or not you are serving. The player who wins the point is awarded the next serve. A player must serve from an area called a service box. The serve must hit the front wall above a service line. It must then rebound to a service area in the opposite rear of the court.

▶ PADDLEBALL

Paddleball is an outgrowth of handball, which was brought to the United States by Irish immigrants in the late 1880's. The one-wall variety is especially popular in New York City. When recreational parks were built in the 1930's, most of them included paddleball courts.

Four-wall paddleball was the creation of a physical education teacher at the University of Michigan in the 1930's. He wanted to keep his tennis team active during the winter months, so he made up a game employing a short paddle and a rubber ball to be played on the university's indoor four-wall handball courts.

Equipment

The official paddle is made of rock maple. It is approximately 20 centimeters (8 inches) wide and 41 centimeters (16 inches) long and weighs about 454 grams (16 ounces). A leather thong is attached to the end of the handle, and it must be worn around the player's wrist at all times. There is no limit on the number or size of holes that may be drilled into the face of the paddle to reduce wind resistance. The same paddle is used for both one- and four-wall games.

The ball for four-wall paddleball is about 5 centimeters (2 inches) in diameter and is made of rubber. The one-wall ball is livelier and slightly smaller—4.8 centimeters (1⅞ inches) in diameter.

The Court

The courts are the same sizes as handball courts. The four-wall court is 6.1 meters (20 feet) wide and high and 12.2 meters (40 feet) long. The back wall, which is often constructed of tempered glass for spectator viewing, must be at least 3.7 meters (12 feet) in height. The walls are made of either cement blocks or plastic panels. The floor is usually made of wood.

The one-wall court is 6.1 meters wide and 10.4 meters (34 feet) long, with the front wall measuring 4.9 meters (16 feet) high. The court is often made entirely of concrete.

Rules and Play

The basic idea of paddleball is the same as that of squash. But in paddleball, the ball may hit the ceiling, and there is no tell-tale.

To win a match, you must win two out of three games. The first and second games are won by the first player who scores 21 points in each. If a third game is required to decide the match, an 11-point game is played. Only the person serving can score points.

In the single-wall version, the players are allowed to transfer the paddle from one hand to the other when making returns. Most one-wall paddleballers have learned to hit the ball equally well and hard using either hand.

Like the other racket sports, racquetball is an enjoyable game that is also an excellent form of exercise.

(9 inches) wide at the broadest part of the hitting head. Rackets vary in weight from 241 grams (8½ ounces) to 276 grams (9¾ ounces). The diameter of the rubber ball may not be larger than 6.3 centimeters (2½ inches) or less than 5.7 centimeters (2¼ inches). The ball weighs 40 grams (1.4 ounces).

The Court

The four-wall and one-wall courts are the same sizes as the paddleball courts.

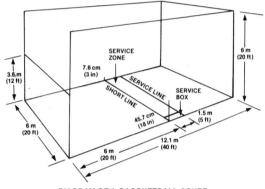

DIAGRAM OF A RACQUETBALL COURT

There is one small difference in scoring between one-wall and four-wall paddleball. In one-wall, the winning side must win by a margin of at least two points. So, for example, final scores of 22–20 or 23–21 are not unusual.

▶ RACQUETBALL

This very simple game is an offshoot of paddleball. It became one of the fastest-growing sports in the United States during the 1970's. Invented by a Connecticut tennis teacher in the 1940's, the sport was first played in community centers and other places that already had handball courts.

Equipment

The loosely strung racket looks like a miniature tennis racket. It is made of either aluminum, fiberglass, carbon, or a combination of these materials. It is approximately 46 centimeters (18 inches) long and 23 centimeters

Rules and Play

The basic idea of racquetball is the same as that of squash and paddleball. As in paddleball, the ball may hit the ceiling, there is no tell-tale, and you must win two out three games to win a match. Twenty-one points decides each of the first two games. If a third game is required to decide the match, an 11-point game is played. Only the person serving can score.

Because of the liveliness of the ball, power has become the key to being an effective racquetball player. The hard-driven **kill shot**, or **roll-out**, which is hit just above the floor on the front wall, is frequently an outright winner.

You can hit any ball harder with a strung racket than with a solid-faced paddle. Racquetball is the same as four-wall paddleball except that racquetball is a faster game simply because of the racket.

▶ PLATFORM TENNIS

The roots of this sport are to be found in Scarsdale, New York. In 1928, the first court

Platform tennis is one of the fastest-growing sports in the United States.

was built at a private home. It was constructed of wood and raised off the ground so that the sport could be played outdoors during the winter months. The sport quickly spread to country clubs that needed a cold-weather activity in order to stay open all year.

Equipment

The oval-faced paddles contain many holes about 1 centimeter in diameter. The paddles are made of either rock maple, plywood, plastic, or aluminum. They are about 43 centimeters (17 inches) long and 20 centimeters (8 inches) wide and vary in weight from 397 grams (14 ounces) to 510 grams (18 ounces).

The ball is either yellow or orange and made of solid sponge rubber. It is about the same size as a tennis ball.

The Court

The overall playing deck is about 9.1 meters (30 feet) wide and 18.3 meters (60 feet) long. The lines within which the ball must land are identical to badminton—6.1 meters (20 feet) by 13.4 meters (44 feet). The framework surrounding the court is 3.7 meters (12 feet) high

and has steel wire screening attached to it. The net that divides the court in half is 86 centimeters (34 inches) high in the center and 94 centimeters (37 inches) at the net posts. The court is usually made of wood or aluminum.

Rules and Play

Scoring is the same as in regular tennis, but only one serve is allowed. "Tie-breaker" sets start when each player has won six games.

The fundamental strokes for squash, racquetball, and paddleball are hit with a loose wrist. But the platform tennis stroke is very much like the more firm, locked-wrist motion of regular tennis. It is not necessary to hit the ball with great power. This is because of the shortness of the court, and because balls that are hit beyond the boundaries of the court may be returned after they have rebounded off the screens that surround the court.

Platform tennis is a unique combination of tennis and the wall games such as squash.

DICK SQUIRES
Author, *The Other Racquet Sports*

See also BADMINTON; HANDBALL; PADDLE TENNIS; TENNIS.

RADAR, SONAR, LORAN, AND SHORAN

Sometimes, when conditions are right, you can hear your own echo. If you shout "Hello!" the sound may bounce back from a large object toward your ears. You then hear your own voice coming back. Your returning voice is called an echo. Sometimes a radio signal, instead of the human voice, is bounced back from an object. This signal is called a radio echo. Producing and receiving radio echoes is called **radar**. The device that makes and picks up radio echoes is called a radar set.

A radar set uses radio echoes to locate aircraft, ships, and missiles. Radar sets can also locate artificial satellites and spacecraft thousands of miles from the earth. They can find such "targets" even in darkness, smoke, clouds, fog, or rain.

Radar can do more than find a target. It can tell how fast and in which direction the target is moving. This information can be used to control the firing of guns and missiles to protect a country against attack. In peacetime, radar can help navigate ships, land planes in a fog, search for storms, and guide astronauts in landing on the moon. Radar can help control street traffic and assist the police in finding speeding automobiles.

The word "radar" was invented by scientists of the United States Navy during World War II. The word comes from the first letters in the term "*radio detection and ranging.*"

Antenna of a tracking radar station. It is used for following the course of aircraft and of space probes.

"Detection," as used here, means to find out whether an object or target is within the range of the radar set. "Ranging" means measuring the distance to the target.

How Big Is a Radar Set?

Radar sets come in many sizes. A small one, made for airplanes, is not much larger than this encyclopedia set. A large one may require a building many stories high. The size of a radar set depends on the job it is expected to do. But all radar sets, regardless of their size, use the principle of the echo.

▶ HOW RADAR WORKS

A radar set produces radio signals. It radiates (sends out) these signals into space by means of an antenna.

When a radio signal strikes an object such as an airplane, part of the signal is reflected back to the radar antenna. The signal is picked up there as a radar echo. A radar set changes the radar echo into an image that can be seen. A radar set also gives the direction of the target and its distance from the set.

How Radar Began

In 1900 a radio pioneer named Nikola Tesla (1856–1943) noticed that large objects can produce reflected radio signals that are strong enough to be picked up. He knew that reflected radio signals are really radio echoes. So he predicted that such echoes would be used to find the position and course of ships at sea. In 1922 Guglielmo Marconi, a great radio scientist, made the same prediction. But nothing was done about it until World War II was about to begin. All big nations had built fast airplanes that could carry bombs. It was necessary to discover a way to detect these warplanes while they were still far away. Then fighter planes could be sent up to keep the planes away or shoot them down.

The big step that made radar possible took place in many countries in 1934 and 1935. The new idea was to send out the radio signals in short bursts, called **pulses**.

Let's see why this was so important. Imagine that you are about to shout across a canyon to make an echo. If you shout a long sentence, the first words will come back before you can finish the last words. It would be impossible to hear the echo clearly, because it

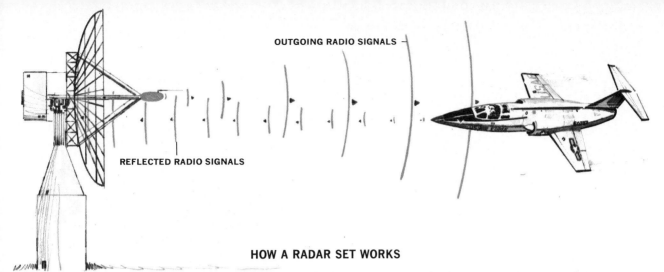

OUTGOING RADIO SIGNALS

REFLECTED RADIO SIGNALS

HOW A RADAR SET WORKS

Radar antenna sends out series of short radio-wave pulses. When radio pulses strike an object, the pulses are reflected. The distance between the antenna and the object is calculated from the amount of time that the pulses take for the trip.

would be mixed with your own speech. But suppose you shout a short word, such as "Hello!" The echo comes back crisp and clear with no interference.

Now suppose a radio signal is given off in a short burst, or pulse, and is reflected from an object. The echo comes back clearly. But if the radio signal lasts a long time, the echo comes back while the signal is still going out. The radar operator cannot detect the echo at all. The outgoing signal is millions of times stronger than the echo. So the weak echo is completely overpowered and cannot be picked up. And if the echo is not detected, the operator will have no warning of the target.

By using echoes, you can find out how far away the reflecting wall of a canyon is. Sound travels about 1,120 feet per second. If the sound takes 1 second to hit the canyon wall and return, it must have gone 1,120 feet. But that is the distance of the round trip to the wall and back. The wall must be half that far away, or 560 feet. So, to find the distance to any echo-making surface, merely count the seconds it takes for the echo to come back. The reflecting surface is 560 feet away multiplied by the number of seconds.

A radar set works on the same principle. It sends out a very short radio signal. Then it counts the time it takes for the echo to come back. Radio signals travel at a known speed—about 186,000 miles per second. If the radio signal comes back in $\frac{1}{1000}$ second, then the round trip is 186 miles. The target must be half that far, or 93 miles, away.

The direction of the target from the radar is found in a different way. The radar antenna sends out radio pulses in a narrow beam, much like the beam of a flashlight. An echo is reflected from a plane only if the narrow beam happens to strike the plane. When an echo comes back, scientists know that the plane's direction must be the same as the direction of the beam. The antenna (and its beam) is slowly rotated through all possible directions, searching the entire sky for targets.

Between 1935 and 1939 a network of radar stations was built around the British Isles. These radar sets gave early warning of attacking planes and missiles. The British used this warning to avoid defeat. Later, the United States also had radar systems. Radar was very important to the Allied victory in World War II.

Radar Systems

A radar set, also called a radar system, has four main parts—a transmitter, an antenna, a receiver, and an indicator. The **transmitter** produces the short radio pulses. Each pulse lasts only about $\frac{1}{1,000,000}$ second. There are usually about 200 or 300 pulses produced each second. The same **antenna** is used both to send out the radio pulses and to pick up the echoes. The returning echoes are sent to the **receiver**, where their strength is increased. The echoes then go to the **indicator**, which shows the range and direction of the target to the operator. On the indicator the echoes appear as bright spots, called **blips**.

The usual type of indicator is the **plan position indicator**, or **PPI**. It has a large tube,

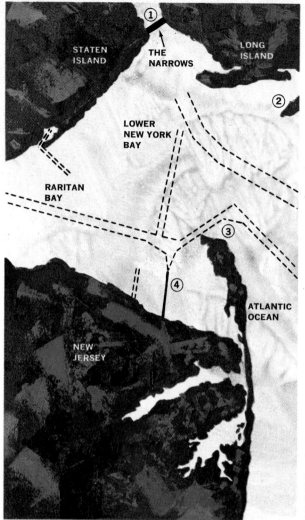

1. VERRAZANO-NARROWS BRIDGE
2. ROCKAWAY POINT
3. SANDY HOOK
4. PIER
A. MOVING VESSELS

Left: Map of Raritan Bay, New York, and surrounding area. Broken lines represent channels. Right: Radar map of same area. Large bright spots indicate land areas. Smaller blips indicate other objects, such as channels (small dots arranged in straight lines), and moving ships (at A).

much like the picture tube in a television set. On the face of this tube the operator sees a maplike picture of the surrounding region. It is as though he were high above the radar set, looking down at the area. The bright spots, or blips, show where land areas are located. Blips also show the position of targets such as planes and ships. It is easy to pick out these targets because they are moving, while the land areas are not.

USES OF RADAR

There are two main military uses of radar. One is called search radar. The other is called fire-control radar. **Search radar** sets are the kind already discussed. They continually search the sky to find targets moving into the region of the radar set. **Fire-control radar** sets are used to aim a gun or missile so that it will hit the target when it is fired. These sets

have to be more accurate than search radar sets. They must be able to pinpoint a target no larger than a basketball at 1,000 miles.

Radar sets are used most often to help navigate ships and planes. These radar sets pick up echoes from other ships and planes and help prevent collisions. They also pick up echoes from buoys in channels when ships enter or leave port.

Radar sets are widely used to help land airplanes when the weather is bad and pilots cannot see the ground. The **ground-controlled approach**, or **GCA**, radar is placed near the end of the runway. The indicator in the control tower shows the operator where the plane is at all times. The operator then talks to the pilot by radio during the landing of the plane. He gives instructions to the pilot, telling him just what to do to follow a safe course while landing.

Radar sets can also be built to get echoes from raindrops. Weathermen use such radar sets to study storms and find the location and movement of hurricanes.

Small radar sets are now used by the police to help catch speeding automobiles. A set placed by the side of the road measures the speed of passing cars. When a speeder goes by, the operator radios ahead to a waiting police car, which picks up the speeder. Other radar sets count the number of cars on busy streets so traffic lights can be changed automatically.

Radar plays a major part in tracking artificial satellites, space probes, and manned spacecraft. Astronauts landing on the moon must use radar to tell them how high they are and how fast they are descending.

One big problem in radar is still unsolved. Engineers call it **discrimination**. The target on a radar screen is not a true picture but a blip of light. All blips look the same. Let's suppose one country plans to fire a missile at another country. The missile can be made to drop harmless pieces of metal, or decoys. Both the decoys and the missile show up as blips on radar, so it is hard to discriminate between them. Scientists are trying to solve this problem.

▶ **SONAR**

The word "sonar" comes from the first letters of "*so*und *na*vigation *r*anging." Sonar is very much like radar. Sonar can detect and locate objects under the sea by echoes. Since radio signals cannot travel far underwater, sonar sets use sound signals instead.

Compared with ordinary sounds, sonar signals are very powerful. Most sonar sets send out sounds that are millions of times more powerful than a shout. These outgoing sound signals are sent out in pulses. Each pulse lasts a short fraction of a second.

Some sonar sets give off sounds that you can hear. Other sonar signals are like sounds from a dog whistle. Their pitch is so high that your ear cannot hear them. But the sonar set has a special receiver that can pick up the returning echoes. The echoes are then used to tell the location of underwater objects.

Sonar is also used in the **fathometer**, an instrument that measures the depth of water. (The fathometer measures depth in fathoms.

Radar set in an airport control tower helps operator guide pilots to safe landings.

One fathom equals 6 feet.) The fathometer measures the time it takes for a sound pulse to reach the bottom of the sea and return to the ship. This length of time is then used to give the water's depth.

Fishermen have found that fathometers often pick up weak echoes from schools of fish. The instruments are now used widely to locate such schools.

Sometimes echoes are received from places beneath the ocean floor. Some of the sound signal enters the mud or sand bottom and strikes a layer of rock underneath. An echo then comes back and gives the distance to the rock layer. Scientists use this information to learn about the ocean floor.

Sonar set on fishing boat sends out short, powerful signals and receives echoes from schools of fish.

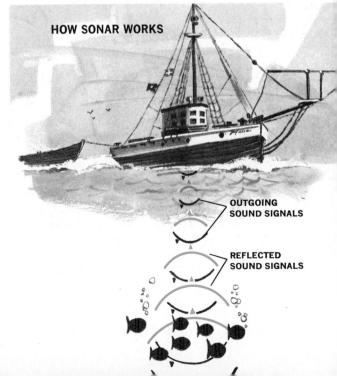

HOW SONAR WORKS

OUTGOING SOUND SIGNALS

REFLECTED SOUND SIGNALS

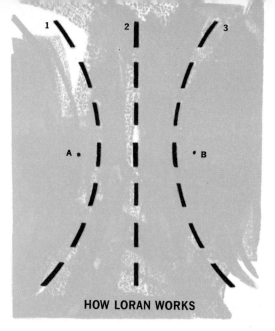

HOW LORAN WORKS

The same idea is used in searching for oil on land. A sonar pulse is sent into the ground. Echoes come back from different layers of soil and rock underneath. This helps geologists predict what may lie deep in the earth.

Sonar is also used in the breeding of livestock. Short sound pulses are sent into an animal's hide. Echoes then return from layers of fat and muscle. The time between echoes gives the thickness of the various layers of fat and muscle tissue. This enables cattlemen to select the meatiest animals for breeding.

Scientists know that bats and porpoises use sonar to navigate and hunt. By studying these

Radio signals sent to loran receiver are used to pinpoint the position of a ship.

animal sound systems, scientists hope to find valuable ideas for better man-made sonar systems.

▶ LORAN

Loran is a special kind of radio broadcasting system used by navigators of planes and ships to find their position on the earth. The word "loran" comes from the first letters of "*long-range navigation*." Loran was first used during World War II, by ships crossing the Atlantic.

Loran stations, on land, send out special radio signals that are picked up by a plane or ship. With these signals the navigator plots his position on a special loran chart. This chart is a map of the region crisscrossed by many curved lines.

In a loran system two separate loran stations work together. One is called a master station because it sends out its signal first. The second, called a relay or slave station, sends its signal out a fraction of a second after receiving the signal from the master station. Because of this time difference, the navigator can tell which signal came from which station. The two stations are usually located a few hundred miles apart.

Here is how the system works. Suppose station A sends out its signal 1 second before station B. (The time is really much less than 1 second, but the principle is the same.) Now imagine that your ship receives the two signals exactly 1 second apart. The signals left their stations 1 second apart and arrived at your ship 1 second apart, so they must have traveled the same distance to get to your ship. This means that your ship must be somewhere on the line marked "2." (Every point on that line is the same distance from each station.)

Now suppose that you pick up station A's signal at a certain time and then you pick up station B's signal less than 1 second later. Signal B must have "caught up" a little with signal A. So your ship must be a little closer to station B than to station A. This puts your ship somewhere on a curved line, like the one marked "3." But if signal B comes in a little more than 1 second later, your ship must be on a line like "1."

A navigator uses a loran receiving set to measure accurately the time difference be-

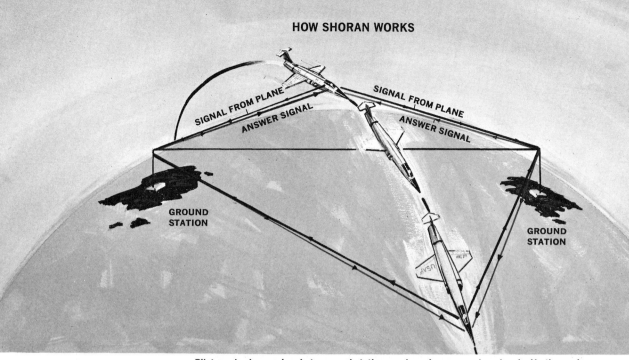

SIGNAL FROM PLANE

ANSWER SIGNAL

SIGNAL FROM PLANE

ANSWER SIGNAL

GROUND STATION

GROUND STATION

Pilot sends shoran signals to ground stations and receives answering signals. He then calculates his distance from the stations and plots his position on a map.

tween the two received signals. This information tells him that his ship or plane lies somewhere on one particular line on the loran chart. The navigator then uses the signals from a different pair of stations to plot a second line on his loran chart. The point where the two lines cross is the position of his craft.

Loran can be used by ships many hundreds of miles from the sending stations. It is valuable to navigators because it enables them to fix their position in bad weather, when the sun and stars are not visible. Even in good weather it is often quicker and easier to use loran for navigation than to use the stars.

▶ SHORAN

The word "shoran" comes from the first letters of "*short-range navigation*." Shoran is a radio system used to help in navigation and map making. It consists of a transmitter and receiver in an airplane and two special radio sets at ground stations up to about 400 miles apart.

The airborne transmitter sends out a radio signal to each of the ground stations. Each ground station automatically sends out an answering signal the instant it receives the signal from the plane. The plane receives the

two answer signals, and the receiving set measures the time it takes for each signal to make its round trip. This gives the plane's distance from each of the stations. The navigator can then plot his position on a map.

Because of its great accuracy, shoran can be used to measure the distance between two places on earth. A ground station is placed at each of the two. Now picture an imaginary line connecting the two stations. The plane starts out at some distance from this line and flies directly toward it. During the flight the shoran system measures the distance from the plane to each station and adds the two distances together. As the plane approaches the line between the stations, the sum of the distances gets smaller and smaller. Then the sum begins to increase again as the plane crosses over the line. When the plane is directly over the line, the distance sum is smallest. That is the distance between the stations.

WILLIAM C. VERGARA
Director of Advanced Research
The Bendix Corporation

See also BATS; ECHO; RADIO AND RADAR ASTRONOMY.

RADAR ASTRONOMY. See RADIO AND RADAR ASTRONOMY.

RADIATION

Switch on an electric lamp. The rays of light spread out from the bulb in all directions. Rays of light, or light waves, as they are called, are a form of radiation.

Turn your radio on. When people speak into the microphone at the radio station, their voices are changed into a form of radiation. Radio radiations, or radio waves, spread out from the station in all directions. When you turn your radio on, you "pick up" these radio radiations.

Stand close to a warm radiator. You can feel the heat coming to your body. The radiator is radiating heat rays. Heat is another form of radiation.

X rays, radar waves, and ultraviolet rays, like the other rays that we have mentioned, are also forms of radiation. All these radiations travel at the same speed—299,728 kilometers (186,251 miles) per second.

Radiation can be detected in different ways. Light can be seen. Heat can be felt. But some radiation, such as radio waves, can be detected only with instruments.

▶ ELECTROMAGNETIC RADIATION

Most kinds of radiation are forms of electricity and magnetism. For this reason, most radiation is known as electromagnetic radiation.

Radiation can have electrical effects. For example, a beam of light can operate an electric device that opens doors.

Magnets have an effect on radiation. The great English scientist Michael Faraday discovered that a beam of light could be twisted if the beam was passed close to a magnet.

▶ HOW RADIATION IS PRODUCED

Most radiation starts inside atoms. Although atoms are far too small to be seen, scientists have found that each atom has a center, called the nucleus. Each kind of atom also contains a particular number of electrons. An atom of iron, for example, has 26 electrons; an atom of hydrogen contains 1 electron; and so on. The electrons circle around the nucleus in orbits, or shells. There may be several shells around the nucleus of an atom, and each shell may have one or more electrons.

Sometimes an electron is hit by another particle. And sometimes the electron is hit by a tiny "bullet" of energy. If the electron is hit, it jumps to another orbit that is farther from the nucleus. But the new orbit is not its natural orbit. The electron does not belong there. So it quickly falls back to its own orbit. As it falls back, it releases a tiny quantity of energy.

When an atom absorbs outside energy, electrons may be forced out of their orbits over and over again very rapidly. And the atom releases energy very rapidly as radiation. The amount of energy that the atom can radiate is the same amount that it has absorbed.

Radiation may also be caused in another way. In some very heavy atoms, such as those of radium or uranium, the nucleus may break up without having absorbed any outside energy. Such atoms, which are said to be radioactive, emit energy on their own.

The Electron Jump

Radiation can be better understood with the help of an example, such as a steam or hot-water radiator. A steam or hot-water radiator gives off heat. Some of the heat warms the air. And some of the heat warms you and other objects in the room.

The radiator is made of iron. The iron is

When an electron is knocked out of its natural orbit into a nearby outer orbit, it falls back to its original position, releasing a small amount of energy.

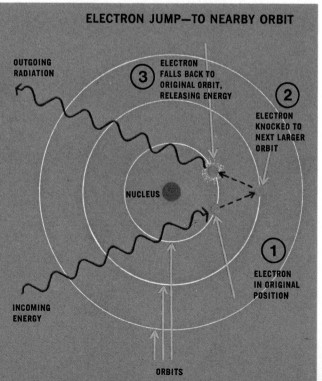

ELECTRON JUMP—TO NEARBY ORBIT

OUTGOING RADIATION

3 ELECTRON FALLS BACK TO ORIGINAL ORBIT, RELEASING ENERGY

2 ELECTRON KNOCKED TO NEXT LARGER ORBIT

NUCLEUS

1 ELECTRON IN ORIGINAL POSITION

INCOMING ENERGY

ORBITS

composed of iron atoms. The steam in the radiator provides heat energy that is taken in by the iron atoms. Some of the heat makes the atoms move about. Some of it is absorbed by electrons within the atom.

The heat energy absorbed by these electrons causes them to become "excited" and jump out of their natural orbits. The electrons do not leave the atom, but jump into larger orbits around the nucleus.

Almost at the same instant, the electrons fall back to their original orbits. As they fall back to their natural orbits the electrons give up the extra energy they absorbed. That energy is emitted from the atoms as heat waves.

Not all the electrons jump to new orbits and fall back to their old ones at the same time. While the radiator is being heated, electrons from some atoms leap into new orbits and others drop back into their old ones. This continues for a while after the furnace is turned off and the steam begins to cool. But now no new energy is being taken in. So the radiator cools, and fewer and fewer electrons jump: less and less radiation is emitted.

The iron atoms of the radiator received energy from the steam. This energy kept knocking electrons into new orbits. As each electron fell back into a lower orbit in the atom, a tiny amount of heat radiation was sent out from that atom.

The steam in a home radiator can provide only a limited amount of heat energy to the iron. The iron atoms absorb enough heat to emit a steady flow of heat radiation.

Before being shaped into a radiator, the iron was probably a solid block or slab of iron. That iron had to receive an enormous amount of heat energy before it could melt and be shaped into a radiator. What effect would such intense heat have on the iron atoms?

▶ HOW RADIATION CHANGES FORM

A slab of iron is placed in a furnace at the foundry, where radiators are made. At first, the iron atoms receive enough heat to radiate heat waves. The foundry furnace, however, provides much more heat than the steam in a radiator does.

Soon the added energy from the furnace fire pushes the electrons farther from their original orbits. The electrons make more vigorous jumps than before. They jump to orbits even farther away from the nucleus. The electrons have a greater distance to fall back, and they release a greater quantity of radiation as they return to their original orbits.

The electromagnetic radiation emitted by the electrons falling a greater distance is different from that of the electrons that jump small distances. The new radiation can be seen. When it reaches your body, it affects the nerves of your eyes. You see a dull red glow in the slab of iron. The tiny amounts of energy emitted from the falling electrons are red light waves.

The slab of iron is still a slab of iron. It cannot be shaped into a radiator yet. It is left in the furnace to absorb more and more heat energy. The iron atoms finally receive so much heat energy that two things begin to happen.

First, the electrons become so excited that they now jump to still larger orbits. They have a longer fall back to their original orbits. This greater fall produces a different form of radiation. It is still light radiation, but it has become yellow-white light waves instead of red.

The second thing that happens is that the atoms themselves move about so quickly and energetically that the iron can no longer keep its shape. It melts.

An object can give off two or more kinds of radiation at the same time. For example, a red-hot piece of iron radiates both heat and light at the same time.

For a long time scientists tried to find out why radiations take different forms. The first clue to this mystery came when they found that all radiation travels outward from atoms in the form of waves.

▶ RADIATION WAVELENGTH

Think of the falling electron as a pebble falling into a pond. When the pebble falls, tiny ripples or waves spread outward in the pond. If the pebble is dropped from a greater height, more energy comes from its fall.

When an electron drops back to its original orbit, waves of radiation are sent out. If the electron has fallen from an orbit near the original one, the waves will carry only a little energy. If the electron has fallen from a more

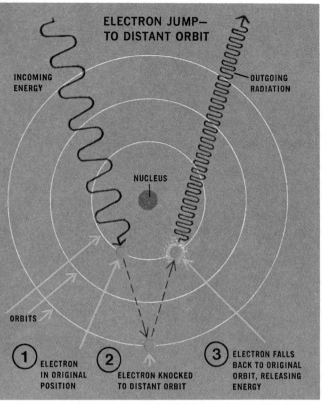

ELECTRON JUMP— TO DISTANT ORBIT

INCOMING ENERGY

OUTGOING RADIATION

NUCLEUS

ORBITS

① ELECTRON IN ORIGINAL POSITION

② ELECTRON KNOCKED TO DISTANT ORBIT

③ ELECTRON FALLS BACK TO ORIGINAL ORBIT, RELEASING ENERGY

When an electron falls back from a distant orbit, the wavelength of the radiation is changed.

distant orbit, the waves will carry more energy. We observe this greater energy as a change in the length of waves that an atom emits. The length of the waves depends upon how far the electron falls.

The length of a wave of radiation is the distance between the crest of one wave and the crest of the next. This is called the **wavelength**.

When steam heats a radiator, the electrons in the iron atoms make short jumps and produce radiation of long wavelength. This is heat radiation. When a furnace fire heats an iron slab, the electrons in the iron atoms make

larger jumps and produce radiation of shorter wavelength. This is light radiation. Whether you feel the radiation or whether you see it depends only upon the length of the radiation's waves.

The color of light also depends upon wavelength. The wavelength of the red light from the iron in the furnace is longer than the wavelength of the yellow-white color produced by the melting iron.

Each color of light has a different wavelength. Therefore, each color is the result of a different-size electron jump. As a matter of fact, most forms of radiation are the result of the distances of electron jumps.

▶ FREQUENCY

Scientists use another measurement, in addition to wavelength, to identify forms of radiation. It is called frequency.

When you sit in front of a campfire, you feel its heat waves and see its light waves. Both radiations reach you at the same time because both travel at the same speed. But the crests of the light waves are closer together than those of the heat waves—that is, the light waves are shorter. About 30 waves of light radiation reach you in the time it takes one wave of heat radiation to reach you. The number of waves that reach a particular spot in one second is called the frequency of the radiation.

We said that the frequency of the light waves is 30 times the frequency of the heat waves. We could also say that the wavelength of the heat waves is 30 times the wavelength of the light waves.

You often hear about frequencies on radio. When announcers say, "We broadcast on a frequency of 750 kilohertz," they mean that 750,000 waves, or vibrations, are reaching your radio each second. (The prefix "kilo" means 1,000, and "hertz" is a unit named after Heinrich Hertz, a German scientist.) To tune in this station, you turn the dial to the number 750. (The final "0" is usually dropped, so that you would turn to the number 75 on the dial.)

Radiation frequencies vary from very low to very high, just as wavelengths vary from very long to very short. Scientists use a special kind of chart to list and identify the wavelengths of electromagnetic radiation.

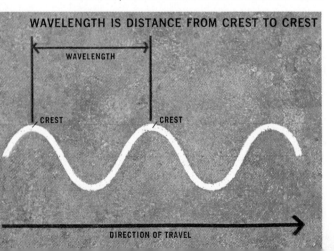

WAVELENGTH IS DISTANCE FROM CREST TO CREST

WAVELENGTH

CREST

CREST

DIRECTION OF TRAVEL

▶ THE ELECTROMAGNETIC SPECTRUM

The electromagnetic spectrum is a chart, or table, of electromagnetic radiation. It is usually made with lines indicating every important radiation wavelength, from the longest waves to the shortest waves.

The whole range of radiation wavelengths covers an amazingly large span. The longest wavelengths on the spectrum are radio waves. Some radio waves are hundreds or thousands of kilometers in length.

Gamma rays, at the other end of the spectrum, have such short wavelengths that hundreds of millions of their waves could fit across your thumbnail.

Visible Light Spectrum

Our eyes can detect waves in one small part of the electromagnetic spectrum. These are light rays, or visible radiation. We can see a thing only when light waves from it reach our eyes.

The wavelength of light waves is about halfway between the longest and the shortest wavelengths in the electromagnetic spectrum. Light waves make up only a tiny part of the spectrum, but there is a big variety of wavelengths among them. Light radiation such as that from the sun is composed of every color. (When all the colors appear together, you see them as white light.)

Each color has a different wavelength. Red light has the longest waves that we can see. About 13,000 of them cover one centimeter of space (about ½ inch). Violet, the color with the shortest visible waves, has about 26,000 waves per centimeter. In other words,

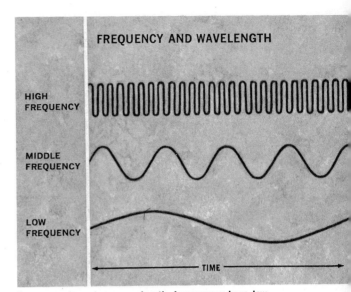

FREQUENCY AND WAVELENGTH

HIGH FREQUENCY

MIDDLE FREQUENCY

LOW FREQUENCY

TIME

Frequency depends on wavelength. Long waves have low frequency, and short waves have high frequency.

people can see electromagnetic radiations that have between 13,000 and 26,000 waves per centimeter.

The second longest wavelength of light is the color orange, followed by yellow, green, blue, and violet. The shadings of these colors have their own wavelengths, which appear in proper order on the spectrum.

All electromagnetic radiation travels through empty space at the same speed. The sun's heat rays, light rays, and other rays all take about eight minutes to reach you from a distance of 150,000,000 kilometers (about 93,000,000 miles).

But when radiation passes through some substances—such as air, glass, or water—its

A large part of the electromagnetic spectrum consists of radio waves. Light rays are only a very small part of the spectrum. There is no sharp line separating one type of ray from the one next to it. Thus, for example, some radio waves and some infrared rays have the same wavelengths and frequencies. Although there is overlap at some points, each type of radiation remains different from the one next to it because each one is generated by a different source.

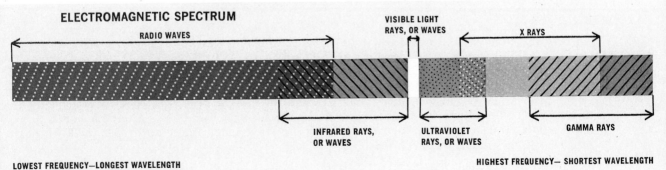

ELECTROMAGNETIC SPECTRUM

RADIO WAVES

VISIBLE LIGHT RAYS, OR WAVES

X RAYS

INFRARED RAYS, OR WAVES

ULTRAVIOLET RAYS, OR WAVES

GAMMA RAYS

LOWEST FREQUENCY—LONGEST WAVELENGTH

HIGHEST FREQUENCY— SHORTEST WAVELENGTH

speed is reduced slightly. Short wavelengths are slowed down by solid substances more than long wavelengths are.

When sunlight travels through drops of rainwater, the different wavelengths move at different speeds. As a result, the various wavelengths, or colors, travel in slightly different paths. They separate. You see these colors dispersed, or spread out, into a rainbowlike band. Scientists call this many-colored band the **visible light spectrum.**

Infrared Radiation

The electromagnetic spectrum extends past both sides of the visible light portion. There are wavelengths both shorter and longer than light waves.

The band of radiation immediately below the visible light portion of the spectrum is called infrared radiation. It has a longer wavelength than red light. You cannot see infrared radiation. But you can feel it. It is heat radiation. Some electrical appliances in the kitchen produce infrared radiation. The toaster browns bread by infrared radiation, and the electric broiler or rotisserie heats by infrared rays.

Below infrared or heat radiation, the next longest wavelengths in the spectrum belong to radiations that cannot be seen or felt. They can be detected only with radio equipment, and you know them as radio waves. Radio wavelengths cover an immense range. The longer radio waves may be thousands of kilometers long. Wavelengths used in television are about one meter long. Shortwaves are also used in radar and radio astronomy and by space probes and artificial satellites.

Ultraviolet Radiation

At the other side of the spectrum, just past the shortest violet-light wavelengths, are the radiations in the ultraviolet range. Ultraviolet rays are emitted by the sun and by certain types of electric lamps. Ultraviolet wavelengths range from just above those of violet light to 1,000,000 waves per centimeter (2,500,000 waves per inch).

Ultraviolet rays are described as penetrating rays. Waves of radiation travel until they strike an object. Light waves are slowed down a little by glass or water, but they are stopped by an opaque object. ("Opaque"

means "not allowing light to pass through.")

Shorter waves of radiation are more penetrating than the longer waves. The penetrating ultraviolet waves from the sun, for example, reach the nerves in your skin.

A long exposure to ultraviolet light makes the skin become dark and in this way prevents too much of this radiation from passing deeper into the body. This darkening of the skin is called a **suntan.** Some ultraviolet radiation is good for you. But too much exposure can be harmful. It can affect the body cells and must be avoided.

Only about one half the ultraviolet rays from the sun reach the ground. Many of them are absorbed high up in the earth's atmosphere. There oxygen atoms absorb the ultraviolet rays and form a different variety of oxygen, called ozone. The ozone layer in the atmosphere acts somewhat like a blanket, keeping many of the ultraviolet rays from reaching the surface of the earth.

Spectrum of the Shortest Waves

Moving across the spectrum to radiation with a shorter wavelength than ultraviolet, you come to X rays. These, as you know, are used in hospitals and by dentists. They are also emitted by the sun. Some X-ray wavelengths are so short that 1,000 of them are not as long as a single ultraviolet wave.

None of the X rays from the sun ever reaches you. This is because the atmosphere acts as a complete blanket, or shield, and does not allow X rays to get through. It is just as well that the atmosphere does this, for X radiation is very penetrating. Too much of it can kill cells in the body and in time kill people.

On the other hand, X rays can be of great help when carefully used. Doctors use them to check internal parts of the body. In fact, because X rays can kill cells, they are sometimes used to destroy cancer cells and thus save lives. X rays also allow engineers to examine the inner parts of metal castings to find any faults within the metal that cannot be seen on its surface.

You see, then, that the whole range of the spectrum of electromagnetic radiation, from radio waves to X rays, is surprisingly large. What you see as light is only a tiny fraction of the whole range of electromagnetic radiation.

RADIOACTIVE RADIATION

There is another form of radiation. It is radioactive radiation. Radioactive radiation is different from other forms of radiation in the way it is generated.

All radioactive radiation is emitted from radioactive atoms. These are atoms that are continually breaking down. As they break down they radiate particles of matter and energy. There are about 50 different atoms in nature that are radioactive. Scientists have created many more.

Radioactive rays are not produced by electron jumps. Two of the three known radioactive rays are actually composed of tiny fragments of the atoms themselves. The third ray is a tiny "bullet" of energy.

Alpha rays are composed of particles of the nucleus of radioactive atoms.

Beta rays are high-speed electrons that shoot out of radioactive atoms.

Gamma rays are bursts of energy emitted from the nuclei of radioactive atoms and from atoms that are broken up in the sun and other stars. They are also produced in nuclear reactors. Gamma rays are very short in wavelength, at least as short as the shortest X rays.

Radioactive radiation is very penetrating. It can be extremely damaging to living things. Properly controlled, however, radioactivity has proved very useful in research, industry, and medicine.

THE NATURE OF RADIATION

Waves on a pond, such as those caused by a pebble, are motions of the water. Sound waves are motions of the air through which they travel. A hundred years ago scientists believed that light waves, too, must be the motion of "something." They called that something ether.

They agreed that you could not feel ether or measure it. But they believed that it must exist, because waves, they said, must have something in which to travel.

Today scientists no longer accept the ether theory. Instead, they have tried to understand more thoroughly the nature of radiation itself. One generally accepted theory is called the **quantum theory**.

Today scientists believe that radiation is emitted in the form of tiny quantities, or

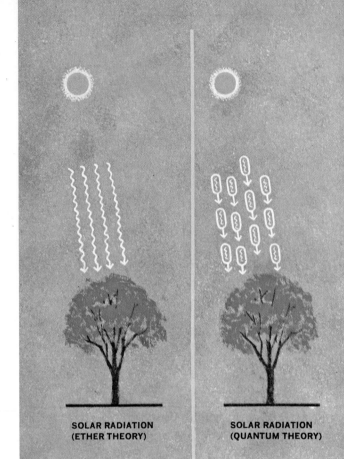

| SOLAR RADIATION (ETHER THEORY) | SOLAR RADIATION (QUANTUM THEORY) |

Old theory held that radiation traveled in the form of waves through the ether. Present theory holds that radiation is emitted in the form of quanta, which travel in packets of waves.

quanta, of energy. ("Quanta" is the plural of "quantum.") Quanta travel in the form of packets, or bundles, of waves. Thus, the tiny quantities of energy are believed to be wave packets.

This theory was developed by scientists to explain two kinds of results they have observed in their research. In some experiments light behaves as though it is made of waves. In others light behaves as though it is made of small packets of energy.

The quantum theory has been very successful in explaining many mysteries about radiation. It is leading scientists to a fuller understanding of the nature of radiation and of the many ways in which radiation can be put to use by mankind.

COLIN A. RONAN
Fellow of the Royal Astronomical Society

See also COSMIC RAYS; HEAT; LIGHT; RADIATION BELTS; RADIOACTIVE ELEMENTS; X RAYS.

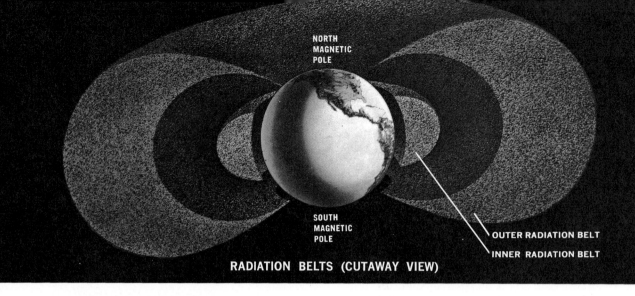

NORTH
MAGNETIC
POLE

SOUTH
MAGNETIC
POLE

OUTER RADIATION BELT

INNER RADIATION BELT

RADIATION BELTS (CUTAWAY VIEW)

RADIATION BELTS

High above the earth's atmosphere is a large region of invisible radiation particles dangerous to life. Most of these radiation particles occur in two belts that circle the earth around the equator. One belt lies inside the other. The belts are thickest above the equator and thin out toward the poles. They are called radiation belts.

The radiation particles consist of electrons and protons. Electrons and protons are usually found as parts of atoms. Both electrons and protons are electrically charged. The electron has a negative charge. The proton has a positive charge. When charged particles exist outside the atom, they are often called **radiation particles**, or simply **radiation**.

Radiation particles are very small. Most of them have a great deal of energy and move very fast.

High-energy radiation particles are a hazard to space travel. Because they are very tiny, these radiation particles can pass through the walls of spacecraft without making a hole. Once inside, the particles may bombard living occupants and cause radiation sickness. This is one reason why scientists are carefully studying these invisible belts of radiation.

Since the discovery of the belts in 1958, certain facts have been learned about them. Scientists have a good idea of the shape of the belts and how far they extend. They know what kinds of particles are found in the belts. They also know some of the effects that the belts produce on the earth. But scientists do not know where the radiation particles come from. Research is being done at present to gain information about the source of the particles.

▶ DISCOVERY OF THE RADIATION BELTS

For many years scientists have been studying a kind of radiation called **cosmic rays**. These are particles that rain down on the earth from unknown sources. Cosmic rays are mostly high-speed protons.

The first United States satellite, *Explorer I,* which went into orbit on January 31, 1958, carried a simple Geiger counter to count these cosmic rays. (A Geiger counter records the number of radiation particles that enter its interior.)

A team of United States scientists, headed by James A. Van Allen (1914–   ), was making a special study of cosmic rays. These scientists expected that the number of cosmic rays would increase at high altitudes because there is less air there. The air acts as a shield that prevents many cosmic rays from reaching the surface of the earth. At very high altitudes the air is so thin that the number of cosmic rays there should be much larger than on the surface of the earth. To the surprise of the scientists, the Geiger counter in *Explorer I* showed that there were fewer cosmic rays at high altitudes. Sometimes the counter showed that there were no cosmic rays at all.

Van Allen's team suspected that something had gone wrong with the Geiger counter. But when another satellite, *Explorer III,* was launched, its counter also found many fewer cosmic rays. The scientists were then convinced that the first counter had not been damaged, as they had suspected. But why, they wondered, did there seem to be fewer cosmic rays at high altitudes than near the earth?

A member of Van Allen's team, Carl McIlwain (1931–   ), gave a possible explanation. Perhaps the number of radiation particles found by the satellites was so great that the counters choked. Perhaps the counters were completely overwhelmed by the great number of particles and could not operate properly.

Later satellites and probes, such as *Explorer IV* and the *Pioneer* moon probes, proved that this was indeed the case. Specially designed radiation counters showed that the earth is surrounded by regions of extremely powerful radiation. This radiation is so powerful that the scientists realized there must be other particles in these regions besides cosmic rays. These are the regions called the radiation belts.

▶ RADIATION AND THE EARTH'S MAGNETISM

Studies of the radiation belts have shown that the belts exist because of the earth's magnetism.

The earth is like a large magnet. Like every magnet, the earth has a magnetic field. It also has a north magnetic pole and a south magnetic pole. The magnetic field consists of invisible magnetic lines that stretch from pole to pole. These lines are called **magnetic lines of force**. The space around the earth is filled with these invisible lines of force.

The earth's magnetic lines of force can change the direction of electrically charged particles such as protons and electrons. In fact the lines of force can act as a trap for these particles.

Imagine a proton or an electron approaching the earth from outer space. If conditions are right, the particle is captured by the earth's magnetism. The particle travels along the lines of force, bouncing back and forth from one pole to the other. At the same time it travels around the earth.

Billions of such particles make up the two doughnut-shaped belts of radiation that surround the earth. One belt is called the inner radiation belt. The other is called the outer radiation belt.

The Inner Radiation Belt

The inner belt is made up of low-speed electrons and high-speed protons. The electrons make up more than 99.9 percent of the particles. The high-speed protons in this belt that choked off the Geiger counters make up only a tiny part of the inner belt's radiation. These fast-moving protons are dangerous to life because of their great speed rather than because of their great numbers.

The belt's lower edge is about 400 miles above the earth. The belt reaches a height of about 3,000 miles. Its strongest radiation is at a height of 2,000 miles. The radiation in the inner belt is extremely dangerous to life because it is very penetrating.

The Outer Radiation Belt

The outer radiation belt consists of high-speed electrons. They are less penetrating than the fast-moving protons in the inner belt, because they are very much smaller than the protons. The electrons cannot gather as much energy as a heavier proton moving at

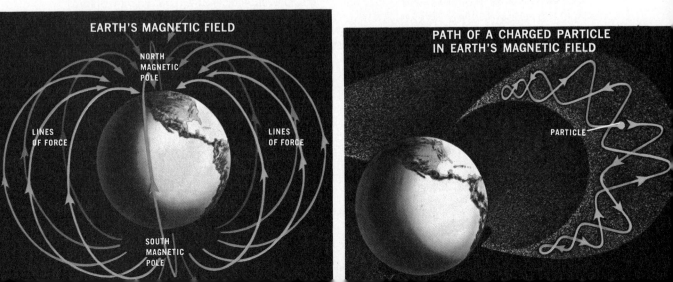

EARTH'S MAGNETIC FIELD

NORTH MAGNETIC POLE

LINES OF FORCE

LINES OF FORCE

SOUTH MAGNETIC POLE

PATH OF A CHARGED PARTICLE IN EARTH'S MAGNETIC FIELD

PARTICLE

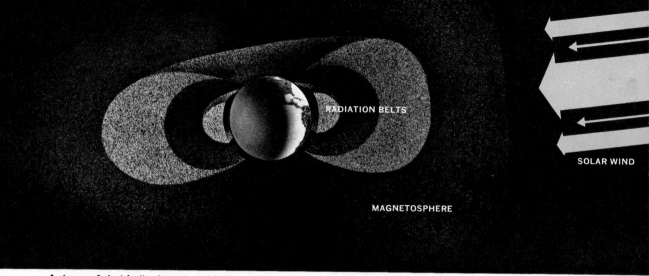

RADIATION BELTS

SOLAR WIND

MAGNETOSPHERE

A stream of electrically charged particles from the sun "blows" against the magnetosphere.

the same speed. Therefore the outer radiation belt is less dangerous to life than the inner belt.

The outer belt extends from about 8,000 to 12,000 miles above the earth. The belt's strongest radiation is at its center, about 10,000 miles above the earth's equator.

▶ THE EARTH'S MAGNETOSPHERE

The two strong radiation belts lie within a much larger region of weaker radiation that surrounds most of the earth. This region is called the magnetosphere. It extends outward for tens of thousands of miles. It consists of low-speed electrons and protons.

The magnetosphere's electrons and protons are also trapped by the earth's magnetic lines of force. At a distance of tens of thousands of miles above the earth the magnetic lines of force are very weak. But the protons and electrons are kept from leaving the magnetosphere because they move slowly. They do not have the energy to escape from the weak magnetic lines of force.

The Shape of the Magnetosphere

The shape of the magnetosphere is determined by the earth's magnetic field. But the shape is distorted by electrically charged particles that stream from the sun to the earth. This **solar wind** of charged particles "blows" against the outermost magnetic lines of force. The solar wind pushes the outermost lines of

force nearer to the earth on the sunlit side. It pushes the outermost lines of force away from the earth on the dark side.

The magnetosphere extends to a height of about 30,000 or 40,000 miles on the sunlit side, depending upon the strength of the solar wind. It rises higher above the dark side of the earth. The lower edge of the magnetosphere comes to within a few hundred miles of the earth.

There is very little radiation near the earth's north and south magnetic poles. The trapped protons and electrons that enter the polar regions are forced to come very close to the earth. This is because the earth's magnetic lines of force enter the earth near the poles. The same lines of force are far above the earth near the equator. If a proton or electron moves too far north or south, it follows the lines of force and comes close to the earth. Once there, it is absorbed by the atmosphere. Most trapped protons and electrons, however, "bounce" away from the polar regions before they come close to the earth, so they are not absorbed. For those reasons the radiation belts do not exist near the north and south poles.

Ever since the discovery of trapped radiation, almost every satellite and space probe has carried instruments to measure this radiation. Great effort has been spent in studying these particles because of their importance to space travel.

MAN-MADE RADIATION BELTS

When a nuclear bomb is exploded about 50 miles up in the atmosphere, artificial belts of radiation are set up around the earth. Most of these artificial belts last a short time—a few days or weeks. But powerful nuclear bombs set up radiation belts that may last for years.

Since scientists know exactly when this radiation is born, they can study the lifetimes of the protons and electrons in the radiation. The **lifetime**, or **rundown time**, is the time it takes for a trapped particle to be knocked out of its orbit around the earth.

In 1958 the United States exploded a number of nuclear bombs high in the atmosphere above the Pacific and South Atlantic oceans. The explosions produced artificial radiation belts that lasted from a few days to several weeks. Scientists gained important information about radiation belts from these explosions, and from others made by both the United States and the Soviet Union in 1962.

The scientists found that the particles in the artificial radiation belts are the same as those in the natural radiation belts. They discovered that the particles in the inner belt are very long-lasting. Those in the outer radiation belt have much shorter lifetimes. Scientists are using this knowledge to develop theories about the origin of the particles in the belts.

RADIATION AND SPACE TRAVEL

Space travel has made the study of the radiation belts more important than ever. If man is ever to travel to the moon or to another planet, his spacecraft will have to travel through the radiation belts.

An astronaut in a spaceship in the heart of the inner radiation belt will receive a death-dealing amount of radiation in a few hours unless he is properly protected. To avoid this danger, his spacecraft must be built so as to provide considerable protection. The spacecraft should pass through the radiation belts at great speed. This will reduce the time it is exposed to radiation.

Solar Flares

Solar flares are eruptions of hot, very bright gas from the surface of the sun. The flares send out high-speed protons and electrons. This radiation can last from a few hours to more than a day. Scientists have observed that radiation in the outer belt becomes stronger than usual a few days after a solar flare occurs. They are not sure why this is so.

Some solar flares produce radiation that is much more dangerous to life than the radiation in the inner belt is. At present no one knows when a solar flare will take place. Therefore it is not possible to plan space trips during safe periods.

Scientists are trying to learn more about solar flares and their connection with the radiation belts. Perhaps they will be able to predict when a solar flare will occur. If this information is known, astronauts can be sent into space during safe periods. But until scientists can predict solar flares, an astronaut must be protected by radiation-absorbent material in the walls of his spacecraft.

AURORAS

The radiation belts produce an effect in the sky called the auroras. Auroras are brilliantly colored lights that appear in the northern sky in the Northern Hemisphere, and in the southern sky in the Southern Hemisphere. They are also called the northern lights, or aurora borealis, and the southern lights, or aurora australis.

Auroras occur most often within a radius of about 1,600 miles from the north and south poles. The auroras usually occur at a height of about 65 miles.

The auroras are thought to be caused by streams of protons and electrons coming from the sun. The earth's magnetism pulls many of these particles toward the poles. There the particles plunge into the atmosphere, causing it to light up.

The auroras are at the northern and southern ends of the outer radiation belt. Scientists therefore know that the auroras and the radiation belts are related, but they are not sure just how. They hope future research will shed new light on the cause of auroras as well as on the source of the trapped protons and electrons in our magnetosphere.

WILLIAM C. VERGARA
Director of Advanced Research
The Bendix Corporation

See also COSMIC RAYS; EARTH AND ITS SUN; INTERNATIONAL GEOPHYSICAL YEAR; MAGNETS AND MAGNETISM; RADIATION.

RADIO

We have all become so used to listening to the radio that we often take for granted the important part it plays in our daily life. It takes a major news event, like a moon shot, to make us realize how much we rely on radio for news and information as well as for entertainment. In the course of just a few decades radio has become the constant companion of millions of people. More people own radios than telephones. In the United States there is more than one radio for every person in the country on the average.

Radio gives people enjoyment in many ways. The average listener spends about 2½ hours each day with his radio. Sometimes he wants background music. At other times he listens carefully to his favorite recording star or symphony orchestra. Many people depend on radio for news of what is happening around the world.

▶ THE USES OF RADIO

Radio was used first to communicate with ships at sea. This is still an important use. Because of radio, ships can keep in touch with one another, and when necessary, call for

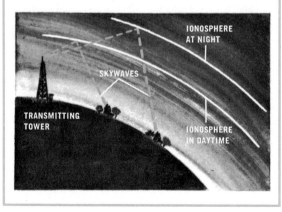

IONOSPHERE AT NIGHT

SKYWAVES

TRANSMITTING TOWER

IONOSPHERE IN DAYTIME

help. Airplanes use radios to keep in touch with the ground.

Two-way radios are used by most police headquarters to keep in constant touch with their patrol cars. Many taxi companies use two-way radios to tell their drivers where passengers are waiting. Short-distance messages can be sent on walkie-talkies—two-way radio sets that are sometimes used by campers and hunters to keep track of one another.

Radio is also used for radiotelephones— telephones without wires. These are used on boats, trains, and airplanes. Villages far away from power lines are sometimes supplied with radiotelephones instead of ordinary telephones, which use wires.

"Hams," or amateur radio operators, use radios to send their own private messages. These operators can send messages hundreds or thousands of miles, sometimes even around the globe.

One very important form of radio communication is television. Radar, too, is a form of radio.

▶ AT A BROADCASTING STATION

A radio broadcasting station is an exciting place. Programs must be broadcast precisely on schedule. To make this possible, the people who work in the station must be alert and observant. These people are vitally concerned with the world about them, and they may work closely with celebrities and other people who make the news.

A radio broadcasting station has three major departments: the program department, the technical department, and the business department. Because the average station employs no more than a dozen people, and often even less, one person may work in two departments. Some of the jobs that are done in a small station by one person may be done in a large station by an entire department.

Program Department

The program department decides what is to be broadcast and how it is to be done. Radio announcers and disc jockeys are part of the program department. The subdepartment called traffic is made up of the people who write and schedule the advertisements to be broadcast at specific times each day.

Because the news-gathering section of the program department has grown so much in recent years, it is in many cases a separate department. News comes into a radio station from many sources. Like newspapers, radio stations have reporters who cover and write local news. National and international news from the large press agencies comes over teletype machines—telegraph machines that print their messages automatically. Some large stations have newsmen in other cities and countries who telephone in news reports. Other stations, trying to fill their newscasts with more information and interest, use a voice news service or network affiliation to provide their listeners with the latest on-the-scene reports from all over the world. These services have made it possible for a radio station to broadcast live or tape-recorded statements by people as important as the president of the United States.

Writing news to broadcast is very different from writing news that will be read. A radio news report must be brief and cannot go into detail. However, the radio newsman can report news events within minutes of their happening. He can use interviews to give the listener a firsthand account of what has happened. The radio news story can be used on more than one broadcast. It can be quickly changed as events develop.

Technical Department

The technical, or engineering, department is responsible for making sure that the announcer's words get from the studio to the transmitter and then to your radio. It is responsible for seeing that the station broadcasts on the frequency assigned to it.

Each station has at least one control room. The most important piece of equipment in it is the control board. To this board come wires from microphones, tape recorders, and record turntables. The engineer is responsible for

---

THE RADIO RECEIVER

The space around you is filled at all times with radio frequency waves from nearby radio stations. They are causing minute vibrations in all the metal objects in the room. But you can hear these vibrations only if you turn on your radio.

The radio picks up the radio waves of the station you want to hear and turns them into sound waves. How does it do this?

(1) The **antenna** (or **aerial wire**) of the radio picks up all the radio frequency currents that are in the air around it.

(2) The **tuner** selects the frequency of the desired station and blocks out the frequencies of other stations.

(3) Now the radio set separates the program current from the carrier current. Special **vacuum tubes** block off the carrier current so that only the program current is left.

(4) The program current, which is very weak, must be amplified (increased) until it can operate the loudspeaker. This is done by vacuum tubes called **amplifiers**. In some radios, transistors are used instead of vacuum tubes to save space. Transistors also use less power than vacuum tubes.

(5) The loudspeaker changes the program current into sound waves. These sound waves are a copy of those in the broadcasting studio.

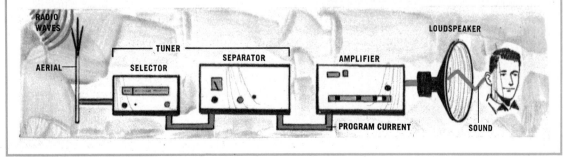

THE IONOSPHERE

The distance that radio waves can travel is determined largely by the sun. The sun sends its energy down toward the earth. This energy electrifies the **ionosphere**—layers of air about 60 to 200 miles above us. The ionosphere layers reflect radio waves back to the earth.

There are layers of the ionosphere high in the sky and layers low in the sky. The more intensely a layer is ionized, the more the path of a wave is bent, or the more that wave is reflected. Bending also depends on the wavelength—the longer the wave, the more the path is bent.

Long waves are usually sent out as **ground waves**. Medium waves are sent out as a combination of **ground and sky waves**. Short waves are **sky waves** that go so far up in the ionosphere that they bounce for long distances. The very shortest waves **(microwaves)** go right through the ionosphere and rarely return to earth at all.

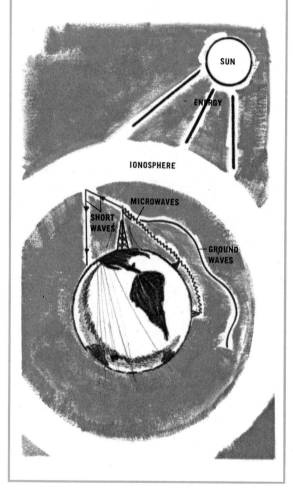

turning on the proper switch at the right time so that continuous sound—voice or music—is sent from the control board to the transmitter.

The microphone also is in the studio. It is the microphone that turns the sound of an announcer's voice into electrical energy that can be sent to the transmitter.

Business Department

The business department is in charge of bringing in the station's money. In it are the accountants who keep the books in order and pay the bills. Also in it are the salesmen who go to local stores and advertising agencies to sell air time on the station.

▶THE EARLY HISTORY OF RADIO

The existence of radio waves was predicted long before they were actually discovered. The prediction was made in 1864 by James Clerk Maxwell (1831–79), the great English mathematical physicist. In 1888 a German physicist, Heinrich Hertz (1857–94), demonstrated that the waves actually do exist and that they travel through space.

Hertz never realized the possibilities for communication by radio waves, even though he made a very simple radio transmitter and receiver to prove the radio-wave theory. However, other men made further experiments with radio waves. An English physicist, Ernest Rutherford (1871–1937), succeeded in sending signals ¾ mile. Another Englishman, Oliver Lodge (1851–1940), developed the basic principles of tuning. But the most successful of all the radio pioneers was Guglielmo Marconi (1874–1937), an Italian who went to England to work. Marconi was the founder of radio communication. In 1896 he took out his first patent. On December 12, 1901, he succeeded, on his first try, in sending and receiving messages across the Atlantic Ocean—from Poldhu in Cornwall, England, to St. John's in Newfoundland, Canada.

Marconi's wireless telegraph could send only dots and dashes; it could not transmit a spoken message. Radio program broadcasting was made possible by the development of the vacuum tube. In 1904 the first vacuum tube was made by John Ambrose Fleming (1849–1945), an English electrical engineer. This tube was a diode—that is, it had two

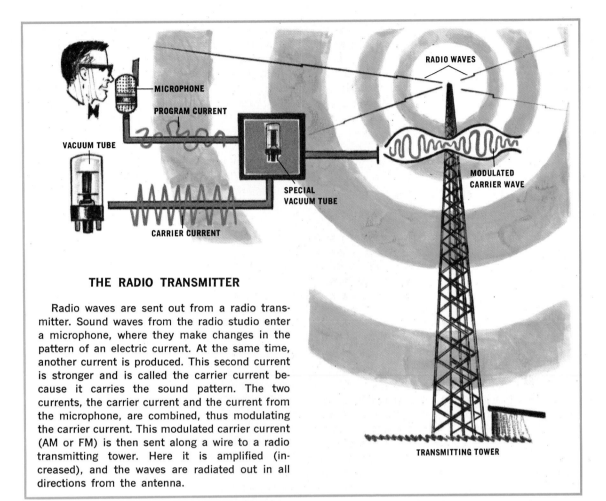

THE RADIO TRANSMITTER

Radio waves are sent out from a radio transmitter. Sound waves from the radio studio enter a microphone, where they make changes in the pattern of an electric current. At the same time, another current is produced. This second current is stronger and is called the carrier current because it carries the sound pattern. The two currents, the carrier current and the current from the microphone, are combined, thus modulating the carrier current. This modulated carrier current (AM or FM) is then sent along a wire to a radio transmitting tower. Here it is amplified (increased), and the waves are radiated out in all directions from the antenna.

electrical parts. In 1906 an American inventor, Lee De Forest (1873–1961), added a third part to Fleming's vacuum tube. This new vacuum tube was called a triode or audion. It was much like the vacuum tube used today.

As time went on, more and more uses for radio transmission were found, and ways in which to improve radio transmission were constantly developed. Today radio waves have even been bounced off the moon. Radio communication with satellites and missiles is being improved. Communications satellites regularly transmit messages and programs.

▶ THE DEVELOPMENT OF RADIO BROADCASTING

The new method of communication developed by Marconi was first known as wireless. The first practical use of wireless was in signaling by ships at sea. The American Navy began to call the wireless the radiotelegraph. From this came the word "radio." The British still use the older term "wireless."

The first radio broadcast was heard on Christmas Eve, 1906. Radio operators on ships at sea suddenly heard a man speaking, then a woman singing and a violin playing. Then came the words "If you have heard this program, write to R. A. Fessenden at Brant Rock."

Fourteen more years went by before broadcasting became practical. Reginald A. Fessenden's broadcasting experiment helped to point out the problems that needed to be solved. As big as any of the technical problems was the problem of getting public and financial approval. The scientists were often called foolish and ridiculous.

But in 1920 a Westinghouse Company engineer, Dr. Frank Conrad, started a series of

RADIO WAVES

Radio waves, like light and heat waves, are electromagnetic. Electromagnetic waves are very mysterious. Men can find them, make them, and control them, but they do not know what they really are.

Like light and heat waves, radio waves radiate in all directions from their source. They travel through space in much the same way as water waves travel out when a pebble is dropped into water. Like waves in water, radio waves get weaker as they get farther from their source.

All electromagnetic waves travel at the same speed—about 186,000 miles a second. Although the waves are invisible, the length of a wave can be measured with scientific instruments. There is no sharp dividing line where long waves become medium waves and where medium waves become short waves. Long waves measure about 6,000 feet from the crest of one wave to the crest of the next. Medium waves measure about 1,800 feet. Short waves are only about 37 to 150 feet long.

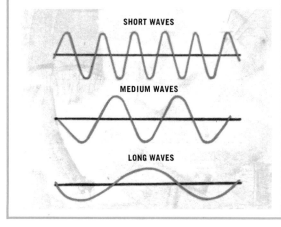

SHORT WAVES

MEDIUM WAVES

LONG WAVES

evening voice broadcasts. The response to his program was enthusiastic, and many radio sets were sold to people who wanted to hear it. An official of Westinghouse decided to build a broadcasting station at Pittsburgh, Pennsylvania. The station was KDKA, licensed by the government. Broadcasting had begun.

International Control of Air Space

Before the radio industry could develop, it had to solve the problems of controlling air space and broadcasting rights. Even when radio broadcasting had not developed beyond the wireless telegraph, people from many countries became aware that problems might develop if there were no rules for the use of air space. Electromagnetic waves do not follow the boundary lines of the countries from which they are sent; they travel out in every direction. Without rules for use, stations might end up sending their electromagnetic waves out on the same frequencies. When one station uses the frequency of another station, none of the waves get through clearly.

In 1909 a central bureau administered by the International Telegraph Union was formed in Berne, Switzerland. The bureau kept on record the frequencies of most of the world's wireless telegraph stations. Using this listing as a guide, new stations could find out which frequencies were free to be used.

As wireless telegraph developed into the wireless broadcasting that we now call radio, the bureau continued to keep international records and rules. Today the bureau is called the International Telecommunications Union. Since 1947 it has been a specialized agency of the United Nations. In accordance with international custom, every important country has set up its own laws to make certain that the international rules will be followed.

By international agreement every radio station is given a first letter or first two letters by which it can be identified. These letters are known as call letters. For convenience, the alphabet is portioned out among the nations. Broadcast stations in the United States are assigned call letters beginning with K or W. Those beginning with K are, with only a few exceptions, all west of the Mississippi River. Stations beginning with W are almost all east of the Mississippi.

Types of Governmental Control

The number of radio stations that can broadcast clearly at one time is limited by the frequencies available. Therefore, radio broadcasting needs some type of control by a central regulatory agency.

There are three basic systems used by governments to control radio. The best examples

Radio communications are essential in modern law enforcement work.

are the control systems used in the Soviet Union, Great Britain, and the United States.

In the Soviet Union all radio stations are owned by the government and operated by government employees. Because of this, the Soviet Government can decide what sort of programs will be broadcast.

Great Britain has a radio system, called the BBC, that is owned and supervised by the government but operated as a private company. In 1970 the British Government decided to allow private broadcasting.

In the United States, radio broadcasting is done by private companies. It is supervised by the Federal Communications Commission, or FCC. The FCC is made up of seven men appointed by the president and confirmed by the Senate. Not more than four members belong to the same political party. Each member is appointed for 7 years.

The FCC was established because, during the early days of radio in the United States, radio listeners often had difficulty with station interference. Too many stations on one chan-

How does a microphone work?

A microphone can turn sound into electrical energy because certain materials, such as carbon granules, will conduct electricity when they are put under pressure. The more pressure put on these materials, the more electricity they will conduct.

The basic parts of a microphone are a diaphragm (a very thin, springy sheet of metal, paper, or plastic) and a capsule, usually containing tiny granules, or grains, of carbon.

When sound waves hit the diaphragm, it presses the carbon granules together. If the pressure is great, the current flow is strong; if the pressure is weak, the current flow is weak. The amount of current always depends on the amount of pressure, which in turn depends on the volume of sound. When the sound stops, the diaphragm snaps back to its original position and the current stops flowing.

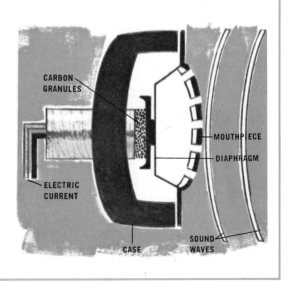

FREQUENCY

Although all radio waves travel at the same speed, the number of radio waves that travel past a point in 1 second can vary greatly. This number is called the **frequency**. The number of waves sent out each second by the transmitter of a radio station is the frequency of that station.

One complete wavelength is called a **cycle**. Frequency can be defined as the number of complete cycles that take place in a second. If wavelength is short, the waves are close together—the crests are close together and follow each other quickly. If wavelength is long, crests are far apart and follow one another slowly. Therefore, long waves are of low frequency, because crests do not come as frequently as those of short (high-frequency) waves.

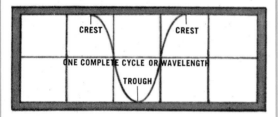

High-frequency waves are measured in **kilohertz** (usually written as **KHz**), or thousands of cycles per second. Very-high-frequency waves are measured in **megahertz (MHz)**, or millions of cycles per second.

On your radio, from left to right, are the numbers 540, 550, 560, and so on to 1600 kilohertz. Each number refers to a wave frequency. A radio station broadcasts its programs only on its own wave frequency.

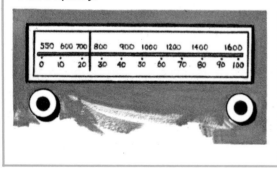

nel gave the listener a babbling noise. It was necessary to have each frequency band assigned to only one station in an area. In 1934 the United States Congress created the FCC and gave it the power to license all radio stations.

The FCC is concerned with more than program broadcasting. It assigns all the frequencies and sees to it that there is no interference on or between broadcast bands. No one in the United States is allowed to transmit any radio signals on any wavelength without a license granted by the FCC. This includes even ham radio operators.

HOW IS RADIO BROADCASTING FINANCED?

There are three main ways to pay for radio broadcasts. One way is to charge the listener directly. This is done by sending listeners a periodic bill, like telephone, gas, and electric bills. This method of paying for radio is used in Great Britain, where all set owners must pay a license fee each year.

Some radio stations are supported by government money that comes from regular sources, such as taxes. This is done in such countries as France, the Soviet Union, Venezuela, Indonesia, and Italy.

In other places, especially in the United States, government support has not been accepted, chiefly because many broadcasters feel that government support would mean government control. Because of this, American broadcasters have developed the commercial advertising system in order to pay their bills. Companies that make such products as cars, soap, soft drinks, and gasoline pay radio stations to broadcast advertisements for their products.

The amount of money that radio stations charge for a minute of advertising time usually depends upon the number of listeners they have. Companies called rating services are hired to measure the size of an audience in each radio station area. The time of day that a radio station has its biggest audience is known as prime time. This is usually between 6 and 10 A.M. and 4 to 7 P.M.

RADIO BROADCASTING TODAY

Radio broadcasting is expanding around the world. New systems that are being developed are more apt to use frequency modulation (FM) than amplitude modulation (AM), because FM has a wide range of pitches as well as less interference than AM.

Broadcasting is expanding very rapidly in the developing areas of Africa and Asia. Many of the stations throughout these areas are government-owned and -operated. They broadcast many educational programs. Many stations send out their programs in three or more languages. In Israel, news bulletins are sent out in 10 languages.

Practically all European countries have local broadcasting stations. Most of the radio stations are publicly controlled. However, a few stations do some advertising. All the major European countries have overseas broadcasting services and school and general education programs.

In the United States, radio has changed a great deal since the 1930's. At that time the major networks—the National Broadcasting Company (NBC), the Columbia Broadcasting Company (CBS), and the Mutual

Interviews with interesting, newsworthy people are a popular form of radio show.

AM AND FM

Radio waves must be modulated to carry a program—that is, the even pattern of the waves must be changed. The wave that is modulated is called the **carrier wave**. It can be modulated in two ways.

If the frequency of the waves remains the same but the **amplitude** (height) varies according to the degree of loudness and the pitch of the original sound, the waves have **amplitude modulation**, or **AM**. Most standard broadcasting uses amplitude modulation. It is also used for long-distance shortwave broadcasting. AM programs can be sent over long distances. However, AM programs are often disturbed by static and similar noises.

AM (AMPLITUDE MODULATION)

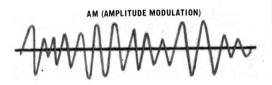

If a radio wave has **frequency modulation (FM)**, the amplitude of the wave remains constant but the frequency varies according to the loudness or pitch of the original sound. Frequency modulation is fairly free from the static that sometimes disturbs amplitude modulation. It is not suited for broadcasting long distances.

FM (FREQUENCY MODULATION)

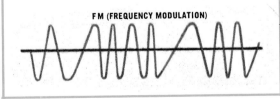

Broadcasting System (MBS)—controlled the nation's most important broadcasting stations. Now the major broadcasting stations are largely independent.

A network is a group of stations across the country linked together by telephone wire. The stations receive entertainment and news programs that are produced in the studios of their network headquarters. A program broadcast in New York or Hollywood can be heard at the same time in large and small cities across the country. The more stations a network has connected with it, the larger its possible audience.

Dramas and live bandstand shows made up much of radio's early programming. But when television became popular in the late 1940's, a change in programming was necessary, for people could now see on television the same sort of thing they could only hear on radio.

So radio stations across the country put emphasis on recorded music and local news, which they produced themselves in their own studios.

Today the networks are a source of expert reporting of worldwide news and entertainment.

▶ RADIO IS A PUBLIC INFLUENCE

Since becoming more and more involved with the affairs of their local communities, broadcasters have started expressing their opinions about public issues. These opinions are presented in editorials. Many stations now editorialize regularly. But this was not always so. It is only since 1949 that the FCC has allowed broadcasters to editorialize.

Before 1949 an American broadcaster could hire a commentator with whom he agreed, or he could produce special programs to point out conditions of which he was critical. But he could not come out himself and call for changes or personally make criticisms. Broadcasters knew that unless they could editorialize they could not compete effectively with newspapers and magazines in advising their audiences. After much discussion over a period of years, the FCC granted broadcasters the right to editorialize. Today almost every serious issue has at one time or another been the subject of a radio editorial.

Although broadcasters are encouraged to editorialize, they are constantly reminded that they must always be fair. Therefore, broadcasters must provide reasonable opportunity for both sides of any public argument to be heard.

Jack Benny, a popular radio and TV comedian.

THE RADIO FREQUENCY BAND

Radio waves may be produced in frequencies as low as 10 kilohertz or as high as 30,000,000 kilohertz. All of these frequencies are a part of the **radio frequency band**—the range of frequencies and wavelengths of electromagnetic radio waves. The band is illustrated with the low frequencies and long waves at one end progressing up to the high frequencies and short waves at the other end.

Government regulating agencies assign the frequencies to all the various radio needs. The lowest frequencies are used by aircraft and shipping. Above this is the wide part of the band, which is used for AM broadcasting. A higher band of frequencies is used for police calls, ships at sea,

taxis, radio hams, and the like. Television uses still higher frequencies. The highest frequencies are used by radar and in experimental work.

There are three broadcasting bands on which stations send out regular programs. The standard AM broadcasting band is the one received by most home and car radios—from 535 kilohertz to 1605 kilohertz. The FM band is in a much higher frequency range than the AM—88 to 108 megahertz. The third broadcasting band is called **short wave**. Since short-wave signals will reach great distances, they are used mainly to beam or direct programs at other countries. For instance, The Voice of America uses short waves to explain the American viewpoint all over the earth.

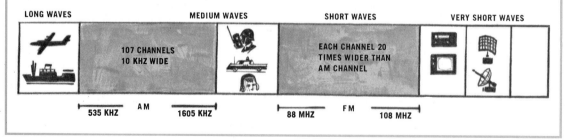

| LONG WAVES | MEDIUM WAVES | SHORT WAVES | VERY SHORT WAVES |

107 CHANNELS 10 KHZ WIDE

EACH CHANNEL 20 TIMES WIDER THAN AM CHANNEL

535 KHZ — AM — 1605 KHZ — 88 MHZ — FM — 108 MHZ

One fact that increases the broadcaster's responsibility is that there are few communities that have their own daily newspapers. Radio stations in cities without local newspapers have a special reason for presenting all sides of the news to their listeners.

R. PETER STRAUS
Chairman, WMCA, New York, N.Y.

RADIO PROGRAMS

From the time of the first round-the-world radio broadcast in 1930, the new wireless wonder began to flourish both as an entertainer and as a means of conveying news.

Events in Europe, as Adolph Hitler rose to power in Germany and moved history toward World War II, drew people to their radios for newscasts. In the depth of the Depression, President Franklin D. Roosevelt began his famous radio fireside chats. In radio entertainment new stars were born: Bob Hope, Jack Benny, James Edward Jordan and Marian Driscoll Jordan (Fibber McGee and Molly), Fred Allen, Freeman F. Gosden and Charles J. Correll (Amos 'n' Andy), Edgar

Above: Renfrew of the Mounted, a popular radio show of the 1930's. Actors deliver their lines at left. Sound-effects men are busy at right. Below: Jimmy Durante (*left*) goes over a script with his producer and band-leader.

Bergen and his saucy ventriloquist's dummy Charlie McCarthy. Drama was developed as a radio art form, reaching its most melodramatic heights in daytime series. These shortly came to be known as soap operas because large soap companies discovered that advertising on these programs reached a vast number of housewives.

Advertising, in fact, was the spur to radio's amazing growth in the United States—as it was later to television's rapid development. In the beginning, radio was largely uncontrolled; the airwaves were in chaos. To correct this, in 1927 Congress set up the Federal Radio Commission (replaced by the Federal Communications Commission in 1934) to give out licenses to use certain frequencies, or wavelengths. Those who received licenses were ordered to operate their stations "in the public interest, convenience and necessity," but they were left to find means of supporting themselves. The broadcasters turned to advertising. It came to them in great volume.

Radio, as does television, leads a dual existence. Like newspapers, both are conveyers of current and general information. Like the theater and movies, they are part of show business. The broadcasters decide, except in countries where there is government control,

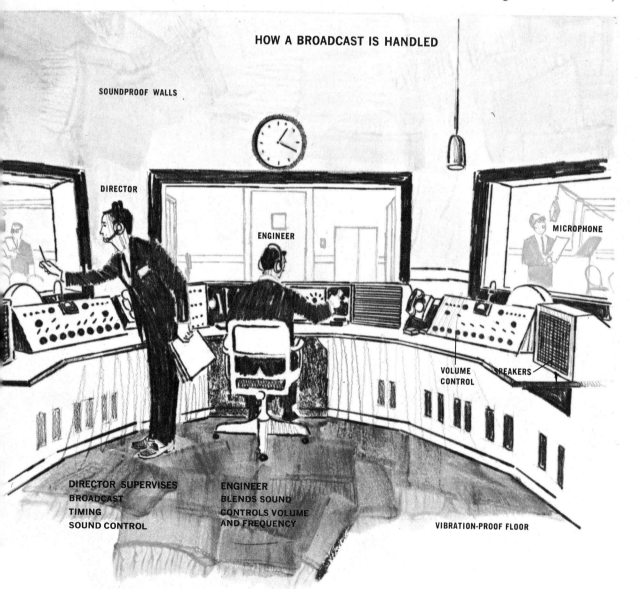

HOW A BROADCAST IS HANDLED

SOUNDPROOF WALLS

DIRECTOR

ENGINEER

MICROPHONE

VOLUME CONTROL

SPEAKERS

DIRECTOR SUPERVISES BROADCAST TIMING SOUND CONTROL

ENGINEER BLENDS SOUND CONTROLS VOLUME AND FREQUENCY

VIBRATION-PROOF FLOOR

At work in a radio studio. Disc jockeys entertain their audiences with talk and music.

how much of each kind of programming shall be put on the air.

In the days before television there was great variety in the programs radio offered. The networks produced dramas, mysteries, comedies, musical varieties, historical documentaries, quiz shows, and other diversions. World War II greatly spurred radio news listening and made famous such war reporters as Edward R. Murrow, later to become director of the United States Information Agency. The war saw the development of magnetic recording tape, which permitted radio to assemble programs in part or in whole in advance of their broadcast. The war also delayed the advent of television. While all industrial effort was bent on waging war, television had to wait.

When peace came, the new wonder of sight plus sound got its green light. It was an immediate and immense hit. The public loved it. Radio, by now portable, fled to the kitchen, the bedroom, the family automobile, the beach, the restaurant, and the store— everywhere but the living room, where the new "home screen" now reigned supreme.

Staggered by the impact of television's overnight dominance, radio fell back on two basic kinds of programming: news and music. The public no longer wanted just to hear drama and comedy and musical variety; it wanted to see them as well. But "old-fashioned radio" still had much in its favor. It could go with its audience wherever listeners went, which television could not.

Even so, television took away radio's big advertisers and big shows. To entertain listeners, radio resorted mostly to spinning phonograph records. The disc jockey became radio's star. Between records he chatted about the newest hit tunes, the weather, the time of day, and whatever else came to mind. Some stations turned most of their attention to younger listeners, who wanted rock 'n' roll, western, and hillbilly music. Others specialized in classical music. Some stations, especially in large cities, began catering to foreign-language groups.

The news-and-music pattern has survived as radio's mainstay. Remarkably enough, radio has prospered.

RICHARD K. DOAN
Television and Radio Editor
New York *Herald Tribune*

RADIO, AMATEUR

How would you like to have your own radio station and have on-the-air conversations with other people? Nearly one million people around the world have and operate two-way shortwave stations from their own homes. They are called radio amateurs, or hams.

Anyone may become a ham, regardless of age or previous experience. But radio amateurs must have a license—that is, permission from the government—in order to transmit and receive messages.

Most amateur stations are set up in the operators' homes, but it is possible to transmit or receive in a car, boat, or airplane. A station consists of a radio transmitter, a receiver, and an antenna. Ready-made equipment is generally available to suit almost every purse. Instructions for assembling the set usually come with the equipment.

▶WHY PEOPLE BECOME HAMS

The hobby means different things to different people. Some hams use their radios to retransmit messages. This is known as handling traffic. The American Radio Relay League, the international headquarters for ham radio, has a network that makes it easy to pass a message to almost anyone anywhere in the world.

Some hams enjoy just talking to each other ("rag chewing") and exchanging QSL cards (written confirmation of a contact). They enjoy contacting nearby hams as well as those who live halfway around the world. Some people play chess by radio. Others share personal experiences or discuss everyday events in their towns. There is one restriction—amateur radio may not be used to transact business.

There are thousands of local and international radio clubs that hold meetings, contests, and other activities during which members can exchange ideas and learn about the latest changes in this field. In the United States and Canada, there are more than 2,000 clubs.

Many ham radio operators have a bit of the experimenter in them. They may try all kinds of communication methods, including solar-powered radios, laser beams, satellites, and computers. Some of the most unique inventions have been developed by blind and deaf hams, and by people who have lost the use of their limbs. Some people use their

AMATEUR ABBREVIATIONS

ABT	About	HI	Laughter
AGN	Again	HP	Hope
ANI	Any	HR	Here; Hear
BCNU	I'll be seeing you	HRD	Heard
BK	Break	HV	Have
BTR	Better	HW	How
CRD	Card	NIL	Nothing
CU	See you	NR	Number
CUD	Could	NW	Now
DX	Distance	OP	Operator
ES	And	PSE	Please
FB	Fine business	RCD	Received
FER	For	RPT	Report
FM	From	RX	Receiver
GA	Good afternoon; Go ahead	SN	Soon
		TNX	Thanks
GE	Good evening	TU	Thank you
GM	Good morning	TX	Transmitter
GN	Good night	WX	Weather
GUD	Good	73	Best regards
HAM	Amateur	88	Love and kisses

equipment to track satellites or to control model aircraft. Pictures from distant planets have been transmitted over ham television.

In addition to being fun, amateur radio has a long history of public service. When an earthquake or other disaster strikes and normal means of communication are not working, ham radio operators can put people in touch with each other through the Amateur Radio Emergency Service. Police, rescue services, and other government groups work closely with hams during these times.

▶ HOW TO BECOME A HAM

To obtain a station and operator's license, you must pass a short written examination that tests your knowledge of operating regulations and simple radio theory. You also must prove that you can send and receive international Morse code at five words per minute.

International Morse code is composed of dots and dashes. It is used by commercial and amateur stations in every part of the world. It is the best way to send a radio signal over a great distance under almost any conditions.

Learning the code requires constant practice. Try to associate each letter with its complete set of sounds instead of its individual dots and dashes.

There are five license levels: Novice, Technician, General, Advanced, and Amateur Extra. Each requires a better understanding of radio technology and a greater proficiency in Morse code than the previous level. The higher your level, the more privileges you have.

Additional information on ham radio, including complete licensing information, can be obtained from the American Radio Relay League, Newington, Connecticut 06111.

▶ WHAT IS CB RADIO?

Citizens band, or CB, radio is another form of radio available to the general public. Any person 18 years or older can get a license to operate a CB radio, without taking an examination. Younger people can use the CB radio if supervised by the licensee.

CB radio is designed for local, or short-distance, communication. The station may not use more than 5 watts of power. This limits a typical home CB station to a distance of about 50 kilometers (30 miles). CB units carried in cars and other vehicles have a range of about 25 kilometers (15 miles). In contrast, amateur radio operators may be licensed to use equipment with as much as 1,000 watts of power input. This enables them to communicate over thousands of kilometers.

Every radio station, commercial or noncommercial, has its own call letters. This is the "name" of the station. WB1ADL is an example of a ham's call letters. The first letters indicate the ham's country. The numeral indicates the geographical region—in this case, New England. The letters after the number are unique for that station.

A CB call sign contains three or four letters and four numbers—for example, KGA-1234. In addition, personal names, or "handles," often are used by CB'ers, who have developed a colorful language of their own that is very different from that used by hams.

BOBBIE CHAMALIAN, WB1ADL
American Radio Relay League

INTERNATIONAL MORSE CODE

A	.—	K	—.—	U	..—		
B	—...	L	.—..	V	...—		
C	—.—.	M	——	W	.——		
D	—..	N	—.	X	—..—		
E	.	O	———	Y	—.——		
F	..—.	P	.——.	Z	——..		
G	——.	Q	——.—	Period (.)	.—.—.—		
H	....	R	.—.	Comma (,)	——..——		
I	..	S	...	Query (?)	..——..		
J	.———	T	—	Error	....		

RADIOACTIVE DATING

In the long history of the earth there have been many changes in the kinds of plants and animals that live on earth. There have also been changes in the earth itself. To have a clear picture of the history of the earth and the life it supports, scientists must have an accurate way of finding when changes occurred. One such way is by radioactive dating. In radioactive dating, the ages of objects are determined by analyzing the amounts of radioactive elements they contain. By using radioactive dating methods, scientists have dated many kinds of objects. For example, wood taken from an old Egyptian tomb was found to be 4,800 years old. Scientists have dated many kinds of rocks, the oldest of which are about 3,000,000,000 (billion) years old. By means of radioactive dating, scientists have estimated the age of the earth itself. It is about 4,500,000,000 years old.

▶RADIOACTIVE ELEMENTS

All elements are made up of atoms. Atoms are the basic units, or building blocks, of matter. Atoms of radioactive elements, such as uranium, break down and radiate (give off) tiny particles.

When radioactive atoms give off these particles, the atoms themselves are changed. Atoms of uranium, for example, break down and eventually form atoms of a certain variety of lead. Another radioactive element, thorium, also breaks down and forms lead. The lead that results from radioactive breakdowns, however, is slightly different from ordinary lead. You will read more about this difference later in this article.

The rate at which a radioactive element breaks down is described by its **half-life**. An element's half-life is the time in which half the element's atoms break down. Thorium has a half-life of 14,000,000,000 (billion) years. It would take 14,000,000,000 years for just half the atoms in a given amount of thorium to break down. It would take another 14,000,000,000 years for half the remaining atoms to break down, and so on.

Uranium has a shorter half-life than thorium. There are three varieties of uranium. One has a half-life of 4,500,000,000 years. Another variety has a half-life of 700,000,000

years. The third variety has a half-life of 248,000 years.

Much of the thorium and uranium that was present when the earth first formed is still present in the earth's rocks.

▶DATING THE ROCKS OF THE EARTH

When the earth was first forming, there were no solid rocks. Uranium and thorium atoms moved about freely in the hot, molten earth.

When solid rocks formed, thorium and uranium atoms were imprisoned within the rocks. Many of the thorium and uranium atoms contained within the rocks still remain there today. Some of the thorium and uranium atoms, however, have since become atoms of lead. This lead, also, has remained imprisoned within the rocks, along with the thorium and uranium.

To determine the age of a rock that contains thorium, scientists measure the amount of thorium now present in the rock. They also measure the amount of lead the rock contains. They know the rate at which thorium breaks down to form lead. They can therefore calculate how long it took the lead to form from the thorium.

Suppose, for example, that when a rock first became solid it contained about a pound of thorium. At the end of a year a small amount of lead—about $\frac{1}{1,000,000,000}$ ounce—would have formed. At the end of 1,000,000,000 (billion) years about an ounce of lead would have formed.

Scientists can also date rocks by comparing the amount of uranium in the rocks with the amount of lead formed from the uranium. This is a bit more complicated, for there are three kinds of uranium and each breaks down at a different rate.

There is another difficulty. Suppose the rock contained some lead to begin with; that is, the rock contains lead that did not come from the breakdown of thorium or uranium. Fortunately, scientists can tell this lead from lead that came from radioactive elements.

There are several kinds of lead. Each kind is referred to by a different number. The numbers represent certain differences in the structure of the nucleus, or central part of the atom. When thorium breaks down, it forms one kind of lead—lead-208. One type of uranium forms lead-206. Another type of uranium forms lead-207. Ordinary lead is a mixture of these three kinds of lead with a fourth kind—lead-204. The presence of this fourth kind of lead enables scientists to tell original lead from lead that came from radioactive elements.

Dating with Other Radioactive Elements

Uranium and thorium are not the only radioactive elements that can be used in dating rocks. Two other types of radioactive elements can be used. These are rubidium-87 and potassium-40. These two elements have certain advantages.

Rubidium-87 is especially useful for dating very old rocks. It has a half-life of 50,000,000,000 (billion) years.

Potassium-40 has the advantage of being found in almost all rocks. It has a half-life of 1,300,000,000 years. It is the most common of all the radioactive atoms.

There are other radioactive atoms that break down more rapidly than uranium. But they are present in such small quantities that they are usually not useful for dating.

▶ RADIOCARBON DATING

Thorium and uranium are used to date the age of rocks. To determine the age of things that were once alive, scientists use another radioactive element, carbon-14.

All living things contain carbon. They also contain small amounts of carbon-14, a radioactive variety of carbon. Using carbon-14, scientists can determine the age of wood and clothing—in fact, anything that was once alive. Dating an object by means of carbon-14 is called radiocarbon dating. Radiocarbon dating is used to date objects up to 50,000 years old. It is of special interest to scientists because it can lead to a better understanding of the history of early man.

Carbon-14 is formed by cosmic rays—energetic particles that bombard the earth. These rays smash into atoms and molecules that make up our atmosphere. The atmosphere contains large amounts of nitrogen. Sometimes a cosmic ray hits a nitrogen atom, changing the atom of nitrogen to a radioactive atom of carbon-14.

If cosmic rays were to stop bombarding the earth, the carbon-14 already formed would slowly break down. After 50,000 years or so, little would be left. But cosmic rays keep on bombarding the earth. New carbon-14 is formed at a rate that just balances the breakdown of old carbon-14. This means that there is always a steady level of carbon-14 in the air. The carbon-14 combines with the oxygen of the air, forming carbon dioxide.

Plants constantly absorb carbon dioxide, using it to make their food. This food is used to build and maintain the tissues of the plant. The carbon dioxide used by plants contains small amounts of carbon-14. Therefore, every bit of a living plant contains a small amount of carbon-14.

Animals feed on plants or on other animals that live on plants. This means that an animal's body also contains a small amount of carbon-14. As the carbon-14 breaks down in the tissues of plants and animals, new supplies of carbon-14 are taken in.

When an animal or plant dies, it no longer takes in carbon-14. The carbon-14 that is in the tissues, however, continues breaking down at a steady rate. This rate is determined by the half-life of carbon-14.

Carbon-14 has a half-life of about 5,500 years. This means that about 5,500 years after a plant or animal dies, half the carbon-14 atoms present at the time of death are left. After 11,000 years one quarter of the original carbon-14 atoms are left. After 16,500 years, the carbon-14 atoms are about an eighth of the original amount, and so on. Because carbon-14 breaks down at this steady rate, scientists can determine the age of objects containing carbon-14.

Dating with Carbon-14

Suppose an old piece of wood is picked up in an ancient tomb and taken to a laboratory. There it can be analyzed. It can be heated and turned to carbon. Or it can be burned to release various gases, including carbon dioxide. The carbon or the carbon dioxide contains a few carbon-14 atoms. These atoms of carbon-14 are breaking down. With each breakdown a tiny particle is sent speeding out of the atom.

The carbon or the carbon dioxide is placed in a sensitive instrument called a Geiger counter. The Geiger counter detects the particles given off by the atoms of carbon-14.

(1) While alive, a tree, like any other living thing, contains a constant amount of radioactive carbon. (Black dots to left of drawings represent atoms of radioactive carbon, or carbon-14.)

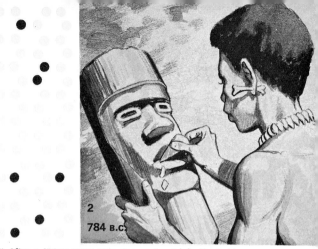

(2) After a living thing dies, the carbon-14 in its tissues continues to break down, or decay. The carving above contains slightly less carbon-14 than the tree from which its wood was taken.

(3) In 1966, 2,750 years after wood was cut from the tree, a scientist using a Geiger counter measures the amount of carbon-14 in the carving. He finds that one fourth of the atoms of carbon-14 have decayed.

(4) After a total of about 5,500 years from the time the wood was cut from the tree, exactly half the atoms of carbon-14 that were present in wood of the living tree will have decayed.

From the number of particles given off, scientists can determine the amount of carbon-14 in the sample.

Scientists know how much carbon-14 is contained in an equal amount of wood from a living tree. This is about the same amount that was contained in the ancient sample at the time of death. From the amount of carbon-14 left in the ancient sample, scientists can tell its age. If, for example, the ancient sample of wood contained half the original amount of carbon-14, it would be about 5,500 years old.

Using radiocarbon dating, scientists have dated wood from old campfires and have estimated when Indians reached various parts of the Americas. Scientists have dated the remains of mammoths and other animals that became extinct, or died out, thousands of years ago. Trees knocked over by glaciers can be dated. This gives scientists an idea of when the continents were covered by these great sheets of ice.

Thus, radioactive dating, including radiocarbon dating, has become a valuable method in the study of the earth's past—and man's past, too.

ISAAC ASIMOV
Boston University School of Medicine

See also RADIOACTIVE ELEMENTS.

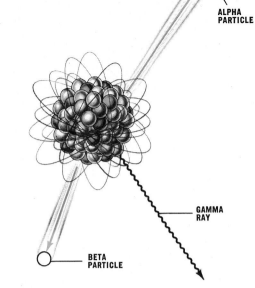

ALPHA PARTICLE

GAMMA RAY

BETA PARTICLE

RADIOACTIVE ELEMENTS

When the element uranium was first discovered in 1789, no one ever dreamed it would become particularly important. For over a century it was just a strange metal with hardly any uses.

Then, in 1896, the French chemist Antoine Henri Becquerel made an interesting discovery. He found that material containing uranium would darken a photographic plate. The uranium seemed to be radiating, or giving off, some sort of penetrating rays. These rays, which are often called radiations, were given off constantly. Uranium was therefore called a radioactive element. In 1898 another French chemist, Marie Curie, found that the metal thorium was also radioactive.

The study of these radioactive elements led to important new ideas about the nature of

HALF-LIFE OF A RADIOACTIVE ELEMENT

SAMPLE OF A RADIOACTIVE ELEMENT (RADIUM—HALF-LIFE: 1,600 YEARS).

AFTER 1,600 YEARS, HALF THE RADIUM ATOMS HAVE BROKEN DOWN.

AFTER ANOTHER 1,600 YEARS, HALF THE REMAINING RADIUM ATOMS HAVE BROKEN DOWN.

AFTER ANOTHER 1,600 YEARS, HALF THE REMAINING ATOMS HAVE BROKEN DOWN.

atoms. (Atoms are the building blocks that make up elements.)

Three Kinds of Rays

Both thorium and uranium are made up of very complicated atoms. At the center of any atom is the **nucleus** (plural: **nuclei**). In complicated atoms, such as those of uranium, the nuclei break down easily and shoot out tiny particles much smaller than the atoms themselves. Some of these particles are fairly heavy. They are called **alpha particles** and are radiated in streams called **alpha rays**. Other particles are very light. They are called **beta particles** and are radiated in streams called **beta rays**.

Finally, there are radiations that are not made up of particles. These radiations consist of very short waves, much like those of X rays, only shorter. These radiations are called **gamma rays**.

When alpha, beta, and gamma rays are given off by nuclei of uranium and thorium atoms, the nature of the atoms themselves is changed. These atoms are no longer atoms of uranium or thorium, but atoms of other elements. These other elements are also radioactive and break down further. After many such changes the atoms become those of lead, an element that is not radioactive. No radiations are given off, and no further changes occur.

The rate at which a radioactive element

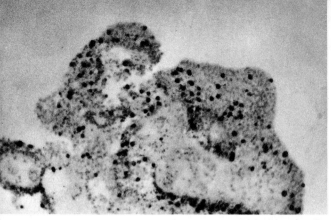

Scientists replace ordinary atoms with atoms of radioactive elements (tracers) to learn more about cell formation. Above: In the photo of human tissue (magnified 100 times) the tracers appear as tiny black dots.

breaks down is called its **half-life**. The half-life of an element is the time it takes for half of its atoms to break down. One variety, or isotope, of uranium has a half-life of 4,500,000,000 years. This means that it takes 4,500,000,000 years for half the atoms in a uranium sample to break down. It also takes 4,500,000,000 years for half the remaining atoms to break down, and so on.

Other elements have much shorter half-lives. One radium isotope has a half-life of less than 1,600 years. The half-life of one of the isotopes of radon is less than 4 days. Such elements are present in very small quantities on earth. In fact, they exist only because they are being formed, very slowly, from uranium and thorium.

The rate at which radioactive elements break down helps scientists determine the age of objects left behind by early man. Such radioactive dating can also help to estimate the age of the earth itself.

RADIOACTIVE ELEMENTS
(by atomic number)

ELEMENT	ATOMIC NUMBER	ELEMENT	ATOMIC NUMBER
Technetium	43	Plutonium	94
Promethium	61	Americium	95
Polonium	84	Curium	96
Astatine	85	Berkelium	97
Radon	86	Californium	98
Francium	87	Einsteinium	99
Radium	88	Fermium	100
Actinium	89	Mendelevium	101
Thorium	90	Nobelium	102
Protactinium	91	Lawrencium	103
Uranium	92	Rutherfordium	104
Neptunium	93	Hahnium	105

Man-Made Elements

The particles given off by radioactive elements can be used as tiny bullets with which to penetrate other atoms. Scientists use these atom-smashing particles to re-arrange the nuclei of atoms. The nuclei can be broken down into simpler nuclei or built up into more complicated ones. In this way scientists can form new elements with atoms even more complicated than those of uranium. Some of these elements, such as neptunium, exist in nature only in very small quantities. Others, like americium, are not found in nature at all. All are radioactive and have very short half-lives. Some of these radioactive elements last only a few seconds before they break down.

Uses of Radioactive Elements

Radioactive elements and radioactive isotopes have many uses. Scientists can replace ordinary atoms in chemical compounds with radioactive atoms. Using special instruments, such as Geiger counters, scientists can follow the particles these tracer atoms leave behind. In this way they can learn much about the details of chemical changes. Radioactive particles can be used to kill bacteria and sterilize food. The particles can also kill cancer cells and can sometimes cure cancer in that way. (However, they must be used carefully, for they can cause cancer as well.)

Radioactive elements are sources of great energy. When a certain particle, called a neutron, bombards an atom of uranium, the uranium nucleus breaks in two. When this occurs, a great deal of energy is released. This energy can be concentrated into a very powerful and destructive nuclear bomb (commonly called an atomic bomb). This same energy release is used for peaceful purposes. For example, nuclear power stations deliver electric current to households without any danger of explosion.

Perhaps in years to come, nuclear power will replace much of the coal and oil now used for energy. Man will then have a better and larger supply of energy for his needs and comfort.

ISAAC ASIMOV
Boston University School of Medicine

See also ATOMS; ELEMENTS; ELEMENTS, SOME FACTS ABOUT; NUCLEAR ENERGY.

One of the world's largest movable radio telescopes is at the National Radio Astronomy Observatory in West Virginia.

RADIO AND RADAR ASTRONOMY

When you look at a clear night sky, you can see the stars. You are able to see them because stars send out light that reaches you across the great distances of space.

Light is a form of radiation. Like all forms of radiation, light travels in waves. Light waves are the only form of radiation that can be seen. When you look at stars and planets through a telescope, you see more of their light waves. Then planets appear bigger and the stars can be seen more clearly.

Besides light, stars send out other forms of radiation. Part of the radiation from stars is sent out as radio waves. Some of these waves can be detected by special radio receivers here on earth. The radio receivers collect and magnify the radio waves, just as ordinary telescopes collect and magnify the picture the light waves give. That is why these radio receivers are called **radio telescopes**.

Radio telescopes are very valuable instruments. Using them, astronomers are learning facts about the universe that could not be known before. Thus, **radio astronomy** has become a very important part of the study of outer space.

There is another kind of radio instrument used by astronomers to learn about objects in space. This instrument, called a radar set, shoots out radio waves in short bursts, like bullets from a gun. When the waves hit an object in space, they bounce back to the radar set on earth.

Radar has been used by astronomers to measure the exact distances to bodies such as the moon and some of the planets and also to track the paths of meteors. Studies like these are called **radar astronomy**.

▶ HOW RADIO ASTRONOMY BEGAN

In 1931 and 1932 an American radio engineer, Karl Jansky (1905–50), was trying to learn what caused the crackling noises that were often heard as static on radios.

Jansky found that some of the static was caused by radio waves given off by thunder-

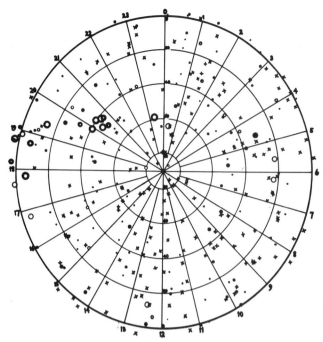

Above: A radio map of the part of the sky than can be seen from the Northern Hemisphere. The map shows the location and strength of sources of radio waves. The strongest sources of radio waves are shown by the open circles, the weakest by the small black dots. Below: Galaxies NGC 4038 and 4039 are part of the constellation Corvus (the crow or raven). These galaxies are a source of intense radio noise. They are either two galaxies in collision or one galaxy splitting in two.

storms. But he also heard strange hissing sounds, even when there were no thunderstorms. This sound was faint and changed its position during the day. Jansky decided that this hissing sound must be caused by radio waves that came from outer space. He noticed that the strongest hissing seemed to come from a part of the Milky Way near the stars of the constellation Sagittarius (the Archer).

Jansky told others about his results, but only one person became interested. He was an American radio ham, Grote Reber (1911–). Reber built a radio telescope in order to study these strange hisses from space. He worked for many years and at last was able to prove that Jansky was correct. Radio waves were coming from the Milky Way. The science of radio astronomy had begun.

▶ RADIO WAVES FROM SPACE

High up in the earth's atmosphere are layers of air that are electrified. These layers of air, called the ionosphere, act like a mirror to most radio waves and reflect them. Only part of the radio radiation is able to pass through the ionosphere. Only those radio waves that pass through the ionosphere can be observed with radio telescopes.

The length of radio waves from outer space is very short compared with the wavelengths used in ordinary radio broadcasting and in television. Radio astronomers must build special radio sets and antennae to be able to receive the short radio waves from outer space.

The short-wave radio radiation can be received by the radio set only if the antennae are pointing in the direction from which the waves are coming. This fact is of great assistance to the astronomer because it shows him the direction in the sky of the source of the radio radiation. He is able to point the antennae at the part of the sky he wants to study and be sure he is receiving the radiation from that part only. Using information gained this way, astronomers have been making "radio maps" of the heavens.

▶ RADIO TELESCOPES

There are many kinds of radio telescopes, but all of them consist of two parts—an antenna and a radio receiver. The antenna is

Radio signals received by a radio telescope are recorded by pen in the form of wavy lines on paper.

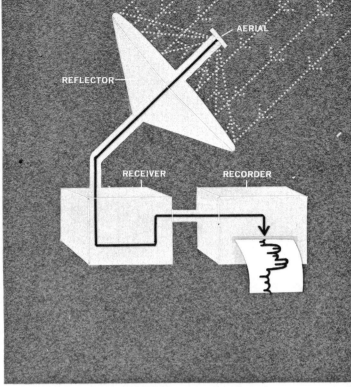

Radio waves striking the reflector of a radio telescope are focused on the aerial and then sent to a recorder.

often a huge, spectacular-looking metal dish. It may be fitted on a movable stand or mounting, so that it can be pointed to any part of the sky. The large metal dish is what people usually think of when they think of a radio telescope. But the radio receiver is an equally important part. Without the receiver the huge antenna would be of no use.

Special kinds of radio receivers are needed to magnify, or amplify, the incoming waves. This is because the radio waves collected by the antenna are often very weak.

After the radio signals are amplified, they may be sent to a loudspeaker that lets the astronomer hear their hissing noise. Usually, however, radio astronomers make a record of the radio waves on paper. A pen recorder attached to the receiver writes down the signals in the form of a wavy line on a strip of paper. In this way radio astronomers have permanent records of their observations. They are then able to study the written record whenever and as often as they wish.

▶RADIO TELESCOPE ANTENNAE

Radio telescopes differ from one another in the kind of antennae they use. The best-known antenna is the steerable paraboloid, which can be pointed to almost every part of the sky.

A paraboloid is a surface shaped like a deep soup bowl. When radio waves hit any part of the surface of the bowl, they are reflected to a certain point in the bowl. This point is called the focus. The waves are all collected at the focus and sent to the receiver.

The antenna of this kind of radio telescope works somewhat like the ordinary reflecting telescope that astronomers use. A reflecting telescope has a large glass mirror to collect the light sent out by the stars and other bodies in space. The mirror reflects this light to a focus.

In the radio telescope the "mirror" is a metal framework. This framework is covered with either wire netting or thin sheets of metal. The wire netting is an excellent reflector for radio wavelengths of a yard or more. These waves are too long to "slip through" the holes in the netting.

There is a small aerial, or antenna, at the focus of the radio telescope "mirror." The antenna passes the collected radio waves to the radio receiver. In most radio telescopes this antenna is a dipole. It is called a dipole because it is made of two metal poles.

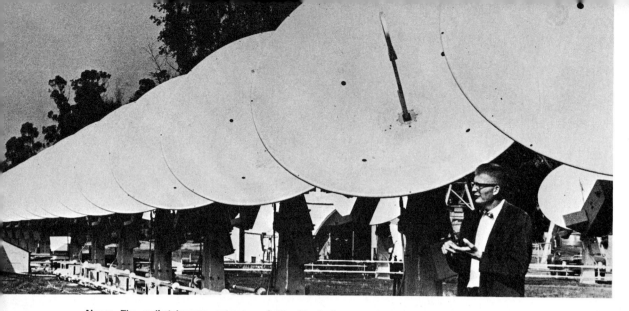

Above: The radio-telescope antennae of the Stanford University interferometer in California. Below: A horn-shaped antenna at Holmdel, New Jersey. The antenna was built to receive radio signals bounced off the Echo I satellite.

If the radio telescope is to receive shorter radio waves, the dipole is replaced by a flat-sided metal tube called a waveguide. The very short radio waves can travel down a waveguide better than down a wire.

Not all radio telescopes have a bowl-shaped antenna to collect radio waves. Some have a long wire frame bent into a curve. Others have two flat screens of wire netting criss-crossing each other. There are even special radio telescopes for studying the sun. The antenna of such a telescope consists of a dipole and many metal rods or a sheet of wire netting to act as a reflector.

Reflectors can be used singly or in arrangements of two or more. A radio telescope using more than one reflector is called an interferometer. The radio waves collected by each reflector interfere with the waves collected by the other reflector. Each antenna is pointed directly toward the source of the radio signals. The interference cancels out some of the radio signals and strengthens others received by each reflector. By using an interferometer, a radio astronomer can pinpoint the locations in the sky from which radio waves are coming.

ADVANTAGES OF RADIO TELESCOPES

In bad weather ordinary telescopes cannot be used to observe or take photographs of the sky. But radio telescopes can operate in all kinds of weather. This is because radio waves are not affected by mist or fog or other kinds of weather that make it impossible for astronomers to see the light waves from stars.

Observatories for optical telescopes are built on high ground and even on mountains, so that they can be above the thicker, dustier air near the ground. Radio astronomers, however, can build their radio telescopes in almost any place they find convenient. The thing they must avoid is electric machinery, such as motors and generators, because it can send out radio waves that might mix with the radio signals from space.

▶ RADAR ASTRONOMY

In radio astronomy the heavenly bodies produce radio signals that are picked up on earth. In radar astronomy scientists themselves produce the radio signals and bounce them off nearby astronomical objects.

Radar Telescopes

A radio telescope can be used as a radar telescope by connecting a special transmitter and receiver to the antenna. The transmitter produces pulses of radio waves. The antenna sends these pulses out into space. Some of the radio pulses hit objects in the sky and are reflected back to earth. When the pulses return again to the antenna, the receiver amplifies them.

The astronomer must measure accurately the time between the sending of the radio pulses and their return. Knowing the speed of the pulses, the astronomer has little difficulty finding the distance to the object from which they have been reflected.

Radar astronomy can be used for studying any of the nearer objects in space, such as the moon, the sun, comets and meteors, and the planet Jupiter.

The stars, however, are too far away for

Above: The giant radio-radar telescope at Arecibo, Puerto Rico. The bowl, set among the mountains, is 1,000 feet in diameter. Below: A 50-foot U.S. Army radar dish at Fort Monmouth, New Jersey, used to track the Explorer satellites.

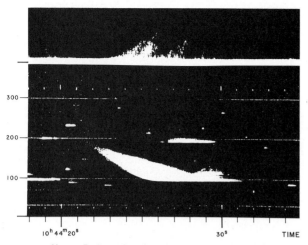

Above: Radar echo of a meteor trail is recorded on meteor radar chart. Below: Giacobini's comet, photographed in 1906. Radar probes of large comets that near the earth may lead to understanding what comets are.

cause these pulses bounce off the electrified gas and are reflected back to earth. This means that astronomers can make very accurate measurements of the sun's distance (or at least the distance to the corona). They can also make studies of the corona itself. The corona keeps changing its shape and size. Radar provides a way of finding out what is happening during these changes.

Radar echoes have been received from the moon and from Venus and Jupiter.

Radar Studies of Meteors

One of the most important uses of radar astronomy has been in the study of meteors. These lumps of rock and metal enter our atmosphere from outer space. They travel at speeds up to 45 miles a second. At that speed they become so hot because of friction against the upper air that most of them are vaporized.

Perhaps you have seen a "shooting star" in the sky at night. What you saw was the faint trail of electrified air particles that a meteor left behind for a second or two after it vaporized.

Before the invention of radar no one could observe a meteor unless it left a bright trail. Now astronomers can map or plot meteor paths more accurately than ever before. They can do this by means of radar pulses that are reflected back by meteor trails. The speeds and sizes of meteors can be measured as well.

Astronomers have found that some meteors are so small that 250 side by side would measure only 1 inch. They have learned that many meteors travel together in swarms that continually orbit the sun in long oval-shaped paths.

Radar astronomy may be used to study comets. Comets orbit the sun and are thought to be collections of ice and dust particles clustered together. Comets come close to the sun in their orbits and also fairly close to the earth. It should be possible, therefore, to probe them with radar, although a large, close comet is needed for this experiment. When such a comet arrives, it seems certain that astronomers will be able to discover new facts about comets. These facts may answer many of the questions scientists still have about exactly what comets are.

radar astronomy to work. For example, a radio pulse sent out to the star nearest our solar system would not return until 9 years later. This is the time a radio pulse takes to make a round trip to the nearest star. The other stars are all very much farther away.

Although radio astronomers cannot use radar to study distant stars, they can use it to learn about the star nearest us—the sun. The sun's outer layer of electrified gas, called the corona, can be studied by radar pulses be-

THERMAL AND NONTHERMAL RADIATION

Radio astronomers have discovered that there are two kinds of radio waves—thermal and nonthermal—produced by bodies in space. Some bodies in space, such as the sun, are so hot that they give off all kinds of radiations—heat, light, radio, and so on.

The radio waves that come from such hot objects are called **thermal radio radiation**. ("Thermal" is from a Greek word meaning "heat.") Radio astronomers observe thermal radio radiation from the sun, from a few other stars, and from clouds of hydrogen gas that surround some of the very hottest stars.

The second type of radio waves that radio astronomers can observe are called **nonthermal radio radiation**. Nonthermal radio radiation is produced when an object gives off almost all its radiation energy as radio waves. The radio waves you receive on your radio set are nonthermal. These waves come from the broadcasting antenna, which never becomes hot as it sends out the radio waves. The broadcasting antenna is an example of a nonthermal radiation source.

Certain bodies in space are sources of nonthermal radio waves. These bodies are called **radio stars**. This does not mean that they are stars like the sun. They may be clouds of gas or other objects in space. These dark gases may not be visible through ordinary telescopes. Radio telescopes, however, are able to locate them. Through the science of radio astronomy much is being learned about these sources of nonthermal radio radiation.

RADIO ASTRONOMY STUDIES OF THE SUN

Studies of the sun by radio astronomers have revealed that the corona is much larger than previously thought. The corona is visible only when the bright disk of the sun is blocked from view. This happens during a total solar eclipse, when the moon is exactly between the earth and the sun.

Astronomers have taken telescope photographs that show that the corona extends out farther than the portion that is visible to you. But it was radio astronomers who were able to prove that the corona extends far beyond the part visible even in telescope photographs. Some astronomers are now suggesting that the corona may extend as far as earth.

A panel of dials and switches controls the radio telescope antenna, seen through the window.

RADIO ASTRONOMY STUDIES OF THE PLANETS

The radio waves from the sun reach the other planets in our solar system. Some of these radio waves are reflected by the planets. From this fact it is possible to learn how hot a planet is. Early radio astronomy observations showed that Venus seemed to be hotter than astronomers had expected it to be. Later, the space satellite Mariner II showed that this seemed to be correct, but more observations are needed.

Occasionally radio telescopes have received radio signals that seem to be emitted from a spot on the giant planet Jupiter. Why this happens is still a mystery. Some astronomers believe that these radio waves may be caused by electrical storms in Jupiter's atmosphere.

RADIO ASTRONOMY EXPLORES THE MILKY WAY

Our sun is one of many billions of stars that are all part of our own galaxy, or island universe. Our galaxy also contains dust and gases. For many years astronomers were trying to learn the exact size and shape of our galaxy. This was very difficult because the dust and dark gases prevented astronomers from seeing the center of the galaxy or the distant regions beyond. But radio waves are not scattered by the dust as are light waves, and so they travel through the dust. The radio waves are plotted by astronomers on a radio map of the sky.

Astronomers have found that our galaxy is spiral-shaped, like a pinwheel. They have

The galaxy containing our solar system is probably shaped like the spiral galaxy above.

The strongest known source of radio noise is thought to be in two galaxies in collision.

found that our galaxy is similar to many millions of other spiral galaxies, which they have already photographed through ordinary telescopes. They have also learned that the sun lies in one of the spiral arms. Without radio telescopes it would not have been possible to make this discovery.

Many radio stars give off little light. Their radiation is mainly nonthermal. Radio astronomers found the strongest of all the radio emitters in the constellation Cygnus. Yet photographs taken with the 200-inch telescope on Mount Palomar in California show only a fuzzy pair of dots where the radio waves seem to come from. Astronomers think these may be two huge galaxies colliding with each other or perhaps an immense galaxy splitting in two.

Radio astronomers have found another strong radio source. Photographs have shown that this also seems to be two galaxies colliding or splitting apart.

Strong radio waves are also coming from a place where two galaxies seem to be orbiting around each other.

These discoveries have shown that radio astronomy is a very powerful means for penetrating into the depths of space. But only certain radio waves can penetrate our atmosphere. Therefore, radio telescopes cannot observe all the sources of radio waves.

One way to overcome this difficulty is to put radio telescopes into space capsules and orbit them. Radio astronomers already have designed instruments for this work. They expect many new discoveries when orbiting radio telescopes receive more radio waves from space.

Radio telescopes are being improved constantly. New ones are being designed to pinpoint the position of objects more exactly and to pick up weaker, more distant signals.

Radio telescopes are now one of the most powerful tools that astronomers have. These instruments are helping scientists probe deeper and deeper into the mysteries of the universe.

COLIN A. RONAN
Fellow of the Royal Astronomical Society

See also ASTRONOMY; ELECTRONICS; QUASARS AND PULSARS; RADAR, SONAR, LORAN, AND SHORAN; RADIO; TELESCOPES.

France's TGV (*train à grande vitesse*—"high-speed train") began regular operations in 1981. It is the world's fastest train. The TGV is powered electrically from overhead lines.

RAILROADS

The sound of a train whistle has always meant adventure and romance. The railroad brought passengers and goods from faraway places. It offered an escape from dreary life on the farm or in the small town. Before railroads, few people were able to travel far from their homes. As a result, people from one village were often regarded as foreigners by people who lived only a few miles away. Railroads, by making it possible for large numbers of people to travel quickly and cheaply, helped break down this isolation. People's horizons were widened. Railroads aided the settlement of the American and Canadian West by giving farmers and ranchers a way to get their grain and cattle to market. Railroads stimulated trade between different parts of countries and so helped to knit countries closer together.

Before railroads, most cities were located on the seacoast or on rivers because people depended on water transportation for their supplies. The railroad made it possible to have cities anywhere rails could be laid.

Railroads were the first kind of quick, cheap mass transportation. Today, in spite of competition from cars, trucks, buses, and airplanes, railroads still play an extremely important part in getting people and goods to their destinations.

▶ **WHAT IS A RAILROAD?**

In its simplest sense a railroad is a set of tracks over which cars can run. In a broader sense a railroad includes the track, roadbed, freight and passenger cars, locomotives, bridges, tunnels, yards and stations, repair shops, and signal systems. All these things are necessary if the railroad is to work smoothly and safely.

Roadbed and Track

The basis of railroad operation is the track and the roadbed beneath it. The track itself consists of two parallel steel rails fastened by spikes and metal tie plates to wooden crossties underneath. The ties hold the track together and keep the rails the proper distance apart. The ties are made of wood rather than a more permanent material, such as metal or concrete, because wood cushions the tracks better.

The rails are joined end to end by a sandwichlike arrangement of steel pieces called angle bars. One angle bar goes on each side of the rails, and the whole arrangement is held together by bolts that go through holes in the angle bars and the rails.

A little gap is left between the ends of the rails because steel expands with heat. If there were no gap to allow for this expansion, the hot summer sun might expand the rails so much that they would push against each other and buckle. These little gaps at the joints are what makes a train's wheels click as they go over the rails. Some railroads use "continuous rail"—that is, standard lengths of rail welded together into lengths of a mile or more. This gives a quieter ride by reducing the clicking of the wheels. The rails are laid during hot weather, when they are fully expanded. They are spiked down extra tight to counteract the effects of contraction.

The distance between the rails is called the **gauge.** In the United States, Canada, Mexico, the United Kingdom, and many other countries, a standard gauge of 4 feet 8½ inches is used. The Soviet Union uses a gauge of 5 feet. Spain and Portugal use an even wider gauge, 5 feet 6 inches. Until 1886 some railroads in the United States used a gauge of 5 feet. There are also a number of narrow gauges, ranging from 3 feet 6 inches down to 2 feet. Narrow gauge became popular in the 1870's because it was cheaper and easier to construct than standard gauge. Narrow-gauge locomotives and cars were also cheaper than those for standard gauge. Many narrow-gauge lines were built in the western United States and other mountainous regions. Most of these lines in the United States have disappeared, but narrow gauge is still important in Latin America, Asia, and Africa.

The track rests on a layer of **ballast,** which is usually crushed rock or gravel. Ballast does several important jobs. It holds the ties firmly in place and cushions the track. It checks the growth of grass and weeds. It lets water drain away freely. Drainage is very important. If water were not drained away from the track, the weight of the trains would churn the ground into soft mud, and the track would sink into it. To avoid this, track and ballast are laid on top of a mound of earth, or embankment, above the ground level.

Preparing the Roadbed. Building a railroad is a great deal of work. Locomotives cannot haul trains up a steep slope, and the track must be made as level as possible. But there are very few places in the world where the ground is level for more than a couple of miles in any direction. The surface of the land is full of hills and valleys, dips and rises. Before the tracks are laid down, an artificial roadbed must be prepared.

Low spots in the ground are filled in with embankments of earth and rock. High ground is dug away to make a cut, or open trench. If a hill is too high for a cut, railroad builders may tunnel through the hill or else run the roadbed around it. Very deep valleys may be crossed on bridges rather than on embankments.

But it is not practical to build a perfectly level roadbed. The cost would be too great. Therefore, most railroad track has a slight grade. The grade is the rate at which the track climbs or falls. A rise or fall of 2 feet for every hundred feet of track is called a 2-percent grade. This is considered a quite steep grade in railroad building. Most mainline tracks in the United States have no grades steeper than 1 percent. In some areas, however, it is impossible to avoid steep grades. In Switzerland, for example, some lines have grades of 7 percent. This is just about as steep a grade as a train can climb without a rack-and-pinion. (A rack is a toothed third rail. A pinion is a toothed, or cogged, wheel that meshes with the rack.)

Curves also are unavoidable, but railroad builders try to keep them as gentle as possible. Sharp curves are dangerous because a speeding train may leave the track if the curve is too sharp.

Much track is laid by machines instead of by hand. Pre-assembled sections of track, ties and all, are lowered into place by railroad cranes. The workers who build and maintain the track and roadbed have many other machines to help them. There are power-driven spike drivers and wrenches for bolting the rails together. There are machines for removing and replacing worn-out ties. Mechanical tampers pack the ballast around the ties. There are even machines that pick up the ballast, clean it, and put it back on the roadbed without disturbing the tracks.

Keeping the track open in bad weather often becomes a problem. Snow may block the tracks. Floods may wash them away. In mountainous country, landslides may block the tracks. While the damaged track is being repaired or the obstruction is being cleared away, a "shoo-fly" track is laid. This is a temporary track over which trains are detoured.

In regions with cold winters, winter storms are the railroads' worst enemies. Switches freeze, snowdrifts block the tracks, and telegraph wires and power lines break. It is a real battle to keep the trains running. To clear the tracks, railroads make use of a small army of machines. For shallow drifts, there are wedge-shaped plows pushed by a locomotive that shoves the snow off the tracks. Power-driven rotary brooms sweep the snow away. Rotary plows are used to cut through high drifts. At the front end these machines have a big wheel that literally chews its way through the snow and flings it off to the side. In yards and terminals, the snow may be melted away from switches by oil-burning machines.

▶ LOCOMOTIVES

There are many kinds of locomotives, large and small, designed for different jobs. Some locomotives are specially designed to pull passenger trains at high speeds. Others are built to haul mile-long freight trains. Some are designed for switching duty. Many loco-

motives are designed for both freight and passenger service.

A locomotive is actually a power plant on wheels. Besides pulling trains, it supplies compressed air for the train's braking system. Steam heat and hot water for passenger trains also come from the locomotive.

For more than 100 years the steam locomotive was the chief source of power on railroads all over the world. Today in many countries the diesel locomotive has taken the place of the steam locomotive, and only a few steam locomotives remain in service. Diesel locomotives are more costly than steam locomotives, but diesels have many advantages. They are cheaper to run, they get much more energy out of their fuel, they cause less wear and tear on the track, and, above all, they need far less maintenance than steam locomotives. The average steam locomotive spends a great deal of its time in the shop for servicing and repairs.

Electric locomotives came into use in the late 1800's but, because of the high cost of electrifying a railroad, never rivaled steam or diesel power. However, Switzerland and a few other countries that are poor in coal and oil but rich in hydroelectric power depend mostly on electric locomotives. Electric locomotives are also well-suited for work in and

Locomotives are serviced and refueled in one time-saving operation at a service depot on the Southern Pacific Railroad.

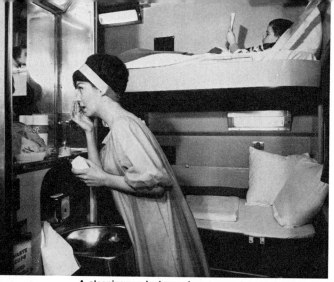

A sleeping-car bedroom has compact accommodations.

near cities, because they create no exhaust fumes.

In recent years new types of locomotives have been developed. The most successful of these has been the gas-turbine locomotive, which is used for long-distance freight service in the mountains of the western United States.

Passenger Service

At the end of World War I there were 6,000 long-distance passenger trains operating in the United States. By 1970 there were fewer than 300 passenger trains in regular service. One of the reasons for this decline was the competition of airlines and private automobiles. Another was rising costs. In fact, railroad managements claimed that they lost money on passenger service.

In 1970, the United States Congress passed the National Railroad Passenger Act. The pur-
pose of this act was to save as much as possible of the United States' passenger rail service, thus relieving pressure on crowded highways and air lanes. The act created a new agency, the National Railroad Passenger Corporation, now called Amtrak, to carry out this mission. Amtrak went into effect in 1971.

Amtrak's plan was to concentrate on improving service on heavily traveled routes while cutting out routes that carried few passengers. Amtrak leased track, equipment, and train crews from railroads that joined the plan, while the railroads handled the actual operation of the passenger trains. Railroads were free to join the plan or not.

Meanwhile, Japan and several European nations were going ahead with plans for new, high-speed rail lines between major cities. Trains on some of these lines were to move at average speeds of 150 miles per hour.

Commuter trains carry people from their homes in the suburbs to nearby city business and shopping centers. These trains have only coaches. Commuter coaches have seats for as many as 125 passengers. On some lines, commuter coaches are double-decked.

Long-distance passenger trains may have 15 to 17 cars, including mail, baggage, and express cars, day coaches, sleepers, dining car, lounge or club car, and observation car.

The dining car is a restaurant on wheels, where passengers can get breakfast, lunch, or dinner. Meals are prepared in a small kitchen at one end of the car. On some railroads the whole car is a dining room, and the kitchen is in a separate car. Electric eyes open the

Left: Dining car on one of Europe's crack express trains. Right: Many long-distance trains provide lounge cars for passengers.

A vista-dome car lets passengers enjoy the scenery.

doors between the two cars as the waiters pass back and forth with their trays.

Sleeping cars are cleverly designed so that the passengers have seats by day and beds at night. Berths (beds) fold down out of the wall, and an attendant called a porter makes them up.

Long-distance trains also carry lounge cars and club cars, where refreshments are served and where passengers can play cards. On railroads in the western United States and Canada, trains often carry vista-dome cars. A vista-dome car has a raised glass-enclosed dome on the roof, giving passengers an excellent view of the scenery in every direction.

At the head (front) end of the train are the mail, baggage, and express cars.

Mail cars are post offices on wheels. Inside them mail clerks sort mail while the train rolls on toward its destination. Mail is picked up and delivered at stations along the way. Express trains can pick up and deliver mail without stopping. The mail sack is hung on an arm beside the track. As the train rushes by, a hook protruding from the mail car catches the mail sack. Another hook by the track catches the mail from the train.

Baggage cars carry travelers' heavy luggage. Express cars are for fast shipment of goods that are too heavy or bulky to be sent by mail.

▶ FREIGHT SERVICE

The big business of most railroads is freight hauling. More freight moves by rail than by any other form of transportation—almost as much as by all other forms combined. To handle this vast movement of goods, American railroads alone have more than 1,800,000 freight cars in service. Through agreements between the railroads, any car of any North American railroad can be sent anywhere in the United States, Canada, and Mexico. That is why cars of many different railroads are often seen in the same train. The cars are so designed that they can all be coupled together and braked together. Even the steps, ladders, running boards, and hand brakes are always in the same place. This system has the advantage of allowing a carload of freight to be sent over many different rail lines without having to be unloaded and reloaded each time it reaches another railroad.

Freight Cars. There are almost as many

kinds of freight cars as there are loads to be carried. There are boxcars for general freight, tank cars for liquids, hopper cars for coal and sand, flatcars for lumber, steel beams, and bulky equipment such as tractors, rack cars for automobiles, and many others.

SOME IMPORTANT DATES IN RAILROAD HISTORY

1804 Richard Trevithick builds and operates the first steam locomotive.

1825 The Stockton & Darlington opens for business.

1826 The first railroad company in the United States begins operations.

1829 George Stephenson's locomotive "Rocket" wins the Rainhill Trials in England; the "Stourbridge Lion" becomes the first full-sized locomotive to run in the United States.

1830 Baltimore & Ohio and South Carolina railroads open in the United States; "Best Friend of Charleston" pulls first steam-drawn passenger train in United States.

1831 Mail first carried by railroad.

1835 Construction begins on first railroad in Canada.

1839 Beginning of Railway Express Service.

1850 President Fillmore signs the first Land Grant Act.

1851 The telegraph is first used in train dispatching; the first refrigerator car is placed in service.

1855 Railroads of the United States and Canada linked by Niagara Suspension Bridge.

1859 George Pullman builds first Pullman sleeping car.

1862 The first post-office car is placed in service.

1868 Eli Janney patents the automatic safety coupler.

1869 Completion of first transcontinental line in United States; George Westinghouse patents his first air brake.

1883 Railroads adopt standard time zones.

1885 Canada's first transcontinental railroad is completed.

1886 Railroads of the United States adopt uniform nationwide gauge.

1887 Interstate Commerce Commission is formed, with power to regulate railroad rates.

1893 New York Central's locomotive "999" reaches a measured speed of 181 kilometers (112.5 miles) an hour—the first locomotive to better 160 kilometers (100 miles) an hour.

1895 Congress passes a law requiring all trains in the United States to have air brakes and safety couplers.

1895 First use of electric locomotive on a main line.

1924 Diesel locomotive first used in United States.

1934 First streamlined passenger trains.

1955 Electric locomotive pulls passenger train at 330 kilometers (205 miles) an hour in France.

1964 Japan opens the New Tokaido Line for high-speed, long-distance passenger service, with express trains averaging 200 kilometers (125 miles) an hour.

1970 United States Congress creates the National Passenger Corporation (Amtrak) to reorganize railroad passenger service.

1981 France begins operating its TGV (*train à grande vitesse*—"high-speed train"). It is capable of a speed of 380 kilometers (236 miles) an hour.

Boxcars are the most important type of freight car. There are more boxcars than any other kind of railroad car. A boxcar is an enclosed car with a big sliding door on each side for loading and unloading freight. It resembles a big windowless box on wheels. Boxcars were formerly built of wood, but today they are built of steel. They carry grain, flour, canned goods, clothing, shoes, refrigerators, stoves, and other goods that must be protected from the weather.

A refrigerator car is an insulated boxcar for transporting fresh fruits, vegetables, meat, dairy products, and other foods that must be kept cold. Most refrigerator cars are cooled by fans blowing air over ice. The ice is stored in big bins, called bunkers, located at each end of the car or in an overhead tank. The ice is loaded through hatches in the roof of the car. Many refrigerator cars have their own mechanical refrigeration systems and do not need ice. Some refrigerator cars are equipped with heating systems to protect their cargoes from freezing in winter.

Cattle, sheep, and pigs are hauled to market in stock cars, which are actually boxcars with sides made of open slats. The slats let in fresh air for the animals to breathe. There are troughs for water and feed. Stock cars for sheep and pigs have two decks.

Gondolas are open-topped cars with low sides and ends. Some gondola cars have hinged ends or sides that drop down for unloading. Gondolas carry heavy, bulky loads, like iron, steel, logs, gravel, and stone. They also carry containers, big waterproof and fireproof boxes of steel that hold up to 5 or 6 tons of freight. Containers are much used for shipments of freight that do not take up a whole carload. They are easily transferred between railroad cars and trucks for door-to-door delivery. Containers cut the cost of freight handling. The goods inside them are not touched from the time they are loaded until they reach their destination. Each time goods are unloaded and reloaded adds to the total cost of shipping them.

Flatcars are open platforms on wheels. They carry logs, blocks of stone, tractors, farm machinery, bulky industrial equipment, and freight containers. Special flatcars with a sunken center, called well-type flatcars, are used for moving very large pieces of equipment, such as giant transformers for electric power plants, that would otherwise stand too high to pass under bridges and tunnels. Some extra-long flatcars have two eight-wheeled trucks at each end—32 wheels in all—to spread the heavy load over the track. Flatcars equipped with three-decker racks carry automobiles.

An interesting use of flatcars is in "piggyback" freight service. Highway truck trailers are loaded on flatcars and sent by rail to distant points. In this way a long haul over a crowded highway is avoided. At their destinations, the trailers are unloaded and sent on to deliver their cargoes at the customers' factories or warehouses.

Hopper cars are open-topped cars with high sides and ends. Their bottoms are equipped with hoppers, or chutes, that can be opened to dump the load. They carry coal, ore, sand, and gravel. Covered hopper cars carry flour, grain, and cement. Hopper cars are unloaded on an elevated ramp. The loads fall down into storage bins underneath the ramp.

Tank cars are steel tanks on wheels. They carry all sorts of liquids: oil, gasoline, acids and other chemicals, wine, milk, and orange juice. Tankers that carry chemicals and food products are lined with glass or porcelain. Specially reinforced tank cars carry gases under high pressure. Other tank cars carry powdered materials. All in all, there are nearly 100 types of tank cars.

At the end of every freight train is the caboose, traditionally painted red. The caboose serves as the conductor's office and the home of the train crew while they are on the road. It has a stove, lockers, bunks, a desk for the conductor, and places to stow flags, lanterns, and emergency tools. There is a raised watchtower, or cupola, on the roof. From the cupola the conductor or a brakeman can watch the train while it is moving and look out for signals from the train crew. Some cabooses have big bay windows on their sides instead of a cupola on the roof. The caboose carries marker lamps on its rear end to show that it is the end of the train.

Just as there are many kinds of freight cars, so there are many kinds of freight trains. Some trains haul just one kind of load in one type of car, for instance, a solid train of hopper cars carrying coal, gondola cars carrying ore, or refrigerator cars carrying oranges. Trains of stock cars carry animals from ranch and farm to the stockyards. "Piggyback" trains are made up entirely of flatcars carrying loaded highway truck trailers. Some trains haul containers only. But the largest number of freight trains haul mixed freight—all sorts of cars and cargoes.

Every freight shipment, large or small, has a ticket called a waybill, which shows the nature of the shipment, where it came from and where it is going, and the number of the car that carries it. The conductor of the train keeps a record of all shipments.

Railroad terminals at seaports and lake ports have amazing machines to transfer freight between ships and trains. There are huge dumping machines that pick up a section of track with a loaded car of coal or ore, turn it over, and dump the load into the hold of a ship. The whole process takes only a minute and a half. Ships are unloaded with giant grab buckets that dip up tons of ore at a single bite. Grain and cement are often sucked up through giant air hoses.

Although most people do not think of railroads as having anything to do with the water, some railroads operate their own fleets of car ferries, tugs, barges, and steamships. Sometimes freight cars are shipped hundreds of miles by water before being delivered to their final destinations by rail.

The Freight Yard. Freight trains begin and end their runs in classification yards, where the trains are broken up and the cars are re-arranged into new trains according to their destinations. These yards are made up of groups of tracks connected by switches. Each track splits up into a number of sidings (side tracks), like the trunk and branches of a tree.

A big freight yard is a busy place. There is always something going on. Trains are continually arriving and departing, day and night. At night, work goes on under floodlights.

When a train arrives with cars to be sorted, the locomotive is uncoupled and a switching engine pushes the cars to the top of a slope called the hump. The cars are uncoupled and allowed to run down the slope to the classification tracks. An operator in a control tower controls the switches so that each car goes onto the correct track. The speed of the rolling cars is controlled by devices called car retarders, which squeeze the wheels against the rails. The operator in the control tower works the car retarders from his control panel. The operator has a list that tells him where each car is to go, and he stops the cars when they have reached their assigned spots. Before car retarders came into use, a man had to ride each car and stop it with the hand brake.

Electronic equipment makes it possible for a single operator in a control tower to run a whole freight yard by pushing buttons on his control panel. An electronic detector spots cracked wheels as the cars roll slowly past it. Another electronic device weighs freight cars while they are moving. Trackside scanners "read" identifying color-coded strips on the sides of freight cars and relay the information to a centralized computer that keeps track of the cars' location. Two-way radios enable the operator in the control tower to speak to engineers in their locomotives. Portable walkie-talkie sets and teletypes enable yard clerks along the track to relay information about cars and their loads to the tower. In some large yards, television helps speed the sorting of cars onto the proper track.

▶ **SIGNALS AND COMMUNICATIONS**

From the earliest days of railroading, various kinds of signals have been used to keep trains from running into each other. One of the first types of trackside signals was a red-painted board placed on a high post at each station. The station agent set the board by a handle on the side of the post. When the line was clear, the board was turned up edgewise. When the broad side of the board faced the oncoming train horizontally, it meant "stop." At night a red lantern was hung from each end of the board to mark its position. The term "board" is still used in railroading. "Clear board," for instance, means "proceed."

Another early signal device was a large white ball hung from a pole. The ball was lowered to indicate "stop" and raised to show that the way was clear ahead. The expression "highball" is used even today to mean a go-ahead signal. (It also means running a train at high speed.)

An early type of signal that is still used is the semaphore, a long arm or blade pivoted at one end to a pole. Like the signal board, the semaphore indicates clear track ahead by a vertical position of its arm. A horizontal arm means "stop," and a halfway position means "proceed with caution." Today's semaphores, often set on special bridges over the track, give their messages by position during the day and by colored lights at night. The lights—green for clear, yellow for caution, and red for stop—are actually colored lenses arranged so that an electric light shines through a different one in each position of the semaphore arm.

Many railroads use lights for signals both day and night. These may be position light signals. These are rows of yellow lights that can be vertical, diagonal, or horizontal. Or they may be red, yellow, and green like traffic lights. Some railroads use a combination of color and position lights.

Before the telegraph came into use, railroad men had no way of communicating with each other between distant stations. When a train left a station, the signalman would set the signals at "stop." After a set amount of time, he would set the signals for "clear." But once the train was out of sight, the signalman had no way of knowing whether the train had passed on safely or whether it had broken down. This meant that the engineer of the following train might find himself bearing down on a stalled train and in danger of a collision.

The invention of the telegraph solved this problem. Stationmasters and signalmen along the line could tell each other when a train reached a station and when it left there. Railroading became safer.

Telegraphic train orders came into use to control train movements. They are still used on many lines today.

The block system of train control is widely used today. Each track is divided into sections called blocks, which are of varying lengths. No train is permitted to enter a block if another train is already in it. Signals at each end of the block show whether it is clear or not. For many years the signals were hand-operated. Modern railroads, however, have an automatic block-signal system. An electric current flowing through the rail sets the signals. When all switches are closed and no train or other obstruction is in the block, the signal shows "clear." When a train enters the block, its wheels and axles short-circuit the current, and the signal changes to "stop." A broken rail or an obstruction across the tracks will also interrupt the flow of current and make the signal read "stop." The signals are usually arranged so that they show "caution" for a block that a train has just left and change to "clear" only when the train is two blocks away.

On some railroads locomotive cabs have a small panel that duplicates the block signal lights. These cab signals can easily be read by the engineer at night or when fog, rain, or snow might hide the trackside signals. Cab signals add greatly to safety at night and in bad weather. Another safety device used on some railroads is an automatic control that stops the train if the engineer fails to obey a stop signal.

An interlocking signal system, in which

Three-decker automobile rack cars.

A traveling crane loads freight containers onto flatcars.

Hauled by four powerful diesel-electric units, a freight train snakes its way across the Nevada desert.

signals and switches are set so as to give one train at a time a clear track, is also used, particularly around terminals.

Centralized Traffic Control. A system of centralized traffic control is in use today on many United States railroads. In this system, the railroad is divided up into a number of territories. All the switches and signals in each territory are controlled from one huge central control board.

The train dispatcher in charge of the territory directs all train movements through this control board. Electric lights on the control panel tell him the position of each train in his territory. By pressing buttons on the panel, the dispatcher can signal any train in his control zone to stop, go slow, or proceed. He can direct a train hundreds of miles away onto a passing track.

CTC, as railroaders call centralized traffic control, is designed so that switches cannot be thrown one way and signals set another. If a train hits an open switch from the wrong direction, it can be derailed. A faulty signal can also send a train roaring through an open switch to hit another train parked on a siding. CTC does away with this danger.

▶ **RAILROAD WORKERS**

To most people the man who most symbolizes the railroad industry is the engineer in the locomotive cab, lifting a gloved hand to wave a friendly greeting as the train thunders through the countryside. But railroads employ hundreds of kinds of workers to keep the trains running safely and smoothly and to handle the paperwork of a giant industry.

The train crews are the men who operate the trains: engineers, firemen or engineer's helpers, conductors, and brakemen.

The engineer and firemen are known as the engine crew. The engineer sits on the right side of the cab and runs the locomotive. On a passenger locomotive, the fireman occupies the lefthand cab seat. Both men constantly watch the signals along the track and the dials and gauges on the control panels in front of them. At present, firemen or helpers are not required on most freight and yard locomotives in the United States.

The man in charge of the train is the conductor. It is his job to see that the crew members do their work properly and that all orders concerning the movement of the train are carried out. The conductor of a freight train, working at his desk in the caboose, keeps a record of all shipments and prepares a "wheel report," listing the cars in his train.

The brakemen assist the conductor. On freight trains there are at least two brakemen. The head brakeman rides in the engine cab. The rear brakeman rides in the caboose, where he helps the conductor keep watch over the train. On passenger trains the brakemen help the conductor collect fares.

The crew of a long-distance passenger train may also include a baggage man, express messengers, railway postal clerks, a special conductor for sleeping cars, Pullman porters, coach porters, club-car attendants, dining-car steward, waiters, and cooks.

Before any train starts out, a car inspector must check all the air-hose connections to make sure that the airbrakes will function properly. Another inspector taps the wheels with a hammer to check for cracks. A cracked wheel gives off a different sound from a good one. Thousands of mechanics are employed in the railroad shops and roundhouses, repairing, reconditioning, and rebuilding cars and engines.

A very important group of railroad workers are the track gangs, who are responsible for keeping the track in good repair. They replace worn and broken rails and ties, level the track, and inspect it regularly.

Running and maintaining the signal systems is the task of another big group of railroad employees.

In addition to these, railroads employ telegraphers, carpenters, boilermakers, electricians, advertising agents, architects, chemists, doctors, lawyers, farm experts, station agents, policemen, office workers, and civil, mechanical, and electrical engineers, and many others.

No matter what his job is, a railroader must

How did 4 feet 8½ inches come to be picked for the width of track?

Railroads were born in England, and the greatest of the early English railroad builders was George Stephenson. When Stephenson was called upon to build the Stockton & Darlington, he made its gauge 4 feet 8 inches, the same as that of the tracks of the railroad at the coal mine where he had formerly worked. Later he added another ½ inch to reduce binding of the wheels by the rails. Stephenson used this 4-foot-8½-inch gauge on all the other railroads he built, and he built more than anyone else in England.

Early railroad companies in the United States and other countries bought English locomotives and laid their tracks to fit the locomotives' wheels. In this way the Stephenson standard gauge became the most common in the world.

be able to accept responsibility. This is true whether his work is operating trains, repairing track and bridges, servicing locomotives and cars, or supervising the work of a whole division. Other people's lives may depend on his vigilance and conscientiousness.

▶HISTORY

Although the railroad industry was born in the 19th century, the idea of tracks is much older. Hundreds of years before the time of Jesus the Greeks built runways of stone slabs with grooves or ruts to guide the wheels of their carts. The Romans, too, built a number of rut roads. During the Middle Ages, miners in Germany and Central Europe built crude wooden tracks along which they pushed their heavily loaded ore carts.

About the beginning of the 17th century, coal-mine owners in northeastern England began building plank railways between the mines and the riverside piers where the coal was loaded onto barges and ships. Horses could pull a loaded coal wagon much more easily along the smooth, firm tracks than over the muddy, bumpy, hole-filled roads of the time. Soon many roads around the English coal mines were turned into railways.

At first the tracks were broad planks. Later, to save wood, narrow rails were used instead. This meant that some way had to be found to keep the wagon wheels from running off the rails. One way was to put a projecting rim, or **flange**, on the rail, making an L-shaped rail. The other way was to put the flange on the wheels themselves. This is the system used today.

To keep the wooden rails from wearing out, iron strips, or straps, were spiked to the tops of the rails. By the middle of the 18th century some rails were being made entirely of iron. The solid iron rails were stronger than the strap-covered wooden ones, but also more expensive. So the old-fashioned strap rails continued to be used for many years.

The steam engine, as well as tracks, was invented before there were railroads. The huge, clumsy steam engines invented by Thomas Newcomen (1663–1729), an English iron merchant, were pumping water out of mines in the early 18th century. Later James Watt (1736–1819), a Scottish instrument maker, improved the steam engine and turned it into a practical source of power for factory machines. Toward the end of the century several men made attempts to hitch the steam engine to wheels for use on highways. Then in 1804 Richard Trevithick (1771–1833), a British mining engineer, built a small locomotive that successfully pulled a string of loaded cars on a mine railway in Wales. This was the world's first steam locomotive.

One of the most important pioneers of railroading was George Stephenson (1781–1848). Stephenson's parents were so poor that they could not afford to send him to school. Instead, he had to go to work as a little boy. When he was a grown man, Stephenson learned to read and write and then taught himself engineering. In 1814 Stephenson built his first locomotive, the "Blucher." After building a number of other locomotives, each one better than the one before, Stephenson was given the job of building the Stockton & Darlington, the world's first railroad that was open to the public. Stephenson also persuaded the directors of the Stockton & Darlington to use steam instead of horses to pull their trains on part of the line. The opening of the Stockton & Darlington in 1825 marked the birth of the railroad industry. Railroading was now a business in its own right instead of just a way of getting coal from the mine to the dockside.

In the fall of 1829 an important locomotive contest was held in England, at Rainhill near Liverpool. Observers from many countries came to watch the locomotives perform. They came away convinced that steam could do the job better and cheaper than horses. Stephenson and his son Robert (1803–59) designed the winning locomotive, the "Rocket." The "Rocket" was the first really practical locomotive, and it set the style of locomotive design for many years.

Men in other countries had been following the success of railroads in England. Bit by bit, railroads spread over Europe. The first railroad in France was opened in 1832, in Belgium and in Germany in 1835, in Russia in 1837, in Spain in 1848, in Sweden in 1856.

Railroads in the United States

In 1825 Colonel John Stevens (1749–1838), a wealthy landowner and amateur inventor, built a tiny experimental locomotive, which he ran on a circular track on his estate in Hoboken, New Jersey. Stevens had long been interested in railroads. In fact, as early as 1815 the state of New Jersey had granted him a charter to build a railroad. However, Stevens was unable to get backing for his project, and the charter ran out before a single foot of track was laid.

The first railroad company in the United States actually to open for business was the Granite Railway Company in eastern Massachusetts. Its 3-mile-long track, built in 1826, was made of wooden rails covered with strap iron. Its horse-drawn cars carried blocks of granite for the Bunker Hill Monument.

A more substantial railroad was built in 1829 by the Delaware & Hudson Canal Company to serve a coal mine. Cars loaded with coal rolled downhill to the canal. The empty cars were pulled back up by horses. Horatio

INVENTION OF THE AIR BRAKE

One of the most important inventions in the history of railroad safety was the air brake, first patented in 1869 by George Westinghouse, a young Civil War veteran. Trains must be able to stop as well as start, and the lack of a good braking system before the air brake was invented caused many serious accidents.

By the middle of the 19th century most locomotives had steam-powered brakes. Steam from the boiler operated a piston that forced curved brake blocks against the rims of the wheels. The steam brake worked very well on locomotives, but it could not be used on train cars because the steam condensed back into water in the pipes that took it from the locomotive to the cars.

Instead, cars were equipped with hand brakes worked by turning a big wheel at one end of each car. When the engineer blew a signal on his whistle, the brakemen would rush to the brake wheels and screw them down one by one. This was dangerous work, especially on freight trains, because freight cars had their brake wheels on top. A brakeman could easily lose his balance and fall off. Hand braking was also slow. If the engineer sighted an obstacle on the tracks just ahead, the train might hit it before the brakemen could set the brakes. Because of this, it was not safe to operate trains at high speeds.

Many attempts were made to develop a fast-acting mechanical brake system for trains. There were hydraulic brakes, electric brakes, and brakes worked by a long chain that passed under all the cars and was wound up on a drum on the locomotive. There were clockwork brakes that the engineer could set by pulling a lever in his cab—but before the train could start again, the brakemen had to wind up the brakes on each car, one by one. There was even an air-brake system invented in England in 1848, but it needed a man on every car to operate it. None of these systems worked well enough to be put into general use.

George Westinghouse became interested in better brakes when a train that he was riding was delayed for several hours because of a wreck on the track ahead. Two trains had collided head on because their engineers had been unable to stop in time.

Westinghouse studied the problems involved in braking a train. He decided that an effective braking system must be controlled by the engineer, must act immediately, and must act on every car in the train at the same time. But he could not find a way to make these ideas work.

Then one day Westinghouse saw an interesting article in a magazine. The article described how compressed air was being used to operate a rock drill deep inside a tunnel through the Swiss Alps. The drill was 3,000 feet from the pump that supplied the air, yet it suffered no loss of power. Here was the answer!

The brake system that Westinghouse patented in 1869 was simple. A compressor on the locomotive pumped air into a tank. A hose led from the tank to the brakes on the cars. When the engineer opened a valve, air rushed from the tank into cylinders on the trucks of the cars, forcing the brake shoes against the wheels.

Westinghouse's first air brake had a dramatic test. As the train sped out of a tunnel, the engineer saw a wagon stalled on the tracks just ahead. Frantically he whistled "down brakes," then applied the air full force. The train bucked and pitched as the brakes took hold—and stopped just a few yards from the stalled wagon. It was proved that air could halt a speeding train.

But the air brake was still far from perfect. If a train broke in half or a bad leak developed in the air line, the brakes would not work. Westinghouse solved this problem by changing the design of his system. Instead of supplying the brakes directly with air from the locomotive, he stored air in a reservoir under each car. A special valve called the triple valve kept the reservoir shut off as long as the pressure in the main air line was kept at a certain level. If pressure in the main line dropped, the triple valve automatically let air from the reservoir into the brake mechanism, setting the brakes. The engineer applied the brakes by letting a small amount of air out of the air line. To release them, he pumped air back into the reservoirs. If a train broke in two, the drop in pressure automatically set the brakes.

Westinghouse's original air brake has been improved many times. Engineers now have much more precise control of the brakes. But the basic principle is the same.

Modern Japanese trains: At left is a commuter train; in the center, an express; and at right, the super-speed train of the Tokaido line, which runs at 125 miles per hour.

Allen (1802–90), a young engineer working for the company, believed that mechanical power was a better method. He went to England and studied railroad operations there, and in 1829 imported four English-built locomotives. One of these, the "Stourbridge Lion," made a trial run on the D & H tracks. The engine performed beautifully, but it was too heavy for the flimsy tracks and could not be used in regular service.

American railroads survived this discouraging start. The next year, 1830, the Baltimore & Ohio opened its first stretch of track for horse-drawn cars. The B & O began steam operation in 1831. Also in 1830 the South Carolina Railroad was completed. On Christmas Day, 1830, the South Carolina Railroad's locomotive, "Best Friend of Charleston," became the first locomotive to pull a passenger train in the United States.

By 1835 some 200 railroad charters had been granted in 11 states, and more than 1,000 miles of track were in operation. Most of these pioneer railroads were little local lines serving small regions. Many of them later became parts of large present-day systems.

The early American railroads were usually poorly constructed. Unlike the well-built railroads of England, the American railroads were full of steep grades and sharp curves. Because of the high price of iron, American railroads at first used wooden rails covered by thin straps of iron. Unfortunately the straps often worked loose and curled up at the ends. Then the wheels of an oncoming car could get underneath the strap and ram it up through the floor of the car. A strap that did this was called a "snakehead," and the unlucky passenger who happened to be sitting over one was usually badly injured. In time, the strap rails were replaced by solid iron rails.

However, the very drawbacks of the bad construction forced American railroad men to take the lead in other ways. They built locomotives that were powerful enough to take the stiff grades, flexible enough to go around the sharp curves without leaving the track, and light enough not to break the flimsy rails. By the 1840's American locomotives were the finest in the world.

At first, passenger and freight cars were mounted rigidly on four wheels. This meant that the cars had to be small in order to go around curves. American railroaders adapted the swivel truck to cars and locomotives. A truck, in railroad language, is a set of wheels held in a frame. The weight of the car rests on a pivot on top of the frame. The pivot lets

Experimental model of a high-speed train proposed for use in the United States.

the truck turn freely when the wheels go around a curve. A big car supported by a swivel truck at each end could take the sharpest curve, yet carry a big load. In Europe, however, the rigid, four-wheeled car was kept for many years.

Because of the great need for cheap overland transportation, railroads developed rapidly in the United States. By 1842 it was possible to ride by train from Boston to Buffalo, with a break for a ferry across the Hudson River at Albany. By 1850 the rail network totaled 9,000 miles, and railroads were operating in every state east of the Mississippi River.

Railroads were building into new territory, opening vast regions to farming, mining, lumbering, and manufacturing. Wherever railroads were built, towns sprang up, trade and industry developed, and farm production increased. Railroads became a part of everyday life, making it easier for people to travel and to ship goods. Distance became less and less of a barrier to trade as railroads improved their service.

To encourage the building of railroads in the unsettled lands of the west, President Fillmore in 1850 signed the first of a series of land grant acts. These acts granted railroads large areas of land along the right-of-way. The railroads expected to sell the land to settlers and then earn more money by hauling their products to market. In return, the railroads agreed to carry government traffic at reduced rates. At the time many people felt that the land grants were an improper giveaway of public property. But by the time the agreements ended in 1946, the railroads that had received land grants had paid back to the government many times the value of the land.

The Civil War halted expansion temporarily, but construction of the first American transcontinental line began even before the fighting ended. Hard-driving construction crews of the Union Pacific pushed west over the Great Plains from the Missouri River, while the crews of the Central Pacific hacked their way through the rugged Sierra Nevada range. The two lines met at Promontory, Utah, on May 10, 1869.

The 1860's also saw important advances in railroad safety. In 1863 steel rails began to come into use. Steel is much stronger than plain iron, pound for pound, and steel rails meant that trains could carry heavier loads at higher speeds than ever before, while the danger of rails' breaking was less. In 1868 Eli H. Janney (1831–1912) patented an automatic "knuckle" coupler—the kind that is used today on railroad cars. In 1869 George Westinghouse patented the first practical airbrake system.

The railroads were responsible for establishing standard time zones in 1883. Before then, each community kept its own time, based on the sun. This meant that no two nearby towns had quite the same time. You can imagine the confusion this caused in railroad timetables. Standard time made things much simpler for travelers.

Safety and efficiency are stressed in modern railroading. Improved signaling systems, safety devices, and electronic push-button freight yards are all part of this drive.

To meet the competition of airplanes and automobiles, railroads are continually looking for ways to improve their equipment. More efficient locomotives are constantly being tested. New, strong, lightweight materials are being developed for cars. New designs have been developed that permit trains to run at very high speeds over ordinary tracks. Some countries are developing trains that will glide on a cushion of air instead of on wheels. For example, Japan is working on a train that will be held up by an electromagnetic field.

WILLIAM H. BUNCE
Association of American Railroads

See also LOCOMOTIVES; TRANSPORTATION.

RAILROADS, MODEL

How would you like to pull back the throttle on a huge steam or diesel locomotive and feel the giant come to life, easily pulling as many as 200 loaded freight cars? Or how would you like to be close to a railroad right-of-way along which roaring expresses speed in the night, bound for destinations perhaps hundreds or thousands of miles away? Few people have the chance to run a real railroad, but most of us can still enjoy the thrills of model railroading. If you're old enough and interested enough to read this article, you're also old enough to build a model railroad system that copies the operation of a real railroad, perhaps the one that passes close to your own home.

▶ GETTING STARTED

Many people who own train sets run their equipment on the floor, often only during the Christmas holiday season. The very first rule of building a real model railroad system is to build your railroad on a table or wooden platform. When your train layout is on a table, you can leave it up all year long in your room or in the basement, attic, or garage. If you live in an apartment where there isn't enough room for a year-round table, build your railroad on a large wooden panel on rollers so that it can be stored under the bed.

The size of a model railroad system depends on how much space is available. An excellent starting size for the small-size HO gauge or TT gauge trains is 4 feet by 8 feet, which also happens to be the standard size in which ¾-inch plywood sheets are sold at lumberyards. For O gauge, O-27 gauge, or S gauge trains, a model railroad system can be somewhat larger, perhaps 6 feet by 8 feet. A 6- by 8-foot table can be made by joining two pieces of plywood measuring 4 feet by 6 feet. If the lumberyard doesn't have this size sheet in stock, the plywood can be cut to order.

Most of the big model railroad club layouts are built to a height of 40 to 42 inches. This height is fine for grown-ups but too high for most boys and girls. It's hard to work on a high table. Your table should be about 2 or 3 feet off the ground. You can use two carpenter's sawhorses as legs or make some wooden or pipe legs.

▶ GETTING EQUIPMENT

There are hundreds of companies that make fine model railroad equipment. Most of the cars and locomotives available are closely modeled after those found on actual railroads.

At Christmastime it is possible to buy model railroad equipment in almost any department store as well as in toy stores and supermarkets. There are also special stores called hobby shops that sell model railroad equipment all year long. Hobby shops carry extra tracks, cars, and new locomotives and all kinds of electrical gadgets to make your trains run better, in addition to various kinds of buildings and accessory items.

The hobby shop dealer is usually able to answer technical questions. He can help you make your railroad better.

▶ A TRACK DESIGN

A real railroad usually runs between two major cities, such as New York and Chicago, Montreal and Toronto, or London and Edinburgh. The run from New York to Chicago is about 1,000 miles. This is far too long a run to model in miniature. Even if you could run track in a straight line in your home, such a length of track could measure at the most about 50 feet. A length of track 50 feet long in O gauge approximates only about one half mile of real railroad. In HO gauge, 50 feet is not quite a full mile. Therefore an HO train traveling at a scale speed of 60 miles an hour would travel the 50 feet of track in 1 minute. That's not a very long run, is it?

To make our model railroad run longer, the railroad line is twisted into curves and grades, and then the two ends are connected. The trains can then run continuously over the same track, and you can pretend that the several stations on your railroad represent many stations. Then you can run your trains as long as you like.

A good layout is perhaps the most important single thing to consider when planning a model railroad. It is possible to have both simple and complicated layouts for both large and small railroads.

In choosing a model railroad layout, you must decide whether to have a giant transcontinental empire or a smaller branch-line type of railroad. Many modelers find that the smaller line is more fun to model and operate. You will need enough sidings and yards to store extra equipment. You will also need a passenger terminal and an engine terminal.

Fortunately in model railroading you don't need everything at once. You can start with a single loop of track and add switches, sidings, and branches as you progress. You never grow out of your model railroad equipment unless you decide to change to a different-size gauge. Even the smallest switching locomotive, which may have been your first locomotive, will continue to be important as your railroad grows.

▶ SCENERY

Scenery will add to the realism of your model railroad. Plastic, wood, and cardboard buildings in easy-to-assemble form are readily available from hobby dealers everywhere. Many modelers prefer to make their own from wood and cardboard, following construction plans to be found in the various model railroad magazines published in the United States and other countries.

Mountains and hills are also easy to make. Old wire screen tacked to a simple wooden framework forms the base on which you can smear a thin coating of plaster or any of the several prepared scenic mixes. Many modelers find papier-mâché to be a handy and economical scenic material.

When they are dry, paint your mountains and hills with such earthy-looking colors as burnt umber or sienna. Avoid shiny enamel paints and very bright colors. Scenery should be subdued and lifelike. After painting the scenery, add trees and shrubs and sprinkle imitation grass material in likely places. Add more life to your railroad by clipping colored ads from magazines for use as store names, billboards, and posters.

▶ LOCOMOTIVES

It wasn't very long ago that the steam locomotive did almost all the hauling of freight and passenger trains. In a few areas where traffic was very heavy and in certain mountain areas, electric locomotives were also used. Steam locomotives are still used by many railroads throughout the world, and many model railroad fans still prefer to collect these.

Recently the diesel has replaced the steam locomotive in many areas. Although the diesel lacks the variety offered by the steam locomotive, it is more colorful. Most model railroads operate both steam and diesel "locos."

You may prefer an old-time railroad layout. If so, you will want only steam locomotives and old-fashioned railway cars.

The modeler will want to have among his locomotives at least the following: (1) a switching locomotive, (2) a small freight locomotive, (3) a local passenger locomotive, (4) a large freight locomotive, and (5) a fast passenger express locomotive. A railroad can use some locomotives for almost any type of service. For example, a GP-9-type general-purpose locomotive, available in HO, S, or O gauge, can be used for switching, passenger, or freight service.

Every layout should have a variety of freight cars, and no layout can have too many. Some hobbyists like to have a number of coal-hopper cars and several refrigerator cars. As president of your own model railroad, run it as you like.

For your passenger trains you will want several coaches and a Pullman, a diner, a baggage car, a mail car, and an observation car. These can be combined to make up almost any type of passenger train, from a local commuter to a speeding express.

▶ OPERATION AND FUN

The fun in model railroading comes from operating your railroad as much as possible like a real railroad. Get an actual railroad timetable and adapt it to your own model railroad. Make up names for your trains, and let them go by real timetable schedules. Such operations can become so involved that you will need the help of your friends to keep the railroad operating on schedule. Your friends can become yardmasters, towermen, station agents, and dispatchers.

You may enjoy starting your own model-railroad club. By pooling equipment, resources, and skills, you can build a much finer layout than you would have had if you built your own railroad without outside help.

HAROLD H. CARSTENS
Publisher
Railroad Model Craftsman magazine

RAIN, SNOW, SLEET, AND HAIL

Rain forms from moisture in the atmosphere. So do snow, sleet, and hail. All, however, have their beginning on the ground, for most of the moisture comes from the surface waters of the earth—its oceans, rivers, and lakes.

Moisture gets into the atmosphere, or air, by a process called evaporation. The word **evaporation** describes the change of a liquid into a gas. Like other liquids, water is made up of molecules, which are tiny particles. Under certain conditions, water molecules escape into the air. That is, water evaporates. The molecules form a gas called **water vapor**.

Evaporation takes place in your own home. In winter, for example, your mother may put a pan of water in a room where the air is hot and dry. The water evaporates, adding moisture to the air and making it more comfortable to breathe. Depending on how hot and dry the air is, the water may disappear in one day or a few days. The warmer the air is, the more water vapor it can hold.

When you take a hot shower, the air in the bathroom becomes cloudy. This happens because water from the shower evaporates and fills the bathroom air with water vapor. Soon the air cannot hold any more vapor. Some vapor then changes back into water droplets. The droplets form around dust particles in the air. You see these droplets as a cloud in the bathroom. Water droplets also form when vapor touches the tiles and mirror, which are cooler. When water vapor changes to water droplets, the process is called **condensation.**

▶ **RAIN**

Day and night the surface waters of the earth are evaporating. The water vapor mixes with the air and is carried high into the atmosphere. There the temperature is colder than it is on the ground. If there is more water vapor than this colder air can hold, some must condense.

The vapor condenses much as it does in the air of your bathroom. In the atmosphere are many billions of tiny particles called **condensation nuclei**. These include dust, smoke from factory chimneys, and salt from the seas, all of which are constantly mixing with the air.

Under certain conditions, some of the water vapor condenses on these tiny particles. Nearly every day we can see these water droplets as a cloud. The cloud droplets are very small and light. Many keep falling out of the cloud toward the earth, but they are so small that they usually evaporate long before they reach the ground. Most droplets, however, are held up in the air by rising air currents.

When enough droplets form and when they grow so heavy that the rising air currents can no longer hold them up, they fall and we feel them as rain. There are at least two ways in which raindrops form.

Raindrops from Ice Crystals. The temperature in some rain clouds is much colder than 32 degrees Fahrenheit. Yet even though the temperature is below the freezing point, the cloud droplets do not freeze. (Water can remain liquid at temperatures below the freezing point if it is free of impurities.) When a cloud contains such low-temperature water droplets, the droplets are said to be supercooled.

Water droplets can reach temperatures as low as −40 degrees without freezing. Supercooled droplets remain liquid until they bump into ice crystals or certain other particles. When this happens, a supercooled droplet freezes. The now frozen droplet bumps into surrounding liquid droplets, collects their water, and grows into a larger ice particle. When many such frozen cloud droplets form and grow heavy enough to fall out of the cloud into warm air, they melt and reach the ground as rain.

Big Drops from Little Drops. Rain also forms in warm clouds, where the temperatures are well above freezing. Several cloud droplets may collide and form a single large droplet. The large droplet now falls through the cloud faster than the surrounding smaller

---

What is the shape of a falling raindrop?

Small droplets of water within a rain cloud are round in shape. These small drops of water join, forming larger drops called raindrops. When raindrops fall through the air, they flatten out. As a result, a raindrop is shaped much like a hamburger bun. A raindrop is not shaped like a pear, as is commonly thought.

ANNUAL WORLD RAINFALL

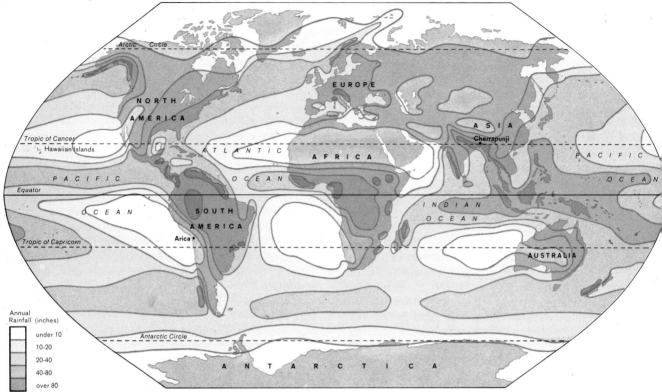

droplets. As it falls, it collides with still more of the smaller droplets, growing larger and heavier with each collision. Gradually it becomes heavy enough to fall out of the cloud as a raindrop.

World Rainfall

As the rainfall map shows you, some parts of the earth receive much more rain or snow than others. Many things—such as temperature and height above sea level—determine

PRECIPITATION AROUND THE WORLD	
CITY	**ANNUAL PRECIPITATION IN INCHES**
New Orleans, Louisiana	50
Boston, Massachusetts	42
Buenos Aires, Argentina	37
Geneva, Switzerland	34
Ottawa, Canada	34
Chicago, Illinois	30
Helsinki, Finland	28
Moscow, U.S.S.R.	25
New Delhi, India	25
Capetown, Republic of South Africa	24
Paris, France	22
Anchorage, Alaska	14

the amount of rain or snow an area receives.

In the United States, New York City expects to get about 40 inches a year. San Francisco receives about 20 inches. About 17 inches falls on Madrid, Spain, while Tokyo, Japan, gets 62.

Cherrapunji, India, is probably the rainiest place in the world. Its average yearly rainfall is 425 to 450 inches. Once 150 inches of rain fell on Cherrapunji in a period of 5 days. In the year 1861 its rainfall added up to 905 inches. At the other extreme, Arica, Chile, is probably the driest place in the world. It averages 0.02 inches of rain a year. The driest area in the United States is Greenland Ranch, Death Valley. There the average yearly rainfall is less than 1.5 inches.

Some large regions of the earth have heavy rainfall throughout the year. This is true along the equator, for example. Almost every point along the equator receives 60 inches or more of rain every year. The equator is the meeting point of two large streams of air. All along the equator air moving down from the north meets air moving up from the south.

There is a general upward movement of hot air laden with water vapor. As this air rises to colder heights in the atmosphere, large amounts of water vapor condense and fall as rain.

Other regions of the earth have very little rain. For example, in the colder parts of the Northern Hemisphere, there is little rain or snow in any season. The reason is that the air is so cold that it cannot hold much water vapor. But the driest (desert) regions are found in the subtropics on the western sides of the continents. (See chart.)

A great deal of rain falls on the windward side of mountain ranges. The other side, which is called the lee, receives much less rain. An example of this is the Cascade Range of California. Here westerly winds laden with water vapor sweep in from the Pacific Ocean. After striking the coast, the air rides up the western slopes of the mountains, cooling as it climbs higher. The cooling of the moist air causes the water vapor to condense and fall as rain or snow.

Having lost most of its moisture, the air continues its journey eastward across the United States. First it plunges down the eastern slopes of the Cascade Range, growing warmer as it descends. It absorbs large amounts of ground moisture as it sweeps down the mountainside. For that reason, this dry, warm, down-the-mountain wind is called a chinook, or snow-eater.

In summer in India much the same thing happens. Air laden with moisture flows off the Indian Ocean toward India's western coast. Then as the air climbs the western slopes of the Western Ghats, the rains fall in torrents.

Rain, snow, sleet, and hail are all called **precipitation**, from a Latin word meaning "to fall." Precipitation is measured in inches. Rain can simply be collected in special containers and measured with a measuring stick. But snow and the ice of sleet and hail are first melted to water and then measured.

Is there such a thing as red snow?

Snow or rain can be red if the air contains red dust particles. Snowflakes or raindrops forming around these dust particles take on a reddish color. Red snows and red rains occur in those parts of Europe—especially Italy—where the air is filled with dust particles from the red sands of the Sahara desert.

A container used to collect and measure rainfall. The white "fence" shields the container from wind.

▶ **SNOW**

Like raindrops, snowflakes begin as water vapor in a cloud. They form when water vapor changes to ice crystals. Each snowflake is made up of a number of ice crystals.

There are two ways in which water vapor can change into ice crystals.

When a cloud is very cold, ice crystals form directly from water vapor. The vapor does not change into water that freezes. It changes into ice crystals. For example, at a temperature of −40 degrees all the water vapor in a cloud changes into ice crystals. This change from a gas (water vapor) directly into a solid (ice) is called **sublimation**. But a cloud does not have to be that cold for ice crystals to form. There is another way this can happen.

Ice crystals can form at temperatures just below freezing (32 degrees). This happens when there are tiny particles, called **sublimation nuclei**, in the cloud. Under certain conditions ice crystals form around these particles, much as water droplets form around condensation nuclei.

Some kinds of particles cause ice crystals to form more rapidly than others. Scientists are not sure which kinds of particles are the best sublimation nuclei. Ice crystals themselves

Snowflakes, greatly enlarged. No two snowflakes have exactly the same shape.

may be. Dust from certain kinds of soils make good sublimation nuclei—clay particles seem to be among the best. Dust from meteor showers may also be important.

When ice crystals form in a cloud, each is a perfect six-sided figure. As far as we know, no two ever have exactly the same shape. (A scientist once photographed more than 1,000 ice crystals. No two were exactly alike.)

Once ice crystals have formed, several may collide and stick together. When they do, a large snowflake is formed. On a very cold day, the crystals in a snowflake do not melt together. You can see individual crystals as flakes fall on your sleeve.

If the air temperature below a snowing cloud is higher than 32 degrees, the snowflakes melt and fall as rain.

▶ SLEET

Sometimes raindrops freeze on their way to the ground. They freeze into ice pellets. In the United States these pellets are called sleet. (The British use "sleet" to describe a mixture of rain and snow.) In winter there is sometimes a layer of warm air sandwiched in between the air at cloud level and the air at ground level. Snow may be falling from the cloud. When the snow passes through the layer of warm air, it melts, turning to rain. When the rain falls through the colder air near the ground, it freezes into sleet.

Trees, coated by freezing rain, bend and break under the weight of the ice.

Hailstone damage to the roof of a house.

Cut hailstone shows layers of ice.

Baseball-size hail fell in 1934.

Sometimes the lowest layer of air is not cold enough to freeze the drops. However, the ground itself may be very cold. The raindrops freeze as soon as they strike the ground. This is called **glaze**, or **freezing rain**.

▶ HAIL

The size of an average hailstone is small—about the size of a pea. But some hailstones reach the size of lemons. In a few minutes, a summer storm of large hailstones can strip bare a fruit orchard or a cornfield.

If you cut a large hailstone in two, you will find that it is made up of rings and looks somewhat like an onion. At the center of a typical stone there may be a ball of small crystals. Air bubbles trapped inside the ball give the ice a milky appearance. Surrounding the center ball is a layer of clear ice. Next may be another layer of milky ice, and so on.

Exactly how a hailstone forms in this way is not wholly understood.

The clear layers of ice seem to be formed by layers of water that freeze slowly. As a result, there is time for the air bubbles to escape. The milky layers may be formed from water that freezes more quickly, and so the air bubbles do not have time to escape.

It is known, however, that where there is hail there is a thunderstorm raging within cumulonimbus clouds. Hail-producing thunderstorms are common over the central parts of continents, such as the Great Plains in the United States. There moist air blowing northward at ground level comes into contact with dry air blowing over the mountains from the western coast. If the moist air is carried high into the atmosphere—45,000 feet or more—towering cumulonimbus clouds and violent thunderstorms may form. These are the conditions that are right for producing hail.

Some hailstones seem to be tossed around within a cloud. Strong upward currents of air may carry a hailstone thousands of feet toward the top of a cloud. Then the stone may fall. It may fall out of the cloud, or it may make several more trips toward the top of the cloud. Somehow, during this up-and-down motion, a layered hailstone is formed.

ROY A. GALLANT
The Natural History Press
Reviewed by JEROME SPAR
New York University

See also CLOUDS; WEATHER AND CLIMATE.

RAINBOW

Rainbows are beautiful bands of color, in the form of a half circle or circle. You can see rainbows in many places—in the spray from a lawn sprinkler, in the mist of a waterfall, and in the sky just after it has rained. You cannot see a rainbow on a cloudy day or when the air is very dry. This is because rainbows are formed from two things: sunlight and drops of moisture in the air.

Sunlight is the source of the rainbow's colors. What you see as white sunlight is really a mixture of all the colors of the rainbow. Sunlight breaks up into these different colors as it hits the surface of a drop of water. The curved inner surface of the drop acts somewhat like a mirror, reflecting these colors to your eyes.

If the rays of color are reflected only once within the drop, a bright rainbow called the primary rainbow is formed. In a primary rainbow the colors are always arranged in the same order. Beginning with the outer, or top, circle, the colors are red, orange, yellow, green, blue, indigo, and violet.

Sometimes the rays of color are reflected twice within the drop. A fainter rainbow, the secondary rainbow, is produced then along with the primary rainbow. In the secondary rainbow the colors are reversed—the outer circle is violet and the inner, red.

A rainbow forms in the mists of Niagara Falls.

This small village occupies a clearing in a rain forest in central Liberia.

RAIN FOREST

"Rain forest" is the name given to the dense growth of trees in very wet climates. The tropical rain forests have a constantly warm and rainy climate. Annual rainfall averages from 1,500 to more than 2,500 millimeters (60 to over 100 inches). In the middle latitudes there are cool rain forests. They also have heavy rainfall, but their climate is much cooler than that of the tropics.

Where Are the Rain Forests?

The largest areas of rain forest are in the lowlands of equatorial Africa and the Amazon River valley of South America. There are other tropical rain forests in Central America, in Southeast Asia, in northeastern Australia, and on the islands of Indonesia. Most of the tropical islands of the world have rain forests on their rainy, windward sides. Cool rain forests are found along the northwestern coast of North America, in southeastern Australia, in New Zealand, and in southern Chile. Small areas of cool rain forest cover some mountain slopes in regions with a wet climate.

Tropical Rain Forests

Trees in tropical rain forests are green all year. Many kinds of trees grow there. The wood of some trees is too heavy to float in water. The wood of others, like the balsa, whose wood is used in model airplanes, is very light. The trees grow close together and reach heights of 30 meters (100 feet) or more in their competition for sunlight. The different species are widely scattered. There are no forests of only one kind of tree, such as the pine forests of the middle latitudes.

In the true rain forest the green foliage of

the branches and treetops spreads out like a huge umbrella to shade the forest floor. Long vines called lianas hang from the tree branches and trunks. Molds, bacteria, and insects attack fallen trees and leaves, causing them to decay rapidly in the hot, damp climate. Because the climate is hot and wet all year, the forest does not change much in appearance from one season to the next.

Along the borders of the rain forest and in places where people have cleared the forest, more light reaches the ground, and there is a dense undergrowth of shrubs, ferns, and grasses. This tangle of vegetation is called jungle.

Animal life in the tropical rain forest is as varied as the plant life. Monkeys and many species of birds and insects live in the treetops. Their food comes mainly from the fruits and seeds of the forest. In the forests of Africa and Asia there are large apes. Reptiles, birds, and such animals as the anteater and the jaguar eat other animals or insects. Only in the grasslands bordering the forest are there many large grazing animals.

Cool Rain Forests

Cool rain forests, like those of the tropics, have dense growths of trees covered with mosses, ferns, and vines. In winter some of the trees lose their leaves. Fallen trees decay slowly. Many lie for years, cluttering the dark forest floor. Animal life in the cool rain forests varies greatly. The rain forest on the western coast of North America has deer, elk, and bears. In southwestern New Zealand there were no mammals until people from Europe brought them in.

People of the Rain Forest

Both the tropical and the cool rain forests have a sparse population. Many primitive peoples in the tropical rain forests live by hunting and fishing. They also gather fruits and nuts in the forest. Their tools are simple, and they use such weapons as bows and arrows or blowguns. They need few clothes in the hot climate. Usually the forest hunters live in small villages. They may move frequently to new areas in search of food. Their houses are of wood with roofs of grass or leaves. Some tribes of Indians in Brazil have large houses in which several families live.

The Pygmies of the Ituri rain forest in Africa live in small shelters and move to new encampments from time to time.

Other peoples of the tropical rain forests are farmers. They cut and burn a patch of forest to grow manioc, bananas, tobacco, and vegetables. Soon the soil is worn out, and jungle plants begin to invade the fields. The farmers must then clear a new place in the forest. Sometimes they move to another area, build a new village, and clear new cropland. From the air their clearings appear as tiny holes in a sea of forest. These people are called migratory farmers. Although they usually keep to themselves, both the hunters and the migratory farmers occasionally trade goods with other people. Many of the rain forest peoples worship trees or other natural objects, and they have mystical explanations for things in nature.

Where the soils are fertile and the people have better tools, the farm settlements are permanent. Many of the rice lands of Southeast Asia were once covered with rain forest. Today they support millions of people. In some rain forest lands, plantations of rubber, cacao, oil palms, bananas, or tea have been developed by foreign investors. Native people work on these plantations, but the products are sold in middle-latitude cities. Today the people of tropical lands are gradually taking over control of the plantations in their countries.

Future of the Rain Forests

For centuries white people knew little about tropical rain forests. They considered the forests barriers to civilization. Only recently have they begun to learn about tropical diseases and how to live in a hot climate and use the forests. They have learned much from the native peoples. Both the tropical and the cool rain forests have valuable timber trees. Some fertile lands could be made to grow more food and fiber crops, although trees are still the best crop for tropical soils. There are probably minerals still undiscovered in these forest lands. With modern machinery and scientific methods, people will make better use of the resources of the rain forests in the future.

HOWARD J. CRITCHFIELD
Western Washington University

See also CLIMATE, TYPES OF; JUNGLES.

RALEIGH, SIR WALTER (1554?–1618)

Sir Walter Raleigh was the most varied in his genius and talents of all the great men of the age of Elizabeth I. He was soldier and sailor, courtier, poet, colonizer, historian, and scientist.

Raleigh was born about 1554 near Budleigh Salterton in Devonshire, England, within sight and sound of the sea. This turned his thoughts to adventure and travel from his earliest days. As a youth he fought in the wars in France, and for a time he attended Oriel College, Oxford. With no money but a great deal of pride, he next went soldiering in Ireland. Having views on Irish policy as on everything else—for he was very much a man of ideas—Raleigh got the chance of presenting them at the English court. There he won the favor of Queen Elizabeth I with his brilliance, eloquence, and good looks. He was made captain of her Guard, knighted, and given various posts in the government. The Queen turned him into a good servant of the state, and he was always a hard worker, full of plans at home and abroad.

The money that came to him from the Queen's favor Raleigh used in planting settlements in America. He sent out the first colony in 1585. It was a group of about 100 men, who lived on Roanoke Island, off the coast of North Carolina, for a year. This was the first English colony to gather experience of life in the New World—all the later colonies flowed from this first attempt. Much of our early knowledge of the Indians, the plant and animal life, and the geography of America we owe to Raleigh's efforts. In 1587 he sent out a second colony of over 100 persons, but all these were lost in the trackless forest of the mainland. Raleigh had spent a fortune on these efforts. Discouraged, he now gave up active colonization in America.

He transferred his attentions to southern Ireland, where he also hoped to establish English colonies. His friendship there with the poet Edmund Spenser (1552?–99), then writing his *Faerie Queene,* was more successful. Raleigh himself was one of the leading poets of the age, though he did not write much in quantity. His best-known lines are from a poem known as "The Nymph's Reply to the Shepherd," written in reply to Christopher Marlowe's (1564–93) famous lyric "Come live with me and be my love":

> If all the world and love were young,
> And truth in every shepherd's tongue,
> These pretty pleasures might me move,
> To live with thee and be thy love.

Raleigh's longest poem, "Book of the Ocean to Cynthia," was unfinished. It tells the story of his devotion to the Queen and its ups and downs. In 1592 he lost Elizabeth's favor by his secret marriage to one of her ladies-in-waiting, Elizabeth Throckmorton. He was exiled from court for some years. In 1595 he made his first voyage to Guiana in South America, where he hoped to find gold. Spain claimed Guiana, but Raleigh hoped to interest England in it. To this purpose he wrote a celebrated book, the *Discovery of Guiana.* Queen Elizabeth was not interested. But in 1596, during the war with Spain, Raleigh played a leading part in the capture of the Spanish city of Cadiz and thus recovered the Queen's favor.

On Elizabeth's death in 1603, King James I came to the throne. James was a personal enemy of Raleigh, who was accused of entering into a conspiracy against him. For this Raleigh was condemned to death. Though the sentence was suspended, he spent most of the rest of his life in the Tower of London.

There he wrote his great *History of the World* and made experiments in chemistry. But his mind remained fixed on Guiana. In 1616 he was allowed out of prison to lead a voyage there. Instead of finding gold he clashed with the Spaniards, and his elder·son, who had accompanied him, was killed. To satisfy Spain, Raleigh was executed on October 29, 1618. There was a great outcry against this. Public opinion in England turned against King James, and Raleigh died a popular hero.

Raleigh's efforts bore fruit after his death. He introduced the potato from the New World into Ireland. He was the first patron of smoking tobacco and made the habit popular; it was this that first set Virginia on its feet. In his eloquent prose and poetry Raleigh still lives in English literature, his name a household word in the English-speaking world.

A. L. ROWSE
Author, *Sir Walter Raleigh*

A chuck wagon brings food to cowboys on the range.

RANCH LIFE

To many people ranch life means the Wild West, with roundups, rodeos, and battles with rustlers and Indians. Many children dream of becoming cowboys or cowgirls and leading romantic, adventurous lives. But ranch life is in reality a hard and grueling business, demanding strength, patience, and a great deal of work.

Ranchers raise cattle for the meat that people eat. Since meat is important in everyone's diet and is a favorite food of people everywhere, ranching is a very important job. Ranching is one of the oldest and biggest industries in the world.

Most ranches are located in flat, open country where there is plenty of grass for the cattle to feed on and room for them to graze. Most of the ranches of the world are on the great prairies of the American West, on the plains (called the Pampa) of Argentina, and in the outback of Australia.

Like all other kinds of farming, ranching is a hazardous job. Dry spells or rainstorms can destroy the food needed for the cattle, or the cattle themselves may become sick and die. The rancher may find that he has lost all his profit through no fault of his own. He must always be on guard against the dangers that nature can create.

History of Ranching

A long, long time ago, at the very beginning of civilized life, people began to keep herds of cattle. These people were called nomads, or wanderers, because they drove their herds from place to place, looking for fresh grass and water. Later, men began to settle in the places where the food and water were plentiful. They built huts for themselves and shelters and yards for their animals. They put up fences to keep their cattle from straying. These were the first ranches.

Cowboys

Ranch life has always centered around the cowboy, one of the most colorful figures in the history of the American West. Stories about cowboys are very popular in America and all over the world. People think of cowboys as free and independent people, unafraid to battle a wild bronco or an angry steer, living close to nature, with the trees and the sky and the stars. Nowadays there are far fewer cowboys, and they no longer live as they did. But their hold on the imagination is still strong. The old-time cowboy is the hero of many books, movies, legends, and songs. He is to Americans what knights and noblemen were to Europeans—a national hero and a treasured part of the national past.

The American cowboy first appeared in Texas around 1836. Soon ranches spread from Texas through the Southwest to the Rocky Mountains, and cowboys were working in almost every part of the West.

Cowboys' lives centered around the roundup and the cattle drive. Every winter and summer the cattle pastured at the ranch. In the spring and autumn the cowboys rounded up the cattle, branded the new crop of calves, and separated the beef cattle from the rest of the herd. Then they took the steers that were to be sold and drove them over many miles of open country to the nearest railroad terminal. From there the cattle were shipped to slaughterhouses and packing plants. In the 19th century, railroads were few and far between. Driving the cattle was a long, hard job. There was danger from Indians or cattle thieves. The cowboys rose before sunup to start the cattle moving. They drove them all day through the heat or dust or wind and dozed around campfires at night, still alert for trouble or for strays (lost cattle). The men were often on horseback 15 hours a day.

Cowboys had to be resourceful and strong. They had to be skilled horsemen and handy with a lariat and a gun. Their distinctive clothing was designed for protection. The wide-brimmed hat was worn to shield them from the sun and dust and to shed the rain; chaps protected their legs from cactus and tumbleweed; the gun and holster provided protection against rustlers or Indian attack.

Now much of the adventure has gone out of the cowboy's life. He no longer has to contend with Indians or thieves. Most ranches are quite close to depots, so the long cattle drive is a thing of the past. Modern inventions have taken many of the cowboy's old jobs. The modern cowboy often must be a technician himself in order to operate the new devices for the care of cattle and for operating the ranch.

Ranching Today

Ranching today is a big business in many countries of the world. Ranches are spread through the West and Southwest of the United States. There are many ranches also in Canada, Mexico, Australia, Argentina, Venezuela, Chile, and Brazil. Argentina, in the southern part of South America, is one of the greatest ranching countries of the world and world-famous for its beef. Great herds roam the Pampa of eastern Argentina, and the cowboys, called gauchos, are as famous as the American cowboys of the Old West.

A modern ranch can cover 500,000 acres of dry, desert country or 100 acres of greener country where the climate is wetter and more grass can be grown. There are big ranches and small ranches; ranches that use modern machines and are run like giant businesses, and ranches run entirely by single families, where each member of the family has a job to do and helps to decide how the ranch should be run. There are ranches in the dry, sandy deserts of Texas, on the cold plains of Montana, and in the green uplands and plateaus of Colorado.

Ranching is healthful outdoor work, but it is sometimes lonely and always very hard. It means putting on a coat and rubber boots to go out in cold winter rain to feed the cows, when a seat by the fireplace would be far more pleasant. It means roping and wrestling husky yearling calves in the hot, dusty summer or getting out of a warm bed in the middle of a winter night to help a baby calf get born. But this hard life is also satisfying. The rancher gladly tolerates the heat and dust for the thrill of pitting his skill and strength against a 500-pound yearling calf. Cold, rainy nights are unpleasant, but the joy of seeing a wobbly-legged newborn calf is worth all the trouble it takes.

Successful Ranching

The most important job of a rancher is seeing that his cattle get enough grass to eat. The amount of grass that can be grown on each acre of land depends on the amount of rain. In dry, desert country 20 or 30 acres of range may be needed to grow enough grass to feed one cow. In high-rainfall areas only 1 or 2 acres may be needed. This is the main reason that ranches vary so greatly in size. A ranch in a dry area has to be very big to feed a herd of cattle, while a ranch in a wetter climate will feed the same herd of cattle on only one tenth the land.

Ranchers are always trying to find new ways to make the soil richer so that it will grow more and better grass. Some ranchers use root plowing to tear out trees and brush and leave more room for pasture. Giant tractors cut off the roots of trees and brush and leave the grass unharmed.

In very dry areas ranchers use irrigation—piping in water from far away. Pipes laid down in the soil have small holes in them to water the dusty ground. This makes it easier to fertilize the soil, since fertilizers will not sink into hard or sandy ground.

Good ranchland costs a great deal of money, and sometimes ranchers find that they cannot afford to buy all the land they need to feed their herds. Then they rent, or lease, the land from the owner until they have enough money to buy the land for themselves. People who want to start ranches of their own and do not have much money often begin in this way.

Winter Feed

Ranchers must make certain that their cattle have enough to eat in the cold winter months. Some ranchers grow a special crop of hay, cut and store it in the summer and fall, and use it all winter to feed the cows. Others plant a special crop of grass, called winter pasture, that can survive cold weather, and they graze their cattle there when the other grasses die. Many ranchers use both methods to feed their herds.

Branding

Everyone who goes to the movies has seen a cattle brand—the brand mark on the side or the back of a steer. Sometimes the hero will look at the brand marks to see which cattle are his. Branding is very important to a ranch operation, for it is the only way the rancher can really know which cows are his own. In branding, the brand mark of the ranch is burned with a hot iron into the side, hip, or back of each calf. Each ranch has a different

New calves are branded so that each rancher can identify his own herd.

brand mark, and some of them have very strange and interesting shapes. They can be signs, pictures, or the initials of the owner's name.

Branding began in the early days when cattle roamed the open range and belonged to anyone who could catch them. Many ranchers in the 1800's got their start by catching these cattle, putting a fence around them, and letting them breed. Even then, some of these cattle would be stolen. Thus, marking the cattle with the owner's brand became a common practice.

Today branding is also used to keep track of cattle by number and age. The number 296/2 on a cow now, for instance, might mean she was the 296th cow born in 1962. On a big ranch with many herds of cattle this quick way of identifying each cow is important to the workers on the ranch.

Roundup

The roundup on a big ranch is a very exciting event. Cowboys ride out into the hills and pastures, round up all the grazing cattle, and drive them all back into a pen. On a big ranch this may mean riding miles and miles over open country and being out several days. The roundup gives the rancher a chance to brand the new cattle, to vaccinate them against blackleg and other diseases, and sometimes to remove the horns from the bull calves to prevent injury. It also enables the rancher to see all his cows together and to separate the bad ones from the herd.

Sheep Ranching

Sheep ranching is practiced in dry areas of the country because sheep eat less grass than cows. In the United States it is practiced mainly in the deserts of Texas, Arizona, and New Mexico. On some ranches the lambs are sold for meat, while other sheep are kept for wool and sheared at the ranch. The fleece, called the wool clip, is sold.

Horses

Good horses are needed on every ranch for the cowboys to ride when they are driving cattle or rounding them up. Some cattle ranches raise their own horses. Others buy them from special horse ranches. Most ranches use quarter horses, which are small but very fast and agile.

Cowboys often have to ride miles to round up all their cattle.

Ranch Families

Thanks to cars and electricity, ranch families are no longer so lonely and isolated as they were in the past. Now most of them live in modern houses, with much the same conveniences that city-dwellers enjoy.

Ranchers today face almost as many challenges as they did when the frontier was opening up. They are trying to develop new breeds of cattle, to cure and prevent animal disease, and to produce better meat at less cost. They also hope to improve the quality of the land so that the number of cattle raised on a ranch can be increased.

The main problem of the rancher is to do more with less. Because the population is increasing and moving outward from the cities, the amount of land available for ranching is decreasing. Fewer people are willing to work on ranches. The modern rancher must try to use less land and less labor to produce more and better meat.

ROBERT C. WELLS
King Ranch, Inc.

RAPHAEL (1483–1520)

Raphael was one of the greatest artists of the Renaissance. His full name was Raffaello Sanzio. Raphael was born in the small town of Urbino, Italy, on April 6, 1483. His father, who was a court painter and a poet, taught Raphael to paint.

By the time Raphael was 12, both his parents had died. Soon after, he was working in Perugia, in the shop of the painter Pietro Perugino. Raphael's early works were influenced by his master's sweet but conservative style.

In 1504, Raphael went to Florence. It was an exciting time to be there. Florence then was the center of the classical style of the Italian Renaissance. Leonardo da Vinci was painting

The roundness and softness of the design add to the beauty of the *Madonna della Sedia* (*Madonna of the Chair*) (1514–15).

the *Mona Lisa,* and Michelangelo had just completed the statue *David.* Leonardo's color techniques and Michelangelo's forceful figures had a lasting effect on Raphael. He painted gentle yet strong figures of the Madonna and Child in jewel-like colors.

Pope Julius II heard of the brilliant work of Raphael and summoned him to Rome in 1508. By that time, Rome had become the art center of the Renaissance. Michelangelo was painting the ceiling of the Sistine Chapel, and Leonardo would come to Rome in 1513. The Pope had frescoes by older painters destroyed so that Raphael could decorate entire Stanze (rooms) in the Vatican Palace. Raphael's dramatic work in the Stanze was done between 1509 and 1517. It shows religious, mythological, and historical scenes. He was also asked to decorate a great loggia (porch) in the Vatican.

In 1514, Raphael was made chief architect of the rebuilding of St. Peter's Basilica. A year later, he became guardian of the ancient ruins of Rome. He was also asked to design ten large tapestries for the Sistine Chapel. These tapestries represent the story of Saint Peter and Saint Paul. During this time, Raphael also painted and designed for private patrons. To accomplish all his commissions, he had to have more and more help from his students. But in spite of their help, he was overworked. He died in Rome on April 6, 1520, at the age of 37, after a week-long bout with fever.

Reviewed by S. J. FREEDBERG
Harvard University

READING

One of man's greatest achievements is the ability to put down in printed or written words his ideas and feelings. The ability to read those words is just as great an achievement.

What Is Reading?

What is this act called reading? Reading can be defined differently by the psychologist, the linguist, and the educator. Each looks at it in a slightly different manner. All would probably agree, however, that reading has to do with the process of attaching meaning to certain written symbols. For example, take the sentence "The little black terrier chased the yellow cat up the tree." As the words meet the eye the reader is stimulated to make a mental picture of the action taking place. He turns the printed words into meaning.

Unlike what many people think and say, reading is not the process of getting meaning from the page. The printed symbols do not have meaning that in some mysterious way is carried to the mind of the reader. Rather, the symbols awaken meaning that is already in the mind of the reader—meaning that has been put there by past experience. If the reader has no earlier knowledge of black terriers and yellow cats, the printed words of the above sentence cannot stimulate meaning. The reader will not have *read,* even though he was able to pronounce every word.

Readiness for Reading

Whether the young child learns to read with success and pleasure depends to a large extent upon whether he is ready to begin.

Preparation in the Home. Much of what is involved in readiness for reading takes place before the child enters kindergarten or first grade. He has experiences that give meaning to the stories he hears. Such experiences as trips to the zoo, to a farm, or to an airport help build up a child's vocabulary of the words that, in time, he will read. He discovers, listening to bedtime nursery rhymes and stories, the pleasure that comes from reading. He senses the importance of reading as he watches older people use it in following the news or in doing schoolwork. If he is lucky, the child is surrounded with a wealth of good books and magazines. This is one of the important ways in which parents can promote readiness for reading.

Preparation in the School. The first-grader will usually begin with a prereading, or reading-readiness, program. In this program the teacher gives attention to the development of oral language. The students learn to distinguish between visual forms that are similar in shape. (Later the ability to tell the difference between similar words, such as *book* and *look,* will depend upon this facility.) Children also learn to listen carefully for sounds at the beginning and end of words. Familiarity with

Children can experience the magic of books long before they are able to read.

sounds of the spoken language is a foundation for phonics, a method of teaching children to read and pronounce words.

Both the home and the school, then, play important parts in promoting readiness for reading. When, through observation and special readiness tests, the teacher finds the pupil ready, she begins the actual reading program. For a few children whose language development is advanced and who have had a rich reading environment in the home, this might take place toward the end of the kindergarten year. Most students, however, will not take the initial step until they are in the first grade. There are a few who may not be ready until still later.

Some educators recommend that children be taught to read in kindergarten or nursery school or even in the home, at the age of 2 or 3, by parents. A few children may learn to respond to words at an early age, and these few may read before they attend school. Parents, however, would be ill-advised to force a child to learn to read. They should answer a child's questions and tell him what a word is if he is curious about it. But let the teacher actually begin the reading program when she has evidence that the time is right.

Some parents ask whether they should teach the ABC's to a preschool child. Children of this age are likely to play with alphabet blocks and look at alphabet books. If they are curious, they will want to know the names of the letters. Eventually they will know that a pictured *drum* begins with *d* (letter name, not sound), that *boy* begins with *b*, and so on.

Actually a child does not need to know the letters of the alphabet in order to learn to read. As he begins reading in school he will probably learn to recognize words as wholes by sight. As he comes to study phonics his teacher will teach him the letters that are associated with the various sounds in words. Still later he will learn the letters of the alphabet in sequence as he begins to use the dictionary.

Teaching Reading

Sight Words. Most children begin the process of reading by learning a sight vocabulary. These are words taught as wholes or as units. The child learns to recognize them by sight. Sight words like *down, jump, look, at, here,* and *get* make it possible for the young child to read at once the story content he finds in the preprimers. Because the child's reading vocabulary is limited, the stories have a limited vocabulary. Although a 6-year-old may speak with a vocabulary of several thousand words, when he begins to read he starts at the zero point and builds up his reading vocabulary by degrees.

No child can become an efficient and independent reader if he depends on someone to tell him what each new word is. He has to acquire skills by which he can recognize new words.

Phonics. One of the techniques used to identify new words is phonics. Phonics is the association of speech sounds with the letter or letters that indicate these sounds. With a knowledge of consonants and vowels and how they function in words, the reader can pronounce a large number of unfamiliar words. He learns to recognize the guides, or cues, to speech sounds that certain letters indicate. As he meets larger words he learns how to divide them into syllables and how to pronounce each syllable.

The teaching of phonics presents many problems because a speech sound can have different spellings in English. For example, the sound indicated by the letter *o* in *no* is found in the words *though, oh, show, yolk,* and *sew.* In each case the sound is indicated by different letters. Because of such inconsistencies, an alphabet called the Pitman Initial Teaching Alphabet has been developed. It originated in England and has 44 characters instead of the 26 letters in the Roman alphabet. Some schools in the United States use the new alphabet for teaching reading.

Structural Units. The young reader also learns to identify new words by dividing them into their structural units. These units are prefixes, suffixes, and word roots and endings indicating plurals, tenses, and the like. This technique is particularly useful in identifying larger and more difficult words. For example, if the reader knows the root word *pack* and has a knowledge of the meaning and function of the added parts, or affixes, he will have no trouble reading *unpack, repack, packing, packer,* or *package.*

Instruction in Dictionary Usage. It is entirely possible for a beginning reader to meet a word that he cannot identify through either phonics or structure. In this case the dictionary is a means of unlocking new words. Instruction in dictionary usage usually comes in the third or fourth grade. A special beginning dictionary, with easily understood definitions and many illustrations, is used. In dictionary training the child is taught how to locate words quickly, to use the pronunciation key, and to select the definition that fits the way the word is used.

A sample of Pitman's Initial Teaching Alphabet.

dan wonted too doo aull the thiŋs coubois did.

hee wonted too ried wield horses.

hee wonted too lassoo wield steers.

Context. "Context" is defined as what comes before or after a word or sentence that helps make the meaning of that word or sentence clear. In the sentence "The mother robin flew to her _____ in the tree," the context of the surrounding words tells the reader that the word is *nest,* if it is not identified immediately as a sight word. In this case the child is not guessing the new word, as one might think at first. The context and phonics and structure, plus his reasoning, tell him the word.

Other Approaches. A teacher may use various approaches to beginning reading instruction. She may, for example, have the children dictate stories of their activities or experiences, which she writes on the blackboard. These are then read by the children. In doing this, they learn to recognize words common to their experiences. Later she may let each child select from a wide variety of materials a book that holds particular interest for him. It may be a narrative tale or a factual account. From these materials each child builds up a sight vocabulary.

However, it is likely that most teachers would build a reading program around a series of **basal readers**. These are graded books that have the special function of teaching reading. The content and the teaching program built into them are designed to promote continuous, step-by-step growth in all the basic aspects of reading. The materials are usually organized so that on the first-grade level there are three small paperback preprimers, a hardcover primer, and a first reader. On the second- and third-grade levels there are usually two readers for each grade, one for each half of the school year. For the fourth, fifth, and sixth grades there is one book for each year. Each book becomes more difficult in terms of sentence length, complexity, and vocabulary. Even the size of type becomes smaller.

Some teachers may supplement their reading program with programed materials. This is a type of material having small sections, or "frames," of reading content followed by a question. The student must answer the question before going on to the next frame. This type of material allows a child to work at his own speed, whether it is fast or slow. It is quite unlikely, however, that programed books or teaching machines will take the place of an enthusiastic reading teacher.

Advanced Reading Skills

It is surprising how rapidly the young reader grows in his ability to perceive words, even by the end of the first year in school. In addition to the words learned by sight, he is able to identify their *s, ed,* or *ing* forms. He can also recognize hundreds of words based upon these known words through using his understanding of phonics. For example, by substituting or by adding and dropping letters and the sounds they represent from the known word *man,* he can form the words *tan, pat, pal, sand, hand,* and *pass.* On levels beyond the first grade, growth is even more rapid as the reader applies more advanced skills.

Understanding Phrase, Sentence, and Paragraph. The ability to recognize words is not the only skill gained in the process of learning to read. In fact, word perception is only the beginning of the reading act. From knowing single words, the reader must go on to understand phrase, sentence, and pararaph meanings. He must learn to make judgments and draw conclusions and sum up a story or article in his own words. He must learn to look behind what a character in a story is doing and saying and to know the character's reasons for behaving as he does. In oral reading the reader must be able to identify with the story characters and project through voice and facial expression the suitable feeling or mood.

Reading Critically. Readers must also learn to evaluate the worth of what is read. A writer may purposely write propaganda. Although propaganda can be used for good causes, it is frequently used to spread a biased point of view. In doing so, the writer may use emotionally charged words, such as *sneaky, rabble, bombastic.* He may be careless of his facts, or he may fail to give evidence for his statements. Unless the reader reads with a critical eye, he may be led to accept warped ideas. He must be able to recognize "loaded" words, to check the reliability of statements, and to raise questions. Only in this way can the reader protect himself from being misled by some of the things he sees in print.

The skills that make one an understanding and critical reader do not come in any certain grade or in any certain length of time. The skills that one uses in mature reading develop slowly, as does the ability to write a good paragraph, to speak correctly, or to listen accurately. The student becomes a better reader with time and with sound, systematic instruction.

Specialized Reading Skills. Recognizing words and understanding them and reading critically are basic skills that apply to all reading situations. These skills, as well as others, are necessary for the specialized reading that students do in the various subject-matter areas, such as science, mathematics, and social studies. The reading of history or geography, for example, requires an intensive type of reading. Science requires the reading of formulas, laboratory manuals, and numerous illustrations and diagrams.

The development of these specialized reading abilities is usually considered the responsibility of the subject-matter teacher. Hence

In individual-reading programs, students choose books related to their own interests.

instruction in these areas is given as part of the teaching of the particular subject. In addition, the student is taught how to engage in study activities. This involves locating reference materials in the library, using encyclopedias, taking notes, and organizing the material for reports, debates, and term papers. These are referred to as work-study abilities, and their development is considered an important part of the reading program.

Learning to read with a high level of efficiency, then, requires instruction beyond the primary and elementary grades. As the student progresses in school the reading content becomes more difficult. More material must be covered, and he must learn to read faster. As a result, the reading begun at the primary level and broadened at the elementary level is extended and refined on the junior and senior high school levels.

Personal and Social Growth Through Reading

What people read and the values they get from reading are as important as learning to read. Signs of reading maturity include the ability to recognize and select quality material and to appreciate fine writing. The young reader who develops permanent interests in reading turns to it regularly. He uses reading as a means of making personal adjustments and of gaining clearer insights into the complex social problems about him.

Personal and social growth through reading is promoted in several ways. Teachers select materials primarily for their quality and for their ability to aid personal growth. Stories subtly point up wholesome family relations, good sportsmanship, and desirable character traits. Teachers guide discussions of stories in order to bring out their values and patterns for behavior.

A program of personal or individual reading is often carried on by the school in connection with the how-to-read program. Students are encouraged to select books or other materials related to their own interests and needs. It does not matter how varied the interests are. They may range all the way from ants to folktales, from xylophones to Zulus.

In order to satisfy these interests, young people need access to books and more books. Elementary schools are now being built with the library as the center of activity. It is the place to go to browse and to select from good literature. Each child should have his own public library borrower's card, and regular trips should be made to the library. The family, too, has a duty to build a collection of children's books and magazines, carefully selected in terms of the maturity of the child.

Reading Problems

Teachers watch for signs of reading difficulties and immediately take steps to help the child before the problem becomes a block to further progress.

In spite of all the precautions to prevent reading problems, some children have difficulties. Problems may arise at any time. Some children have ear or eye defects that are not detected before they enter school. These children may find it hard to see print clearly or hear spoken sounds distinctly. School absences due to illness or other causes may be a stumbling block, for it may be that while a child is absent from school, a new reading skill is introduced.

With population increasing as rapidly as it is, many teachers lack enough classroom space to give good instruction. A teacher with an overcrowded classroom cannot serve the individual needs of children learning to read.

There may be times when reading instruction is begun before the child is ready. Perhaps he cannot distinguish between sounds and words that are similar, or he may see no purpose or value in learning to read. His background of experience may be so limited that the printed words do not stimulate meaning. Instruction given before the child is ready to profit from it may have only negative effects.

Many schools now provide special reading teachers trained to make diagnoses of reading difficulties and provide corrective help for children who have reading problems. If a school does not have such a teacher, a nearby state college or university may provide the help needed. Parents who feel that a child requires special help should go to a teacher or principal who can advise appropriate action.

A. STERL ARTLEY
University of Missouri

See also INITIAL TEACHING ALPHABET; PHONICS.

RONALD WILSON REAGAN (1911–)

40TH PRESIDENT OF THE UNITED STATES

REAGAN, RONALD WILSON. The life of Ronald Wilson Reagan is a story of unlikely successes. Reagan was born of poor parents in a small town in Illinois. He graduated from college during the Depression of the 1930's. Yet he became a successful actor in motion pictures and on television. When his entertainment career began to decline, he began a new career—in politics. In 1966 he ran for governor of California as a Republican. He won, despite the fact that most California voters were Democrats.

In 1968 and again in 1976, Reagan sought the Republican nomination for president. He lost both times. After that, many people thought that Reagan's age—then 65—would prevent his party from nominating him. But he worked hard for the nomination in 1980. And he demonstrated to the voters' satisfaction that he could stand up to the stress of a job that is perhaps the most difficult in the world.

▸ **EARLY YEARS**

The 40th President of the United States was born in Tampico, Illinois, on February 6, 1911. His father, John Edward Reagan, was an Irish-American shoe salesman. His mother,

Nelle Wilson Reagan, was of English and Scottish ancestry. Neither parent had more than an elementary school education. Ronald had one brother, Neil, who was two years older. Neil picked up the nickname Moon, and Ronald was called Dutch.

Reagan's father often moved the family around the state in search of a better-paying job. But life in the small towns of Illinois was pleasant. "My existence turned into one of those rare Huck Finn–Tom Sawyer idylls," Reagan recalled in his autobiography, *Where's the Rest of Me?* "Those were the days when I learned the riches of rags."

Dixon, a small town to which the family moved when he was 9, was the place where Reagan got most of his schooling. He was not an outstanding student. But his interests in drama, sports, and politics began early. His mother gave dramatic readings before clubs and in prisons and hospitals, and he was first exposed to acting before he started school. He began to play football—one of the great loves of his life—before he was 10 years old, in neighborhood games arranged on the spur of the moment.

"There was no field; no lines, no goal. Simply grass, the ball, and a mob of excited youngsters," he later wrote. "Those were the happiest times of my life." Reagan graduated from that kind of football to action as a guard and end on the Dixon High School team. He also participated in basketball and track, acted in school plays, and was president of the student body. During most of his high school and college summers, he worked as a lifeguard at a summer resort near Dixon.

After his high school graduation in 1928, Reagan enrolled at Eureka College, a small college in Eureka, Illinois. He majored in economics; joined the college football, track, and swimming teams; and acted in school plays. He washed dishes at his fraternity house and saved money from summer jobs to help pay his expenses. His grades were not exceptional. But he earned acceptable marks through "quick studies" before tests. He also served for one year as president of the student body.

As a freshman, Reagan took part in a student strike that resulted in the resignation of the college president, who had proposed cutting back the curriculum and the teaching staff because of a shortage of funds. Reagan made the main speech at a rally that won support for the strike from nearly all the students. He later said that he learned then what it was like to succeed with an audience. His skill with audiences was to be a major factor in his successes in later life.

▶ HIS ACTING CAREER

Reagan earned a B.A. degree from Eureka in 1932, at a time when the Depression had left many people without jobs. He spent one last summer as a lifeguard. Then he set out to obtain a job as a radio announcer. He won a tryout for a job announcing football games at WOC in Davenport, Iowa, not far from Dixon. His tryout consisted of making up a play-by-play broadcast for an imaginary football game. He did well enough, and he was signed on. That job led to work at WOC's larger affiliate, WHO in Des Moines. By the time he was 25, he was one of the top sports broadcasters in the Middle West.

In 1937, Reagan traveled with the Chicago Cubs to their spring training camp near Los Angeles, California. While there, he managed to obtain a screen test from Warner Brothers, and he was offered an acting contract. He quickly accepted. Reagan's movie career spanned more than 20 years and over 50 movies. His most successful roles were in *Knute Rockne—All American* in 1940 and in *King's Row* in 1941. In *Knute Rockne,* Reagan played star halfback George Gipp, who died imploring his coach to have his teammates "win one for the Gipper."

In 1942, during World War II, Reagan entered the Army as a second lieutenant. He was disqualified for combat duty because of poor eyesight, and he spent the next four years making military training films. He then re-

Ronald Reagan as a young child (*right foreground*), with his parents and his older brother, Neil.

In the movie *Knute Rockne—All American,* Reagan drew on his love of football to play star halfback George Gipp.

As governor of California in 1967, Reagan signs a bill into law. Members of the state legislature look on.

turned to the motion picture industry. Until this time, Reagan had been a Democrat and had supported many liberal causes. But after the war his views became more conservative. This change was caused in part, he later said, by government inefficiency that he had witnessed when he was in the Army.

Reagan served as president of the Screen Actors Guild, the labor union for actors and actresses, from 1947 to 1952. And he became a strong opponent of Communism. In 1947 he went to Washington, D.C., to testify before the House Committee on Un-American Activities about Communist influence in Hollywood.

By 1954, Reagan was less in demand for leading-man roles in films. He accepted a job with the General Electric Company, as the leading personality on the firm's television show, "General Electric Theater." Between shows, he traveled around the nation for the company, making speeches about the dangers of big government and the blessings of free enterprise. When "General Electric Theater" went off the air in 1962, Reagan became host of another show, "Death Valley Days." Meanwhile, the high salaries he earned in movies and on television, together with real estate investments, had made him wealthy. He had married Jane Wyman, an actress, in

1940. They had two children—a daughter, Maureen, born in 1941, and a son, Michael, who was adopted as an infant in 1945. The marriage ended in divorce in 1948. Four years later, Reagan married another actress, Nancy Davis. They had two children—Patricia (Patti), born in 1952, and Ronald, born in 1958.

▶ GOVERNOR OF CALIFORNIA

Reagan's entry into politics was hastened by a speech he gave in October, 1964, on behalf of the Republican presidential candidate, Senator Barry Goldwater of Arizona. The nationally televised speech, "A Time for Choosing," won Reagan a national following. It was credited with drawing more political contributions than any other speech in the nation's history. The speech also brought Reagan to the attention of powerful figures in the Republican Party. They urged him to seek the governorship of California.

Reagan announced his candidacy early in January, 1966. He easily won the Republican primary. In the election, he faced Edmund G. (Pat) Brown, who had been a popular Democratic governor for eight years. Reagan was critical of government spending and welfare payments that he believed were too high. He won by nearly 1,000,000 votes. Four years later, Reagan easily defeated Jesse Unruh, the speaker of the state assembly, for a second term. He served as governor through 1974.

Government spending increased considerably during Reagan's two terms as governor. In his first term, he was forced to seek a large income tax increase. But it was generally thought that he kept costs below what they might have been. He fought with the state legislature through much of his first term. But he learned to work well with the lawmakers. He regarded the passage of welfare reform legislation as his biggest accomplishment as governor. The law meant considerable savings for California taxpayers.

IMPORTANT DATES IN THE LIFE OF RONALD WILSON REAGAN	
1911	Born in Tampico, Illinois, February 6.
1932	Graduated from Eureka College, Eureka, Illinois.
1937	Acted in his first film, *Love Is on the Air*.
1942–1946	Served in the United States Army.
1947–1952	Served as president of the Screen Actors Guild.
1967–1975	Served as governor of California.
1980	Elected president of the United States.

The Reagans wave to supporters at the 1980 Republican convention. From left: son Ronald; Patti; Nancy and Ronald Reagan; Michael with his wife, Colleen, and son, Cameron; and Maureen.

▶ THE PRESIDENCY

Reagan first sought the Republican presidential nomination in 1968. He presented himself as a representative of conservative elements in the party. But his effort was too little and too late. Richard M. Nixon was nominated and eventually won the office. In 1976, Reagan waged a strong campaign for the nomination. But he lost narrowly to Gerald R. Ford, who had become president when Nixon resigned in 1974. The Democratic candidate, Jimmy Carter, won the 1976 election.

Reagan started the 1980 campaign not long after his 1976 fight had been lost. In the 1980 primary contests, he called on his skills as a speaker to win support. His views seemed to reflect growing conservatism in the country, and he won the nomination in an overwhelming victory. His nearest opponent, George Bush, was chosen as his vice-presidential running mate. Another Republican contender, U.S. Representative John B. Anderson of Illinois, ran against both Reagan and Carter as an independent candidate.

In the campaign, Reagan took solidly conservative positions. He favored reducing total government spending while increasing the amount spent on national defense. He also supported large tax cuts and state or local control of programs such as welfare. And he felt that the United States should take firmer stands against Communism and in support of friendly governments. Some of Reagan's critics said that his stand on foreign policy might be seen as warlike. Others pointed out that at 69, he would be the oldest person ever elected president. But Reagan campaigned hard. He presented himself well in a televised debate against Carter. And he found widespread support for his positions. He won the election with 489 electoral votes, to 49 for Carter. His share of the popular vote exceeded Carter's by 10 percent.

Reagan's presidency began dramatically in 1981. Minutes after he was sworn in, Iran released 52 U.S. citizens who had been held hostage there for over 14 months. The release had been negotiated by the Carter administration. Then, in March, Reagan was shot in Washington, D.C., by John W. Hinckley, Jr., a 25-year-old drifter. Reagan recovered, and a jury later found Hinckley insane and not responsible for his act.

Congress passed Reagan's early requests for cuts in taxes and government spending. In 1982, he proposed turning many federal welfare programs over to the states. The states did not support the plan. Meanwhile, the economy was in a recession, and some people began to criticize Reagan's economic policies.

Reagan imposed trade sanctions against Poland and the Soviet Union in 1982, after Poland's Communist government had declared martial law to silence dissent. Later that year, he began a new round of strategic arms talks with the Soviets. In the Middle East, Reagan's policy was to improve relations with Arab countries while giving strong support to Israel. But in 1982, Israeli troops entered Lebanon to drive out Palestinian fighters based there. Reagan criticized the Israeli action strongly. U.S. officials helped work out a truce, and U.S. troops joined in an international peacekeeping force in Lebanon.

JAMES O. BELL
Los Angeles Times

A group of houses on the same piece of land, all built and sold by one firm, is called a development. Housing developments have sprung up around many big cities to take care of a growing population.

REAL ESTATE

Real estate (also called real property) is land and all things that are attached to the land. This includes the minerals, such as coal or iron, that may lie beneath the surface, the trees and crops that grow on the land, and the houses and buildings on it.

In the past the landowners were nobles, the richest and most powerful people in society. The people who lived on their lands had to perform certain services and give part of their crops to the landowner. The

nobles were truly lords of the land, and this is the origin of our word "landlord."

The feudal system during the Middle Ages in Europe was based upon land ownership. Under the rule of the landowning nobles were two main groups: vassals and serfs. Vassals were tenants of a landlord's estates who either rented land or were allowed to live on the land in return for rendering services to the nobles. Nobles, in turn, were vassals of the king. Serfs were slaves who were considered part of the property. When land was sold or traded, the serfs usually were included as part of the property. Gradually the feudal system ended, and more and more people obtained land of their own. Anyone who could manage to buy land could own it. Many people wanted land because it was a basic source of wealth.

Some of the greatest fortunes in the United States have been made from buying and selling land. John Jacob Astor (1763–1848), who emigrated from Germany to the United States, made millions of dollars in New York real estate. Astor used the money he made in the fur trade to buy land in Manhattan. He often paid only a few hundred dollars for a piece of land. As the city developed, the value of Astor's land multiplied and his fortune grew. Nicholas Longworth (1782–1863) in Cincinnati and Marshall Field (1834–1906) in Chicago also made fortunes by buying real estate in those cities. These men sometimes held their land for a few years and then sold it for many times the price they had paid for it. They put up buildings on the land and rented them out. Or they leased, or rented, the land to someone who wanted to put up a building.

The rights of real estate owners are pro-

SOME TERMS USED IN REAL ESTATE

Amortization—The paying off of a debt, usually in periodic installments.

Assessed value—The value set on a piece of property by the local government for the purposes of taxation. Assessed value is different from **market value**, which is the price the property would sell for.

Broker—A real estate person who handles sales and purchases of property. Most real estate people are brokers.

Commercial property—Property reserved by law for business use.

Commission—The fee paid to real estate brokers or agents for their services. It is a percentage of the money involved in a sale or lease of property.

Deed—A written document that is proof of the ownership of a piece of property.

Escrow—A written agreement between two persons that is held by a third person until certain conditions are fulfilled.

Lease—A legal contract between a property-owner and a person who uses the property. It states the terms under which the property is to be used, how much rent is to be paid, and how long the property is to be used.

Mortgage—A legal document by which a person borrows money for the purchase of property and promises to pay it back. If the money is not repaid, the lender can take over the property.

Realtor—A real estate broker who is a member of the National Association of Realtors.

Residential property—Property reserved for homes.

Title search—An investigation of records to make certain there are no claims against a piece of property.

Tract—A defined area of land or water.

Zoning—The method by which a local government divides its area into residential, commercial, and industrial property.

tected by law. No one can use land without the consent of the owner. This includes building roads across the property or using the waterways on it.

Real estate can be bought, sold, traded, given away, or left to heirs at the death of the owner. Whatever way the property changes hands, the new owner usually has the same rights that the old owner had.

Real estate may not be transferred from one owner to another without written agreement. There are two types of documents connected with the transfer of property. A **lease** is a contract between an owner and a tenant (a person who uses the property). The lease contains the terms agreed upon by the owner and the tenant, such as the amount of rent the tenant agrees to pay and the length of time the property may be used. A **deed**, or title, is a document showing that a landowner legally owns the property. When someone buys a piece of real estate, he or she receives a deed to the property from the previous owner.

A person who acts as the intermediary in the buying and selling of property is called a real estate broker. The broker is an important person in a community. When a new home, apartment house, or office building is to be built, a broker finds the proper site and handles the purchase of the land. When purchasing land for the client, the broker (or a lawyer) makes a **title search**, to be sure that no one except the seller has any claim to the property. The broker may also help arrange for a mortgage from a bank or an insurance company, so the client can obtain the money to buy the property. A **mortgage** is a legal agreement by which a person borrows money for the purchase of land and promises to pay it back. Under the terms of the mortgage, the lender can take over the property if the money is not repaid.

When a large number of houses or apartment buildings are erected in a new area, stores, restaurants, and other business establishments are needed to serve the new tenants. A real estate broker handles the arrangements for buying or renting land for these purposes. In a short time an empty section can become a thriving small city. Much of the credit for this must go to the real estate broker.

Real estate people usually specialize in some particular branch of real estate. Special-ists in industrial property obtain land and buildings for manufacturing plants. They bring in new businesses and factories, which provide jobs for the people living in the area.

Property management is another specialty in real estate. The property manager's duties include collecting rents on the land or buildings, supervising the upkeep of the property, and keeping the accounts and tax records.

Many real estate people specialize in buying and selling residential property for houses and apartments. When a homeowner decides to sell property, a real estate broker will help the owner set a price and find a buyer for the property. The broker advertises the property for sale and notifies people on his or her customer list who have expressed interest in buying a home. The broker usually shows prospective buyers the property and acts as the go-between for the owner and the buyer. A broker may also handle the leasing of property. For these services a broker is paid a fee called a commission. It is a percentage of the money involved in the sale or leasing of the property.

Property in a city or in the suburbs outside a city usually is divided into zones for residential use and zones for commercial and industrial use. Community officials make the zoning laws of an area. These laws prevent factories or other unwanted business establishments from being located too close to people's homes. Real estate people must know the zoning laws thoroughly, so they can advise prospective buyers.

Besides being an expert in property and zoning, a real estate person must be familiar with economics, insurance, finance, and general business methods. To provide this training, many colleges and universities offer courses and degrees in real estate. Many states require that a person pass an examination and get a license before working as a real estate broker.

There are many professional real estate organizations. One of the largest in the United States is the National Association of Realtors. Members of this organization are called realtors and realtor-associates. These terms are registered marks.

Reviewed by DAVID MURRAY
National Association of Realtors

RECESSIONS. See DEPRESSIONS AND RECESSIONS.

RECIPES

In great-grandmother's time, recipes were not much help if you didn't know how to cook. "Add a handful of flour," the recipe said. How much flour this turned out to be depended on how big your hand was. Fortunately this is no longer so. Today's recipes have been tested; measurements are exact. Oven heat controls can be set correctly for baking or roasting. Anyone who can read can cook.

Like all skills, cooking requires practice and experience. Don't let a failure keep you from trying again. Few cooks ever did everything perfectly the first time.

▶ COOKS MUST BE CLEAN AND TIDY

Cleanliness is very important for anyone handling food. Always wash your hands with warm water and soap before you start cooking. See that your apron, the tabletops where you will be working, and all utensils are spotlessly clean. Rinse all the foods that you will use—meat (except chopped meat), poultry, fish, vegetables, and fruits, for example—in running water. Get into the habit of replacing boxes of ingredients on the pantry shelf when you are finished with them. Wash the bowls and pots used and put them away.

▶ PREVENT FOOD SPOILAGE

Foods can spoil quickly, particularly in warm weather. This is both wasteful and dangerous to health. The hour or so on the dinner table will do no harm, but do not leave foods out, uncovered, for long periods of time or overnight. Place all cooked foods in the refrigerator as soon as possible if they are not to be eaten right away. Uncooked meat, fish, poultry, and dairy products should be refrigerated as soon as they are brought home.

▶ COOKING VEGETABLES

Some of the important vitamins in vegetables dissolve in water (are water-soluble). In order to prevent the loss of these vitamins, vegetables should be cooked as quickly, and in as little water, as possible. Always place the vegetable in water that is already boiling. This will shorten the cooking time.

Never overcook vegetables. A crisp, undercooked vegetable is more colorful, better-tasting, and better for you than a limp, soggy one. Cooking time for vegetables will vary, depending on how fresh they are. The best way to tell whether they are done is to taste them as they cook. As soon as they are tender but not limp, remove the pan from the heat. Drain the liquid (there should be very little).

▶ READY TO COOK?

First read the recipe carefully. Be sure you understand it. Prepare the ingredients, measuring cups and spoons, and pans you will need. Make all measurements level unless the recipe calls for a "rounded" or "heaping" measurement.

Here is an easy dinner for four:

Apple Juice or Cranberry Juice

Hamburgers

Baked Tomatoes   String Beans and Mushrooms

Heavenly Hash

Bread and Butter   Brownies   Milk

Hamburgers

1½ pounds chopped beef	1 tablespoon fat
½ teaspoon salt	(butter, margarine,
pinch of pepper	or oil)
1 egg	

Place the chopped beef, salt, pepper, and unbeaten egg in a mixing bowl. Mix well with a large spoon. Shape into 4 meat patties.

Grease a heavy skillet with fat. Heat over a medium flame for 2 minutes or until skillet is hot. Place meat patties in pan and cook for 8 minutes on each side. For well-done hamburgers, cook a few minutes longer.

Baked Tomatoes

4 small, firm, ripe tomatoes	2 tablespoons chopped parsley
salt and pepper	2 tablespoons vegetable oil
¼ cup bread crumbs	

COOKING TERMS

Bake—To cook in heated oven with dry heat.

Baste—To spoon fat, liquid, or gravy over food while it is roasting.

Blend—To mix ingredients together until smooth.

Boil—To cook in liquid heated until bubbles rise and break on the surface.

Broil—To cook uncovered on a rack under or over direct heat.

Cream—To mash or mix one or more foods together until they are soft and creamy.

Fry—To cook in hot fat, uncovered, on top of the stove.

Panbroil—To cook uncovered in a heated skillet with little or no fat.

Pinch—Less than 1/8 teaspoon.

Preheat—To set heat control of oven to proper temperature before placing food in oven.

Roast—To cook uncovered without water in oven.

Simmer—To cook in liquid below boiling point (when bubbles form slowly and break below surface).

Preheat oven to 400 degrees. Wash tomatoes and cut off stem ends. Cut tomatoes in half crosswise. Sprinkle them with salt and pepper. Mix the bread crumbs, parsley, and oil together in a small bowl. Spread each tomato half with bread-crumb mixture. Place tomatoes in greased baking dish. Bake 10 to 15 minutes or until bread crumbs are golden brown.

String Beans and Mushrooms

1 package frozen string beans	½ teaspoon salt
½ cup boiling water	1 4-ounce can sliced mushrooms

Place beans in boiling salted water. Cook for 7 or 8 minutes. Add drained mushrooms to beans 3 minutes before end of cooking time, just long enough to heat them through. Drain beans and mushrooms. Season with additional salt and pepper and a lump of butter if desired.

Heavenly Hash

1 No. 2 can pineapple tidbits	3 tablespoons confectioner's sugar
1 cup marshmallows, diced	juice of 1 lemon
1 banana, diced	½ cup walnuts, coarsely chopped

"Diced" means cut in small pieces. Be sure to use the pineapple tidbits—not the crushed or chunk pineapple. Drain pineapple and save juice.

Place drained pineapple, diced marshmallow and banana, sugar, lemon juice, and nuts in a glass bowl. (Use marshmallow miniatures if you can; they are just the right size.) Add enough pineapple juice to moisten the mixture. You will need about ⅓ cup or so. Mix ingredients lightly. Place in refrigerator to chill for 2 hours.

Brownies

¼ pound (1 stick or ½ cup) butter or margarine	1 heaping tablespoon cocoa
1 cup sugar	2 tablespoons heavy cream
2 eggs, lightly beaten	1 tablespoon vanilla
pinch of salt	⅔ cup sifted flour
	1 cup walnuts, coarsely chopped

Leave the butter or margarine out of the refrigerator a few hours to soften. To measure a half-cup of butter, fill a measuring cup one-half full of water. Add butter until the water reaches the 1-cup level. Pour off water.

Preheat oven to 375 degrees. Grease an 8-inch-square baking pan. Place the butter and sugar in a bowl and cream together until smooth. Beat in eggs. Add salt, cocoa, cream, and vanilla. Beat until smooth. Add flour and beat until blended. Add nuts and mix well. Spread batter evenly in baking dish. Bake 35 to 40 minutes or until a cake tester (or toothpick) comes out dry. Cut into 16 squares while still warm.

SWEETS AND SNACKS

French Toast

Use bread that is not quite fresh—about 2 days old. French bread cut into slices about ½ inch thick will do very well.

1 cup milk	pinch of pepper
1 egg	½ teaspoon sugar
¼ teaspoon salt	butter or margarine for frying
4–6 slices French bread	

Beat milk, eggs, salt, pepper, and sugar together in a shallow bowl. Heat a large, heavy skillet. Melt about 2 tablespoons butter or margarine. When fat is hot and sizzling, soak slices of bread in egg-milk mixture. Leave them in liquid until they are wet through but do not fall apart. Fry bread quickly until golden brown. Turn and brown other side. Add more fat as you need it. Serve as soon as possible with jam, powdered sugar, or maple syrup. Serves four.

Fudge

2 cups sugar	1 teaspoon vanilla
6 tablespoons cocoa	1 cup walnuts, coarsely broken
¾ cup milk	
2 tablespoons butter	

Place sugar, cocoa, and milk in a heavy, good-sized saucepan. Cook slowly, stirring, until the sugar dissolves. Continue to cook over medium heat, stirring occasionally. To tell when the mixture has cooked enough, test by dropping a few drops into a glass of cold water. When it forms into a soft ball in the water, it is done. Remove the pan from the heat and add the butter, but do not stir. Allow to cool until lukewarm, add vanilla, and beat the fudge until it loses its shiny look and becomes thick and creamy. Fold in nuts and distribute them evenly. Pour fudge into a lightly greased 8-by-8-inch pan. When hardened, cut into squares.

Television Nibbles

½ cup butter or margarine (1 stick)	2 cups each: Wheat Chex, Rice Chex, Corn Chex, thin pretzel sticks
1 tablespoon Worcestershire sauce	1 cup peanuts or walnuts
½ teaspoon salt	
¼ teaspoon garlic salt	

Place butter or margarine in shallow baking pan (15 by 10 by 1 inch). Put pan in oven preheated to 275 degrees until butter melts. Add seasonings to melted butter and mix well. Add cereals, pretzel sticks, and nuts. Stir thoroughly until all are coated. Return pan to oven for 45 minutes, stirring every 15 minutes. Remove from oven, and spread cereal mixture on brown paper or paper towels to cool. Store in screw-top jars to keep crisp.

Spice Squares

1 cup dark brown sugar
1 cup water
1½ cups seedless raisins
⅓ cup vegetable oil
1 teaspoon cinnamon
¼ teaspoon each of cloves, salt, nutmeg
1 teaspoon baking soda
1 tablespoon warm water
2 cups sifted flour
½ teaspoon baking powder
½ cup walnuts, coarsely chopped
confectioner's sugar

Preheat oven to 350 degrees. Boil sugar, water, raisins, oil, cinnamon, cloves, salt, and nutmeg in a medium-sized saucepan for 3 minutes. Cool mixture for 10 minutes. Dissolve soda in warm water and add to boiled mixture. Sift flour and baking powder together and add to mixture in saucepan. Fold in chopped nuts. Grease an 8-inch-square baking dish. Spread batter evenly in baking dish. Bake 30 to 35 minutes or until cake tester comes out dry. When cool, sprinkle with confectioner's sugar and cut into 16 squares.

Chocolate Chip Oatmeal Cookies

¾ cup butter or shortening, soft
½ cup sugar
1 cup dark brown sugar
1 egg
¼ cup water
2 teaspoons vanilla
1 teaspoon baking soda
1 cup sifted flour
1 teaspoon salt
3 cups uncooked oats, regular (not quick-cooking)
1 cup chocolate chips

Preheat oven to 350 degrees and grease cookie sheet. Place shortening, sugars, egg, water, and vanilla in mixing bowl and beat thoroughly. Sift together flour, salt, and soda and add to shortening mixture. Mix well. Blend in oats and drop by teaspoons onto cooky sheet. If you wish, you may also add ⅓ cup chopped nuts, raisins, or shredded coconut to the batter. Bake for 12 to 15 minutes, until slightly brown at the edges. Remove from cooky sheet with spatula. Makes 5 dozen.

Taffy

1 cup sugar
½ cup water
¼ cup light corn syrup
⅛ teaspoon salt

Place sugar, water, corn syrup, and salt in a saucepan. Boil over medium heat until the mixture, when tested in a glass of cold water, forms a brittle ball like a marble. Remove the mixture from pan and let it cool until you can comfortably handle it. Butter your hands and firmly grasp the ends of the taffy. Pull it as far as it will go. Fold the two ends together and pull again. Repeat the folding and pulling until the taffy becomes snowy white. Pull out and twist into a long, thin rope. Cut into bite-size pieces. Wrap each piece in waxed paper or kitchen plastic.

Popcorn Balls

7 cups popped corn or cereal, like Kix or Cheerios
1 cup sugar
⅓ cup water
⅓ cup light corn syrup
1 teaspoon salt
¼ cup butter
1 teaspoon vanilla

Place corn or cereal in a large bowl. Place sugar, water, syrup, salt, and butter in saucepan, and mix. Cook over medium heat until a few drops form a hard ball when dropped into cold water. Remove from heat. Stir in vanilla. Pour syrup in a thin stream over corn or cereal, stirring constantly to mix well. Butter your hands and shape the glazed popcorn or cereal into balls. Makes 12 to 15 large balls.

Butter Cookies

½ cup butter (1 stick)
⅓ cup sugar
1 egg
¾ cup flour
½ teaspoon vanilla
⅓ teaspoon salt

Preheat oven to 375 degrees. Cream butter and sugar. Mix in egg, slightly beaten. Sift flour and salt and combine with egg mixture; add vanilla and mix until batter is smooth. Drop batter by teaspoonfuls onto greased and floured baking sheets, leaving some space between cookies. Bake 10 to 15 minutes or until the edges of the cookies turn brown. Makes about 2 dozen cookies.

Cupcakes

1 cup sugar
½ cup butter, soft
2 eggs
1¾ cups cake flour
1½ teaspoons baking powder
⅛ teaspoon salt
½ cup milk
1 teaspoon vanilla
1 cup nuts, coarsely chopped, or 1 cup raisins

Preheat oven to 350 degrees. Grease 2-inch muffin tins, or use paper liners. Beat softened butter until fluffy and add sugar, a little at a time, beating until mixture is light and creamy. Add eggs, one at a time, beating well. Sift flour and sprinkle a little over nuts or raisins to coat them. Beat flour, baking powder, and salt into butter mixture. Add milk and vanilla, and beat until smooth. Fold in flour-coated nuts or raisins. Pour batter into cupcake tins, filling them about two-thirds full. Bake for 25 minutes or until they are light brown and a toothpick inserted in the center of a cupcake comes out dry. Remove from oven, and cool for 10 minutes. Remove from tins, and sprinkle tops with confectioner's sugar. Makes 28 2-inch cupcakes.

SYLVIA ROSENTHAL
Author, *Live High on Low Fat*

See also FOOD SPOILAGE AND CONTAMINATION; OUTDOOR COOKING AND PICNICS.

The Freedmen's Bureau set up free public schools throughout the South.

RECONSTRUCTION PERIOD

In United States history "Reconstruction" has two meanings. One is political. It means the way in which the Confederate states, which seceded (withdrew) from the Union in 1860 and 1861, were brought back into the Union at the end of the Civil War. The other meaning refers to the building of a new social order in the postwar South.

▶ PRESIDENTIAL PLANS FOR RECONSTRUCTION

The North, under President Abraham Lincoln's leadership, had never admitted that a state had the right to leave the Union. But the end of the war did not automatically restore the states of the Confederacy to their former places in the nation. Even, Lincoln would not go so far as to say that it did. The states that had seceded would have to be punished in some way and meet certain conditions before they would be taken back into the Union.

In the last 18 months of his life, Lincoln gave much thought to the problem. On December 8, 1863, he presented his ideas for the first time when he issued the Proclamation of Amnesty and Reconstruction. In this he offered a general **amnesty** (official pardon) to all Confederates—except high army officers and officials—who would swear to support the federal government and the Constitution of the United States. Lincoln also promised that he would recognize the government in any state where persons equal in number to one tenth of the votes cast in the presidential election of 1860 took the oath and set up a government.

Lincoln's proclamation was not well received in Congress. Many members believed that Congress, not the President, should lay down the terms of reunion. Many also wanted to impose much harsher measures on the South. These members were called Radical Republicans.

▶ CONGRESSIONAL PLANS FOR RECONSTRUCTION

By July, 1864, Congress had worked out its own plan of Reconstruction. This plan, set forth in what was called the Wade-Davis bill, required that a majority of voters in a state that had seceded (rather than only 10 percent) must take an oath to support the Constitution. The bill also imposed much stricter qualifications upon voters. Both houses passed the bill, and it was presented to Lincoln on the last day of the session. But he kept it from becoming law by not signing it.

Four Southern states organized governments under Lincoln's plan of Reconstruction. But Congress, which is the final judge of the qualifications of its members, refused to receive their representatives and senators. Thus the political problem still existed when Andrew Johnson succeeded Lincoln as president on April 15, 1865.

The Radical Republicans believed that Johnson would be much harder on the former Confederate states than Lincoln had planned to be. Many were surprised, therefore, when the new president, on May 29, 1865, issued a proclamation much like Lincoln's proclamation of December 8, 1863. On the same day, in a proclamation relating to a new government for North Carolina, Johnson avoided any numerical requirement concerning the number of voters and gave the right to vote to the loyal "portion of the people." Within six weeks the President had issued proclamations like this for six other former Confederate states.

Under these proclamations Southern states set up their own governments. They agreed to meet some of the conditions the President had laid down. They canceled their ordinances, or laws, of secession, refused to pay the bonds they had issued to raise money during the war, and did away with slavery. But they would not give any signs of being sorry for having left the Union. Instead, they elected to office many high officials of the Confederate Government and former Confederate officers of high rank. They refused to give blacks the right to vote. Both Lincoln and Johnson had urged that qualified blacks and those who had fought for the Union should be given this right. Instead, the Southern states passed laws, known as Black Codes, that were intended to keep blacks in a lower position. The South had been forced to free the slaves. But the Southern states did not intend to make the black people equal to white people.

The refusal of the South to act like a defeated enemy angered the Republican majority in Congress. When Southern senators and representatives presented themselves for the new session, which began in December, 1865, they were refused seats. Then, in April, 1866, the Republicans passed a civil rights bill. This bill made citizens of "all persons born in the United States . . . of every race and color," whether or not they had been slaves. Blacks were to have the same rights to property that white people enjoyed. President Johnson vetoed the bill. But on April 9, 1866, Congress passed it over his veto.

On July 16, Congress passed another bill over the President's veto. This bill continued for two years the existence of the Freedmen's Bureau, which was first created on March 3, 1865. Various acts of Congress continued it until 1872. The purpose of the bureau was to aid freed slaves by furnishing supplies and medicines, setting up schools, and seeing that blacks were treated fairly by their former owners. The bureau accomplished much, but the South looked on it almost as a tool of a foreign government.

So far, the Radical Republicans had shaped Reconstruction as they wanted it. But they knew that laws could be reversed by the courts. They decided to amend the Constitution, which was beyond the reach of the courts. By June 13, 1866, both houses had passed the Fourteenth Amendment. The first section defined citizenship to include blacks and entitled them to equal protection of the law. The second section proposed, in effect, to cut down the number of representatives in Congress from any state that did not allow blacks to vote. The third section closed many federal offices to former Confederates. The fourth made it unconstitutional for the United States or any state to pay the Confederate debt or to pay anyone for freed slaves. The amendment was ratified (approved), and it became part of the Constitution in 1868.

By the summer of 1866, relations between the President and Congress had come close to the breaking point. The Radical Republican leaders wanted to end the power of the Southern aristocracy and the Democratic Party and to give blacks the vote and legal equality with white people. The President, himself a Southerner, sympathized with the South even

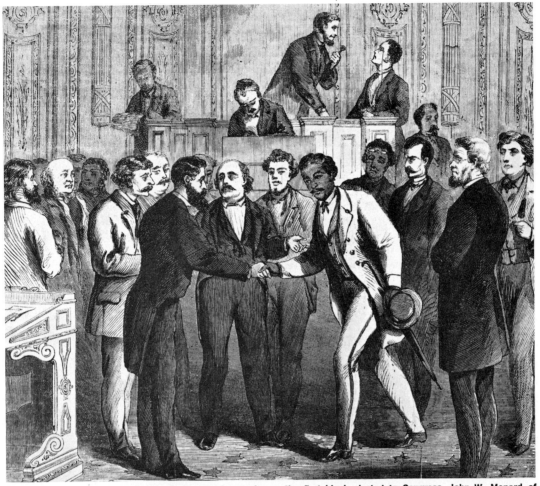

Radical leaders welcome the first black elected to Congress, John W. Menard of Louisiana, in 1868. His right to be seated was challenged, and he never served.

though he despised the old, wealthy planter class. He also believed firmly in states' rights. He insisted that the South should be left alone to deal with blacks and that the President rather than Congress should decide when the Southern states should be readmitted to the Union. But Johnson was not tactful. He was always sure that he was right, and he was unable to yield even a little when others did not agree with him.

In the late summer of 1866, Johnson decided to go beyond Congress and appeal to the people. He spoke in the principal cities of the East and Middle West in support of his policies. By his bad temper and loose statements, he made more enemies than friends.

Feeling stronger than ever, Johnson's opponents in Congress now decided to put their own plan of Reconstruction into law. In March, 1867, the First and Second (or Supplementary) Reconstruction Acts divided into five military districts the former Confederate states that had not ratified the Fourteenth Amendment. Each district was to be in the charge of an army officer commanding enough troops to keep the peace and oversee elections so that blacks could vote. When a majority of the voters had accepted a constitution that Congress would accept and when the state had ratified the Fourteenth Amendment, its representatives and senators would be seated, and it would be back in the Union. Johnson refused to approve this Reconstruction plan on the ground that it invaded states' rights, but it was soon passed over his veto.

The President and the Radical Republicans were now openly at war. That same year the Republicans passed the Tenure of Office Act. It forbade the President to dismiss cabinet members and lesser government officials without the consent of the Senate. When Johnson dismissed his secretary of war, Edwin M. Stanton, without the consent of the Senate, the Radicals decided to act. On February 24, 1868, the House of Representatives adopted a resolution that President Johnson be **impeached,** or charged with "high crimes and misdemeanors in office." Actually, the chief reason for impeachment was that Johnson had blocked all of Congress' efforts to pass laws for an intelligent plan of Reconstruction for the South. After a trial before the Senate, the vote stood 35 to 19, one short of the two-thirds majority needed to find Johnson guilty.

▶ **RECONSTRUCTION IN THE SOUTH**

Meanwhile, the Reconstruction Act of 1867 and several similar bills had gone into effect. With soldiers standing at the polls, the clerks had registered blacks as well as eligible whites. In the ten states of the former Confederacy, 1,330,000 voters were enrolled. Of these, 703,000 were blacks. The new voters elected delegates, among them many blacks, to the conventions that would frame new state constitutions.

The new state governments quickly approved the Fourteenth Amendment. This they had to do if they were to be re-admitted to the Union. By midsummer, 1868, seven states had acted and were back in good standing. The remaining four—Virginia, Texas, Georgia, and Mississippi—were re-admitted in 1870.

Thus, the old Union was restored. But in the South a new order prevailed. Between 1870 and 1881, 16 blacks represented Southern states in Congress. Many others sat in the state legislatures. The blacks never controlled any state government. But they were accused of lack of responsibility, spending too much money, and dishonesty. The mere fact that they held public office angered a great mass of white citizens. Many whites turned to violence in hopes of keeping the freed slaves from enjoying their new rights. The best known of the white groups that set about "putting the blacks in their place" was the Ku Klux Klan. Founded in 1866, this secret body soon spread throughout the South. The members—masked, clothed in white robes, riding only at night—singled out blacks who had displeased the old ruling class. By threats, whippings, and even lynchings, they made their point. Less often the Klan taught a lesson to white people, called **carpetbaggers** and **scalawags,** who had joined with the blacks in the new state government. Scalawags were Southern whites who supported the Republicans for the purpose of directing black votes. Carpetbaggers were Northern whites who went south, usually for their own gain, and who were willing to give the blacks what they wanted. The name came from their traveling bags made of carpeting. Today, people who are active in the politics of a city or state where they do not live are called carpetbaggers.

▶ **THE END OF RECONSTRUCTION**

By 1870, with all the Southern states back in the Union, the North began to have a change of heart. Several of the Radical Republicans had died. Others were losing interest in the black cause and in reform. In the South, farmers and business people were recovering from the effects of war. More and more of the old leaders were being pardoned and given the vote again. State by state the Democrats took over the governments. In 1877, the last federal troops were withdrawn from the South. Reconstruction had come to an end.

In law the South had been reconstructed. Secession was dead, the Union was restored, and slavery was ended. But in fact, it had not been reconstructed. After a few years, blacks had their right to vote restricted and were kept out of office by economic power, fear, court decisions, and other means. Even more than that, they could not travel in the same railroad cars, eat in the same restaurants, or sleep in the same hotels as white people. Black people had been given freedom but not equality.

PAUL M. ANGLE
Author, *The Lincoln Reader*

See also CIVIL WAR, UNITED STATES; CONFEDERATE STATES OF AMERICA; IMPEACHMENT; JOHNSON, ANDREW; LINCOLN, ABRAHAM; NEGRO HISTORY.

RECORDER

The recorder is one of the most ancient of instruments. Even the most primitive societies had some form of it. The great composers of the baroque period were particularly fond of it. Claudio Monteverdi used it in his operas. Henry Purcell, François Couperin, Johann Sebastian Bach, and George Frederick Handel all composed for the recorder. So did many of their contemporaries, such as George Philipp Telemann, whose music is now being played again after having long been forgotten.

The recorder itself was almost forgotten for more than a century after Bach and Handel. The great pioneer who revived it in modern times was Arnold Dolmetsch (1858–1940). He felt that early music should be played on the instruments it was written for. The recorder is now as popular as it ever was.

How to Play the Recorder

At the top of the recorder there is a slot. When you blow into this, it guides your breath across a sharp edge and into the instrument. This edge makes little whirlpools in the air. These reach your ear as sound vibrations, and you hear a clear, pure sound of lovely quality.

Before the sound vibrations travel to your ear, they must pass through the instrument. Finger holes are spaced along the recorder. When you cover all these with your fingers, the sound vibrations must pass down the full length of the instrument before escaping into the air. This gives the lowest note. When you take your fingers off certain holes, the sound vibrations can escape without passing down so much of the instrument. This gives higher notes.

There is one hole on the opposite side of the instrument from the other holes. This is kept covered by one thumb, except when you want still higher notes. Then you uncover it or half uncover it, and this allows each note to jump up to the octave above. Since you must blow a little harder as well, this technique is called overblowing.

You do not lift your fingers in the same order as the notes of the scale. (Some instruments are made with a simplified fingering that allows you to do this, but they are never quite in tune.)

There are five sizes of recorder in common use. The smallest and highest is the sopranino. It sounds an octave higher than the written notes. Then come the soprano (called the descant in England), the alto, or treble, and the tenor. The largest and lowest is the bass. Its notes are written in the bass clef, but it sounds an octave higher.

Since these recorders have the same basic fingering, a player can soon master all sizes. It is chiefly a matter of how wide the player stretches his fingers. A good stretch is needed for the bass recorder. The easiest sizes on which to start are probably the soprano and the alto. Perhaps they are also the most pleasant to play as solo instruments. In an

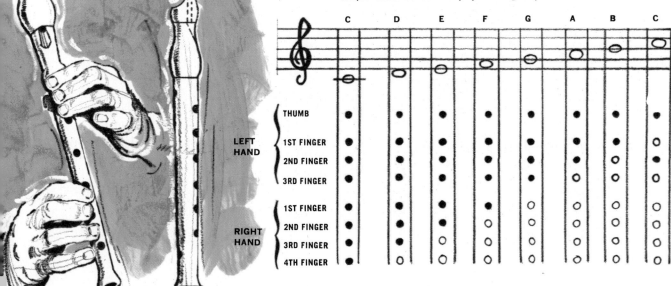

German fingering for the C-major scale on a soprano recorder. Black means covered; white means uncovered. Many simple melodies can be played using only these notes.

	C	D	E	F	G	A	B	C
THUMB	●	●	●	●	●	●	●	●
LEFT HAND 1ST FINGER	●	●	●	●	●	●	●	○
2ND FINGER	●	●	●	●	●	●	○	●
3RD FINGER	●	●	●	●	●	○	○	○
RIGHT HAND 1ST FINGER	●	●	●	●	○	○	○	○
2ND FINGER	●	●	●	○	○	○	○	○
3RD FINGER	●	●	○	○	○	○	○	○
4TH FINGER	●	○	○	○	○	○	○	○

ensemble of recorders all sizes are equally enjoyable.

The recorder is not at all hard to learn. These are the chief points to watch:

(1) The finger or thumb must completely cover its hole. Any leak of air will spoil the note. When air escapes, try finger by finger (from the bottom upward) until you find one that is not covering properly. You do not have to press hard. Light but firm fingering gives the best results. Let your fingers move comfortably.

(2) Use your tongue to separate notes you do not want to slur together. Tonguing interrupts the breath between one note and the next. The standard method of tonguing is to put your tongue behind your teeth and quickly take it away again. Keep your tongue and fingers well in step with one another by thinking of your movements a little ahead of the music.

(3) Listen all the time to be sure you are well in tune. You can lower the pitch a little by relaxing the breath or raise it by stressing the breath. The most important point of good recorder playing is keeping in tune.

(4) Let your breath flow into the recorder in a deep and steady stream. This is the secret of making a beautiful tone. Take a full breath before you start and a new breath whenever there is a rest in the music or a break in the phrasing. Your breath is the life of the recorder.

ROBERT DONINGTON
Author, *The Instruments of Music*

RECORDS AND RECORD COLLECTING

People have been collecting recordings in one form or another ever since the early 1890's. At that time a few of the best-known performers of the day were persuaded to record for Thomas Alva Edison's new phonograph. Early recordings were in the shape of cylinders. Some of the most popular cylinder recordings were made by the United States Marine Band, conducted by John Philip Sousa (1854–1932). There are collectors today who have large libraries of early cylinder recordings. Some can still be found in antique shops.

The first sound heard on many early cylinder recordings was the announcer's voice introducing the material that followed. These "masters of ceremonies" were the very first disc jockeys. The sound of the cylinders is primitive by modern standards. Yet one gets an idea of the musical tastes and performing styles that were popular at the time.

Music was by no means the only form of entertainment provided by the early cylinder recordings. Specialty acts, such as whistlers, storytellers, bird imitators, and comedians, were also very popular. There were even some poetry readings, including brief excerpts from the plays of Shakespeare.

Flat Discs

A man named Emile Berliner (1851–1929) developed the flat, circular disc that became the standard shape of phonograph recordings. He began manufacturing his machine, called a Gramophone, in 1894.

One of the most important events in the growth of recording and record collecting occurred on a March day in 1902. A young tenor named Enrico Caruso (1873–1921) stepped up to a bell-shaped tin recording horn in a studio in Milan, Italy, and recorded 10 operatic arias on wax blanks. The blanks were then rushed to Hanover, Germany, to be transferred to discs. The recordings became sensations overnight. Thousands upon thousands were sold. They carried the name of Caruso to the far corners of the world.

Thanks largely to his recordings, Caruso was soon the best-known singer in the world. He became the biggest star at New York's Metropolitan Opera, and until his death in 1921 he returned regularly to the recording studios. The list of Caruso recordings is staggering in number. Interestingly, the Caruso recordings still excite collectors everywhere. Many of Caruso's records, including all those made at the very first recording session, have been reissued on modern long-playing records and are still available. It seems safe to predict that the Caruso recordings will always be prized by lovers of great voices and great singing.

If recordings made Caruso a household name, it is also true that Caruso's recordings gave the whole recording medium a respectability that it might not have achieved otherwise for many years. Other leading performers of the day agreed to make recordings, chiefly because of Caruso's success.

Piano Rolls

At about the same time that Caruso was making his first recordings, a different kind of process was being developed for recording the piano. Strips were inserted into an apparatus built into an ordinary concert grand piano. When these strips, or piano rolls, were played back on a player piano, or pianola, the sound that came out was remarkably lifelike. Maria Terese Carreño (1853–1917), Vladimir de Pachmann (1848–1933), and many other leading pianists of the time performed for the piano-roll process. The medium also attracted some of the leading composers. Claude Debussy recorded several of his works; so did Edvard Grieg, Camille Saint-Saëns (1835–1921), Gustav Mahler, and others. Many of these performances have been transferred to long-playing records and are available today. Opinion is divided about the quality of the recordings. Some experts believe that the piano-roll recordings distort the original performances. Others hold that a reliable and accurate image of the playing comes through.

Orchestras

The first symphony-orchestra recordings were made in Europe a few years later, but it was not until 1916 that symphony-orchestra recordings were made in the United States. The Chicago Symphony, the Boston Symphony, and the Philadelphia Orchestra all made recordings in Camden, New Jersey. The orchestras played before large recording horns in tents set up outdoors. Many of the instruments could not be recorded by the primitive equipment. Clarinets and piccolos often had to reinforce the string parts, and percussion was usually omitted completely. The recorded sound bore little resemblance to the actual sound of an orchestra. Yet one can get at least an idea of the performances of great conductors of many years ago, such as Arthur Nikisch (1855–1922) and Karl Muck (1859–1940). These recordings, by and large, have not been transferred to long-playing discs.

Electrical Recordings

When radios first appeared in 1923, sales of records began to slump badly. Then, in 1925, came the next great development in recordings. Electric power was used for the making of records. One of the first American recordings made electrically—that is, with microphones, tubes, and other paraphernalia—was a performance of 15 glee clubs (about 900 voices) in New York's Metropolitan Opera House on March 31, 1925. When the disc was put on sale a few weeks later, it disclosed a brilliance and resonance never before heard on a phonograph record. The recording art had come of age.

Records came from the pressing plants in ever growing numbers for more than 20 years. The range of recorded material expanded enormously. Symphonies, operas, jazz, folk songs, popular music, plays, specialty acts, religious music, and many other kinds of sounds were recorded. It was clear that recordings were playing a growing role in social and cultural life.

Long-Playing Records

For nearly 50 years the standard phonograph record was a disc 10 or 12 inches (25.4 or 30.5 centimeters) in diameter that revolved 78 times per minute. The playing time was approximately 4½ minutes for a 12-inch side and 3 minutes for a 10-inch side. One of the most revolutionary events in the entire history of recording took place in 1948. This was the introduction of the long-playing record, with closely compressed grooves and a slower turning speed of 33⅓ times per minute. The long-playing record could fit as much as 30 minutes onto a single 12-inch side. During the early 1950's a battle was fought between supporters of the long-playing format and those who favored a new 7-inch (17.8 centimeter) record with a large hole in the middle. This smaller record, called the 45 disc, revolved 45 times per minute. The 45 disc was less expensive. It took less storage space, and it was especially good for short pieces. The 33⅓ long-playing disc won out for most forms of recorded music, and the 45 format became standard for 3-minute single records.

Stereophonic recording, which made musical performances more lifelike, was introduced to the public in 1955. The first releases were on tape, but by the end of 1957 the first stereophonic discs, in long-playing format, were made available.

Record Collecting as a Hobby

The collecting of recordings has been a popular worldwide hobby ever since the 1890's. In those early days many a pleasant social evening was spent listening to the latest cylinder recordings. It was in the early years of the 20th century, however, after the changeover to flat discs, that the real collector "bug" came into being. Those early Caruso recordings, and others of the period, were collected and treasured. Even today many a family has a collection of old 78 discs that is a family heirloom, passed from one generation to the next.

As the years have passed, record collecting has become more and more refined and specialized. There are collectors interested only in the recordings of pre-1925 tenors. Others seek out as many recordings as they can find of one particular artist. Still others want to have every recording ever made of a particular selection.

In the days before long-playing records some rare recordings were sold for fantastically high prices. Out-of-the-way Caruso 12-inch single discs were sold for as much as $50 and more. Record shops specializing in out-of-print and rare recordings did a flourishing business. Some shops set themselves up as record collectors' exchanges, with merchandise purchased from private collectors.

This whole picture was changed dramatically with the introduction of long-playing discs. Along with the great rush to record new material for the newly developed medium, there were many reissues. Great performances from the past were reprocessed and re-released. This was especially true of some of the recordings made by the leading singers and instrumentalists of the early 20th century. A Caruso performance that had once brought a very fancy price was put with perhaps a dozen other immortal Caruso performances and sold at a fraction of the original cost. Thus, the development of long-playing records had a double advantage: the technical improvement was enormous, and the price of the finished product was lowered.

Records, however, are not the only way to collect music. Since they were first developed in the 1950's, tape recordings have become increasingly popular. Eight-track, cassette, and reel-to-reel tapes are being used to record all styles of music, and they now are widely used by collectors.

Basic Record Library

Here is a list of works that belong in any basic record library of serious music.

SYMPHONIES
Beethoven: Symphony No. 3 in E flat, "Eroica"
Symphony No. 5 in C minor
Symphony No. 6 in F, "Pastoral"
Symphony No. 7 in A
Symphony No. 9 in D minor
Brahms: Symphony No. 1 in C minor
Symphony No. 4 in E minor
Bruckner: Symphony No. 7 in E
Dvořák: Symphony No. 9 in E minor, "From the New World" (Old number 5)
Franck: Symphony in D minor
Haydn: Symphony No. 94 in G, "Surprise"
Symphony No. 101 in D, "Clock"
Mendelssohn: Symphony No. 4 in A, "Italian"
Mozart: Symphony No. 40 in G minor
Symphony No. 41 in C, "Jupiter"
Schubert: Symphony No. 8 in B minor, "Unfinished"
Symphony No. 9 in C, "Great"
Tchaikovsky: Symphony No. 5 in E minor
Symphony No. 6 in B minor, "Pathétique"

CONCERTOS
Bach: *Brandenburg* Concerto No. 5 in D
Beethoven: Piano Concerto No. 5 in E flat, "Emperor"
Violin Concerto in D

Brahms: Piano Concerto No. 2 in B flat
Violin Concerto in D
Chopin: Piano Concerto No. 1 in E minor
Dvořák: Cello Concerto in B minor
Grieg: Piano Concerto in A minor
Mendelssohn: Violin Concerto in E minor
Mozart: Piano Concerto No. 20 in D minor
Piano Concerto No. 24 in C minor
Violin Concerto No. 4 in D
Paganini: Violin Concerto No. 1 in D
Rachmaninoff: Piano Concerto No. 2 in C minor
Schumann: Piano Concerto in A minor
Tchaikovsky: Piano Concerto No. 1 in B flat minor
Violin Concerto in D

OPERAS
Bizet: *Carmen*
Mozart: *Don Giovanni*
The Marriage of Figaro
Puccini: *La Bohème*
Madama Butterfly
Rossini: *The Barber of Seville*
Verdi: *Aïda*
Rigoletto
La Traviata
Wagner: *Die Meistersinger von Nürnberg*

CHAMBER MUSIC
Beethoven: String Quartet No. 9 in C ("Rasoumovsky" No. 3)
Trio in B flat, "Archduke"
Brahms: Piano Quartet No. 1 in G minor
Dvořák: Piano Quintet in A
Haydn: String Quartet in C, "Emperor"
Mendelssohn: Octet in E flat
Mozart: Clarinet Quintet in A
String Quartet No. 15 in D minor
String Quintet in C
String Quintet in G minor
Schubert: Piano Quintet in A, "Trout"
String Quintet in C
Trio No. 1 in B flat
Schumann: Piano Quintet in E flat
Tchaikovsky: String Quartet No. 1 in D

CHORAL WORKS
Bach: *Mass in B minor*
St. Matthew Passion
Beethoven: *Missa Solemnis*
Handel: *Messiah*
Haydn: *The Creation*
Mozart: *Requiem*
Verdi: *Requiem*

MARTIN BOOKSPAN
Music Director, WQXR (New York City)

See also HI-FI AND STEREO; PHONOGRAPH; TAPE RECORDERS.

RED CROSS

In 1859, a Swiss traveler named Henri Dunant (1828–1910) was passing through northern Italy. He arrived at the town of Solferino the day after a fierce battle had taken place. Austrian troops under the command of Emperor Francis Joseph I had fought French and Italian troops led by Napoleon III. Thousands of dead and wounded lay on the battlefield, receiving no attention. Dunant and a group of volunteers quickly set up emergency hospitals, where they took care of the wounded soldiers from both armies.

Back in his native city of Geneva, Dunant could not forget the picture of the wounded men left to die on the battlefield for lack of medical assistance. Three years after the experience, he published a book. In it he outlined his idea for the formation of a neutral organization of volunteers in every country, who would be trained and ready to help the wounded in time of war.

Public interest in Dunant's book resulted in the appointment of a Committee of Five, of which Dunant was a member. The committee's job was to study ways of achieving Dunant's dream. The outcome of its work was the founding of the Red Cross in 1863. Today the Red Cross is an international movement, joining people in more than 100 countries in service to people in need.

A New Idea in Service

The Red Cross is made up of national Red Cross societies throughout the world. In most countries its symbol is a simple red cross on a white background. Nearly all Muslim countries use a red crescent (quarter-moon shape) symbol. Iran uses a red lion and sun.

The Red Cross performs its services through the national Red Cross societies, the League of Red Cross Societies, and the International Committee of the Red Cross. There is no single program for Red Cross activity or organization. Each of the national Red Cross societies is independent and bases its program on the particular needs of its nation's people.

The League of Red Cross Societies is an international organization through which the individual societies help one another. It acts as a clearinghouse for Red Cross information from all parts of the world. It sends its specialists to national societies everywhere to help them establish new service programs or improve old ones. When an emergency arises that is too big for one Red Cross society to handle by itself, the league can call in help from other societies.

With this kind of worldwide co-operation, Red Cross societies have been able to bring help to millions of people, including displaced persons, refugees, and victims of floods, fires, earthquakes, and other disasters.

The International Committee of the Red Cross, another international organization, is the successor to the original Committee of Five. The International Committee continues to guard Red Cross ideals and to give help during wars and other conflicts. It acts whenever a neutral group is needed. The work of the Red Cross in wartime is carried out under four international treaties called the Geneva Conventions, or Red Cross treaties. Under the terms of the treaties, the life and dignity of a helpless person must be respected, regardless of race, nationality, political allegiance, or station in life. The treaties protect the war-wounded, prisoners of war, civilian populations of occupied countries, and military hospitals and their staffs and supplies.

Red Cross Services

Over the last 100 years the Red Cross has changed from an organization with a program of wartime services alone to one that serves at all times. In some European countries the Red Cross owns and operates hospitals and clinics that serve as nurse-training centers. It also helps to train community public-health workers. Part of the daily work of Red Cross societies in the new African and Asian nations is to educate people to good habits of health and hygiene. In Canada, the Red Cross Society has programs for children and adults that include water safety, first aid, and general health care.

A large number of societies have, or take part in, blood service programs. Blood is collected from volunteers, processed, and distributed to civilian and military hospitals and doctors. Most Red Cross societies have Junior Red Cross branches and disaster-relief programs. The disaster-relief program is a broad one, covering community preparedness, emergency relief activities, and finally the care of the disaster victims until they are able to care for themselves. Several countries have trained Red Cross ambulance corps.

All Red Cross societies take part in an international search in order to bring together members of families who have become separated or have been lost to one another through wars or other disasters.

United States Red Cross

The United States Red Cross is a private voluntary organization supported mostly by contributions from the public. It was founded in 1881 largely through the efforts of a former New England schoolteacher, Clara Barton, who had worked voluntarily among the Civil War wounded. It was first chartered by Congress in 1900. The second charter, still in force, was granted in 1905. Under the charter the Red Cross is required to serve members of the Armed Forces and their families. The organization must also carry on a disaster preparedness and relief program. In addition, the Red Cross must provide assistance in carrying out the terms of the Geneva Conventions whenever such assistance is requested by a government.

Other Red Cross activities include collecting and processing blood from volunteer donors (people who give blood) and maintaining a reserve of nurses, who volunteer their services during emergencies. The Red Cross gives courses in home nursing and preparation for parenthood. It trains volunteers for service in Red Cross chapters, hospitals, clinics, and other agencies. It gives training in first aid and in swimming, boating, and other water skills. It takes part in international Red Cross training conferences and arranges study visits to the United States for officials from other Red Cross societies all over the world.

Young People Are a Red Cross Strength

Most of the world's 125 Red Cross societies have child and youth memberships, called Junior Red Cross in most countries. The Junior Red Cross movement started during World War I, when educators asked the Red Cross for a program that would allow young people to help in the war effort. In the United States, the junior branch of the Red Cross is now called Youth Services. It is made up of young people of elementary and high school

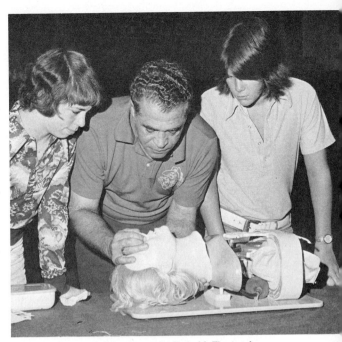

Students take a Red Cross course in first aid. The teacher uses a model to show mouth-to-mouth resuscitation.

age. In Canada, the Junior Red Cross was first organized in 1922. Today this branch of the Canadian organization is known as Red Cross Youth.

The aims of the Red Cross services for young people are the same throughout the world. They seek to give the youth of many countries an opportunity to serve others, to teach the ideals of giving service to those in need, to encourage understanding and compassion, and to give young people a greater knowledge of the world they live in.

The League of Red Cross Societies urges all national Red Cross societies to expand their service opportunities for young people, particularly those for teenagers.

Among the many projects carried out by young Red Cross members around the world has been the exchange of gift boxes. To promote friendship and understanding among children of all nations, young Red Cross members have also exchanged paintings done by students and exhibits relating to school and community life. Children in disaster areas particularly have been sent chests of classroom and recreational supplies.

AMERICAN RED CROSS

RED SEA. See OCEANS AND SEAS.

REED, WALTER (1851–1902)

Yellow fever used to cause thousands of deaths a year. Although a tropical disease, it did not always stay in the tropics. Boston and New York both suffered epidemics of yellow fever. Philadelphia once lost a tenth of its population to the same disease.

In 1900 an epidemic of yellow fever broke out in Cuba. It struck the United States troops who were still stationed there as a result of the Spanish-American War. The United States Army sent a group of doctors to disease-ridden Cuba. Heading the group was Dr. Walter Reed, whose work led to the control of yellow fever.

Reed was born in Belroi, Virginia, in 1851. He received medical degrees from the University of Virginia and from Bellevue Medical College in New York City. After working as a public health doctor in Brooklyn and New York City, Reed joined the army in 1874 as an assistant surgeon.

After 15 years of duty in the western United States, Reed moved to Baltimore, Maryland. Returning to his studies, he specialized in epidemic diseases at Johns Hopkins University. Later, in Washington, D.C., he became a professor at the Army Medical College. Reed was dedicated to his work. A brilliant man, he soon ranked as one of the leading scientists in the United States. He was often sent by the government to investi-

Dr. Walter Reed's brilliant research led to the control of the dreaded disease yellow fever.

gate outbreaks of typhoid, yellow fever, and other diseases.

When he was sent to Cuba, Reed faced what seemed an impossible job. The hospitals were full of patients with high fevers and yellowish-colored skins—victims of yellow fever. Hundreds had died of the disease.

Reed decided to follow up a clue he had found in earlier work on the disease. Yellow fever, he suspected, was carried by a certain type of mosquito. He could test this idea by capturing some of these mosquitoes and allowing them to bite yellow-fever patients. If these mosquitoes could give the disease to healthy persons, his idea would be right.

Yellow fever seemed to affect only human beings. Reed knew that he would need human volunteers—persons who would be willing to risk catching the disease. One of his co-workers—Dr. James Carroll—volunteered in spite of the great danger. When bitten by an infected mosquito, Dr. Carroll fell ill with yellow fever. He recovered but remained in poor health for the rest of his life. Another of Reed's co-workers—Dr. Jesse W. Lazear—died of the fever after being bitten accidentally by an infected mosquito. Other brave men volunteered despite the risk.

Reed worked patiently. He set up many careful experiments that soon proved his theory. He showed that yellow fever was carried by a mosquito. The disease could therefore be wiped out by destroying the carrier mosquitoes.

Military forces set about exterminating the mosquitoes and destroying their breeding places. As a result, yellow fever was controlled in Cuba and was no longer a threat to the United States itself.

Although his work led to the control of yellow fever, Reed could not identify the germ of the disease itself. Other scientists later identified the cause as a virus—a particle so small that it cannot be seen under an ordinary microscope.

In 1901 Reed returned to Washington and his position as professor in the Army Medical College. He died the following year, after an attack of appendicitis. The army hospital in Washington, D.C., was later named in his honor.

DAVID C. KNIGHT
Author, science books for children

REFERENCE BOOKS

What are reference books? In what section of a library are they found? Are they difficult to use? Why should we know something about them?

Reference books provide information arranged in such a way that it can be located easily. They are not meant to be read through. Some reference books, such as the standard encyclopedias, offer general information; others give specific information. Libraries keep them in reference sections, where people can refer to them easily.

Reference books are not difficult to use. Once you learn to check certain parts of a reference book—the table of contents, index, glossary, copyright date, and text—you will understand the purpose of the book and will easily find the information you need. However, in order to develop independent study habits, you should be familiar with the basic types of reference books.

Kinds of Reference Books

Encyclopedias. "Encyclopedia" comes from two Greek words, *enkyklios* (meaning "in a circle") and *paideia* (meaning "education"). A loose translation of the two Greek words is "instruction in the circle of arts and science." For most people "encyclopedia" means a set of books containing general information, written either for adults or for younger readers. *The New Book of Knowledge,* the encyclopedia you are now reading, was prepared especially for young people. *Encyclopedia International* and *Merit Students Encyclopedia* are written on an intermediate level. *Encyclopedia Americana* and *Encyclopaedia Britannica* are written on a more adult level. All of these sets are general-information encyclopedias.

There are also many encyclopedias that cover only one subject: law, sports, art, or some other single field. Encyclopedias deal with things, ideas, and subjects rather than with words and meanings only, as dictionaries do.

How do you use an encyclopedia? Choose a subject you want to learn about—rockets, for example. In the R-volume index to this encyclopedia the subject heading "Rockets" will list the pages and volumes where the article ROCKETS and related facts about rockets appear.

Encyclopedias differ in their methods of indexing. Some have an index in each volume. Others have a single-volume index, while a few have no index. The article on INDEXES AND INDEXING in Volume I gives more information on this subject and on the use of cross-references. Additional information about encyclopedias can be found in the article ENCYCLOPEDIAS.

Dictionaries. Dictionaries list words in alphabetical order, giving their spelling, definition, and pronunciation. There are two types of dictionaries—the abridged, or shorter version, and the unabridged. Some dictionaries deal with only one field of knowledge, such as art or science. There are also two-language dictionaries, such as an English-Spanish dictionary, which lists English words alphabetically and gives their translation in Spanish. A second section of the dictionary lists Spanish words and gives their translation in English. Most dictionaries have very helpful information aside from the definitions—forms of address, abbreviations, biographical names, and a gazetteer of geographical terms. (Historical data about dictionaries is in the article DICTIONARIES.)

Atlases. An atlas is a collection of maps in book form. The number and type of maps vary with the publication. Most atlases include political and physical (or relief) maps. The political maps show such man-made boundaries as country, state, and county lines. The physical maps indicate elevation and land surface. Other maps often show resources, climate, and population. (The article MAPS AND GLOBES in Volume M explains how to use a map.)

Gazetteers. A gazetteer is another form of dictionary. It lists geographical places, such as cities, lakes, mountains, towns, and so on, with their location and other vital facts. Indexes in atlases are really gazetteers.

Biographical Dictionaries and Directories. Biographical sources give information about people. *Webster's Biographical Dictionary* contains thousands of brief biographies of internationally famous people of both the past and the present. *Current Biography* is an excellent reference source if more detailed information is required. It has articles on living people in the news and of international fame. *The Junior Book of Authors, More Junior*

Authors, *Third Book of Junior Authors,* and *Fourth Book of Junior Authors and Illustrators* feature authors of young people's books. Remember also that the card catalog is useful in locating biographies that are available in your library.

Information about important living Americans may be found in *Who's Who in America.* (It also has some listings of non-Americans.) The British *Who's Who* contains biographies of important people, with emphasis on British people. In the scientific field, *American Men and Women of Science* is helpful. There are also directories of people in education, law, and other professions.

Indexes. Occasionally the information you seek will not be in a reference book. If it is too recent, it will be found only in a magazine. To locate this kind of information, use the index to magazines entitled *The Reader's Guide to Periodical Literature.* This publication is an author-and-subject index to about 175 magazines. Here is a sample author entry:

DUNSTAN, Thomas C.
    Our bald eagle: freedom's symbol survives. il
        Nat Geog 153:186-99 F '78

The author's name is followed by the title of the article. It appeared in the *National Geographic,* volume 153, pages 186–99, in the February, 1978, issue.

Articles are also listed by subject:

EAGLES
    Our bald eagle: freedom's symbol survives. T.
        C. Dunstan. il Nat Geog 153:186-99 F '78

Note that both of the entries use the abbreviation "il" to tell you that this article is illustrated.

Abbreviations of names of periodicals indexed are found in the front of *The Readers' Guide.* In this index and others there are symbols and guides for finding the information you want.

There are also indexes to educational magazines, to books, to poetry, and to many other subjects. Bibliographies, or lists of books on certain subjects, are like indexes in that they help to locate additional sources of information. The *Children's Catalog* is a much-used bibliography.

Almanacs, Handbooks, Manuals, and Yearbooks. These reference books are difficult to classify. They contain statistics, instructions on how to do or make things, quotations, and miscellaneous facts.

The earliest almanacs were crude calendars used over 2,000 years ago by the Egyptians for keeping track of religious holidays. Roger Bacon, an English scientist-philosopher, compiled an almanac in the 13th century that showed the movements of the sun, moon,

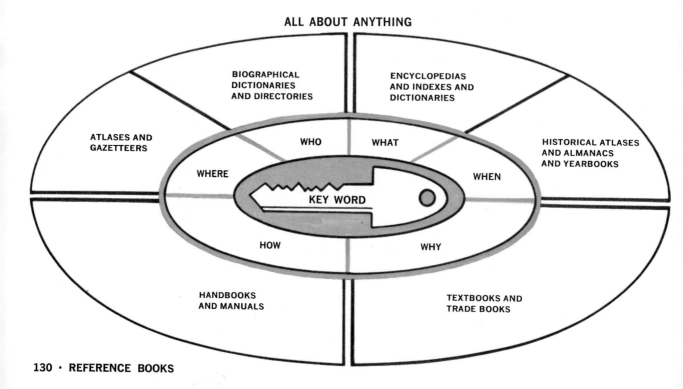

ALL ABOUT ANYTHING

and planets. In the 15th century, with the invention of printing with movable type, printed almanacs became popular and have remained so. At first they only forecast weather and offered a variety of fact and fancy. Benjamin Franklin's *Poor Richard's Almanack,* published in America between 1732 and 1757, is remembered for its witty sayings. Since 1792 the *Farmer's Almanac* has been published annually in the United States. Two popular present-day almanacs are *The World Almanac and Book of Facts* and the *Information Please Almanac.* Both contain a wide range of information.

The terms "handbook" and "manual" are often used interchangeably. But most authorities agree that a handbook contains facts on one central subject, while a manual usually instructs. References such as Langer's *Encyclopedia of World History* or the *Statistical Abstract of the United States* would fall into the handbook category. The *Complete Book of Running* is an example of a manual.

The purpose of a yearbook, as its name suggests, is to provide its readers with a summary of events of a single year. For example, the *Yearbook of the United Nations* is published each year to provide a summary of the work of that organization. Some encyclopedias publish annual supplements, or yearbooks.

Some references contain specialized information. Bartlett's *Familiar Quotations* lists well-known quotations and their authors, and Roget's *Thesaurus* gives synonyms and antonyms. The *Guinness Book of World Records* lists records in hundreds of categories.

Locating and Recording Information

Before you can start locating information, you must decide what questions you want answered. Into what subject area do the questions fall—history, science, or some other branch of knowledge?

Next, pinpoint the information with a key word or words—"space travel," for example, if the general area is science. Go directly to this heading in a reference book or in the card catalog. Remember to check for related subjects noted in the cross-references. Information on space travel might also be listed under "outer space," "astronauts," and "satellites." Write down the call number, author, and title for the books you select.

When you have found the book you want, look at its index or table of contents for the topic you are tracking down. Once you have the desired pages, use chapter titles and subheads as further signposts to the facts you need.

Be sure to use the guides to locating information that are in each book—the table of contents, index, chapter titles, and subheads. Read the entire article first before you take notes on the main ideas.

How to Judge a Reference Book

A reference book must be accurate. Experts in various fields of knowledge prepare the articles, statistics, charts, and other matter that go into a reference book. Writers, editors, copy editors, and proofreaders try to make the content as readable as possible.

Artists and designers arrange the text and illustrations in an appealing format. A reference book, however, must offer more than facts and a pleasing makeup. It must present the facts in such a way that readers can easily find what they are looking for.

No one book or set of related books can embrace all knowledge. A good reference book, however, has a definite aim. It tries to reach a certain age group. It limits itself to covering only material that is important and useful. It is selective both in what it includes and what it omits.

Examine a book's front matter and back matter. In the front matter look on the title page for the copyright date to make certain you are using an up-to-date volume. The table of contents and any "how to use" instructions should also be clear. In the back matter the index is most important. Check several subject entries for exactness and completeness. The index, like the body of the book, should be attractive in layout and easy to read.

At times the information you need will be found in a trade book. Trade books differ from reference books and textbooks in that they are intended for general readership. If the book you are using was written by an expert and if it has been kept up-to-date, it is safe to use it for reference.

EILEEN CONLON
Author, *Books Lead the Way*

See also LIBRARIES.

REFORMATION

The Reformation was a religious movement in the Christian Church in Europe during the 16th and 17th centuries. It was an attempt to renew and reform the Church of the Middle Ages by a return to the ideas of the New Testament. It was also a serious protest against certain abuses and tendencies within the medieval Church. So it is often called the Protestant Reformation.

▶ BACKGROUND AND CAUSES

The Reformation was also part of a changing world situation. It was not so much a revolution as an evolution. The seeds of unrest, of change, and of new ideas about truth and freedom had been sown many years before. The Reformation broke out in scattered areas all over Europe. It was directed and encouraged by many kinds of religious leaders. Reform and protest were common to all Reformation groups. But there was also a wide variety of opinion. The movement developed into many kinds of Protestant churches.

The Changing World

The unity of the Middle Ages in philosophy, science, and religious ideas (theology) was threatened during the 14th and 15th centuries by the new questioning spirit of the times known as the Renaissance (rebirth). By the beginning of the 16th century, this unity was broken as men began to explore new worlds. Up to the time Christopher Columbus discovered America in 1492, men had a very limited idea of the size of the world. They were astonished to hear of the vast areas of sea and land that had been discovered.

As trade developed, man's views of the world and of himself widened. In science Galileo Galilei and Nicolaus Copernicus greatly enlarged man's idea of the world around him and of the natural laws that govern it. In philosophy a revival of ancient classical studies in Greek and Latin laid the foundations of the modern European schools and universities. Printing with movable type, an invention attributed to Johann Gutenberg, made the new ideas available to a wider audience. A new spirit of national awareness was emerging in France, England, and else-

Martin Luther

where. Feudal lords and local rulers gave way to princes and kings. A new sense of political freedom and responsibility was in the air.

Forerunners

Certain forerunners of the Reformation noticed the changes that were taking place all around them. They dared to suggest changes in the Church as well. John Wycliffe (1324–84) of Oxford translated the Bible from Latin into English, but it was never printed. He urged the Church of his day to return to the simple life and faith of the first Christian centuries. In Bohemia (modern Czechoslovakia) John Huss (1369–1415) called for reform within the Church, to allow for more individual freedom and less rigid control by priests. The Council of Constance (1414–18) decided against Huss, and he was burned at the stake in 1415. The council also declared Wycliffe to be a **heretic** (one who holds certain views that Church authorities consider to be questionable or untrue). Although he had been dead some years, his body was dug up and burned.

The Religious Protest

The need for religious renewal within the medieval Church was widely recognized a cen-

John Calvin

John Knox

tury or more before the Reformation. The Church had become more and more like a small state. The pope, the head of the Church on earth, directed its affairs very much like a national or sovereign ruler. Much of the new spirit of learning, of science, and of personal freedom passed unnoticed by the Church. The ignorance, immorality, and luxury of many of the priests became a scandal. Through the pope and the priests church members had to pay large taxes to the Church at Rome. In this way the Church became a major financial power in Europe. Official papal documents known as indulgences, which promised forgiveness of sins, were sold throughout Europe to the poor and ignorant. The relics and sacred objects associated with the saints and especially with the Virgin Mary were often unduly worshiped. Long and expensive pilgrimages to the sacred shrines of the Church were encouraged. The sacrament of the Lord's Supper was often denied to the people. Much was made of the required confession of sins to a priest, the doing of penances (acts to show repentance for wrongdoing), and the need for priestly absolution, or freeing from the guilt of sin.

Although there were many fine, devout priests, the hierarchy of the Church began to suffer a loss of prestige toward the close of the 14th century. The power of the pope was questioned as the countries and states of Europe developed their own sense of nationality. This questioning of the pope's authority, and through him of the Church itself, reached a crisis when a succession of popes tried to rule in Avignon, France, as well as in Rome. For 40 years and into the first 10 years of the 15th century, the papacy was thus divided.

▶ MEN, IDEAS, AND CHURCHES

These conditions lasted many years. For this reason the religious protest against the abuses of the medieval Church grew in strength and unity to become the movement known as the Protestant Reformation.

Luther and Germany

Martin Luther was the major prophet and foremost leader of the Reformation. Although he was a friar in the Church, he was troubled by the high demands of the Christian faith and the moral regulations of the Church. He was troubled, too, by his own feeble efforts to make himself righteous. Try as he would, Luther could not be sure that he had fulfilled God's requirements for a holy life. At last it dawned on him that God is not a terrible Judge but a comforting Father. Luther realized that salvation was assured by true repentance and faith in God's love and mercy. This meant for Luther the working out of a completely new religious philosophy of salvation based on the apostle Paul's notion of justification by faith.

Luther discovered the basis of this doctrine of God's grace and free forgiveness in the Bible. From Greek, Latin, and Hebrew versions he translated the Bible into German, the common language of his countrymen.

Luther believed that the new life of the Christian was the gracious gift of God to the faithful believer. Thus, much of the previous value of popes, priests, sacraments, indulgences, pilgrimages, and worship of saints now seemed to Luther completely worthless. The individual believer, he declared, can be in direct contact with God through Jesus Christ. It is not necessary to bother with the elaborate structure of religion, which for centuries had been taken for granted in the medieval Church. To be freely forgiven in Christ by a merciful God did not mean for Luther that the believer became a saint; he still remained a sinner. Now, however, he was a forgiven sinner, eager not only to serve Christ but to spread the good news of the Christian faith.

Taking up the fight with Rome and the Pope, Leo X, Luther prepared a list of 95 theses, or topics for debate. These he publicly nailed to a church door in Wittenberg. The year, 1517, is usually taken as the birth date of the Protestant Reformation.

After a long series of debates with papal representatives, Luther was **excommunicated** (deprived of the sacraments and the rights of church membership) from the Catholic Church in 1520. He still had some idea of remaining with Rome. But as time passed he began to organize an independent church based on the principles of his revolt against Rome. At the Diet (Parliament) of Worms in 1521, when asked to deny his Protestant faith, Luther replied: "Here I stand; I cannot do otherwise." Luther's many books and essays spread his ideas far beyond his own land. People everywhere who were searching for help and comfort welcomed the new movement with enthusiasm. Luther's original views, planted in German soil, soon became the seedbed for many later varieties of Reformation beliefs. The Reformation protest made by Luther spread quickly during the next few decades, chiefly into northern Germany and Scandinavia.

Calvin and Knox

The most successful organizer of Protestant thought and life was a French-born theologian, John Calvin, who lived in Geneva, Switzerland. Calvin was more logical than Luther. He was interested in applying Reformation beliefs to the whole of life, including politics and the state. Calvin developed a variety of Protestantism in Geneva that became known as the Reformed (as distinct from the Lutheran) faith. Luther made the personal search for faith the cornerstone of his thought. Calvin, on the other hand, emphasized the glory of God as shown in the creation of the world. Because God is the supreme ruler of the universe, man is a mere creature, a sinner in the sight of God's holiness. Yet salvation, as with Luther, is available in God's free, forgiving love through Jesus Christ.

Calvin believed that God had predestined (determined in advance) salvation for some people, but others were less fortunate and were lost or damned forever. Sad as this may be, Calvin argued that it is a mystery of God's purpose and that sinful man cannot begin to understand it. Calvin's views were arranged in systematic form in his textbook on theology, *The Institutes of the Christian Religion* (1536–59), which had great influence on the later development of Reformation teachings. Calvinism spread to France, Germany, the Netherlands, and Great Britain.

At the same time in Geneva, a Scotsman, John Knox (1505–72), became Calvin's coworker. Knox had been exiled from England by Catholic Queen Mary (1516–58) because of his Protestant views. The two men had much in common. When Knox was permitted to return to his native Scotland, he carried with him the Calvinistic, or Reformed, faith. In Scotland the Reformation took the form of the Presbyterian Church, and later it spread to the United States, Canada, Australia, New Zealand, and wherever Scotsmen migrated.

Anglicans and Puritans

The Reformation in England lasted longer and involved more varieties of churches than had either the Lutheran movement in Germany or the Calvinistic faith in Switzerland. At first the Reformation protest in England was more political than religious. Henry VIII (1491–1547) broke with the pope over the question of divorce. He set himself up as the supreme head on earth of the Church of England. From that time on, the Anglican view has been a practical one of striking a middle ground between a too radical Protestant emphasis on one hand and the Roman Catholic tradition from the past on the other.

The history of the Reformation in England is tangled with the rise and fall of kings and queens. Under Henry's son, Edward VI (1537–53), the classic English *Book of Common Prayer* was prepared. Ever since, it has bound together Anglicans the world over in a common way of worship. Under Mary (1516–58) the Protestants were persecuted and exiled. Under Elizabeth (1533–1603) the Reformation was renewed and made secure. Under James I (1566–1625) the so-called King James, or Authorized, Version of the Bible was translated from Hebrew, Greek, Latin, and German versions into English. The work was begun by William Tyndale (1492?–1536) and completed by Miles Coverdale (1488?–1569). Under Oliver Cromwell (1599–1658) the more active Protestant group in England, the Puritans, debated with leaders of the Church of England over such questions as the power of bishops. In 1689 a Toleration Act was passed. It gave all religious views and churches the legal right to exist.

The Puritan tradition of Protestantism spread into Scotland, where it merged with Knox's Presbyterian and Calvinistic views. Later it was brought to America. In New England the Puritans were variously known as Separatists, Independents, and Congregationalists.

In the 18th century in England, John Wesley split with the Church of England. He began what is known as the Evangelical Revival of Bible preaching in the streets and in the open air. This variety of Protestantism became the Methodist Church. It grew rapidly in America and elsewhere.

▶ **THE CONTINUING REFORMATION**

One of the basic principles of the Reformation was that the Christian Church should continue reforming itself in its beliefs, practices, and organization. In the same way, it is a principle of Protestantism to protest not only against abuses of all kinds but even against the errors and imperfections within itself.

But after the first years of the Reformation, when the various church traditions became established in Europe and Great Britain, Protestantism was not always true to its own principles of reform and inner renewal. Lutherans argued with Calvinists on the correct interpretation of the sacrament of the Lord's Supper. Some churches flourished under government support; others sought complete separation from the state. Some Protestants insisted on certain creeds, and others made the Bible the only authority. Some worshiped according to set forms of prayers, and others were more open and free.

Small groups of devout Protestants formed their own independent churches in protest against the more highly organized churches such as the Lutheran, Reformed, and Anglican. Two such groups were the Mennonites and the Quakers (or members of the Society of Friends), both of whom stressed simplicity of life and doctrine. The Mennonites had a great influence on the development of the various Baptist churches. The Quakers became identified with nonviolence, pacifism, and aid to needy people.

By the middle of the 20th century the Protestant churches began to seek ways and means for healing their differences. The older disputes had lost much of their original meaning. A new spirit of toleration and mutual understanding became evident in such organizations as the World Council of Churches. Even the basic differences of opinion between the leaders of the Reformation and the Roman Catholic Church moved toward a new level of discussion when Pope John XXIII convened a Roman Catholic Ecumenical Council in the Vatican in 1963. In the 19th century the effect of the Reformation took the form of many different Protestant churches, all apparently in competition with each other. The tendency in the 20th century, in Catholicism as in Protestantism, is toward greater unity.

HUGH T. KERR
Princeton Theological Seminary

See also BIBLE; CALVIN, JOHN; LUTHER, MARTIN; PROTESTANTISM; QUAKERS; WESLEY, JOHN.

REFRIGERATION

Refrigeration is the process of cooling. Refrigeration usually means cooling below room temperature. The most important use of refrigeration is in keeping food fresh. Refrigeration is also used to keep medical supplies from spoiling. Air conditioning is still another important use of refrigeration.

For thousands of years people living in cold regions have used ice and snow to keep food cold and fresh. The Greeks and Romans, who lived in lands with hot summers, built snow cellars. These were underground rooms packed with snow brought from the mountains during the winter. The snow melted so slowly that food was kept cold all summer.

Although natural ice and snow kept things cold, they were not a dependable source of refrigeration. In most parts of the world there is not enough ice and snow to keep whole cities supplied. And in warm climates there is none at all.

By the middle of the 19th century, scientists had learned a great deal about heat. Inventors began using this knowledge to develop refrigeration machines. The first such machine was patented in England in 1834 by Jacob Perkins (1766–1849), an American inventor. In 1851 a doctor named John Gorrie (1803–55) was granted the first American patent for a refrigeration machine. With the invention of these machines it was no longer necessary to save ice from winter. Ice could be manufactured when it was needed.

▶ HOW REFRIGERATION WORKS

Cold is simply the absence of heat. A refrigerator does not add cold to food; it removes heat. A refrigeration system absorbs heat in one place and gives it off somewhere else.

Most refrigerators work on the principle that an evaporating liquid absorbs heat. When a liquid evaporates (changes to a gas), it absorbs a great deal of heat from the surrounding air and from nearby objects. If you have ever stood in a wet bathing suit when the wind was blowing, you have experienced cooling by evaporation.

The refrigerant (the substance that does the cooling) used in refrigerators is a gas under normal conditions. But under high enough pressure, with cooling, the refrigerant turns to a liquid. When this happens, the refrigerant gives off heat. When the pressure is released, the refrigerant changes back to a gas. In doing so, it absorbs heat.

The Compression Refrigerating System

The compression system is the most common type of refrigerating system. A good example of a compression system is the kind used in most home refrigerators. The heart of this system is a motor-driven pump called a **compressor**, which pumps the refrigerant gas into the **condenser**, a long, coiled metal tube over which air is blown by a fan. At the far end of the condenser is a very small tube called the **capillary tube**. The capillary tube prevents the refrigerant from passing through too freely. As the compressor pumps more and more gas into the condenser, the pressure of the gas builds up quickly because the capillary tube holds the gas back. As the pressure increases, the temperature of the gas rises too. (You can see this principle at work when you pump up a bicycle tire or a basketball. After a few strokes, the barrel of the pump becomes hot to the touch.) When the temperature of the gas trapped in the condenser pipes becomes higher than the temperature of the air being blown over the pipes, heat is given off to the air. When the refrigerant loses enough heat, it turns from a gas into a liquid.

The capillary tube leads to another pipe, called the **evaporator** or cooling coil. In a home refrigerator this pipe is built into the walls of the freezing compartment.

The evaporator tube is much wider than the capillary tube. When the liquid refrigerant passes from the capillary tube to the evaporator, its pressure is suddenly lowered. As a result, the refrigerant turns back to a gas. This process absorbs heat and makes the evaporator—and the space around it—cold. The refrigerant then goes back to the compressor, and the process is repeated.

Compression systems are used in home refrigerators and freezers, air conditioners, refrigerated trucks and railroad cars, cold-storage warehouses, and ice-making plants. The most commonly used refrigerants are pure ammonia and a group of chemicals called Freons. Ammonia is a gas at room temperature. The "ammonia" used as a household cleaner is really a solution of ammonia and water. A Freon is usually used as the refrigerant in home refrigerators.

The Absorption System

The absorption system was developed in 1859 by the French inventor Ferdinand Carré (1824–94). It is based on the fact that certain gases are easily absorbed by certain liquids. The system is used in some home refrigerators, but it is used mainly in industry. Ammonia is the refrigerant most often used in the absorption system.

In the absorption system there is no compressor to turn the refrigerant gas into a liquid. Instead, there are two tanks partly filled with water. One tank is called the **absorber**. The other is called the **boiler**. Energy is supplied by a gas flame.

The water in the boiler is full of dissolved ammonia. As the flame heats the boiler ammonia gas is driven off. The ammonia gas, at high temperature and pressure, passes into a condenser, where it loses heat. The pressure in the condenser is very high. This high pressure, together with the loss of heat, makes the ammonia gas turn into a liquid. The liquid ammonia then passes through the evaporator, where it does its work of cooling.

As the ammonia is driven off, the water from the boiler flows through a cooling coil and is then sprayed into the absorber tank. There it absorbs the ammonia coming from the evaporator. The ammonia solution that results is pumped back to the boiler tank, and the cycle begins again.

Air Cycle System

Another type of system, the air cycle system, is widely used to air-condition airplanes, particularly jet airplanes. This system depends on the fact that expanding air absorbs heat. Expanding air does not absorb as much heat as an evaporating liquid, but an air-conditioning system does not have to produce very low temperatures.

In the engine of a jet airplane air is pumped up to a high pressure before it enters the engine's combustion chamber. In the air cycle system some of this compressed air is made to flow through a coil, where it is cooled.

Then it is allowed to expand. As it does so, it becomes very cold. This cold air is used to air-condition the cabin of the airplane.

▶ INSULATION

A refrigerator must be insulated to keep out heat from the outside; otherwise the refrigeration system would have to work constantly, using up power and wearing out quickly. A home refrigerator is a metal cabinet with a hollow double wall. The space inside the wall

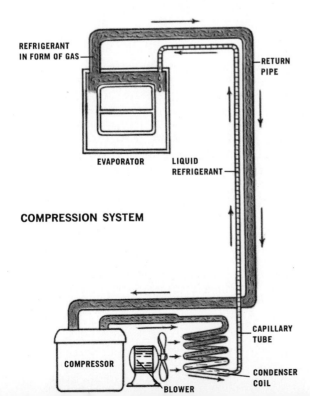

COMPRESSION SYSTEM

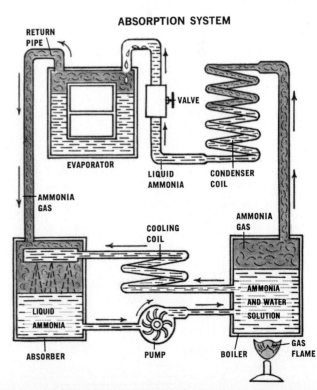

ABSORPTION SYSTEM

is filled with an insulating material, such as cork, wool, fiber glass, or foamed plastic. Heat does not pass readily through these materials. Thus, the refrigerator system does not have to work so hard to keep the inside of the cabinet cool. Cold-storage rooms and refrigerated freight cars and trucks are insulated in the same way.

▶ USES OF REFRIGERATION

Home Refrigerators and Freezers. The most familiar use of refrigeration is in refrigerators and freezers. Refrigerators have a freezing compartment, where ice-cube trays and frozen foods are kept. Since the evaporator coils are built into the walls of this compartment, it is colder than the rest of the refrigerator. The temperature in the freezer is usually kept at about –18°C (0°F), and the food compartment is kept at about 4°C (40°F). In a home freezer used for the storage of frozen foods, the entire inside of the cabinet is kept at about –18°C. The temperature is kept steady by means of a thermostat. The thermostat turns the machine on when the temperature gets too high. It turns the machine off when the desired low temperature is reached.

Transportation. All types of transportation equipment—trucks, railroad cars, and ships—that carry food and other perishables are refrigerated to prevent spoilage. One refrigeration method makes use of manufactured ice. This method is somewhat old-fashioned, but it is still used a great deal. The ice is stored at one end of the truck, railroad car, or ship's hold. A powerful fan forces air through the ice. The chilled air then refrigerates the storage space and the goods that are stored there.

When a compression system is used, the evaporator takes the place of the stored ice. The compressor (driven by a gasoline engine) and the condenser are mounted outside the space that is to be refrigerated.

Warehouses. Large refrigerated warehouses are used for storing food and other perishable goods. The walls of these buildings are well insulated. Large refrigeration machines cool pipes containing brine (salt water). Brine can be made very cold without freezing. The cold brine is pumped through pipes that line the walls of the warehouse building. This produces a more even cooling than is possible by cooling the building directly from the evaporator.

Air Conditioning. Air conditioners are simply refrigeration machines with fans that circulate the cooled air through a room or building. A small home air conditioner, located in a window or an opening in the wall, cools one or two rooms. Air conditioning systems that are used to cool big buildings may be as large as several rooms. They are usually located in the basements or on the top floors of these buildings.

Other Uses. Refrigeration has many other uses. It is used in the manufacture of rubber tires and some plastics and in treating certain metals. Liquid oxygen, used in rocket fuels, could not be made or stored without refrigeration.

An interesting use of refrigeration is in tightly fastening together parts of precision machines—shafts to gears or wrist pins to pistons, for example. The shaft or pin is made a tiny bit larger than the hole into which it is to fit. It is chilled in liquid air or dry ice. This shrinks it. It will then slip into the hole easily. When it warms up, the shaft or pin expands and is locked tightly in place.

Reviewed by W. T. SANDERS
Columbia University

See also AIR CONDITIONING.

REFUSE DISPOSAL. See SANITATION.

SIMPLE HOUSEHOLD REFRIGERATION SYSTEM

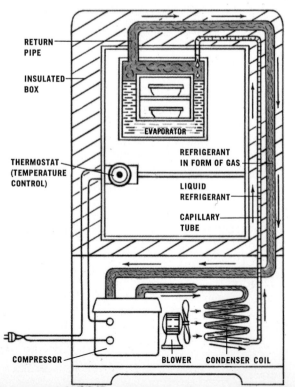

RETURN PIPE

INSULATED BOX

THERMOSTAT (TEMPERATURE CONTROL)

EVAPORATOR

REFRIGERANT IN FORM OF GAS

LIQUID REFRIGERANT

CAPILLARY TUBE

COMPRESSOR

BLOWER   CONDENSER COIL

RELATIVITY

Most scientists believe that the universe is a very orderly place. They believe that all the forces and motions in it are regulated by a few simple rules, or laws of nature. These rules, when fully understood, explain and tie together many apparently unrelated things. For example, the rules explain the earth's gravity, which pulls a well-hit baseball to the ground; the forces that keep a man-made satellite in orbit; the constant speed of light; and the way the planets and stars move in the sky.

The theory of relativity, first published by Albert Einstein at the beginning of this century, is such a set of rules. It explains all the events mentioned above and many more. In addition, the theory of relativity has helped scientists to predict, with great confidence, many things about the universe that they cannot yet see or measure with telescopes or other instruments. Finally, the theory of relativity gives many clues to the great mysteries of how the earth, the planets, and the stars were formed and what will eventually happen to them billions of years from now.

Einstein was not the first scientist to try to pin down the basic laws of nature in words and mathematical equations. (Words and equations that define basic laws are called **theories**.) Many men, throughout recorded history, have developed theories of the universe. Some of these theories had great value. The theories helped astronomers measure accurately the size of the earth's orbit around the sun, for example. The theories gave practical ideas to inventors and engineers who designed weapons and machines. But although many of these theories were accepted for a time, scientists usually found that the theories had two fatal failings: (1) the theories ignored or failed to explain facts that did not fit the theory; and (2) one or more of the key ideas in the theory proved wrong as better scientific measuring equipment was built and new mathematical tools were developed.

▶ THE PARTS OF RELATIVITY

There are two major parts to Einstein's theory. The first part, called the special theory of relativity, was published in 1905. The second part, called the general theory of relativity, was published in 1916. Both parts of the theory have been questioned and tested again and again by top scientists all over the world. While there have been some changes and modifications (several suggested by Einstein himself), his basic ideas now constitute one of the accepted explanations of how all forces and motions operate in the universe.

As is true with most creative basic research, Einstein's theory of relativity was developed with no practical reason in mind. As with all important scientific developments, however, relativity eventually came to affect almost everyone on earth.

The most dramatic use of relativity was in atomic energy. The theory of relativity helped lay the scientific foundation for the atomic and hydrogen bombs. In fact, Einstein's famous letter to President Franklin D. Roosevelt in 1939—written after he emigrated from his native Germany and became a United States citizen—was instrumental in convincing the President that an atomic bomb could be built.

The theory of relativity has also played a vital role in **cosmology**, which is the study of the structure of the universe and what happens to bodies that move through space. The United States Apollo program to send men to the moon, and all the other space exploration programs also use many parts of the theory of relativity.

Even our efforts to find out if there is life on other planets in the universe depend in large measure on relativity. The reason: to fully interpret any light or radio signals we send to or receive from millions of miles out in space will require a knowledge of the theory of relativity.

▶ EVOLUTION OF RELATIVITY

The best way to understand the theory of relativity is to follow part of the same train of thought that led Einstein to it. Like all scientists, Einstein based his new ideas on the work of many earlier researchers and thinkers all over the world. Even their errors often provided useful information.

His approach was what is usually called the scientific method. This can be thought of as a four-step process: (1) Study all the available facts and theories that are currently in use; (2) look for errors or inconsistencies—this

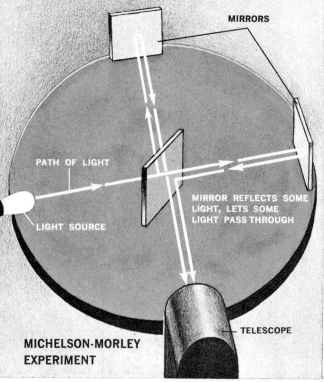

MICHELSON-MORLEY
EXPERIMENT

MIRRORS

PATH OF LIGHT

LIGHT SOURCE

MIRROR REFLECTS SOME LIGHT, LETS SOME LIGHT PASS THROUGH

TELESCOPE

Experimenters used interferometer to compare speeds of light beams and found that light traveled at the same speed regardless of the direction of travel.

search can be a mental process or a set of experiments or both; (3) if the old ideas don't work well, create a new hypothesis, or explanation; (4) test the new hypothesis in all possible ways, correcting it or abandoning it if it does not stand up. Einstein's genius was in step 3, where he created a new hypothesis that both corrected the errors of the older theories and explained many newly discovered facts. The theory also predicted phenomena, such as atomic energy, that were unknown before the theory was published.

Before the theory of relativity, the accepted laws of force and motion were developed by Sir Isaac Newton, the great English mathematician and philosopher. Through all the 18th and most of the 19th century, Newton's laws of gravitation and motion were the foundations of physics and cosmology.

As scientists continued working in the mid-19th century, however, they began finding more and more situations that did not fit in with the Newtonian laws, which they had always accepted. By far the greatest problem concerned light. Scientists could not understand how light travels through space. As scientists experimented with light, they found that the only way they could understand how

light traveled was to say that it was carried along in an invisible material. They called this material **luminiferous ether**. They assumed that the ether must exist all over the earth and throughout the universe. By accepting the ether, the physicists could explain how light energy traveled through space. Light, they said, traveled in the form of waves. The light waves traveled through the ether much as water waves travel through water.

There was one major difficulty with the ether, however. Its properties conflicted with the laws of mechanics.

▶ **THE MICHELSON–MORLEY EXPERIMENT**

The ether concept came under attack in the late 19th century. Scientists were becoming dissatisfied with it because they were unable to detect any ether. Finally, in 1887, two American physicists, named Albert A. Michelson (1852–1931) and Edward W. Morley (1838–1923), devised an experiment to detect the invisible ether.

Their experiment was basically very simple. They reasoned that if ether filled the universe, the earth must be passing through it very rapidly as it revolved around the sun each year. Therefore, if light traveled through the ether, it should be affected by the motion of the earth through the ether.

An easy way to understand this experiment is to think of a boy standing on the shore of a stream, watching a boat out in the current. Suppose the current flows at 2 miles an hour and the boat moves at 20 miles an hour. If the boat heads downstream, it moves at 22 miles an hour (the speed of the current plus the speed of the boat). If the boat moves upstream, it travels at 18 miles an hour (the speed of the boat less the speed of the current). If the boat moves in some other direction, it goes at some speed between 18 and 22 miles an hour.

In the Michelson-Morley experiment the earth is the stream's bank, the ether is the water current, and a light source is used instead of the boat. In their experiment Michelson and Morley mounted a light source on the edge of a large platform. A mirror at the center of the platform split the light into two beams. One part of the beam traveled parallel to the earth's motion through the ether.

The other part traveled at right angles to the earth's motion. A mirror arrangement on the edge of the platform reflected the light beams to a device that compared the arrival times of the beams. The experimenters expected to find a difference in the arrival times.

The amazing result was that no matter in which directions the beams of light were aimed, they always bounced back at exactly the same instant.

This convinced Michelson and Morley that the ether did not exist. The results of the Michelson-Morley experiment were checked repeatedly and confirmed by other scientists.

Since the ether concept was dead, scientists began searching for an alternative to it. Early in the 20th century Albert Einstein announced a new theory. It not only accounted for the motion of light but also explored the very nature of motion itself and of space and time.

▶ THE SPECIAL THEORY OF RELATIVITY

Einstein's theory of relativity provided a new framework for the old ideas about force, motion, and gravitation. Let's examine now the two parts of the theory of relativity to see how they changed many of science's major ideas about the whole physical world.

In creating the special theory of relativity, Einstein made two basic assumptions about the universe.

To understand the first assumption, think again about the boat in the stream and the boy on the bank who is observing and measuring its motion. Assume that he can see nothing but the boat. If he can measure how far it is from him and can accurately figure its direction, he can make many calculations about its motion and other physical properties.

Now, suppose that there is another boy, flying overhead in a jet plane. He, too, is aware only of himself and the boat—he cannot see the movement of the stream or the banks of the river or the other boy, and he has no real information about the direction and speed of his plane. But he can measure the distance to the boat, figure its speed, and make a full set of calculations about it.

The point is this: both boys, using the same laws of force and motion, will come up with different answers to questions about the movements of the boat and its physical properties. Each boy's measurements will take into account automatically, without his even being aware of it, his own position and motion. The position and motion determine his point of view. Technically, each point of view is called a **frame of reference**. The first assumption, then, is that the same laws of force and motion hold true in different frames of reference.

The second assumption is that the speed of light—186,272 miles per second—is the same in each frame of reference.

Using these assumptions, Einstein developed mathematical equations that describe the motion and speeds of any body of matter, from a tiny grain of sand to a planet or a star. When the speeds involved are those that scientists on the earth were used to dealing with, the results of calculations with Einstein's equations were about the same as those obtained by using the Newtonian laws. This explains why Newton's laws were so useful and stood so long.

When the speeds involved approach the speed of light, however, the equations give many seemingly strange results. The many

Boat's speed and direction of travel vary, depending on observer's frame of reference.

BOAT SEEMS TO MOVE AWAY FROM OBSERVER IN PLANE

BOAT SEEMS TO MOVE TOWARD OBSERVER ON SHORE

predictions made possible by these equations are difficult even to imagine. It is not necessary to understand the mathematics or all of the theory of relativity to appreciate how revolutionary these new ideas were when they were introduced and still are even today.

Changes in Physical Properties

According to the special theory, all three of the fundamental quantities of mechanics—length, mass, and time—undergo surprising changes when things move at a speed near that of light. The length shrinks, the mass increases, and the passage of time slows down.

As the speed of an object approaches that of light, the length of the object shrinks in the direction it is moving. But its width and depth (at right angles to the length) do not shrink at all. If the object is traveling at almost the speed of light, it will have almost no length in its direction of motion. Many experiments in laboratories have confirmed this shrinkage. The first experiments on changes in mass were made in 1909 by a physicist named A. Bucherer. He noted that beta particles, which are fast-moving electrons emitted by radioactive substances, exhibited just the increase in mass predicted by the special theory. The time slowdown was demonstrated in the early 1920's by an American scientist named Herbert Ives (1882–1953).

The time-slowing idea has important implications for the world's growing space program. A clock, for example, that is traveling rapidly through space should slow down.

Much more dramatic, however, is the fact that an astronaut in a spaceship traveling near the speed of light would not age as fast as the men he left behind on earth.

Another important finding of the special theory is that neither matter nor energy can move at a speed faster than the speed of light. The reason is that as the object moves close to the speed of light, its mass increases. The mass becomes infinitely great. Since there is no infinite force available to make the object go any faster, its speed levels off, and it approaches the speed of light as a limit.

The final major consequence of the special theory is the equivalence of mass and energy, shown by the famous formula $E = mc^2$. In this equation E stands for energy, m stands for mass, and c represents the speed of light. The key point of the equation is that energy and mass are two forms of the same physical thing, and under the proper circumstances, can be changed from one form to the other. This equivalence is one of the reasons it was possible to develop most of the uses of nuclear energy. In many of these reactions a material such as uranium 235 can develop great quantities of energy. In the case of an atomic bomb, the reaction is fast. In the case of a nuclear power station, the reaction is controlled and relatively slow.

▶ GENERAL THEORY OF RELATIVITY

The general theory of relativity, published 12 years after the special theory, attempts to explain within a single framework many of the

The special theory of relativity predicts that objects gain in mass, shrink in the direction of their travel, and keep slower time as their speed nears that of light.

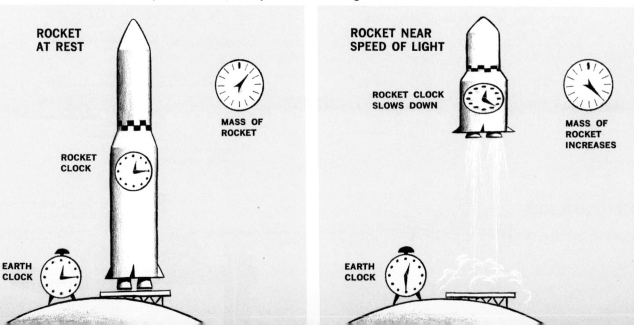

ROCKET AT REST

ROCKET CLOCK

MASS OF ROCKET

EARTH CLOCK

ROCKET NEAR SPEED OF LIGHT

ROCKET CLOCK SLOWS DOWN

MASS OF ROCKET INCREASES

EARTH CLOCK

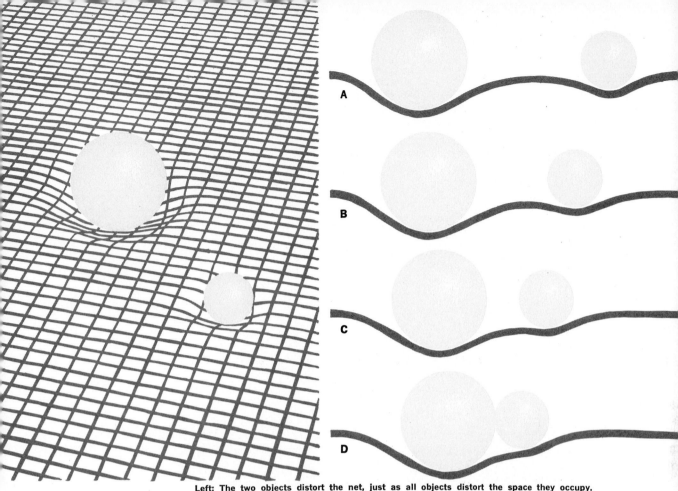

Left: The two objects distort the net, just as all objects distort the space they occupy. Right: Figures A through D illustrate how this distortion causes bodies in space to gravitate, or move, toward one another.

laws of the physical universe. In fact, the special theory can be considered as a part of the general theory.

One of the key ideas in the general theory is that gravitation is a distortion of space. This concept of gravitation can be illustrated by thinking of space as a flat network of crossed rubber bands. If a large stone is placed in the middle of the rubber bands, it produces a depression. Near the stone the rubber bands stretch from their flat surface, while farther away the surface of the bands very nearly retains its flat shape.

Just as the stone distorts the rubber bands, so does matter distort, or warp, space. This distortion of space is called gravitation.

If two large stones are placed close to each other on the rubber-band network, they will tend to move toward each other. The distortion of the rubber bands forces the two stones to move toward each other. Similarly, if two large objects in space are close to each other,

they will tend to move (gravitate) toward each other. The distortion of space, or gravitation, forces the two objects to move toward each other.

If space is not distorted, then the distance between the two points, measured along the rubber bands, will be a straight line. But this straight line becomes a curved line when matter is present, for matter distorts the space.

Is this strange picture anything like reality? Can the distortions of space that were predicted by the general theory be proved by experimentation and observation? Most scientists would now say Yes to both questions. The following facts seem to confirm the general theory of relativity:

(1) The planet Mercury revolves about the sun in an elliptical orbit, as do all the planets. The point in the ellipse at which the planet is closest to the sun is called the perihelion. According to the general theory of relativity, the perihelion should rotate slowly about the sun because of the

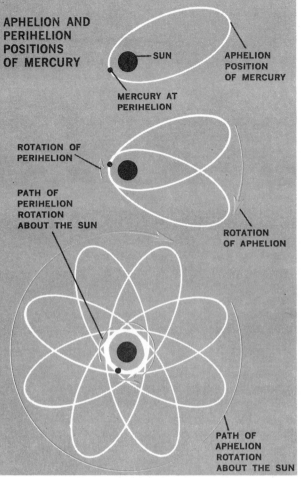

APHELION AND PERIHELION POSITIONS OF MERCURY

SUN

APHELION POSITION OF MERCURY

MERCURY AT PERIHELION

ROTATION OF PERIHELION

PATH OF PERIHELION ROTATION ABOUT THE SUN

ROTATION OF APHELION

PATH OF APHELION ROTATION ABOUT THE SUN

As predicted by the general theory of relativity, the sun's distortion of space causes the perihelion and aphelion position of Mercury to change slightly with each orbit the planet makes about the sun.

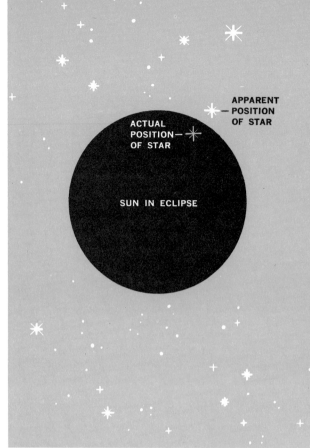

APPARENT POSITION OF STAR

ACTUAL POSITION OF STAR

SUN IN ECLIPSE

Light bends as it passes through the sun's gravitational field, and star appears to shift its position. This effect—seen during a solar eclipse—confirms the general relativity theory.

distortion of space by the sun. Careful observations by astronomers show that the motion of Mercury is close to what is predicted by the general theory.

(2) Light from distant stars deviates slightly from a straight line as it passes close to the sun, according to the general theory. This already has been illustrated by taking photographs, during an eclipse of the sun, of stars that appear to be directly behind the edges of the sun. When the same stars were photographed later and the two photographs matched, the stars did not line up. The light from the stars had apparently been shifted while moving through the distorted space near the sun's surface.

(3) The general theory of relativity predicted that light from certain very dense stars, called white dwarfs, would be changed in frequency by their extra-high gravitational field. When the light from these stars was measured, the shift was found.

(4) The distortion of space was recently de-

tected in the laboratory. The distortion is just what the general theory predicted it would be.

All these experiments indicate very strongly that the general theory of relativity presents a more accurate model of nature than any previous theory. Does this mean simply that Einstein was right and Newton was wrong? A "yes" answer would be an oversimplification. The truth is that all physical theories are only approximations of nature. None is perfect. In this case, Einstein's is more accurate than Newton's and therefore will be used by scientists where needed, until it eventually is replaced with something better.

SERGE A. KORFF
New York University

See also EINSTEIN, ALBERT; ENERGY; GRAVITY AND GRAVITATION; LIGHT; MATTER; NEWTON, ISAAC; PHYSICS; SCIENCE, HISTORY OF.

RELIEF, PUBLIC. See WELFARE, PUBLIC.

RELIGIONS OF THE WORLD

Our early ancestors lived in tribes of closely related families. Each tribe developed its own language, its special type of dress, and its particular weapons for securing food and withstanding enemies. Each had its own code of courage and group loyalty and its own way of life—depending on the geographic surroundings and the dangers they presented. And as far back as these primitive tribes have been studied, each has been found to have had a set of beliefs that made up a form of religion.

Very, very early our primitive ancestors tried to understand the mystery of death. The one great change they could notice when a fellow human died was that he had stopped breathing. And when he stopped breathing, he stopped living. Our primitive ancestors concluded that a human being has a visible body and an invisible "breath" (or "wind" or "spirit" or "soul," as it is called in different languages). And when the breath, or the soul, left the body, the individual died.

They observed that this was also true of animals, big and small. And they concluded that all living things had souls—just like men. Slowly they extended this belief to include everything in nature.

▶ RELIGIONS OF PRIMITIVE AND ANCIENT MAN

It is believed that from this idea the earliest religion, known as **animism**, was developed. According to this religion, all natural objects in the universe (as well as the universe itself) have souls that cannot be seen, and this is what animates all things in the world. To primitive men this belief seemed to be confirmed by their dreams. For in their dreams they saw men and animals that were not there when they were awake. Such dreams confirmed them in the conviction that disembodied spirits, or souls, could move and be wherever they pleased after they had left the bodies they had inhabited. Not only could they be wherever they pleased, but they could act as they pleased, for good or evil.

From these beliefs in souls of many kinds arose the belief in all-powerful spirits, later called gods. First, primitive men worshiped the spirits of departed ancestors. Then they worshiped the spirits of various animals that

they feared or admired. These animals were made gods by certain tribes and were represented by totems, or emblems. The most powerful of all were the spirits of natural forces, such as the sun, the moon, and the rain. These were feared most, and their goodwill was sought after.

The number of gods multiplied rapidly. Each tribe worshiped its own nature gods, giving preference to some while ignoring others. Each tribe developed its own rituals and forms of worship. In the early tribal days the group into which a man was born was not only a community of kinsmen, or relatives. It also included a number of divine spirits, to whom each tribesman belonged and who belonged to him. These people recognized a dual relationship within each tribe. The group into which a man was born was his kin by blood. He was also related to them in their common belonging to their tribal gods.

Primitive man regarded his particular faith as people today regard their nationality. Today a man is born into a given family, whose members are his kin by blood. He is also born in a given nation, to which he is loyal and which offers him protection. When members of one tribe came in contact with members of another tribe, they did not try to win them over to their beliefs. They could not. For their god belonged only to them, and their tribe belonged only to their particular god. In fact, none of the early religions tried to win converts or followers.

From the worship of nature spirits, or world souls, which could not be seen, men were led in time to the worship of the visible images, or idols, representing these gods. The idols were revered for the spirits they represented. They themselves were also considered powerful beings, and it was believed they could be influenced in a great variety of ways by means of magic.

Countless ways of practicing magic were developed by primitive man. These included casting spells, singing chants, attempting to foretell the future, using protective charms, and endowing various kinds of objects with powers of good and bad luck. When primitive man stepped onto the first rung of the ladder that was to take him up to civilization, he took with him many of his early beliefs in magic. The Chaldeans, an ancient Semitic

A Hindu at evening prayer. He is burning incense before a small statue of the god Siva.

people of the Middle East, had an extensive system of foretelling the future. The Sumerians, the earliest inhabitants of what is now Iraq, were great idol-worshipers. The ancient Egyptians believed there was an essential magic in names and numbers.

The earliest civilizations—of which we are the inheritors—also incorporated some of the primitive dependence on magic. The early Greeks, for instance, devoutly believed in **oracles**, the replies of a god through an inspired priest whom they consulted for advice in critical situations. The Romans also used magic as a system of political prophecy. Some of the primitive beliefs in magical numbers (often associated with the influence of the stars), names, and chants have survived in our own times among both civilized and tribal peoples. Most of them have gone through many changes and have been given new interpretations as to their meaning and value.

When we trace any religious belief to its beginnings, we find it rooted in some primitive belief of the days of animism. The belief that everything in nature has a soul gave rise to

polytheism, or the belief in many supernatural powers. A later development was **monotheism,** or the belief in one god. Upon these beliefs are based all the living religions.

▶ **GREAT LIVING RELIGIONS**

There are many religions in the world today. They may be divided into several groups, all related to each other because all developed from earlier faiths and influenced other religions with which they came in contact. In one large group are the faiths that originated in India and from there spread throughout the greater part of Asia. The most important in this group are **Hinduism, Buddhism,** and **Jainism**.

A second important group of related religions originated in China and Japan. To a great extent they remained in the lands of their birth. These religions are **Confucianism, Taoism,** and **Shintoism**. It is not really correct to describe these as religions in the Western sense. To their followers they chart a way of life based on time-honored traditions.

Nearly one third of the more than 4,422,000,000 people in the world today are followers of one of the three religions that make up the third related group: **Judaism, Christianity,** and **Islam**. One of their bonds of kinship is monotheism.

Hinduism

The largest and most important of the religions originating in India is known to the Western world as Hinduism. Its origins go back thousands of years. Hinduism has no bible in the Western sense. Instead, it has many sacred books, the oldest being the Vedas. These sacred books contain epics, myths about the creation of the world and the history of India, and hymns and prayers to accompany sacrifices or to be used as magic.

Traditional Hindu society is divided into higher and lower castes, each of which is divided into many subcastes. According to the Hindu religion, people are **reincarnated,** or reborn, after death. At that time they are rewarded for their good deeds or punished for their evil deeds. This is known as **karma,** the law of the deed: From good must come good, and from evil must come evil. The article HINDUISM in Volume H tells more about this religion and its nearly 480,000,000 followers.

Buddhism

In the 6th century B.C. a new religion was born in India. It accepted the basic beliefs of Hinduism that existed in India at that time. It accepted the belief in reincarnation and in karma, for example. But it just as strongly rejected the Hindu caste system. According to tradition, the founder of this religion was Prince Siddhartha Gautama (called the **Buddha**). The Prince renounced his kingdom so that he could devote his life to the study of the nature of reality and of how people ought to live according to their moral beliefs. More information about this religion of over 250,000,000 people is contained in the article BUDDHA AND BUDDHISM in Volume B.

Jainism

About the same time, another prince, Vardhamana, of a neighboring kingdom in India, began to preach what at first seem to be the same reforms of Hinduism. He, too, accepted karma and believed in reincarnation. He, too, rejected the caste system and the sacredness of the Hindu Vedas. But unlike the Buddha, Prince Vardhamana did not go on to teach moderation. He urged upon his followers the extreme path of asceticism, or self-denial. Vardhamana became known as Mahavira, the Great Hero. Mahavira was a most unusual kind of hero. He was honored not because he had conquered others but because he had conquered himself.

The religion founded by Mahavira is called Jainism, the Religion of the Conquerors, and its followers are called Jains. After Mahavira's death his teachings were gathered in many books. These became the sacred scriptures of the Jains. Most of them teach how to give up all worldly pleasures and how the educated person should live and behave. The sum of his teachings is given in one word: **ahimsa**. "Ahimsa" literally means "noninjury" or "nonviolence," and it implies a reverence for all life.

All Jains are vegetarians. Jains cannot take part in war. They cannot be butchers or engage in any work in which they might kill or injure any living thing. They cannot even be farmers, for in tilling the soil they might kill worms. Jainism exists mainly in India. Today there are about 3,000,000 Jains, who are divided into two major sects: the Svetambaras, whose priests are clad in white, and the Digambaras, whose priests are "sky-clad," wearing only loincloths in public. Because of the limitations placed upon the Jains by their religion, many of them become teachers, merchants, or bankers.

Confucianism

For untold centuries the Chinese were ancestor worshipers and nature worshipers. Around their beliefs they wove a tapestry of rites, traditions, and mystic symbols that were handed down as a heritage from one generation to another.

About the same time that the two princes Gautama and Mahavira were born in India, a child was born in China, not far from the

A statue of the Great Buddha in Kamakura, Japan.

Yellow Sea. His name was K'ung Ch'iu. He became known as K'ung Fu-tzu (K'ung the Philosopher). We call him Confucius. The article CONFUCIUS in Volume C will tell you more about him.

We can dimly realize from the mountain of legends and myths under which he lies buried that Confucius was a great teacher of tradition and ethics (moral principles). Most of his life was devoted to studying and re-interpreting ancient records, which he organized into the Four Books. To these he added a fifth book of his own, called *The Autumn and Spring Annals*. At his death he willed these books to his followers. Confucius' disciples added to his books selections from the master's sayings, known as the *Analects* of Confucius.

In all of these Confucius clarified the disciplines and behavior of what he called the superior individual, but he avoided the topic of religion. It was not that he wished to appear an unbeliever. He stated that anyone who does not recognize the existence of a divine law cannot be a superior person. Yet nowhere in his writings do we find any discussion of heaven or any theories about God. Most people therefore consider Confucianism a philosophy or a system of ethics, rather than a true religion.

Confucius influenced generation after generation of Chinese with his idea of the outstanding individual. Followers of Confucianism often follow also the teachings of Buddhism or Taoism—or both of these. For this reason, the exact number of Confucians is not known. But it is estimated that there are nearly 160,000,000. Most of them are found in China.

Taoism

When Confucius was a young man, there lived in another part of China a remarkable teacher whose work became the foundation of a great mystic religion. About this man we know very little outside of legends. We do not even know his real name, for he is remembered only as Lao-tzu, which simply means "the Old Philosopher." The Old Philosopher may well have been the keeper of the archives in the Imperial Library in the ancient city of Loyang. Legend tells how the Old Philosopher wished to leave the province of Honan. The border guard, a great admirer of the old

man, would not permit him to cross the frontier until he had written down his basic teachings. These were known to people only by word of mouth. Lao-tzu submitted to the wish of the devoted guard and wrote down his teachings. These were contained in 81 short poems, which he called the *Tao Tê Ching*. Then he crossed the border and was never heard from again. These short poems, written some 2,500 years ago, have been studied, translated, and interpreted ever since. They have become the "bible" of a great mystic religion.

The *Tao Tê Ching* is a short book and a puzzling one. Many books in many languages have been written about it, but its full meaning is disputed to the present day. *Tao* has been translated or interpreted as "the Way," "the Path," "the Word," "the Great Beginning," "Reason," "Virtue," and "God," or "God's Way." Although parts of the *Tao Tê Ching* are difficult to understand, other parts are quite clear, and the teachings are inspiring. In it Lao-tzu wrote: "A truly good man loves men and hates none." Goodness, he taught in many ways, is more important than wisdom or knowledge. "Little faith is put in those who have little faith," he observed. Confucius devoted his life to clarifying the behavior of the "superior man." Lao-tzu devoted himself to the behavior of the "good man."

Around the *Tao Tê Ching* the disciples of Lao-tzu developed a great mystic faith known as Taoism. This faith is confined almost entirely to China. It is difficult to learn the exact number of Taoists, for China is known as the Land of Three Teachings (Confucianism, Taoism, and Buddhism) and one person may belong to all three at the same time. But it is estimated that there are more than 31,000,000 followers of Taoism.

Shintoism

The religion of the Japanese people is best known by its Chinese name, Shintoism, which means "The Way of the Gods." In Japanese it is called *Kami-no-michi,* which means the same thing. Shintoism had its beginning in primitive times, when the Japanese thought that their islands were the only inhabited places on earth. They believed in a number of nature gods and goddesses. Until recently they believed that their emperor was descended from these deities. The myths of those early days when the world was young and the gods mingled with the Japanese people were assembled as recently as the beginning of the 8th century A.D. One volume is called *Kojiki* (*Record of Ancient Events*), and the other volume contains the *Nihongi* ("Chronicles of Japan"). These are the most important sacred books of Shintoism.

About the same time the ancient records were assembled, Buddhism became well established in Japan. But it was not the same Buddhism that had arisen in India. It had traveled from India to Tibet, from Tibet to China, from China to Korea, and finally from Korea to Japan. By that time Buddhism had changed greatly. In Japan, Buddhism merged with Shintoism, from which it adopted certain rites and beliefs. Meanwhile, Confucianism also had reached Japan. The three religions merged and produced a new way of life, governed by **bushido**, the code of the knight. This code encouraged love of justice and praised courage, loyalty, and love of wisdom and learning. Above all, it instilled the love of nature. Today close to 60,000,000 people still hold to the beliefs and practices of Shintoism. They are free to join other religions, too, if they wish.

Judaism

The oldest of the world's living religions is Judaism, which had its beginnings over 5,000 years ago. Like many ancient faiths, it begins with stories of the Creation and of a devastating flood. Then the ancient record continues with the story of Abraham. Although Abraham objected to the worship of idols, he was not a monotheist (believer in one god) in our sense of the word. This idea of one god who created and ruled the universe was developed much later by the prophets of Israel. From the days of the prophets the belief in one god became the core and foundation of Judaism.

Differences arose very early among Jewish religious leaders on the interpretation and practice of their faith. But it was not until the 19th and 20th centuries that three major divisions of Judaism appeared: Orthodox, Conservative, and Reform. Judaism does not attempt to gain converts, and its followers have consequently remained small in number.

Today there are more than 14,000,000 Jews, who are dispersed throughout the world. The article JEWS AND JUDAISM in Volume J tells about their long history, their beliefs, and their practices.

Christianity

The faith with the largest following in the world today is Christianity. It sprang from Judaism. It accepts the Jewish Bible (the Old Testament) and the teachings of the proph-

A modern Protestant church in Stockholm, Sweden.

Indians at prayer in a Catholic church in Bombay.

Muslims in Friday noon prayer at the Kano Mosque in Nigeria.

ets. But to these it adds new teachings, known as the New Testament. In the New Testament is told the story of Jesus of Nazareth, who challenged the orthodoxy of his day for holding the law more important than the people it was supposed to serve. He went out among the people and preached a return to old ideals: integrity, righteousness, peace, and, above all, love. Soon he gathered a great following among the poor, the sick, the discouraged, and the outcast.

Wherever his disciple Saint Paul (?–A.D. 67?) went as a missionary, he organized Christian churches. Soon after the death of Saint Paul the Christian Church became firmly established among the Greeks and Romans. Later, great conflicts arose between the fathers (or patriarchs) in Constantinople and the Church leaders (or popes) in Rome. The Church of the East became known as the Orthodox Church. The Roman Church of the West became known as the Roman Catholic Church. The rift between them gradually widened. Finally, in the 11th century A.D., the Orthodox Church and the Roman Catholic Church became completely separated. In recent years there have been some attempts at closer relationships between the two branches.

Early in the 16th century a German priest named Martin Luther (1483–1546) challenged certain practices of the Roman Catholic Church. This led to the Protestant Reformation. Since that time many new sects have arisen within the Protestant Church. Today over one fifth—nearly 1,000,000,000—of the world's people belong to the many divisions and sects of Christianity. Their story is told in the article CHRISTIANITY, HISTORY OF, in Volume C.

Islam

The youngest monotheistic religion is Islam. It was greatly influenced by its predecessors, Judaism and Christianity. Islam (often incorrectly known in the Western world as Mohammedanism) was founded in Arabia early in the 7th century by Mohammed (570–632). The followers of Islam are known as Muslims ("those who give themselves to God"), and they have spread throughout the world, particularly the countries of Africa and Asia. Today about 590,000,000 people—just over one eighth of the world's population—are Muslims.

Like other religions that have survived for a long time and spread to other countries, Islam has divided into different sects. Almost from the beginning there were two camps: the Sunnites and the Shi'ites. The Sunnites follow the teachings of the Koran, the sacred book of Islam. Meditation and mystic exercises are intended to unite them with Allah—not after their death but while they are still alive. The Shi'ites believe that the leadership of Islam was willed by Mohammed to his son-in-law Ali. They do not recognize any of the caliphs (heads of Islam) who succeeded Mohammed. They have developed a number of rituals and traditions of their own wherever Islam is followed. The most important Muslim beliefs and practices are described in the article ISLAM in Volume I.

The gateway to a Shinto temple is called a *torii*.

Zoroastrianism

One religion that is rapidly dying out has only about 140,000 followers, chiefly in a limited area in India. Yet it must be mentioned because of its influence on the monotheistic religions. This religion teaches

Buddhist monks in meditation before the gold-leafed Shwe Dagon Pagoda in Rangoon, Burma.

Interior of the Central Synagogue in New York City.

that the world is ruled by two forces, one good and one evil. It was founded by the prophet Zoroaster, who lived in Persia about the 6th century B.C. Driven from its native land, Zoroastrianism found refuge in India some 1,300 years ago. There its followers are known as Parsis or Parsees ("Persians"). They believe that by dedicating themselves to good deeds, they will help Ahura Mazda, the One Wise Lord, overcome the spirit of evil in the world. They sum up their beliefs in a short prayer: "I praise aloud the thought well thought, the word well spoken, and the deed well done." To learn more about this religion, consult ZOROASTRIANISM in Volume Z.

▶ LATER RELIGIONS

In the world today there are many sects within each religion. There are also religions that are mixtures of two or more faiths. Most of them are of recent origin, for they arose after the great religious movements began to spread. Many people were dissatisfied with some of their teachings. They were attracted to the new teachings and yet were unwilling to give up their own entirely. The result was new religions, which attracted new followings. Among these are **Sikhism**, a mixture of Islam and Hinduism; **Sufism**, a mixture of Islam and Christianity; **Bahá'í Faith**, which accepts the prophets of Judaism, Christianity, and Islam. The followers of the Bahá'í Faith believe in the brotherhood of man and favor a universal language, so that all men may have a common medium of communication.

While all these divisions in the religions of the world have taken place and are still taking place, about 500,000,000 people in the world still follow the many varieties of tribal faiths. This seems to emphasize the point that there are really no religions. Rather, there is *religion,* which has many paths. All these paths are directed to the summit, where man hopes to find an answer to the mystery of life and death and the purpose of being.

JOSEPH GAER
Author, *How the Great Religions Began*

See also ORTHODOX EASTERN CHURCHES; PROTESTANTISM; ROMAN CATHOLIC CHURCH; articles on individual continents and countries.

RELIGIOUS HOLIDAYS

Since the beginning of time, people have set aside certain days for giving thanks to a divine being for the good things in their lives. The earliest peoples held feasts and festivals in honor of events that were important to them in their daily lives. The change of seasons, the planting time and harvest, and the summer and winter solstices were celebrated with joyful ceremonies. Offerings were made to the gods for the first fruits and grains of the harvest. As civilizations advanced, some of the pagan customs were taken over by the church and given new religious meanings. The word "holiday" really means "holy day."

Each of the world's religions has its important holidays. Often these holidays celebrate the same event, but at different times and in different ways. Many countries and religions use the Gregorian calendar, in which the year begins in January and ends in December. The Russian Orthodox Church uses the Julian calendar, which is 13 days behind the Gregorian. Thus, the Russian Orthodox Church celebrates the New Year on January 14. The Jewish people begin their religious year in the Hebrew month of Tishri. Tishri starts in September or October on the Gregorian calendar. In Asia and Africa some people use the lunar calendar, which is based on the movements of the moon.

Holidays that fall at different times each year, such as Easter, are called movable holidays. Holidays that always fall on the same date, such as Christmas, All Saints' Day, and Candlemas, are called immovable holidays.

In many countries each little town and village has its own special festivals and **saints' days**. They may be unknown in the next village. Among the saints who occupy a high place in the Christian Church everywhere is Saint John the Baptist. His birthday, June 24, is widely celebrated with special church services and processions. Bonfires are lighted on the eve of the feast. With the exception of Saint John's, all saints' days celebrate the anniversary of the death of the saints. The day of death is thought of as the time the saints are born again to glory.

The first day of the week, **Sunday**, is a holy day for most Christians. It was the day of Christ's Resurrection. Churches hold services, and most people rest from their usual work. It is generally a legal holiday throughout the United States. The Seventh-Day Adventists, a Christian sect, observe the seventh day of the week, Saturday, as their **sabbath**.

The Jewish sabbath also falls on Saturday. It begins at sunset on Friday and lasts until sunset on Saturday. *Shabath* is Hebrew for "to rest."

The Mohammedans keep Friday as their day for special services. They are not expected to rest from work except during mid-day prayer.

Ember Days are periods of fasting and special prayers in the calendars of the Roman Catholic and Protestant Episcopal churches. Ember Days come at the beginning of each quarter of the church year—in the spring, summer, fall, and winter.

Long ago, ministers could be admitted to holy orders only during Ember Days, but this is no longer so. Nor are the exact dates and observance of Ember Days firmly established. The decision as to when and if Ember Days are to be observed is left to the discretion of the conference of bishops in each locality.

▶ SPRING AND SUMMER HOLIDAYS

Easter is the most important movable feast of the Christian Church. Its date fixes the dates of the holidays connected with it—Lent, Shrove Tuesday, Ash Wednesday, Holy Thursday, Palm Sunday, and others. **Shrove Tuesday** falls on the day before Ash Wednesday, which marks the beginning of Lent. At one time people confessed their sins before Lent. They were pardoned, or "shriven." The day has many other names. In England it is sometimes called Pancake Tuesday. In France and in some southern cities of the United States it is called **Mardi Gras**. "Mardi Gras" is French for "Fat Tuesday." This name came from the custom of housewives' cleaning their cupboards of the fats, eggs, and other foods that are not eaten during the fast days that follow. They used up the forbidden ingredients in pancakes, doughnuts, and other rich foods. Since Shrove Tuesday is the last day before the fast, it is a time for feasting and fun.

Ascension Day, also called **Ear of Wheat**

Thursday, falls on the 40th day after Easter—always on Thursday. It is considered the oldest feast of the Christian Church. It commemorates Jesus' Ascension, or rising, from earth into heaven. Some churches call the day Holy Thursday, but it is not to be confused with the Holy Thursday that falls just before Easter.

Ten days after Ascension Day, or 50 days after Easter, is **Pentecost**, or **Whitsunday**. Pentecost comes from the Greek word *pentekoste,* meaning "50th day." Many new Christians were baptized at Pentecost. They dressed in white clothing for the ceremony. For this reason the day came to be called White Sunday in England. It was later shortened to Whitsunday. Pentecost ranks with Christmas and Easter among the great feasts of Christianity, for it marks the birthday of the Christian Church. It commemorates the coming of the Holy Spirit with his gift of faith to the Apostles and Disciples. Some European countries observe the Monday following Whitsunday as a legal holiday.

At about the same time, the Jewish people celebrate **Shabuoth**, or **Pentecost**, also known as the **Feast of Weeks**. It, too, is called Pentecost, because it falls on the 50th day after the second day of Passover. It is a time for giving thanks for the spring harvest and the Ten Commandments. Boys and girls are confirmed on this holiday. The Christian Church had its beginning on the feast of Shabuoth.

Trinity Sunday is the Sunday after Whitsunday, 57 days after Easter. The **Feast of Corpus Christi** (the feast of "the body of Christ") is celebrated the following Thursday. Catholics in many countries hold colorful religious processions on this day. Priests in beautiful robes carry the Blessed Eucharist through streets that have been strewn with flowers.

Annunciation Day, also known as Lady Day, March 25, usually falls during Lent. This church feast commemorates the angel Gabriel's message to the Virgin Mary that she was to become the mother of Jesus.

The Jewish Arbor Day, Hamishah Asar B'Shevat, is celebrated on the 15th day of the Hebrew month of Shevat. Shevat marks the beginning of spring in Israel and falls in January or February on the Gregorian calendar. The children in Israel plant trees on this day.

The Hindu fire festival, known as **Holi** or **Basant**, is celebrated in India in March or April. In Bengal the Holi festival honors Krishna, a Hindu god. Thailand honors its Lord Buddha in a 3-day religious festival called **Visakha Puja**. **Wesak**, in Ceylon, is like the Christian Easter and Christmas. This great festival in honor of Buddha takes place at the time of the full moon. Homes are decorated with lanterns, and thousands of people go to the temples to pray. **Id-Al-Adha** is a Muslim holiday marking the end of the pilgrimage to Mecca, the birthplace of Mohammed.

▶**FALL AND WINTER HOLIDAYS**

The most sacred period in the Jewish religious calendar, the High Holy Days, begins with **Rosh Hashanah**, the New Year, and ends with **Yom Kippur**, the Day of Atonement. Rosh Hashanah falls on the first day of the month of Tishri in the Hebrew calendar. Orthodox Jews observe Rosh Hashanah for 2 days. Tishri may come anytime between about September 5 and October 5. According to Jewish belief it is during this period that God remembers the good and evil deeds of men and decides on rewards and punishments. Yom Kippur, 10 days after Rosh Hashanah, is the most solemn day in the Jewish calendar. The Jewish people fast from sundown on the eve of Yom Kippur until sundown the next day. Yom Kippur eve and the day of Yom Kippur are spent in prayer in the synagogues.

The Jewish **Feast of the Tabernacles**, or **Sukkoth**, comes in September or October. In many places boys and girls build small huts or tabernacles of branches. This is in memory of the huts in which the Jews lived during their years of wandering through the wilderness. The festival lasts 8 or 9 days and is a thanksgiving for the fall harvest.

Feast of All Saints, November 1, also known as All Hallows or Hallowmas, is an important feast of the Roman Catholic Church. It honors all the saints—particularly those who do not have a day of their own.

All Souls' Day, November 2, is observed by the Roman Catholic Church. Requiem masses are said for the souls of the faithful.

Martinmas, on November 11, honors Saint Martin and is a harvest feast in many European countries. It was the Thanksgiving Day of the Middle Ages. Harvest foods and roast goose are eaten. Often the new wine is tasted.

The **Feast of the Immaculate Conception**, on December 8, is a time of great celebration in Spain. It is also Mother's Day in that country.

The **Day of Our Lady of Guadalupe**, December 12, is Mexico's greatest religious holiday. It commemorates the Virgin Mary's appearance before a humble Mexican peasant. A church was built on the spot where she appeared. Thousands of people visit the shrine of Our Lady of Guadalupe.

Advent (from the Latin *adventus,* meaning "a coming") is observed by Christian churches in honor of the coming of Christ. It covers a period that includes the four Sundays before Christmas. It is marked by solemn observances, prayer, and fasting.

Epiphany, on January 6, marks the end of the Twelve Days of Christmas. "Epiphany" is from the Greek word for "manifestation." It is the day when Jesus manifested, or showed, himself to the Magi. Epiphany was a church festival before Christmas was observed. It is also known as Twelfth Night, Three Kings' Day, Little Christmas, and Festival of the Kings, and by other names. It commemorates the visit by the Magi, or three kings, to the manger at Bethlehem where Jesus was born. In many countries it is a day for presenting gifts.

Id-al-Fitr marks the end of the Mohammedan month of Ramadan. During Ramadan, Muslims fast from sunrise to sunset. Id-al-Fitr is like the Christian's Christmas. Dressed in new clothes, people go to the mosques to pray. They then visit with family and friends.

Candlemas, on February 2, is also known as the **Purification of the Virgin Mary**. It celebrates the presentation of the infant Jesus in the temple 40 days after his birth, and the purification of his mother. On this day the year's supply of candles for the church is blessed.

Reviewed by Lavinia Dobler
Author, *Customs and Holidays Around the World*

See also Calendar, History of the; Carnivals; Christmas Customs Around the World; Easter; Hanukkah; Holidays; Passover; Purim.

REMBRANDT (1606–1669)

The paintings of Rembrandt touch something deep in almost everyone. His great skill and his sympathetic understanding of people have given him a place in art history that few others enjoy. Perhaps Rembrandt understood people so well because he himself experienced much misfortune, as well as happiness. He was rich during some periods of his life and poor during others. Ten years of happy marriage ended in tragedy. At first his work was praised, then violently attacked, then ignored.

Rembrandt Harmenszoon van Rijn, one of seven children, was born in Leiden, Holland, on July 15, 1606. His father was a miller, and his mother was a baker's daughter. The simple, religious Harmenszoon family was called van Rijn ("of the Rhine"), for the Rhine River flowed near their mill.

When Rembrandt was 7, he was sent to the best local school. At 13 he was enrolled in the University of Leiden. Shortly after this he convinced his parents to allow him to study art with a local painter. After 3 years he went to Amsterdam, where he spent 6 months studying with Pieter Lastman (1583–1633). Lastman had studied in Italy and had been influenced by the work of the Italian artist Caravaggio (1573–1610). Though Rembrandt never went to Italy, he, too, through the teaching of Lastman, was affected by Caravaggio's work.

In 1625 Rembrandt returned to Leiden, where he shared a studio with his friend Jan Lievens (1607–74). Both men worked hard, and Rembrandt had several pupils. From his many self-portraits we know that he was a vigorous young man with a broad face, big nose, and unruly hair. His small eyes had an alert, piercing look.

During his 7 years in Leiden, Rembrandt painted many pictures of his family. In this

Detail of Rembrandt's *The Night Watch* (1642), which is in the Rijksmuseum, Amsterdam.

period he tried several techniques but was always concerned with showing how light changes the appearance of subjects.

As his work came to the attention of collectors Rembrandt was often invited to Amsterdam to paint portraits for rich patrons. In 1632 he settled there. In that year he painted his first group portrait, *The Anatomy Lesson of Dr. Tulp,* a picture of the Amsterdam Guild of Surgeons. His reputation established, he received many more commissions.

The next 10 years were Rembrandt's happiest and most prosperous. In 1634 he married the beautiful and wealthy Saskia van Uijlenburgh. Many of their friends were prominent citizens of Amsterdam. Yet Rembrandt was somewhat unsociable. He worked long hours in his studio, producing works of art and teaching his many pupils.

Rembrandt was extravagant and impulsive. He spent money recklessly. He bought fine clothes and jewels for Saskia and himself. He filled their home with paintings, drawings, and other works of art. His studio was crowded with costumes, helmets, and old weapons. In 1639 he bought a big house—bigger than he could really afford.

Then suddenly, in 1642, Rembrandt was plunged into deep sorrow. His beloved Saskia—whom we see in so many of Rembrandt's paintings—died. She left him with their little son, Titus. At the same time, his group portrait *The Night Watch* was severely criticized. Rembrandt's popularity began to decline. He withdrew even more from people and worked longer in his studio. He received and accepted fewer portrait commissions. People did not like his use of **chiaroscuro**—contrasts of light and dark. They thought the technique was old-fashioned. They simply wanted good likenesses. Rembrandt began to paint more subjects of his own choosing—especially illustrations of Bible stories.

Earlier, Rembrandt had painted people in the midst of dramatic action. He had made them look like actors in a spotlight. Now he became more interested in people's inner feelings. As his own suffering increased, so did his understanding of the suffering of Biblical characters. He had always sympathized with poor people, whom he now began painting in restful poses. The light in his paintings became a golden-brown haze surrounding the figures. His paintings reflected his new understanding of the human soul.

Most Dutch artists of the 17th century were specialists in one kind of painting, but Rembrandt excelled in many. Besides portraits, he painted landscapes, religious subjects, and **genre**—scenes of everyday life. He painted more self-portraits than any other known artist. Rembrandt was also a great master of etching, a printmaking technique.

As Rembrandt continued to paint to please himself his fortunes dwindled. In 1656, in spite of the efforts of his son and of his devoted housekeeper, Hendrickje Stoffels, Rembrandt went bankrupt. He had to sell all his belongings and move to a poorer neighborhood. Yet Rembrandt's most creative period was the last 10 years of his life. He cared for little except his art and was usually seen in a smock covered with paint. Forgotten by many art collectors, Rembrandt received only a few commissions. One of these was his greatest group portrait, *The Officers of the Draper's Guild,* painted in 1661 and 1662.

In 1663 Hendrickje died. Five years later Titus died. Old and in failing health, Rembrandt could not recover from this shock. He died the following year on October 4, 1669, in Amsterdam.

Reviewed by AARON H. JACOBSEN
Author, *The Baroque Sketchbook*

RENAISSANCE

The period that began in Italy about 1300, developed at a later date in other European countries, and ended about 1600 is known as the Renaissance. The early part of the Renaissance is sometimes called the late Middle Ages.

Renaissance is a French word meaning "rebirth." The period received this name because of a rebirth of interest among Italian scholars in the learning and arts of ancient Greece and Rome. There was a reawakening of the classical concern for beauty and for man and his destiny on earth. But this time of rebirth was also a time of birth—of the appearance of new things. In these years Europeans developed new scientific ideas and inventions, produced new literature and art, and discovered new lands and trade routes. They began to think about man and his world in new and different ways.

▶THE RENAISSANCE BEGAN IN ITALY

Following the Crusades, the Mediterranean Sea was the main route for trade between Europe and the East. The Italian states were leaders during the Renaissance. Italians traveled to foreign lands. Italian merchants and bankers did business all over Europe. Cities grew, and wealth increased. The ancient ruins of Rome, the source of inspiration for the Renaissance, were in Italy. Italian scholars led the revival of interest in ancient learning. Artists from Italy set the fashions in painting, architecture, and sculpture. Italian explorers discovered new lands.

Growth of City-States

Italy at the time of the Renaissance did not have a unified government. It was divided into a number of independent states that competed with each other for leadership. The Kingdom of the Two Sicilies (or Kingdom of Naples) in the south was the largest but also the poorest. In central Italy the pope ruled the city of Rome and a group of states called the Papal States. He was their **secular** (earthly) leader as well as their spiritual leader. Northern Italy was divided among several city-states, of which the most important were Venice, Milan, and Florence.

Venice. Situated on the Adriatic Sea, Venice was the main port during the Renaissance. Spices and other products of the East passed through the port of Venice before the discovery of the sea routes around Africa. In theory Venice was a republic, whose government was headed by an official called the doge. In fact it was aristocratic, ruled by a grand council whose members belonged to noble families. Surrounded by lagoons, the island city of Venice was protected from the struggles of other Italian cities. Peaceful and wealthy, it devoted itself to the development of commerce and art.

Milan. Situated on the main trade routes that ran through the Alpine passes, Milan profited from trade and also manufactured fine cloth and arms. The city had once been a republic, but in the 14th century a series of strong rulers, or despots, took over its government. Foremost among these were Gian Galeazzo Visconti (1351–1402), Francesco Sforza (1401–66), and Ludovico Sforza (1451–1508).

Florence. Florence was an active city of merchants, craftsmen, artists, and scholars. With some justice the Florentines called their city the Athens of Italy. Learning, art, and business flourished together. Rich patrons employed architects to build fine town houses, which they filled with paintings and statues. They paid for the building and decoration of churches and monasteries. They collected libraries and supported scholars. Noble families competed for glory as well as power. From this long struggle the Medici family of bankers emerged victorious in 1434. They ruled Florence with an iron hand. Lorenzo de' Medici (1449–92), known as Lorenzo the Magnificent, brought the city to a height of artistic glory achieved only by a few civilizations in history.

▶THE RENAISSANCE SPREAD NORTHWARD

As Italian trade with other parts of Europe increased, Italian ideas spread. A young gentleman of England, France, Flanders, or Germany did not consider his education complete until he had traveled in Italy. Artists traveled to Italy to learn from the works of the great masters.

Increasing trade brought great changes in European life. Even though most people lived on the land, the wealthy and powerful

SOME IMPORTANT DEVELOPMENTS DURING THE RENAISSANCE

The revived interest in classical culture began in Italy and spread all over Europe.

Voyages of discovery and exploration changed popular ideas about geography.

Cities grew in size and wealth as trade and the merchant class became more important.

Reform movements stirred the Christian Church.

New weapons changed methods of warfare.

New discoveries about the physical world, and the growth of independent thought, encouraged the development of scientific ideas and method.

Printing with movable type made possible a wide reading of national literatures. A growing interest in all kinds of learning spread throughout Europe.

class was no longer made up only of feudal landlords. Great merchants and bankers in the cities of northern Europe as well as in those of Italy were beginning to play important roles. The worldly influences of the new rulers took hold. Monuments, statues, and portraits were commissioned in their honor. The new rulers no longer were interested only in God and God's world but also in man and his world.

▶ THE HUMANISTS

The scholars who created the new interest in Greek and Roman antiquity were known as **humanists**. The word "humanism" comes from the Latin *humanitas,* meaning "culture." But it has also come to express the concern with human life that characterized the ancient Greeks and Romans.

Francesco Petrarch (1304–74), one of the first humanists, wrote an imaginary conversation between himself and Saint Augustine, the great medieval church scholar. This conversation was a discussion of whether a man should concern himself with this life or with the hope of heaven. Petrarch insisted that it was perfectly reasonable for men on earth to seek the good things of this life and leave the glories of heaven until "we shall have arrived there." The humanists had little interest in theology (knowledge about God). Instead they studied history, the story of men, and they read poetry that praised men's deeds or expressed their feelings.

A New Interest in Ancient Scholars

Petrarch revived the interest in ancient scholars. The humanists read about how Rome became a great republic, as told by the historian Livy. They delighted in the poetry of Vergil, which told of ancient heroes. They read Cicero's letters and orations, filled with advice on how men should conduct both private and public affairs. The early humanists also read Greek authors, for the Greeks had been the teachers of the Romans. Professors from Greek lands of the eastern Mediterranean were encouraged to come to Italy to teach.

Growth of National Literature

The humanists took the ancient authors for their models. They copied the Latin of ancient times rather than the style of Latin, called Vulgate, used during the Middle Ages. The humanists particularly admired Cicero, and they copied his writings. Some of the humanists modeled their speeches after those once given in the Roman Senate. They tried to write letters like those of Cicero and to write histories as they imagined Livy would have done.

But the humanists did more than copy ancient Latin authors. They also wrote in the **vernacular**, the everyday language of the people. Petrarch wrote sonnets in Italian to the lady Laura, and his pupil Giovanni Boccaccio (1313–75) was the author of a collection of stories entitled *The Decameron*. In his most famous work, *The Prince*, Niccolò Machiavelli (1469–1527) told how a ruler could acquire and hold power.

The Dutch scholar Desiderius Erasmus, in his *Praise of Folly*, and the French author François Rabelais (1494?–1553), in his tales *Pantagruel* and *Gargantua*, poked fun at man's follies. In England, Geoffrey Chaucer wrote *The Canterbury Tales* and Edmund Spenser (1552?–99) *The Faerie Queene*. William Shakespeare, creator of *Hamlet*, *Macbeth*, *The Tempest*, and a host of other plays, was the outstanding dramatist of the Renaissance in England. In *Don Quixote* Miguel de Cervantes Saavedra created one of the most famous characters in literature.

Religion and the Humanists

Although the humanists were not very interested in theology, they were interested in ancient books, and the Bible was an ancient book. Men who learned to read Greek could read the New Testament in its original language. A few learned Hebrew and studied the Old Testament in its original language.

Some humanists thought that men's devotion to their religion would increase if they studied the scriptures in the original languages. Erasmus had an edition of the New Testament printed in its original Greek. He thought that a Christian should read and study "the philosophy of Christ" as a follower of Plato would study Plato's books. The philosophy of Christ, as Erasmus understood it, included little theology. As a humanist, he was much more interested in Christ's teachings about how men should treat each other.

Martin Luther, the great German leader of the Protestant Reformation, and men like him began to question the books they studied. They began to question accepted beliefs as well.

▶ **NEW DISCOVERIES AND SCIENCE**

The Renaissance was an age when men made new discoveries about the physical world. It was a time when restless European explorers found sea routes to Asia and lands unknown to them in the Western Hemisphere. The voyage of Christopher Columbus to the New World changed popular ideas about geography. Ferdinand Magellan sailed around the world. Vasco da Gama found a new route to India around the Cape of Good Hope.

These new discoveries and the growth of independent thought encouraged the development of scientific ideas and method. But most people still clung to medieval ideas. Many humanists believed that the authority of ancient writers was as great in the realm of nature as in other matters. They continued to accept the theories of the Greek astronomer Ptolemy and the medical tradition of the Greek physician Galen, even though both these men lived before A.D. 200. Other men were laying the foundations of modern scientific method by direct observation and experiment.

Philippus Aureolus Paracelsus (1493?–1541), a Swiss-born physician and philosopher, studied diseases among his contemporaries. He held that the functions of the body are chemical in nature and so can be treated by chemical processes. Andreas Vesalius (1514–64), a lecturer at the University of Padua, insisted that surgery should be performed by skilled men trained in anatomy and not by ordinary barbers, as was usual up to that time. He dissected human bodies in his laboratory, and in 1543 he published the first complete treatise on human anatomy, *De Humani Corporis Fabrica* (*Concerning the Structure of the Human Body*).

The same year, Nicolaus Copernicus, a Polish-born astronomer living in Italy, published his astronomical observations, *De Revolutionibus Orbium Coelestium* (*Concerning the Revolutions of Heavenly Bodies*). Copernicus rejected Ptolemy's theory that the sun and other heavenly bodies revolve about

Portrait painting flourished in the studios of Renaissance artists.

the earth. But, being a true man of the Renaissance, he first turned to other ancient writers to see if any of them had held ideas about the movement of the heavenly bodies that differed from those of Ptolemy. He did in fact find that several ancient Greeks had stated that the earth moved about the sun. Starting from this point, Copernicus went on to develop his own theory that the earth and other planets move about the sun and that the earth rotates on its own axis.

Before the 1440's all copies of books had to be made by hand. The invention of printing with movable type, often attributed to Johann Gutenberg, made it possible to produce many copies of a book at a time and thus spread interest in all types of learning. The new developments in navigation, warfare, mining, trade, and commerce encouraged advances in mathematics, physics, metallurgy, and other sciences. Weights, measures, and coinage were standardized to meet the growing needs of bankers and merchants.

▶ A GOLDEN AGE IN THE ARTS

Renaissance artists turned for inspiration to science, nature, and antiquity. They looked directly at man and his surroundings. They borrowed classical forms and used them in new and different ways.

Filippo Brunelleschi (1377?–1446) was the most famous architect of Florence. He used the domes, round arches, and columns of classical architecture to create a new Renais-

sance architecture. Brunelleschi was commissioned to complete the cathedral in Florence. The Florentines wanted it crowned with a cupola, or dome. Brunelleschi based his design on the ancient Pantheon at Rome. He created a high-rising dome that blended surprisingly well with the Gothic style of the rest of the cathedral.

St. Peter's Basilica in Rome is probably the most famous building of the Renaissance. Donato Bramante (1444–1514) and a number of other architects contributed to the design of this great church, which took 120 years to complete. As his last great work, Michelangelo Buonarroti designed the cathedral's famous dome, which rises to a height of 435 feet.

By the 16th century as many castles, palaces, and civic buildings as cathedrals were being built. In France châteaus (castles) of kings and nobles sprang up along the Loire river near Paris.

Renaissance artists sometimes borrowed their subject matter from Greek and Roman mythology, but although the subject matter was old, the way of painting was new. Painters such as Masaccio (1401–28), Paolo Uccello (1397–1475), and Andrea Mantegna (1431–1506) and sculptors such as Lorenzo Ghiberti (1378–1455), Donatello (1386?–1466), and Antonio Pollaiuolo (1429–98) wished to give their work the appearance of reality. They studied the interplay of light and shade, perspective (the illusion of depth), and the human body. Improvements in painting techniques allowed painters to work in new ways. The Flemish painter Jan van Eyck (1370–1441) discovered that painting with slow-drying oils instead of with quick-drying egg tempera permitted him to work more slowly and in greater detail.

Artists of the Renaissance painted worldly subjects, as well as religious ones. Leonardo da Vinci painted a fresco of *The Last Supper* on the "fresh" (wet) wall of a monastery refectory, or dining hall, in Milan. But his famous *Mona Lisa* was the portrait of a wealthy man's wife. Titian, a Venetian, painted portraits of many powerful and wealthy patrons, including kings and princes. Sometimes an artist painted his patron in a mythological or even sacred scene. In *Adoration of the Magi* Sandro Botticelli pictured Cosimo de' Medici as one of the wise men kneeling before the infant Jesus. The artist even included himself in the painting.

Renaissance popes were great builders and patrons of the arts, and many gifted architects, painters, and sculptors were attracted to the papal court. When Leo X (1475–1521), a member of the Medici family, became pope in 1513, Rome replaced Florence as the center of Italian art.

Raphael, famous for his paintings of madonnas, was commissioned by Pope Julius II in 1508 to decorate the walls of various rooms in the Vatican. About the same time, the Pope also commissioned Michelangelo, the greatest artist of the age, to decorate the arched ceiling of the Vatican's Sistine Chapel. In this remarkable work, scenes from the Book of Genesis seem to come to life. Michelangelo worked 4 years to complete the ceiling, often lying on his back on a high scaffold. A sculptor, poet, painter, and architect, Michelangelo has dominated the art of many centuries. His statue of David the youthful warrior became the symbol of the strength and vigor of Florence.

Although the fullest flowering of the arts took place in Italy, northern Europe learned from and contributed to the Renaissance. The German artist Albrecht Dürer was influential in bringing the ideas of the Renaissance to the north, and the portraits painted by Hans Holbein the Younger were known throughout Europe.

Music

The development of the violin, the flute, and the organ gave rise to a demand for new musical forms. The most important of these were the opera and the oratorio, in which voices were accompanied by instruments. The madrigal, a form of nonreligious song usually unaccompanied by instruments, was also popular. Music in general became more secular, more worldly. It was written for theater and court entertainment, as well as for the church.

▶THE RENAISSANCE IDEAL OF THE ALL-AROUND MAN

Leonardo da Vinci's name would appear often in any account of the Renaissance, for he was a man of many talents. He was a painter, sculptor, writer, architect, inventor, engineer, and even something of a scientist. Leonardo was not a typical man of his time, but many Renaissance men would like to have done the many kinds of things that Leonardo did. The many-sided man was the ideal of the age.

Baldassare Castiglione (1478–1529) wrote a book, *The Courtier,* about the Renaissance ideal. According to Castiglione, the true gentleman should be able to do many things. He should be witty and able to entertain at a party. He should be skilled in arms and such vigorous sports as hunting, swimming, and wrestling. In addition, a true gentleman was a humanist scholar who knew the best Latin and Greek authors. But he must do more than read the poets, orators, and historians. A gentleman must himself be a writer, an orator, and a poet. It was also good if he could set his verses to music and sing them. It was not enough to be just a scholar, a soldier, or a poet. A man should be all these things and a great deal more. To be sure, few men could actually do all these things, let alone do them well. But this was the ideal, and it was an ideal that tells much about the spirit of the Renaissance. It was an age when men believed in their ability to achieve great things.

KENNETH S. COOPER
George Peabody College

See also EXPLORATION AND DISCOVERY; ITALY (Italian Art and Architecture); LEONARDO DA VINCI; MICHELANGELO; RENAISSANCE ART AND ARCHITECTURE; RENAISSANCE MUSIC.

Giotto painted the fresco *Meeting at the Golden Gate* about 100 years before the Renaissance. His natural portrayal of people and their emotions influenced the painters of the Renaissance.

RENAISSANCE ART AND ARCHITECTURE

In the early 1400's a new movement in art and literature began in Italy. This movement was known as the Renaissance. It spread all over Europe, and its influence has been felt to this day. The spirit of the Renaissance affected not just the arts but all phases of life. As a result, the name of this artistic movement has been given to the whole period of history of the 15th and 16th centuries.

▶ THE SPIRIT OF THE RENAISSANCE

The word "renaissance" means "rebirth" or "revival." In the 14th century many Italian scholars believed that the arts had been declining in quality for 1,000 years. They admired the art and writing of the Classical Age (400 B.C.–A.D. 400), the time of the Greek and Roman empires. To revive the glory and grandeur of the ancient past, these scholars eagerly studied classical literature, architecture, and sculpture.

But the Renaissance was much more than a rebirth of classical art. It was a rejection of the Middle Ages, which were just ending. During medieval times, the arts were concerned mainly with religion, with the life of the spirit, with the hereafter. Little importance was given to life on earth except as a preparation for the next world. But as the 15th century began, Italians were turning their attention to the world about them. People started to think more about secular, or non-religious, matters. They began placing faith in their own qualities and their own importance. This new spirit was called **humanism**. Discipline, unquestioning faith, obedience to authority—these medieval virtues were no longer blindly accepted. People asked questions and wanted to find their own answers.

Artists were among the first affected by the new spirit of humanism. In their work they began to focus on human life on earth.

▶ THE EARLY RENAISSANCE IN FLORENCE

The spirit of humanism was expressed by the painter Giotto di Bondone (1267?–1337) a century before the Renaissance actually began. Giotto's religious pictures were painted with great sympathy for the human qualities of his subjects. Holy figures are shown in countryside settings, dressed in worn and commonplace clothing. Giotto's lovely paintings seem to have been created especially for the common people of his time. Never before in Christian art had viewers been reminded that the saints of their religion were peasants like them.

Soon after Giotto died, a terrible plague, followed by small but destructive wars, swept through Italy. Progress—including the progress of art—was slowed. At least 50 years passed before Giotto's ideas became popular. But then it became clear that Giotto had been the forerunner of Renaissance painting.

The First Generation

Early in the 15th century, Florence, where Giotto had worked, became the first great center of the Renaissance. There a group of young artists experimented with new techniques. The architect and sculptor Filippo Brunelleschi (1377?–1446) was a leader of the group.

Attempting to break with the Gothic traditions of building, Brunelleschi looked to classical architecture for inspiration. After studying Roman buildings, he developed a new approach to architecture. In 1421 he designed the first Renaissance building, the Ospedale degli Innocenti (Foundling Hospital) in Florence. The facade (front) of the building has a **colonnade**—a series of wide arches separated by slender Corinthian columns like those used in classical architecture. Between the arches are colored terra-cotta (hard-baked clay) medallions of babes in swaddling clothes made in the workshop of Luca della Robbia (1400?–82). Harmonious proportions distinguish Brunelleschi's architecture.

Brunelleschi devised a mathematical method for creating the illusion of depth on a flat surface. This method, called **perspective,** is based on the principle that objects appear smaller as they go farther into the background. It became a valuable tool to painters.

Brunelleschi was less successful as a sculptor than as an architect. In 1401 he competed with Lorenzo Ghiberti (1378–1455) for the commission to design a pair of bronze doors for the Baptistery of Florence Cathedral. The doors were to be carved in **relief** sculpture, in which the figures remain attached to a background. The subject chosen for the competition was the *Sacrifice of Abraham.* Ghiberti's design won.

Later, about 1435, Ghiberti designed reliefs for a second pair of doors for the cathedral. Impressed with the great beauty of the doors, Florentines called them the Gates of Paradise. A comparison of the two pairs of doors shows how the new ideas of the Renaissance influenced Ghiberti. In the earlier doors his designs are closer to the flat, patterned compositions of the Gothic style. The reliefs on the Gates of Paradise look much more realistic and are done in perspective. The human figures look more like classical sculptures.

Tommaso Guildi, nicknamed Masaccio (1401–28), was another member of the early Florentine group. He was one of the first painters to use perspective as a device to make his painting look more real. Masaccio went much further than Giotto in giving his subjects dignity and emotion. His compositions were always very simple, usually built up in geometric arrangements.

The most famous sculptor in the group was Donato di Niccolò di Betto Bardi, known as Donatello (1386?–1466). He studied human anatomy and classical sculpture. He was not content to follow formulas handed down from the Middle Ages. He and other Renaissance artists went directly to nature itself. Donatello's sculptures have a realism and freshness that came from his studies of live models.

The Second Generation

The revolution begun by Brunelleschi, Masaccio, and Donatello was continued in the second half of the 15th century. The Florentine architect Leon Battista Alberti (1404–72) followed Brunelleschi's example of imi-

The Foundling Hospital in Florence was designed by Brunelleschi in 1421.

tating the forms used in classical architecture. But Alberti's buildings are much heavier and actually closer in form to ancient Roman buildings than Brunelleschi's. St. Andrea, a church in Mantua begun in 1470, shows how Alberti took over the motif of the Roman triumphal arch and made it the main theme of the facade. A triumphal arch has three sections, with a large central opening. St. Andrea's facade is divided into three similar parts, with an enormous central archway forming a dramatic entrance to the church.

Many 15th-century Italian painters continued some of the Gothic traditions of painting

Right: The Gates of Paradise (1435?), a pair of doors for the Baptistery of Florence Cathedral designed and executed by Lorenzo Ghiberti. Below: *Isaac, Jacob, and Esau,* one of the panels on the doors.

The Expulsion from Paradise, painted by Masaccio about 1424. Church of the Carmine, Florence.

while also using such new discoveries as perspective. Fra Angelico (1387?–1455), a Dominican monk, was one of these painters. His work is a blend of the old and the new. His figures are rather flat, as in medieval painting. It was entirely natural for a monk, schooled in the medieval traditions of the Church, to continue using older methods. One of the important things to understand about the Renaissance is that its new ideas did not immediately replace all the other traditions but took hold gradually.

Paolo Uccello (1397–1475) was one of a group of artists who were fascinated by perspective. His paintings of battle scenes contain crowds of figures arranged according to the rules of perspective. However, Uccello, like Fra Angelico, emphasized flat patterns and tiny details much as medieval artists had done.

Sandro Botticelli (1444?–1510), a masterful painter of graceful, rhythmic line, was another of those who combined the old and the new. For subject matter, Botticelli often turned to the myths of the ancient Greeks.

Piero della Francesca (1416?–92), from the town of Borgo San Sepolcro, in central Italy, went to Florence. There he became interested in perspective. When he returned to Umbria, he applied the knowledge that he had gained in perspective, lighting effects, and anatomy to his painting. Most of his pictures are constructed with the same precision as a work of architecture. Each form was simply drawn, with no unnecessary details. Piero used light and shadow to model his figures and to help give the illusion of depth.

Angel **(1450?), by Fra Angelico. Louvre, Paris.**

THE HIGH RENAISSANCE IN ROME

In the 16th century the center for Renaissance artists shifted from Florence to Rome. Almost every great name in 16th-century art went to Rome either to work on some project for the popes or the nobility or just to see what was going on. It was a time of splendor, and it was called the High Renaissance.

The climax of church architecture in the High Renaissance was St. Peter's Basilica. It was built to replace an early Christian church on the same site. Donato Bramante (1444–1514) and Michelangelo Buonarroti (1475–1564) were the main architects, although their original plans were altered by others. The basic plan of 1506, by Bramante, called for a central-type building. Bramante's plan was not carried out, and the church was lengthened. Michelangelo designed the huge dome.

Leonardo da Vinci

The climax of late 15th-century painting came in the work of Leonardo da Vinci (1452–1519). Leonardo studied painting in Florence, but he spent much of his life working in Milan. The last few years of his life were spent in France in the service of King Francis I.

Leonardo is the perfect example of the "Renaissance man" because he was interested in and well informed about a great many subjects: literature, science, mathematics, art—almost everything about man and nature. Like many artists of the time, he was a sculptor and an architect as well as a painter. His paintings, particularly *The Last Supper,* the *Mona Lisa,* and *The Madonna of the Rocks,* have made him famous. The unique way he handled light and shadow is his most unusual characteristic. Leonardo's remarkable ability to grasp and express the mysteries of man and nature made him one of the greatest of all painters.

Raphael

The talented painter Raffaello Sanzio, known as Raphael (1483–1520), from

Detail from *The Battle of Constantine* (1465?), by Piero della Francesca. Church of San Francesco, Arezzo.

The School of Athens (1510–11), by Raphael. Stanza della Segnatura, Vatican.

Ginevra de' Benci (1474–78), by Leonardo.
National Gallery of Art, Washington, D.C.

Madonna and Child (1504?), by Michelangelo.
Bruges, Belgium.

Urbino, was called to Rome by Pope Julius II. Many influences went into the formation of his beautiful style of painting. From his early training in Urbino he developed a feeling for spaciousness and open landscape. When he was 21 years old, he went to Florence, where he absorbed the achievements of the Florentines. From them, especially from Leonardo, he learned how to group figures in space. Michelangelo's influence can be seen in the twisting postures of his human figures.

Everything Raphael painted—especially his madonnas—has an air of serenity and dignity. His famous madonna painting, *La Belle Jardinière* ("The Beautiful Gardener"), painted in 1507, has an unusually pleasing composition. Raphael envisioned man as the ruler of his environment, not as its servant, a High Renaissance idea beautifully expressed in this painting.

Michelangelo

One of the greatest 16th-century artists was Michelangelo Buonarroti (1475–1564). In sculpture, architecture, and painting he was so outstanding that he was called divine. He was born in Caprese, and as a young man moved to Florence, where he studied the works of Giotto, Masaccio, Donatello, and the Greeks and Romans. He became fascinated with the problems of representing the human body, and he devoted himself completely to mastering them.

In 1505 Michelangelo was called by Pope Julius II to Rome, where he was commissioned to work on a number of projects. The most important were the Pope's tomb, the decoration of the ceiling of the Sistine Chapel in the Vatican, and the new basilica of St. Peter's.

The Sistine ceiling, which took 4 years to paint under difficult conditions, is composed of hundreds of figures from the Old Testament. In all his representations of the human figure, whether in sculpture or in painting, Michelangelo strove for monumentality.

With the art of Michelangelo the High Renaissance came to its climax. His work, in fact, betrayed signs of a changing attitude in the art of the day. The twisted, tormented figures and the flattened space of his painting of *The Last Judgement,* for example, already displayed a new direction in European art.

Venice was the most important northern Italian city of the Renaissance. The Venetians lived a gay and luxurious life. Enjoying the benefits of an active trade with the east, they imported silks, jewels, slaves, and exotic foods. Close connections with Eastern art and a naturally colorful location inspired the Venetian painters to use bright color. They were influenced by the new "scientific" developments in Florentine art. But their use of anatomy and perspective was combined with their love of color and pageantry.

One of the most important north Italian painters was Andrea Mantegna (1431–1506). Born in Padua, a city not far from Venice, Mantegna introduced many Florentine characteristics into north Italian painting. He particularly admired the realism of Donatello's sculptures, and like Donatello, he studied ancient Roman art. He used perspective to create the effect of a stage on which his figures perform. Mantegna's scientific approach to painting is like Piero della Francesca's. His solid, sculptural figures are similar to Masaccio's.

The greatest of the 15th-century Venetian painters was Giovanni Bellini (1430?–1516). Mantegna's friendship with Bellini had a direct influence on Venetian painting. Bellini's rich, mellow color and warm lighting bring out the human qualities of his serene madonnas and saints. He was one of the first Italians to use oil paint on canvas.

▶ THE HIGH RENAISSANCE IN VENICE

Two of Giovanni Bellini's pupils became the most outstanding Venetian painters of the High Renaissance. They were Giorgione (1478?–1510) and Titian (1488?–1576), whose full name was Tiziano Vecelli. Giorgione's colorful and poetic pictures attracted a large following of artists known as Giorgionesque painters.

Titian began as a Giorgionesque painter but developed far beyond this style. He achieved such mastery in the handling of bright, warm color that he was considered to be the equal of Michelangelo. Titian's huge canvases are full of sweeping movement and rich color. In his late works figures and objects melt into a glow of light and color—a treatment of painting that seems very modern.

Self Portrait (1498), by Dürer. Prado, Madrid.

Andrea Palladio (1518–80) was the major north Italian architect of the period. The Villa Rotonda, begun in 1550 near Vicenza, a city near Venice, shows how closely Palladio followed Roman architecture, without becom-ing dry or too scholarly. Built as a country home, it has a symmetrical plan, with porches on all four sides that allow a full view of the countryside. Colonnades, resembling Greek temple fronts, surround a square building topped by a dome. The superb proportions of this and all Palladio's buildings make them very attractive.

▶ THE NORTHERN RENAISSANCE

Oil painting had become popular in Venice by the end of the 15th century. The Venetians learned a great deal from Flemish artists. The Flemish painter Jan van Eyck (1370?–1440?) is often given the credit for developing an important oil technique.

The Flemish and German styles of the early 15th century were completely different from the early Renaissance style of the Florentines. Instead of simple geometric arrangements of three-dimensional figures, as in Masaccio's paintings, the northern Europeans aimed at creating realistic pictures by rendering countless details—intricate floor patterns, drapery designs, and miniature landscapes. This intricate style of the north did not develop from a humanistic classical art (ancient Roman and Greek) but from the Gothic tradition of mysticism and tormented realism.

The Harvesters (1565), by Brueghel. Metropolitan Museum, New York.

Flemish Painting

Van Eyck's *Madonna of the Canon van der Paele,* painted in 1436, is an excellent example of Flemish realism. All the details of the room—the patterned carpet, the armor of Saint George, the architecture—make this picture seem very real. There is no sign of the Italian sense of beauty here: the figures are not idealized. In the faces of the people can be seen the wrinkles and imperfections of real life.

One of the best-known Flemish artists of the second half of the 15th century was Hugo van der Goes (1440?–82). When the Florentine painters saw Hugo's work, they were impressed by its lifelike quality. This Flemish influence can be seen in later Florentine paintings. There were many such interchanges between Italy and Flanders in the course of the century. Gradually the hard outlines of the Flemish style became softer because of Italian influences, and by the middle of the 16th century the ideas of the Renaissance had been absorbed into Flemish art.

German Painting

The German artist Albrecht Dürer (1471–1528) went to Italy, where he was impressed by the countryside and by the art he saw. While in Venice, he came to know and admire Giovanni Bellini. Bellini, in turn, admired Dürer's work. Dürer had been trained in the Gothic tradition of German art. He had learned to imitate nature accurately and painstakingly. He was a master in the use of sensitive line in drawings, woodcuts, engravings, and paintings.

As a result of his contact with Italian art, Dürer came to share many of the ideals of the Renaissance. He devoted himself to studies of anatomy, to the rules of proportion, perspective, composition, and to the effects of light and color. He passed on to German art all that he learned from the Italians.

France: the School of Fontainebleau

Francis I, who reigned from 1515 to 1547, brought the Renaissance to France when he imported such artists as Leonardo da Vinci and Benvenuto Cellini (1500–71), a famous bronze-worker and goldsmith, to decorate his château (castle) at Fontainebleau. Other Italians who came were Giovanni Battista Rosso (1494–1540), Francesco Primaticcio (1504–70), and Niccolò dell'Abbate (1512?–71). They began a school of painting known as the School of Fontainebleau. The style of the school was an outgrowth of the Italian style of about 1520–50 known as mannerism. The term "mannerism" was intended as a criticism because the art was thought to have put too much stress on technique, or the "manner" in which it had been created.

French artists of the Fontainebleau School adopted the elegant and refined mannerism of Cellini and Primaticcio. Jean Goujon (1510?–68?), a French sculptor, did several fountain reliefs about 1548 that are clearly mannerist. They are long figures of graceful nymphs with their draperies clinging and swirling.

▶ THE END OF THE RENAISSANCE

During the second quarter of the 16th century, mannerism began to take hold in European art. This was the first truly international European style. Renaissance art had been typically Italian in style, but mannerism developed throughout Europe and combined many traditions. The art of northern painters such as Pieter Brueghel the Elder (1525?–69) and Dürer can be considered part of this school. So can the work of Michelangelo and Tintoretto and many other 16th-century Italian artists. The work of the French painters of Fontainebleau and that of El Greco in Spain is also part of the mannerist style.

Mannerism was both a reaction against and an outgrowth of the High Renaissance. It was typified by abnormally lengthened or distorted figures and the replacement of perspective with a flatter and less organized type of space.

By the end of the 16th century the High Renaissance in Italy had given way to late mannerism and the early baroque. But the discoveries and ideals of the Renaissance remained as a permanent heritage to all artists who came afterward. Perhaps the most important contribution of the Renaissance was its vision of man as beautiful, noble, and independent.

SARAH BRADFORD LANDAU
Department of Fine Arts
New York University

See also ARCHITECTURE; ITALY (Italian Art and Architecture); PAINTING; SCULPTURE.

RENAISSANCE MUSIC

The court of Burgundy was very important to the history of music during the first part of the 15th century. The patronage of the dukes of Burgundy, Philip the Good (1396–1467) and Charles the Bold (1443–77), brought about many new developments.

Guillaume Dufay (1400?–74) was a famous musician in the court of Philip the Good. He wrote compositions of many different kinds. Some of his pieces are known as *chansons,* the French for "songs." Chansons are songs for several voices or for a voice with two or more instruments. The songs often deal with love. Sometimes they were sung at festive court entertainments. The banquet hall was hung with splendid tapestries, the nobles were garbed in silk, and the air was scented with sweet perfume.

Dufay also wrote masses for use in the Roman Catholic Church. These masses were often based on a particular melody, which was used throughout. Such a tune was called in Latin a *cantus firmus* ("fixed melody"). A mass based on such a melody is called a *cantus firmus* mass. The melody might be drawn from the Gregorian chant, or it might be a popular tune, perhaps a love song, of the day. One tune Dufay used was called "If I Have a Pale Face." Another was called "The Armed Man." Today popular music is often used in religious services, such as weddings and folk masses.

Another important musician at the Burgundian court was Gilles Binchois (1400?–60). Like Dufay, he composed both sacred music and chansons.

Flemish Composers

During the second half of the 15th century Flemish composers had the greatest influence on the art of music. Jean d'Ockeghem (1425?–95) wrote some excellent chansons, but his finest work is found in his masses. One remarkable mass is the *Missa Prolationum.* In this, every voice has a different time signature. Also, the two upper voices and the two lower voices are in strict canon. That is, one voice begins alone, and the other, coming in later, imitates it strictly throughout.

A little later came Jacob Obrecht (1452–1505). He was especially famous for his masses. In fact, more than two thirds of his works are in this form. One particularly beautiful mass is based on the tune "Maria Zart," an old German song honoring the Virgin Mary. He wrote love songs, too. Gustave Reese (1899–1977), a great authority on Renaissance music, said of Obrecht's music, "Its sheer loveliness makes him one of the greatest figures in a great generation."

But the peak of achievement was reached with Josquin des Prez (1450–1521). He was a great personality, a great teacher, and a great composer. A student of his wrote that Josquin "never gave a lecture on music or wrote a theoretical work, and yet he was able in a short time to form complete musicians, because he did not keep back his pupils with long and useless instructions, but taught them the rules in a few words, through practical application in the course of singing." After his death Cosimo Bartoli, in a book printed in Venice in 1567, compared him to the artist Michelangelo: " . . . as there has not thus far been anybody who in his compositions approaches Josquin, so Michelangelo, among all those who have been active in these his arts, is still alone and without a peer; both one and the other have opened the eyes of all those who delight in these arts or are to delight in them in the future."

Josquin wrote many fine chansons and a great deal of religious music, both masses and smaller works. A five-voiced *Miserere* (a setting of Psalm 51) is especially eloquent and powerful. His music is often very profound and serious, but he sometimes shows a delightful sense of humor. For a while he was master of the chapel music in the court of King Louis XII of France. He was asked to write a piece in which the King could perform. But the King had a very poor voice. So Josquin wrote a piece containing a part marked *vox regis* (the Latin for "the king's voice"). This consisted of just one note repeated all the way through. History does not tell us what the King thought of this joke.

An outstanding Flemish composer who lived at about the same time as Josquin was Heinrich Isaac (1450?–1517). After he became court composer to Emperor Maximilian I at Vienna, he often traveled to the beautiful little town of Innsbruck in the

Austrian Alps, where Maximilian had one of his several palaces. One day Isaac had to leave Innsbruck. He was so sad that he wrote a lovely song of parting, "Innsbruck, ich muss dich lassen" ("Innsbruck, I now must leave thee"). It became almost as popular as a folk song. It was turned into a chorale of the German Lutheran Church. The music is still used today in Episcopal hymnals, but the words have been changed to "Come see the place where Jesus lay."

In a lighter vein were the songs of Clément Janequin (1485?–1560?). This clever French composer delighted in musical tone painting. One of his most famous pieces is "Le Chant des Oiseaux" ("The Song of the Birds"), in which the voices imitate many different kinds of birdcalls. In another chanson, "La Bataille" ("The Battle"), he imitated the sounds of war: drumbeats, fanfares, and battle cries. No wonder that a poet friend of his wrote about him:

> If he with heavy chords motets compose,
> Or dare to reproduce alarms of battle,
> Or if in song he mimic women's prattle,
> Or imitate birds' voices in design,
> Good Janequin in all his music shows
> No mortal spirit—he is all divine.

Madrigals

In a publication of 1530 the term "madrigal" is used probably for the first time in the 16th century. Madrigals of that period were vocal settings of Italian poems of high quality. As in the chansons, the verses often told of unrequited love. The emotions were intense, so the music, too, had to be very expressive. Philippe Verdelot (?–1550?), a Flemish composer who lived many years in Italy, may have been the first man to write madrigals of this kind. Others who composed madrigals at this time were Jacob Arcadelt (1505?–60?), Adrian Willaert (1490–1562), and Cypriano de Rore (1516–65). Luca Marenzio (1553–99) brought the madrigal to a high degree of sophistication. In the late 16th and early 17th century men such as Claudio Monteverdi (1567–1643) and Carlo Gesualdo (1560?–1613) were still writing very emotional and expressive madrigals.

This form was taken over in England at the end of the 16th century. Composers such as Thomas Morley (1557–1602), Thomas Weelkes (1575?–1623), and John Wilbye (1574–1638) wrote many beautiful madrigals to English texts. Some of these were very sad and doleful, but others were gay and dancelike.

Ayres

Another popular vocal form in England was the ayre. The ayre was a song for solo voice with lute or viol accompaniment. Some of these songs were very serious and emotional. John Dowland (1562–1626) wrote a great many of this type. Other ayres were light and gay, such as Morley's "It Was a Lover and His Lass."

Instrumental Music

In England at this time, instrumental music as well as vocal music was very popular. Some of the best composers of keyboard music were William Byrd (1543–1623), John Bull (1562?–1628), and Orlando Gibbons (1583–1625). Byrd was particularly famous in his own day. A contemporary, Father William Weston, referred to him as "the most celebrated musician and organist of the English nation." Although he was a loyal Catholic and wrote great music for the Roman Catholic Church, he also held important positions in the Church of England—a very unusual state of affairs. Of his lighter music for the virginal (a small rectangular instrument belonging to the harpsichord family), the pavanes and galliards are especially charming. (The pavane was a slow dance. The galliard, which usually followed it, was a faster dance that used the same theme in different meter.)

Religious Music

Often considered the most typical Renaissance composer of sacred music is the Italian Giovanni Palestrina (1525?–94). Though he composed a number of different kinds of music, it was as a composer of masses that he particularly excelled. In fact, he was one of the greatest mass composers that ever lived. As many as 105 of his masses have survived —an amazing number. He is famous for the purity and serenity of his unaccompanied vocal music.

Two great contemporaries of Palestrina were the Fleming Roland de Lassus (1532–94) and the Spaniard Tomás Luis de Victoria (1549?–1611). Like Palestrina, Victoria is famed for his church music. Less serene than Palestrina's, it is filled with an ardent and intense mysticism. Lassus led a most varied career. When a young boy soprano, he was kidnapped three times because of the beauty of his voice. In later years he traveled a great deal, finally settling in Munich, Bavaria. He wrote many different kinds of music, ranging all the way from lively or tender chansons to the powerful and profound *Penitential Psalms* of 1565. A versatile, active person, he presents a vivid contrast to the more contemplative Palestrina.

For still another type of religious music, it is interesting to turn to the work of the Venetian composer Giovanni Gabrieli (1557–1612). A fine example is the brilliant piece for so-loists, double chorus, and brass ensemble (with one violin) *In ecclesiis benedicite Domino* ("Bless ye the Lord in His sanctuaries"). It glows with all the pomp and circumstance of the wealthy city of Venice, where it was written. He also wrote fine instrumental music.

The musical language of the Renaissance was spoken with many different accents. The people of Italy, France, the Netherlands, and England all had their own individual dialects. Yet underlying these differences was the spirit of newness—of rebirth. The composers themselves felt this spirit, and that is why the best of their music is still so vital today.

DIKA NEWLIN
Virginia Commonwealth University

RENOIR, PIERRE AUGUSTE (1841–1919)

The painter Pierre Auguste Renoir was born in Limoges, France, on February 25, 1841. When he was 4, his family moved to Paris. As a boy, Renoir drew on the floor with chalk from his father's tailor shop. To stop his chalk from disappearing, his father gave the young artist pencils and paper.

At 13, Renoir became an apprentice in a porcelain factory. He decorated plates for 4

Color and light are important elements in impressionist paintings, as in Renoir's *Two Sisters* (1910).

years, and then he painted fans and blinds and drew scenes on the walls of cafés. In 1862 he entered the studio of the Swiss artist Charles Gleyre (1808–74) to study art.

Renoir and his friends gradually found new ways of painting. They liked to show the fleeting changes of light on figures and landscapes by using small dabs of pure color. This kind of painting, later called **impressionism**, was not popular, but he began to earn a little money from doing portraits. In 1879 his picture of Madame Charpentier and her daughters was greatly admired.

About 1883, Renoir changed his technique somewhat and painted figures with careful outlines and harsh colors. In the 1890's, he developed another style, using rich colors and flowing brushstrokes. Throughout his career Renoir liked to paint women and children. His wife, Aline, and their three sons were favorite later subjects. One of the sons, Jean, became a well-known filmmaker.

Because of Renoir's arthritis, the family moved to the warmer climate of southern France around 1903. But even in that climate he became so crippled that he could not leave his wheelchair. In spite of his suffering, Renoir never lost his love for life and painting. He painted a picture of flowers on the day he died—in Cagnes, December 3, 1919.

REPORTS

News columns, magazine articles, news broadcasts, and television documentaries are all reports. There are many ways to report information. A report may be oral or written. It may be a demonstration or an exhibit. Students are often asked to report their own research on some topic connected with a class study.

For example, in a class study of Mexico there might be written reports on Aztec or Mayan culture or on the causes of the Mexican War. A report on the music and dance of Mexico might be illustrated by having several students perform a Mexican dance, accompanied by students playing the guitar. A report on the handicrafts of Mexico might be an exhibit of various examples of these handicrafts.

To prepare any type of report, the student needs to understand clearly the reporting assignment, to find and use the best sources of information on the topic, to take notes and organize them, and to outline the report. If the report is to be written, the student must then write and revise the report.

Finding Information. In his search for information the student may wish to visit a certain place, talk with certain people, or watch a certain process. He may refer to maps, pictures, books, magazines, newspapers, encyclopedias, filmstrips, and recordings. His teacher or librarian can help him locate information in reference materials.

In a source such as an encyclopedia several articles may relate to a topic. For example, if the student plans to write on Paris, he will find information under Paris and under France. These articles probably mention important men and events. The entries under the names of the men and events should also be read. The Seine River runs through Paris, so it might be a good idea to look up the article on rivers. Sometimes five or six related articles are found in one encyclopedia.

Taking Notes. For each reference the student should write three things at the top of a page in his notebook or on a card: the name of the author, the title of the book or article, and the date when it was published. While reading, the student should jot down important ideas or facts. Notes on a historic event might include causes, dates, persons, and perhaps something about the place. Just the key words are enough: "Settlers arrive, 1810—Indians friendly—six cabins—trees cut—river deep, ferry needed—surprise attack, March, 1812—new buildings, fort, 1813."

Sometimes the reader finds an especially good sentence he thinks he will want to quote in his paper. This should be copied exactly, word for word, with punctuation, capitalization, and spelling as in the original. Such a quotation should be clearly indicated by quotation marks. The name of the author and of the book, as well as the numbers of the pages quoted, should be given in parentheses or in a footnote.

When the student feels he has all the information he needs, he is ready to organize his notes. He puts all the information about each point together. He weeds out information that repeats itself. Contradictory information is checked. As the various items take on a certain order of importance in the student's mind, he is ready to make an outline.

Outlining. A long outline is not necessary, but it is always helpful to arrange the paper's topics in their best order. This takes a little time, but it makes a better paper.

Writing. The student writes the report much the same way he would write a composition of any kind. His introductory paragraph must catch the reader's attention. It introduces the reader to the topic and makes him want to learn more about it.

Since most reports need a good deal of rewriting and correction, rough drafts are usually written in pencil. After the ideas are down, the paper should be read over and improved. Reading aloud is helpful. A sign (¶) indicates where each paragraph should begin. Sometimes a whole paragraph may need to be moved to a new place. Scissors and Scotch tape help. Words and even whole sentences may have to be cut if they seem repetitive. Sometimes wording should be changed. This account is monotonous: "Here the settlers cleared the forest. Then they planted grain. Then the settlers began building fences. Next they made better houses for themselves." It would be better this way: "After clearing some forest and planting grain, the settlers turned to making fences and building better shelter."

After making the corrections, the writer should decide which ideas the readers should remember. These are put into the final paragraph, called the conclusion.

If possible, put the report aside, then reread it. A fresh look often uncovers errors.

The report is now ready to be copied. Typewriter-size paper is preferred. Write the title at least 25 millimeters, or 1 inch, from the top of the first page. Capitalize the main words. The writer's name goes below the title. Leave an even margin of about 25 mm, or 1 in, at the left side of the page; a narrower one at the right. Number each page.

A bibliography—a list of books and articles used in preparation—is often added.

A final reading is necessary. Any errors in spelling, punctuation, or grammar can often be neatly corrected without recopying.

Lou LaBrant
Dillard University

See also Bibliography; Outlines; Research.

REPRODUCTION

In the spring, poppy seeds sprout. Poppy plants burst into leaf. They flower and produce seeds. In the fall, with the coming of frost, the poppies die. But their seeds survive and sprout the following spring. A new generation of poppies replaces the one that has died. Poppy plants continue to exist.

Every kind of living creature, from tiny bacteria to enormous whales, makes new living things like itself. In other words, it **reproduces**. An individual plant or animal may fail to reproduce, but that does not hurt the individual. Nor does it hurt the species (kind) of animal or plant, so long as enough other individuals of that kind reproduce.

Among living creatures there are two main types of reproduction. In one type the new individuals, or young, come from a single parent. Bacteria, for example, grow to a certain size and then divide into two equal parts. Each new bacterium is a small copy of the parent. This type of reproduction is called **asexual reproduction**.

The other main type is called **sexual reproduction**. In this type, young are produced by two parents or from two different parts of the same parent. When two deer mate, for example, living material from both animals is joined, or fused. In time a fawn is born, looking like its parents but not exactly like either one.

Some living things can reproduce sexually at some times and asexually at others.

▶ **ASEXUAL REPRODUCTION**

There are three main ways that living things reproduce asexually. They may divide like bacteria, they may form buds, or they may create spores. The simplest is dividing.

Dividing

Bacteria, amoebas, and many other tiny one-celled creatures reproduce by dividing in half. Some larger creatures, too, may divide in half. This is true, for example, of a freshwater relative of the earthworm. The body of this worm slowly pinches in around the middle. Finally the body separates in two. The front end grows a hind end, while the hind end grows a front end.

New plants may grow from pieces of an older plant. For example, if you set a sweet-potato root (the part you eat) in water, the root will sprout leafy shoots and new roots. In time you will have a sweet-potato vine.

Budding

A number of living things, such as yeasts, sponges, corals, and grasses, can reproduce by forming buds. Unlike flower or leaf buds, these buds develop into complete new individuals. The threadlike hydra will serve as an example. This is a tiny water animal related to corals and jellyfish.

Sometimes a hydra develops a bulge on its side. This bulge—which is a bud—slowly grows into a complete new animal just like the parent. The new hydra may separate from the parent and take up life on its own. Or it may remain attached to the parent and, in turn, produce buds. In some creatures entire colonies, or groups, may form this way, each individual a descendant of the one original parent.

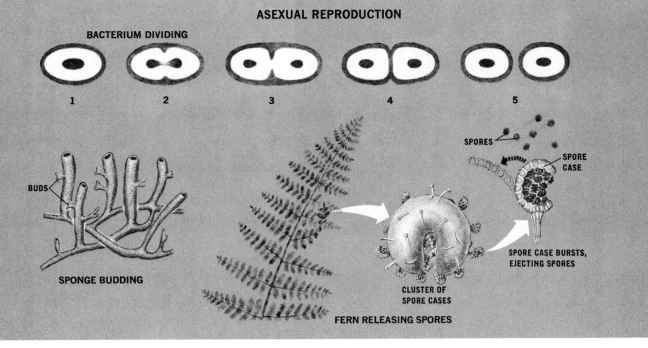

ASEXUAL REPRODUCTION

BACTERIUM DIVIDING

1   2   3   4   5

BUDS

SPONGE BUDDING

FERN RELEASING SPORES

SPORES

SPORE CASE

SPORE CASE BURSTS, EJECTING SPORES

CLUSTER OF SPORE CASES

Spores

Some plants reproduce by means of tiny specks of life called spores. You may have seen tiny black dots on the undersides of fern leaves. These dots are spore cases filled with spores. When the spores are ripe, they fall. Those that land on moist, cool ground sprout into tiny new plants.

Mosses and a number of other plants reproduce by forming spores. So do yeast cells and certain one-celled creatures.

▶ SEXUAL REPRODUCTION

Most creatures, even those that can reproduce asexually, reproduce by sexual means. For example, let us look again at the tiny hydra. A bud develops on the parent hydra. This time the bud does not develop into a complete new individual. This bud contains sperm if the hydra is a male or eggs if the hydra is a female. Eggs and sperm are special reproductive cells.

When the eggs or sperm are ripe, the bud bursts open and sheds its contents into the water. The eggs, as in all creatures, are bigger and rounder than the sperm. Eggs contain a food supply that will nourish the new individual as it develops. Unlike sperm, eggs have no means of moving about.

Hydra sperm, like those of most species, have thin, whiplike tails that enable them to swim toward an egg. A sperm is very much

smaller than an egg. It lacks a food supply of its own.

Hydras produce many eggs or sperm in a single bud. Some of the sperm from the male hydras meet some of the eggs from the females. When a sperm fuses with an egg, the egg is said to be **fertilized**. A fertilized egg contains living material from two parents. It grows and develops into a new individual combining the traits of both parents.

Sexual reproduction in most creatures is more complicated than in the hydra. However, it involves the same basic steps. First, reproductive cells must form. In most species the two sexes are separate. Eggs are formed by females, and sperm are formed by males. Next, eggs must be fertilized. Sperm need a fluid in which to swim to the egg. If sperm are not shed into water, the body must produce the necessary fluid. Finally, some sort of food and protection for the developing egg must be provided until the young can care for itself.

Care of Eggs Shed in Water

Hydras and many other animals shed their eggs and sperm directly into water. They do little if anything to ensure the survival of their offspring.

Many other animals have special ways of making sure that their eggs and sperm meet and that their fertilized eggs are protected.

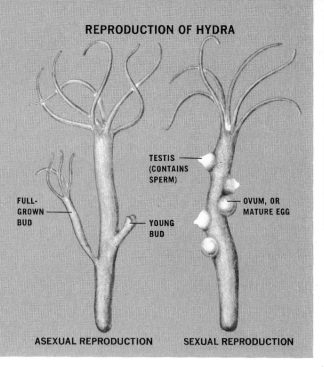

REPRODUCTION OF HYDRA

FULL-GROWN BUD

YOUNG BUD

TESTIS (CONTAINS SPERM)

OVUM, OR MATURE EGG

ASEXUAL REPRODUCTION   SEXUAL REPRODUCTION

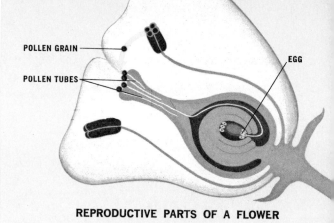

POLLEN GRAIN

POLLEN TUBES

EGG

REPRODUCTIVE PARTS OF A FLOWER

Sperm, contained in pollen grain, fertilizes egg.

A female trout, for example, makes a nest. She uses her tail fin to scrape a hollow in a stream bottom. There she sheds her eggs. The male swims along beside her and covers the eggs with sperm. The female then scrapes gravel over the fertilized eggs. This helps prevent enemies from eating the eggs.

The eggs of some water animals are protected with a thick jellylike coating. In such species the sperm fertilizes the eggs just as they leave the female's body and before the coating is formed. A male horseshoe crab, for example, clasps the female's shell and sheds his sperm directly over the eggs. The pair usually dig into the sand before depositing their eggs and sperm. As the mating pair withdraws, the sand drifts over the eggs, giving them extra protection.

In many lobsters, crabs, and shrimps, the male clasps the female and fertilizes the eggs as they are shed into the water. Frogs and toads mate in a similar fashion.

Fertilization Inside the Body

In salamanders, which are related to frogs and toads, eggs are fertilized inside the female. The male courts his mate and then deposits one or more jellylike packets of sperm on the ground or the pond bottom. The female squats over a packet and draws it up into an opening beneath her tail. The sperm fertilize the eggs before the eggs are shed.

Male squids also produce packets of sperm. A male uses a special tip on one of his tentacles to place the packet inside the body covering of the female.

Snails, guppies, sharks, rays, some crabs, and other water animals also fertilize their eggs internally. In some the eggs remain inside the female until they hatch.

Among land animals, fertilization usually occurs internally. If eggs and sperm were shed directly onto the ground, they would soon dry out in the air. Moreover, the sperm would have no way of swimming toward the eggs unless dew or rainwater happened to be present.

Male spiders deposit their sperm in a drop of fluid. Then they place the drop of fluid in an opening on the body of the female. She later spins a cocoon in which she lays the fertilized eggs.

In most land creatures, however, fluid containing sperm is inserted directly from the body of the male into the body of the female. This is true of insects, reptiles, birds, and mammals, including man.

In seed plants, such as pine trees and daffodils, both eggs and sperm have heavy coatings that keep them from drying out. The sperm, contained in tiny pollen grains, may be transferred by wind or by insects to the female part of the flower. Although the sperm have no tails, they are carried down into the egg in a special pollen tube. The fertilized egg is protected inside a tough seed coat and by the fruit.

Care of Eggs Fertilized Internally

Most insects lay their eggs in protected places where the newly hatched insects will find food. Insect eggs are very small and contain very little food. Insects hatch before they are fully developed, and most species pass through several stages before they look like their parents.

The eggs of both birds and reptiles are well supplied with yolk and protected by shells. With a large yolky egg the young develop into small copies of their parents before food is needed from outside.

Snakes, lizards, and turtles lay their eggs in holes in the ground, and many cover the nests with mud or sand. The eggs of some lizards and snakes remain inside the mother until the young hatch.

Most birds build nests of some sort and hatch the eggs with the warmth of their own bodies. The parents take turns feeding and guarding the young.

In most mammals the eggs are small and have little yolk. The developing individual gets the nourishment it needs from its mother's body. After birth the young suckle milk from the mother. The result is that the offspring are large before they have to fend for themselves.

Small mammals, such as mice and foxes, may have from two to a dozen or more offspring at a time. Few of these offspring manage to grow up. Large mammals, such as horses and elephants, usually have only one offspring at a time. The parents feed and guard the young for a long time. Each offspring has a good chance of growing to full size and of reproducing in turn.

Human beings usually produce babies one at a time. Their babies are helpless at birth. But they are so well taken care of that each has a better chance of growing up than any other kind of creature.

N. J. Berrill
McGill University

See also CELL; EGGS AND EMBRYOS; FLOWERS AND SEEDS; GENETICS; METAMORPHOSIS.

HUMAN REPRODUCTION

One of the marvels of nature is the ability of living beings to reproduce themselves. Humans belong to the class of living beings known as mammals. All mammals reproduce by the mating of a male with a female of the same species. This is called sexual reproduction.

The human male and female, unlike most other mammals, have no special mating season. Humans are unique in having the ability to plan their reproduction. The mating of grown-up male and female humans marks the beginning of a family. A family that grows out of love and marriage is the most important feature of our civilization. A family must be planned with much thought and care, since the production of a new human life is a great privilege and even greater responsibility.

In the human as in other mammals, the body structure of the male and female is specially adapted for the part each has in mating. The male's contribution is the sex cell known as the sperm. The female's is the ovum, or egg. When the two sex cells combine, the process is called fertilization. The fertilized egg is the very beginning of a human life.

As boys grow into their teens, the parts of the body that have to do with reproduction grow and develop. The sex cells, or sperm, are contained in the testes, a pair of oval-shaped structures over an inch long. They are located in a pouch called the scrotum, under the penis, outside the body. The tubular-shaped penis serves as the passageway for urine and also for the sperm cell fluid.

In the female, the main parts of the body involved in reproduction are the uterus and the ovaries. The uterus is the womb or nesting place for the fertilized egg. The uterus is a small, hollow, pear-shaped organ located in the lower central part of the abdomen.

On both sides of the uterus is an ovary that contains the ova, or eggs. When a girl is reaching her teens, the ovaries become active. About once a month an ovary discharges an egg that reaches the uterus through a connecting tube on each side of the uterus. The egg is a tiny speck, hardly visible to the naked eye. Unless fertilized by a sperm, the egg dries up and is expelled about 2 weeks later from the uterus. The uterus throws off this dried-up egg mixed with some blood and mucus through the vagina and then out of the body. The vagina is a small tunnel-shaped structure that has an opening between the one for the urine and the one for the bowel movement. This discharge lasts 4 or 5 days and occurs usually once a month. Known as menstruation, it is nature's cleansing process of the uterus. It starts at the period of development known as puberty and indicates that the body is maturing to make future reproduction possible.

In the mating process in humans, a small amount of special fluid containing sperm cells is deposited by the penis into the vagina. The sperm cells have a remarkable ability to travel rapidly up the vagina into the uterus. The tiny sperm cannot be seen by the naked eye. But under a microscope one sees the tiny tadpole-shaped cell with a long threadlike tail that acts as a propeller. If an egg has been discharged from the ovary about this time and is moving toward the uterus, the sperm and ovum unite, resulting in a fertilized egg.

In the uterus, this fertilized egg undergoes a series of changes. Within a month, it grows and develops into an embryo about a quarter inch long. As it continues to grow, it becomes the fetus, soon developing all the necessary organs—heart, lungs, brain, nervous and digestive systems. It obtains nourishment from the mother through the placenta, a disk-like structure, which connects the blood supply of the mother to the fetus through a ropy-looking cord from its belly button (navel). Every human being has a belly button, which is a reminder of how each of us began life.

In about 9 months, this tiny fertilized egg has become a baby ready to be born and leave its mother's body for the outside world. Then the muscular uterus squeezes down on the baby, pushing it out through the vagina, which at this time is described as the birth canal. The baby is usually born head first and is expelled with its cord and the placenta, or afterbirth. This completes the miracle of reproduction. A new human life has appeared.

JEAN PAKTER, M.D., M.P.H.
Director, Bureau of Maternity Services
and Family Planning
New York City Department of Health

See also GENETICS.

REPTILES

Crocodiles, lizards, snakes, and turtles are all reptiles. They are grouped together because they are alike in many ways, sharing many important features. Although other animals have some of these features, only reptiles have all of them.

Reptiles are vertebrates. This means that they have bodies supported by a framework of bone—the skeleton. A reptile's body is covered by dry, scaly skin. Most reptiles have four legs. Each foot ends in five clawed toes. All reptiles breathe air through their lungs.

A reptile's body temperature varies. Reptiles regulate their body temperatures in many ways: by changing their color to absorb or reflect heat; by moving to the shade when the sunlight is too hot; by retreating into a burrow when it is too hot or too cold above ground; and in other similar ways.

The eggs of most reptiles dry easily. Because of this the eggs must be laid in moist places in the earth or sand or in rotten wood.

Young reptiles look much like their parents, although they may be colored differently.

History of Reptiles

The first reptiles walked on the earth about 300,000,000 years ago. These early creatures flourished and branched out—over millions of years—into many different kinds of animals. Scientists say that the first birds developed from certain of these reptiles. Other reptiles developed into the first mammals (animals that nurse their young on their milk).

Reptiles themselves developed along many separate lines. Huge dinosaurs, flying reptiles, and reptiles of the sea spread throughout the earth in great numbers. Today there are about 6,000 kinds of reptiles.

Living Reptiles

There are four main groups of living reptiles.

The first group is made up of crocodiles, al-

TUATARA

ALLIGATOR

SEA TURTLE

COBRA

Representatives of the four main groups of living reptiles.

ligators, gavials, and caymans. These are the largest of the reptiles. They are long-bodied creatures with tough skin and strong jaws. Each has a powerful tail.

The second group is made up of turtles and tortoises. Many turtles have bodies that are almost entirely enclosed within a hard, two-layered shell. When threatened, many can withdraw completely into this shell.

The third group is made up of lizards and snakes. These animals are generally easy to tell apart. Snakes, for example, are legless and cannot close their eyes. Most lizards are four-legged and are able to shut their eyes.

The fourth group contains only one kind of animal—the tuatara. This creature looks somewhat like a lizard. The tuatara has three eyes, as do many lizards. The third eye, located on top of the head, is covered by a thin layer of skin. It does not function as a normal eye, and no one knows what its function is. The tuatara can remain active at 52 degrees Fahrenheit—a temperature at which most reptiles move about slowly, if at all. The tuatara is the last remaining reptile of a group that was once widespread. Today it is found only on islands off the coast of New Zealand.

Reviewed by RICHARD G. ZWEIFEL
The American Museum of Natural History

See also CROCODILES AND ALLIGATORS; DINOSAURS; LIZARDS AND CHAMELEONS; SNAKES; TURTLES AND TORTOISES.

REPUBLICAN PARTY. See POLITICAL PARTIES.

RESEARCH

Research is a quest for information. Sometimes the purpose of research is the solution of a specific problem. And sometimes the purpose of research is to add to man's store of knowledge. In searching for information, a researcher looks in libraries to find out what is already known and perhaps forgotten. He works in a laboratory or a planetarium. He digs into the earth to study ancient ruins or rock formations. He may travel into space.

History of Research

Research was born when the first men on earth began to ask questions and search for answers. Men who invented the wheel and discovered how to record time by the movement of the stars were very great researchers. Modern research, based on study and experimentation, got its true start in the 1500's with the work of Galileo.

Researchers used to work alone. Of course they could exchange information with each other through learned societies, journals, and letters. But they seldom joined forces to work together in the same laboratory on the same problem. Today much research is organized. Research projects may cost millions of dollars and need many workers.

Kinds of Research

Every branch of learning has developed special methods of discovering knowledge. In the natural sciences, such as chemistry, physics, medicine, and biology, the methods of research are very exact. Scientists have developed very accurate tools, such as electronic microscopes.

The social sciences, which study how and why people act as they do, do not have such accurate instruments. Research in these sciences is a fairly new development. Anthropology is the study of how man lives. To carry on research, an anthropologist may live with a primitive tribe in order to study its customs and language. Cameras and tape recorders are tools of research in anthropology.

Psychology, the study of man's mind, depends on careful observation of people acting or learning under certain conditions. Researchers in psychology use interviews, questionnaires, and tests to collect information. Compared to the research tools used by chemists, physicists, and biologists, these are very crude measuring devices.

One branch of psychology investigates what people buy and how they spend their leisure time. This is called market research. You may have taken part in this kind of research by answering an investigator's questions.

Educational research is concerned with how people learn, especially in schools. This is another kind of research in which you have probably taken part. For instance, you may have learned to read with a new alphabet, called i/t/a (initial teaching alphabet). If so, you were given tests from time to time. The results of your tests were studied, along with many hundreds of others, to determine how well pupils using this special alphabet learned to read.

Still another kind of research is historical research. Sources include all kinds of written reports, such as diaries, letters, documents, laws, treaties, bills of sale, certificates, newspapers, magazines, and books. Researchers also examine objects, such as tools, jewelry, vases, and furniture, especially in studying ancient times. This kind of research is conducted by archeologists.

The scientific study of how people use spoken language is called linguistic research. Linguists study samples of speech. They may analyze these samples to find out what particular speech sounds a certain group of people uses. Or they may investigate how people who live in a certain locality use words.

Basic and Applied Research

Basic research is aimed at discovering more about the laws of nature, including human

ATLAS   GLOBE   INTERVIEW

nature. In basic research a scholar pushes into the unknown, often with very little idea of what lies ahead. He may be trying to find out why birds migrate or whether plants grow on Mars or how the first people arrived on this continent. He seeks answers to these questions simply because he is curious. He does not care whether the knowledge he uncovers is useful in any practical sense. He wishes only to add to the world's knowledge.

Applied research is aimed at a practical goal. The researcher sets out to discover or invent new and useful products or better ways of doing something. For example, the first synthetic plastic, called Celluloid, was the result of research done by John Hyatt during the 1860's. He hoped to win a prize offered for a substitute for ivory in the manufacture of billiard balls. Celluloid paved the way for today's enormous plastics industry.

Basic and applied research work hand in hand. Ideas from basic research are the foundation upon which practical, or applied, research can be built. In turn, the basic-research scientist depends on applied research for the invention of instruments that make further investigations possible.

In the social sciences, too, basic and applied research work together. Psychologists have set up laboratory experiments with rats and pigeons to discover laws of learning. They have tested these principles in human learning. Now researchers are applying these principles to methods of teaching and are testing them in classrooms. If you use a programed textbook in mathematics or are learning a foreign language in an electronically equipped laboratory, you are using results of applied research in education.

Your Research

Someday you may become a researcher in industry, government, education, medicine, or another field. In the meantime, as a student you often use research methods to collect information for oral or written reports.

Like all researchers, you begin with a clear

understanding of the topic of your report or the problem you are to solve. You gather information from many sources. You use the library, visit a museum, interview experts, or conduct an opinion poll. You may make observations or perform an experiment and record data accurately.

It is usually best to begin with reference books. Reference books contain information about general and specific topics.

Dictionaries and encyclopedias give descriptions of a great many topics. The topics are arranged alphabetically or in categories. Large topics are often divided into subtopics. If you have a clear idea of your subject, you can tell quickly what topics and subtopics you should read. Usually you will need to look under several topics to get all the information you want.

Yearbooks tell about new events and recent progress in different fields. They also include up-to-date information and statistics of the type that change frequently.

Atlases contain maps of various kinds. Political maps show location, and physical maps show elevation and land surface. Maps often give information on climate, resources, and population.

Indexes are lists of such things as magazine articles, musical works, short stories, essays, plays, and poetry.

You should write down the important points you find in reference books. Keep these notes in a notebook or on index cards. They should include only the things you want to remember.

When you have gathered all the necessary information, you are ready to organize it into a clear explanation. What are the subtopics in the information you have collected? What details are included under each subtopic? In what order should these be arranged? An outline is a good way to organize information. From this outline you can compose a clear and accurate report of your research.

MARGARET EARLY
Syracuse University

RESINS

There are two kinds of resins, natural and synthetic (man-made). Resins are used in paints, varnishes, printing inks, and plastics, to name only their most important uses. They have a wide range of hardness, color, flexibility, strength, and elasticity. Some are gummy and soft. Others are hard and rigid.

Natural resins come mostly from trees. When the bark of certain trees is injured, a thick, sticky material oozes out of the wound. This sticky material, which is sometimes called pitch, is made up of two parts, an oil and a resin. The oil gradually evaporates, leaving the resin. The resin itself is a mixture of materials. Each kind of tree makes its own resin, which is different from the resins of other trees. Many trees produce resins, but only a few are used commercially.

Most resins are gathered by cutting, or slashing, the bark of a tree and collecting the liquid in cups. After the liquid is collected, the oil is separated from the resin by distillation. Perhaps the best-known resin is rosin, which comes from certain pine trees. The oil that is separated from rosin is known as spirits of turpentine. Rosin is used in making printing inks, paper coatings, and varnishes. It is also used in some kinds of soap, in linoleum, and in flotation agents that separate valuable ores from worthless rock. Plain rosin is used to stop unwanted slipping. Baseball players use powdered rosin on their hands to get a better grip on the bat or on the ball. Boxers, ballet dancers, and tightrope walkers use rosin on their footgear to keep their feet from slipping. Violinists use it on their bows, so that the bows will "bite" the strings better.

Stumps of trees that have fallen or been cut down also produce resin. This resin may be obtained by grinding up the stumps and treating the wood chips with hot steam. This drives off the turpentine as a vapor. The resin remains in the wood chips and is dissolved out with a solvent, such as gasoline. The solvent is then distilled off, leaving the useful resin.

Under certain conditions the resin of ancient trees has been preserved and can still be found in the ground. Such resins are called fossil resins. They are much harder than other resins. Amber is the best-known fossil resin. It is often used in jewelry.

Many resins give off a pleasant odor when they are burned or heated. For this reason, resins have long been used for incense. Myrrh and frankincense (also called olibanum), two resins used in incense, are mentioned in both the Old Testament and the New Testament of the Bible. Resins were once thought to have curative properties and were often used as medicines. Very few resins are still used as medicines, but some are used in cough drops and cough syrups.

Certain resins contain dyes that were once very important, though now they have largely been replaced by less expensive man-made dyes. A reddish dye that has been used to color varnish for violins comes from a resin called dragon's blood. Turmeric, a resin used to season and color food, is the source of a yellow fabric dye that was once important.

Today the most important use of natural resins is in varnishes. Even in ancient times resins were used as coatings to preserve wood. At first, the resin was simply smeared on or melted on with a hot iron. The resin was then rubbed until a smooth, hard, shiny surface was formed. In Roman times, it was found that the resin could be dissolved in a solvent and painted onto a surface. The solvent evaporated, leaving a smooth, shiny film of resin. Varnishes are made in much the same way today. Other modern uses of natural resins are in the manufacture of printing inks, polishes, and coatings for paper.

Lac is a resin produced by the lac insect, which feeds on the sap of certain trees. These insects swarm twice a year. The lac that they secrete forms a thick layer over the twigs they feed on. The lac is collected by scraping it off the trees and drying it. It contains many impurities, such as twigs, bark, and the bodies of the insects. Most lac comes from India. Lac is the source of a red dye that was formerly important, and of shellac, which is purified lac. Shellac dissolved in alcohol is used in the same way as varnish. White shellac is bleached orange shellac.

▶SYNTHETIC RESINS

Synthetic resins are made by man from chemicals containing carbon, hydrogen, and other substances. Some of them are similar chemically to natural resins; others are quite different. Because synthetic resins are less expensive and more uniform in quality, they have largely replaced natural resins for many uses.

One of the most important uses of synthetic resins is in plastics. Resins are the chief ingredients of plastics. The resin gives a plastic most of its qualities, such as strength, durability, and hardness.

Synthetic resins are also used in paints, varnishes and lacquers, and printing inks. Extremely strong adhesives are made from synthetic resins.

One unusual use for resins is in purifying water. Water is made hard by small amounts of metals, such as calcium, magnesium, and iron, dissolved in the water. These metals are present as electrically charged particles called ions. Ions are much too small to be seen, but they make themselves very noticeable. When soap is dissolved in hard water, the metal ions in the water combine with the soap and form a useless material called soap curd. Soap curd is what makes the familiar bathtub ring. Certain resins, called ion-exchange resins, can remove the metal ions that make the water hard. These resins are bristling with hydrogen ions. When hard water passes over the resin, the metal ions stick to the resin and hydrogen ions take their place. This makes the water become an acid. The water is then passed over another type of resin that takes out nonmetallic ions, such as those of chloride and sulfate, and gives off hydroxyl ions in exchange. A hydroxyl ion consists of one atom of hydrogen plus one atom of oxygen. It has a negative electric charge. (Hydrogen ions have a positive charge.) The hydroxyl ions combine with the hydrogen ions from the first resin to form pure water. Water treated by the ion-exchange process is very soft and contains hardly any impurities.

Ion-exchange resins can be made to pick certain kinds of metal ions out of a solution and let others pass by. This helps chemists find out what is in the solution.

The resins lose their ability to exchange ions after a while, but they can be "recharged" by soaking them in inexpensive chemicals.

▶ **GUMS**

Gums are hardened sticky juices from plants. Some plants form gums that are mixed with resins. Many different sorts of gums are found in nature. Many plant gums swell in water. Others dissolve in water, making a gluelike liquid.

Gum arabic comes from acacia trees. There are many varieties of acacia trees, and each may produce a different gum. Gum arabic dissolves in water, forming a sticky liquid. This gum is used in making candy and medicine and in printing designs on textiles. Some inks contain gum arabic to make the ink stick to paper or cloth. Most gum arabic comes from Africa.

Tragacanth gum is a yellowish powder. It comes from a shrub that grows in the Middle East. Tragacanth gum is used to make mixtures of oil and water called emulsions and to preserve food.

Agar, sometimes called agar-agar, is obtained from seaweeds that grow mostly in the Pacific and Indian oceans. When dried, agar is a light-brown flaky material. It swells and dissolves in hot water. Agar is used as a substitute for gelatin and for egg whites. Even sausage casing can be made from agar. One of agar's uses is in science. So that scientists can study bacteria easily, the bacteria are raised in small glass dishes of agar.

Chewing gum is made from chicle, the dried juice of sapodilla trees, which grow in Mexico, Central America, the West Indies, and parts of Africa. Chicle does not dissolve in water, but it does dissolve in many other liquids, such as kerosene and ether. The gum is purified by dissolving it and filtering out bark, insects, and other impurities. The liquid is then evaporated, leaving clean chicle. The chicle is mixed with sugar, starch, and flavoring to make chewing gum.

Gutta-percha is made from the milky juice of trees found chiefly in the Malay Peninsula. For many uses it has been replaced by less expensive synthetic resins. But it is still used for electrical insulation, especially to protect underwater cables.

Balata is a rubberlike gum from a tropical tree. The gum is treated with chemical solvents, and the part that dissolves is recovered and used with chicle to make chewing gum. The part that is left, called gutta balata, is used to make the coverings of golf balls.

ELBERT C. WEAVER
Phillips Academy (Andover, Mass.)

See also PLASTICS; TURPENTINE.

RESTAURANTS

A restaurant is a public eating place. The word "restaurant" was first used in France in 1765. Because the word has been used for a long time, it has become the popular way to refer not only to a place where full meals are served but also to snack shops, drive-ins, cafeterias, hotel dining rooms, and cafés.

Historical records of restaurants go back many hundreds of years. In Egypt in 512 B.C. there was a public dining place where a single dish was offered—a combination of wildfowl, onions, and cereal. The first lunch for business people is said to have been prepared by a Roman innkeeper in 40 B.C. for ship agents who were too busy to go home.

During the Middle Ages, travelers could find meals as well as lodging at inns and taverns. Where there were no inns, monasteries and manor houses sometimes served food to travelers.

By 1650, England had coffeehouses, where people met to discuss politics and literary affairs. Customers of the coffeehouses were expected to drop coins into a box on which was written "To Insure Promptness." The initials of that phrase, T.I.P., are said to be the origin of the modern word "tipping."

The French tradition of fine restaurants began after the French Revolution of 1789. During the Revolution many aristocrats who were in hiding were said to have been fed in secret by their former servants. Other wealthy citizens were willing to pay a charge for these well-cooked meals. By the time the Revolution was over, many of the chefs had gained great reputations. They continued to serve meals to paying guests.

In Colonial America wayside taverns and inns, patterned after those in England, were the only public eating places. Many of the famous old inns—such as Raleigh Tavern in Williamsburg, Virginia, and Wayside Inn in Sudbury, Massachusetts—still exist.

The first restaurant in the United States that was not a part of an inn or a tavern was Delmonico's, opened in New York City in 1827. The demand for food service away from home grew, and many other restaurants were soon started.

The cafeteria, where the guest stands in a line and picks up food at a counter, was de-

A chef at work in the kitchen of a French restaurant.

veloped by John Kruger in Chicago. He had seen smorgasbord, a buffet meal offering many different dishes, served in Sweden and decided to design an eating place that served meals in a similar way.

As early as 1762, an innkeeper in America started curb service for people on horseback. A person could ride up to a window and be served without dismounting. This was the forerunner of the modern drive-in.

▶ TYPES OF RESTAURANT SERVICE

There are many kinds of eating places available to suit the needs and tastes of everyone. The following are some of the main types of restaurant service. Many of these may be found combined in one restaurant.

Cafeteria and Buffet Service. Cafeterias display their food selections. The customers pick up their food at a counter and carry it to individual tables to eat. There is usually a wide variety of food items. The prices are somewhat lower than they are in restaurants where the food is brought to the table and served to the customer. Cafeterias are popular not only because of the prices but also because a meal can be obtained quickly.

Counter Service. In some restaurants the customer eats at a counter. Many snack shops, luncheonettes, coffee shops, and sandwich-soda fountains have counters.

Table Service. In a great many restaurants the customers sit at tables and are served by a waiter or waitress. This type of service may be quite informal. But in many restaurants and hotel dining rooms, the atmosphere is formal. The floor is carpeted, the lights are dimmed, and the tables are covered with heavy white linen.

Drive-In Service. A drive-in restaurant serves quick meals that customers may eat in their cars. Many drive-ins also have a counter and tables inside.

Take-Out Service. In some restaurants the customers may order portions of food to take out and eat elsewhere. Take-out places often specialize in such foods as chicken and pizza. Many also have dining areas.

▶STYLES OF COOKING

Restaurants are classified according to the foods they serve, as well as according to the type of service they provide.

In general, restaurants prepare food according to typical national eating habits. In North America and most of Europe, this would mean a variety of appetizers, main dishes (entrées), vegetables, salads, and desserts or fruit. In Asian countries, soup, rice, and dishes to accompany rice are popular.

Some restaurants feature one general kind of food, such as seafood, steaks, pancakes, or sandwiches. The featured foods generally are the best-prepared dishes on the menu (the list of dishes served).

Some restaurants serve food of only one national origin. For example, a restaurant may serve only French, Greek, Chinese, Mexican, or Italian food. Restaurants that serve French or Chinese food are especially popular and may be found all over the world.

Some restaurants specialize even more and serve food typical of only one area of a country. Food typical of New England, the South, or Hawaii may be served in restaurants found in many parts of the United States. Similarly, there are restaurants specializing in foods from northern Italy and others that specialize in southern Italian dishes.

▶BEHIND THE SCENES IN A RESTAURANT

Restaurants and the companies that supply restaurants with food, linens, and other items employ large numbers of people in most countries of the world. In the United States, more than 8,000,000 people work in the food-service industry. About 250,000 new employees must enter the industry each year to meet the need for personnel at all levels. Before a meal can be served to a customer in a restaurant, there are many jobs that must be done.

Planning Menus and Food Purchases. The first decision concerns the food items to be served. In large eating places, preparing the menu is a full-time job.

Once the menu has been chosen, food must be bought in the amounts needed. It may be bought in quantities to last a week, a month, or even several months. It is difficult to predict the number of customers who will eat in a restaurant on any one day and what dishes they will choose.

Storing and Preparing the Food. When the food arrives at the restaurant, it must be stored. Freezers must be available for frozen foods. Other foods, such as meats, fruits, and vegetables, must be refrigerated.

Most foodstuffs need some preparation before the actual cooking is done. Vegetables and fruits must be cleaned and perhaps cut. Meats must be sectioned into the needed cuts for cooking. Sauces, too, are usually prepared ahead of time. The actual cooking of the food is done as close as possible to the time the customers arrive.

Serving the Food. Once the food is cooked, it must be kept tasty until it is served. Warm foods must be kept warm, and cold foods, cold.

When customers enter a restaurant, they usually are given a menu. They make a selection and give their order to a waitress or waiter, who serves the food.

Cleanup and Maintenance. When the customers have finished their meal, the dishes must be removed, washed, and stacked for reuse. Crumbs must be swept up, spills must be wiped away, and everything must be freshened for the next customers.

Sanitation laws for restaurants differ from country to country. In the United States, the U.S. Food and Drug Administration has approved a uniform national plan for the training of food-service managers.

CHARLES H. SANDLER
National Institute
for the Foodservice Industry

RETAIL STORES

Almost all the food we eat, the clothes we wear, and the things we need for our homes are bought in retail stores. Goods are gathered from the four corners of the world and made available to us in retail stores.

There are many kinds of retail stores. A retail store may be a small shop run by one or two people or a large department store with hundreds of employees. In addition to department stores, there are specialty shops, variety stores, clothing and food chain stores, supermarkets, and discount houses. The grocery, bakery, drugstore, and candy shop are all retail stores. Department stores bring under one roof almost every kind of merchandise a customer might want. Specialty stores specialize in certain kinds of merchandise, such as women's and men's clothing, hardware, or furniture. Variety stores are engaged mainly in selling many kinds of goods in a low price range—stationery, toilet articles, and housewares, for example. Chain stores have many units, sometimes in different cities, all under one management. A discount house is a store that offers merchandise, often of standard brands, at lower than usual prices.

Customers are apt to take retail stores for granted. They are pleased when they find what they want at the right price. They are annoyed when they don't or when they think the price is too high or the service is poor. They probably do not realize how much foresight, imagination, and effort are required to satisfy people's shopping needs.

▶ IMPORTANCE OF RETAILING

Retailing is the business of buying goods in large quantities from producers and wholesalers and then selling these goods in smaller quantities to the consumer. In the chain of distribution of goods from the producer of raw materials to the manufacturer to the customer, the retail store plays an important part. It is in the retail store that customers have a chance to examine goods and say, "I don't like this" or, "I'll take that." Thus the merchant knows what the public wants and needs.

The orders the retailer sends to the manufacturer are based on his knowledge of his customers' likes and dislikes. Naturally the retailer orders those items that are in demand and does not order items that he cannot sell. The manufacturer also wants to sell as much as possible, so he increases the manufacture of the popular items ordered by the retailer. To increase the manufacture of these items, the manufacturer needs a larger quantity of the raw material from which these things are made. The producer of the raw material, in turn, increases his production of the desired material.

Retailing is one of the largest industries in the United States (there are about 2,000,000 retail stores). This represents 42 percent of all the country's businesses. More than 11,000,000 men and women work in stores in the United States—about one out of every eight persons in the labor force.

▶ RETAILING AROUND THE WORLD

Retail stores of one kind or another are to be found in countries all over the world. But they are not all the same by any means. In the United States, Canada, England, Scotland, France, Germany, and Japan, for example, department stores that sell everything from pins to pianos are quite common. Russia has several department stores too, GUM being its largest and most famous. Variety stores, formerly called dime stores, are a big business in England, Canada, France, Italy, Belgium, and the United States.

Specialty stores are perhaps the most universal type of retail establishment. They specialize in one kind of merchandise—jewelry, hardware, shoes, or children's clothes, for example. You will find them everywhere. The same can be said about grocery stores. But if you want to find a supermarket, you will have to look in such countries as the United States, Canada, and England.

Many stores, especially in these countries, use credit extensively as a selling tool. But in Japan, Hong Kong, and the Philippines purchases are mainly cash transactions.

The department stores in Japan differ considerably from those in other countries. The "bargain," or "budget," floor, instead of being the basement, is usually the top floor. The roof of the store is a giant playground for children, with fishponds, merry-go-rounds, and slides. Sometimes, as in Tokyo, Japan, a department store is built right over the top of a railroad station.

There are hundreds of different kinds of jobs in retailing. There are promising careers in stores of all kinds for the person who wants to be his own boss, for the person who likes to work in a big organization (or a small one), and for the person who wants to be a jack-of-all-trades as well as for those who prefer to be specialists. You can be the all-around man or woman who runs a local store, or you can work in any of the dozens of departments of a large store or a chain store.

A typical large department store usually has about 800 jobs, involving different skills, duties, and opportunities. There are more selling jobs, of course, than anything else. But 30 to 40 percent of employees in even the smaller stores perform duties other than selling. You can choose from an almost unlimited number of jobs no matter what your special talents may be.

Retailing offers greater executive opportunities than does almost any other trade or industry. It has a high proportion of executive positions (there is one executive for every 10 employees). In other industries there are often hundreds of people under one supervisor.

Women, especially, fit into the retailing picture. They can find more and better opportunities in retailing than in almost any other field. Women hold about 46 percent of all retail jobs today.

In retailing the road to success is neither easy nor short. However, for the hardworking, the interested, and the talented it holds great rewards.

J. GORDON DAKINS
Executive Vice President
National Retail Merchants Association

See also DEPARTMENT STORES; DRUGSTORES; MARKETING; SUPERMARKETS.

RETARDATION, MENTAL

All through infancy, childhood, and adolescence the mind and the body are growing and developing at the same time. The person whose body stops growing before it has reached its full size becomes a dwarf. The person whose mind stops growing before it has reached its full powers is mentally retarded.

Retardation is not a single disease. It is a **symptom**, or sign, that something is wrong. It has many causes, not all of which are understood. Because mental retardation occurs during the course of a person's growth and development, this condition must begin before the 17th year of life. For that is when the mind of the average person reaches its full growth. Some retarded people have a particular appearance that sets them apart, but most do not look different from anyone else.

No one knows exactly how many retarded people there are. Studies show that about 2 to 3 percent of the world's population may suffer from retardation. Only the more severe retardation is recognized before the child enters school. A child's slowness may not show until he begins to fall behind in the first or second grades in school. However, many who are mildly retarded during their adolescence are able to hold jobs when they are adults. They are therefore no longer considered retarded. It is generally estimated that 3 percent of the population, or over 5,000,000 people in the United States, are suspected of being retarded at some point in their lives. Today there are about 200,000 retarded people in institutions in the United States, but most of the retarded live at home.

Mental retardation is a major health, education, and welfare problem. But until recently it received little attention. Like the mentally ill in the past, the retarded were looked down upon and avoided. They were not given the help and sympathy they needed. Many were gathered together in overcrowded state institutions, with not enough trained people to take proper care of them.

Now, however, the increasing interest of professional people, government officials, and parents of the retarded have brought this condition to the attention of the public. Federal funds for education and job training for the retarded have been increased. More work is being done in research, treatment, and care of the retarded, but much remains to be done. The institutions that take care of the retarded have improved their programs. There is a move toward providing education and care in each community.

Many different kinds of specialists are needed in the treatment of the retarded. Doctors, psychologists, nurses, teachers, social workers, vocational counselors, and other professionals have a contribution to make. But none can be expected to solve the problem of retardation alone.

▶ CLASSIFICATION

Mental retardation is usually classified by severity, cause, and symptoms. Although there is no complete agreement among experts, many believe that a person's intelligence may be measured with certain tests. The results of these mental-ability tests are known as the Intelligence Quotient, or IQ. An IQ of 100 is considered average. A person whose IQ is below 70 and who does not seem to understand how to get along in everyday life is considered mentally retarded.

There are four classes of retardation: mild, moderate, severe, and profound. For practical purposes the severely and profoundly retarded can be combined. The IQ's of the severely and profoundly retarded are below 35. Their mental ability is not above that of a normal 5-year-old. Most of them cannot care for their personal needs. They do not know how to protect themselves from common dangers. Someone must always take care of them.

The moderately retarded may reach the mental ability of 8-year-olds and have IQ's up to 50. When taught with patience and special teaching methods, they can learn useful skills. They may then be able to work in special workshops where they are watched over. They have difficulties in reading, writing, and arithmetic.

The mildly retarded may have IQ's as high as 70 and reach a 12-year-old's level of mental ability. They can learn elementary-school subjects. As adults they are often successful in simple jobs. About 90 percent of all retardation is mild. The remaining 10 percent is divided among the other three groups.

▶ CAUSES

Retardation can be caused by something going wrong in the mind, the body, or the surroundings in which the child grows up. Much has been learned about some types of retardation. A few types can now be prevented, although there is a great deal that is still unknown. About 200 specific causes have been identified. These include infections and injuries to the brain that occur before, during, or immediately following birth. Some poisons, brain tumors, lack of oxygen, and imbalance in hormones (chemical substances formed by some of the glands in the body) can also cause retardation. An unusual blood condition in newborn babies that might cause retardation can now be recognized in advance and prevented. In this condition the baby's red blood cells are harmed by a substance in the mother's blood known as the Rh factor. Damage to the baby's brain results. Premature birth also increases the chances of retardation. Thus it is important for pregnant women to receive good care early in their pregnancy. Another cause is infection with certain viruses, such as German measles, early in the mother's pregnancy. In recent years the development of vaccines offers hope in preventing these conditions.

A few types of mental retardation are inherited—passed from parents to the child. Phenylketonuria, known as PKU, is an example. A test has been discovered that makes it possible to recognize this disease when the baby is only a few days old. When the baby's diet is strictly regulated, the baby grows and develops normally.

Down's syndrome is a common type of retardation, affecting about 10 percent of all the retarded in institutions. Slanted eyes give these individuals an Oriental look. For this reason, in earlier days the condition was called mongolism. Scientists have learned much about its complicated causes.

A large number of retarded show no signs of damage to the brain. It is believed that poor environment, such as slum surroundings, may affect a child's intelligence. Without books or home teaching, the slum child who starts school at 5 or 6 may feel so handicapped that he believes he can never catch up. This kind of mental retardation might be prevented if these deprived children could be given the missing opportunities for learning. Pre-kindergarten classes for deprived children are being set up in some American communities to see if a child's brainpower can be increased with early teaching.

SERVICES FOR THE RETARDED

With so many differences in symptoms, severity, and ages among the retarded, many kinds of services are needed. It is desirable that the retarded be given care in the same way and in the same places as other children and adults. The professional people who take care of them—doctors, nurses, teachers, social workers—should therefore be specially trained to deal with the retarded. Unfortunately, too few communities offer a complete program of services that can take care of the retarded person's present needs and plan for his future. As more retardation centers are established this problem will decrease, giving the retarded a continuity of care.

A complete program of community services recognizes the following basic needs of the retarded person and his family:

Diagnosis. When retardation is suspected, careful examination should be made to establish the type, severity, and if possible, the cause. Planning for the future of the retarded person should follow. The services of doctors—particularly pediatricians, psychiatrists, and neurologists—and other professional people are needed for this planning. Clinics for the examination of the retarded should be located in hospitals for the retarded or in large medical centers where many kinds of specialists are at hand.

Parent Counseling. Many parents feel guilt, shame, fear, and even desperation at having a retarded child. It is most important that the retarded child have happy, healthy home surroundings. He needs the same protection, love, and understanding at home as the normal child. But parents cannot create a healthy home environment if they are too anxious or over-protective or if they make the child feel unwanted. Parents of a retarded child need outside help and advice. They may find these at local organizations made up of other parents of retarded children. They can benefit from the experience of these parents who have had to face the same difficulties.

Education. Most retarded children can benefit from schooling, which should be provided by local school systems. Regular school attendance can help retarded children to extend their knowledge. These children require specially trained teachers and small classes. In most large communities there are classes for the mildly retarded, who are known as "educable." The moderately retarded are described as "trainable." There are fewer classes for them, but the school experience can help them learn to do a number of things for themselves.

Treatment. There are specific treatment methods for a few types of retardation. But in all cases it is important to maintain the health of the retarded at the highest possible level. The retarded are easily subject to physical and emotional illnesses and often suffer from other handicaps. Family doctors and other specialists, particularly psychiatrists and pediatricians, whether seen in their offices or at a clinic or hospital, can be of help to the retarded and his family.

Work Opportunities. The retarded want to work. They should have the chance to earn a living or have a job of work to do, under supervision in a special, or "sheltered," workshop, as it is called. An important part of the community program should concern itself with preparing the person for a job, training him, and placing him. Even the simplest work can give him satisfaction.

Other Services. The retarded, like everybody else, need opportunities for worship, recreation, and social life. There are clubs, bowling leagues, and other activities for the retarded. Parents also need rest and a change from the constant task of caring for a retarded child or adult. Housekeeping, baby-sitting, and vacation relief services are important to the family's mental and physical health.

Medical knowledge about retardation is increasing. With this increase comes the need for more trained teachers and other specialists to work with the retarded. But everyone has the responsibility of being sympathetic and understanding toward the people who are mentally limited through no fault of their own. Public understanding, sympathy, and interest in the retarded offer help for their future.

GEORGE TARJAN, M.D.
Professor of Psychiatry
The Neuropsychiatric Institute
University of California at Los Angeles

See also MENTAL ILLNESS.

REVERE, PAUL (1735–1818)

Paul Revere, a silversmith and American Revolutionary patriot, was born in Boston, Massachusetts, on New Year's Day, 1735. His father, Apollos Rivoire, was born in France. Because Apollos Rivoire was a Huguenot (Protestant), his religious beliefs were not tolerated in France. In 1716, he emigrated to America. He served as an apprentice silversmith in Boston and then opened his own shop. To make his name easier to pronounce, Apollos Rivoire changed it to "Paul Revere."

His son, young Paul Revere, attended the North Writing (Grammar) School. There he learned to read well enough to understand a newspaper or book without difficulty. He also learned to write reasonably well. While in his early teens, he was taught his father's trade. Paul was 19 when his father died, and he took over the family business. In 1757, he married Sara Orne.

Revere was a skilled artisan, and he carried on a thriving business. He won a reputation as the leading silversmith in Boston and one of the best in America. Many examples of his work have been saved and can be seen in museums throughout the United States.

▶ REVOLUTIONARY PATRIOT

Revere was an influential figure among the artisans of Boston, and he took an active part in the events leading up to the Revolution. He joined the North End Caucus, a group of colonists organized to protect the rights of the American colonists against the actions of the British Government. He became friendly with such colonial leaders as James Otis, Dr. Joseph Warren (1741–75), Samuel and John Adams, and John Hancock. Along with the majority of other Massachusetts colonists, Revere protested the Stamp Act of 1765. This act placed a tax on newspapers, legal and business documents, and many other items. Later, he was asked by the Sons of Liberty, who led the opposition to the British, to make a silver punch bowl in honor of the members of the Massachusetts legislature who had defied the Stamp Act. Revere also made many engravings celebrating the exploits of Massachusetts patriots.

In 1773, Revere took part in what became known as the Boston Tea Party. Angered

---

The following excerpts are from Henry Wadsworth Longfellow's poem "Paul Revere's Ride." Note that in the second stanza Revere is incorrectly described as being "on the opposite shore."

PAUL REVERE'S RIDE

Listen, my children, and you shall hear
Of the midnight ride of Paul Revere,
On the eighteenth of April, in Seventy-five;
Hardly a man is now alive
Who remembers that famous day and year.

He said to his friend, "If the British march
By land or sea from the town to-night,
Hang a lantern aloft in the belfry arch
Of the North Church tower as a signal light,—
One, if by land, and two, if by sea;
And I on the opposite shore will be,
Ready to ride and spread the alarm
Through every Middlesex village and farm,
For the country folk to be up and to arm."

. . .

So through the night rode Paul Revere;
And so through the night went his cry of alarm
To every Middlesex village and farm,—
A cry of defiance and not of fear,
A voice in the darkness, a knock at the door,
And a word that shall echo forevermore!
For, borne on the night-wind of the Past,
Through all our history, to the last,
In the hour of darkness and peril and need,
The people will waken and listen to hear
The hurrying hoof-beats of that steed,
And the midnight message of Paul Revere.

because the British Government had placed a tax on tea without the consent of the colonists, Revere and over 100 other patriots from Boston and neighboring towns disguised themselves as Indians. They boarded three British ships, loaded with tea, in Boston Harbor and dumped the tea chests overboard.

Revere served as a courier for the patriots' Committee of Safety. He also was appointed official courier from the Massachusetts Provincial Congress to the Continental Congress. Communications were poor, and the role of the courier on horseback was a vital one. Revere rode to New York and Philadelphia several times to carry news of important events. But his most famous ride took place on the night of April 18, 1775.

A group of patriots, fearing a clash with the British soldiers, had stored ammunition and other military supplies at Concord, Massachusetts, about 35 kilometers (22 miles) from Boston. But they began to suspect that the British military governor, General Thomas Gage (1721–87), was planning a secret raid on the supplies. On April 16, Revere was sent to warn John Hancock and Samuel Adams, who were at nearby Lexington.

Upon his return, Revere and other patriots arranged for a warning system to indicate the British plan of attack. If the British came by land, one lantern would be hung high in the steeple of Boston's North Church; if they came by sea, two lanterns would be placed there. The signal would be flashed to patriots waiting at Charlestown, Massachusetts, across the Charles River.

▶ REVERE'S RIDE

Revere knew the North Church well, for when he was 12, he and some friends had rung the bells for church services. On the night of April 18 he was summoned by Dr. Joseph Warren. The British were planning to cross the Charles River by boat and then march to Concord. Revere was told to give the signal—two lanterns—and to ride for Lexington, rousing the Minutemen. A second rider, William Dawes (1745–99), was dispatched by another route.

Revere alerted the church sexton, who lighted the lanterns. Meanwhile, Revere returned home, put on his riding boots, and headed for the river, where his boat was hidden. Two friends accompanied him. The boat's oars were wrapped with a woman's flannel petticoat to muffle their sound in the water. Cautiously, the three men rowed past the *Somerset,* a British man-of-war guarding the bay. Finally they reached Charlestown. The local patriots had seen the signal and had one of their best horses waiting.

The countryside was thick with British soldiers as Revere galloped off. He eluded two of them guarding the road to Cambridge. He entered Medford, alerted the Minutemen and, then, in his own words, "I alarumed [alarmed] almost every house till I got to Lexington." Dawes and another rider, Dr. Samuel Prescott (1751?–77), joined Revere in Lexington, and together they rode on to Concord. About halfway there, the three were stopped by British soldiers. In the chase that followed, Revere was captured. Dawes fell from his horse and escaped into the woods. Only Prescott rode on to Concord, where he alerted the patriots.

Later that night, Revere was released— without his horse. He walked back to Lexington, arriving just as the first shots of the Revolution were being fired.

During the war Revere was given a number of assignments. He made copper plates for printing money. He designed the seal of the state of Massachusetts. And he was sent to the Continental Congress in Philadelphia to arrange for the manufacture of gunpowder, which was badly needed. He then helped to set up a powder mill in Canton, Massachusetts. At the same time, he served in the Massachusetts militia, rising to the rank of lieutenant colonel.

▶ LATER YEARS

When the war ended in 1783, Revere returned to his work as a silversmith. He also set up a bell foundry and in 1792 cast the first church bell made in Massachusetts.

After his first wife died in 1773, Revere married Rachel Walker. He had 16 children, but many of them died in infancy.

Paul Revere died in Boston on May 10, 1818, at the age of 83. In tribute one newspaper declared: "Seldom has the tomb closed upon a life so honourable and useful."

CLARENCE L. VER STEEG
Author, *The American People: Their History*

REVOLUTIONARY WAR

April 19, 1775, marked the end of an era. On that day the first shots of the Revolutionary War were fired at Lexington, Massachusetts. Some 6½ years later, on October 19, 1781, the British forces surrendered at Yorktown, Virginia. What had started as a fight for the rights of Englishmen in the 13 colonies ended in the creation of an independent nation—the United States of America.

▶ BACKGROUND OF THE REVOLUTION

Life in the 13 colonies had been going on undisturbed by the English for over 100 years. The great distance between the colonies and the mother country was one reason for this. Another was British involvement in wars on both the European and the American continents. The pressure of these wars gave the British very little time to concern themselves with what was going on in the colonies. During this period the colonists learned to manage their own affairs.

Life in the colonies differed in many ways from life in England. Englishmen who went to the colonies for a visit found it difficult to understand the new way of life that the colonists were leading. The independent spirit and the attitude of the colonists toward the British Government was also puzzling to the Englishmen. King George III (1738–1820) was another Englishman who did not understand the colonists. He was a well-meaning monarch, but he was shortsighted in his approach to the colonists and their problems.

The people who had journeyed to America from Europe had come in search of the opportunity to lead a better life and earn a better living. Many had come to escape the political and religious persecution and the lack of economic opportunity that existed throughout Europe at that time. And in the beginning, America was a land of opportunity. Restrictions existed in the colonies as they did in most countries then, but the colonists did not find them especially oppressive.

Opposition to British Policies

British policy toward the 13 colonies changed abruptly in 1763 after the French and Indian War. As a result of winning this war, England was the dominant power on the North American continent. The war, however, had been an expensive one, and the English people were heavily taxed. Now, in addition to the war expenses, there was a vast new territory that England had to govern.

It was at this time that the British Government began to feel that the colonists should pay their share of the costs of the colonial administration, including the postwar army. Britain wished to avoid the possibility of any further trouble between the colonists and the Indians and Spanish. It was therefore decided to maintain a standing army in the colonies. Because this army would protect the colonists, the British Government believed that the colonists should help pay for it. To reduce the possibility of trouble on the western frontier even further, the British issued the Proclamation of 1763. This closed the lands west of the Allegheny Mountains to further settlement or colonization.

Both these measures angered the colonists, who felt that they were now being taxed unfairly and that their freedom of movement was being unjustly curtailed.

Sugar Act. In 1764 the Revenue, or Sugar, Act was passed by Parliament. The molasses trade between the colonies and the French and Spanish West Indies had been extremely profitable for the colonies. This act made the tax on molasses from the French and Spanish West Indies much higher than that on molasses from the British West Indies. It was hoped that the colonists would buy from the British islands or pay the tax. Customs officials were given more power. They were expected to enforce the tax on molasses as they had not done before.

The colonists felt that these measures and those that followed violated their colonial charters and their rights as Englishmen. They argued that they were being taxed by a parliament in which they had no representative. "No taxation without representation" was the cry that echoed throughout the colonies. The British Government, on the other hand, argued that the interests of all Englishmen were represented in Parliament, whether they had a representative there or not. The colonists rejected this argument and said that their only legal allegiance was to George III and not to Parliament.

Quartering and Stamp Acts. In 1765 the

Angry colonists burn official British stamps in a protest against the Stamp Act.

British Prime Minister George Grenville (served 1763–65) persuaded Parliament to pass the Stamp Act and the Quartering Act. The Quartering Act required colonial authorities to provide certain supplies for the British troops stationed in the colonies. The colonists were angered by this—especially by a provision of the act saying that under certain circumstances, they would have to quarter British soldiers in their homes.

The Stamp Act required the colonists to pay for stamps on all legal documents, business forms, and even newspapers. This stamp on legal documents and business forms was really not so unusual. In fact, even today legal documents, playing cards, and cigarettes must be stamped. However, the colonists were not used to being taxed and especially resented being taxed by a parliament that did not represent them.

The British Government never expected the storm of protest that the Stamp Act created in America. The Stamp Act was denounced in every colony. Never had Americans felt themselves so oppressed. In the past, there had been objection to other taxes, tariffs, and duties, but not to the extent evoked by the Stamp Act.

Royal agents attempting to enforce the act were beaten by angry colonists. A Bostonian named James Otis agitated strongly against the Act. "Taxation without representation is tyranny!" he declared.

Boston became the center of colonial defiance of England's tax policies. A mob of Bostonians ransacked the home of Thomas Hutchinson (1711–80), the royal lieutenant governor. Rioters burned the barge used by the royal tax collector. Tempers ran high in Boston, and discontent boiled up in each of the 13 colonies. Samuel Adams became the chief spokesman against the British, and other Bostonians rallied around him. Adams found an able associate in John Hancock, a wealthy merchant.

Citizens' groups called the "Sons of Liberty" sprang up in all the colonies to protest the Stamp Act. By October, 1765, opposition to the tax served as the basis for a congress. The Stamp Act Congress, with delegates from 9 colonies, met in New York. It was the first intercolonial meeting summoned by the colonists themselves.

Among the speeches delivered, one suggested the new idea of colonial unity. Christopher Gadsden (1724–1805), a South Carolina merchant, proclaimed, "There ought to be no New England man, no New Yorker, known on the continent, but all of us Americans!"

If the delegates were not yet ready to accept that proposition, they displayed enough solidarity to draw up a Declaration of Rights. This declaration suggested to the King that the colonies could do their own taxing, since they were not represented in Parliament.

Townshend Acts. The Stamp Act proved unenforceable and was revoked after a year. But any colonial jubilation over the repeal soon ended. For at the same time, Parliament passed the Declaratory Act, which said that Parliament had every right to tax the colonies. New, more hateful taxes were passed by Parliament in 1767. These were the Townshend Acts (named after the British Chancellor of the Exchequer), which placed a duty on many products brought into the colonies from England, particularly lead, glass, paint, paper, wine—and tea.

Colonial reaction to the Townshend Acts was furious, since the new law provided for a blank warrant known as a writ of assistance, which empowered any officer of the King to search a man's home for taxable goods. To counter the Townshend Acts, nonimportation agreements were reached among the colonial merchants. The merchants agreed not to import any goods from England.

Boston Massacre. It became quite respectable, especially in busy Boston, to smuggle goods taxable under the Townshend Acts. In 1768 King George, annoyed by the widespread flouting of the law in Boston, ordered 4,000 troops under General Thomas Gage (1721–87) to be sent there, along with a flotilla of warships. The Americans would be shown their place.

The Redcoats, or "Lobsterbacks" (as Bostonians nicknamed the British soldiers), received a cold welcome. Townsmen and soldiers brawled in taverns and on the streets.

Matters grew more tense, and serious violence seemed imminent. To prevent riots in the streets of Boston, British authorities shipped several battalions out of the city, hoping that with fewer soldiers around, the situation might become calmer. But shifting a few hundred Redcoats did not pacify the Bostonians. They wanted all the soldiers to go.

Matters came to a head on March 5, 1770. Some boys taunted a British sentry walking his post at the Customs House on King Street. A group of local toughs gathered and began snowballing the sentry. The guard called for help. A squad of soldiers came with bayonets fixed on their loaded muskets. The crowd, which had swelled into a mob, grew ugly. Sticks, brickbats, and snowballs showered upon the troops.

Suddenly a British musket went off; then a ragged volley raked the threatening mob. When the gunsmoke cleared, five civilians lay dead in the snow—among them, a free Negro laborer named Crispus Attucks. Several Bostonians were wounded by Redcoat bullets. The ugly affair was labeled the Boston Massacre.

Committees of Correspondence. In June, 1772, a royal revenue vessel, the *Gaspée,* was chasing smugglers near the coast of Rhode Island. The naval vessel ran aground in Narragansett Bay, and a band of citizens of Providence rowed out to the cutter and burned it. The British Government threatened to take the guilty colonists back to England for trial.

It was at this time (November, 1772) that Sam Adams proposed that the colonies form "Committees of Correspondence." In this way people in each of the 13 colonies would be kept informed through letters of what was going on in the other colonies.

Tea Act and Tea Party. In 1770 Lord Frederick North, Prime Minister of Great Britain (served 1770–82), had repealed all the Townshend Act taxes except that on tea. Because there was still a tax on British tea, the colonists refused to buy it. As a result, the British East India Company was in trouble and asked Parliament for help. In 1773 Parliament passed the Tea Act. Although this Act made the price of British tea lower than any other, there was still a tax on the tea. The colonists, on the principle of no taxation without representation, refused to buy the tea. Sam Adams called for an American boycott of tea. The Sons of Liberty enforced the boycott, often with violence against offenders.

Lord North, however, was not to be intimidated. On the night of December 16, 1773, there were three tea-laden cargo ships from England at anchor in Boston Harbor. Several hundred Bostonians, disguised as Indians, raided the vessels and dumped 342 cases of tea into the water. This event is known as the Boston Tea Party. A similar occurrence took place in New York Harbor, but the Boston Tea Party resulted in serious consequences, while the affair in New York has been nearly forgotten.

Intolerable Acts. The tea dumped into

Boston's harbor was valued at $75,000, and the British reacted vigorously to this act of defiance. Lord North's government drew up the so-called Intolerable Acts (1774). One of these Acts was the Boston Port Bill, which closed Boston Harbor to all shipping. Warships of the Royal Navy patrolled the harbor mouth. Boston was effectively blockaded, except for a narrow neck of land that connected the city to the mainland. Only over that route could supplies reach Boston. The wealthy port faced both hunger and economic ruin. Massachusetts was also limited in its practice of self-government.

This punishment was to continue until the citizens of Boston paid for the tea that had been dumped. To prevent mob violence, General Gage placed the city under martial law and brought in hundreds of troops.

The Bostonians proved more stubborn than the British. They refused to pay a cent. Word of Boston's plight was sent out to the other colonies through the Committees of Correspondence. The people of New York, Connecticut, Philadelphia, Baltimore, and Charleston rushed food and money to the surrounded, besieged, and beleaguered town. Every colony rallied to Boston's support.

First Continental Congress

In September, 1774, the First Continental Congress was held at Philadelphia. The delegates drew up a list of rights and grievances addressed to the people of Great Britain. At the same time they pledged support for Boston.

One of the most important accomplishments of this Congress was the **Association**.

This was an agreement among the colonies to refrain completely from importing or exporting British goods. However, it was at this time that George III declared, "The dye is now cast, the colonies must either submit or triumph. . . . There must always be one tax to keep up the right, and as such I approve of the Tea Duty."

The winter of 1774–75 brought growing discontent to Boston. The Port Bill had turned the once prosperous harbor into a desert. Ships lay rotting at anchor, commerce was at a standstill, and unemployment grew each day. In April, 1775, Parliament passed the **Restraining Act**, which forbade the colonists to trade with any country other than England and the islands of the British West Indies. It also barred the colonists from fishing in the waters off Newfoundland.

Preparations for War

Recruits swelled the ranks of the Sons of Liberty. Flames of revolt were rising in Boston, but the British ignored the obvious military preparations of the Americans. Neither Gage nor his officers could seriously consider "bumpkins, peasants, and illiterate plowboys" a threat.

Boston Tea Party. Disguised as Indians, Bostonians raid British ships and dump their cargoes of tea overboard.

Not only did Gage deride the American militiamen, but he was fully convinced that the Port Bill would eventually humble Boston into submission. This viewpoint was supported, not only in Boston but in every colony, by persons called Tories or Loyalists. These individuals remained faithful to King George III and considered the Patriots (those colonists who were critical of British rule) traitors and rebels. Obviously, ill will existed between Tories and Patriots. This bad feeling was to cause much bloodshed in the coming years.

In February, 1775, General Gage began to take the military activities of the Patriot group called the Minutemen more seriously. His men began looking for hidden weapons, and on several occasions they narrowly avoided clashes with the Minutemen.

The main American arms storehouse was at Concord, about 32 kilometers, or 20 miles, from Boston. To protect the guns, shot, and powder concealed there, the Americans decided that if any large British force was sent out of Boston, all available militia would assemble to block the foe.

▶ THE WAR BEGINS

On April 15, 1775, a leading Patriot, Dr. Joseph Warren (1741–75) received word that Gage planned to send 700 infantry troops toward Lexington and Concord. Sam Adams and John Hancock were hiding at a home in Lexington (Gage had issued warrants for their arrest). Dr. Warren sent a messenger to warn them. Word was passed to move the arms from Concord, and the courier returned to Boston. He was Paul Revere, an engraver, silversmith, coppersmith, cartoonist, artist, and goldsmith. In addition to having all these talents, Revere was a superb horseman.

Gage did not strike on the 15th. But on April 18 rebel spies warned Warren that Gage was ferrying troops across the Charles River for a swift march against Lexington and Concord. Warren sent Paul Revere and William Dawes to rouse the Minutemen. All that night Revere and Dawes rode, in the words of Longfellow's poem, "through every Middlesex village and town," spreading the alarm that the British were coming.

Patriots leaped from bed, grabbing their powder horns, cartridge boxes, and flint-locks. Then they dashed into the darkness to mobilize at pre-arranged points.

Lexington and Concord

At dawn on April 19 the British column reached Lexington. Fewer than 100 Minutemen had gathered to face the Redcoats. The British commander, Major John Pitcairn (1722–75), ordered his troops to spread out. Awed by the sight of so many soldiers, the Americans, under Captain John Parker (1729–75), broke ranks and began to straggle away. Suddenly a shot rang out, and then others followed. Eight Americans fell dead; 10 others were wounded by the firing. The American Revolution began at that moment and in that place.

Later, at Concord, Minutemen drove the Redcoats from the town with sniping fire. From behind every rock, tree, and hill, men and boys blasted away at the British. The hated Lobsterbacks withdrew from Concord and retreated toward Boston. Their march was plagued almost every foot of the way by American marksmen. Before the day was over, more than 70 Redcoats were dead and 173 were wounded.

Lexington and Concord unleashed a terrible storm over the 13 colonies. Patrick Henry of Virginia had voiced the sentiments of most Americans in March when he thundered, "I know not what course others may take, but as for me, give me liberty or give me death!"

The colonists were divided among themselves at the start of the war; thousands still supported the Crown. Before long, neighbor fought neighbor and brother turned against brother in a bitter civil war between Tory-Loyalist and Patriot-Rebel.

General Thomas Gage soon realized that what the Americans lacked in military skill they made up for in bravery and determination. He soon found himself in an unenviable position. Some 6,000 militiamen commanded by General Artemas Ward ringed Boston and kept Gage locked up inside the city. The only route open to the British was by sea.

Day by day, Ward's army grew more numerous as detachments marched in from Rhode Island, Connecticut, and Vermont (then known as the New Hampshire grants).

Americans open fire on British troops in retreat from the battle of Concord.

Leaders who had some military training also joined the forces besieging Gage. Israel Putnam (1718–90), a veteran Indian fighter; John Stark (1728–1822), veteran of many frontier battles; and young Nathanael Greene (1742–86) were among the leaders.

The Americans did not sit still. On May 10, 1775, a detachment led jointly by Ethan Allen of Vermont and Benedict Arnold, who commanded the Connecticut governor's Foot Guard, surprised and captured the British stronghold of Fort Ticonderoga on the southern tip of Lake Champlain. Allen's "Green Mountain Boys" swarmed into the enemy fort with hardly a shot fired.

Bunker Hill

On June 17, 1775, a major clash took place between the Americans and the British. General Ward had some troops dig in on heights overlooking the British lines. The Patriots entrenched themselves on Breed's Hill next to Bunker Hill.

General Gage could not allow the Americans to hold a fortified position that dominated his. He held a meeting with three newly arrived officers—General Sir William Howe (1729–1814), General Sir Henry Clinton (1738?–95), and General John Burgoyne (1722–92)—who advised him to blast the Americans off the hill with artillery.

A furious bombardment by naval and field guns failed to dislodge the Yankees. Gage sent several regiments under General Sir William Howe to do the job. The British regulars started up Breed's Hill as though on parade. But their perfect alignment was shattered by a murderous volley from the militiamen on the hilltop, who had been ordered by one of their commanders—William Prescott (1726–95)—"Don't fire until you see the whites of their eyes."

Again and again the Redcoats tried to storm the crest, only to be beaten back. It was not until the Americans had run out of powder and shot that they yielded the posi-

The colonists hold the crest of Breed's Hill against advancing British soldiers.

tion. Taking the hill cost the British 1,054 dead and wounded out of the 2,300 men assigned to the task. American casualties numbered about 500. (Among the fallen was Dr. Joseph Warren, who had sent Paul Revere off on his immortal ride.)

When the battle was over, a young British officer exclaimed, "I can't believe it! Those bumpkins fought like Englishmen!" "Of course they did," another officer said. "After all, they *are* Englishmen!"

Second Continental Congress

At the very moment the fighting was raging on Breed's Hill, a less spectacular but more momentous event was taking place in Philadelphia, where the delegates to the Second Continental Congress were gathered.

A Massachusetts delegate had proposed to the Congress the formation of an army responsible to Congress and not to the colonial legislatures. This was a novel idea and a stirring one. With such an army in the field—a trained, disciplined force—the British would not be facing raw militiamen.

Such leading Rebels as John Hancock and John Adams thought that a Continental Army would be a good thing. They argued in favor of the proposal, and Congress voted to create a 20,000-man regular army, which would incorporate in its ranks those militia forces then serving against the British.

Selecting a commander in chief for the new army called for much consideration. At last, after much debate, Congress chose a 43-year-old Virginian, a man of wealth and position named George Washington, already a colonel in the Virginia militia. Washington had fought in the French and Indian War. He was a good organizer, a man of quiet strength, who had inspired confidence.

Washington Takes Command. The newly appointed commander in chief went up to Boston and took over the Continental Army at Cambridge, Massachusetts, on July 2, 1775. The troops he inherited were more an armed rabble than a disciplined military group. The American camps were unruly. But after Washington came, the men began to behave in a more soldierly manner. He worked and drilled them relentlessly.

There was little action for the army around Boston that winter. The American forces had the British penned up in Boston, but Washington did not know how long he could keep them hemmed in. There were rumors that reinforcements were on the way for General Howe, who had replaced Gage as commander at Boston. Washington knew that a determined assault by superior British forces would break his siege lines. He needed cannon to bombard the British positions. Someone remembered that at Fort Ticonderoga there were heavy guns, and Washington's chief of

artillery, Colonel Henry Knox (1750–1806) offered to bring this equipment from the captured British fort.

Knox had undertaken a difficult job. It was now November. Hauling the cannon overland in the dead of winter seemed impossible. But Henry Knox was a determined man. He gathered a party of volunteers and began the 275-mile haul from Ticonderoga to Boston after loading the guns on ox-drawn sleds.

Defeat in Canada

Progress was slow and tedious; but the guns were inched toward Boston over ice-slick trails in bone-chilling cold. As Knox made his painful way with the cannon an American military expedition under the command of General Richard Montgomery (1736–75) captured Montreal in Canada on November 13, 1775. The colonists hoped to gain the aid of the French Canadians and to prevent the British from using Canada as a base for attack. However, the American adventure in Canada ended disastrously.

The attempt to capture Quebec was a debacle for the Americans. Montgomery fell during the fighting, and only a handful of survivors stumbled back under the leadership of Colonel Benedict Arnold, who assumed command after Montgomery's death. The Americans abandoned Montreal. Their dreams of conquest in Canada were over.

1776–77: War in the East

But the fortunes of war turned for the Yankees in March, 1776. Henry Knox finally reached Boston with the cannon. Washington mounted the guns on Dorchester Heights. The fear of a devastating American bombardment was so great that General Howe evacuated Boston (March 17, 1776) by sea. Some thought he was sailing for Halifax, Nova Scotia, but others, including Washington, believed that Howe intended to attack New York City by land and sea in a major effort to capture that great port.

The loss of New York and its fine harbor would be a stunning blow to the Americans. To forestall the possibility, Washington rushed troops there from Boston. His men were set to work digging entrenchments and gun emplacements from one end of Manhattan Island to the other.

Washington correctly guessed Howe's intentions. Late in June a British fleet numbering 130 warships carrying thousands of Redcoats arrived in New York Harbor. It was followed in July by another fleet of 150 ships carrying more Redcoats and Hessians (German soldiers hired by King George III to fight for England).

Fighting in New York. The British landed on Staten Island, ferried over to Brooklyn, and drove the outnumbered Americans from one defensive position to another. A succession of battles in Brooklyn, Long Island, Manhattan, and White Plains ended in American defeat. The major battle took place on Long Island on August 27, 1776. All Rebel resistance around New York City and Westchester was broken. During this campaign Captain Nathan Hale was executed by the British for crossing their lines to get information for Washington. The British occupied New York in mid-September, 1776. Shortly afterward a mysterious fire—probably set by Patriots—destroyed most of the city.

Meanwhile, Washington, pursued by strong enemy forces under General Lord Cornwallis (1738–1805), retreated to Peekskill, New York. From there he crossed the Hudson and began a long and grueling march through New Jersey. He crossed the Delaware River near Trenton and paused to rest his exhausted men. At the time, Washington had only 5,000 troops; they were thinly clad, hungry, poorly armed, and disheartened. Never had the American cause been at such a low ebb.

Declaration of Independence. The Second Continental Congress meeting in Philadelphia passed the Declaration of Independence on July 4, 1776. The motion for a declaration of independence had been made on June 7 by Richard Henry Lee (1732–94) of Virginia. Virginia's great statesman Thomas Jefferson wrote the text of the Declaration of Independence. The Patriots were now fighting for their freedom as a nation—the United States of America. The Declaration of Independence gave a new dignity to the American cause.

But in the winter of 1776 the fate of the United States seemed sealed; the army had been defeated. A bleak future stretched before the Americans. But all did not lose hope. A writer named Thomas Paine penned a stirring series of pamphlets called *The Crisis,* in which he wrote: "These are the times that try men's souls. The summer soldier and the sunshine patriot will, in this crisis, shrink from the service of their country; but he that stands it NOW, deserves the love and thanks of man and woman."

Trenton and Princeton. George Washington was no "summer soldier," and the tattered men he led were not "sunshine patriots." They longed to strike a blow at the enemy. The opportunity to hit the foe came on Christmas Eve, 1776. Scouts brought word to Washington that in Trenton, on the opposite shore of the Delaware River, 1,400 Hessians under Colonel Johann Rall were celebrating the holiday.

Washington decided to break up the Hessian party. On Christmas night his men crossed the ice-choked Delaware during a sleet storm. Rugged fishermen from Marblehead, Massachusetts, handled the boats, which transported troops and cannon to the enemy side of the river.

At daybreak the Americans were in position. They fell on the Hessians with such fury that Rall and most of his troops were killed. The victory at Trenton was a fine Christmas present for the young American nation.

General William Howe was furious over the Trenton affair. He ordered General Charles Cornwallis to "run Washington into the ground." On January 2, 1777, Cornwallis had apparently succeeded. Washington's troops were surrounded in Trenton by 8,000 British regulars.

But the Americans slipped out of the British trap and escaped to Morristown, New Jersey, where the Continental Army went into winter camp. Before encamping, Washington scored another triumph over the enemy at Princeton, New Jersey. There he suddenly turned on the pursuing British and scattered some of the King's best troops in a sharp battle (January 3, 1777).

Somehow the American Army survived the grueling winter at Morristown. With the coming of spring the men's spirits lifted. Congress had managed to purchase supplies in Europe. Guns, muskets, powder, shot, shoes, and clothing were distributed to the troops.

A British Plan

The British also stirred with the coming of good weather. A bold plan had been conceived to end the revolution at one stroke. General John Burgoyne was to strike south from Lake Champlain in an advance to Albany, New York. Another column, under Colonel Barry St. Leger (1737–89), reinforced by Mohawk Indians and Tories, would move from Fort Oswego on Lake Ontario and meet Burgoyne at Albany, while General Howe was to head north from New York and join the others.

This maneuver would take the Hudson Valley and probably end the war—if it was successful. But something went wrong. Instead of marching to Albany, Howe moved against the American capital at Philadelphia.

Fighting in Pennsylvania

To counter this thrust, Washington brought his troops from Morristown into Bucks County, Pennsylvania, where he could interpose his forces between Howe and Philadelphia. While awaiting the enemy, Washington was joined by a young French nobleman who had volunteered to serve the American cause. He was the 19-year-old Marquis de Lafayette. Lafayette was assigned as an aide to Washington and did memorable service for the rest of the war.

Lafayette was one of many foreign volunteers who aided the Americans in their struggle for liberty. Others were Baron de

Kalb (1721–80), a German; Count Casimir Pulaski (1748?–79), a Pole; Thaddeus Kosciusko (1746–1817), another Pole; and Friedrich, Baron von Steuben (1730–94), a Prussian officer, who drilled the Continentals and forged them into a disciplined army.

Howe sailed from New York, loading his 15,000 men into 260 ships. The fleet landed at a point about 50 miles south of Philadelphia, and the struggle for the American capital began. The Yankees fought bravely but were defeated at Brandywine Creek. The way to Philadelphia was open. On September 26, 1777, Howe took the city, and members of the Second Continental Congress fled, first to Lancaster and then to York, Pennsylvania.

Although he had been beaten, Washington struck back at the British in the battle of Germantown on October 4, 1777. Again the British triumphed, but the Americans fought so well that foreign military men praised Washington's troops. "No army with such spirit is a defeated army," a French officer told the American commander in chief. "You will yet prevail."

Articles of Confederation

On November 15, 1777, shortly after Germantown, the 13 colonies took a step that brought them much closer to unity as a nation. Congress adopted the Articles of Confederation, which had been drafted by a committee headed by John Dickinson (1732–1808) of Pennsylvania. The Articles served as a set of regulations by which the colonies agreed to be ruled until the war ended. The aim of the Articles was to give Congress the necessary powers for winning the war. However, the Articles did not go into effect until 1781, when all the colonies had ratified them.

In the field Washington pulled back to Valley Forge, Pennsylvania, where he set up winter quarters only 20 miles from Philadelphia. His troops suffered agonies in the coldest weather in many years. The soldiers wrapped themselves in rags to keep warm. Disease spread through the camp. The men endured starvation, scurvy, and frostbite, while only a score of miles away the British lived in comfort and plenty.

But the ordeal of Valley Forge hardened the core of Yankee resistance. To that awful camp came the Prussian Baron von Steuben. He took the sick and hungry Americans and made them into crack soldiers. A topnotch drillmaster, von Steuben whipped Washington's "band of scarecrows" into topnotch troops comparable to any army in the world. "Give them enough to eat and they'll whip the Lobsterbacks at will," von Steuben bragged.

Saratoga Victory Brings France into the War

In July, 1777, General Burgoyne started southward from Lake Champlain, and he captured Ticonderoga on July 6. He knew that

Baron Friedrich von Steuben, saber in hand, drills American troops. Many of the colonial soldiers wore homemade uniforms and had little idea of military discipline.

Howe was not marching to meet him. But he did not know that Colonel Barry St. Leger's mixed force of Tories and Indians would be smashed by Benedict Arnold on August 22, 1777.

Burgoyne continued his advance toward Albany. He sent a force of Hessians into Vermont, where, he heard, the Rebels had stored supplies of food and had many horses. Burgoyne wanted both the food and the horses. His Hessians were crushed on August 16, 1777, at Bennington, Vermont, by the American General John Stark, who led a force of hardy Vermonters.

This setback did not deter Burgoyne. He pressed ahead to Bemis Heights, just north of Albany. On September 19, 1777, in the first battle of Freeman's Farm, he ran into an American army under General Horatio Gates (1728?–1806). The brilliant work of Colonel Henry Dearborn (1751–1829) and Virginia riflemen under Daniel Morgan (1736–1802) brought an American victory.

Burgoyne dug in to await St. Leger while Gates surrounded him. At last the British general realized that help was not coming. On October 7, 1777, he tried to cut his way through the encircling Americans. The attempt failed in the second battle of Freeman's Farm, which saw Benedict Arnold emerge as the hero of the day. Arnold fought furiously until his left leg was smashed by a sniper's bullet.

Burgoyne resisted stubbornly until October 17, 1777, when he saw that further fighting was useless. He surrendered his 5,000 men to General Gates at Saratoga. It was the turning point of the American Revolution. The great victory at Saratoga encouraged the Rebels, and even more important, brought France openly into the war as an American ally. Burgoyne's defeat convinced King Louis XVI of France that the British could be beaten. Even before this, France had given the Rebels secret military aid on a large scale. France now recognized the independence of the United States, and the two countries formed a military alliance.

▶ YEARS OF HOPE: 1778–81

Americans faced 1778 with new hope and courage. On May 5, Washington announced to his troops that an alliance had been formed with France. General Sir Henry Clinton, who had succeeded Howe at Philadelphia, was worried by France's entry into the hostilities. Clinton believed that Howe had blundered by occupying Philadelphia. But Clinton could not change what had been done.

Concerned that a French fleet might bottle Clinton up in Philadelphia, the British Government ordered him to ship some troops to defend the British West Indies against a French raid and march the rest of them overland to New York.

On June 18, 1778, Clinton began his withdrawal to New York. He was hampered by rains, supply wagons, and American raiders. Washington decided to launch a full-scale attack on Clinton's troops, against the advice of his senior officer, Major General Charles Lee (1731–82).

However, on June 28, when Lee learned that young Lafayette was to be given 6,000 troops for the attack, he insisted on leading it. A great battle erupted at Monmouth Court House, New Jersey. British regulars fell back, astounded by the disciplined tactics of von Steuben's trained men.

But General Lee did not prove up to the ability of the troops he led. He missed many opportunities to rout the enemy and ordered a withdrawal, which spread confusion in the American ranks. An angry Washington countermanded Lee's command to retreat. Lee was later court-martialed and dismissed from the service for his conduct at Monmouth.

The battle ended at nightfall on June 28. Clinton retreated, but Washington could not pursue with his tired men. Clinton reached New York in disarray. No one then knew that Monmouth was to be the last major battle in the north. Clinton stayed in New York City. The American forces crossed the Hudson River to New York from a point near Paramus, New Jersey, moving to White Plains, New York. For the rest of the war, only minor clashes took place in that region, but in other areas the struggle continued with unabated fury and bloodshed.

The War in the West

From the very beginning of the Revolution a vicious side war was fought in the border territories beyond the Alleghenies and on the New York frontier. The British armed bands of Indians, who raided the pioneer settlements of Kentucky.

A frontiersman named George Rogers Clark (1752–1818) recruited a force of hardy woodsmen. They destroyed the main British centers, Kaskaskia and Cahokia, from which the hostile Indians were supplied with arms. Clark also took Vincennes and other enemy posts in the Illinois country. In December, 1778, the British recaptured Vincennes. Clark mobilized his forces and led 200 men through the bitterest cold, fording streams and pressing over frozen swampland, to complete an incredible march that covered 180 miles in 18 days.

Clark's tough pioneers fell on the British, took Vincennes, and broke the enemy's hold on the huge tract known as the Northwest Territory. But even as Clark quieted the trouble in his territory, trouble exploded in the Mohawk Valley of upper New York State. It spread to the Wyoming Valley of eastern Pennsylvania. Death and destruction came to the Wyoming Valley in 1778, when the Tory colonel Sir John Butler (1728–94) led Loyalists and Indians on a raid through that fertile region. Butler and his men joined forces with the Mohawk chief Joseph Brant (1742–1807) and his braves and later marauded through the rich Cherry Valley of New York state. The Tories and Indians left behind a trail of burned cabins and murdered settlers.

General Washington sent generals John Sullivan (1740–95) and James Clinton (1733–1812) to deal with the Tories and Indians. The Patriot troops left a path of destruction through the Indian Territory, but the fighting continued through 1780 and 1781. Not until American troops under Colonel Marinus Willett (1740–1830) defeated the main force of the enemy at Jerseyfield, New York (December, 1781), did the New York frontier have any peace.

The War at Sea

While great battles raged on land, the American Revolution, almost from the beginning, was also a maritime war. The Americans had no navy to match the strength of British sea power and so resorted to using daring sea captains as privateers. Such bold sea dogs as John Barry (1745–1803), Joshua Barney (1759–1818), and John Paul Jones preyed on British shipping with outstanding success.

The most successful of the American naval heroes was John Paul Jones. He struck at the heart of the British Isles and in a daring raid actually landed his men at Whitehaven

Who was Molly Pitcher?

Molly Pitcher was a heroine of the Revolutionary War. She won her nickname and her fame in 1778 at the battle of Monmouth, New Jersey. Her real name was Mary Ludwig Hays McCauley.

Molly was born October 13, 1754, on a dairy farm near Trenton. Her father, John Ludwig, was a German immigrant. Molly grew up to be a short, stocky farm girl, not pretty but kind and hardworking. When she was 15, she went to Pennsylvania to work as a housemaid, and soon afterward she married John Hays.

John fought in the Revolution with the American artillery. Molly went to the army camp to take care of him. She cooked, sewed, and washed for John and the other soldiers.

The battle of Monmouth started on June 28, a very hot day. All day long Molly ran back and forth from a well, bringing water to the hot, thirsty fighters and helping the wounded. Seeing her, the soldiers cried thankfully, "Here comes Molly with her pitcher! Molly, bring the pitcher here." Soon they were just calling, "Molly! Pitcher!" And so she won her battle name.

During the battle Molly's husband was overcome by the heat and fell beside his cannon. Molly stepped up to the cannon and took his place. As long as the battle raged, Molly loaded and fired with the rest of the soldiers. Today there are monuments at Monmouth and at her grave, honoring her as a brave fighter. There are songs about her too.

The rest of Molly's life was not exciting. After her husband died in 1789, Molly married again. Her second husband was George McCauley (or M'Kolly). They were poor and not very happy. Molly earned her living scrubbing floors, washing, and taking care of children.

Many years later, in 1822, people remembered that this humble scrubwoman had fought for independence like a soldier. So the Pennsylvania General Assembly passed "An act for the relief of Molly M'Kolly." The act gave Molly a soldier's pension. Until she died in 1832, Molly received $40 a year from her grateful country, in honor of her services.

(1778), captured a British sloop of war, and looted the Earl of Selkirk's castle on St. Mary's Isle in Solway Firth.

Jones carried out his most noted feat on September 23, 1779, as captain of the *Bonhomme Richard,* a merchantman converted into a 42-gun warship. Although his ship was slow and clumsy, Jones attacked a British convoy off Flamborough Head in the North Sea. The merchant ships were escorted by a 50-gun man-of-war, the *Serapis,* which promptly engaged the *Bonhomme Richard.* In the furious fight that followed, the American ship was blasted to splinters but still managed to keep afloat. When the captain of the *Serapis* called on the Americans to surrender, Jones replied, "I have not yet begun to fight!"

Eventually the *Serapis* was forced to surrender, and Jones boarded the enemy vessel, which had been fearfully battered, her mainmast felled and her decks "slippery with blood," according to an eyewitness.

Although no national navy of any size opposed the traditional British rule of the seas, the Americans sent out almost 2,000 privateers during the war. These vessels sank a number of royal merchant vessels and war-

The American ship *Bonhomme Richard* (left) was badly damaged in its battle with the British man-of-war *Serapis* (right). But the Americans won the battle because of the bravery of John Paul Jones and his crew.

ships. The confiscated goods were valued at more than $18,000,000.

The balance of sea power shifted to the Americans when France entered the war as an ally. The French fleet was the deciding factor. Its frigates and men-of-war played the decisive role in 1781 by keeping the British army under Cornwallis bottled up at Yorktown, Virginia, and repulsing a British relief expedition.

War in the Hudson Valley

As the war dragged on, General Henry Clinton, the British commander in New York, decided to revive Burgoyne's old plan to overrun the Hudson Valley. His first blow in that operation was to take the American stronghold of Stony Point, New York, located a few miles south of West Point, in May, 1779.

West Point, which dominated the Hudson River, was powerfully defended. Clinton had to conquer that American bastion before the Hudson Valley could be made British. His scheme received a setback when the Yankees regained Stony Point in a daring night assault on July 15, 1779, led by General "Mad Anthony" Wayne (1745–96).

Benedict Arnold's Betrayal. As a result of this Rebel victory, Clinton changed his tactics. Instead of storming West Point, which would have meant great cost in men and equipment, the wily British general sought an American traitor who could help him get it through stealth. Clinton found his man. He was Benedict Arnold, hero of Quebec and Saratoga, veteran of a dozen Revolutionary War battles. Arnold was Washington's favorite combat officer; and the commander in chief regarded him with respect and affection.

After Arnold was wounded at Saratoga, Washington made him military commandant of Philadelphia, where he met and married a beautiful Tory, Peggy Shippen. The new Mrs. Arnold was used to high living. Arnold tried to match his wife's mode of life. However, he was not a rich man. Probably driven to desperation by his need for money, Arnold offered his services to the British. He negotiated with General Henry Clinton through Major John André (1751–80), the Redcoat general's adjutant.

In January, 1780, Arnold was relieved of duty in Philadelphia by Washington, and in August he was put in command of West Point. Arnold now had the plans of the fort, showing defensive positions and gun emplacements. Working through André, he made a deal with the enemy.

A British sloop of war, the *Vulture,* sailed up the Hudson to a point where André and Arnold could meet. The papers were turned over, but André was caught by an American patrol while carrying the secret documents to New York. At the last moment André had decided to travel overland and not by ship. His capture exposed the treasonable plot. André was convicted and executed as a spy.

Arnold fled to the *Vulture* and went to New York. The British gave him a brigadier general's commission and a cash settlement of 6,315 pounds sterling. He served his former enemy with skill and daring. He led raids into his native Connecticut and on the Virginia coast.

War in the South

During the time that battles raged in Massachusetts, New York, New Jersey, and Pennsylvania, the war hardly touched the southern colonies. Not since 1776, when a British attack on Charleston, South Carolina, had been repulsed, had any large-scale fighting taken place in the South, although Tories and Patriots clashed in numerous skirmishes.

That situation changed in 1778. The British high command switched its strategy and decided to conquer the southern colonies. In December, 1778, a mixed force of British, Hessian, and Tory troops captured the important seaport of Savannah, Georgia.

A combined Franco-American army made a belated attempt to recapture Savannah almost a year later (October 9, 1779), only to meet with disaster. After the defeat French naval and military forces were withdrawn, and only a weak American army commanded by General Benjamin Lincoln (1733–1810) was left to oppose the foe.

Carolina Campaigns. General Henry Clinton rushed a powerful army from New York to invade the South. The British overwhelmed Charleston. On May 12, 1780, the Americans there surrendered, and the Redcoats marched into the city with bands playing and flags flying. After the fall of Charleston those Rebels and their sympathizers who would not take an oath of allegiance to the crown were arrested.

In June, 1780, Clinton delegated the task of conquering the South to General Charles Cornwallis, who promptly smashed an American army marching to attack the British munitions store at Camden, South Carolina. This force had as its leader General Horatio Gates, the victor of Saratoga. Gates stumbled into a British trap at Camden (August 16, 1780), and his militia fled in a disgraceful manner. Only a few regiments of Continental regulars were left to face Cornwallis.

After Camden the American situation was a grim one. Gates could rally only 700 of the 3,000 men with whom he had originally set out—the rest had been killed, wounded, or taken prisoner.

Some Carolinians engaged in partisan warfare. Francis Marion, a planter, conducted a guerrilla campaign against isolated British outposts and supply depots. Marion, soon nicknamed "Swamp Fox" because he retreated into the swamps after each raid, kept alive the fires of the Revolution. The "Swamp Fox," with Thomas Sumter (1734–1832) and Andrew Pickens (1739–1817), kept Cornwallis off balance. The Americans also scored a victory over a Tory army at King's Mountain, South Carolina, on October 7, 1780.

But it was not until December that real hope came to the South—in the form of General Nathanael Greene, who had replaced Gates. Greene inspired the discouraged remnants of the American army. He sent out a call for "men who love their homes, wives, and children . . . and will fight to protect them." The men came to him. Lieutenant Colonel "Light Horse" Harry Lee (1756–1818) brought in 300 well-equipped troopers. Colonel William Washington (1752–1810) added another fine cavalry troop.

On January 17, 1781, American troops under the command of Brigadier General Daniel Morgan defeated the British in a cleverly fought battle at Cowpens, South Carolina. Then followed a series of engagements that overextended the guerrilla-plagued British. Greene and Morgan made a masterful retreat into Virginia, with Cornwallis always dogging them. After receiving some reinforcements, Greene doubled back into North Carolina. By now the British Army was exhausted from chasing the elusive Americans.

Cornwallis fought and won a bruising battle with Greene at Guilford Courthouse, North Carolina (March 15, 1781). Cornwallis then retired to Wilmington, North Carolina, to gather men and supplies hauled by the Royal Navy.

Meanwhile, with Cornwallis out of the scene, Rebel partisan activity in South Carolina broke out everywhere. Greene fought successive battles with the British until they were confined to the areas around Savannah and Charleston. The countryside in between teemed with partisans aiding Greene in the field. It was only a matter of time before the foe would have to give up both cities. Meanwhile events elsewhere were bringing matters to a climax.

Yorktown

Cornwallis marched into Yorktown, Virginia, and awaited his orders from Clinton. They never arrived. On September 5, 1781, a French fleet under an admiral, the Comte de Grasse (1722–88), defeated a Royal Navy squadron in Chesapeake Bay.

This French victory ended the last chance Cornwallis had to save his army, which was already penned in Yorktown by Franco-American troops. The Americans, led by Washington, and the French, under General Jean Baptiste de Rochambeau (1725–1807), had marched to Yorktown, where they surrounded Cornwallis. For the first time in the war, the British, not the Americans, were on short rations.

Cornwallis held out, even after he learned what had happened to the British Navy in Chesapeake Bay. Although the outcome was settled, he fought on. The Yankees took British positions at bayonet point, and the sea swarmed with French warships, which kept up a merciless bombardment.

On October 9 Washington and Rochambeau brought up heavy guns. A hundred mammoth cannon blasted the Redcoats for 8 days. Cornwallis finally asked for terms. Surrender negotiations lasted until October 19. On that morning the defeated British marched out of Yorktown. General Charles O'Hara, acting for Cornwallis, handed his sword over to General Benjamin Lincoln, and the surrender was complete. The British band played a tune called "The World Turned Upside Down."

In accordance with the capitulation agreement, the Redcoats stacked arms. Except for a few minor skirmishes in the South, the American Revolution was over.

When news of Cornwallis' surrender at Yorktown reached King George, he wanted the British to keep on fighting. But the British Government and the people were weary of the war. Lord North's Cabinet fell, and a new one was chosen to negotiate the peace.

▶ PEACE

Peace talks began in Paris in April, 1782. Congress ratified a preliminary treaty on April 19 of the following year. The final version of the treaty was signed in Paris on September 3, 1783. John Adams, Benjamin Franklin, John Jay, and Henry Laurens (1724–92) were the American representatives. David Hartley represented the British side. Richard Oswald had worked on the preliminary peace for the British. The treaty extended the westward boundary of the United States from the Allegheny Mountains to the Mississippi River, the northern boundary to the Great Lakes, and the southern boundary to the 31st parallel. The Americans were also guaranteed fishing rights in the northern waters off Newfoundland. The treaty also contained a provision that stated that Congress would "recommend" to the states that they return property seized from the Loyalists (Tories) during the war and also pay any debts owed to British subjects.

Results of the Revolution

The end of the Revolution brought complete independence to the 13 colonies, now the United States of America. The success of the American Revolution brought about the first break in the European colonial system and set in motion a chain of revolutions (beginning with revolutions in the Spanish colonies of South America) that has continued to this day. The firm establishment of republican government was finally secured in the United States in 1789 with the adoption of the Constitution, which replaced the Articles of Confederation as the basis of American government.

IRVING WERSTEIN
Author, *1776: The Adventure of the American Revolution*

▶ **JOHNNY TREMAIN**

Johnny Tremain is the teen-age hero in the historical novel of the same name by Esther Forbes (1894?–1967). *Johnny Tremain* is the story of Boston in revolt as seen through the eyes of a young Bostonian. The story takes place during the exciting year of the Boston Tea Party (1773) and ends after the battle of Lexington (1775).

Johnny Tremain and Rab worked for a newspaper, the *Boston Observer*. They were right in the thick of things when Paul Revere, Samuel and John Adams, John Hancock, James Otis, and other Boston patriots were plotting independence from Britain. The following passage tells what happened when they were chosen to dress up as Indians for the Boston Tea Party.

The day had started with rain and then there had been clouds, but as they reached Griffin's Wharf the moon, full and white, broke free of the clouds. The three ships, the silent hundreds gathering upon the wharf, all were dipped in the pure white light. The crowds were becoming thousands, and there was not one there but guessed what was to be done, and all approved.

Rab was grunting out of the side of his mouth to a thick-set, active-looking man, whom Johnny would have known anywhere, by his walk and the confident lift of his head, was Mr. Revere. 'Me Know You.'

'Me Know You,' Johnny repeated this countersign and took his place behind Mr. Revere. The other boys, held up by the crowd, began arriving, and more men and boys. But Johnny guessed that many who were now quietly joining one of those three groups were acting on the spur of the moment, seeing what was up. They had blacked their faces, seized axes, and come along. They were behaving as quietly and were as obedient to their leaders as those who had been so carefully picked for this work of destruction.

There was a boatswain's whistle, and in silence one group boarded the *Dartmouth*. The *Eleanor* and the *Beaver* had to be warped in to the wharf. Johnny was close to Mr. Revere's heels. He heard him calling for the captain, promising him, in the jargon everyone talked that night, that not one thing should be damaged on the ship except only the tea, but the captain and all his crew had best stay in the cabin until the work was over.

Captain Hall shrugged and did as he was told, leaving his cabin boy to hand over the keys to the hold. The boy was grinning with pleasure. The 'tea party' was not unexpected.

'I'll show you,' the boy volunteered, 'how to work them hoists. I'll fetch lanterns, mister.'

The winches rattled and the heavy chests began to appear—one hundred and fifty of them. As some men worked in the hold, others broke open the chests and flung the tea into the harbor. But one thing made them unexpected difficulty. The tea inside the chests was wrapped in heavy canvas. The axes went through the wood easily enough—the canvas made endless trouble. Johnny had never worked so hard in his life.

He had noticed a stout boy with a blackened face working near him. The boy looked familiar, but when he saw his white, fat hands, Johnny knew who he was and kept a sharp eye on him. It was Dove. He was not one of the original 'Indians,' but a volunteer. He had on an enormous pair of breeches tied at each knee with rope. Even as Johnny upended a chest and helped get the tea over the rail, he kept an eye on Dove. The boy was secretly scooping tea into his breeches. This theft would come to several hundred dollars in value, but more important it would ruin the high moral tone of the party. Johnny whispered to Rab, who put down the axe he had been wielding with such passion and grabbed Dove. It wasn't much of a scuffle. Soon Dove was whining and admitting that a little of the tea had happened to 'splash' into his breeches. Johnny got them off and kicked them and the many pounds of tea they held into the harbor.

'He swim good,' he grunted at Rab, for everyone was talking 'Indian' that night.

Rab picked up the fat Dove as though he were a rag baby and flung him into the harbor. The tea was thicker than any seaweed and its fragrance was everywhere.

Not a quarter of a mile away, quite visible in

the moonlight, rode the *Active* and the *Kingfisher*. Any moment the tea party might be interrupted by British marines. There was no landing party. Governor Hutchinson had been wise in not sending for their help.

The work on the *Dartmouth* and the *Eleanor* finished about the same time. The *Beaver* took longer, for she had not had time to unload the rest of her cargo, and great care was taken not to injure it. Just as Johnny was about to go over to see if he could help on the *Beaver*, Mr. Revere whispered to him. 'Go get brooms. Cleam um' deck.'

Johnny and a parcel of boys brushed the deck until it was clean as a parlor floor. Then Mr. Revere called the captain to come up and in-spect. The tea was utterly gone, but Captain Hall agreed that beyond that there had not been the slightest damage.

It was close upon dawn when the work on all three ships was done. And yet the great, silent audience on the wharf, men, women, and children, had not gone home. As the three groups came off the ships, they formed in fours along the wharf, their axes on their shoulders. Then a hurrah went up and a fife began to play. This was almost the first sound Johnny had heard since the tea party started—except only the crash of axes into sea chests, the squeak of hoists, and a few grunted orders.

See also DECLARATION OF INDEPENDENCE; articles on Revolutionary War leaders.

REYNOLDS, SIR JOSHUA (1723–1792)

One of England's great portrait painters, Joshua Reynolds was a well educated, deep-thinking man who considered carefully every stroke of his brush. His scholarship included not only art but history, literature, and philosophy as well.

The son of Samuel Reynolds, a schoolmaster, Joshua was born in the town of Plympton Erle, not far from the navy port of Plymouth. He began drawing at an early age, and when he was 17, he studied portrait painting. From 1743 until 1749 he worked alone in London and in Devon. Then he went to Italy to study the masters of that country. Copying and analyzing the works of these great painters and working out his own methods slowly and carefully, he became an expert artist.

In 1752 Reynolds moved back to London and won quick success as a portrait painter. He had remarkable talent for capturing the character of his models, who included such celebrated men as the writers Samuel Johnson and Laurence Sterne. He painted portraits of women and children too, with delicacy and taste.

As time passed, Reynolds became a friend of most of the important men of his day. In 1764 he founded a literary club, which often met at his house. Before he was 40, he became deaf, but he did not allow this handicap to discourage him. He continued to lead a full social life and was increasingly sought after as a portraitist.

Reynolds was always willing to try something new. He was constantly experimenting with methods and materials. Unfortunately some of the paints he used have not lasted well. For example, the foreground of *The Age of Innocence* has cracked. A visit to Holland and Flanders in 1781 affected his way of painting. He was especially influenced by the vigorous painter Rubens. Even though he was 58 and successful, he was willing to accept new influences and to change his own style.

Meanwhile, in 1768, the Royal Academy, an exhibiting society and school, had been founded in London. Reynolds was made its first president and received the honor of knighthood. Sir Joshua wrote a controversial series of essays on the principles of art for the students of the Royal Academy. These essays, called the *Discourses,* are still read and argued about today.

A good-natured, calm, and pleasant-mannered man, Sir Joshua was kind to young students. His powers of work were remarkable, and it is estimated that he painted over 2,000 portraits. Among the best are *Nelly O'Brien, Miss Bowles,* and *Mrs. Siddons as the Tragic Muse.*

HERBERT B. GRIMSDITCH
Former Executive Editor
Fleetway Publications (London)

RHEUMATIC FEVER. See DISEASES.
RHINE RIVER. See RIVERS.

A white rhinoceros nurses her baby. Young rhinoceroses are called calves.

RHINOCEROSES

Rhinoceroses have huge, heavy bodies and one or two large horns above their nostrils. They usually move about slowly, paying little attention to their surroundings. They do not hunt other animals for food but eat only grass and other plants. Though usually quiet and retiring, they may become very fierce if cornered. They can charge at speeds of about 50 kilometers (30 miles) an hour. Then their strong, pointed horns and large size make them powerful and dangerous.

The smallest rhinoceros, the Sumatran, usually weighs less than 1 metric ton. At the shoulder, it may measure somewhat more than 1 meter high. The largest rhinoceros, the African white rhinoceros, weighs about three times more than the Sumatran and is about twice as high at the shoulder.

The great body of the rhinoceros rests on four short legs. Each foot has three toes. Rhinoceroses are hoofed animals and are related to horses.

The horns of some kinds of rhinoceroses are often very long—as long as 1 meter or sometimes more. The animal may have one or two horns, depending on the kind of rhinoceros. The horns are made up of closely packed masses of tough hairs. The rest of the body is usually hairless except for patches of hair about the ears and at the tip of the tail. Because the tough, thick skin has no sweat glands, rhinoceroses must cool themselves in baths of water, mud, dust, or ash.

Rhinoceroses usually travel alone, but they are sometimes found in small family groups. A female bears only one young at a time. The calf is born about 18 months after mating and remains with the mother for several years.

There are five different kinds of rhinoceroses living today. Two of these—the black rhinoceros and the white rhinoceros—are found in Africa. Both African kinds have two horns.

The other three kinds live in Asia. Indian and Javan rhinoceroses have one horn. (Females of the Javan kind usually lack horns.) Deep folds divide the skin of these Asian rhinoceroses into great shieldlike sections. The Sumatran rhinoceros has two horns, and its skin is not so deeply folded. Its body has a thin covering of short hair.

Reviewed by ROBERT M. McCLUNG
Author, science books for children

See also HOOFED MAMMALS.

RHODE ISLAND

"For happily the government of the United States . . . gives to bigotry no sanction, to persecution no assistance. . . ." These words on tolerance come from a letter written by George Washington to a Jewish congregation in Newport. The date was 1790, shortly after Washington had visited the lovely white synagogue now known as Touro Synagogue.

The Touro Synagogue, built in 1763, is the oldest synagogue building in the United States. It has been called one of the most perfect works of colonial architecture. This historic house of worship was built by a congregation founded originally in 1658. Its members were mainly Spanish and Portuguese Jews who had fled intolerance. One of the interesting features of Touro Synagogue is a secret door and stairway, which lead from the speaker's platform to the basement. It was designed by men who had suffered a long history of terror and persecution. But Washington's words to the congregation proved to be true, and the secret door never was used. In 1946 the Touro Synagogue was designated as a national historic site.

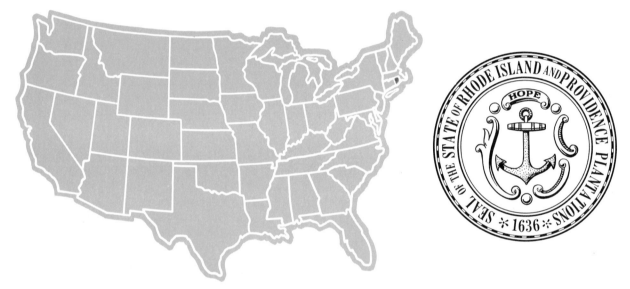

Rhode Island is the smallest of the 50 states. It has the shortest state motto ("Hope") and the longest official name (State of Rhode Island and Providence Plantations). It also has more people for every square mile of land area than any other state except New Jersey. But its single greatest distinction is the principle on which it was founded in 1636—religious freedom.

Independent spirit also has been an important part of Rhode Island's heritage. This spirit is memorialized by a statue, the *Independent Man,* atop the dome of the state capitol. It is dedicated to the spirit that made Rhode Island one of the first of the 13 colonies to declare its independence.

Roger Williams, founder of Rhode Island, displayed this spirit of independence. He came to the Massachusetts Bay Colony from England in 1631. Soon he found himself in trouble with the authorities of that colony because of his views on religious worship. He fled from Massachusetts and went to what is now Providence. There he established a settlement, from which Rhode Island traces its beginnings.

Rhode Island's nickname, Little Rhody, refers to the small size of the state. Delaware, which ranks 49th in size, is nearly twice as large as Rhode Island. It would be possible to fit 483 Rhode Islands into Alaska, the largest state. In spite of its small size, Rhode Island long has been an important industrial state. Its many industries turn out a variety of products, from silverware, jewelry, and fine lace to heavy machinery.

In agriculture Rhode Island is famous for a breed of poultry, the Rhode Island Red, which traces its beginnings to a farm in Little Compton in the 1850's. Another, quite different product that came into being in Rhode Island is the Quonset hut, which was first built at a Quonset Point naval air station in 1941. Quonset huts were used by United States armed forces in all theaters of war during World War II. As a result "Quonset" is now a familiar word in many of the languages of the world.

Rhode Island calls itself the nation's first vacationland. As early as the 1700's wealthy planters from the South and from the West Indies began to come to Rhode Island to spend the summer at Newport. Since that time Rhode Island's shore resorts, historic sites, and woodlands have attracted an ever-increasing number of visitors.

▶ THE LAND

Rhode Island is one of the New England States. It is located in the southeastern part of New England, between Massachusetts and Connecticut. Block Island Sound and the Atlantic Ocean form the southern boundary of the state.

STATE FLAG.

STATE TREE: Red maple.

STATE FLOWER: Violet.

STATE BIRD: Rhode Island Red.

RHODE ISLAND

CAPITAL: Providence.

STATEHOOD: May 29, 1790; the 13th state.

SIZE: 3,140 km² (1,212 sq mi); rank, 50th.

POPULATION: 947,154 (1980 census); rank, 40th.

OFFICIAL NAME: State of Rhode Island and Providence Plantations.

ORIGIN OF NAME: The early settlements were referred to as plantations. The earliest one—Providence, founded in 1636—was named by its founder Roger Williams "in commemoration of God's merciful providence." In 1644 the settlements of Providence, Warwick, Portsmouth, and Newport were incorporated under the name Providence Plantations. In that same year Aquidneck Island, the largest island in Narragansett Bay, was officially renamed Rhode Island, possibly after the Isle of Rhodes in the Aegean Sea. In 1633 the names Rhode Island and Providence Plantations were combined.

ABBREVIATIONS: R.I.; RI.

NICKNAME: Little Rhody.

STATE SONG: "Rhode Island," by T. Clarke Brown.

STATE MOTTO: "Hope."

STATE SEAL: The seal is an anchor, with the state motto above it. The name of the state and the date of its founding, 1636, appear in the outer border.

STATE FLAG: The flag is white, sometimes edged with a yellow fringe. In the center is a gold anchor, with the state motto inscribed on a blue banner beneath it. Thirteen gold stars representing the original colonies surround the anchor and motto.

Landforms

The work of the great ice sheet that once covered Rhode Island is very much in evidence today. This mass of ice left rolling hills in the western part of the state and long, narrow ridges in the south. It also created waterfalls and changed the courses of rivers and streams.

Rhode Island lies within two major natural regions of the northeastern United States. The higher western part of the state belongs to the New England Upland. The lower eastern section is part of the Seaboard Lowland.

The Seaboard Lowland is occupied mainly by Narragansett Bay. Once this lowland stood above sea level, and sand and gravel were washed into it from nearby mountains. Later the area sank, and the sea came up onto the land to form the bay. Today the higher parts stand out as islands in the bay. The largest are Rhode Island (Aquidneck Island), Conanicut Island, and Prudence Island. The land portion of the Seaboard Lowland is generally flat. It lies close to sea level except in the east, near Massachusetts, where the land is higher and gently rolling.

The New England Upland covers nearly two thirds of the state. It begins just to the west of Providence. There the elevation is about 200 feet above sea level. The land continues to rise toward the west, where it reaches its highest point (812 feet) at Jerimoth Hill near the Connecticut border. A long, low ridge extends across southern Rhode Island from Westerly to Wakefield. This ridge, called a moraine, was formed at the edge of the ice sheet. It changed the river drainage and created some marshes and swamps. There is evidence of another such moraine on Block Island, an island about 10 miles offshore, between Block Island Sound and the Atlantic Ocean. The southern coast of Rhode Island is lined with sandy beaches and peninsulas. Behind these are shallow saltwater ponds, marshes, and swamps.

Rivers, Lakes, and Coastal Waters

Rhode Island's most important body of water is Narragansett Bay, an arm of the Atlantic Ocean that extends inland a distance of 30 miles and almost divides the state in two. The bay varies in width from 3 to 12 miles.

The largest river in the state is the Blackstone, which rises in Massachusetts. It flows south through Rhode Island to empty into the Seekonk River, then into the Providence River, and finally into Narragansett Bay. The Providence River is an estuary, or an arm of the bay, about 8 miles long. The northern part of this river is the harbor of Providence. Rivers that empty into the bay south of Providence include the Pawtuxet and the Potowomut. The Pawcatuck River forms the extreme southwestern border of the state. It flows into Block Island Sound.

The largest inland body of water is Scituate Reservoir and its several tributary reservoirs. This reservoir system provides water for the city of Providence. Throughout central and northern Rhode Island there are many other smaller reservoirs, or man-made lakes. The natural lakes usually are called ponds. The largest of these—which include Worden Pond, Watchaug Pond, and Stafford Pond—are in the southern half of the state.

Rhode Island has 40 miles of general coastline on the Atlantic Ocean. The tidal shoreline, including the shoreline of sounds and bays, is 384 miles long.

Climate

The climate of Rhode Island is characterized by changeable weather, with warm summers, mild winters, and relatively even amounts of precipitation throughout the

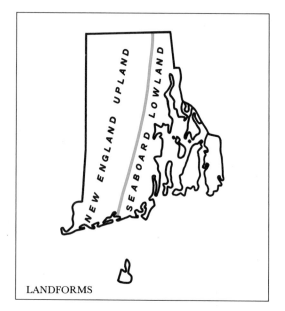

LANDFORMS

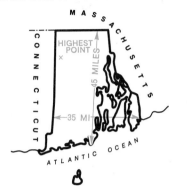
year. July temperatures average about 72 degrees Fahrenheit, and January and February temperatures about 30 degrees.

Nearness to the bay and the ocean and the relatively large coastal area have a great influence on Rhode Island's climate. These conditions tend to moderate the temperatures in winter and often to bring rain instead of snow. The total amount of precipitation averages somewhat over 40 inches a year throughout the state. The average snowfall is 40 to 55 inches a year in the western part of the state and about 20 inches in the southeast. Usually snow does not cover the ground for long periods.

From time to time severe tropical storms have caused much hardship and damage to the state. The hurricane of 1938 killed more than 250 persons and caused damage estimated at $100,000,000. Other hurricanes causing great damage occurred in 1944, 1954, 1955, and 1960. Recently the Army Corps of Engineers has built the Fox Point Hurricane Barrier Dam on the Providence River. This dam will be closed during hurricanes to protect downtown Providence from flooding.

Natural Resources

Rhode Island's greatest natural resources are water and the marine life in the water. Other resources include woodlands, soils, and minerals.

Water. The numerous waterfalls in the rivers provided power for Rhode Island's first industries. Dams on these rivers provide hydroelectric power for the factories and homes of today. In the 19th century the waters of Narragansett Bay made the city of Providence an important seaport for commercial fishing and whaling vessels. Today the waters of the bay and the ocean draw tourists from all over the United States to enjoy fishing, swimming, surfing, and boating.

Marine Life. Rhode Island's waters contain more than 200 species of fish and shellfish. Among the most abundant fish near shore are flounder, porgy, striped bass, and mackerel. The deeper waters offshore provide swordfish, tuna, bluefish, menhaden, and cod. Shellfish are especially important. The most abundant is the quahog, which is called clam in the South and hard clam, or cherrystone, in the Middle Atlantic States. Other shellfish are crabs and lobsters.

Vegetation. About two thirds of Rhode Island's land area is woodland. The trees are little used for lumbering, although some sawtimber and pulpwood are produced. Much of the woodland is included in state forests, which are carefully managed for conservation of trees, wildlife, soil, and water. The forests are especially important also as places for recreation.

Soils and Minerals. The soils throughout the state are not particularly rich. The best soils are around Narragansett Bay, especially in the north.

In early times Rhode Island became known for three mineral resources. One was a very strong granite called Westerly granite because it came from the vicinity of Westerly. Another was coal, mined in the area around Narragansett Bay. This coal was so hard that it did not burn well. The other mineral resource was iron ore from Iron Mine Hill in the northeastern corner of the state and bog iron from the Cranston area. These deposits supported busy ironworks in the 1700's. But higher-grade ores were available in other parts of the country by the early 1800's, and it was no longer profitable to mine ore in Rhode Island. Today the most important mineral resources are sand and gravel and various crushed stones, such as limestone and granite. These are used for construction purposes.

▶ **THE PEOPLE AND THEIR WORK**

The earliest settlers of Rhode Island came from neighboring colonies or directly from Europe, chiefly from the British Isles. In 1774 the population of Rhode Island was about 60,000. Newport was one of the largest cities in the colonies. The Revolutionary War was a time of heavy losses of population, and by 1782 Rhode Island had fewer people than in 1774. But the first federal census, which was taken in 1790, showed a population of almost 69,000. After that, the population increased steadily until 1980, when the census showed a slight decline.

The first large wave of migration came in the period 1840–50. At this time Rhode Island's industries were growing rapidly, and there were many opportunities for jobs. This also was the time of a famine in Ireland, and large numbers of Irish emigrated to the United States. People came from other European countries as well. But the Irish made up the largest single group. A second wave of newcomers in the late 1800's was made up chiefly of Canadians, especially French-Canadians. Italians made up the largest group in the third wave of migration, which took place up to 1920. Today the people represent many different ancestries. Members of a special group, the Narragansett Indians, trace their ancestry to the native peoples of the area.

Where the People Live

Rhode Island has an average of about 350 people for every square kilometer (nearly 900 for every square mile). But the population is unevenly distributed. More than four fifths of the people live in the Providence-Warwick-Pawtucket area.

Industries and Products

Up to the year 1700 agriculture was the main occupation in Rhode Island. For the next 100 years—up to 1800—agriculture was still important, but commerce grew rapidly, and the sea took on special significance. Fishing, shipbuilding, whaling, and commerce became increasingly important during the 1800's. The first factory was established in 1790, and manufacturing began to grow as the numerous waterfalls were harnessed to provide power.

Today dams in the rivers provide hydroelectric power, and the rivers and streams provide fresh water for home use and industrial purposes. But just as important are the salt waters of Narragansett Bay and the Atlantic Ocean. These waters make Rhode Island a major vacationland, and vacation services are a major industry in the state.

Manufacturing. Rhode Island is one of the most highly industrialized states in the nation. About one third of all its workers are engaged in manufacturing. The textile industry once employed the largest numbers of workers. This industry began in Pawtucket in 1790, when a young Englishman, Samuel Slater, built the first successful waterpower textile machinery in America. A larger mill was needed, and in 1793 another one was built.

POPULATION

TOTAL: 947,154 (1980 census). **Density**—346.7 persons to each square kilometer (897.8 persons to each square mile).

CHANGE SINCE 1790

Year	Population	Year	Population
1790	68,825	1910	542,610
1830	97,199	1960	859,488
1850	147,545	1970	949,723
1880	276,531	1980	947,154

Loss Between 1970 and 1980—0.3 percent.

CITIES: Population of Rhode Island's largest incorporated places (cities) according to the 1980 census.

Providence	156,804	East Providence	50,980
Warwick	87,123	Woonsocket	45,914
Cranston	71,992	Newport	29,259
Pawtucket	71,204	Central Falls	16,995

This one, known as the Old Slater Mill, still stands in Pawtucket. It is a museum, with exhibits of early industrial machines and tools.

Employment in the textile industry reached a peak of 75,000 in 1919. Today only a fraction of that number work in textile plants. The movement of the textile mills out of Rhode Island began in the 1920's, and it has continued to the present. Most of the departing mills move to the South, drawn there by lower wages, newer markets, and nearness to raw materials. But the textile industry is still one of the major industries in the state. Rhode Island produces about half of the nation's lace. Fabrics, both natural and synthetic, are other important textile products.

Today the metal trades—primary and fabricated metals, machinery, and electrical equipment—employ the greatest number of workers in Rhode Island. The metal industry was started by the demand for machinery to be used in the textile mills. One of the most important early inventors and manufacturers was Joseph R. Brown, who was born in Warren. He designed precision instruments (calipers and protractors) of extreme accuracy and invented precision gear cutters and other machine tools. The Brown and Sharpe Manufacturing Company, established in the late 1860's, became one of the nation's major machine-tool plants. Machine tools are machines that are used to make other machines or machinery. Products of the metal trades in Rhode Island today include wire and cable, precision instruments, electrical machinery, electronics equipment, and transportation equipment, especially boats. The building of ships and boats began in Rhode Island before 1650. Today this industry produces a variety of commercial vessels—tugs, cargo carriers, and fishing vessels—as well as yachts and other pleasure boats.

Jewelry and silverware make up a third major group of manufactured products. The jewelry industry was started in Providence in 1794 by Nehemiah Dodge, a goldsmith and watch repairer. He perfected a process for gold-plating base metals and made jewelry to be sold at popular prices. Today the jewelry industry is centered in the Providence-Attleboro (Massachusetts) area, where a large part of the costume jewelry of the United States is made. The silverware industry was founded by Jabez Gorham, an apprentice of Dodge's.

Another major industry of Rhode Island is the making of rubber and plastic goods. Rubber products include footwear and rubber-coated yarns. Plastics are used in a variety of products, including pleasure boats. Other kinds of manufactured goods include processed foods, clothing, and industrial chemicals.

Agriculture. The climate and the soils over much of the state are well suited to production of hay and pasture, and dairying is a leading agricultural activity. Poultry raising, like the keeping of dairy cows, has been important for many years. The Rhode Island Red, a world-famous breed of poultry, is noted both for eggs and for meat. In the Narragansett Bay area there are many truck farms and greenhouses and nurseries. Potatoes have long been the main commercial crop, but the truck farms grow a variety of vegetables for city markets. The greenhouses and nurseries produce flowers, plants, and shrubs. Fruits, especially apples, are grown in central Rhode Island.

Fisheries. The value of fish and shellfish caught commercially each year is usually more than $35,000,000. Because the price of fish has gone up in recent years, the value of the state's commercial catch has increased greatly. More than half the total catch is inedible fish, chiefly menhaden, which is used to make fish oil and fish meal. The chief edible fish are scup, whiting, butterfish, flounder, and fluke. Quahog, or hard clam, is by far the most important shellfish.

WHAT RHODE ISLAND PRODUCES

MANUFACTURED GOODS: Fabricated metal products, jewelry and silverware, primary metals, textile mill products, nonelectrical machinery, electric and electronic equipment, rubber and plastic products, products of printing and publishing, instruments and related products.

AGRICULTURAL PRODUCTS: Greenhouse and nursery products, milk, potatoes, poultry and eggs, miscellaneous vegetables, hogs, cattle and calves, apples.

MINERALS: Sand and gravel, stone.

Transportation and Communication

In Rhode Island's early days, water provided the most important means of transportation. Providence and Newport sent goods by sea to the West Indies, South America, Africa, and China. Foreign commerce through Rhode Island ports declined rapidly after the 1830's, when improvement of inland transportation made it easier for goods to be shipped from Boston, New York, and Philadelphia. But Providence, the major seaport of Rhode Island, has continued to be an important port. Most of its trade is coastal traffic, chiefly tankers carrying fuel oils and gasoline. Other important cargoes are coal, lumber, chemicals, and cement.

Land transportation was little used in the early days because the bay area and the numerous rivers made overland travel difficult. After industries began to develop in 1790, roads had to be built or improved to carry materials to the factories. Turnpikes were the most important land routes until 1835, when a railroad line was completed from Boston to Providence. During the rest of the 1800's the railroad was king. But when the automobile came into use in the early 1900's, the railroads began to feel the competition. The number of tracks and trains declined until at present only one major railroad and several short feeder lines are operating. An extensive system of roads and highways has been built, and trucks and buses have taken over much of the passenger and freight business.

The state operates several airports. The largest and most important is the Theodore Francis Green Airport, located at Warwick, just south of Providence. It is named for Theodore Francis Green, governor of Rhode Island from 1933 to 1937 and United States senator from 1937 to 1960.

The first newspaper in Rhode Island, the *Rhode Island Gazette,* was published at Newport in 1732 by James Franklin, brother of the famous Benjamin Franklin. It existed less than a year. In 1758 James Franklin's son, also named James, established the Newport *Mercury.* This paper still appears weekly. At present there are approximately 20 newspapers in Rhode Island, about a third of which are dailies. The largest dailies are the *Journal* and the *Bulletin,* both published in Providence.

The first radio station in Rhode Island was established in Providence in 1922. Today there are more than 20 AM and FM stations in the state and four television stations.

▶ EDUCATION

In colonial times children learned to read and write in dame schools (private elementary schools taught by women) or in other private schools. Wealthy families often hired tutors for their children. In 1640, the town of Newport attempted to establish a public school but did not succeed.

Schools and Colleges

The first statewide public school law was passed in 1800. It provided for a school in each town to be supported by local funds. This law was repealed in 1803, but Providence continued to build a public school system. New school laws, passed in 1828, provided for state funds to be distributed to local schools. After that time the number of schools increased throughout the state.

Higher education started in Rhode Island in 1764 with the establishment of Rhode Island College in Warren. In 1770 the college was moved to Providence, and in 1804 it was renamed Brown University in honor of Nicholas Brown, a chief benefactor. Brown is the seventh oldest college in the United States. Its women's college, Pembroke College, was merged with its undergraduate college for men in 1971. Other private colleges in Rhode Island include Barrington College in Barrington, Roger Williams College in Bristol (with a branch in Providence), Salve Regina College in Newport, and Providence College, Rhode Island School of Design, and Johnson and Wales College, all in Providence.

The University of Rhode Island in Kingston was chartered as Rhode Island College of Agriculture and Mechanic Arts in 1892. The name was changed to Rhode Island State College in 1909 and to the University of Rhode Island in 1951. The other state college is Rhode Island College in Providence. A system of state-supported junior colleges was authorized in 1960. The first one opened in Providence and later moved to Warwick.

The Naval War College, founded at Newport in 1884, offers advanced training to officers of the United States armed services.

Libraries and Museums

Rhode Island has more than 70 free public libraries that receive state aid. The largest is the Providence Public Library, which was established in 1878. Among the notable collections in this library are books and documents on the Civil War and slavery and on Irish culture.

The earliest libraries in Rhode Island were private, for the use of members only. The first of these was the Redwood Library in Newport, built in 1748–50. It was designed by the colonial architect Peter Harrison, who also designed the Touro Synagogue. Another well-known private library, the Providence Athenaeum in Providence, was founded in 1753 by the merger of older library companies. Both of these libraries are still in use.

Numerous other libraries are maintained by historical societies, colleges, and universities. The John Hay Library at Brown University has one of the largest Lincoln collections in existence. This library is a memorial to the distinguished statesman John Hay, a graduate of the university, who served as private secretary to President Lincoln, 1860–65. Later, he became United States secretary of state under presidents William McKinley and Theodore Roosevelt. The Rhode Island Historical Society in Providence and the Newport Historical Society in Newport have extensive library collections as well as exhibits of art and historical objects.

The Museum of Art of the Rhode Island

University Hall, the original structure housing Brown University after it was moved to Providence in 1770.

School of Design in Providence is the largest art museum in the state. It contains many collections of American, European, Oriental, and primitive art, as well as galleries for special exhibits of prints and drawings. The Roger Williams Park Museum and Planetarium in Providence includes a museum of natural history as well as a planetarium. It also maintains the Betsey Williams Cottage, a colo-

Rhode Island Reds at feeding time on a chicken farm.

Commercial fishing in Narragansett Bay.

The lighthouse on Mohegan Bluffs, cliffs on the southern shore of Block Island overlooking the Atlantic Ocean.

nial house built in 1773 and last occupied by Betsey Williams, a descendant of Roger Williams.

The South County Museum near Wickford exhibits early Rhode Island tools and vehicles, housed in a large barn. The Haffenreffer Museum of Anthropology near Bristol has American Indian, Eskimo and Arctic, and other collections. The many other special museums include the Old Slater Mill Museum in Pawtucket, the National Lawn Tennis Hall of Fame and Tennis Museum in Newport, and the Varnum Military and Naval Museum in East Greenwich.

▶ **PLACES OF INTEREST**

Rhode Island long has been known for its many resorts and recreation areas along Narragansett Bay and the Atlantic Ocean. More recently the woodland areas of the state have been developed for camping and freshwater sports. Rhode Island also is interesting for its many historic places—homes, houses of worship, and other buildings and sites—which exist side by side with the most modern accommodations for visitors.

State Areas

The state maintains numerous parks, forests (called management areas), and beaches as well as several historic buildings.

Arcadia State Park near Arcadia consists of 19 hectares, or 48 acres, with facilities for picnicking, swimming, hiking, and fishing. It is part of the Arcadia State Management Area. Other parks in this area are **Beach Pond State Park** and **Dawley Memorial State Park**.

Block Island State Beach covers about 8 ha,

or 20 acres, on eastern Block Island. It is popular for surf fishing and swimming.

Burlingame State Park, surrounding Watchaug Pond, includes more than 800 ha, or 2,000 acres, of woodland, with campsites and other recreational facilities.

Casimir Pulaski Memorial State Park is located in the Pulaski Memorial Management Area in the northwestern corner of the state. The park provides for water sports in summer and skating in winter.

Diamond Hill State Park in the northeastern corner of the state is popular for skiing, tobogganing, and other winter sports.

Lincoln Woods State Park, north of Providence, includes more than 240 ha, or 600 acres, of beautiful woodland and rock formations. The park surrounds Olney Pond.

Misquamicut State Beach is located on Block Island Sound near the western border of the state. Other state beaches, all at or near the eastern end of the sound, are **East Matunuck State Beach**, **Sand Hill Cove State Beach**, and **Scarborough State Beach**.

Kent County Courthouse in East Greenwich was built in 1750. Until 1854 the building was used as one of Rhode Island's five statehouses (one in each of the five counties). A constitutional convention met there to prepare the state constitution of 1842. The **Bristol County Courthouse** in Bristol and the old **Washington County Courthouse** in Kingston also were once used as statehouses from time to time. The other old statehouses, in Providence and Newport, were the principal capitol buildings from 1854 until 1900.

Old State House in Newport, also known as Old Colony House, was built in 1739. During the Revolutionary War, General George Washington met in this building with the French general Comte de Rochambeau to plan the strategy that led to victory for the colonies. The first Roman Catholic masses in Rhode Island were held there by French army chaplains.

Old State House in Providence was built in 1762. In this building the colony of Rhode Island declared its independence from England on May 4, 1776—2 months before the Declaration of Independence.

Other Places

The following are among other places that attract many visitors each year.

Block Island is a picturesque summer resort with some year-round residents. The island was named for the Dutch explorer Adriaen Block, who visited it in 1614.

INDEX TO RHODE ISLAND

Anthony (Kent) B3
Aquidneck Island (Washington) ...C3
Arcadia (Washington) ...B3
Barrington (Bristol) ...C3
Beach Pond ...A3
Block Island (Washington) ...B5
Bristol • (Bristol) ...C3
Central Falls (Providence) ...C2
Charlestown (Washington) ...B4
Conanicut Island ...C3
Coventry (Kent) ...B3
Cranston (Providence) ...C2
Diamond Hill ...C2
East Greenwich • (Kent) ...C3
East Providence (Providence) ...C2
Foster (Providence) ...B2
Galilee (Washington) ...B4
Gaspee Point ...C3
Grants Mills (Providence) ...C1
Great Swamp ...B4
Jamestown (Newport) ...C4
Jerimoth Hill ...A2
Keech Pond ...B2
Kingston (Washington) ...B4
Lafayette (Washington) ...C3
Limerock (Providence) ...C2
Lincoln (Providence) ...C2
Little Compton (Newport) ...D3
Lonsdale (Providence) ...C2
Middletown (Newport) ...C3
Narragansett (Washington) ...C4
Newport • (Newport) ...C4
Ninigret Pond ...B4
North Providence (Providence) ...C2

Pascoag (Providence) B2
Pascoag Reservoir (Providence) ...B2
Pawtucket (Providence) ...C2
Peace Dale (Washington) ...C4
Point Judith (Washington) ...C4
Point Judith Pond ...B4
Ponaganset Reservoir (Providence) ...B2
Portsmouth (Newport) ...D3
Providence ★ (Providence) ...C2
Prudence Island (Providence) ...C3
Quonset Point (Washington) ...C3
Sakonnet Point (Washington) ...D4
Saunderstown (Washington) ...C3
Saylesville (Providence) ...C2
Scituate Reservoir (Providence) ...B2
Smith and Sayles Reservoir (Providence) ...B2
Smithfield (Providence) ...B2
South Kingstown (Washington) ...B4
Stafford Pond (Newport) ...D3
Tiverton (Newport) ...D3
Wakefield (Washington) ...C4
Warren (Bristol) ...C3
Warwick (Kent) ...C3
Watchaug Pond (Washington) ...B4
Westerly (Washington) ...A4
West Glocester (Providence) ...B2
West Kingston (Washington) ...B4
West Warwick (Kent) ...B3
Wickford (Washington) ...C3
Woonsocket (Providence) ...C3
Worden Pond (Providence) ...B4

• County Seat   Counties in parentheses
★ State Capital

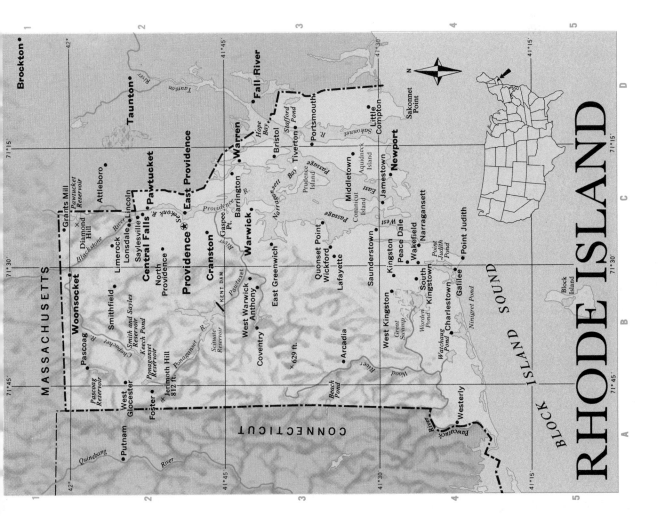

RHODE ISLAND

MASSACHUSETTS

CONNECTICUT

BLOCK ISLAND SOUND

Brockton •
Taunton •
Taunton River
Fall River •
Warren •
East Providence •
Pawtucket •
Grants Mill •
Pawtucket Reservoir
Attleboro •
Lincoln
Diamond Hill ×
Blackstone River
Limerock •
Lonsdale •
Saylesville •
Central Falls •
North Providence •
Providence ★
Cranston •
Hope Bay
Bristol •
Barrington •
Gaspee Pt.
Providence River
Seekonk R.
Narragansett Bay
Portsmouth •
Tiverton •
Stafford Pond
Little Compton •
Sakonnet Point
Sakonnet R.
Middletown
Aquidneck Island
Newport •
Jamestown •
Prudence Island
Conanicut Island
East Passage
West Passage
Quonset Point •
Wickford •
Lafayette •
Saunderstown •
Kingston •
Peace Dale •
Wakefield •
South Kingstown •
Narragansett
Point Judith Pond
Galilee •
Point Judith
Block Island
Woonsocket •
Pascoag •
Smithfield •
Smith and Sayles Reservoir
Keech Pond
Chepachet R.
Ponaganset Reservoir
West Glocester •
Foster •
Jerimoth Hill 812 ft. ×
Pascoag Reservoir
Putnam •
Quinebang River
Scituate Reservoir
Ponaganset R.
Pawtuxet River
KENT DAM
West Warwick •
Anthony •
Coventry •
× 629 ft.
Arcadia •
Wood River
Beach Pond
East Greenwich •
Warwick •
Great Swamp
Worden Pond
West Kingston •
Watchaug Pond
Charlestown •
Ninigret Pond
Westerly •
Pawcatuck River

N

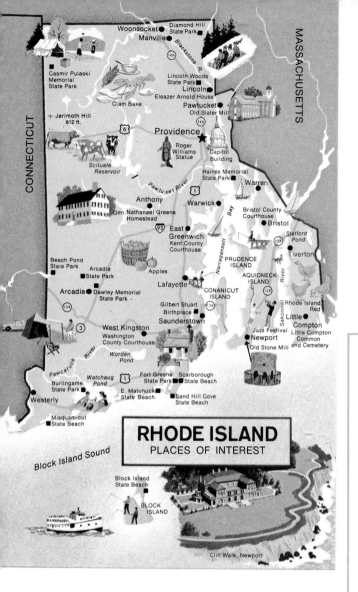

RHODE ISLAND
PLACES OF INTEREST

Cliff Walk, Newport

nomination in North America. It was designed by Joseph Brown, one of the four Brown brothers of Providence, and was dedicated in 1775. Recently the building has been beautifully restored through a gift of a well-known Brown alumnus, John D. Rockefeller, Jr.

Little Compton Common and Cemetery in Little Compton is typical of early New England villages. The cemetery contains the burial place of Elizabeth Pabody, daughter of John and Priscilla Alden and first non-Indian child born in New England.

Old Stone Mill in Touro Park, Newport, is an old gristmill believed to have been owned by Benedict Arnold, great-grandfather of the Revolutionary War traitor. Arnold served as the first governor of Rhode Island under the charter of 1663. The actual origin of the mill is unknown.

What was the "Black Regiment"?

The 1st Rhode Island Regiment was organized in 1778, during the Revolutionary War. It was known also as the "Black Regiment," because it was made up of black soldiers. The members fought valiantly in the battle of Rhode Island, which took place on August 29, 1778, at Portsmouth, north of Newport. And they served with distinction in the Yorktown campaign of 1781.

In memory of those brave soldiers, the 1st Rhode Island Regiment was reorganized in 1976 as a state Bicentennial project. The new 1st Rhode Island Regiment is a fife and drum corps, dressed in colonial uniform. It is made up of black youths, aged 13 to 18, from all over Rhode Island. The organizers think of the regiment as more than a parade unit. It was formed to help young people from the black community learn about their heritage and about the contributions that black people have made to Rhode Island and to the nation.

▶CITIES

Seven of the eight cities in Rhode Island are located in the Narragansett Bay area. The other, Woonsocket, is located on the northern border of the state.

Providence

Providence is the capital of Rhode Island and one of the largest cities in New England. It was settled on a site chosen in 1636 by Roger Williams. Providence became the sole capital of Rhode Island in 1900, and in 1901 the General Assembly began to meet there in

Cliff Walk in Newport is an impressive 3-mile walk along the shores of the Atlantic. On one side are the steep, rocky cliffs that face the ocean. On the other are some of the largest and most beautiful homes in the United States, including **The Breakers** and **The Elms**. The Breakers is considered the most magnificent of all. It was built in 1895 for the New York railroad magnate Cornelius Vanderbilt. The Elms was built in 1901 for Edward J. Berwind, a Philadelphia coal magnate.

Eleazer Arnold House in Lincoln is one of the best-preserved "stone-ender" buildings in the state. An enormous stone chimney forms one entire end of the structure. It was built in 1687 and was used as a tavern as well as a place where Arnold held court with the Indians.

The First Baptist Meeting House in Providence is the mother church of the Baptist de-

The state capitol in Providence, with the statue *Independent Man* atop the dome.

the new capitol building. The capitol is an impressive structure of white marble. It contains many prized works of art and historical objects, including the original parchment charter granted by King Charles II on July 8, 1663.

For many years Providence was mainly a seaport town. It is still an important port for coastal traffic. But today it is chiefly a financial, business, and manufacturing center with a variety of industries. The city lost population during the 1970's, while suburban areas and coastal towns grew.

Providence is a cultural and educational center, with important museums, libraries, and art galleries and most of the state's institutions of higher education. The city is also well known for its many historical sites, including houses of worship, public buildings, and homes.

Pawtucket

Pawtucket, one of Rhode Island's largest cities, lies immediately north and east of Providence. It is located at falls of the Blackstone River. Below the falls the river is known as the Seekonk River. The Pawtucket area was granted to Roger Williams by the Narragansett Indians in 1638. But the area remained a part of Massachusetts until 1862, when it was added to Rhode Island.

Pawtucket is an important manufacturing center. It has been called the cradle of the cotton-manufacturing industry in the United States because the first successful water-powered cotton-manufacturing machinery in the nation was built there in 1790.

Newport

Newport is located on the island in Narragansett Bay known both as Aquidneck Island and as the island of Rhode Island. William Coddington and others from the Massachusetts colony settled Newport in 1639. In the 1650's and later, Newport attracted many Quakers, Jews, and other groups who sought refuge from persecution.

Newport's early prosperity was based on shipbuilding and trade by sea. After the Revolutionary War, Newport began to attract wealthy tourists, and it has continued to be a major resort area. It reached its peak and became known as the Queen of the Resorts in the late 1800's, when many elegant residences were built.

Other Cities

Warwick, one of the four original settlements, is located on the western side of Narragansett Bay, south of Providence. It has experienced the greatest growth since World War II of any Rhode Island city or town and,

COUNTIES

as a result, in 1970 became the second largest city in the state. It is primarily a residential area, but new and growing industries have located there, and Rhode Island's two largest shopping malls have been built there. Cranston joins Providence in the southeast. It is a residential suburb with various manufacturing establishments. Originally it was a part of Providence. In pre-Revolutionary War days Cranston was known for its beds of bog iron ore. East Providence is located across the Seekonk River from Providence. Roger Williams first came to what is now East Providence. Today the city is a residential center with some manufacturing. Woonsocket, the only city outside the Providence area, was an early textile-manufacturing center. It attracted many French-Canadians and today the people are largely of French-Canadian descent.

▶ GOVERNMENT

Rhode Island is governed by its second constitution, which was adopted in 1842. The first was the royal charter of 1663.

The governor is the chief executive officer. Other elected officers are the lieutenant governor, secretary of state, attorney general, and treasurer.

The state legislature is called the General Assembly. This lawmaking body is made up of the Senate and the House of Representatives. It holds annual sessions.

The highest court is the state Supreme Court. Others are the superior court and the district, family, and probate courts.

Rhode Island is divided into five counties. But the counties are geographical divisions rather than political units for the purpose of local government. In Rhode Island, as elsewhere in New England, the entire state is divided into units called towns, which include every woodland and farm. Many places in a town have their own post offices, stores, and industries, but they do not have their own local governments. They share in the town government. There are 31 towns in Rhode Island. In addition, there are eight large centers of population known as cities. Each city, like each town, has its own local government.

▶ FAMOUS PEOPLE

Rhode Island has produced many leaders in government and military affairs, industry, and the arts. All but two of the following were born in the state.

Roger Williams, founder of Rhode Island, was born in London, England. He arrived in the Massachusetts Bay colony in 1631 and remained there until he was banished in 1635 because of his independent views. A biography of Roger Williams is included in Volume W.

Stephen Hopkins (1707–85), born in Providence, served 10 terms as governor of Rhode Island, beginning in 1755. He was also one of Rhode Island's signers of the Declaration of Independence. His signature on that document is visibly shaky. According to tradition, he remarked that his hand trembled but that his heart did not. His home, known as the Stephen Hopkins House, is one of the important places of interest in present-day Providence. It is owned by the state.

Moses Brown (1738–1836) was the youngest of four distinguished brothers, all born in Providence. He is remembered as a manufacturer, a leader of the movement to abolish slavery in Rhode Island, and a generous benefactor of educational institutions, including Brown University. **Nicholas Brown** (1729–91), eldest of the brothers, was a merchant, a Revolutionary War patriot, and a principal benefactor of Brown University. **Joseph Brown** (1733–85) was a manufacturer known especially for his interest in physical science and in architecture. **John Brown** (1736–1803) is remembered as a patriot and as a merchant engaged in the East

India and China trade. His house, built in 1787, is considered a notable example of 18th-century architecture. It now houses the Rhode Island Historical Society.

Nathanael Greene (1742–86)—Revolutionary War general, second in command only to General Washington—was born in Potowomut, now Warwick. He is remembered especially for his campaigns in the Carolinas in 1781. The house that he built in Anthony, known today as the General Nathanael Greene Homestead, is preserved as a historic shrine.

Robert Gray (1755–1806), born in Tiverton, was a sea captain, fur trader, and explorer. On a voyage during the years 1787–90 he became the first person to carry the United States flag around the world. On a second trip around the world, 1790–93, he discovered Grays Harbor (an inlet of the Pacific Ocean in western Washington) and named the Columbia River after his ship, the *Columbia*. This discovery formed the basis of the United States claim to the Oregon country.

Gilbert Stuart (1755–1828), portrait painter, was born at his father's snuff mill near present-day Saunderstown. The building, known as the Gilbert Stuart Birthplace, is preserved as a historic shrine and museum. At the time of Stuart's birth the snuff factory occupied the lower floor of the building, and the family lived on the upper floors. While Stuart was still a child, the family moved to Newport. Stuart studied painting in London, England, under Benjamin West, the famous Pennsylvania-born painter of historical subjects. Gilbert Stuart painted portraits of many famous persons, but he is best known for his portraits of George Washington, three of which were painted from life.

Oliver Hazard Perry, naval officer, was born at Rocky Brook in the town of South Kingstown. He is remembered especially for a famous message, "We have met the enemy and they are ours," which he sent after the battle of Lake Erie during the War of 1812. His brother **Matthew C. Perry**, born in Newport and also a naval officer, commanded the expedition to Japan in 1852–54 that opened Japan to trade with the United States. Biographies of the Perry brothers are included in Volume P.

Ambrose Burnside (1824–81), a Union Army general, commanded the Army of the Potomac in the battle of Fredericksburg in 1862. Burnside, who was born in Indiana, came to Rhode Island in 1852 to manufacture a rifle of his own invention. After the Civil War he returned to Rhode Island, where he served three terms as governor, beginning in 1866. From 1874 to 1881 he represented Rhode Island in the United States Senate. Burnside wore a type of side-whiskers that have since been called burnsides (or sideburns).

George M. Cohan (1878–1942)—actor, playwright, producer, and writer of popular songs—is Rhode Island's best-known native son in entertainment and music. He was born in Providence. His song "Over There" is recognized as the best song of World War I. This song and the song "You're a Grand Old Flag" brought him a Congressional Medal for building and maintaining national morale. Cohan told the story of his life in his book *Twenty Years on Broadway and the Years It Took To Get There.*

▶**HISTORY**

When Roger Williams came to Rhode Island, the land was inhabited by several Indian tribes. The best-known were the Narragansett, who lived to the north and west of Narragansett Bay. Much of our knowledge of these Indians comes from a book written by Roger Williams, entitled *A Key into the Language of America.* It is a description of Indian life as well as a dictionary of Indian terms.

Exploration and Early Settlement

It is believed that Norsemen may have been in the Narragansett Bay area around the year 1000. But the first European known to have visited Rhode Island was Giovanni da Verrazano, who came to Narragansett Bay in 1524 and wrote a description of it. Adriaen Block, the Dutch explorer, sailed along the coast in 1614. After the coming of the Pilgrims in 1620, some of the English settlers moved into what is now northern Rhode Island, but this area remained a part of Massachusetts for some time.

From 1636 to 1642 four settlements were

Exterior view (*above*) and interior (*below*) of Touro Synagogue in Newport, the oldest synagogue building in the United States and a fine example of colonial religious architecture.

established—Providence and Warwick on the mainland and Portsmouth and Newport on Aquidneck Island in Narragansett Bay. Roger Williams insisted that all land should be purchased from the Indians, whom he considered the rightful owners. But the colonists of Massachusetts felt that the title to the land should come from the English king. To protect the title to their lands, the Rhode Island colonists chose Roger Williams to go to London to obtain a charter. He did so in 1644. In 1651 William Coddington, one of the founders of Portsmouth and Newport, obtained a parliamentary grant to all of Aquidneck and Conanicut islands, in direct violation of the 1644 charter. To prevent this grant from becoming effective, the colonists obtained another charter—this one from King Charles II in 1663.

Except for a few minor skirmishes, the

IMPORTANT DATES

1000   Norsemen may have been in the Rhode Island area.

1524   Giovanni da Verrazano, exploring for France, visited Narragansett Bay.

1614   Adriaen Block, the Dutch navigator, explored the coast and gave his name to Block Island.

1636   Roger Williams fled from Massachusetts and founded Providence.

1638   Portsmouth founded on Aquidneck Island.

1639   Newport founded.

1644   Royal charter granted to Roger Williams for Providence Plantations; Aquidneck Island renamed Rhode Island.

1663   Second charter granted to the colony by Charles II of England.

1675   Settlers defeated the Indians in the Great Swamp Fight during King Philip's War.

1732   Rhode Island's first newspaper, the *Rhode Island Gazette*, published in Newport.

1764   Brown University established in Warren as Rhode Island College; moved to Providence in 1770 and renamed in 1804.

1772   British ship *Gaspee* sunk by Providence residents.

1776   May 4, Rhode Island renounced its allegiance to King George III.

1790   May 29, Rhode Island ratified the United States Constitution; Samuel Slater built a cotton mill in Pawtucket.

1828   Public schools established throughout the state.

1835   Rhode Island's first railroad completed.

1842   Dorr's Rebellion led to adoption of a liberalized state constitution.

1892   University of Rhode Island in Kingston chartered as Rhode Island College of Agriculture and Mechanic Arts.

1895   Rhode Island Red hen officially recognized as a new poultry breed.

1900   Providence became the sole state capital.

1971   First permanent state income tax enacted.

1973   The U.S. Navy announced plans to close several of its important installations in Rhode Island.

1978   The Narragansett Indians won their claim to land in Charlestown.

Indians lived at peace with the colonists until 1675, when a war broke out in Massachusetts. The chief battle in Rhode Island, known as the Great Swamp Fight, took place near present-day West Kingston. King Philip (Metacomet), the leader of the Indians, was killed the next year, and the power of the Indians was ended.

Revolutionary War Days

Before the outbreak of the Revolutionary War, there was strong feeling in Rhode Island against the Stamp Act and the high levies placed on imported goods. In 1765 a mob in Newport seized and burned a British boat. In 1769 another group from Newport burned a British sloop. Most important was the burning of the *Gaspee,* a British ship grounded at what is now Gaspee Point in Warwick, by a group of Providence men. Feelings continued to run high. On May 4, 1776, the Rhode Island General Assembly, meeting in Providence, passed an act renouncing allegiance to King George III—a full two months before the Declaration of Independence was adopted by the Continental Congress.

The only Revolutionary War battles in Rhode Island were fought in Narragansett Bay and on Aquidneck Island. During the years 1776–79 the British occupied Newport and some surrounding areas. They burned houses, attacked Bristol and Warren, and forced the American troops from Aquidneck Island in what was called the battle of Rhode Island. It was at this battle that the distinguished French volunteer General Lafayette made his appearance. The British evacuated Newport in 1779, and in 1780 General Rochambeau and his forces came to Newport from France to aid the American cause. In 1781 he marched from Newport to join the main body of the American Army on its way to Yorktown.

Statehood and Later Times

Rhode Island ratified the United States Constitution on May 29, 1790. The Charter of 1663 served as the state constitution until 1842. The charter was considered a liberal document when it was first issued. But it became a source of disagreement, mainly because men who did not own property were not allowed to vote. In 1842 Thomas W. Dorr,

Old Slater Mill in Pawtucket, where Samuel Slater built the nation's first successful cotton textile mill.

a native of Providence, led a rebellion against the state government in order to win voting rights for all adult males. He was put into prison but later released. Through his actions a new state constitution was adopted the same year. That constitution, with amendments, is still in effect.

About 24,000 Rhode Islanders served in the Union forces during the Civil War. Between the time of that war and 1910, Rhode Island's population grew by 25 percent every 10 years. Industries grew rapidly, too, as electricity became available to run the mills and the factories.

After World War I the textile mills began to move from the state, but slowly other industries came to replace them. At the end of World War II, people began to move from the older cities, and the suburbs grew.

The Future

Rhode Island's location as the gateway to southeastern New England will continue to make it an important transportation and industrial center. Industries that provide services of many kinds will grow as older industries decline. Narragansett Bay—with its inlets, islands, and resorts—will remain an attraction for visitors and residents of the nation's smallest state.

CHESTER E. SMOLSKI
Rhode Island College

RHODES, CECIL (1853–1902)

Cecil John Rhodes was one of the great empire builders of the 19th century—a time when powerful nations tried to extend their rule to distant parts of the world. He acquired enormous wealth and power, which he used to build what amounted to a private empire in southern Africa. Recognizing the great natural wealth of the vast continent, he spent his life trying to bring about a union of southern African states under the British flag. Rhodes was both praised and condemned for his activities. But he played an important role, for good or bad, in the history of Africa.

Rhodes was born on July 5, 1853, in Bishop's Stortford, Hertfordshire, England. He was one of twelve children of the local vicar. His father hoped that Cecil would enter the church. But the boy's health was poor, and doctors advised that he be sent to live in a warm climate. At the age of 17, he joined his oldest brother, Herbert, a cotton farmer in the British colony of Natal, now a province in the Republic of South Africa.

During the diamond rush of 1871, the brothers staked a claim in the Kimberly diamond fields. Almost overnight, Cecil Rhodes became a rich man. From 1873 to 1881, he divided his time between England and southern Africa. In England he studied at Oxford University. In Africa he continued to build his fortune and to advance his plans for a British-

controlled union. After graduating from Oxford, he returned to Africa to live.

In 1881, when he was 28 years old, Rhodes became a member of the legislature of the British Cape Colony (now part of South Africa). In this position he continued to further his dream of union. In 1884 he urged the British to take over Bechuanaland (now Botswana). They did so the following year.

Rhodes obtained mining rights in an area northeast of Bechuanaland from the Ndebele people. This enabled him to form the British South Africa Company (B.S.A.C.), which was granted a charter to rule the area in 1889. The area was named Rhodesia, after Rhodes, and is also known as Zimbabwe.

Rhodes became prime minister of the Cape Colony in 1890. He was a strong and sometimes ruthless ruler, but he did much to further mining and agriculture. He improved the railway system, and thousands of kilometers of track were added to it.

In 1895, Rhodes played a key role in an attempt to organize an uprising in the neighboring Boer (Dutch-speaking) state of the Transvaal (now part of South Africa), where he had gold-mining investments. There was no uprising. But B.S.A.C. police under Leander S. Jameson invaded the Transvaal. They were quickly captured by the Boers. In the scandal that followed, Rhodes was forced to resign as prime minister. Jameson's raid increased the growing hostilities between the Boers and the British and was one of the factors leading to the Boer War of 1899–1902.

Rhodes devoted the rest of his life to developing Rhodesia. He encouraged the British to settle in the area. When the Ndebele revolted against B.S.A.C. rule in 1896, Rhodes met with the chiefs and arranged a peace.

Rhodes died near Cape Town on March 26, 1902, at the age of 48. He left his home, Groote Schuur, to be used as a residence by future prime ministers of South Africa. The famous Rhodes scholarships—which provide funds for outstanding students from the Commonwealth countries, the United States, and Germany to study at Oxford University—are supported by a grant set up by his will.

JOHN E. FLINT
Author, *Cecil Rhodes*

See also ZIMBABWE (RHODESIA); SOUTH AFRICA.

RHODESIA. See ZIMBABWE (RHODESIA).

RICE

When the Chinese greet one another, they do not say, "How do you do?" Instead they say, "Have you eaten your rice today?" This expression is used because rice is very important to the Chinese. It is important to many other people as well. Nearly half the population of the world lives partly or almost entirely on a rice diet. In some countries of Asia each person eats from 90 to 180 kilograms (200 to 400 pounds) of rice a year. In the United States, each person eats about 3 kilograms (7 pounds) of rice a year. In South America, the amount eaten is nearly twice this much. Wheat is the only grain that is more important as a human food, and it is only slightly more important.

An advantage of rice is its high yield when it is cultivated properly. The average yield per hectare is much higher than for wheat. Because of this high yield, rice has long been a symbol of fertility. Rice is thrown at a bride and groom after a wedding ceremony to wish them many children.

Rice probably originated in southern India, where it has been grown for thousands of years. From there it spread eastward into China more than 5,000 years ago. Soon afterward it spread westward into Persia (Iran) and Egypt. Rice was not taken to North America until the 1600's. Today the leading rice producers are China, India, Indonesia, Bangladesh, Thailand, and Japan. In the United States rice is grown chiefly in Arkansas, Texas, California, and Louisiana.

▶ THE RICE PLANT

The rice plant belongs to the grass family. It has long, narrow leaves and several stems. At the top of each stem, a head of flowers forms. The grains, or seeds, develop from the flowers. Each head produces 50 to 150 grains of rice. Most rice plants grow 60 to 150 centimeters (2 to 5 feet) high. Rice is considered to be an annual plant. Most varieties take five or six months to ripen. But where the growing season is long enough, a second crop develops from the plants.

Rice thrives only where the weather is warm and the soil is wet. Most rice is **lowland rice**. It is grown on level land and is kept flooded in 10 to 20 centimeters (4 to 8 inches)

Left: A head of rice. Right: A rice plant ready for harvest.

of water for part or all of the growing season. **Upland rice** is grown in areas where the land is too rugged for flooding but where the rainfall is heavy enough so that flooding of the fields is not needed. Upland rice yields much less grain than lowland rice.

▶ GROWING AND HARVESTING RICE

In Asia and other parts of the world, rice seed is sown in seedbeds by hand. When the plants are 18 centimeters (7 inches) high or more, they are pulled from the bed, trimmed, and transplanted to a muddy field. The fields then are flooded. Later they usually are drained for weeding, which is done by hand. The fields are flooded again and are drained a short time before harvesting.

In the southern United States rice usually is seeded by a machine called a grain drill. The field is flooded when the plants are 15 to 20 centimeters (6 to 8 inches) high. In California and some other places, the seeds are scattered on flooded fields from airplanes. Weeds are controlled chiefly by the use of chemical sprays.

Most of the world's rice is harvested by hand, using sickles and knives. The grains are knocked free from the straw by threshing. Threshing is done by machines that beat the rice heads or by animals that trample on them. In some countries rice is cut and threshed in one operation by machines.

In Japan young rice plants are transplanted to the paddies by hand labor.

▶ MILLING

The threshed grains of rice are called **rough rice** or **paddy rice**. (The word "paddy" is also used for the flooded field where rice is grown.) Rice in this rough state is still covered with coarse hulls that must be removed before the rice is cooked. Hulling may be done by machine in a rice mill, or the rice may be pounded by hand in a mortar.

Rice with the hulls removed is called **brown rice**. It is covered with a brownish outer skin called the bran. Most of the vitamins and minerals of the rice grain are stored in the bran. But brown rice does not keep as long as white rice. Most people prefer white polished rice to brown rice. Polished rice can be enriched by adding vitamins and minerals.

When rice is milled, the bran and the germ are removed by sending the kernels through a hulling machine that gently grinds the surface of each grain. Some rice is also scoured in a special machine called a pearler. As the kernels go through the milling process, the whole or slightly broken grains are separated from the broken grains, the flour, the bran, and the germ. After milling, the kernels are white and have a polished surface.

Converted rice is a slightly darker milled rice that has more B vitamins and minerals than ordinary polished rice. Before converted rice is milled, it is soaked in water that is just under the boiling point. Then it is steamed under pressure. This process is called **parboiling**. Vitamins from the bran soak into the grain during parboiling.

▶ RICE PRODUCTS

Rice is used in many ways. It supplies abundant food energy, but other foods are needed to provide a well-balanced diet. In North America, there are three classes of rice —long grain, medium grain, and short grain. All have the same food value. But long-grain rice tends to cook dry. Medium- and short-grain rice cook moist, yet firm.

Rice may be eaten boiled or baked or in the form of a breakfast cereal. Rice flour, a by-product of milling, is used to make bread, sugar, starch, face powder, and glue. Wine can be made by fermenting rice. Such wine is called sake in Japan, samshu in China, and arrack in India. Rice also can be used to make malt—an ingredient of beer.

Hulls and bran from milled rice can be fed to farm animals. The hulls also are used as bedding for farm and laboratory animals, as packaging around fragile items, and as a fuel. In Asia, rice straw is used to make paper and for mats, hats, baskets, and roof thatching.

▶ WILD RICE

The wild rice of North America is not really rice at all but a native grass. For many years it was an important food of Indians of the Great Lakes region. The people gathered the harvest by slipping through the water in their light canoes. The stalks were tilted over the canoes, and the grains were gently knocked off with sticks. Because wild rice grows in water and is also harvested in water, it has never been grown in large quantities. Most of the wild rice that is produced in the United States today comes from Minnesota. Wild rice is delicious and nourishing, but it is much more expensive than ordinary rice.

JOHN H. MARTIN
Oregon State University

See also GRAIN AND GRAIN PRODUCTS.

RICHELIEU, CARDINAL (1585–1642)

Cardinal Richelieu was one of the leading figures in French history. He was chief minister to Louis XIII, king of France from 1610 to 1643. His full name was Armand Jean du Plessis, Duc de Richelieu, and he was born in Paris on September 9, 1585. His father was a member of the French nobility.

As a youth Armand planned to follow his father's career as a soldier. But at the age of 21 he was persuaded by his family to accept an appointment as Bishop of Luçon. He acquired the necessary training and served at Luçon until 1614, when he was elected to the Estates General, the French assembly. There his brilliance brought him to the attention of Marie de Médicis (1573–1642), queen mother of the young Louis XIII. He became the king's secretary of state for war and foreign affairs. But when Marie de Médicis was exiled from court by her enemies, Richelieu left with her. During this period he was made a cardinal.

In 1624 Marie de Médicis was allowed to return to Paris. Richelieu returned with her, and through her influence, became the king's chief minister. For the next 18 years, until his death, Richelieu worked to establish a strong, centralized France under a powerful monarchy. He did this by curbing the power of the great nobles and by capturing the city of La Rochelle, stronghold of the Huguenots, the French Protestants. The Huguenots, who had controlled their own area of France, were forced to accept the sovereignty of the king.

Richelieu was now the most powerful man in France. But he had made many enemies, and they tried several times to overthrow him. Marie de Médicis turned against him and became his most bitter opponent. King Louis himself disliked his chief minister but knew that he could not govern without him.

Outside France the Thirty Years War (1618–48) was raging. Originally a religious and political conflict between Catholic and Protestant powers in Europe, it had become a struggle for European supremacy. France's great enemy, the Hapsburg monarchy of Austria and Spain, was the leader of the Catholic powers. To thwart the Hapsburgs, Richelieu allied Catholic France with the Protestant forces of Sweden and the north German states.

Richelieu died in Paris on December 4, 1642. He did not live to see the French victory; but because of his policies, France became the leading power of Europe under Louis XIV, who came to the throne in 1643.

RIDDLES. See JOKES AND RIDDLES.

RIDING. See HORSEBACK RIDING.

RIFLE MARKSMANSHIP

Rifle marksmanship is a good sport for teen-agers. Young people usually have the very good reflexes and steady nerves that are needed. Although adults may have greater shooting experience and more expensive equipment, young people often have the advantage of better eyesight. Championship matches, national as well as local, are held by junior shooters.

▶ **ORGANIZED JUNIOR MARKSMANSHIP**

Rifle shooting as an organized activity for junior marksmen began in New York City about 1903. Rifle practice for boys over 13 was introduced there in the Public Schools Athletic League. In 1907 the National Board for the Promotion of Rifle Practice approved a program of training in high schools and colleges, and a national championship trophy was created for private and public secondary school competitors. The .22-caliber (small-bore) rifle became standard for junior shooting. (Caliber refers to the diameter of the bore of a rifle—in this case $2\frac{22}{100}$ inch.)

The National Rifle Association (Washington, D.C.), founded in 1871 by a group of National Guard officers to promote civilian interest in marksmanship, created a junior membership in 1926. It is open to people under 19. The N.R.A. sets standards for shooting, conducts national championship matches, and promotes safety with firearms.

▶ **LEARNING TO USE A RIFLE**

If you have a rifle, you must have a safe place to shoot it. And you need skilled adult

Four standard positions are used in rifle marksmanship. They are prone (lying flat on one's stomach), sitting, kneeling, and standing. A good position depends on relaxed muscles and the use of the bones for support. Any position may be difficult at first, but it becomes comfortable with practice. Your body serves only to hold the rifle while it is being fired. You are acting as gun mount, and the mount should be as stationary as possible. A sling helps to make a rigid brace for the arm that supports the rifle under the barrel.

In each position the rifle should point naturally at the target. If it doesn't, muscles are strained. If you find this to be the case, shift your body so that no part of it is under strain or pressure.

The prone position is the steadiest and the best for a beginner. You can most easily learn to shoot in this position, and you certainly can make the best scores. Lie on the ground so that the rifle barrel (which is pointed at the target) forms an angle of 30 to 45 degrees with your body. Your left elbow should be on the ground, directly under the barrel. (All directions are for a right-handed marksman.)

When you get into position, aim your rifle at the target and close your eyes. When you open them, in a few seconds, the sights should still be on the target. If they aren't, move your body until you are aiming naturally. For safety and accuracy you should load and shoot one round at a time. So have your ammunition close enough for you to load without getting out of position.

Sitting is the next steadiest position. Face halfway to the right in relation to the target, and then sit down. With your feet spread, lean forward so that your elbows are braced just over your knees. The left elbow should be directly under the barrel, as in the prone position. The sling may need shortening to make it tight enough. In a variation of this position the ankles may be crossed. But it is important that your knees and thighs not touch the ground.

For kneeling, the basic principles are the same. The sling should be tight. Face half right with your right knee on the ground. Either you should have your right leg flat on the ground as you sit on the side of your foot,

supervision. You must learn the trigger squeeze and correct breathing. Trigger squeeze calls for slow, steady pressure on the trigger until the rifle fires. Jerking or yanking the trigger will never give good results. When you breathe, the rifle moves. So take a full breath and let out about half of it. Then you can hold your breath without effort while you squeeze the trigger. If you wait too long, your pulse beat will become strong enough to make the rifle move. If this happens, take another breath and start again.

Learn to put all of your shots close together in a tight group. You learn to "sight," or focus on the target, by looking at it through the rifle sights—adjustable devices with small openings. These help the rifleman find the precise direction in which to shoot. You learn the right sight picture—the way the target, front sight, and rear sight look with every shot. When you can shoot a tight group, move the sights, if necessary, to put that group exactly in the center of the target.

Peep sights are best for junior target shooting. But the principle of lining up the sights with the target is the same with any kind of sights.

which is turned in, or you should sit on the heel, which is in a raised position. Your left knee supports the left arm just above the elbow, and that arm should be directly under the rifle.

The offhand, or standing, position is the most difficult, because body support is limited to the feet. Good trigger squeeze and breathing are most important, because you cannot hold the rifle as steady as you can in other positions. Since much informal shooting, as in hunting, is done from this position, it is worth practicing. Stand facing a little to the right of the target with your feet far enough apart to form a steady base for your body. The rifle should rest on the heel of your left hand. The left elbow should again be under the barrel. In the army standing position the left elbow is not allowed to rest against the body; the body weight should be almost equal on both feet. In the N.R.A. standing position the left hand is placed closer to the trigger guard and the left arm against the body; the weight is mostly on the left leg, and the left hip is thrust forward to support the elbow.

▶ HOW SAFE IS RIFLE SHOOTING?

Under proper shooting rules and range controls, such as those of the National Rifle Association, rifle shooting is a safe sport. This is why it is important to learn to shoot with the guidance of a trained instructor.

The general safety rules are easy to understand and to follow. Learn and practice them. Just one accident in a lifetime, even a slight one, can ruin your enjoyment of a very fine sport. These safety rules make good sense:

(1) Treat every gun as if it were loaded. Never ask if a gun is loaded. The owner might be wrong. See for yourself.

(2) Keep the muzzle pointed in a safe direction. This always keeps you from shooting something you don't want to shoot.

(3) Always keep the breech action open when not shooting. Other people have a right to know that your rifle is safe.

(4) Keep your finger out of the trigger guard until your sights are on the target. This one rule, practiced at all times, will guarantee that you will never hit anything except the target. It is an excellent rule for hunting.

(5) Know your gun and ammunition and what they can do. Some people have no idea that a .22 long rifle cartridge is dangerous up to 1 mile away.

(6) Be sure of your backstop. Remember that a bullet has to have a safe place to stop.

(7) Be sure of your target. You must be able to identify it to be sure that it is safe to shoot at.

(8) Obey every firing-line command at once. This makes organized shooting a safe sport for everybody.

▶ TAKING CARE OF YOUR RIFLE

A good rifle is a finely made mechanism. It deserves good care. It should not be dropped or banged against hard objects.

Carry your rifle in a case when you travel and when other objects might damage its sights and action. Store it in a dry place—preferably not in a case, where moisture might collect. Small children and careless persons of any age should not be able to get their hands on your rifle, and ammunition should be stored away from the rifle itself.

Modern ammunition is not in itself harmful to rifle barrels. But occasional cleaning is necessary to make sure that there is no deposit of lead in the bore. A light coating of oil in a clean barrel will protect it from rust for several weeks. When you are going to store your rifle for a long time, grease all metal surfaces lightly, inside and out.

Remove moisture and dirt as soon as possible after firing. Wipe the bore with a dry patch, or cloth, perhaps using a powder solvent. Use the dry patch in a good cleaning rod several times, to make sure that the bore is clean and dry. Then run an oily patch through the bore once or twice. Wipe the outside of the rifle dry and oil it very lightly. Put it away in a level position. If you stand it up in a corner, any excess oil running down from the bore may clog the action and stain the stock.

If you want to learn to shoot or to improve your skill, get in touch with a rifle club near your home. You are likely to find that adults are very interested in teaching young people to shoot safely and accurately. The nearest hardware or sporting-goods store where guns are sold should be able to tell you where there is such a club in your community.

G. E. DAMON
Author, *Gun Fun With Safety*

RIGHTS, BILL OF. See BILL OF RIGHTS.

RINGWORM. See DISEASES.

PACIFIC OCEAN

BOLIVIA

PARAGUAY

CHILE

ARGENTINA

URUGUAY

BRAZIL

RIO DE JANEIRO

ATLANTIC OCEAN

RIO DE JANEIRO

Rio de Janeiro, Brazil's second largest city and until 1960 the nation's capital, is one of the most beautiful cities in the Western Hemisphere. To Brazilians, Rio is "the city of a thousand delights."

Rio is a bustling business and cultural center. This city of over 5,000,000 is a major port on the Atlantic coast. Most of Brazil's imports and a good many exports pass through the city's vast and busy harbor. Rio is the home of the nation's leading cultural institutions and of many of Brazil's artists and writers and business and political leaders.

Rio's setting is one of the most attractive in the world. To the east is Guanabara Bay, a deepwater inlet of the Atlantic Ocean. To the west are the Serra dos Orgãos ("Organ Mountains"), which give the city a magnificent background.

Pão de Açúcar ("Sugar Loaf" Mountain), at the entrance to the bay, is a cone-shaped rock about 400 meters (1,300 feet) high. A trip to the top of Sugar Loaf by aerial cable car affords the visitor an unforgettable view of the city. Nearby is Corcovado ("Hunchback"), a sharp rocky peak 700 meters (2,300 feet) high. Upon its summit rises a monumental statue of Christ the Redeemer.

The best known of Rio's golden beaches is Copacabana, but Ipanema, Leblon, and Leme, among others, are equally popular with Brazilians in summertime. The island of Pa-queta, the Rodrigo de Freitas Lagoon, and Tijuca Forest add to Rio's natural beauty.

A Modern City

Rio is an old city, but it is also one of the most modern on the continent. The oldest part is on lowland adjoining the bay. The modern suburbs extend along the shore and sprawl up the hillsides. Locked as it is by sea, mountains, and forests, Rio cannot expand horizontally and so it is a city of tall buildings. Avenida Rio Branco, a wide boulevard, extends through the central district from Guanabara Bay to Mauá Plaza. Parks, theaters, residential buildings, sidewalk cafés, and hotels line the avenue. Although much of Rio's architecture is modern, there are many old colonial buildings, such as those found in Aguas Ferreas Square and along Rua do Ouvidor, a narrow street lined with fashionable shops. Many of Rio's hills are crowded with makeshift shacks, known as *favelas*. These homes of the desperately poor are the cause of much concern to the government and the Church. Much is being planned and done to replace many of the *favelas* with modern homes.

Way of Life

Although Rio is not primarily an industrial city, many of its people are engaged in manufacturing textiles, furniture, pharmaceuticals, glass, clothing, and electrical and household appliances. Two miles of docks line the waterfront to the north. Many of the city's commercial houses, factories, and warehouses are found in this area.

The University of Brazil, the Pontifical Catholic University of Rio de Janeiro, the Rural University, the School of Fine Arts, and

A view of Rio de Janeiro, showing Guanabara Bay and Sugar Loaf Mountain jutting into the bay.

the National Museum and National Library (the largest in all Latin America) make Rio the nation's cultural center. The city has many fine art galleries, theaters, and concert halls. The Botanical Garden, on the outskirts of the city, is famous for its collection of native and foreign plants.

With the sea and mountains at their disposal, the *cariocas,* as the natives of Rio are called, enjoy swimming, sailing, fishing, deep-sea diving, and horseback riding. As in the rest of Brazil, the favorite sport is soccer, played at Maracaña Stadium, one of the largest in the world. Carnival, celebrated 4 days before Lent, is Rio's gayest festival. *Cariocas* from all walks of life, rich and poor, take part in the festival.

History

Rio was discovered in 1502 when a Portuguese navigator led an expedition into Guanabara Bay. He thought the bay was the mouth of a big river, and because he found it on January 1 he called it Rio de Janeiro ("River of January"). In 1567 the Portuguese won a battle against French Huguenots who had settled in the area. The battle took place on January 20, the Feast of Saint Sebastian. In thanksgiving to the saint as well as to honor Dom Sebastião, King of Portugal, the victors called the city Saint Sebastian of Rio de Janeiro.

Rio's fine bay and very favorable climate attracted many settlers. The city was made the capital of the Portuguese colony in 1763. When Napoleon invaded Spain and Portugal, the Portuguese king and court fled to Rio and made the city the capital of the empire itself. In 1822 Brazil became independent of Portugal, and Rio became the capital of an independent empire. In 1889 it became the capital of the newly formed republic of Brazil.

Because Rio was the national capital for so many years, its growth paralleled that of Brazil itself. This growth and the need to give Brazil a more centrally located capital led the federal government to create a new capital at Brasília.

Today Rio de Janeiro is the capital of Rio de Janeiro state. Although no longer the capital of Brazil, its cultural and commercial vitality make it the heart of everything Brazilian, and when people think of Brazil it is usually Rio that they think of.

Reviewed by ZORA SELJAN
Ministry of Education, Brazil

RIVERS

A river is any natural stream of fresh water that flows in a definite channel. But what makes a river begin? Why do rivers flow in some places and not in others?

▶ HOW RIVERS FORM

No place on the surface of the earth is perfectly level. Wherever rain falls, some water flows downhill. Some water evaporates. Some seeps through the soil into the ground. But some rainwater remains on the surface. As rainwater flows across the land, it follows the shortest and steepest way downslope. Sometimes a gully is gouged out of the earth by fast-flowing rainwater. With every new rainfall, shower, or storm, the gully becomes larger, deeper, and wider.

Some rivers start as little gullies or rivulets high up in the mountains. There the snow melts and follows the easiest way into the valley. Whenever it rains in the mountains, there is even more water for the rivulets to carry, and the river becomes bigger. With each new rainstorm millions of little rills are born and flow in countless numbers downslope. Many of these rills grow until they become rivers that flow all the time.

▶ THE STRUCTURE OF RIVERS

Rivers come in all sizes, shapes, and forms. Some flow lazily and very slowly. Others flow swiftly—sometimes fiercely. Little rivers that are narrow and not very deep are sometimes called streams, creeks, or brooks. Small rivers that join bigger rivers are called **tributaries**. A large river and its tributaries form a **river system**.

We call the beginning of a river its **source**. The place where a river ends its flow is the river's **mouth**. The mouth of a river is usually

San Juan River in Utah has carved weird shapes in the landscape.

the place where the river flows into another river, a lake, or the sea.

Every river flows through a **river valley**. The part of the valley covered by water is called the **bed** or **channel**. A **river bank** is the land on either side of the river.

Rivers are separated from each other by heights of land. These heights, called **divides**, decide the slope of the land and the direction in which the water will flow. Sometimes divides are called **watersheds**, because they decide in which direction the rainwaters will flow. A **drainage basin** is the land area that is drained by a river and its tributaries.

▶ RIVER MOUTHS

Some rivers empty into a quiet sea or lake, where there are no great waves or tides or currents to disturb the water. In such places a river's load is deposited at its mouth in the form of a **delta**. A delta is a fanlike deposit at the end of the river. It is usually made of fine, rich topsoils that the river picked up miles away. Some of this material is carried to the mouth of the river to form a delta. Deltas may be very large, especially if more than one river empties into the sea in the same place. For example, the Netherlands is for the most part a large delta made by the Rhine, Meuse, and Scheldt rivers.

Delta soils tend to be fertile. In such countries as Egypt, Pakistan, and India millions of people live on delta land. They raise crops and build cities on deltas, though they know that every year may bring another flood. The delta plain may be the one place with fertile soil and enough water for farming.

Where tides, currents, and waves are strong, no delta is formed. The ocean waters carry away the silt that the river empties into the sea. As a result, the seawater may be muddy for 160 kilometers (100 miles) offshore as the silt is carried into the ocean.

Other rivers, such as the Hudson in New York and the Thames in England, have no deltas. Instead they have **drowned mouths**. For some reason, in the past the land sank and the waters of the oceans rose. The lowest portions of the rivers were submerged. These drowned mouths are called **estuaries**.

▶ HOW RIVERS FLOW

The way a river works depends on the slope of the land, the quantity of water that flows in its channel, and the kind of surface material it flows across. The amount of **precipitation** (the moisture that falls to the earth as rain, snow, hail, or sleet) determines the amount of water in any river. The amount of water also depends on underground springs. Water seeps and trickles underground after each shower or melting of ice and snow. It collects in cracks and crevices inside the earth, and much of it finally reaches a river.

In places that are very dry, a river may disappear underground or evaporate into the air. Then the riverbed is dry and fills with water again only when it rains. Such rivers are called **intermittent** rivers or streams. In some countries (Algeria, Libya, Israel, and Saudi Arabia, for example) the beds of intermittent rivers are called **wadis**. In the southwestern United States the same kind of dry riverbed is called an **arroyo**. In the western United States and Canada they are sometimes called **washes**. These intermittently dry streams are usually found in desert regions.

Some rivers have their sources in highlands or mountains where there is heavy precipitation. Sometimes these rivers cross vast desert regions. Despite the loss of water by evaporation from the hot desert sun, these rivers often have plenty of water to spill into the sea. They receive so much water at their source that they can cross hundreds of kilometers of desert without going dry. The Nile and the Colorado rivers are examples.

▶ THE WORK OF RIVERS

Many familiar land features are mainly the result of the never ceasing work of rivers. Running water can carve the landscape or deposit new features on the land. As water flows within a channel or riverbed, it carries sand, silt (fine soils), pebbles, gravel, and even large stones. This assortment of loose material is gathered as water runs downslope. These materials in turn push along other pieces that are in their way. With their sharp edges they gouge out or scratch away more soil or scrape off parts of rocks and stones over which the water flows. In this way a river deepens or widens its channel.

Usually, the muddier the stream, the more material it is carrying. The heavier materials are rolled along the bottom of the river, while the finer sands and silts are carried in suspension, within the water itself. A stream may lose part of its carrying power because it lacks water or because its slope becomes more gentle. Then it flows more slowly and deposits the heaviest materials.

▶ RIVER FLOODS

If a river channel receives more water than it can hold, the water spills over onto the land on either side of the river. This is called a **flood**. As the river overflows, it deposits some of the heavier gravel and sand on the valley floor next to the river bank. This ridge-like deposit is called a **natural levee**. Then the overflowing water continues to spread over the valley floor beyond the levees and deposits the finer silt and sand.

Material that is deposited by rivers is called **alluvium**. The flat valley floor on either side of the river is called a **floodplain**.

Flood Control. People use the rich soils of the floodplain for growing crops. They often build cities and factories near a river and use the river for water supply or for shipping cargo. When a river overflows its banks, serious damage may be done to artificial structures that are in the path of floodwaters. Sometimes artificial levees of stone or concrete are built on top of the natural levees to hold the river in its channel. Sometimes the water level is controlled by the construction of dams that store water in reservoirs during the high-water period and release this stored water for use during the time of low water.

▶ LIFE CYCLE OF A RIVER

Rivers can be classified in three ways—young rivers, mature rivers, and old rivers.

Columbia River, Washington, in flood.

Feluccas on the Nile River, Egypt.

Hamburg, a busy port on the Elbe River.

Neches River, Port Neches, Texas.

Rio Grande forms part of the boundary between the United States and Mexico.

These names do not refer to the age of a river in years. Instead, they describe certain features in the appearance of a river.

A **young river** flows rapidly. Its bed is steep and irregular. Its flow is often interrupted by rapids and waterfalls. There are few tributaries. The valley through which a young river flows is often steep-sided. There is no broad floodplain nor any natural levees.

In a **mature river** most of the rapids and waterfalls have disappeared. Mature rivers flow more slowly than young rivers. The slope of the riverbed is gradual. The river valley is broad, and the mature river often meanders (winds) across a wide floodplain. Natural levees and swamps are sometimes present; and the river often has tributaries.

Old rivers meander slowly back and forth through broad, flat valleys and wide floodplains. The sides of the river valley are worn down to gentle slopes. An old river often builds a delta where it empties into the sea.

Some rivers which grew old over the ages have been rejuvenated (made young again) by uplifting of the earth's crust. A river may be youthful at its source, be mature farther downriver, and end up as an old river at its mouth. The Mississippi is such a river.

HISTORICAL IMPORTANCE OF RIVERS

People have always used rivers for transportation. In the early history of many countries, rivers served people by providing water for growing crops. The ancient Egyptians used the waters of the Nile to aid in growing crops as early as 3400 B.C. The ancient Babylonians, Chinese, and American Indians all used river water for irrigation. People have often coaxed the river to turn wheels and so give them power to grind grain.

RIVER COMMERCE AND TRADE

Some rivers provide natural transportation routes for the movement of large quantities of goods. River barges carry heavy cargoes on the Illinois, Mississippi, Ohio, and Hudson rivers. In Europe many rivers are crowded with barges moving from country to country.

Not all rivers are suitable for navigation. Not all rivers have enough water throughout the year. Some rivers in the Soviet Union and North America freeze in the winter. Waterfalls and rapids may prevent navigation.

In some cases large navigable rivers, such as the Mackenzie in Canada and the Lena, Ob, and Yenisei in the Soviet Union, flow northward into the Arctic Ocean, where there is little or no trade. Though they are navigable for part of the year, not much freight is shipped on these rivers. There are few cities or people to carry on trade. Therefore, there is not much transportation. In the tropical rain forests of the Congo and Brazil there are also many navigable rivers but few people to use them. If these areas are developed, the rivers will be used in many ways.

RIVER BOUNDARIES

Many rivers serve as boundaries between nations. Rivers are easy to describe in treaties and are usually fixed in their location. Rivers that serve as partial international boundaries include the St. Lawrence, Yalu, and Rio Grande. Provincial and state boundaries also follow the courses of some rivers. Examples are the Ottawa in Canada, the Murray in Australia, the Ganges in India, and the Ohio and Mississippi in the United States.

RIVERS AS SOURCES OF POWER

People have always used the force of falling river water to provide power. A river must have rapids or a waterfall to supply this energy. In the past, factories using waterpower had to be located near the rapids or falls. Since the development of electricity the pressure of the falling water is used to turn a turbine. This, in turn, runs electric generators. The electricity can be sent many kilometers over wires. It is no longer necessary for factories to be situated at the waterfalls.

If natural falls do not exist, dams are built to back up the water. Gates in the high dam are opened. As the river water rushes through the openings, it drops down to the river below the dam and turns the turbines that have been built there.

WATER FOR IRRIGATION

Much of the earth's land is too dry to produce crops. People have therefore developed methods of using rivers to irrigate the soil.

Today rivers are used for large irrigation systems. Dams are constructed across rivers to store water. When water is needed for growing crops, the water in the reserve or reservoir is piped into fields. Electric generators supply power to pump water hundreds of kilometers through pipes. Dams conserve water that collects during rainy seasons.

▶OTHER USES OF RIVERS

A map of any country shows at a glance that people like to live near rivers. Hundreds of cities throughout the world are built on the banks, floodplains, and deltas of rivers. Rivers not only provide water for home use, but furnish water for industry and supply sources of food and recreation.

Water for Use in Industry

Industries use vast quantities of water. Paper factories use much water to wash the wood and to mix the wood pulp into a mash that is pressed into paper. Iron and steel mills use enormous quantities of river water each day to cool and wash the various iron and steel pieces that are being formed.

Industries also use rivers as places to dump their waste materials. And people discharge the sewage and waste of their homes through pipes into the rivers nearest them. In today's world there are so many cities and people and industries that many rivers are badly polluted. Pollution kills fish and animal life. It destroys the recreational value of rivers. Polluted rivers are a health hazard. If the polluted water is to be used for drinking or washing, it must be purified by chemical means in water-treatment plants near the rivers. This is an expensive process. Not all river water used by people today is purified.

Rivers as Sources of Food

Rivers have long provided people with food in the form of fish. Millions of people in South America, Africa, and Asia fish for their food every day. In North America and Europe large industries are based on river fishing. The salmon industry is one example of a large river-fishing industry in Canada and the United States.

Recreation-Area Rivers

Rivers are valuable for recreation. People camp and picnic near rivers. Rivers are used for swimming, boating, and water-skiing. State and national parks that have been created near rivers are favorite places for people to spend holidays and vacations and enjoy water sports.

You will find articles relating to rivers in several other volumes of this encyclopedia. There are separate articles, for example, on dams, erosion, floods, irrigation, water pollution, and waterpower.

▶SOME RIVERS OF THE WORLD

The Amazon River in Brazil. See AMAZON RIVER.

The Amur River in Asia rises in northern Mongolia and empties into the Sea of Okhotsk. The Amur, with its headstream, the Onon, is about 4,350 kilometers (2,700 miles) in length.

The Brahmaputra River of southern Asia rises in the Himalayas and empties into the Bay of Bengal. It is 2,900 kilometers (1,800 miles) long. The delta formed by the Brahmaputra and Ganges rivers in Bangladesh is one of the world's largest.

The Colorado River rises in Rocky Mountain National Park and empties into the Gulf of California. The Colorado is more than 2,330 kilometers (1,450 miles) in length and drains areas in both the United States and Mexico. Hoover Dam in Black Canyon, on the Arizona-Nevada border, is an important unit in the Colorado River flood control, irrigation, and power programs.

The Columbia River rises in the Canadian Rockies in British Columbia. It is 2,000 kilometers (about 1,240 miles) long and drains a basin in Canada and the United States. The Grand Coulee and the Bonneville dams on the Columbia supply water for irrigation and power and help to control floods.

The Congo River in Africa. See CONGO RIVER.

The Danube River, the second largest river in Europe, is about 2,800 kilometers (1,750 miles) long. It rises in the Black Forest of Germany and empties into the Black Sea. It flows through or borders a number of European countries. On its banks are three capitals —Vienna (Austria), Budapest (Hungary), and Belgrade (Yugoslavia). The Danube is controlled by the countries bordering it. Each nation takes care of its own riparian rights (rights to the use of a river and its banks). Dams and power plants may be built as long as they do not interfere with navigation.

A houseboat on the Amazon River, Brazil.

The **Delaware River** rises in the Catskill Mountains in southeastern New York. It is 507 kilometers (315 miles) in length and empties into Delaware Bay. The river is used to produce hydroelectric power. The Delaware Aqueduct system is one of the sources of water for New York City.

The **Dnieper River,** the third longest river in Europe, rises in the Valdai Hills of the Ukraine in the Soviet Union and empties into the Black Sea. It is about 2,300 kilometers (1,420 miles) in length. The river is a source of hydroelectric power. Canals link the Dnieper to the Baltic Sea, forming a continuous north-south waterway.

The **Don River** rises in the central uplands of the Soviet Union. It flows for about 1,970 kilometers (1,220 miles) and empties into the Sea of Azov, which connects with the Black Sea. The Don is navigable for most of its length, except in the winter months. The river carries boats loaded with timber, coal, building materials, and grain.

The **Ebro River** rises in the Cantabrian Mountains of northern Spain. It flows for 800 kilometers (500 miles) before emptying into the Mediterranean Sea. It is the longest river lying entirely within Spain. The Ebro supplies much of Spain's hydroelectric power.

The **Elbe River** rises in the Sudetes, mountains between Czechoslovakia and Poland. It is about 1,165 kilometers (725 miles) long and empties into the North Sea. It forms part of the border between East and West Germany.

Parker Dam on the Colorado River between California and Arizona.

The river is navigable for ocean liners as far as Hamburg, the largest port in West Germany. Canals connect the Elbe with the Rhine, Weser, and Oder rivers and with important Baltic ports.

The Ganges River in India. See GANGES RIVER.

The Garonne River of southwestern France rises in the Pyrenees mountains of Spain and flows through the famous Bordeaux wine region. It is about 650 kilometers (400 miles) long and empties into the Bay of Biscay. Below Bordeaux, the Garonne is joined by the Dordogne River to form the Gironde estuary.

The Guadalquivir River rises in the mountains of southern Spain and empties into the Atlantic Ocean. It irrigates olive groves and fruit orchards of the Andalusian plain. Cordoba and Seville are on its banks. It is about 600 kilometers (375 miles) long.

The Hudson River rises in the Adirondack Mountains of New York and empties into upper New York Bay at New York City. Part of the river forms a boundary between New York and northeastern New Jersey. It is 507 kilometers (315 miles) long. The New York State Barge Canal system links the Hudson to the Great Lakes and Lake Champlain. The Richelieu Canal connects it with the St. Lawrence River. The lower Hudson (the North River) is part of New York Harbor.

The Hwang Ho (Yellow River) in China. See CHINA.

The Indus River, Pakistan's greatest river, rises in Tibet and empties into the Arabian Sea. The Indus is about 3,200 kilometers (2,000 miles) in length. It irrigates a large cotton and grain area.

The Irrawaddy River, Burma's major river, flows south through the length of Burma and empties into the Andaman Sea. It is about 2,100 kilometers (1,300 miles) in length and is navigable for small ships along part of its course. The Twante Canal links the river to Burma's main port and capital, Rangoon. The river's delta is one of the world's great rice-producing regions.

The Jordan River in Israel and Jordan. See ISRAEL; JORDAN.

The Lena River in central Siberia is about 4,260 kilometers (2,648 miles) in length. It rises in the Baikal Range and empties into the Laptev Sea through a wide delta. Between the months of May and November, the Lena is navigable for most of its course. Ships carry coal and lumber. But during part of the year, the river is clogged with ice. Traffic on the Lena connects with the Trans-Siberian Railroad at Kirensk.

The Liffey River rises in the Wicklow Mountains of Ireland, flows through Dublin, and empties into Dublin Bay on the Irish Sea. Canals connect the 80-kilometer (50-mile) Liffey with the Shannon River, making a waterway across Ireland.

The Loire, the longest river in France, rises on Mont Gerbier de Jonc in southeastern France. It flows for 1,005 kilometers (625 miles) and empties into the Atlantic Ocean. Only the lower Loire is navigable.

The Mackenzie River in northwestern Canada is Canada's greatest river and part of a large river system. It rises in Great Slave Lake and empties into Beaufort Sea, an arm of the Arctic Ocean. The total length of the system, which includes several rivers, is more than 4,000 kilometers (2,500 miles).

The Magdalena River, about 1,600 kilometers (1,000 miles) long, is Colombia's chief river. It rises in the mountains of southwestern Colombia and empties into the Caribbean Sea.

The Manzanares is the river of Madrid. It rises in the Sierra de Guadarrama in Spain and flows 90 kilometers (55 miles), emptying into the Jamara, an arm of the Tagus. It is noted for the beautiful bridges that span it at Madrid.

The Mekong River rises in China and flows through Southeast Asia before emptying into the East China Sea. It is about 4,200 kilometers (2,600 miles) long and forms a vast delta in Vietnam. This was one of the world's most important rice-producing regions.

The Meuse River rises in eastern France. It flows for about 900 kilometers (560 miles) through France, Belgium, and the Netherlands and empties into the North Sea. The river forms part of the Dutch-Belgian border. It is linked to the Rhine, Moselle, Marne, Scheldt, and Oise rivers by canals. The lower course of the river is an important shipping route for coal and iron ore.

The Mississippi River in the United States. See MISSISSIPPI RIVER.

The Missouri River in the United States. See MISSOURI RIVER.

Jebba, a fishing village on the Niger River, Nigeria.

The Murray River, the chief river of Australia, is 2,575 kilometers (1,600 miles) long. The Murray rises in the Australian Alps in New South Wales and empties into the Indian Ocean at Encounter Bay.

The Niger River, one of the longest rivers in Africa, is 4,200 kilometers (2,600 miles) long, with a drainage basin of about 1,500,000 square kilometers (600,000 square miles). Its waters irrigate an enormous area of West Africa. It empties into the Atlantic Ocean.

The Nile River in Egypt. See NILE RIVER.

The Ob River, with its tributary the Irtysh, rises in the Altai Mountains of Siberia and empties into Ob Bay, on the Kara Sea. It is 5,200 kilometers (3,230 miles) long. Most of the river is navigable several months of the year. It is an important source of hydro-electric power.

The Oder River rises in the Oder Mountains of Czechoslovakia, flows about 900 kilometers (560 miles) through Poland, and empties into the Stettin Lagoon, an arm of the Baltic Sea. The Oder is connected with the Vistula, the Elbe, and other rivers by a series of canals and tributaries. This system is an important trade route for iron, coke, and coal.

The Ohio River, in the United States, rises at the junction of the Allegheny and Mononga-hela rivers at Pittsburgh, Pennsylvania. The river, 1,578 kilometers (981 miles) long, is one of the chief tributaries of the Mississippi. Dams, reservoirs, and levees have been built on the Ohio to control seasonal floods and to aid navigation. Coal, petroleum products, sand and gravel, and steel products are shipped by river barge on the Ohio.

The Orange River in southern Africa is 2,100 kilometers (1,300 miles) long and rises in the Drakensberg, the main mountain range of South Africa. The river empties into the Atlantic Ocean. Diamond deposits are located near the mouth of the Orange River.

The Orinoco River is one of South America's greatest rivers. It rises in the Sierra Parima near the Venezuelan-Brazilian border and flows 2,160 kilometers (1,340 miles) across Venezuela to the Atlantic. The Orinoco is navigable for 1,600 kilometers (1,000 miles). The mouth of the delta was sighted by Columbus in 1498.

The Ottawa River forms part of the boundary between Quebec and Ontario provinces in Canada. It is 1,271 kilometers (790 miles) long, rises in Grand Lake Victoria in the Laurentian Plateau, and empties into the

The Rhine River at Oberwesel, West Germany.

St. Lawrence River near Montreal. The lower Ottawa is navigable for a distance of about 400 kilometers (250 miles).

The Paraguay River rises in Brazil and flows south about 2,170 kilometers (1,350 miles) to join the Paraná at the Argentine border. It is an important means of transportation.

The Paraná River, about 3,300 kilometers (2,050 miles) long, is second in size in South America to the Amazon River. It rises in southeastern Brazil and empties into the Río de la Plata near Buenos Aires in Argentina. It drains a vast area. The river forms part of the Río de la Plata estuary.

The Platte River is formed by the joining of the North and South Platte rivers, which rise in the Colorado Rockies. The North Platte–Platte River is 1,094 kilometers (680 miles) long. The Platte joins the Missouri River at Plattsmouth, Nebraska. It supplies hydro-

Tower Bridge, Thames River, London.

electric power and water for irrigation but is too shallow for navigation. Pioneers followed the Platte Valley westward.

The Po River, Italy's longest river, rises in the Italian Alps and flows eastward 652 kilometers (405 miles) to the Adriatic Sea. The Po is navigable for small boats for much of its length. The river irrigates crops in the Lombard fields and provides hydroelectric power for Italy's leading industrial area.

The Potomac River rises near Cumberland, Maryland, flows for 460 kilometers (285 miles), and empties into Chesapeake Bay. Just above Washington, D.C., are the Great Falls of the Potomac. The Potomac is navigable for small vessels for some distance downstream from Washington, D.C.

The Red River (Song Ca) in Vietnam rises in China and empties into the Gulf of Tonkin. It is about 1,175 kilometers (730 miles) long. Its red color is due to iron oxide in the silt the river carries. The Red River ends in a great delta below Hanoi. The delta was an important rice-producing area. Dikes for flood control line the channels of the delta.

The Rhine River rises in the Swiss Alps. It flows about 1,320 kilometers (820 miles) through Switzerland, Germany, and the Netherlands and empties into the North Sea. The Rhine flows along the Swiss-Austrian, Swiss-German, and French-German borders. Below Bonn the river passes through the Ruhr iron and coal district. Economically, it is the most important river of western Europe.

The Rhone River rises in the Swiss Alps. It flows for 815 kilometers (505 miles), passes through France, and empties into the Mediterranean. The Rhone supplies hydroelectric power and irrigates vineyards and olive groves.

The Río de la Plata is the 275-kilometer (170-mile) estuary on the Atlantic Ocean between Argentina and Uruguay, formed by the junction of the Paraná and Uruguay rivers. It is a vital waterway to inland South America. Its chief ports are Buenos Aires in Argentina and Montevideo in Uruguay. The name Río de la Plata is often given to the entire river system that includes the Paraná, Paraguay, and Uruguay rivers.

The Rio Grande, 3,033 kilometers (1,885 miles) in length, rises in the San Juan Mountains of Colorado. It flows through parts of Colorado, New Mexico, and Texas and emp-ties into the Gulf of Mexico near Brownsville. The river forms part of the boundary between the United States and Mexico. Dams on the Rio Grande create reservoirs and provide irrigation for crops, hydroelectric power, and flood control.

The Saint John River is 673 kilometers (418 miles) long. It rises in northern Maine and empties into the Bay of Fundy at St. John, New Brunswick. The river forms part of the border between the United States and Canada. High tides in the Bay of Fundy cause the river to reverse its flow, resulting in the famous Reversing Falls.

Saint Lawrence River. See SAINT LAWRENCE RIVER AND SEAWAY.

The Salween River of Southeast Asia rises in China (Tibet) and flows through Burma to empty into the Andaman Sea. The Salween is 2,820 kilometers (1,750 miles) long and forms part of the Burma-Thailand border.

The São Francisco River rises in Brazil and flows about 2,900 kilometers (1,800 miles) to the Atlantic. It is the main transportation route into the interior of eastern Brazil. The river supplies hydroelectric power for part of northeastern Brazil.

The Saskatchewan River with its tributaries is 1,939 kilometers (1,205 miles) long and rises in eastern Alberta in Canada. The river empties into Lake Winnipeg in Manitoba.

The Scheldt River rises in northeastern France. It flows across Belgium and empties into the North Sea through two estuaries in the Netherlands. About 435 kilometers (270 miles) long, it is part of an important network of waterways. Antwerp, Belgium's chief port, is on the Scheldt.

The Seine River, France's most navigable river, rises in the Plateau of Langres and enters the English Channel at Le Havre. The river is 775 kilometers (482 miles) long. It flows through Paris and divides the city into the "Left Bank" and "Right Bank."

The Shannon River, Ireland's chief river, is about 355 kilometers (220 miles) long. It rises near the border of Northern Ireland and empties into the Atlantic. Canals link the Shannon with Dublin on the Liffey.

The Si Kiang (West River) is southern China's longest river. It is about 2,000 kilometers (1,250 miles) long. It empties into the South China Sea through the Pearl River.

The **Sungari River** in Manchuria rises near the Chinese–North Korean border and flows into the Amur River. It is about 1,850 kilometers (1,150 miles) long. Its waters provide power for northeastern China's largest hydroelectric plant.

The **Tagus River,** a major river of Spain and Portugal, rises in eastern Spain. It flows for about 910 kilometers (565 miles) to Lisbon in Portugal, where it enters the Atlantic. The river cuts through mountains and deep gorges marked by falls and rapids.

The **Tennessee River** is formed by the joining of two rivers, the Holston and French Broad rivers, east of Knoxville, Tennessee. It is 1,049 kilometers (652 miles) in length and empties into the Ohio River. The chief cities on the Tennessee are Knoxville and Chattanooga, Tennessee. The Tennessee Valley Authority (TVA), a government-owned agency, has constructed reservoirs, dams, and hydroelectric power plants on the Tennessee River and its tributaries.

The **Thames River** is England's chief water highway. It rises in the Cotswold Hills of Gloucester and flows about 340 kilometers (210 miles) before emptying into the North Sea. Famous communities on the banks of the river include Eton, Oxford, Henley—scene of the Royal Regatta—Windsor, and Reading. The Thames flows through London, passing the Houses of Parliament and the Tower of London.

The **Tiber River** in central Italy rises in the Etruscan Apennines. It flows 345 kilometers (215 miles) across the Sabine Mountains, through Rome, and into the Tyrrhenian Sea. Dams and reservoirs provide irrigation.

The **Tigris and the Euphrates** are two great rivers of southwestern Asia. They rise in Turkey, flow roughly parallel, and join in Iraq. The Euphrates is about 2,700 kilometers (1,700 miles) long. It is broad and too shallow for navigation except by small boats. The Tigris is 1,850 kilometers (1,150 miles) long. It is swifter, carries more water, and is more navigable. The rivers are linked by irrigation canals. The region between them was called Mesopotamia ("land between rivers"). It is considered one of the birthplaces of civilization.

The **Ural River** in the Soviet Union rises in the Ural Mountains and empties into the Caspian Sea. It is 2,530 kilometers (1,570 miles)

long. The Ural supplies water to the dry steppes of Kazakhstan. It is partly navigable but freezes over in winter.

The **Uruguay River** rises in the mountains near the southeastern coast of Brazil. It flows along the Brazil-Argentina and the Argentina-Uruguay borders. It is about 1,600 kilometers (1,000 miles) long and forms part of the Río de la Plata estuary.

The **Vistula River,** Poland's longest river, rises near the Czechoslovakian border and flows 1,090 kilometers (678 miles) to the Baltic Sea. Warsaw is on its banks. Canals link the Vistula with the Oder River.

The **Volga River,** Europe's largest, is the chief water highway of the Soviet Union. It rises in the Valdai Hills west of Moscow and flows for 3,690 kilometers (2,290 miles), emptying into the Caspian Sea near Astrakhan. It drains one third of the European Soviet Union. Canals connect the upper Volga with Moscow and the Baltic and White seas. The Don-Volga canal permits shipping to reach the Black Sea and the Mediterranean. The Volga has several large dams and hydroelectric plants.

The **Weser River** in West Germany is formed by the joining of the Fulda and Werra rivers, which rise in the Rhön Mountains. The Weser flows 480 kilometers (300 miles) and enters the North Sea near Bremerhaven.

The **Western Dvina River** in the Soviet Union rises in the Valdai Hills and flows 1,020 kilometers (635 miles) through Belorussia and Latvia to empty into the Gulf of Riga.

The **Yalu River** rises in northeastern China and flows southwest about 800 kilometers (500 miles) to Korea Bay in the Yellow Sea. The river is a source of hydroelectric power for China and North Korea. The Yalu forms the border between China and North Korea.

The **Yangtze River** in China. See YANGTZE RIVER.

The **Yellow River** (Hwang Ho) in China. See CHINA.

The **Yenisei River,** one of the world's longest rivers, rises in the Eastern Sayan Mountains. It flows through Siberia for about 3,800 kilometers (2,360 miles) to empty into the Yenisei Gulf of the Kara Sea. The Yenisei is navigable during the ice-free season. Boats carry grain and lumber to Krasnoyarsk.

The **Yukon River,** one of the longest rivers in North America, is 3,185 kilometers (1,979

Victoria Falls on the Zambezi River between Zambia and Zimbabwe (Rhodesia).

Twenty-five bridges cross the historic Tiber River in Rome.

miles) long and rises in the Yukon Territory, Canada. The river flows through Alaska, passes the Arctic Circle, and empties into the Bering Sea. During the summer months the river is navigable as far as Whitehorse in the Yukon Territory. Gold was discovered along the banks of the Yukon during the Klondike gold-rush days (1897–98).

The Zambezi River in southern Africa is about 2,600 kilometers (1,600 miles) long and drains a large area. It rises in Angola, flows through Zambia and Mozambique, and empties into the Indian Ocean. The Zambezi forms part of the boundary between Zambia and Zimbabwe (Rhodesia). Only the lower Zambezi is navigable. The spectacular Victoria Falls are on the middle Zambezi.

FRANK SEAWALL
California State University—Chico
VERA L. HERMAN
Ohio State University

RIVETS. See NAILS, SCREWS, AND RIVETS.

Junks on the Yangtze River, Shanghai.

Cloverleaf interchange on a highway near Toronto, Canada.

ROADS AND HIGHWAYS

When we speed along a modern highway, we rarely stop to think what it is we are riding on. To understand what a road is, we must study the ways in which people have traveled in the past.

The very first roads were really tracks beaten in the ground by wild animals in prehistoric times. People followed these winding trails because they provided an easy and quick way to get through thick forests. In time, people began to improve the paths by filling holes with earth and laying logs across soft, boggy spots. These attempts were crude, but they were the beginning of road construction.

As people began to transport goods over longer distances, they developed new ways of traveling. First they packed their wares on animals. Then they invented various kinds of sleds. Finally, after the invention of the wheel, they built wagons. Each advancement brought a need for better traveling routes.

Later in history, when well-traveled routes were made sturdier with rocks and stones, the path was raised above the surrounding land; it became a "high way." (The word "road" comes from the same root as the word "ride.")

Roads in Ancient Civilizations

The great civilizations throughout history were also the great road builders. Roads were necessary to control and extend empires, to permit trade and travel, and to move armies. As early as 3000 B.C., roads were built in Mesopotamia, and later in Egypt, India, and China. Most of these early roads were simply hard-packed dirt; but some were paved with stone blocks or burnt bricks.

The Romans were the most impressive road builders of the ancient world. Over 80,000 kilometers (50,000 miles) of roads, many of them well paved, stretched in a vast network all over the Roman Empire, from Britain through Europe into Asia and down to North Africa. Some of the Roman roads are still in existence today. And many modern highways follow the ancient Roman routes.

The New Era

For over 1,000 years after the Roman era, Europe's road system was neglected. Wars were being fought, countries were poor, and people had little interest in travel. Roman roads were forgotten and left to decay. Then, as Europe slowly recovered, strong rulers seized power and created new countries. Trade and travel became important for the growth of the new countries, and their rulers turned their attention once more to the building of roads.

During the 18th and early 19th centuries, France and England took the lead in road building. Pierre-Marie Jérôme Trésaguet (1716–94) was the most prominent French road builder. He built roads in three layers, putting very large rocks at the bottom and smaller stones in each following layer.

The most influential British road designer was John Loudon McAdam (1756–1836). McAdam believed that the most important thing in road building was to make sure the foundation was well drained. On this dry and firm bed he put a thick layer of small stones. This layer was packed down by allowing traffic to pass over it. Then another layer of fine rock was added. McAdam's method was so successful that his roads were soon built even in the United States.

At about the same time, private English companies began to build roads and charge tolls to pay for building and maintenance costs. The roads were called turnpikes, and they helped greatly to further road building.

When Napoleon, in 1800, began an extensive road-building project to move his armies around, he laid the foundation for modern organized road building in Europe.

But in rural areas roads were still poor. When it rained, the roads were slippery, and in dry weather they were dusty. People using horses and wagons accepted this. But with the beginning of the 20th century a new invention, the automobile, began to take over the road. To keep up with the new vehicle and its demands, roads had to be built ever better and stronger. As a result, the modern superhighway was eventually developed.

▶ BUILDING MODERN ROADS

The first step in building a road is to plan the route. Sometimes the route has been decided by the nature of the land, but today nature can often be conquered. With powerful modern machinery, whole mountains can be removed and valleys filled in to make the route as direct as possible.

Then the details are planned: the width of the highway, the number of driving lanes, the number and location of entrances and exits, and how strong the road must be. All these depend on the amount of traffic that is expected. Modern roads are usually planned for the next 20 years' traffic.

The next step is the testing of the earth foundation on which the road is to rest. Engineers carefully study the soil to learn how solid it is, how much moisture it contains, and how well it drains. Then they decide how the soil should be prepared and packed to provide a good, sturdy foundation, or **roadbed**. They prescribe the thickness of the road layers, the size of the rocks in them, and the other materials that should be used.

While the testing is under way, a group of **surveyors** begins to measure the land to find out exactly how much work needs to be done and how much it will cost. Then the construction crew can finally move in.

Giant bulldozers clear the path for the roadbed. They knock over trees and tear large rocks out of the ground. Other powerful earth-moving machines, such as loaders and scrapers, follow in their tracks, scoop up earth and rocks, and dump them into low spots. These filling materials are pressed down tightly with power rollers, and gradually the roadbed becomes a long, level band of hard-packed dirt.

Proper drainage is essential in road building, because if the foundation became soggy, the heavy road would sink into it. And if the water were to freeze in the ground, it would expand and crack the road. To protect the highway from such damage, drainpipes called **culverts** are laid across the roadbed wherever a strong flow of water is expected. The roadbed itself is shaped so that the middle of the finished road will be higher than the sides. Then water and melting snow will easily drain off its surface into the drainpipes or ditches. The roadbed is given a final **grading** (smoothing) and is now ready to receive the road itself.

Almost all roads are built in two or more layers, or **courses**, of rocks or stones. The bottom layer is 10 to 20 centimeters (4 to 8 inches) thick and usually made up of larger stones. The upper course has smaller stones and is about 8 centimeters (3 inches) thick. In most roads the lower course is wider so that the edges, or shoulders, of the top course do not break off or sink into soft dirt. After each course is laid, it is compacted (pressed together) by heavy power rollers.

The top, or surface, layer of a road must withstand the weight of heavy vehicles. It must also prevent water from seeping into the roadbed and destroying it. Modern highways are therefore surfaced either with concrete or with **bituminous materials**, such as asphalt, tar, or heavy oils.

Asphalt is the most commonly used bituminous material. It can be found in its natural state or it may be manufactured from crude oil. It is well suited for road surfaces because it needs no water for mixing and will not let water get through. It is generally poured on the road in a layer 5 centimeters (2 inches) thick. Since asphalt has a dark color, roads surfaced with it often are called **blacktop** roads.

This basic rock-layer method for building up roads can be varied in a number of ways. Sometimes hot asphalt is sprayed on each layer to fill any spaces between the rocks. Tar is often used in the same way. Roads built this way are generally called macadam roads, because they are like the original McAdam layer roads with tar, or sometimes oil, added as a binder.

Ready-made mixtures of asphalt, rock, and cement are also used as surface layers. These mixtures may be applied either hot or cold. Often water alone is used as a binder. It is sprinkled over a surface of fine dust and is rolled until it is pressed into the layer below. This method is likely to be used for country roads with little traffic. Highways that have to carry heavy, high-speed traffic usually are surfaced with concrete.

This section of interstate highway I-95 in Virginia has many safety features. Some of these features are a wide center strip between traffic going in opposite directions, long sight distances, gentle curves, entry and exit lanes, and wide paved shoulders.

Concrete Highways

Concrete is a mixture of cement, sand, gravel or broken rock, and water. It can be poured easily as a thick liquid, and it dries into a hard mass.

When used for surfacing, the concrete is poured on a solidly packed layer of stones or gravel. To keep the concrete from spreading out while drying, bars of steel are laid along each side of the section that is being poured. Concrete is mixed right at the construction site in huge machines called **pavers**. As the paver moves along the road, it drops load after load of wet concrete on the lane. A **spreader** follows behind and spreads the piles evenly between the steel forms. Then **vibrators** shake the concrete to get out all the air bubbles. A concrete layer may be from 20 to 30 centimeters (8 to 12 inches) thick.

Concrete expands (swells) in hot weather and contracts (shrinks) in cold weather. This means that if it were laid in one long, uninterrupted band, the road would buckle and crack in the summer. In the winter, the buckled-up places would crumble and become holes. To prevent the weather from causing damage to roads and highways, concrete is laid in slabs from 3.5 to 9 meters (12 to 30 feet) long. To connect the slabs—and to keep water from entering—tar or asphalt is poured between them. These narrow strips across the driving lane are called **expansion joints**.

Concrete is often strengthened, or re-inforced, with metal. Steel rods or a mesh of steel wire is placed on a layer of wet concrete, and another layer of concrete is then poured over it.

Safety on Highways

Roads and highways are built for fast travel in high-speed vehicles and must therefore be as safe as possible. Some safety devices can be built right into the road; others are added when the road is finished.

For instance, steep hills are lowered so that the road rises gradually. Curves are designed to be wide and clear. This allows the driver to see well ahead, and it prevents cars from skidding, especially on wet or icy roads. To be safe, roads should be fairly straight. But if there are too many long, straight stretches, a driver may get drowsy. Highways are therefore deliberately constructed with a gentle curve now and then. On concrete roads, motorists have sometimes been lulled to sleep by the regular thudding noise that tires make when rolling over the expansion joints. This is why new highways are built with slabs of irregular sizes.

When a car makes a turn, its speed and weight combined tend to push it outward and off the road. To counteract this force, the road is tilted, or **banked**, so that the outside curve is higher than the inside curve. This tilt is shaped into the roadbed and repeated in every layer up to the surface.

Road crossings are often constructed in several levels in order to permit traffic to flow quickly and to avoid collisions. Sometimes entry and exit roads are curved in a regular pattern of circles to and from each level. Such crossings are called **cloverleaf** crossings.

The safety devices added to the finished highway include warning signs, lights, painted lines to mark traffic lanes, guide rails, and many others. Warning signs for curves, hills, turn-offs, merging traffic, and a number of other dangers are a must on modern highways. Signs have to be clear and simple so that the driver can recognize them quickly. Travel lanes are usually divided by lines painted on the road surface, sometimes in a paint that reflects light. Light-reflecting paint is also used on guide rails at the side of the road. At intersections or at dangerous stretches, overhead lighting is often installed. Reflecting lights may be spaced along the side of the road, especially in curves.

The glare from the lights of oncoming traffic at night can be a great danger. To block out this glare, trees and bushes are planted on the center strip between opposing traffic lanes.

GEORGE N. BEAUMARIAGE, JR.
Formerly, California State University—
Sacramento

See also BULLDOZERS AND OTHER CONSTRUCTION EQUIPMENT; PAN AMERICAN HIGHWAY.

ROBIN HOOD

Robin Hood is one of England's most famous legendary heroes. No one knows whether he really lived, but he is very much alive in story and ballad.

According to legend, Robin Hood was an outlaw who lived with a large company of followers in Sherwood Forest, near Nottingham. They were a carefree band who spent their time hunting the king's deer, testing their skill at archery, and robbing the rich to give to the poor. They loved the greenwood and a free life, were brave and adventurous, and protected women and children.

Robin's right-hand man was Little John. He got his name because he was tremendously tall and strong. Friar Tuck was Robin's chaplain and confessor. Others in his band were Will Scarlet, Arthur-a-Bland, Will Stutely, Much, and the minstrel Allen-a-Dale. Robin's sweetheart was Maid Marian.

Toward the close of the Middle Ages, Robin Hood was the hero of the common people. Here was a man of action, a man of humor, who was at the same time a champion of the poor against the tyranny of the wealthy nobility. Robin and his band risked everything to see that simple folk were treated justly. One of his great enemies was the Sheriff of Nottingham, who defended the rich and oppressed the poor. In the same period, the nobility found their ideal in King Arthur and his Knights of the Round Table.

The oldest mention of Robin is in an edition of *Piers Plowman* published about 1377. One legend says Robin was the Earl of Huntingdon and lived from 1160 to 1247. A grave at Kirklees Priory, Yorkshire, is supposed to be his.

After the 15th century, May Day celebrations turned into Robin Hood plays. The May king and queen were called Robin Hood and Maid Marian. Young men in the archery contests took the names of Robin's merry men. The ballads about Robin were sung and dramatized. This Robin Hood may be a combination of the English Robin Hood and a Robin that came from France. Plays given at Whitsuntide in France in the 13th century had a shepherd hero called Robin. French minstrels may have brought the name to England in their ballads.

Robin Hood appears in Sir Walter Scott's novel *Ivanhoe.* More than 30 ballads about him still exist.

Many great writers have retold the stories of Robin Hood for young readers. One of these was Howard Pyle, whose book *The Merry Adventures of Robin Hood* was published in 1883, with strong, clear illustrations by Pyle.

More recently, in 1959, Orville Prescott wrote *Robin Hood: The Outlaw of Sherwood Forest,* a collection of seven stories. One of the Prescott stories is given below.

NANCY LARRICK
Author, *A Parent's Guide to Children's Reading*

▶ THE ARCHERY CONTEST

The longer Robin Hood and his band dwelt in Sherwood Forest the more famous did they become, and the proud Sheriff of Nottingham gnawed his mustache and pulled his beard in rage. No matter what he did he could not catch the merry outlaw. His troops searched the forest, but no sign of Robin Hood could they find. Few men dared to try to capture Robin Hood by themselves. And some of those who did, instead of claiming a reward of 200 pounds, stayed in Sherwood Forest with Robin Hood instead. The Sheriff swore to hang any member of Robin Hood's band as a traitor to the King, but nothing he did could stop the sly smiles and mocking jokes of the people who loved Robin Hood.

So off to London town rode the Sheriff to see the King. If he could not capture Robin Hood with the troops he had, he would ask for more. And, because he was afraid of Robin Hood, he took most of his own armed guard with him to keep him safe upon the road. In London town when the Sheriff finished complaining about Robin Hood and asking for help, knights and squires, pikemen and archers, the King sat silent for a while glaring at the Sheriff. Finally he said, "Are not you my Sheriff in Nottingham? Have not you stalwart armed men of your own as I have seen with mine own eyes? Can not you maintain the King's justice against a few paltry outlaws without a suit of armor or even a horse to call their own? If you cannot, I must soon find me a new Sheriff of Nottingham who can. Go hence and see that you capture that bold thief right quickly."

Sad and perplexed was the Sheriff of Nottingham as he rode home from London town. And bitterly angry was he, and ashamed. But what was he to do? Finally he remembered that Robin Hood was said to be the finest archer in all England and doubtless, like other men, he was

proud of his skill. If, then, another archery contest were held in Nottingham and a fine prize were offered—an arrow made entirely of gold for instance—could Robin Hood resist competing for it? And if he came and shot, could he not be captured by the Sheriff's men? The gloomy Sheriff began to smile.

Only a few days later, as Robin Hood sat on a mossy bank under the greenwood tree, young David of Doncaster came trotting up to him. "Master," he said. "I have news. Our good friend the Sheriff of Nottingham has proclaimed a great archery match and invites all who wish to try their skill to come and shoot. The prize will be a bright golden arrow made of solid gold."

"How I would like to win the Sheriff's arrow!" said Robin Hood. "It is a temptation hard to resist. Shall I see what I can do?"

"Nay, Master," said Little John. "Would you put your head in the lion's mouth? It is but a trick to capture you. If you must shoot in the Sheriff's archery match, at least disguise yourself."

"Well spoken, good Little John," said Robin Hood. "It is a measure of reasonable caution which keeps brave men alive. Let us then take off our suits of Lincoln green. Let some of us dress as monks and some as peasants, and some as tinkers and some as butchers, and some as yeomen and some as beggars. And I myself will dress in scarlet, those tattered rags we took from that poor beggar yesternight when we gave him a much better suit. And I will wear a patch over my left eye and shave my beard. And if none of you begrudges me the privilege, I alone will shoot in the contest. But you must all mingle with the crowd, and stand ready to come to my aid if I should need you."

So after three days had gone by, Robin Hood and his men went off to Nottingham town on the day of the great archery match. A gay crowd all dressed in holiday clothes was there. Benches had been erected for the better sort, and ropes were nailed to posts to keep the common people from crowding in too close. From the high plat-

form where the Sheriff sat, he could see the targets and could watch the archers as they took their turns.

There were thirty archers waiting, stout men famous for their skill in Nottinghamshire, and in Derbyshire and Lincolnshire, too. The Sheriff glared at them all, but none looked like the outlaw he had heard described so often.

As the match continued and fewer archers remained to shoot their arrows, the Sheriff's smiles turned to scowls. "I thought that surely he would be here," said he to the captain of his guard. "He's supposed to be a bold fellow who likes an archery match above all things. The best of these archers are all known to me, or, if they are not, they are too big or too small, too dark or too freckled. He did not dare to come, and I have wasted my money on that golden arrow."

Now only six contestants were left, and the excited crowd cheered loudly for a man in tattered scarlet with a patch over his left eye. All shot well. But he shot better. The others hit the bull's-eyes. But he hit the center of the bull's-eyes. Such mastery of the yew bow had never been seen before in Nottingham town, and never had such loud cheers been heard there as when the Sheriff presented the golden arrow to the archer in scarlet who refused to tell his name.

Back went Robin Hood and his merry men to their home in the thickest and most secret part of Sherwood Forest. Happy and gay were they, and the men shouted and laughed and sang. But Robin Hood was strangely silent.

"Master, what is the matter?" asked good Little John. "Have not you shot bravely today? Have not you tricked the Sheriff of Nottingham who thought to trick you? Why then so solemn?"

"It vexes me," said Robin Hood, "that the Sheriff of Nottingham knows not to whom he gave this golden arrow. I will hang it on our greenwood tree, but half the pleasure of beholding it there will be lost to me if the Sheriff thinks that Robin Hood did not dare shoot in his archery contest."

"As for that," said Little John, "let's write a letter and tell our friend the Sheriff all about it."

"But how shall we deliver it so that we can be sure the Sheriff will read it?" asked Robin Hood.

"Leave it to me," said Little John. "I cannot shoot quite as well as you do, Master, but I can shoot quite well enough to send an arrow through the window of the Sheriff's dining hall with a letter wrapped around its shaft and neatly tied there with a bit of bow string."

On the following day, as the Sheriff sat at dinner in his castle, no one noticed a tall man in a friar's dress who strolled in pious meditation beneath the castle wall. And no one noticed either when he drew forth from beneath his robe a bow and arrow and shot through the window of the great hall. But the Sheriff of Nottingham, when he read Robin Hood's letter thanking him for the gift of a golden arrow, was more furiously angry than ever before. And he swore by all the saints that somehow he would contrive to hang bold Robin Hood.

But to hang Robin Hood the Sheriff had first to catch him. And how to do that when he had never knowingly laid eyes upon him? "Dearly would I like to have that saucy rogue right here in my own hall," thought the Sheriff. "If I could have him here but once, how joyful I would be. He would not trouble me long thereafter." Little did the Sheriff know how soon Robin Hood would feast at his own table and how little joy he would have of it.

ROBINSON, JACK ROOSEVELT (JACKIE) (1919–1972)

January 23, 1962, was a big day in the life of Jackie Robinson. On that day he was elected to the Baseball Hall of Fame—the first black ever to achieve this honor.

Jack Roosevelt Robinson was born on January 31, 1919, in Cairo, Georgia. When he was a baby, his family moved to Pasadena, California. During his school days Jackie excelled in all sports. He set a broad-jump record, he was a star basketball and baseball player, and he made the second team in All-American football.

During World War II, Robinson served in the Army, first as an enlisted man and later as a commissioned officer. After his release from active duty he coached basketball. Then he turned to baseball, playing shortstop with the Kansas City Monarchs, a team in the Negro American Baseball League.

Baseball at that time was a segregated sport. During World War II, Branch Rickey, president of the then Brooklyn Dodgers, decided that the time had come for a change. Robinson was signed by Brooklyn in 1945 and was sent to the Montreal Royals, a Dodger farm team, in 1946. In 1947 he joined the parent club. He encountered much prejudice his first year. But he still excelled and was chosen Rookie of the Year in 1947.

Robinson was an aggressive and thrilling baserunner and a determined player. He compiled a career batting average of .311. In 1949 he was named the National League's Most Valuable Player. During the ten years that Robinson played with the Dodgers, they won six National League pennants and the 1955 World Series. He retired from baseball in 1957 and was active in business and civil rights until his death on October 24, 1972.

Reviewed by MONTE IRVIN
Member, Baseball Hall of Fame

ROCKEFELLER, JOHN D. (1839–1937)

John D. Rockefeller founded the Standard Oil Company and amassed such a fortune that his name came to stand for wealth and power.

John Davison Rockefeller was born near Richford, New York, on July 8, 1839. He was the second of six children. In 1853, the family moved to Cleveland, Ohio, where he attended high school. At 16, he went to work for a firm of farm-produce shippers. Four years later, he went into that business for himself.

In 1863, Rockefeller bought an interest in an oil-refining company. In 1870, he founded the Standard Oil Company with his brother William and three other partners. By the 1880's, the company was one of the largest and richest manufacturing concerns in the world.

Besides his business, Rockefeller's main interest was his family. He had married Laura Celestia Spelman in 1864. They had three daughters—Bessie, Edith, and Alta—and one son, John D. Rockefeller, Jr. (1874–1960).

Starting from the first Standard Oil Company in Ohio, the Rockefeller business grew into a large combination of companies, called a trust, that almost monopolized the oil business. Growing criticism of the Rockefeller trust led to investigations. In 1911, the U.S. Supreme Court ruled that the Standard Oil Company was a monopoly in restraint of trade and ordered it broken up. It was replaced by 38 separate companies, many of them controlled by Rockefeller and his associates.

In spite of his great wealth, Rockefeller lived a simple, thrifty life. He seldom went to the theater or concerts and paid little attention to clothes or food. One of his favorite dishes was bread and milk.

Rockefeller founded the University of Chicago in 1892. He received so many requests for gifts that he needed help in planning his philanthropy. Four organizations were set up to help give his money to worthy causes—the Rockefeller Institute for Medical Research (founded 1901), the General Education Board (1903), the Rockefeller Foundation (1913), and the Laura Spelman Rockefeller Memorial (1918).

Rockefeller died at the age of 97 on May 23, 1937, in Ormond, Florida. He was buried in Lake View Cemetery, Cleveland, Ohio.

Reviewed by GERALD KURLAND
Author, *John D. Rockefeller*

ROCKETS

Although rockets were invented in China about 700 years ago, only in the past 20 to 30 years have they been used widely. This is because the modern rocket can travel faster than any other vehicle yet invented. It is also because the rocket is the only kind of vehicle that can operate in the near-emptiness of outer space.

When you think of a rocket, you probably picture a complete vehicle of some kind. Perhaps you think of a bullet-shaped missile or a giant spacecraft launcher. But "rocket" is really the name for a kind of engine. Rockets can supply power to anything that must be propelled—a spacecraft, a boat, an automobile, or a missile. In fact, rocket power has been used to propel all of these.

▶ HOW A ROCKET WORKS

In its simplest form a rocket is a tube of fuel closed at one end and open at the other. When the fuel burns, it turns to a gas. Hot gas expands and pushes outward in all directions. In a rocket the expanding gas rushes out at the open end. The action of the rushing gas causes the container to move in the opposite direction. The faster the gas rushes out, the faster the container moves.

By experimenting with a garden hose, you can see for yourself how rockets work. Put the hose on a fairly smooth surface, and turn the water on full force. Adjust the nozzle until you get the most powerful jet. See how the hose twists and turns as the water rushing out forces the nozzle backward.

When a gas or liquid is forced out of an opening at high speed, the container out of which it rushes is pushed in the opposite direction. Even the largest rockets work on this principle. The push, in rocket language, is called **thrust**. Thrust is measured in pounds.

Rockets and Newton's Laws of Motion

The way rockets and garden hoses behave can be explained by three laws of motion. These laws were first discovered by the great English scientist Sir Isaac Newton and published in 1687.

Newton's third law describes the force that gives the rocket its power. The law states that

Hot gas shoots upward as rocket engine is test-fired.

for every action there is an equal reaction in the opposite direction.

A good example of action and reaction is swimming. When a person swims, he pushes the water backward with his hands and arms, and his body is propelled forward. The same thing happens in paddling a canoe. The paddle pushes the water backward, and the canoe shoots forward. The backward motion of the arms or the paddle against the water is the action. The forward motion of the body or the canoe is the reaction.

Water rushing from a hose is action. The movement of the hose nozzle is reaction. In a rocket, burning fuel inside the rocket gives off exhaust gases. The gases rush out through an opening in the rear of the rocket. The rocket's forward motion is the reaction to the backward motion of the escaping gases.

Once a rocket is launched, it accelerates—that is, its speed increases as long as its engines fire. This is in accordance with Newton's second law of motion. The law says that acceleration depends on the amount of force applied. The greater the force produced by the rocket's exhaust, the faster the rocket will go.

Newton's first law is called the law of inertia. It states that a body at rest remains at rest unless acted upon by some outside force. A body in motion in a straight line continues such motion unless acted upon by some outside force. Another way of saying this is:

Bodies at rest or in motion resist change. This resistance is called inertia.

In launching a rocket, force must be applied to it in order to overcome its inertia. This force comes from the thrust produced by the exhaust gases. A bigger rocket needs more thrust than a smaller one. The amount of thrust required depends on the weight of the rocket.

Rocketry is based on these three laws of motion. An understanding of these laws will enable you to understand how rockets behave as they do.

Rockets Work in Space

Airplanes need air in order to fly. But a rocket does not need air. In fact, a rocket works best in outer space, where there is no air. Near the earth's surface the rocket must cut its way through the air. The air creates friction, or drag, against the rocket and tends to slow it down. At higher altitudes the air becomes thinner. As the rocket rises there is less air to create a drag. In outer space there is almost no drag against the rocket to slow it down.

Rockets are the only engines that can operate in outer space. In order to burn, fuels must combine with a type of chemical called an oxidizer. Oxygen is the most common oxidizer. Large quantities of oxygen are present in the air. Airplanes take in air and use its oxygen to burn their fuel. But rockets carry their own oxidizer, in liquid or solid form, inside their cases. They do not need oxygen from the air.

▶ ROCKET POWER

Have you ever seen firemen using a big fire hose? It reacts violently to the rush of the water. Two or more firemen must hold the hose to keep the water going in the right direction and the nozzle from whipping around. Can you see why it is harder to control a fire hose than a garden hose? The pressure is the same in the water main that supplies water to both hoses. Therefore, it must be the greater amount of water rushing through the fire hose that makes the big hose react as it does.

In the same way, a large amount of gas rushing out of the exhaust of a rocket gives the rocket a large thrust. And a large amount of

March, 1926: Robert Goddard prepares to launch the world's first liquid-fuel rocket.

exhaust gas is produced when a large amount of fuel is burned each second.

Increasing Rocket Power

If a rocket is to go very fast, its engines must be in operation long enough to accelerate it to the proper speed. This may take one to several minutes, depending on the rocket's weight. Large rockets must carry large amounts of fuel. At the same time, the weight of the rocket shell must be kept down.

To keep the rocket's weight down, lightweight metals and strong, lightweight plastics are used for the shell. Rockets have been made with "skins" so thin and light that they

are like collapsible stainless-steel balloons. One rocket has a stainless-steel skin that is thinner than a dime. When the fuel tanks are empty, pressure must be maintained inside the rockets. Otherwise they would collapse and break. When the fuel tanks are filled, the pressure of the fuel and oxidizer keeps the rockets rigid.

The Payload

A rocket is a vehicle designed to carry something. Whatever it carries is called its payload. Large rockets are made to carry large payloads. Small rockets carry small ones.

The payload's destination is also important in the planning of the rocket's design. A larger and more powerful rocket is needed to launch a satellite into orbit 600 miles above the earth than to carry a missile to a height of 50 miles. One type of rocket can place a 6,500-pound payload into an orbit about 150 miles above the earth. But it can carry only about 750 pounds to the moon or 450 pounds to Mars.

▶ ROCKET FUELS

The amount of fuel a rocket burns each second is important in giving a rocket its power. But the kind of fuel that the rocket burns is just as important.

Some fuels produce more thrust than others. The most energetic rocket fuel known is hydrogen. Hydrogen is the lightest of all gases. A gas is not suitable as a rocket fuel, however, because it takes up too much space. For use as a rocket fuel, hydrogen is compressed until it becomes a liquid. Liquid

Cutaway view of a liquid-fuel rocket. Pumps drive fuel and oxidizer to combustion chamber.

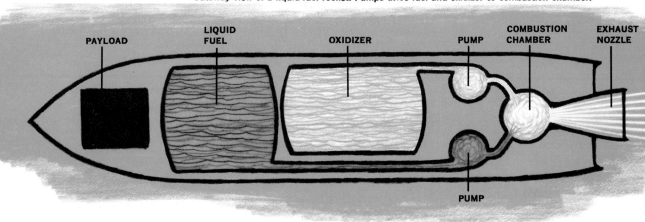

PAYLOAD   LIQUID FUEL   OXIDIZER   PUMP   COMBUSTION CHAMBER   EXHAUST NOZZLE   PUMP

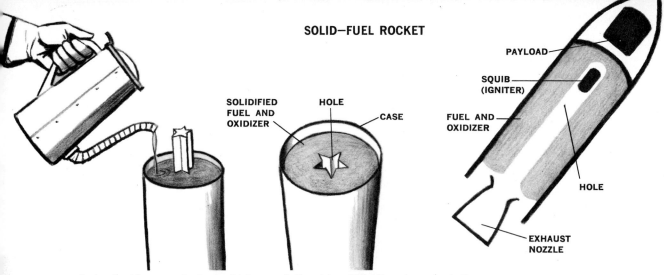

Fuel and oxidizer are mixed around a form and allowed to solidify. Form is removed after propellant has hardened. (Shape and size of hole help determine the amount of thrust of the rocket.) Case containing propellant is then installed in rocket.

hydrogen has a temperature of −423 degrees Fahrenheit. Because it is so cold, it is very difficult to handle even with the greatest care. It is also very expensive. Therefore it is used in rockets only when its high energy is absolutely necessary.

There are several hydrogen-rich fuels that are liquid at ordinary temperatures. Two important ones are kerosene and hydrazine. Certain hydrogen-rich solids also are used as fuels. Some types of rubber and plastics are such solids.

Oxidizers for Rocket Fuels

Fuels must be burned to release their energy. They must therefore be combined with an oxidizer. Pure oxygen is one of the best to use because it combines so readily with fuels. It is a very energetic oxidizer. In liquid form, pure oxygen is called **lox**, from the first letters of "liquid" and "oxygen." Lox is frequently used as the oxidizer in liquid-fuel rockets.

Fluorine, a gas, is a more energetic oxidizer than pure oxygen. But fluorine is dangerous and very hard to work with. At present, scientists are able to use only a little liquid fluorine, which they add to lox to make an "oxidizer-fluoridizer" called **flox** (fluorine-lox). Flox is a better oxidizer than lox.

Lox and flox cannot be stored very long in a rocket. One reason for this is that they boil constantly, turning back into a gas. Rockets that use them must be "loxed" or "floxed" at the last moment before launching.

Besides lox and flox, other oxidizers are often used. Nitric acid and nitrogen tetroxide are liquid oxidizers. Ammonium nitrate and ammonium perchlorate are solid oxidizers.

The combination of a fuel and an oxidizer is called a bi-propellant, or simply propellant. In general, liquid propellants produce a greater thrust than solid propellants.

▶CHOOSING PROPELLANTS

The rocket engineer chooses propellants according to the job the rocket is to do. He usually chooses a solid propellant for small military rockets. Rockets that use solid propellants can be fueled, then stored for long periods of time. They are always ready for use.

In fueling a solid-propellant rocket, the fuel and oxidizer are first mixed together outside the rocket. Other chemicals are added to make the mixture burn evenly and to make it stick to the rocket case.

At first, the mixture is a thick liquid, like molasses. While still soft, the mixture is poured into the rocket case around a form set into the case. The fuel hardens inside the case. The form is then pulled out, leaving a hole in the solid fuel. The size and shape of the hole left in the mixture determine how fast the fuel will burn.

Most solid fuels are not as energetic as liquid fuels, but solid-fuel rockets can be ready for action at all times, so most military rockets use solid fuels. Some military rockets use a special type of liquid propellant that can be stored in the rocket. The rocket can then be fueled and kept ready for action.

Different liquid propellants are used if the rocket does not need to be ready at all times and if it needs exceptionally great power. Such rockets, for example, are used to put a spacecraft into orbit. These rockets are fueled just before they are launched.

Liquid-propellant rockets are more difficult to design and operate than solid-propellant rockets. One reason for this is that liquid-propellant rockets have a complicated system of tanks, pumps, valves, and pipes. The liquid fuel and the oxidizer must be carried in separate tanks. Hoses and pumps are needed to feed the liquids to the rocket engines.

Because this "plumbing" is so complicated, it can easily get out of order. When something goes wrong with big rockets, a faulty plumbing system is usually the reason.

▶ ROCKET STAGES

A single enormous rocket could be built to carry a heavy payload into space. But it would not be economical or efficient, because the weight of the fuel and the fuel tanks would be very great. Tremendous thrust would be needed to lift such a rocket and accelerate it to the proper speed.

A rocket needs the most thrust at launching in order to overcome its inertia. Once started, the rocket becomes lighter as its propellants are burned. This means there is a constant decrease in the amount of weight the thrust must accelerate, and so the rocket gains speed very fast.

After a few seconds of flight a rocket's fuel tanks are no longer full. But the tanks themselves are very heavy. The empty part of the tanks is unnecessary weight in a rocket. The rocket would be more efficient if there were a way to get rid of the extra weight.

Rocket engineers have solved the problem of useless rocket weight after takeoff. They mount one or more rockets on top of one another. The smallest rocket is on top, and the largest rocket is on the bottom. The bottom rocket is the main launching rocket. This method of mounting rockets is called **staging**, and each rocket is called a **stage**. Each stage is complete with its own engine and propellants. The combination of stages is called a **multistage rocket**. The main launching rocket is called the first stage or **booster**. The next stage is called the second stage, and

so on to the topmost rocket, which is called the final, or upper, stage.

The booster is cut loose when it has used up all its fuel, usually within 2 minutes. The engines of the second rocket stage begin to fire. When its fuel is used up, it too is cut loose and the engines of the third stage start firing.

Each stage is lighter in weight than the one before it. It carries less fuel because it needs less thrust to accelerate it. And each stage

A multistage rocket is fired from earth. The largest engine—the first stage—launches rocket.

The first stage, emptied of its fuel, is cast off. The second stage now provides rocket power.

Then the second stage is cast off. The engine of the final stage will deliver rocket to its destination.

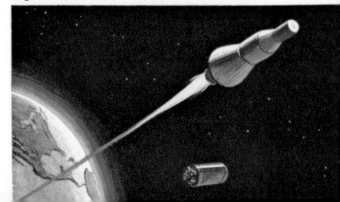

goes faster than the one before it because of constant acceleration. The last stage goes the fastest. It also goes the farthest distance. This is because it has been carried much of the way by earlier stages before its own engines begin to fire.

The multistage rocket's payload is carried in the last stage. The speed of the last rocket stage and its distance from the earth may be great enough to place a satellite into orbit or send it to another planet.

▶HOW ROCKETS ARE IGNITED

When a rocket is launched, its fuel must be ignited. To ignite something means to make it start burning. To ignite skyrockets used in fireworks, it is only necessary to touch a lighted match to a fuse attached to the outside of the rocket. But starting a large rocket that carries a payload is more complicated. This is because the fuel is contained in tanks that have a number of valves and other controls.

There are several methods of igniting the fuel in a large rocket. The method used depends on the particular combination of propellants in the rocket. In each method the ignition must take place inside the rocket engine itself.

Solid rocket fuels may be ignited by means of a powder that burns readily. A small packet of this powder, called a **squib**, is set inside the hollow of the propellant mixture. The squib is ignited by an electric spark. The burning powder ignites the solid fuel.

In large solid-fuel rockets the squib may set off another powder charge that burns like a fireworks display. Burning particles spray down the inside length of the rocket, igniting nearly the entire burning surface at once. This causes a tremendous amount of exhaust gases to be given off at one time. In this way the rocket builds up quickly the thrust it needs for launching.

Igniting Liquid-Propellant Rockets

Some liquid propellants produce a highly inflammable gas when mixed. The combination of liquid hydrogen and lox is an example. The mixture may be exploded into flame with the spark from a large spark plug inside the rocket or by a fireworks device like a flaming pinwheel.

There are propellants that burst into flame the moment they come together. They are called **hypergolic liquids**. Hydrazine and nitric acid are two such liquids. Rockets that use these propellants are able to stop and start again in space. Controls shut off the flow of propellants at a certain point and start the flow again later.

▶HOW ROCKETS ARE STEERED

A liquid-fuel rocket is sometimes steered by an automatic device that tilts the engine. The engine is mounted in a round frame called a **gimbal**. The gimbal is pivoted in such a way that it allows the engine to tilt in any direction. When the engine tilts, the exhaust changes direction and the rocket also changes its direction.

Steering Vanes

Some liquid-fuel rockets are steered by control surfaces, called steering vanes, placed in the rocket's exhaust. When the vanes move, the exhaust is turned in a different direction and the rocket changes its course. Solid rockets too can be steered by vanes in the rocket's exhaust. They can also be steered by a movable "collar" around the nozzle through which the exhaust flows.

Jets

One possible way of steering a rocket is by causing the exhaust to be hit with a jet of gas or liquid. The gas may be steam obtained from a liquid called hydrogen peroxide. (This is the same peroxide that you may find in your medicine cabinet. But the hydrogen peroxide in your medicine cabinet has been diluted with water. The kind used in rockets is much more concentrated.)

In the rocket a stream of hydrogen peroxide passes through a screen made of platinum or silver wire. The metal causes the hydrogen peroxide to break down into oxygen and steam. When the steam hits the exhaust gases, it changes the direction of the exhaust flow. This in turn changes the direction of the rocket.

External Control Surfaces

Rockets used as antiaircraft missiles operate within the earth's atmosphere. They can therefore be steered by control surfaces on the outside of the rocket. These control surfaces are much like those used on an airplane. This method of control is not used in most modern rockets because the control surfaces drag against the air and slow down the rocket.

Steering by "Command"

Steering devices in most modern rockets are operated by "command." This means that the devices may be started and stopped by radio or radar signals beamed to the rocket from the ground. "Command" may also mean that the steering devices are set before the rocket is launched.

The commands may be preprogrammed— that is, they may be put on special magnetic tape. As the tape unwinds, it sends signals to the steering controls. The tape may be connected to a clock that gives the signals at the proper time.

One type of command is called **inertial command** or **inertial guidance**. In this type, gyroscopes are placed in the rocket when it is built. These gyroscopes are able to sense any change in the rocket's direction. Each change is converted into an electric signal. The signal sends corrections to the steering mechanism.

In some command systems, information from gyroscopes and other devices in the rocket is sent to a computer at the ground stations. The computer figures out what steering corrections should be made. It then transmits the corrections to the steering apparatus by radio or radar beam.

▶ ROCKETS OF THE FUTURE

In the future some rockets will probably still use chemical propellants. But scientists are developing rockets that will use electrical or nuclear energy. These rockets will no doubt be much more efficient than those using chemical propellants.

Rocket Propulsion by Electricity

One form of electric propulsion is the ion engine. The fuel used is mercury or cesium. The atoms of the fuels are changed into charged particles called ions. Electromagnets accelerate the ions to tremendous speeds. The ions rush out through the exhaust nozzles of the rocket, giving the rocket its power.

The big advantage of this kind of rocket is that it needs very little fuel to operate. If it carries as much fuel as a chemical rocket, it

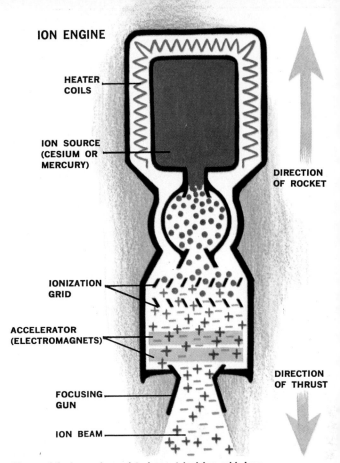

ION ENGINE

HEATER COILS

ION SOURCE (CESIUM OR MERCURY)

DIRECTION OF ROCKET

IONIZATION GRID

ACCELERATOR (ELECTROMAGNETS)

DIRECTION OF THRUST

FOCUSING GUN

ION BEAM

Atoms of fuel are changed to ions at ionizing grid. Ions are accelerated, forced into narrow beam by focusing gun, and shoot out at tremendous speeds from rocket.

can travel a much longer distance. It can travel to a distant planet much more economically than a chemically fueled rocket can.

There is a disadvantage, however, to the ion rocket. It does not have enough thrust to lift it off a launching pad. It must be launched by a powerful booster rocket, or it must start its journey from an artificial satellite in orbit. Once it is moving, it gains speed gradually. It may take a few months of travel to reach its greatest speed. But it can travel on at that speed for years.

The Hydrogen-Fuel Nuclear Rocket

It is possible to obtain rocket power from a small nuclear reactor. One type of nuclear rocket of the future will use liquid hydrogen as a fuel. A nuclear reactor produces great amounts of heat. The heat of the rocket's reactor is used to turn the hydrogen to a very hot, energetic gas. The hot hydrogen gas rushes out through the exhaust nozzles and gives the rocket its power.

A rocket-powered airplane—the X-15—has its landing gear ready and skids down for a landing. This research plane has reached record speeds of over 4,000 miles an hour.

Model of hydrogen-fuel nuclear rocket engine. Hydrogen from globes is pumped to nuclear reactor and heated. The hot gas is then ejected through nozzle, providing thrust.

Since the exhaust gas is not the result of burning, the hydrogen-fuel nuclear rocket does not need to carry an oxidizer. This kind of rocket can be twice as efficient as a rocket that burns hydrogen with an oxidizer. Nuclear rockets are launched as the upper stage of a chemical rocket, to avoid danger from radioactivity if the rocket fails on takeoff.

Recovering Launch Vehicles

Scientists hope to make another change in rocket operation. Today rockets are used only once. Some fall back to earth and crash when their fuel is used up. The heat caused by friction against the air makes the other rockets burn up as they fall.

The rockets of tomorrow may return to earth safely, perhaps on wings, perhaps by a special kind of parachute or paraglider. It may be possible to send a pilot up in a rocket. He would fly the rocket back after it had delivered its payload.

Some years in the future there may also be what engineers call an aerospaceplane. This vehicle is a combination airplane and rocket—that is, it contains both jet and rocket engines. The jet engines work while the aerospaceplane is in the atmosphere. As the vehicle climbs high in the atmosphere, it becomes a rocket-powered vehicle that goes into orbit or perhaps to a space station circling the earth.

HAROLD LELAND GOODWIN
Author, *All About Rockets and Space Flight*
See also MISSILES; SATELLITES; SPACE TRAVEL.

A scene from the film *Grease* (1978), a rock musical about growing up in the 1950's.

ROCK MUSIC

Rock music is a part of popular music today. It is played and listened to in almost all the countries of the world.

Until the 1950's, American popular music was divided into three separate styles, each with its own performers, musical content, and audience. One style was called pop, and it served most Americans. Pop songs came from movies, Broadway musicals, and pop composers. The songs were mainly simple 32-bar melodies with lyrics about love. They were played by bands in dancehalls, restaurants, and nightclubs and on radio. The bands consisted of anywhere from six to more than twenty musicians playing combinations of trumpet, trombone, saxophone, and clarinet, with a rhythm section of drums, guitar, string bass, or piano. Soloists or small vocal groups generally accompanied the bands.

In the late 1930's and 1940's, there were hundreds of "big bands." The most popular included the white bands of Artie Shaw, Benny Goodman, Glenn Miller, Tommy and Jimmy Dorsey, Harry James, and Woody Herman. There were also the more jazz-style black bands of Jimmie Lunceford, Fletcher Henderson, Count Basie, Duke Ellington, and Lionel Hampton. After World War II, individual singers such as Frank Sinatra, Perry Como, Nat ("King") Cole, Doris Day, Patti Page, and Jo Stafford, most of whom had been band singers, became much more popular than the bands themselves.

The second style, rhythm and blues, came from the blues sung by black performers, along with the fast dance music that had grown out of ragtime and boogie-woogie. It was the popular music of the black people of the United States, played and sung in taverns and clubs or listened to on records in jukeboxes. Later, it was called soul music. A few of the most popular rhythm and blues performers of the 1940's and early 1950's were Chuck Berry, Fats Domino, B. B. King, Dinah Washington, and Willie Mae Thornton. Both the white pop bands and the black rhythm and blues musicians were influenced by jazz and by black spirituals and gospel music.

The third style is now called country and western, or country music. But before World War II it was often called hillbilly music. It includes the commercialized folk music of the rural southern and southwestern parts of the United States. The main center of this music has always been Nashville, Tennessee.

▶HOW ROCK BEGAN

Rock and roll was the name given to the music that developed when these three separate styles came together in the early 1950's. It is widely believed that the term "rock and roll" was first used by a Cleveland disk jockey, Alan Freed. He was one of the first persons to bring rhythm and blues to white audiences. He did this on his radio program and through concerts he produced, beginning in 1952, which presented both black and white performers to audiences of black and white teenagers. But not any one person created rock and roll. Rock was born as a result of changes in the music, broadcasting, advertising, and entertainment industries.

Before World War II the music industry was centered in New York. Music publishers printed the words and music of songs, and people all over the country bought this sheet music to play the songs on their guitars, pianos, or accordions. A hit song might sell 1,000,000 copies, but most songs made little or no money. No one really knew what made a hit, but most people believed in a few rules. One was that success in the immediate past meant success in the immediate future. If last week's hit was about apples, then next week's songs would be about oranges or pears. If last week's hit was sung by Perry Como, next week the music industry would have new songs for him or would be looking for someone who sounded just like him. Another rule was just the opposite—find a new and different song; find a new and different performer.

But finally, only public response could make a hit. Enough of the public had to hear a song often enough to distinguish it from the rest and become familiar with it. So the publishers brought songs to bands playing in and around New York—especially bands that had radio programs. In that way, not only would more people hear the songs, but the newspapers of the entertainment industry could keep count of how often they were played. The publishers also arranged for as many recordings of their songs as possible. Sheet music was still more important than records, but by the early 1950's several things had happened to change this.

First came the disk jockeys. Just before World War II, the Federal Communications Commission, which regulates United States broadcasting, authorized the licensing of new radio stations. These stations needed three things to be successful—inexpensive, interesting material; advertisers who would buy time from them; and a large audience. The answer was found in disk jockeys. They designed programs consisting of pop records with a playing time of about three minutes. They also read "spot" commercials and held the program together with talk.

The disk jockeys soon had local audiences loyal to their stations, products, and musical tastes. This weakened the control of the net-

Elvis Presley combined rhythm and blues with country and western. He became one of the top rock stars of all time.

work stations and of the bandleaders over what songs became hits. The disk jockeys appealed mainly to young people in their teens who were more interested in dancing and listening to music than playing it themselves.

The disk jockeys also held "record hops" (dances) in high schools and invited teenagers into radio studios to listen to new records. The teenagers made it clear which songs they liked and which they did not. Now the music industry could find out more quickly what kind of songs to do next. Now, too, records became more important than sheet music.

Several other things happened in the early 1950's to set the stage for rock and roll. The big dance bands were losing popularity, and dancehalls were closing as record companies followed the charts and recorded individual singers and small groups. Television was replacing radio, and soon disk jockeys had television programs of their own.

Rhythm and blues was expanding, too. During and after World War II many black people moved to northern cities in search of jobs. Because the war improved their economic position, the music industry was responsive to their tastes. This led to an increase in the production of rhythm and blues records. Radio stations played more rhythm and blues and had black disk jockeys. But white teenagers also listened, even in the South, because there was no segregation of the radio audience.

Country and western music was also being more widely heard. At first, rhythm and blues and country and western hits were copied by white pop singers. They used black or hillbilly material, but they often changed the lyrics and smoothed out the "roughness" of the music.

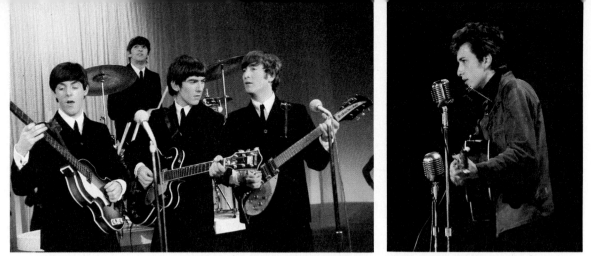

Left: The Beatles—Paul McCartney, Ringo Starr, George Harrison, and John Lennon—revolutionized pop music. Right: Bob Dylan sparked folk rock.

▶ HOW ROCK DEVELOPED

In 1955, records by a young singer from Tennessee, Elvis Presley, were heard across the country. After he appeared on nationwide television, Elvis Presley's singing—a combination of rhythm and blues and country and western—and his performing style came to mean "rock and roll" all over the United States. Presley's many hits, including "Heartbreak Hotel" and "Hound Dog," made him an all-time star of pop music. Bill Haley and the Comets—with songs like "Rock Around the Clock"—were a country and western group that also became a rock pacesetter.

At first it was mainly the fast, strong beat of rock songs that appealed to young audiences. Musically, the songs were simple, too, following a one-four-five chord pattern similar to that used in the blues, with chords based on the first, fourth, and fifth notes of the scale. For example, in a song written in the key of C, the first chord would consist of the notes C, E, G, and C; the second of F, A, C, and F; and the third of G, B, D, and G.

Young people identified with the music, and soon songs especially aimed at the lives and problems of teenagers were being written. These included such hits as Chuck Berry's "Sweet Little Sixteen" and "Teen Age Prayer" by Gale Storm. Within a short time, young singers began to replace older entertainers. Ricky Nelson, Paul Anka, Leslie Gore, Bobby Darin, and Dion and the Belmonts were just some of these. New black groups also became successful—the Drifters, the Platters, and the Clovers were typical. But older performers such as Dinah Washington, Bo Diddley, and Fats Domino were also popular.

Rock became mainly the music of the young. They understood its beat and sound, and its lyrics spoke to them. By the early 1960's, rock had spread across the Atlantic to England, and new groups began to emerge there as well. The one that rapidly became most popular was made up of four boys from the industrial port city of Liverpool, on England's west coast. Calling themselves the Beatles, John Lennon, Paul McCartney, George Harrison, and Ringo Starr had been playing together since 1960. At first they did songs by other composers, but John and Paul soon began to write the Beatles' songs. By 1964, when the Beatles were introduced to U.S. audiences, they had revolutionized pop music.

PHILIP H. ENNIS
Wesleyan University
MICHAEL SAHL
Composer

▶ ROCK IN THE 1960's

In the mid-1960's, rock music began to be influenced by certain new and surprising forces. Folk rock brought the gentler sounds of folk ballads into rock. Bob Dylan is generally acknowledged to have sparked folk rock when his song "Mr. Tambourine Man," recorded by the Byrds, became a tremendous hit. This was followed by the release of Dylan's own album, *Bringing It All Back Home*. Other folk rock artists included Donovan and the Mamas and the Papas.

Among black musicians, the 1960's brought about a polishing and speeding up of old rhythm and blues forms. The Supremes, the Temptations, and Stevie Wonder were among the best and most popular of soul music artists.

The Supremes. Diana Ross, center, was the lead singer.

The Bee Gees, a popular rock group of the 1970's.

Major British groups—including the Beatles, the Rolling Stones, and the Who—confirmed their earlier promise by producing mature reflective music. In the United States, bands on the West Coast, such as the Grateful Dead and the Jefferson Airplane (later Jefferson Starship), were influenced by the free-form techniques of jazz.

In the 1960's, too, young people began to think of themselves as a new and "different" generation because they were the first to grow up with rock and roll. Concerts, dances, and rock festivals—such as the one held at Woodstock, New York, in 1969—were part of this trend.

Rock went into musical theater with such shows as *Hair* (1968) and *Jesus Christ, Superstar* (1971). Rock musicians also became interested in experimental music, notably electronic music, and in the sound language of modern composers. Once a breakthrough had been made, rock could move in new directions. There was no longer any way of telling what was rock except by the community it served.

▶ ROCK TODAY

The 1970's were a time of tremendous expansion within the rock industry. Rock became a very big business, earning more money annually than any other form of entertainment, including the film industry. One reason was that the number of rock music fans grew larger all the time. People who were originally excited by it in the 1950's and 1960's continued to buy records and attend concerts. Their children, in turn, were also attracted to this music of youth.

Until the 1970's, a rock performer would have been proud to earn a "gold record," an album that achieved $1,000,000 in sales. But the 1970's brought about the "platinum record," awarded when 1,000,000 copies of a record are sold. Among those who have platinum records to their credit are the singers Elton John and Peter Frampton and the groups Fleetwood Mac and the Bee Gees.

In the late 1970's, the Bee Gees became the most popular performers of disco, an offshoot of soul music of the 1960's. It had a steady, almost mechanical beat that was easy to dance to. The most important instrument in the development of disco was the electronic synthesizer, a complex machine with a keyboard. It could be made to sound like anything from a single snare drum to an entire orchestral string section.

The increasing sophistication of rock music—in terms of both business and technology—sparked a cry of protest within the rock world itself. Many struggling rock bands were beginning to resent rock's new maturity. They felt that this youthful music was becoming a music of business people and millionaires. They believed that the smoothness and polish of modern recording techniques had drained rock of much of its vigor and daring.

These musicians formed rock bands that rejected extensive musical knowledge and elaborate equipment. They chose to play short tunes at high volume. This music, harsh and direct in sound, became known as punk, or new wave, music. In England, it was played by such bands as the Clash. In the United States, well-known groups included the Ramones and Blondie.

Rock's energy, its expression of the concerns of young people, and its ability to speak through many musical forms make it a living part of our musical world.

KEN TUCKER
Music Critic, Los Angeles *Herald Examiner*
See also COUNTRY AND WESTERN MUSIC.

ROCKS, MINERALS, AND ORES

Rocks are everywhere around you. Mountains are great masses of rock. Stones and pebbles are small pieces of it. When you pick up a handful of sand, you are picking up tiny grains of rock. Soil is mostly broken-down rock, mixed with decayed plant and animal material. In fact, our earth is a great ball of rock about 6,600,000,000,000,000,000,000 (6.6 sextillion) tons in weight.

Rocks are made of one or more **minerals**. A mineral is a naturally occurring chemical substance that is neither a plant nor an animal. There are different kinds of rocks. The kind of rock is determined by the kinds of minerals in it, how the minerals are arranged, and the amount of each mineral.

A rock is dark-colored if it is made up mostly of dark minerals. A rock is light-colored if the minerals in it are mainly light-colored. Some rocks are harder than others because the minerals in them are harder. Some rocks are heavy because their minerals are heavy.

Many rocks have minerals from which useful metals can be extracted. If a metal can be extracted from a mineral profitably, the mineral is called an **ore**. However, it may cost too much or be too difficult to get a metal from a mineral. In that case the mineral is not considered an ore.

▶ ROCKS

See how many different kinds of rock you can find. A good place to look for them is at the bottom of a shallow stream or where a road has been cut. You might want to separate the rocks you find into groups according to color. Or you might separate them into those that contain bands or layers and those that do not. You might group them according to where you found them.

Geologists (scientists who study the earth) divide all rocks into three main groups, according to how the rocks were formed. But when geologists speak of rock, they usually do not mean a small stone. They mean the great mass that makes up a mountain or that underlies a large region. Geologists will speak of the rock of the Appalachian Mountains or the Sierra Nevada or of the rock lying beneath the Great Plains.

The geologist groups rocks under three main headings: igneous, sedimentary, and metamorphic. All rocks you can ever find belong to one of these three main groups.

Igneous rock was formed from rock material so hot that it was liquid. In fact, "igneous" means "fiery." Most of the liquid rock material cooled and hardened below the surface of the earth. Some of the liquid rock broke through to the surface, flowed out, and then hardened.

Sedimentary rock was usually formed from sand, mud, or clay that was deposited in the ocean. These deposits are called sediments. "Sedimentary rock" means "rock made from sediment." Some kinds of sedimentary rock were made from the shells of tiny sea animals. Some were made from dissolved minerals that settled out of ocean or lake waters.

"Metamorphic rock" means "rock that has been changed." It was made from solid rock that was bent, folded, squeezed, twisted, or heated so that the form of the rock changed.

▶ IGNEOUS ROCK

Igneous rock underlies all other rock of the earth. It forms the base of the continents and the cores of mountains. It lies beneath the sediments of the ocean floor.

In some places sedimentary rocks lying above the igneous rock have been worn away, and the base has been exposed. An igneous rock mass that can be seen on the surface may once have been the core of a mountain. It may be rock that reached the surface in a molten state. But whether it was formed deep within the earth or on the surface, all igneous rock was once liquid.

Liquid rock lies in huge underground pockets. This liquid underground rock is called **magma**. Magma is lighter in weight than the colder, hard rocks around it. Therefore it is slowly pushed upward by the pressure of the rock around it. In many places the magma never does reach the surface but slowly cools and hardens underground. It takes many thousands of years for magma to harden into rock. In other places the cold, hard rocks near the surface cannot withstand the pressure of the magma beneath them. They crack a little bit, and the magma rises up along the cracks.

The liquid rock may extend upward in the cracks and form dikes in the surrounding rock. You may have seen such dikes in rock exposed at the surface.

Magma often remains hot enough to stay in liquid form until it reaches the surface of the earth. It then flows through the cracks and spreads out on the ground. Magma that reaches the surface of the earth is called **lava**.

The type of igneous rock formed depends on which minerals are in the magma. It also depends on where the liquid rock cools and on how big the mineral grains grow as the mineral cools.

Rock from Lava

Compared to magma, lava cools quickly. Most lava hardens within a few weeks after coming to the surface. Lava forms into certain kinds of rocks that are quite different from the igneous rocks that cool slowly underground.

When lava cools exceptionally fast, it forms a natural glass called **obsidian**. Obsidian is usually black. Because it is glass, its broken edges are very sharp. This is why American Indians used to chip obsidian into points to make their arrowheads, spear points, and knives.

Sometimes lava froths and bubbles while it is still hot. A great deal of gas from within the lava rises to the top. The escaping gas puffs up the top of the lava into a spongy mass. When this spongy mass cools, it becomes rock that is full of holes and small pockets of gas that have not been able to escape.

Light-colored lava rock with many small holes and pockets in it is called **pumice**. It is thrown out during some volcanic eruptions. Pumice is light gray or cream-colored. It floats on water because it is so full of holes and gas pockets. Pieces of pumice have been found on shores many miles from the volcano in which the pumice was formed. Pumice is often ground up into a powder and is used for fine polishing. Dentists use it to polish teeth.

Black or dark-red porous lava rock is called **scoria**. It is heavier than pumice, and its holes and pockets are usually bigger. In some countries it is used as a building stone. It is also used to decorate rock gardens.

Basalt is the rock that makes up most lava flows. It is nearly always dark gray or black. The mineral grains in basalt are so tiny that you cannot see the individual grains with the unaided eye. For this reason scientists say basalt has a very fine-grained texture. Basalt is sometimes called trap. It is crushed and used in road building.

Felsite is a different type of very fine-grained lava rock. It is lighter in color than basalt. Felsite can be white, pink, gray, or yellow. One kind of felsite, called yellow rhyolite, gives Yellowstone National Park its name.

Basalt and felsite make up the main rocks of lava flows. Obsidian is a rarer lava rock. Pumice and scoria are frothy lava. All these rocks are **extrusive** rocks. This means that the magma from which they were formed was extruded, or flowed out onto the surface.

Crystals Grow in Magma

Magma that is to become extrusive rock usually starts cooling while it is still being pushed upward. As the magma slowly rises, certain minerals in it grow into big crystals sooner than the other minerals do. The crystals float in the magma. When this magma reaches the surface of the earth, the liquid rock turns to a solid in a short time. The big crystals carried in the liquid are "frozen" into the fine-grained lava rock. The whole rock is then made of many large crystals embedded in a very fine-grained rock, such as basalt.

Such a rock is called **porphyry**. It is a very attractive rock, especially when it is polished. For this reason it has been used as a building stone since the time of the early Egyptians.

Granite, a Slow-Cooling Rock

Granite is the most common igneous rock at the earth's surface. Whole mountains of granite, once the core of much bigger mountains, lie exposed on the surface. The mountains in northern New England, the Sierra Nevadas in California, the Black Hills in South Dakota, parts of the Scottish Highlands, and most of the mountains of northern Sweden are some of them.

The three main minerals in granite are quartz, feldspar, and mica. The color of granite is either gray or pink, depending on the color of its feldspar.

The mineral grains in most granite are small

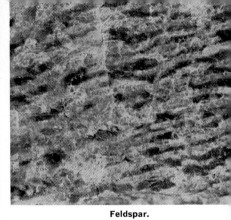

Rose quartz.

Mica crystals.

Feldspar.

COMMON MINERALS

Hematite.

Calcite.

Gypsum crystals.

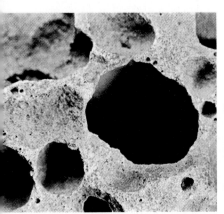

Lava rock, showing gas bubbles.

Obsidian.

Pumice.

IGNEOUS ROCKS

Basalt.

Felsite (yellow rhyolite).

Porphyry.

Granite.

Magnified view of granite under polarized light.

and are all about the same size. But sometimes granite magma cools very slowly. Then the mineral grains grow large. Scientists call this kind of rock **coarse-grained**. If you find a piece of coarse-grained granite, you should have very little trouble noting the different minerals in it.

Granite is a very beautiful rock, especially when it is polished. Granite porphyry, with large crystals of quartz or feldspar, is particularly beautiful. All granite is also very hard. Because of these qualities it is used a great deal as a building stone, for decoration, and whenever hard rock is needed. In some European cities streets were paved with granite cobblestones hundreds of years ago. The cobblestones are still in good condition.

▶SEDIMENTARY ROCK

About three fourths of the earth's land surface is covered with sedimentary rock. Many mountains are made of sedimentary rock, sometimes thousands of feet thick, lying above a granite core.

Most sedimentary rock was once part of some other, older rock. As the older rock was worn down, its particles were carried away by water, wind, or ice. The particles were finally deposited as layers of sediment on the floor of a lake, a river, or an ocean.

Pressure caused by the weight of overlying sediments squeezed the particles closer together. Ocean water deposited cementing minerals between the particles. Slowly, over hundreds of thousands of years, the sediments became solid rock. The kind of sedimentary rock formed depended on the particles from which it was made and the cementing minerals.

Because it was made of layers of sediment, sedimentary rock is usually in bands, or layers. You can often find layers of different kinds of sedimentary rock lying one above the other.

Sandstone

Sandstone is a common sedimentary rock. As you might guess from its name, it is made of grains of sand cemented together. The sand is made mostly of quartz grains. The minerals that cement the grains together are usually limonite, hematite, or calcite. Sandstone takes its color from the cementing material that stains the grains of sand. Sandstone may be yellowish, green, brown, pink, orange, or red. Some sandstone is light gray or almost white. Sandstone is often used as a building stone. The brownstone houses seen in many cities are made of sandstone.

Conglomerate

The word "conglomerate" means "uneven mixture." This is just what the rock called conglomerate is—a mixture of pebbles and gravel cemented together by sand and minerals carried by water.

The pebbles in conglomerates are smooth and rounded. This shows that they were worn down by and carried by water. Because pebbles and gravel are heavy for their size, water cannot carry them far out into the ocean. The water drops them near the shore or near the mouths of rivers. Therefore, conglomerates are formed fairly close to the shore or near the mouths of rivers.

The color of conglomerates comes from the pebbles, the gravel, and the cementing material. Some conglomerates have a reddish-brown background with white quartz pebbles showing clearly. Most conglomerates are different shades of gray.

Shale

Tiny particles of mud and clay squeezed together for hundreds of thousands of years become shale. The minerals in shale are flat little grains. They lie one on top of the other in thin layers. As sediments pile up, pressure on the lowest layers causes these layers to harden into rock.

Shale splits apart easily into flat layers or flakes and is often identified by the way it splits. Most shale occurs in various shades of gray.

More than half of all sedimentary rock is shale. Although it is abundant, it is not used as a building stone because it wears away easily. It is used for its clay. Shale is crushed or ground to make tile, bricks, and cement.

Limestone

Limestone is made almost entirely of the mineral calcite. Calcite is a form of calcium carbonate. The calcium carbonate came from the shells of millions of tiny sea animals. In most cases the shells have been broken down into bits even smaller than the mud and clay that make up shale. If you see a piece of limestone, you cannot tell that the tiny mineral grains in it were once part of animal shells.

Tiny powdered shell fragments settle on the bottom of the ocean and form a layer there. The layer is called limy ooze. In time, the limy ooze is covered by other sediments. The weight of the sediments above it presses the limy ooze into solid rock.

Most limestone is gray. But it can also be so light that it is almost white or so dark that it is almost black.

To test a rock for limestone, scientists use hydrochloric acid. They put a few drops of the acid on the rock. Little bubbles appear in the acid if the rock is limestone.

Chalk is a form of limestone. So are the beautiful rock formations found in many caves. One type of limestone, coquina, is made of small animal shells cemented together by minerals from seawater. You can see individual shells in coquina. This rock is common in eastern Florida. The early Spanish settlers in Florida built some of their forts of coquina.

Limestone is one of the world's most im-

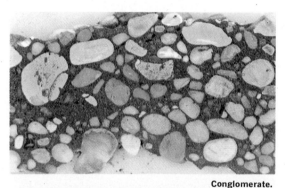

Conglomerate.

Shale.

Limestone.

SEDIMENTARY ROCKS

Sandstone, showing ripples caused by wave action.

Sandstone, showing imprint of fossil fish.

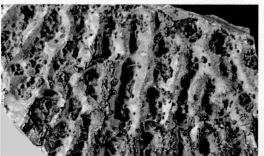

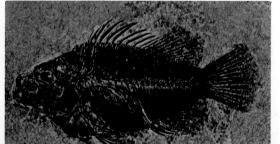

Slate.

Mica schist.

METAMORPHIC ROCKS

Gneiss.

Quartzite.

Pink marble.

portant rock materials. When crushed and heated to a high temperature, it becomes a white powder called **lime**. Bricklayers use a mixture of lime, sand, and water to make the mortar between bricks. Lime is used in glass-making, in extracting metals from ores, and for many other purposes.

Limestone is widely used as a building stone. For example, the Pentagon near Washington, D.C., is made of limestone.

Fossils in Sedimentary Rocks

Sedimentary rocks are like a book in which scientists can read the story of life on earth.

This is because traces of ancient plant and animal life are sometimes found in sedimentary rock.

These traces are called **fossils**. The fossils may be the shells of sea animals or the bones of animals buried in sand, mud, or limy ooze that later became rock. Or they may be the print of a leaf or the footprint of an animal made before the sediment hardened.

Fossils are common in shale. The soft mud that became shale held the impression of a bone, a leaf, or a footprint better than other sediments.

The only sedimentary rocks in which fossils are never found are halite (salt) and gypsum. These rocks were made when the water of very large lakes evaporated. As the water evaporated, the lakes became so salty that no animals or plants could live in them. After the dried-up lakes had changed to rock, there were no fossils in the rock.

▶ METAMORPHIC ROCK

Powerful forces are present within the earth. These forces produce great pressures on all rocks. Masses of rock are lifted up, folded, and wrinkled. This wrinkling and folding bring about changes in the rocks. For example, in some rocks the minerals are crushed and broken into smaller ones. In other rocks the minerals are stretched into long, thin, flat grains.

Underground heat coming near the surface also brings about changes in rocks. Rock changed by heat or pressure, or both, is called metamorphic rock. Sedimentary rock can be changed to metamorphic rock when the cementing materials are replaced by other minerals.

Most metamorphic rock was once either igneous or sedimentary. But metamorphic rock itself can also be affected by heat and pressure and changed into other types of metamorphic rock.

Some fairly common rocks are metamorphic. Slate, schist, gneiss (pronounced like the word "nice"), and marble are all in this group.

Slate

Slate is a metamorphic rock made from shale. Slate breaks into very thin slabs. These slabs are used as roofing material and as flagstones. Blackboards in many classrooms used to be made of slate.

Slate has a shiny luster like that of satin. The luster is very different from the dull look of the shale from which it was made. Most slate is gray, just as most shale is gray. But there is brown slate, which comes from brown shale, and reddish slate, which comes from reddish shale.

Schist

Schist is made almost entirely of minerals that are thin and flat. Most schists are made of mica combined with other minerals.

A schist gets its name from the most abundant mineral in it. Thus there is mica schist, hornblende schist, chlorite schist, and so on. Much of the rock of Manhattan in New York City is mica schist. Schist is also abundant in northeastern Minnesota near Lake Superior and in Finland, Sweden, and Norway.

Schists occur in layers that look alike. The layers split easily into scaly pieces. Usually the easiest way to identify a schist is by the thousands of flat mineral grains showing as thin lines throughout the rock. The color of each kind of schist is the color of its chief mineral.

Gneiss

The name "gneiss" is used for any metamorphic rock that has light-colored and dark-colored bands next to each other. Gneiss therefore has a distinct banded appearance. The original rock may have been any kind of rock.

A gneiss is usually given the name of the main mineral in its dark bands. Gneiss sometimes gets its name from the rock from which it was made. Thus there is biotite gneiss, hornblende gneiss, granite gneiss, and so on. The over-all color of a gneiss depends on the minerals in its light bands. It may be pink, gray, white, or even green.

Marble

The metamorphic rock you are most likely to see is marble because it is so widely used. Marble is metamorphosed limestone and is mostly calcite. The calcite of the marble may be in the form of crystals.

Most marble is white or gray, like the limestone from which it was formed. Sometimes, however, it is in shades of brown or pink because of small amounts of other minerals in it.

The original limestone may have had layers of shale or other rock in it. When the limestone was changed to marble, the shale or other rock became twisted into dark streaks. Marble with such streaks has a very pleasing appearance. Polished streaked marble is used to decorate the lobbies of many big buildings.

Marble can be broken into big solid blocks. It can be worked with a chisel. When polished, it gleams and flashes in the light. For these reasons it has been used to make statues since the time of the early Greeks. Many of the world's most beautiful statues are made of white marble.

Quartzite

Another common metamorphic rock, quartzite, is made from sandstone. Most kinds of quartzite were made by great pressure and heat. Some kinds were made when quartz grains, carried by water, slowly replaced the cement in the sandstone that held the sand grains together. Thus, quartzite is a rock made of quartz sand cemented by quartz. It is one of the hardest rocks known.

The color of quartzite depends on what other minerals besides quartz are in the rock. Some quartzite is milky white, but most is light brown or pink. Quartzite is too hard to be worked very much as a building stone. It is sometimes crushed and used in building roads.

▶ MINERALS

It is usually easier to identify a rock than to identify a mineral. The main reason is that rocks are in big masses. Their overall appearance is a good clue to the type of rock. Minerals, however, are generally in small pieces. This makes it hard to identify a mineral just by looking at it. It is often necessary to test the mineral for certain **properties**, or characteristics, before you can know what kind it is.

Altogether, about 1,500 different kinds of minerals have been found, many of them quite rare. About 30 minerals are common in rocks. They are called rock-forming minerals.

▶ IDENTIFYING MINERALS

If you find a mineral, split it with a hammer. Geologists use a special hammer to break rock or minerals into pieces. It is best to examine the freshly broken surface of a mineral in order to identify it. A rock or mineral that has been exposed for a long time may become discolored and hard to recognize. Besides showing the true color of a specimen, a freshly broken mineral shows other things. One of these is the mineral's luster—how it shines when light is reflected from it. You can also see how the mineral breaks—whether in straight planes, slanting surfaces, or uneven chunks.

These three properties of a mineral—color, luster, and how it breaks—can be observed easily.

Color

The color of a mineral helps identify it. Color is not always a good clue to a mineral's identity, because many minerals are found in several colors. But most minerals are never found in certain colors. For example, quartz may be clear, milky white, smoky gray, or pink. It is never truly black. Hornblende is very dark green or black, but never light-colored.

Luster

One of the easiest things to notice about a mineral is its luster. Minerals that shine like metal have a metallic luster. All other minerals have a nonmetallic luster. There are several ways of describing nonmetallic luster—pearly, glassy, silky, or dull.

Some minerals have such a distinct luster and color that these are all you need to identify them. Pyrite is such a mineral. It has a distinct metallic luster, and its color is silvery yellow, like brass. Once you have seen a piece of pyrite, you will have no trouble recognizing it thereafter.

Cleavage

Certain minerals break in a very definite way. This is called a mineral's cleavage.

Galena, the mineral from which lead is extracted, cleaves into little cubes. Mica cleaves easily into very thin sheets, almost like paper. Calcite cleaves into pieces that look like little slanting bricks. Feldspar cleaves in two directions. It splits into pieces with surfaces that join each other almost at right angles. A broken piece of feldspar looks as if it had little steps on its surface.

Many minerals have no definite cleavage. They break into irregular chunks. Quartz is one of these minerals.

Hardness

Some minerals are harder than others. Some are so soft that they can be scratched easily. A diamond is so hard that it cannot be scratched by any other known substance.

Geologists use a standard scale of hardness, called **Mohs' scale**, to describe a mineral's hardness. The scale was developed about 100 years ago by a German scientist, Friedrich Mohs. In Mohs' scale, 10 standard minerals are given a number from 1 to 10. Talc is number 1, quartz is number 7, and diamond is number 10. Talc is the softest mineral on the scale, and diamond is the hardest.

A mineral on Mohs' scale can scratch any other listed below it. For example, topaz can

MOHS' SCALE OF HARDNESS

(10)	Diamond	(5)	Apatite
(9)	Corundum	(4)	Fluorite
(8)	Topaz	(3)	Calcite
(7)	Quartz	(2)	Gypsum
(6)	Feldspar	(1)	Talc

scratch quartz, and quartz can scratch feldspar and every other mineral below it on the
scale. In turn, a mineral can be scratched by
every mineral above it on the scale. Talc can
be scratched by every other mineral on Mohs'
scale. Corundum can be scratched only by
diamond.

Thus, an unknown mineral that cannot be
scratched by fluorite, hardness 4, but can be
scratched by feldspar, hardness 6, has a hardness in between and may be 5. The mineral
may be apatite. Its color, luster, and cleavage
will further help to identify the mineral.

You can make your own scratch test by
using this simple scale:

a good steel knife blade	**hardness 6**
window glass	**hardness 5½**
a copper penny	**hardness 3**
a fingernail	**hardness 2½**

Streak

Sometimes the powder of a mineral has a
color different from that of a large piece of the
mineral. You can best see the powder by
scratching the mineral across a hard, dull-
white surface. A material with such a surface
is called a **streak plate**. The back of a
bathroom tile makes a good streak plate. So
does the broken edge of a china dish. The
trail of powdered mineral that is made on the
streak plate is called the **streak** of the mineral.

The color of the streak of certain minerals
is important in identifying them. Streaking is

Iceland spar is identified by its double refraction—objects
seen through calcite appear double.

used mostly to identify dark-colored minerals.

Other Ways of Identifying Minerals

Color, luster, cleavage, hardness, and
streak are important in identifying most minerals. Sometimes, however, a mineral can be
positively identified only by laboratory
tests.

Some minerals are identified by special
properties. For example, halite is best identified by its taste. If you touch a clean piece of it
with your tongue, you get a salty taste. The
mineral kaolin (sometimes called kaolinite)
is identified by its earthy smell. It has the
distinct smell of dry, freshly plowed earth.
Talc has a greasy, slippery feel that no other
mineral has. Weight helps in identifying some
minerals. Those with iron or lead in them are
much heavier than most other minerals.

Pure clear calcite, called Iceland spar, has

Galena cleaves, or breaks up, into little cubes. Its cleavage helps identify the mineral.

Pyrite, or "fool's gold," can be recognized easily by its
distinct color and luster.

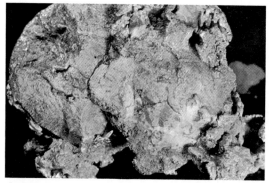

Copper ore.

Bauxite—aluminum ore.

ORES

Cinnabar—mercury ore.

double refraction. If you look at a pin through a piece of Iceland spar, you will see two pins on the other side. Print seen through clear calcite appears double. Calcite has one other property that no other mineral has. It effervesces, or bubbles, in hydrochloric acid. This is why limestone and marble are tested with acid—they are almost entirely calcite.

Some minerals always grow as crystals. Garnet is such a mineral. Other minerals never do. Still others grow as crystals under certain conditions. The study of crystals is a science in itself. It is called **crystallography**. Learning to recognize the crystal of a mineral is another way of identifying the mineral.

▶ **ORES**

Ores—minerals from which useful metals can be extracted—usually occur in layers or in veins in the rock. The ores were deposited in cracks or cavities in underground rock by rising magma. By the time the magma reached the surface, it had already deposited most of its ore-bearing material. This is why mines must usually be dug underground to get at an ore deposit.

A few metals, such as gold, are not very active chemically—that is, they do not readily combine with other elements. When the rock in which they occur wears away, bits of the metals are washed into streams and deposited in the stream beds. Sand and gravel in which such metals are found are called **placer deposits**. The miners in the American West who

Gold crystals.

Silver crystals.

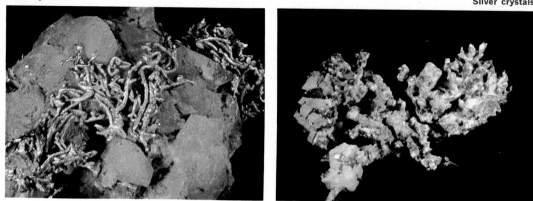

panned for gold were trying to separate gold grains from sand and gravel in placer deposits.

Recognizing Ores

Sometimes a metal is found in an almost pure state. It is then called a **native ore**. Native ores are rare but quite easy to recognize. If you are lucky enough to find native silver or copper, you will have no trouble identifying it. Or you might find little flakes of native gold in gold-bearing quartz.

It takes special knowledge and experience to recognize most ores. Some ores can be recognized by their weight or their color. For example, iron and uranium ores are always heavy.

The ores of some metals can be recognized by their streak. One of the best ways to recognize galena, the ore of lead, is by its cleavage. It breaks into perfect cubes.

But by looking at most ores or by lifting a piece of their rock, you cannot easily tell what metals are in them. Bauxite, an aluminum ore, gives no hint that it contains aluminum. Some silver ores are black. Mining prospectors and mining geologists spend years learning the different kinds of ores. You can learn a few common ones, such as iron ore, in much less time.

SIDNEY E. WHITE
The Ohio State University

See also CRYSTALS; EARTH, OUR HOME PLANET; GEOLOGY AND GEOPHYSICS; VOLCANOES.

ROCK AND MINERAL COLLECTING

Rocks, minerals, and ores can be collected almost anywhere, even in the city. When a new building goes up, steam shovels dig rocks out of the earth. When an old building is torn down, you often can find samples of limestone, marble, granite, and other building stones. Along the seashore you can find sand and pebbles, but you also may find rocks that have come from distant countries. In earlier days, when a ship had no cargo, rocks were used as ballast to steady the ship. They were discarded when cargo was taken on. You may find chunks of rock blasted away where hills have been cut through to make level beds for roads or railroad tracks.

YOUR KIT

A knife or steel file for scratching the stones.

A piece of glass to make scratches on (be sure that it has smooth edges, or bind the edges with adhesive tape so that you won't cut yourself).

A magnifying glass for examining the stones closely.

A copper penny.

A piece of unglazed white tile.

A hammer for breaking rocks open (the hammer should have a flat end for breaking stones and a sharp end like a chisel for splitting them).

A chisel for chipping small pieces of stone from bigger ones. It should be a special rock chisel. Wood chisels will be spoiled if you use them on stone.

▶ A COLLECTING TRIP

On a collecting trip you'll need a hammer, a chisel, and a strong canvas shoulder bag in which to put your specimens. Take along a supply of plastic bags for specimens, such as small crystals, that are easily lost and for soft stones that are easily scratched.

You also will need adhesive tape for labeling specimens as you find them. Before you start from home, cut a long strip of adhesive tape into small pieces and stick the pieces on a sheet of waxed paper. Number the pieces in ink.

Most collectors chip or hammer off specimens about the size of a fist. But a small stone can be very good, too. Sometimes you may want a larger chunk because of some especially interesting feature, such as the wavy bands of color in a piece of gneiss.

As soon as you get a specimen, put a numbered piece of adhesive tape on it. And immediately write in your notebook the number of the stone and where you found it. If you wait until you get home to do it, you may forget where you found the stone.

If you can, take home two specimens of each stone, one for your collection and one for testing or trading.

MARIBELLE CORMACK
Author, *The First Book of Stones*

See also ROCKS, MINERALS, AND ORES.

ROCKY MOUNTAINS

The Rocky Mountains are part of the great North American Cordillera (western mountain system). The Rockies extend from northern Alaska to New Mexico—a distance of about 3,000 miles. These mountains form the great Continental Divide, which separates river systems flowing to opposite sides of North America.

The Northern Rockies begin in the Brooks Range of Alaska, facing the Arctic Ocean ice pack. They wind inland through western Canada across the Montana border to Yellowstone National Park. The Middle Rockies spread across Wyoming in a bewildering maze of peaks and gorges. The Southern Rockies are found in Colorado, New Mexico, and southern Wyoming.

The highest peaks in the Rockies are found in Colorado. Over 50 peaks tower more than 14,000 feet above sea level; and 300 more are between 13,000 and 14,000 feet.

During the 16th century, Spanish conquistadores under Coronado became the first Europeans to explore the Southern Rockies. From 1804 to 1806 Meriwether Lewis and William Clark crossed and recrossed the Northern and Middle Rockies in their exploration of the Louisiana Territory. Beaver trappers led by Jedediah Smith explored the Middle Rockies in 1824. They established the Rocky Mountain Fur Company in 1830, inaugurating the era of the "Mountain Men" in American history.

Until mountain passes were discovered, the Rockies were an obstacle to settlers eager to reach the Pacific Coast. For a long time it was easier to reach California by sailing around South America or by crossing the Isthmus of Panama.

Some mountain passes used by settlers to cross the Continental Divide are still important. The old Missouri River trail followed by Lewis and Clark crosses the Rockies into Idaho and Washington. The Northern Pacific Railroad and several highways follow the same route. The Union Pacific Railroad takes advantage of the old Mormon Trail used by Brigham Young and the Latter-Day Saints on their journey to Utah. Part of Coronado's Spanish Trail through the Southern Rockies is used by the Southern Pacific Railroad. Today nine railroads cross the Rocky Mountains.

The rugged mountains act as a barrier to man, but they provide him with opportunities as well. The Rockies are highly mineralized. They yield gold, silver, lead, zinc, copper, molybdenum, and tungsten. In addition, the mountain landscapes are enjoyed in many American and Canadian parks, forests, and wilderness areas.

GEORGE W. CAREY
Teachers College, Columbia University

See also FUR TRADE IN NORTH AMERICA; MOUNTAINS; OVERLAND TRAILS.

RODENTS

Rodents are gnawing mammals. The very word "rodent" comes from a Latin word that means "to gnaw." House mice and rats, squirrels and chipmunks, beavers and porcupines, hamsters and guinea pigs—all are familiar rodents. And all are famous for their gnawing abilities. They are just a very few of the many, many kinds of rodents that live in the world today.

In both variety and total numbers the great order Rodentia is the most successful of all the orders of mammals. There are thousands of different kinds of rodents in the world—nearly as many as all other kinds of mammals added together. And individual rodents probably outnumber all other individual mammals together. Hardy and adaptable, rodents flourish all over the world.

▶ CHARACTERISTICS OF RODENTS

Most rodents are the size of a rat or smaller. The biggest rodents are the beaver and the South American capybara. The capybara sometimes measures 4 feet in length and weighs 100 pounds or more.

Rodents are most easily identified by their teeth. Every rodent has four chisel-shaped front teeth—two in the upper jaw and two in the lower. These are its gnawing teeth, or incisors. The incisors grow throughout the animal's lifetime, but they wear away against each other and so remain a constant length. The front surface of the incisor is hard enamel. This is backed by softer dentine. As the teeth grind against each other the dentine is worn away, and the enamel is ground to a keen cutting edge.

All rodents eat plant food—roots, bulbs, leaves, stalks, fruit, seeds, and nuts. Many rodents have cheek pouches in which they transport food to storage places. Many species—squirrels, rats, and mice, for example—also eat eggs as well as insects and other small animals.

Most rodents do not live very long. But as a group they mature quickly and have many big litters of young. Rodents must have big families in order to survive, for they have many enemies. Most of the flesh-eating mammals, birds, and reptiles hunt them as their main prey.

Chipmunks, like many rodents, eat mostly plant food, such as leaves, stalks, and seeds.

▶ HARMFUL RODENTS AND HELPFUL ONES

Various rodents do vast amounts of damage to grain and fruit and other crops that man grows. Rats and mice invade man's buildings, where they ruin stores of food and other products. Porcupines kill many trees by eating the bark, through which sap flows. Many rodents are infested with fleas that carry various diseases.

Many rodents, on the other hand, are of use to man. Beavers and muskrats are valued for their fur. Rats, mice, guinea pigs, and hamsters are raised as laboratory animals. Many rodents in the wild eat large quantities of insects and weed seeds, thus helping to control them. Squirrels aid in the job of tree planting by burying nuts, acorns, and pine seeds. Millions of burrowing rodents help to turn over and condition the soil.

Scientists have separated the many rodents into 32 or more families. These, according to their characteristics, can be grouped into three main divisions:

(1) Squirrels and their relatives
(2) Rats and mice
(3) Porcupines, cavies, and their relatives

A woodchuck's chisel-like front teeth are typical of all rodents.

SQUIRRELS AND THEIR RELATIVES

This group includes many of the most appealing and familiar rodents—the bushy-tailed tree squirrels, the engaging little chipmunks and ground squirrels, the roly-poly woodchuck, and the sprightly prairie dog.

Tree Squirrels

The familiar tree squirrels are characterized by their thick, plumed tails. The tail acts as a balancer when a squirrel leaps from branch to branch, as a parachute if the squirrel should fall, and as a snug blanket when it curls up to sleep.

Tree squirrels live in holes in trees or in bulky leaf nests, which they build high in the branches. They are usually active throughout the year. Their main diet is seeds and nuts and fruit, but many of them eat insects and other small animals as well. Many squirrels gather hoards of nuts for winter use.

A great number of different kinds of squirrels live in Eurasia, Africa, and the Americas. The gray squirrel is the most common species in the eastern United States. It is usually colored a grizzled gray, lighter underneath. In certain areas many individuals are almost pure black. Once in a while you may see a white one.

The largest of the American tree squirrels is the fox squirrel. Some individuals are mostly rust-brown and tan. Others are gray and black.

The red, or pine, squirrels are smaller than either the gray or the fox squirrels. They are found from coast to coast and usually live in evergreen forests. They are great hoarders and sometimes store several bushels of cones in one hiding place. The seeds from the cones are their main food.

The little flying squirrels are seldom seen. They live in hollow trees and are active only at night. Flying squirrels have furred membranes of skin joining their front and hind legs. Spreading these like wings, the squirrels glide from tree to tree. Sometimes they travel 150 feet or more in one downward leap.

Chipmunks and Ground Squirrels

The eastern chipmunk is common throughout southeastern Canada and the eastern United States. It is a small, reddish-brown ground squirrel with dark and light stripes on its face and sides. Its tail is not so bushy as the tails of tree squirrels. The chipmunk can climb trees but usually prefers to hunt food on the ground. Darting back and forth, it stuffs seeds and nuts into its cheek pouches. Looking as though it had mumps, it whisks down its burrow and unloads its cheeks in an underground storeroom.

Three to five young are born each spring in an underground nursery, about a month after the parents have mated. By autumn the young are nearly full-grown and on their own. They dig burrows, which they fill with stores of food. Then they sleep away most of the winter underground. Occasionally they wake up, eat some of the food, and then sleep again.

Other species of chipmunks live in western North America. All of them look much like the eastern chipmunk and have similar habits. Many other kinds of ground squirrels are found throughout the West, too. Some of these are plainly colored, without the chipmunk's stripes. Others have striking patterns. One of the best-known is the thirteen-lined ground squirrel. It has a number of alternating light and dark stripes on its back and sides. Some of the dark stripes have center rows of whitish spots. The thirteen-lined ground squirrel hibernates all winter long, as do many other ground squirrels.

Marmots and Prairie Dogs

Marmots are large, heavy-bodied relatives of the squirrels. They have short legs and tails. Several species of them live in Europe and Asia, and others in the Rocky Mountains of western North America. The most familiar marmot in eastern North America is the groundhog, or woodchuck.

The woodchuck digs its burrow in fields or clearings. There are usually two or more entrances. A strict vegetarian, the woodchuck stuffs itself with clover and other plant foods all summer long. By early autumn it is very fat. Retiring to its underground sleeping chamber before the first frost, it hibernates there until the following spring.

Prairie dogs look very much like small marmots and have similar habits. They live on the western prairies and plains. They dig fairly deep burrows, often with entrance shafts going almost straight down for 10 or 12 feet.

Left: A flying squirrel glides through the air. Right: A chipmunk, its cheek pouches stuffed with seeds.

Sociable animals, prairie dogs live in colonies and often form large towns. Because they damage crops and range grass and because their holes are hazards for horses, prairie dogs have been killed off in many areas.

Rodents with Fur-Lined Cheek Pouches

The pocket gophers are among the strangest of all rodents. A number of different kinds of these small burrowing animals live in North America. Equipped with short, stout legs and long, powerful claws, pocket gophers are expert diggers. Various individuals have been known to tunnel as much as 200 to 300 feet in a single night. Most of their lives are spent underground, where they feed on roots, bulbs, and other vegetable matter.

The most remarkable thing about the pocket gopher is the fact that on the outside of each cheek it has a slit that leads to a fur-lined pocket. The animal stuffs seeds and other food into its pockets with its front paws. Then it goes off to a storage or eating place and pushes the food out by rubbing its cheeks with its paws.

The kangaroo rats and pocket mice that live in western desert areas also have fur-lined cheek pouches. These attractive little rodents have tiny front legs, long tails, and long hind legs on which they hop about like miniature kangaroos. They live in burrows, where they retire during the day, often plugging the entrance behind them. Many of them do not drink during their entire lives but obtain moisture from seeds and juicy vegetation.

The *Aplodontia,* or Mountain Beaver

The *Aplodontia,* or mountain beaver, looks something like a miniature beaver with a stubby tail. This stocky little rodent, usually 12 to 18 inches long, lives along the Pacific coast from southern Canada into California. It has short legs and very small ears. It lives in colonies and builds extensive tunnels. Bark, twigs, and green plant material form the *Aplodontia*'s main food. During the summer it busily stockpiles such food for winter use.

▶RATS, MICE, AND THEIR RELATIVES

Thousands of kinds of rats and mice and their relatives populate the earth in untold billions. They are the most abundant of all the abundant rodents. Besides the familiar

A woodchuck peers cautiously about before emerging from its underground burrow.

A pocket gopher, feeling its way with its tail, can move backward as quickly and easily as it can forward.

The mountain beaver, or *Aplodontia*, has short legs and a stubby tail.

The collared lemming lives in far northern tundra areas. It usually has a band of brownish fur about its neck.

house mouse and rat, there are multitudes of field mice, lemmings, deer mice, pack rats, jumping mice, and many other kinds. The best-known, however, are the house mouse and the brown, or house, rat.

The House Mouse and Brown Rat

These two rodents are among the most successful of all animal species. Along with the housefly—and man—they have populated most of the world. Hardy and resourceful, these two rodents have followed man practically everywhere he has gone.

Originally natives only of the Old World, house mice are little gray-brown rodents with long, nearly naked tails. They usually live in houses and buildings, where they build their nests between walls or in holes. They often do great damage to stored foods and other materials. One reason for their success is their high rate of reproduction. Female house mice may mate when they are 40 days old. Their young—four to seven in a litter and sometimes more—are born only 19 or 20 days

Rats do great damage to stored foods and other materials.

after their parents have mated. Sheltered from the weather, house mice breed all year round.

The brown rat, also called the house rat or the Norway rat, is much larger than the house mouse and reproduces almost as much. Breeding throughout the year, brown rats bear seven to nine young at a time, about 3 weeks after mating. The young are ready to become parents when they are about 4 months old. The brown rat is the most destructive of all mammals, as far as man is concerned. It not only destroys hundreds of millions of dollars' worth of foodstuffs and other products yearly, but also spreads disease. The only kind thing that can be said for the brown rat is that its domesticated strains are used as experimental laboratory animals the world over. As such, they also help man in conquering various diseases.

Field Mice and Lemmings

Field mice—or voles, as they are sometimes called—are small, stout mice with short tails and short legs. They have small eyes and ears. There are many different kinds. Mainly seed- and plant-eaters, they make mazes of tiny runways and shallow tunnels across fields and woodlands. They build globe-shaped nests of grass under logs or rocks. Here several litters of five to eight young are born during the warm months. When the weather is favorable and food is plentiful, field mice tend to have more families and larger ones than usual. Then thousands of mice per acre overrun the area and do great damage to crops.

Ready to defend itself, a porcupine raises its sharp quills and gives a warning rattle.

A prairie jumping mouse, using its long tail for balance, can leap as far as 12 feet in a single jump.

Lemmings are closely related to field mice. They live in far northern tundra areas of the Northern Hemisphere. They also multiply very fast in favorable years. It is then that their famous travels, or migrations, take place. Moving away from their birthplace in search of less crowded areas, brown lemmings gather into great hordes—sometimes numbering many millions—that sweep across the land. Coming to a river, the tiny rodents swim across. Coming to a cliff, they plunge over. Many swim out to sea—when they reach it—and are drowned. Huge numbers of flesh-eaters—foxes, wolves, weasels, owls, hawks, and the like—follow the hordes of lemmings and feast on them. Finally, the lemming population drops sharply. For several years lemmings are quite scarce in the area. Eventually, however, the survivors build up to another peak. Then another lemming migration occurs.

Muskrats, Hamsters, and Other Kinds of Rats and Mice

There are hundreds of other kinds of rats and mice. One of the largest is the muskrat. Equipped with partly webbed feet, it lives in ponds and marshes. There it builds snug, dome-shaped houses of cattails and other marsh plants. The muskrat is an important fur animal.

Many different varieties of attractive little deer mice, or white-footed mice, inhabit North America. These mice have fawn-colored upperparts and white underparts. They have enormous dark eyes and big ears. Clean and dainty, they build their nests in hollow trees or under logs. Here they store seeds for winter use. Sometimes they invade houses during the winter.

Pack, or wood, rats inhabit woodlands, mountains, and desert areas of North America. Some of them build huge nests of twigs and brush. They are called pack rats because they collect buttons, bits of glass, and other shiny objects, which they carry to their nests.

Jumping mice are tiny American mice with very long tails and long hind legs. They sometimes cover as much as 12 feet in one leap. The jerboas form another family of rodents that also hop about on their hind legs. They live mainly in dry or desert areas of the Old World.

The golden hamster, a familiar pet, also belongs to the group of mouselike rodents. It was originally a native of Syria and neighboring areas. It is now kept the world over as a pet and laboratory animal.

▶ PORCUPINES, CAVIES, AND THEIR RELATIVES

The third large group of rodents has only a few species, comparatively speaking. Many of these are fairly large. Unlike most other rodents, most species in this group bear young that are active, fully furred, and have their eyes open at birth.

Porcupines—Rodents with Quills

The North American porcupine is a large, clumsy-looking rodent with short legs. A big porcupine may measure 3 feet in length and weigh 20 or 30 pounds. It is famous for its

The capybara, largest of the rodents, is about the size of a domestic pig.

Domestic guinea pigs' coats show a variety of patterns and colors.

protective covering of long, sharp quills—as many as 30,000 on a single individual.

Porcupines cannot shoot their quills. The quills are loosely attached, however. They come out on contact with an attacker's skin. Then they work their way deeper and deeper into the flesh. Each quill has many tiny barbs at its tip. These dig into the flesh like the barbs on fishhooks. The barbs make it very difficult to take out the quill. A sudden, quick pull with pliers or tweezers works best.

Many meat-eating mammals that attack porcupines get quills in their faces and mouths. The quills work their way deeper and deeper. Eventually the animal may be unable to eat and may die as a result.

Porcupines live in wooded areas. They make their homes in burrows or in hollow trees. Their main food is the bark of trees. They kill many trees by stripping off rings of bark. A single young porcupine is born in the spring, about 7 months after mating.

The prehensile-tailed porcupine lives in tropical North and South America. It has a long tail with a bare spot near the end. It uses the tail to hold onto branches.

Crested porcupines live in Africa and Asia. They are usually a bit larger than North American porcupines and have even longer quills. Those on the neck and back may measure 20 inches in length.

Guinea Pigs and Their New World Relatives

The domestic guinea pig was originally a native of South America. A rat-size rodent, it has short legs, no tail, small ears, and a rabbitlike face. Wild guinea pigs are reddish or gray-brown. Domestic guinea pigs, however, come in many assorted colors and patterns. They may be white, black, brown, reddish, or buff-colored. Or they may be spotted with several different colors. Guinea pigs usually bear two to four young at a time. Several litters may be born each year. The baby guinea pigs, born 60 days after mating, are fully furred and active at birth.

Agoutis are another group of tropical New World rodents. They have sleek, reddish or golden fur, small ears, fairly long, slender legs, and practically no tails. They are burrowers, as are their relatives the pacas and the Patagonian cavies.

The South American capybara is the largest of all rodents. About the size of a good-size pig, it has a blunt face, a stout body covered with brownish fur, rather long legs, and partly webbed feet. The capybara lives near water and is an expert swimmer.

The chinchilla is a native of the high Andes of South America. With a 10-inch body and 5-inch tail, it is thickly covered with smoky-blue fur that is as soft as thistledown. It is now quite rare in the wild. In the 1920's about a dozen chinchillas were captured in Chile and brought to the United States. The little animals were bred in captivity, and now many thousands are raised on fur farms.

Another famous South American rodent is the coypu, or nutria. It looks very much like a big muskrat and has similar habits. The coypu has been introduced into the southern United States and into Europe, where it is trapped for its fur.

ROBERT M. McCLUNG
Author, science books for children

See also BEAVERS; RABBITS AND HARES.

RODEOS

In rodeos cowboys and cowgirls try their luck and riding skill on unbroken horses called bucking broncos. They risk their lives riding raging bulls. And they test the speed and training of their horses in calf roping and team roping.

"Rodeo" is a Spanish word that means "roundup." Rodeos started in the western United States more than 100 years ago as a celebration after the work of roundup had been done. Gradually some cowboys began to choose rodeo as a profession. The competition became more difficult as rules and regulations were made. In 1936, contestants began organizing themselves. In 1945 the Rodeo Cowboys Association—later renamed the Professional Rodeo Cowboys Association (PRCA) —was formed. The association governs procedures and makes the rules for professional rodeos.

The rodeo today is a big business. More than 500 rodeos are held each year in Canada and the United States. They are attended by millions of spectators, and the prize money exceeds several million dollars. Every rodeo has five standard events—bareback bronco riding, saddle bronco riding, bull riding, calf roping, and steer wrestling.

▶ BUCKING EVENTS

Usually the first thing you think of when rodeo is mentioned is the bucking bronco. The bronco is a wild, untamed horse. It fights anyone who tries to saddle or ride it.

In bareback bronco riding, the contestant rides with one hand holding onto a thick leather cinch that is strapped around the horse behind its shoulders. The rider must stay on the plunging, bucking horse for eight seconds and must spur the horse continuously during the ride. (Dull spurs are used.)

Saddle bronco riding requires the use of a special saddle. In this event, the rider's balance and timing are more important than physical strength. With one hand, the rider holds onto a soft woven rein that is attached to the horse's halter. As in bareback, the rider must stay on the horse for eight seconds and must keep on spurring. Riders must also keep their feet in the stirrups.

Two judges score the bucking events. Each

A bucking bronco does its best to throw its rider. The rider must stay on the horse for eight seconds.

gives points to both horse and rider. Riders may lose points for not spurring or for simply riding poorly. Horses lose points for not bucking enough. The point scores are added together, and the highest total wins. Riders are disqualified for touching the horse with the free hand or for falling off before eight seconds are up.

Bull riding is considered by many to be the most dangerous rodeo event. The contestant rides bareback with one hand holding onto a rope that is tied around the bull behind its shoulders. Again, the rider must stay on the animal for eight seconds. If a rider falls, rodeo clowns run out and distract the bull so that the rider can get safely out of the arena.

Scoring in the bull-riding event is the same as in bronco riding, except that the contestants do not lose points for not spurring.

▶ TIMED EVENTS

The two timed events in a rodeo are calf roping and steer wrestling. In calf roping, the goal is to rope a running calf, throw it on its side, and tie three of its legs together.

To be successful, the contestant must be good with a rope. But teamwork between the horse and rider is just as important. The horse must stand quietly and alertly and must be able to move quickly as soon as the calf is let out of the chute. Once the calf is roped, the horse must stop quickly and try to keep the rope taut while the contestant makes the tie.

Contestants are disqualified for missing the calf with the rope. If they start out of the box too soon, a ten-second penalty is added to their time.

In steer wrestling, the contestants ride up beside running steers, leap off their horses, and grab the animals' horns. They get the steers off balance by twisting the horns and forcing the animals to fall flat.

As in calf roping, good horses are important to success in steer wrestling. The horses must be fast. They are trained to run up next to the steers so that the riders can make their jump.

There is another rider—called a hazer— in the steer-wrestling event. The hazer rides along the other side of the steer and tries to keep the animal running in a straight line. This makes it easier for the contestant to catch the steer.

In both calf roping and steer wrestling, the rider who takes the least amount of time to complete the event is the winner.

Team roping is another timed event that is seen at many rodeos. Two contestants work together. One throws a rope around a steer's horns, and the other ropes the animal's hind legs. Time is called when the steer is roped and the two contestants have pulled their ropes taut and are standing away from the steer facing each other.

▶ RODEO SKILLS

Different skills are required in each event. In fact, in competition today you seldom find contestants who ride and rope equally well. They must concentrate on one or the other. Usually the best ropers come from the southwestern part of the United States, where cattle are still roped on the range. In the north, outdoor roping cannot be done during the winter. But a great many indoor or covered arenas have been built so that the northerners can continue their practice sessions unhampered by the cold. Bronco riders are more numerous in Canada and the northwestern United States, where more emphasis is put on their event. There are also more horses broken to ride in those areas. Canadian rodeos always have an amateur bronco-riding event as well as the professional contest. This serves as schooling for the young bronco riders. As a general rule, the horses raised in the northwest and in Canada are heavier than those raised in the southwest. They provide a little more action when they are being "gentled." This factor contributes to the northerners' riding skill.

▶ WOMEN IN RODEOS

In most rodeos, women compete only in an event called barrel racing. Each cowgirl races her horse around a course marked by three barrels, weaving in and out among them. The rider with the fastest time is the winner. Penalty time is added for knocking over barrels.

There are all-cowgirl rodeos. In these rodeos, cowgirls compete in calf roping, bareback bronco riding, and bull riding, as well as other riding and tying events.

▶ JUNIOR RODEOS

The rodeo is not for adults only. The National Little Britches Rodeo Association sponsors several hundred rodeos a year for youngsters between the ages of 8 and 17. These young people compete in all the rugged events of adult rodeos. The Little Britches Rodeos provide good training for young people who want to go on to become professional rodeo performers.

At the high school level, the National High School Rodeo Association holds about 600 rodeos a year. Each state has championship elimination trials among the various teams. Rodeos are also held at the collegiate level, under the auspices of the National Intercollegiate Rodeo Association.

These college and junior organizations are spread over more than half the United States. They are organized in the same manner as professional rodeos, ending in national finals and annual championship awards. Each year, gold and silver trophy buckles are given to championship winners.

RODEO NEWS BUREAU
Association of Professional Rodeo Cowboys

RODIN, AUGUSTE (1840–1917)

François Auguste René Rodin—the greatest of French sculptors—was born in Paris on November 12, 1840. At the age of 14 he began taking drawing lessons, and in 1857 he tried to enroll in the École des Beaux-Arts (School of Fine Arts). The admissions director of the school thought that Rodin's work was crude, and he rejected the young artist.

Rodin then took odd jobs making plaster ornaments and casting other sculptors' works. His skill increased, and he was given the opportunity to carve figures on buildings.

By 1875, when he was 35, Rodin had not yet worked on his own. He borrowed money from a friend and went to Italy. The sculpture of the great Italian masters, especially Michelangelo, stirred Rodin. When he returned home, he began to work independently, and the influence of Michelangelo touched all of Rodin's sculpture.

Rodin's first life-size statue was *The Age of Bronze*, a male nude figure. Using a technique new to sculpture, Rodin modeled the surface of the figure with many small, flat areas. Each of these planes acts as a mirror, catching and reflecting light. As the viewer walks around the figure, the light shifts, and the surface appears to be real skin.

The Age of Bronze was first shown in an exhibition in Paris in 1877. Visiting critics were so startled by the lifelike effect of the statue that they accused Rodin of having made a mold of a living person. Although this accusation was ridiculous, the sculpture was not widely admired until 1884, when it was shown in London.

Rodin soon began to win recognition because a great many people disagreed with the critics. In 1880 he was commissioned to make a bronze door for the Museum of Decorative Arts in Paris. The door, called *The Gate of Hell*, was never cast during his lifetime. But some of Rodin's later works—*The Thinker*, for example—were based on figures first planned for the door.

Rodin constantly experimented with new techniques and new ideas. He created sculptures of expressive hands alone. Several times Rodin carved part of a body out of a block of stone, leaving much of the original block uncut and unpolished. He was also a portrait sculptor who made busts of some of the most

When critics saw *The Age of Bronze* (1877), they thought Rodin had made a mold of a living person.

important people of his time. Many young artists were inspired by Rodin to take up sculpture—a neglected art form that had been used chiefly for public monuments for 200 years.

In 1916, Rodin gave all his work to the people of France. One year later, on November 17, 1917, he died. He was buried near his home at Meudon (near Paris), with *The Thinker* as the headstone on his grave. (A photograph of *The Thinker* is included in the article FRENCH ART AND ARCHITECTURE in Volume F.) The Rodin Museum in Paris, which houses much of his work, was built in his honor.

Reviewed by JOSEPH RISHEL, JR.
Philadelphia Museum of Art

ROLLER-SKATING

People started skating in Scandinavia more than 2,000 years ago, as a means of transportation over ice. The first recorded instance of skating on rollers was in 1760, in England. This might not have been remembered but for the fact that the skates could go only straight ahead. The inventor of the skates, Joseph Merlin, crashed into a mirror at one end of the ballroom where he was giving a demonstration. In 1819 a French inventor named Petitbled devised a skate that had two, three, or four wheels in a straight line.

In 1863, James Plimpton, an American, made a four-wheeled skate, and the sport became popular. His skates permitted movement sideways as well as forward and backward. When it became apparent that roller skaters could do all the movements that ice skaters could do, arenas for roller-skating were built. These attracted many people to the sport.

Roller-skate wheels used to be made of steel, but they are now made of plastic. Skates no longer clamp onto shoes. They are riveted, bolted, or screwed to skating boots or bootlike shoes. Skating boots are cut higher and give greater support to the ankle than shoes. As in all sports, there is a variety of equipment for sale, from the most basic to the frivolous. Safety accessories, such as knee pads, are also available.

The first contests in roller-skating were held in racing. This is similar to ice-skating racing, in which you follow a rectangular track with two corners and two straightaways. In racing, the skill lies in turning corners as swiftly as possible and in passing another skater.

Another form of competition is roller hockey, which is popular in Europe. It is played on a court similar to an ice-hockey rink. The game is very fast, since body contact is not allowed. Two teams of five people attempt to move a ball into the opposing team's cage. The ball is handled by a stick with one end curved to enable a player to control the ball. A good player must have skating skill and stick-handling ability. The United States Olympic Committee featured roller hockey in the Summer Sports Festival Program in Colorado Springs in 1979.

Roller Derby is a popular United States sport involving contests of speed, skill, and endurance between two teams of roller skaters. Each team is made up of five men and five women. Women compete only against women, and men against men. Roller Derby contests usually take place in an arena with a specially constructed track. Points are scored when a member of one team overtakes and passes an opposing player. It is a rough game, and players wear protective helmets and padded clothing.

The most popular form of competition throughout the world is the artistic form of roller-skating. The skater is judged on artistic skills such as form, carriage, timing to music, grace, and beauty of movement. Contests are held in singles (men against men, women against women), pairs, and dance.

Roller disco developed from the dance styles popular at discotheques. Some disco dance patterns have been choreographed for skaters. But for the most part, roller disco is a freestyle form of dance that is spontaneously developed by the individual skater. Special roller disco rinks have elaborate lighting and sound systems.

Roller-skating requires a flat, fairly smooth surface. The area must be rather large and uncrowded because the ease of rolling makes you travel far. Sidewalks are inappropriate because pedestrians can be hit. It is better to skate in either indoor or outdoor rinks. Outdoor rinks usually have a skating surface of smooth concrete. Indoor rinks have floors of flake board, which is a pressed, wood-type substance that is plastic-coated. Indoor rinks are heated and well lighted.

In skating, you control your balance differently from the way you do in walking. Roller-skating differs from walking in that you place your foot flat, rather than heel followed by toe. To maintain good balance, bend your knees whenever you take a step. Always try to keep your body in line between your head and the foot that is off the floor.

The basic movements in roller-skating are starting, which is what you do when you begin any skating move; rolling forward, which requires practice in keeping your balance on one foot; stopping, which is necessary whenever something or someone gets in your path; and skating a curve, the part of roller skating that makes it so much fun. You will find it necessary to try the basic movements over and over until they feel natural.

Roller-skating provides good muscular exercise. Since no strenuous movements are required, roller-skating is suited for people of all ages and physical conditions.

GEORGE F. WERNER
Former United States Dance-Skating Champion

ROMAN ART AND ARCHITECTURE

The Romans were a practical people. They wanted their art and architecture to be useful. They planned their cities and built bridges, aqueducts, public baths, and marketplaces, apartment houses, and harbors. When a Roman official ordered sculpture for a public square, he wanted it to tell future generations of the greatness of Rome. Although the practical uses of art were distinctly Roman, the art forms themselves were influenced by the ancient Greeks and Etruscans.

In the late 7th century B.C., the most powerful people in Italy were the Etruscans, who had come from Asia Minor and settled in Tuscany, an area north of Rome. Although the Etruscans imported Greek styles of art, they achieved much by themselves. They developed a very realistic type of portrait sculpture. They were also the first to introduce the use of the stone arch into architecture.

▶ARCHITECTURE

The Romans put the lessons of the Etruscans to practical use. The baths and arenas are tributes to the skill of Rome's great builders. Because of the use of the arch, the Romans could build on a greater scale than the Greeks, who used the post and lintel (a beam supported by two columns). Roman aqueducts were often three levels of arches piled one on top of another. And their buildings, such as the Baths of Caracalla, enclosed huge open areas.

In the 1st century B.C. the Romans developed the use of concrete. It could be poured into any shape for arches, vaults, or domes. Concrete enabled architects to build structures of immense size. One such gigantic construction was the Temple of Fortune at Praeneste, built by the ruler Sulla about 80 B.C. The architect used concrete to support terraces

The Pont du Gard, an aqueduct near Nîmes, France, was built by the Romans in 19 B.C.

Detail of a statue of Antinoüs (A.D. 110?–130), who was famous for his grace and beauty.

In A.D. 79, an eruption of the volcano Vesuvius covered the city of Pompeii with layers of lava that hardened into rock. The wall paintings preserved in this rock tell us nearly everything we know about Roman painting.

Painting was usually done as a form of decoration. In Pompeii, for example, paintings were executed on the inside walls of the houses in fresco (painting on wet plaster). Often these murals were used to make the room seem larger, by giving the illusion of depth, or to create a pastoral landscape where there was no window or view.

Columns and other forms of architecture were often painted into the compositions or used to frame the murals and add to the feeling of depth. A system of perspective was known and used by the Romans. Red, black, and cream-white were among the most popular colors.

Roman painting achieved a high degree of naturalism through the artists' understanding of perspective and use of light and shade. It also had within it a streak of romanticism. The Romans painted many charming scenes from nature and portraits of children and beautiful young men and women. Religion, too, inspired their art.

and to build what was in effect a skyscraper. To build their open-air theaters, the Greeks had scooped out the sides of hills, using the hills to support the sloping tiers of seats. But the Roman engineers used concrete to support the three gigantic tiers of the Colosseum, their main stadium for public entertainment. The tiers held seats for more than 45,000 spectators. A picture of the Colosseum is included in the article on Rome.

▶ SCULPTURE

The Romans used a great deal of sculpted decoration to embellish their architecture. Columns were often placed on the walls of buildings as part of the decoration. (They actually supported no weight themselves.) Many of these decorations were copied from Greek styles. In fact, many Greek forms were simply placed on the facades of Roman buildings without any practical reason for being there.

In portraying their gods, the Greeks had been influenced by their ideas of form and beauty. Roman sculptors were greatly influenced by the Greeks. But the Romans showed their skill and originality in their portraits. They portrayed their emperors, generals, and senators with a degree of realism unknown to the Greeks. Thinning hair, double chins, crooked noses—all the physical traits that make one person look different from another —can be found in Roman portraiture.

Narcissus, a fresco in a Pompeian home. Narcissus was a youth who fell in love with his own reflection in a pond.

The Delivery of the Keys, by Pietro Perugino, shows the first pope, Saint Peter, receiving the keys of the kingdom of heaven from Jesus Christ.

ROMAN CATHOLIC CHURCH

The history of the Roman Catholic Church began in an upper room in Jerusalem almost 2,000 years ago. About 120 persons were gathered there. They were followers of Jesus Christ, and they were awaiting the coming of the Holy Spirit he had promised to send them from heaven. The day on which the Holy Spirit came down is considered the birthday of the Church. The Church may be described as the society that Jesus founded, which is vitalized by the Spirit of God and organized according to a structure which he established. The history of the Roman Catholic Church traces the destinies of that society from its beginning until now.

The earliest written record of the Church is the New Testament, a collection of books composed by the Apostles of Jesus or their disciples ("followers"). The four **Gospels** ("good news") contain the message preached by the Apostles in written form. They relate the story of Jesus from his birth to his death and his resurrection and ascension into heaven. Jesus founded the Church to carry his message of salvation to all men. From his followers he chose 12, whom he called Apostles (Luke 6:14). "Apostle" means "one who is sent on a mission." Jesus appointed one of the Apostles head of the group. He was called Simon, but Jesus changed his name to Peter (the Greek word *petra* means "rock") and said to him, "Upon this rock I will build my Church" (Matthew 16:18). The Acts of the Apostles follows the Gospels in the New Testament. It tells the history of the Church's early years, especially the deeds (*acta*) of the great Apostles Peter and Paul. Following the Acts of the Apostles are 14 letters by Paul written to the churches, seven letters written by others, and finally a prophetic book about the ultimate destiny of the Church.

This collection of writings is called the New Testament to distinguish it from the books in

Early Christians were persecuted by the Romans.

the message of Christ to Asia Minor and Greece and perhaps as far as Spain. The Greek tongue was spoken throughout the empire, and the splendid Roman roads made long journeys possible.

The conversion of gentiles in great numbers brought about the first crisis in the Church. Male converts from Judaism had been circumcised in infancy, according to the Law of Moses. Some of them felt that the gentiles should also be circumcised before entering the Church. Saint Paul was opposed to this. To settle the question, the Apostles came together in Jerusalem in the year A.D. 50. This Council of Jerusalem was the first council of the Church (although it is not numbered among the general councils). It was decided not to require circumcision of the gentiles (Acts 15).

With the spread of the Gospel, churches were founded in the cities of the empire. The churches were presided over by the clergy, of which there were three degrees: bishops, priests, and deacons. The Christians met in weekly assembly on the Lord's Day, the first day of the week. The Eucharist ("thanksgiving") was offered in memory of the death of Jesus. A systematic course of instruction was given to those who desired to become Christians, and they were also prepared by special rites for the sacrament of Baptism, by which they became members of the Church.

During the first 3 centuries of the Christian era, Christians lived under the threat of persecution or actual oppression by the Roman emperors. This period is properly called the Age of the Martyrs. The reason for the persecutions was that Christians would not worship the emperor and the state. Roman religion made gods of the state and the emperor. The refusal of Christians to pay religious homage to the emperor and to the state was looked upon as civic disobedience and disloyalty. Christians were considered dangerous to the state, and as such they were put to death. There were 10 persecutions in all, according to the classical reckoning: the first under Nero, and the last and the greatest under Diocletian (245–313). In 303 Diocletian began a war of extermination against the Church. Constantine the Great emerged victorious from the civil wars that followed the resignation of Diocletian. He was the first

the Bible that precede it, which Christians call the Old Testament. Jesus used the expression at the Last Supper when he instituted the **sacrament** ("the sign of a sacred thing") of the Eucharist. Taking the chalice of wine, he said, "All of you drink of this, for this is my blood of the New Testament" (Matthew 26:28). **Testament** means "covenant" or "alliance." God had made a covenant with Israel at Mount Sinai in the days of Moses, over 1,000 years earlier. He made the new covenant with all mankind through Christ. The Church of Christ is the fulfillment of the promise of the Old Testament. Jesus said, "I have not come to destroy [the Old Testament] but to fulfill [it]" (Matthew 5:17).

▶THE CHURCH OF THE MARTYRS

The Apostles first preached Christ's message to their own people, the Jews, and then to non-Jewish people, called gentiles, who were pagans. Slowly and steadily the Church spread beyond Judea, Samaria, and Galilee across the Roman Empire. Jerusalem was the center of the mission to the Jews. Antioch became the center of the mission to the gentiles. From there Saint Paul set out to bring

emperor to be converted to Christianity. By the Edict of Milan (313) he ended the persecution of Christians.

THEOLOGY AND THE GROWTH OF DOCTRINE

With the Edict of Milan a new era in the history of the Church began. The next few centuries were times of great theological (religious) debate and dispute. Men tried to express the mysteries and truths of the Christian faith in exact terms. All men, not just bishops and priests, were deeply interested in theology. People then were as stirred by theological debates as we are by political and social issues today. The disputes were often accompanied by riots and street fighting. Clergy and people were divided, and the emperors were disturbed by the public disorders.

The religious dispute that caused the greatest conflict and public disorder was created by Arius (?–336), a priest of Alexandria. He taught that Christ was not God, but a man like other men. This **heresy**, or departure from accepted beliefs, was called Arianism. It was condemned, and Arius' teachings were rejected by the Council of Nicaea in 325. This first **ecumenical**, or general, council of the Church also drew up a statement of Roman Catholic belief that is still in effect today. It is known as the Nicene Creed. The greatest champion of the teachings of the Council of Nicaea was Athanasius, Bishop of Alexandria (293?–373).

The Golden Age

During the next 500 years eight general councils were held. All were called by the emperors and were held in the eastern part of the empire. This period has been called the Golden Age because of the important role played by these councils in the life of the Church.

The second general council was held at Constantinople (Istanbul) in 381. The third was held at Ephesus in 431; and the fourth, at Chalcedon in 451. These four councils are important for the **doctrine**, or body of defined truths, set forth concerning Christ, the Holy Trinity, and Mary, the Mother of Jesus.

The Council of Constantinople declared that after the bishop of Rome, the bishops of Constantinople ranked above all the other bishops of the Church. This was because Constantinople was the "new Rome." The other ancient churches of the east were not happy with this declaration. Antioch was noted as the first **see** (seat of a bishop's power or authority) of Saint Peter and the main center of gentile Christianity. Alexandria in Egypt was famous for its theological school. Jerusalem was the city where the Church was born. Conflicts and power struggles among these sees, and especially between Constantinople and Rome, marked this period. They finally led to a break between the Church in the east and the Church in the west. The split has continued even into the 20th century.

FALL OF THE ROMAN EMPIRE

In the west the Roman Empire was entering its last days. The downfall of the central government was brought about by what historians call the barbarian invasions. The barbarians were people of different tribes—Goths, Huns, and Vandals—who lived beyond the borders of the Roman Empire. They began to enter the Roman armies, first as soldiers, then as officers. Finally, they married into the imperial family. Theodosius was the last ruler of the united empire. In 410 Rome itself was plundered by Alaric (370?–410) and the Visigoths. By the end of the 5th century the Roman Empire in the west had collapsed.

Survival of Ancient Thought and Civilization

The Church was the only great institution to survive the downfall of the western empire. Three of its great saints proved to be the means by which the heritage of ancient thought and civilization was brought to Europe. Saint Augustine, Bishop of Hippo in North Africa, was the father of Latin theology. His writings became the source of the new Christian culture. Saint Ambrose (340?–397), Bishop of Milan, set down the principle by which the Church came to be more independent of civil powers in the west than in the east. Saint Jerome (340?–420), translator of the Bible into Latin, laid the foundations of Biblical scholarship within the Church. His translation was the commonly accepted, or Vulgate, text of Christian Europe for almost 1,000 years. Illuminated manuscripts of the Latin Vulgate are among the finest masterpieces of Christian art. An out-

What are holy days?

Roman Catholics (along with members of the Orthodox Eastern Church, Anglicans, and some Protestants) keep certain days and seasons of the year as religious observances. The Church year contains two great cycles, or seasons, of holy days. Other holy days are scattered throughout the year. Some of the days celebrate events in the life of Jesus and Mary. Others honor the saints, usually on the day of their death. A few commemorate doctrines or mysteries of the Christian religion.

The Christmas Cycle

Advent—a period of about four weeks in preparation for Christmas. It begins on the Sunday nearest November 30.

Christmas (December 25)—celebrates the birth of Christ.

Solemnity of Mary (January 1)—honors Mary as Mother of God, her oldest title.

Epiphany (January 6 or the Sunday nearest that date)—commemorates the coming of the Magi (Wise Men) to the infant Christ.

Lent and Easter Cycle

Ash Wednesday—introduces the 40 days of Lent, a period of preparation for Easter.

Holy Week (the week before Easter)—commemorates Christ's entry into Jerusalem (**Palm, or Passion, Sunday**), the Last Supper (**Holy Thursday**), and the crucifixion of Christ (**Good Friday**).

Easter—celebrates Christ's resurrection, or rising from the dead. The 50 days from Easter to Pentecost are an especially joyous season, known as **Paschal**, or **Easter, Time.**

Ascension (40th day after Easter, or the following Sunday)—celebrates the ascent of Christ into heaven.

Pentecost, or **Whitsunday** (50th day after Easter)—commemorates the descent of the Holy Spirit upon the disciples of Christ.

Days Throughout the Year

Corpus Christi (second Thursday or Sunday after Pentecost)—honors the body and blood of Christ in the Eucharist.

Saint John the Baptist (June 24)—commemorates the birth of Christ's cousin and forerunner.

Saints Peter and Paul (June 29)—honors two martyred Apostles.

Assumption of the Blessed Virgin Mary (August 15)—celebrates the taking up into heaven of the Virgin after her death.

All Saints' (November 1)—celebrates all Christian saints, known and unknown.

All Souls' (November 2)—commemorates souls of faithful departed.

standing example of an illuminated manuscript is the Book of Kells in the Trinity College library, Dublin, Ireland.

One of the most important accomplishments of the Church in this period was the Christianizing and civilization of the barbarians themselves. From this came medieval Christian culture and Western civilization. Many great men of the Church arose during this period. Saint Benedict (480?–543?) founded an order of monks that transformed the rural areas by the principle "to labor is to pray."

The monasteries were the centers in Europe where the flame of learning and culture burned. Saint Patrick, called the Apostle of Ireland, converted a whole nation. By the time of his death he had established a bishopric (territory administered by a bishop) in each of the provinces. Ireland became a place of holiness, learning, and culture. The conversion of the Anglo-Saxon invaders of England was begun by Saint Augustine (?–604) of Canterbury and 40 monks whom Gregory I (540?–604), pope from 590 to 604, sent from Rome in 597. From Catholic Ireland monks crossed to Europe to kindle the light of faith. Saint Columbanus (543–615) set out with 12 companions in about 585 to convert the heathens and restore Christian life. Everywhere they went in Europe, monasteries sprang up. Hundreds of Irish monks followed the example of Columbanus. One of the greatest figures of the period was the English Benedictine monk Winfrid (680–754), or Boniface, known as the Apostle of Germany.

In the early 7th century, events were taking place that were to have a terrifying impact on the Church. The tribes of Arabia had never been converted to Christianity. They remained pagan until Mohammed came, proclaiming that he had been named God's prophet by the Angel Gabriel. His creed, called Islam, was taken from Jewish and Christian sources. It held that there was but one God and Mohammed was his prophet. By the time Mohammed died, all of Arabia had been converted to Islam. Mohammed's successors undertook a "holy war" against the Christian world. The Muslims, as the followers of Islam were called, conquered most of the eastern world except Constantinople. They entered

Spain in 711 and invaded southern France. But their attack on France was halted by the victory of the Frankish ruler Charles Martel (689?–741) at Tours in 732.

The son and successor of Charles Martel, Pepin (714?–768), was consecrated king by Saint Boniface in 751 and reconsecrated by Pope Stephen III in 754. This crowning marked the beginning of the friendly relations between the papacy and France that became a dominant force in shaping medieval Europe. A generous gesture of Pepin decided much of the later history of the papacy. When Rome was threatened by the Lombards, the pope called upon the Franks for help. They invaded Italy and drove out the Lombards. Pepin handed over the conquered lands to the pope. This was the origin of the Papal States. The papacy was now a temporal, or worldly, state as well as a spiritual institution, and the pope was also a king. The papacy now was assured independence as a sovereign state. But the new territory brought with it grave dangers. In a society that was still harsh and violent, the papacy became a prize sought after by greedy men. For such men the easiest road to power and wealth was to put a friendly baron on the papal throne.

▶**THE MIDDLE AGES**

Charlemagne, Pepin's son and successor, built up the vast Frankish kingdom. On Christmas Day in the year 800 he was crowned emperor of the Holy Roman Empire by Leo III (750?–816), who was pope from 795 to 816. The goal of Charlemagne was to build a truly Christian state, revive education and learning, reform Church life, and advance the interests of the Church. The shadow cast across these great plans was the domination of the court over the affairs of the Church. The Emperor named the bishops. Another unfortunate policy was introduced by Charlemagne: converting people to Christianity by force. When Charlemagne died, all his plans for the Christian world died with him. But the Holy Roman Empire came to life again in 962 with the coronation of Otto I (912–73), and it lasted until 1806.

Breakdown and Revival

The 9th century brought confusion and a breakdown of civilization in Europe. The Danes overran England, Ireland, and northern Europe, wrecking monasteries and murdering Christians. For 100 years the Danes remained a threat to Christendom. Muslim hordes invaded France and Italy. In 846 they plundered the Roman basilicas of Saint Peter and Saint Paul. Europe was laid waste by political disorder and civil war. Education and discipline all but disappeared among the clergy. Bishops were little more than brutal, greedy, and immoral noblemen. Laymen (persons who do not belong to the clergy) took to naming bishops. The roots of the evil lay in the system of feudalism. Under this system bishoprics and monasteries were in the domain of overlords. This meant that they had not only a religious position but a civil and military one as well. The practice of **lay investiture**, the act by which the overlord or sovereign granted titles and possessions to bishops, led to many abuses. It seemed to suggest that the bishop also received his spiritual power from the sovereign. Therefore it was opposed by the Church. During this period the papacy itself became the prize of ruthless nobles, especially rival Roman families. For 150 years the chair of Saint Peter was mainly occupied by wicked popes.

With the election of Leo IX (1002–54), who was pope from 1049 to 1054, a new age dawned for the Church. Pope Leo attacked **simony** (the sale of sacred things), immorality of the clergy, and lay investiture. The beginning of the reform can be traced to the Benedictine Monastery of Cluny, founded in 910. Cluny was blessed with a succession of holy abbots, who had a great influence on popes and kings. The struggle between pope and emperor reached its peak under Gregory VII (1020?–85), who was pope from 1073 to 1085, and Henry IV (1050–1106). The Pope excommunicated the Emperor (cut him off from communion with the Church) and deposed him. At Canossa, Italy, in 1077 the Emperor asked for, and was granted, the Pope's forgiveness. The investiture dispute was settled by the Concordat of Worms in Germany in 1122.

The centuries-old tension between Rome and Constantinople reached the breaking point in 1054 with the excommunication of the Patriarch of Constantinople, Michael Caerularius. From that time the two patriarchates and the sees dependent upon them drifted apart.

In 1071 Jerusalem fell into the hands of the Turks, who savagely persecuted the Christians. The conscience of western Christianity was aroused. Pope Gregory VII planned to organize a crusade to win back the holy sepulchre, the tomb of Christ in the holy city. The investiture struggle prevented this crusade. But his successor, Victor III (1027–87), pope from 1086 to 1087, aided by the preaching of Peter the Hermit, launched the First Crusade (1095–99). This was followed by the Second Crusade in 1147 and the Third Crusade in 1189.

Only the First Crusade achieved its goal. The holy city was taken by the Crusaders in 1099, and the Latin Kingdom of Jerusalem was established. But it was soon weakened by lack of unity, need for money, and the continued rivalry and treachery of the emperors of Constantinople. The end of the kingdom came when the Turks, under Saladin (1138–93), sultan of Egypt and Syria, recaptured Jerusalem in 1187, leaving the Latin Kingdom only Tyre, Tripoli, Antioch, and some distant outposts.

The reform of Pope Gregory VII was followed by a great revival of religion and culture that included law, theology, and philosophy. The papacy had regained its position of influence and spiritual leadership. Priests, as well as bishops, began to preach. Popular devotion was marked by a great interest in the humanity of Jesus. New religious orders sprang up—notably the Cistercians, or Order of Citeaux, which was named after the place in France where it was founded in 1098. The best-known monk of this new order was Saint Bernard (1090–1153). Works of Christian charity included new hospitals, orphanages, and homes for the aged. Reverence for marriage and Christian behavior were restored. The great cathedrals of Europe that still stand as symbols of the faith of the Middle Ages were largely products of this period.

The worldly power of the papacy reached its peak under Innocent III (1161–1216), who was pope from 1198 to 1216. Medieval Christian society embraced both worldly and spiritual power. At the summit stood the pope, from whom the emperor received his imperial power. The sacred coronation of the emperor was the exclusive right of the pope. As vicar of Christ on earth, the pope was considered the head of all Christendom, which combined Church and state in one universal community. The most brilliant presentation of medieval Christianity was the fourth Lateran Council, held in 1215.

Under Pope Innocent the Church had its own laws, its own courts and civil service, and its own armies. One of the Pope's major efforts was stamping out the Albigensian heresy, named after the city of Albi in southern France, where it began. Albigensianism taught that all matter (marriage, for example) was evil. It was a serious threat to the civilized world as well as to the Church. Courts were set up to try Catholics accused of the heresy and later even those who were only suspected of it. During the pontificate (1227–1241) of Gregory IX (1147?–1241) this became the Papal Inquisition. The priest-judges appointed to make the inquiry were called inquisitors. Torture was often used to force confessions, and persons found guilty were given to the state for execution.

Two great religious orders came into being at this time. The Friars Preachers, also known as the Order of Preachers or the Dominicans, was founded by Saint Dominic (1170–1221). Its purpose was to provide a corps of priests who were prepared to go anywhere to preach the Christian truth. In order to preach the faith with knowledge, Dominicans devoted themselves to study. One of the greatest theologians of the Church was Saint Thomas Aquinas, a member of this order. The order of the Friars Minor (Lesser Brethren) was founded by Saint Francis of Assisi. Its members are familiarly called Franciscans. Poverty was the spiritual ideal of Saint Francis, one of the most appealing saints of all time. His mission was to bring Christ to the common people by simple word and shining example in order to fight the worldliness of the Church.

It was in this period that the great European universities came into being. A university was a grouping together of a number of schools—for example, law, medicine, theology—to form a universal school of all studies. Among the earliest universities granted their charters by the popes were those of Paris, Bologna, Oxford, and Cambridge.

Several factors contributed to the steady decline of the Church during this period. To rid the Church of interference by laymen, Pope Gregory VII had introduced a system for the appointment of bishops and abbots by election. There was strong competition for positions under this system, leading the competitors to seek the support of lay powers. This, in turn, led to a weakening of the system and to an increase in the influence of Rome. The trend toward centering power in the papal court continued. The patronage, or backing, of the Roman Curia, the highest administrative body of the Church, became the all-important factor in appointments. From this situation grew the **benefice system** (appointments to ecclesiastical offices with income provided by wealthy patrons). This proved troublesome to the Church in the 14th and 15th centuries and created many scandals.

Taxation by Rome was another source of evil. Church property everywhere was taxed, and officials of the popes went about collecting taxes from the local clergy to meet the expenses of the papal court. It became papal policy during this period to play off one state against another in order to protect the Papal States. Aided by the growing spirit of nationalism in Europe, this led to bitter feelings against the papacy. Finally, the worst situation of all arose with **nepotism** (giving special favors to relatives). Popes appointed members of their families to the Sacred College of Cardinals, made them princes, and married them into the royal houses of Europe.

The honor and position of the papacy suffered a damaging blow with the struggle between Boniface VIII (1235?–1303), who was pope from 1294 to 1303, and Philip the Fair of France (1268–1314). This dispute arose when Philip taxed the clergy and ordered all shipments of money to Rome to stop. The Pope threatened to depose him. Philip sent an army into Italy to take the Pope captive. But the Pope was saved by the people of Anagni—only to die a month later.

Exile and Division

The political independence of the papacy was further lessened with the election of a Frenchman, Clement V (1264–1314), who was pope between 1305 and 1314. He never went to live in Rome; instead, he took up residence in Avignon in southern France. Of the 24 cardinals he created, 22 were French. In this way began the exile of the papacy in Avignon, and it lasted for 70 years. All seven Avignon popes were Frenchmen. The papacy had become almost a puppet of France.

In 1346 a great plague called the Black Death struck Europe, and millions perished. Its damaging effect upon the Church cannot be measured. The ranks of the clergy were seriously reduced. In the effort to replace the fallen, men who had little preparation were ordained priests. With the decrease in the number of monks, the great monastic estates fell into ruin. The effect of the Black Death on the people of Europe was a lessening of religious feeling and a lowering of moral standards. An uneducated and greedy clergy was unequal to the task of spiritual restoration.

In 1377 the pope returned to Rome. The chief credit for the return goes to Saint Catherine of Siena (1347–80), a lay member of the Dominican Order. The exile in Avignon had greatly weakened the papacy, but it had yet to face the great disaster known as the Western Schism (division). Urban VI (1318–89), who reigned from 1378 to 1389, was elected by the cardinals assembled in Rome. They later protested that it was not a valid election because the Roman people had used pressure on them to elect an Italian. In September the cardinals set about electing a new pope, who took the name of Clement VII (1342?–1394) and reigned from 1378 to 1394.

With two rival popes and the general uncertainty about their claims, Christians were divided in their loyalties. In an effort to solve the problem, the cardinals met at Pisa in 1409 and elected Alexander V (1340?–1410), who reigned between 1409 and 1410. To end the situation of three popes, a general council was held at Constance from 1414 to 1418. The council demanded the resignation of the three popes and elected Martin V (1368–1431), who reigned between 1417 and 1431, bringing the schism to an end.

▶ RENAISSANCE AND REFORMATION

The change from the Middle Ages to modern times is known as the Renaissance, a

French word meaning "rebirth." It began in Italy in the 14th century and reached its height in Europe in the 15th and 16th centuries. Growing from a revival of interest in the art and literature of ancient Greece and Rome, the Renaissance brought about a new emphasis on the individual. This gave man a new importance and an almost pagan reverence for the purely human. It had a very serious impact on the Church.

Under Nicholas V (1397?–1455), who reigned from 1447 to 1455, Rome became the center of art, learning, and culture. Unfortunately, it also became a center of vice. The Renaissance popes lived as worldly princes rather than as spiritual shepherds. They were guilty of personal immorality, nepotism, simony, and bribery. The papacy became a prize to be competed for by the Borgias and the Medicis, two notorious aristocratic Italian families. Alexander VI (1431?–1503), a Borgia, stands in history as the symbol of the decline of the papacy in that period. During his reign (1492–1503) the influence of the papal court was at its lowest point. Everywhere men recognized the crying need for reform. The fifth Lateran Council, the 18th ecumenical council, met from 1512 to 1517, but no reform resulted.

Six months after the close of the council, Martin Luther, a German Augustinian friar, started a religious revolution. Known as the **Protestant Reformation**, it was to change the face of Europe. Soon most of Germany broke with the Roman Catholic Church. In the following generation the reform of John Calvin cut off Switzerland, the Low Countries, Scotland, and parts of France. Under Henry VIII, England broke with Rome.

On the Roman Catholic side the cry went up for a general council. Emperor Charles V (1500–58) of the Holy Roman Empire favored a council because he was interested in restoring peace between warring Roman Catholics and Protestants in Germany. King Francis I (1494–1547) of France was against a council because he feared that the settlement of the religious disputes would add to the political power of the Emperor. After many attempts and delays the general council met at Trent in 1545, thanks to the energy and patience of Paul III (1468–1549), who was pope from 1534 to 1549.

▶THE CHURCH IS REFORMED AND THEN CHALLENGED

The Council of Trent (1545–63) was a turning point in the life of the Church. The decisions of Trent were directed toward doctrines and discipline. The doctrinal decisions concerned articles of faith or belief that were attacked by the Protestants, the relationship of the Bible to tradition in the Church, the doctrine of original sin and justification, the sacraments, purgatory, veneration of saints, and indulgences. The disciplinary decisions concerned the duties of bishops and parish priests to live in their dioceses or parishes, the education of priests, and the rules for religious orders.

Reform was accomplished within the Church not only by the Council of Trent but by a series of great popes and saints who founded religious orders. The best-known order is the Society of Jesus, the Jesuits, founded by Saint Ignatius of Loyola (1491–1556). The order was perfectly in tune with the needs of the time. It was marked by fine intellectual training, strict military discipline, and individual initiative. Foreign missionary activity was another mark of the spiritual renewal within the Church. Alexander VI (1431?–1503) became pope the year Columbus discovered America (he reigned from 1492 to 1503). Spanish missionaries brought the gospel to the New World. Jesuit missionaries reached Africa, India, Japan, and later, China.

The program of reform of the Council of Trent, however, did not touch the Roman Catholic princes. They continued to think of their worldly power as absolute, and they treated the Church as their subject. This is seen in the actions of Philip II of Spain (1527–98). His loyalty to the Roman Catholic faith was beyond question. But his policies tended to reduce the Church, including the papacy, to a dependency of the state. After the Treaties of Westphalia (1648), following the Thirty Years War, the pope and the Church were no longer forces in the public life of Europe, even in Catholic states.

In the 17th century a system of thought called Deism arose in England. It denied that religion was revealed by God and defended natural religion based on human reason. Deism spread to France, where it drew to itself the most brilliant writers of the time. Among them was the French writer Voltaire. By the middle of the 18th century the Church found itself cut off from the life of Europe as never before. Then, in 1773, the strongest arm of the Church, the Society of Jesus, was suppressed by the intrigues of Roman Catholic rulers.

▶THE FRENCH REVOLUTION AND ITS AFTERMATH

The trend toward royal dictatorship, which was such a threat to the independence of the Church, was ended by the outbreak of the French Revolution in 1789. In the next few years what was left of the physical structure of medieval Roman Catholicism was destroyed. The revolutionaries took over Church property and imprisoned priests. Hundreds of priests were put to death in the September Massacres (1792). During the Reign of Terror (1793–94) an all-out effort was made to de-Christianize France. The effects of the Revolution on the Church were disastrous. They were made more serious by the division of the clergy into wealthy bishops and poor priests.

After a time, the Roman Catholics of western France rebelled against the republic that the Revolution had created. In 1795 freedom of worship was again granted to Roman Catholics. In 1801 Emperor Napoleon Bonaparte signed a concordat, or agreement, with Rome, recognizing the freedom of the Church in France. However, the Emperor soon broke the concordat by his actions. A long struggle began between Napoleon and Pius VII (1742–1823), who was pope between 1800 and 1823, and it led finally to the imprisonment of the Pope. The French Revolution marked the end of the old regime, for Napoleon's conquering armies carried the ideas of the Revolution with them across Europe.

In the turmoil of the French Revolution the Church had lost two of its greatest supports: its religious orders and its great universities. An enormous task of restoration lay ahead. New religious orders for women were formed to carry on the work of Christian education. In 1814 the Society of Jesus was restored. Other orders, such as the Dominicans and Franciscans, slowly regained their lost strength. The era that followed the Revolu-

tion was the age of democracy and industrialization. In these surroundings the old Church faced new problems and new threats.

Democracy and Growth

By the middle of the 19th century, liberalism was firmly rooted in every country of Europe. This was a movement that drew upon the ideals of the age of Voltaire and the ideas of the French Revolution. It favored democracy and opposed the absolute monarchies and the established state churches. The liberalists worked hard and almost alone for the social and economic betterment of individuals. But some of their basic principles could not be accepted by the Church. This was especially true of the liberalists' refusal to accept the place of the Church in society. The popes, as worldly rulers, were caught in the struggle between the liberalists and the monarchists (persons who wish to restore a monarchy). The worst of the struggle was felt in Italy. Here the presence of the Papal States divided the country.

In 1869 the 20th ecumenical council was called to meet at the Vatican. After much dispute the council decreed that the pope was infallible. This means that the pope cannot be wrong when he teaches a matter of faith or morals to be held by the whole Church. By this decree the papacy acquired great spiritual influence throughout the Catholic world. The outbreak of the Franco-Prussian War in 1870 prevented the first Vatican Council (Vatican Council I) from completing its work. The French protective garrison was withdrawn from Italy, and in the struggle to unify Italy, Rome was taken by patriot forces. The papacy lost its lands and ceased to be a worldly power. Pius IX (1792–1878), who was pope between 1846 and 1878, expressed his protest

---

THE APOSTLES' CREED

I believe in God, the Father Almighty, Creator of heaven and earth; and in Jesus Christ, His only Son, Our Lord; Who was conceived by the Holy Spirit, born of the Virgin Mary, suffered under Pontius Pilate, was crucified, died, and was buried. He descended into hell; the third day He arose again from the dead; He ascended into heaven, and sits at the right hand of God, the Father Almighty; from thence He shall come to judge the living and the dead. I believe in the Holy Spirit, the Holy Catholic Church, the communion of saints, the forgiveness of sins, the resurrection of the body, and life everlasting. Amen.

by becoming a voluntary "prisoner of the Vatican." The issue, called the Roman Question, was long a problem between united Italy and the Church. It was settled finally by the Lateran Treaty of 1929. This established the state of the Vatican City—a small separate and independent territory around Saint Peter's Basilica.

The 19th century also brought many glories to the Roman Catholic Church. Around the middle of that century the Church was again fully accepted in England. In John Henry, Cardinal Newman (1801–90), England gave to the Church one of the most learned and distinguished converts of its history. The United States saw a tremendous increase in its

POPES OF THE ROMAN CATHOLIC CHURCH

The pope's titles are bishop of Rome, vicar of Jesus Christ, successor of Saint Peter, prince of the Apostles, supreme pontiff of the Universal Church, patriarch of the West, primate of Italy, archbishop and metropolitan of the Roman Province, and sovereign of the State of Vatican City.

The names of doubtful popes and antipopes, or pretenders, are in italics.

YEAR OF CONSE-CRATION	NAME OF POPE	YEAR OF CONSE-CRATION	NAME OF POPE	YEAR OF CONSE-CRATION	NAME OF POPE
42?	St. Peter	432	St. Sixtus III	708	Constantine
67	St. Linus	440	St. Leo I	715	St. Gregory II
76	St. Cletus (Anacletus)	461	St. Hilarius	731	St. Gregory III
88	St. Clement I	468	St. Simplicius	741	St. Zachary
97	St. Evaristus	483	St. Felix II (III)	752	Stephen (II) (died before consecration)
105	St. Alexander I	492	St. Gelasius I		
115	St. Sixtus I	496	Anastasius II	752	Stephen II (III)
125	St. Telesphorus	498	St. Symmachus	757	St. Paul I
136	St. Hyginus	498	*Lawrence*	767	*Constantine*
140	St. Pius I	514	St. Hormisdas	768	*Philip*
155	St. Anicetus	523	St. John I	768	Stephen III (IV)
166	St. Soter	526	St. Felix III (IV)	772	Adrian I
175	St. Eleutherius	530	Boniface II	795	St. Leo III
189	St. Victor I	530	*Dioscorus*	816	Stephen IV (V)
199	St. Zephyrinus	533	John II	817	St. Pascal I
217	St. Calixtus I	535	St. Agapetus I	824	Eugene II
217	*St. Hippolytus*	536	St. Silverius	827	Valentine
222	St. Urban I	537	Vigilius	827	Gregory IV
230	St. Pontian	556	Pelagius I	844	*John*
235	St. Anterus	561	John III	844	Sergius II
236	St. Fabian	575	Benedict I	847	St. Leo IV
251	St. Cornelius	579	Pelagius II	855	Benedict III
251	*Novatian*	590	St. Gregory I	855	*Anastasius*
253	St. Lucius I	604	Sabinian	858	St. Nicholas I
254	St. Stephen I	607	Boniface III	867	Adrian II
257	St. Sixtus II	608	St. Boniface IV	872	John VIII
259	St. Dionysius	615	St. Adeodatus I (Deusdedit)	882	Marinus I (Martin II)
269	St. Felix I	619	Boniface V		
275	St. Eutychian	625	Honorius I	884	St. Adrian III
283	St. Caius	640	Severinus	885	Stephen V (VI)
296	St. Marcellinus	640	John IV	891	Formosus
308	St. Marcellus I	642	Theodore I	896	Boniface VI
309	St. Eusebius	649	St. Martin I	896	Stephen VI (VII)
311	St. Miltiades	654	St. Eugene I	897	Romanus
314	St. Sylvester I	657	St. Vitalian	897	Theodore II
336	St. Mark	672	Adeodatus II	898	John IX
337	St. Julius I	676	Donus	900	Benedict IV
352	Liberius	678	St. Agatho	903	Leo V
355	*Felix II*	682	St. Leo II	903	*Christopher*
366	St. Damasus	684	St. Benedict II	904	Sergius III
366	*Ursinus*	685	John V	911	Anastasius III
384	St. Siricius	686	Conon	913	Lando
399	St. Anastasius I	687	*Theodore*	914	John X
401	St. Innocent I	687	*Paschal*	928	Leo VI
417	St. Zozimus	687	St. Sergius I	928	Stephen VII (VIII)
418	St. Boniface I	701	John VI	931	John XI
418?	*Eulalius*	705	John VII	936	Leo VII
422	St. Celestine I	708	Sisinnius	939	Stephen VIII (IX)

Roman Catholic population with the large-scale immigration from Europe. In 1800 there were only about 40,000 Roman Catholics in the United States. By 1890 there were more than 10,000,000; today there are about 49,000,000. They came from Ireland, Germany, Poland, Italy, and other lands. Before long the immigrants set about building churches and schools. The school system built by the Roman Catholics of the United States is considered to be unequaled in the history of the Church.

▶ **MODERN POPES**

The long reign (1878–1903) of Pope Leo XIII opened another era of progress for the

YEAR OF CONSECRATION	NAME OF POPE	YEAR OF CONSECRATION	NAME OF POPE	YEAR OF CONSECRATION	NAME OF POPE
942	Marinus II (Martin III)	1143	Celestine II	1458	Pius II
946	Agapetus II	1144	Lucius II	1464	Paul II
955	John XII	1145	Eugene III	1471	Sixtus IV
963	Leo VIII	1153	Anastasius IV	1484	Innocent VIII
964	Benedict V	1154	Adrian IV	1492	Alexander VI
965	John XIII	1159	Alexander III	1503	Pius III
973	Benedict VI	1159	Victor IV	1503	Julius II
974	Boniface VII	1164	Pascal III	1513	Leo X
974	Benedict VII	1168	Calixtus III	1522	Adrian VI
983	John XIV	1179	Innocent III	1523	Clement VII
984	Boniface VII (second time)	1181	Lucius III	1534	Paul III
985	John XV	1185	Urban III	1550	Julius III
996	Gregory V	1187	Gregory VIII	1555	Marcellus II
997	John XVI	1187	Clement III	1555	Paul IV
999	Sylvester II	1191	Celestine III	1559	Pius IV
1003	John XVII	1198	Innocent III	1566	St. Pius V
1004	John XVIII	1216	Honorius III	1572	Gregory XIII
1009	Sergius IV	1227	Gregory IX	1585	Sixtus V
1012	Benedict VIII	1241	Celestine IV	1590	Urban VII
1012	Gregory	1243	Innocent IV	1590	Gregory XIV
1024	John XIX	1254	Alexander IV	1591	Innocent IX
1032	Benedict IX (deposed)	1261	Urban IV	1592	Clement VIII
1045	Sylvester III	1265	Clement IV	1605	Leo XI
1045	Benedict IX (second time)	1271	Gregory X	1605	Paul V
1045	Gregory VI	1276	Innocent V	1621	Gregory XV
1046	Clement II	1276	Adrian V	1623	Urban VIII
1047	Benedict IX (third time)	1276	John XXI	1644	Innocent X
1048	Damasus II	1277	Nicholas III	1655	Alexander VII
1049	St. Leo IX	1281	Martin IV	1667	Clement IX
1055	Victor II	1285	Honorius IV	1670	Clement X
1057	Stephen IX (X)	1288	Nicholas IV	1676	Innocent XI
1058	Benedict X	1294	St. Celestine V	1689	Alexander VIII
1059	Nicholas II	1294	Boniface VIII	1691	Innocent XII
1061	Alexander II	1303	Benedict XI	1700	Clement XI
1061	Honorius II	1305	Clement V	1721	Innocent XIII
1073	St. Gregory VII	1316	John XXII	1724	Benedict XIII
1080	Clement III	1328	Nicholas V	1730	Clement XII
1086	Victor III	1334	Benedict XII	1740	Benedict XIV
1088	Urban II	1342	Clement VI	1758	Clement XIII
1099	Pascal II	1352	Innocent VI	1769	Clement XIV
1100	Theodoric	1362	Urban V	1775	Pius VI
1102	Albert	1370	Gregory XI	1800	Pius VII
1105	Sylvester IV	1378	Urban VI	1823	Leo XII
1118	Gelasius II	1378	Clement VII	1829	Pius VIII
1118	Gregory VIII	1389	Boniface IX	1831	Gregory XVI
1119	Calixtus II	1394	Benedict XIII	1846	Pius IX
1124	Honorius II	1404	Innocent VII	1878	Leo XIII
1124	Celestine II	1406	Gregory XII	1903	St. Pius X
1130	Innocent II	1409	Alexander V	1914	Benedict XV
1130	Anacletus II	1410	John XXIII	1922	Pius XI
1138	Victor IV	1417	Martin V	1939	Pius XII
		1431	Eugene IV	1958	John XXIII
		1439	Felix V	1963	Paul VI
		1447	Nicholas V	1978	John Paul I
		1455	Calixtus III	1978	John Paul II

Source: Annuario Pontificio (Pontifical Yearbook).

Roman Catholic Church. The genius of Leo XIII lay in an understanding of his times and an ability to deal with them. In his letters to the whole Church, called **encyclicals**, he revealed himself to be a true world teacher. One of the most significant of his encyclicals is *Rerum Novarum* (*Of New Things*), written in 1891. It is a statement of the social teachings of the Church. A conflict between religion and science arose in the mid-19th century. It was due chiefly to Darwin's theory of evolution. The faith many Christians had in the Bible was disturbed by the new scientific discoveries. In 1893 Pope Leo issued his famous encyclical on sacred scripture, *Providentissimus Deus* (*The Most Provident God*). He stands at the head of a series of outstanding popes who have brought the Church to its greatest honor in many centuries.

Pope Leo's successor was the saintly Pius X (1835–1914), who reigned from 1903 to 1914 and was canonized (declared a saint) by the Church. Pope Pius brought about a renewal in **liturgy**, or ritual, and church music. He is remembered for favoring frequent Communion and allowing children to receive the Holy Eucharist (Holy Communion) at an early age. Benedict XV (1854–1922), who was pope from 1914 to 1922, devoted himself to the effort of bringing World War I to an end and of establishing a lasting peace. He is noted for his charity toward the victims of war, and he founded the Vatican service to aid war prisoners.

An event of great historical significance in the pontificate (1922–39) of the next pope, Pius XI (1857–1939), was the settlement of the Roman Question by the Lateran Treaty of 1929 between the Holy See and the Kingdom of Italy. The treaty's importance lay in the new freedom it gave to the Vatican in the appointment of bishops in Italy and in the teaching of religion. The founding of many new Roman Catholic universities and institutes gave great force to learning. Missionary work was reorganized, and the selection of native priests as bishops of the Church was a significant advance. Pope Pius strongly defended the freedom of the Church against the political dictatorships in Italy and Germany.

Eugenio Pacelli took the name Pius XII and reigned from 1939 to 1958. The new pope was an aristocrat by birth and a diplomat by experience. He left to the Church a great intellectual heritage in his many encyclicals. After World War II the gains of Communism increased its danger to the Church. The Pope threatened to excommunicate all Roman Catholics who willingly supported Communism. In the critical elections in Italy in 1948, he called on all Roman Catholics to defeat the Communists at the polls. In 1956 Pius XII published the reform of the Holy Week liturgy. He made Holy Communion more readily available to the people by simplifying the laws of fasting and increasing the hours available for the celebration of Mass.

In 1958 Pius XII was succeeded by Cardinal Roncalli, a man of peasant stock who was to become the most loved pope of modern times. He took the name John XXIII. The emphasis of his pontificate (1958–1963) was, in his own words, pastoral (concerned with the direction of souls) and ecumenical (concerned with the reunion of Christians). As spiritual shepherd, he was especially concerned for the working classes and the poor. He issued two great social documents, the encyclicals *Mater et Magistra* (*Mother and Teacher*) and *Pacem in Terris* (*Peace on Earth*). He gave new life to the ecumenical spirit in the Church. In December, 1960, for the first time in 400 years, the Archbishop of Canterbury, head of the Church of England, visited the Vatican. The high point of Pope John's brief reign came when he called the second Vatican Council in October, 1962.

Vatican Council II

The purpose of the second Vatican Council was to bring about a spiritual renewal of the Church and to work for unity among Christians. The Pope also described its purpose as bringing the form of the Christian message up to date, to meet the needs of modern man. Pope John opened a new age in the history of the Church.

Why is it called the Roman Catholic Church?

The Roman Catholic Church is the branch of Christianity that looks upon the pope, the bishop of Rome, as its spiritual head on earth. The title most often used officially is Holy Catholic and Apostolic Church. "Catholic" means that it is universal, or general. "Apostolic" means that it is in direct succession from Saint Peter. The term "Roman Catholic Church" is more generally used to distinguish it from other Christian churches that are Catholic (sharing a historical and continuous tradition of faith and practice).

The first session of Vatican Council II (the Ecumenical Council) met at St. Peter's in Rome in November of 1962.

After Pope John's death in 1963, Cardinal Montini, Archbishop of Milan, was elected pope and took the name Paul VI. He reopened Vatican Council II and continued the program of reform and renewal begun by Pope John. In 1968 he issued an encyclical, *Humanae Vitae* ("Of Human Life"), upholding the traditional ban on artificial birth control. Pope Paul traveled all over the world in the cause of peace and social justice.

Pope Paul VI died in August, 1978. He was succeeded in the same month by Cardinal Luciani of Venice, who took the name John Paul I. Pope John Paul I died after only 33 days in office. A month later, Cardinal Wojtyla of Poland was elected pope and took the name John Paul II. He was the first non-Italian pope in 455 years.

BISHOP JOHN J. DOUGHERTY
First Scholar in Residence
Seton Hall University

▶ **BELIEFS AND PRACTICES OF THE ROMAN CATHOLIC CHURCH**

The Roman Catholic faith is based on sacred scripture, tradition, and the teaching authority (*magisterium*) of the Church. The Church, under the guidance of the Holy Spirit, draws from scripture and tradition the truths God has revealed and the laws—such as the Ten Commandments—that he wants people to follow. The Church also makes its own laws. They are called **precepts** and have to do with such things as when one should fast and attend Mass. The Church makes these laws, and so the Church can change them. Roman Catholics believe the Church has the right and duty to make such laws.

Doctrine and Morality

In exercising its teaching authority, the Church has defined certain truths when the time seemed right. This body of defined truth is called doctrine. It includes truths about God, such as the Trinity (that God is one in three equal persons), and truths about man, such as original sin (that every human being, except Mary, is born in a state of sin and remains in that state until he or she is baptized).

The Church's teaching about morality (how we should behave) is based on its beliefs about God and humanity. Jesus summed up all the commands in two: to love God above everything and to love our neighbor as ourselves. Roman Catholics believe that God has told us, through the Church, how he wants us to put that love into practice.

All Roman Catholics are supposed to live by this law of love of God and love of neigh-

BAPTISM

CONFIRMATION

THE SEVEN SACRAMENTS

PENANCE

HOLY ORDERS

HOLY COMMUNION

MATRIMONY

SACRAMENT OF THE SICK

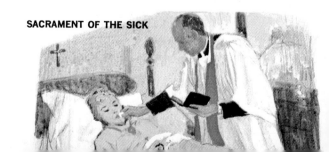

bor. But some people feel that they are called by God to show that love in a special way. These men and women make the decision to devote their lives to the service of God and neighbor by entering religious orders as priests, brothers, or sisters.

The Creed and the Sacraments

The main points of Christian belief are expressed in the Apostles' Creed, which was in use as early as A.D. 150. The creed shows, for example, that Roman Catholics believe in one God, who is in the form of three persons (Holy Trinity). The Holy Trinity is composed of the Father, the Son (Christ), and the Holy Spirit (Holy Ghost). It is believed that the Father sent his Son, the second person of the Trinity, to teach humanity the truth. Christ was born as a human to the Virgin Mary. He spent his time on earth preaching and then died on the cross for humanity's sins. Christians believe that Christ will return again to pass judgment on all people. The Holy Spirit, the third person of the Trinity, is believed to dwell in the world, both within the Church and in all Christian souls. Through the belief in the communion of saints, each Christian is spiritually united with Christ and with all other faithful Christians.

The way God helps people attain eternal salvation is by the gift of grace (a sharing in the divine life through Christ). Grace is given in many ways. For Roman Catholics, the most important way is through the sacramental system. There are seven sacraments—Baptism; Confirmation; Holy Eucharist (Holy Communion, or the Lord's Supper); Penance (the Sacrament of Reconciliation); the Sacrament of the Sick; Holy Orders; and Matrimony. The sacraments confer grace from the beginning of a person's life as a Christian (Baptism) to the day of death (Sacrament of the Sick). Confirmation is administered to a baptized person, usually by a bishop. Through it, the person receives the Holy Spirit and is strengthened to bear witness to Christ by word and example. In the Holy Eucharist, Roman Catholics believe, the body and blood of Jesus Christ are truly present through the presence of bread and wine. By Penance one's sins are forgiven and one is reconciled to God and one's fellow Christians. By Holy Orders a man is ordained to the priesthood forever. In Matri-

mony a man and a woman become Christian husband and wife.

Adult Roman Catholics are obliged to receive the sacrament of Penance once a year if they have committed a mortal (serious) sin and to receive the Holy Eucharist every year during the Easter season. But most Roman Catholics receive both these sacraments many times during the year. According to Roman Catholic belief, the sacraments of Baptism, Confirmation, and Holy Orders confer a special gift, or character, in addition to grace. This character makes a permanent change in the soul that cannot be undone. Therefore, these three sacraments cannot be repeated. But the others may be received more than once.

Prayer and Worship

The first Christians met once a week on the Lord's Day, the first day of the week. They offered the Eucharistic sacrifice in memory of the death of Jesus Christ. This was a ceremony in which Christians consecrated bread and wine by repeating the words Jesus had spoken at the Last Supper (I Corinthians

---

What are sacramentals?

Sacramentals are certain objects or actions instituted by the Church, in imitation of the sacraments, to obtain spiritual or temporal blessings for the faithful. Sacramentals include **holy water, palms, blessed ashes,** the **stations of the cross,** the **sign of the cross,** and a number of similar practices and objects.

Holy water is water that has been blessed for certain religious purposes (such as symbolic cleansing on entering a church and at the beginning of Mass) and to which blessed salt has been added. Palms are symbols of Christ's victory over death. They are blessed and carried on Palm Sunday—the Sunday before Easter—which marks the beginning of Holy Week. On Ash Wednesday, the first day of Lent, the burned ashes of palms left from the Palm Sunday of the previous year are placed on the foreheads of clergy and people to remind them of their mortality and of the need for penance. The stations of the cross are 14 pictures, carvings, or symbols representing the last journey of Christ from Pilate's house to his death and entombment. They are usually arranged around the walls of a church and are visited in order by the faithful, who recite prayers and meditate on each incident. The sign of the cross is used partly as making holy every action in daily life, partly as encouragement in temptation and trial.

Since Vatican Council II, the Mass regulations require that the priest face the people. Most of the Mass is said in the language of the country in which it is celebrated, and the congregation takes an active part in the service.

11:23–25). The bread and wine, thus changed into the body and blood of Jesus Christ, were consumed by all the people present. This sacred meal usually took place in the house of one of the Christians. During the meal there were readings from the Old Testament and the chanting of psalms, according to the Jewish practice. The letters, called Epistles, written by Saint Paul to the various Christian communities also were read aloud to the assembly.

This Sunday observance of the early Christians is the basis of the Roman Catholic Mass. The ceremony of the sacred meal has changed over the centuries to meet the ever-changing needs of the Christian community. But the essential elements remain: the consecration of the bread and wine, the partaking of it by the faithful, and the readings from the Old Testament and the New Testament. As it was from the beginning, the Mass is today the central act of the Roman Catholic Church. All Roman Catholics are obliged to come together once a week on the Lord's Day and be present at the celebration of the sacrifice of the Holy Eucharist.

The Mass and certain other forms of prayer are liturgical. This means they are the officially prescribed, or ordered, forms of public worship in the Church. After the Mass, the chief liturgical prayer is that called the Liturgy of the Hours. Priests and monks, and some sisters, have always said it. But Vatican II encouraged the laity to say at least some parts of it too. The Psalms form the chief part of the Liturgy of the Hours.

Other forms of prayer and worship practiced by Roman Catholics are nonliturgical. They are private expressions of devotion. A well-known example of nonliturgical prayer is the rosary. The Lord's Prayer and the Hail Mary are repeated a certain number of times while the worshiper meditates upon certain events in the life of Christ and the Virgin. The prayers are usually counted on a string of beads held in the hand.

The Roman Catholic Church is composed of the faithful, or laity, and the clergy. It is governed by a hierarchy composed of priests and bishops and headed by the pope. A pope is elected by members of the Sacred College of Cardinals on the death of his predecessor. According to Roman Catholic belief, the bishops are the successors of the Apostles, and the pope is the successor to Saint Peter, prince of the Apostles and first bishop of Rome. The pope is known by various titles that reflect this succession. The pope's residence, from which he exercises his spiritual authority over the universal Church, is the Vatican.

MARGARET O'CONNELL
National Council of Catholic Women

See also CHRISTIANITY, HISTORY OF; CRUSADES; HOLY ROMAN EMPIRE; INQUISITION; JESUS CHRIST; MARY, VIRGIN; ORTHODOX EASTERN CHURCHES; PROTESTANTISM; REFORMATION; TEN COMMANDMENTS; VATICAN CITY; articles on individual saints and popes.

A street in ancient Rome.

ROMAN EMPIRE

For over 400 years the Roman Empire governed all the lands around the Mediterranean Sea—and most of the rest of Europe. Much of what is now England and France, Belgium and the Netherlands, Spain and Portugal, Switzerland, Austria, Hungary, part of Germany, Rumania, Bulgaria, Greece, Turkey, Israel, Syria, Arabia, the United Arab Republic, Tunisia, Algeria, and Morocco was ruled by the Romans from their base in Italy.

Rome at first was a small city on the Italian peninsula, with territory that stretched only a few miles in each direction. Little by little, Rome began to control the other cities around it. Soon it was able to unite all of the Italian peninsula into a strong nation, with Rome as the leading city. Then the Romans conquered some of the territory nearest them—Sicily, Spain, France, Greece, and North Africa.

The government of this large territory was run by noblemen, from 300 to 900 in number, who were members of the Roman senate. This organization is called the Roman Republic. Julius Caesar made himself dictator in 49 B.C. and ruled the republic for 5 years. Many people began to fear the power Caesar had acquired. And so, on the ides (15th) of March, 44 B.C., he was murdered by a band of conspirators led by Brutus (85–42 B.C.) and Cassius (?–42 B.C.). Caesar's great-nephew Caesar Augustus (Octavian) (63 B.C.–A.D. 14), Mark Antony (83?–30 B.C.), and Lepidus (?–13 B.C.) ruled together for a few years. Gradually Caesar Augustus gained control of the government.

The Empire Is Established. In 27 B.C., Caesar Augustus was recognized as Rome's leader. He brought peace and prosperity to the Romans after many years of strife. Although Augustus said that he held no unusual office, he had as much power and influence as any king. He became the first Roman emperor. Rome at this time was ruled by one person, and it continued to be so after Augustus. The Roman rulers were called emperors because they ruled a growing empire beyond the Italian peninsula.

▶ **THE EMPERORS**

The emperors did a great deal to improve the management of their large empire.

The Army. The emperors developed a permanent army in which men from all over

THE ROMAN EMPERORS

NAME	REIGNED	NAME	REIGNED	NAME	REIGNED
THE CAESARS		Macrinus	217–218	Constantine the Great	306–337
Augustus (Octavian)	27 B.C.–A.D. 14	Heliogabalus,		Constantine II	337–340
Tiberius	A.D. 14–37	or Elagabalus	218–222	Constans	337–350
Caligula	37–41	Alexander Severus	222–235	Constantius II	337–361
Claudius	41–54	Maximinus	235–238	Julian the Apostate	361–363
Nero	54–68	Gordianus I	238	Jovian	363–364
Galba	68–69	Gordianus II	238	Valentinian I (West)	364–375
Otho	69	Balbinus and Pupienus	238	Valens (East)	364–378
Vitellius	69	Gordianus III	238–244	Gratian (West)	367–383
Vespasian	69–79	Philip the Arabian	244–249	Valentinian II (West)	375–392
Titus	79–81	Decius	249–251	Theodosius the Great	
Domitian	81–96	Gallus	251–253	(East)	379–394
		Aemilianus	253	Maximus (West)	383–388
THE GOOD EMPERORS		Valerian	253–260	Eugenius (West)	392–394
Nerva	96–98	Gallienus	253–268	Theodosius the Great	394–395
Trajan	98–117	Claudius II	268–270		
Hadrian	117–138	Aurelian	270–275	**ROMAN EMPERORS OF THE WEST**	
Antoninus Pius	138–161	Tacitus	275–276	Honorius	395–423
Lucius Aurelius Verus	161–169	Florian	276	Valentinian III	425–455
Marcus Aurelius	161–180	Probus	276–282	Petronius Maximus	455
		Carus	282–283	Avitus	455–456
MILITARY DESPOTS		**LATER EMPERORS**		Majorian	457–461
Commodus	180–192	Carinus and		Severus	461–465
Pertinax	193	Numerianus	283–285	Anthemius	467–472
Didius Julianus	193	Diocletian	284–305	Olybrius	472
Septimius Severus	193–211	Maximian	286–305	Glycerius	473
Geta	211–212	Constantius	305–306	Julius Nepos	473–475
Caracalla	211–217	Galerius	305–311	Romulus Augustulus	475–476

the empire could serve. The soldiers had to learn Latin, the official language of the Romans, in addition to their own local language. Because they belonged to the Roman Army, these men felt more Roman than Egyptian or Spanish or Greek. The Army defended the empire from people on the outside, such as the Germanic tribes, who sometimes tried to invade it. The soldiers also built good roads everywhere, so that armies could move about more swiftly. The roads could be used also by travelers or by wagons carrying freight. The Roman Navy kept the sea free of pirates.

The Civil Service. The emperors also developed the civil service—the group of men who managed the nonmilitary activities of the government. These men looked after the collection of taxes, the construction of government buildings, the farming of land that belonged to the government, and the building of dikes where rivers were likely to overflow. The emperor Claudius (10 B.C.–A.D. 54), who ruled from A.D. 41 to 54, did much to improve the civil service.

But not every emperor was hardworking and good. Nero, who followed Claudius, paid little attention to his official duties after the first 5 years of his reign. He spent much time practicing singing and competing in singing contests. He spent a great deal of money on presents for his friends and on a huge palace in the middle of Rome. In 64 there was a great fire in Rome. Nero blamed it on the Christians and tortured some of them to death. The next year some of the noblemen formed a plot to murder him, but the plot was discovered and most of them were put to death. Vespasian (9–79), who reigned from 69 to 79, was an experienced and sensible man, who governed carefully. The Colosseum was begun during his reign.

The Provinces. Hadrian (76–138) tried to improve conditions in the provinces, as the parts of the empire outside Italy were called. Not only did he take men from the provinces into the Army, as earlier emperors had done, but he also took them into the civil service. He even made them noblemen, who could sit in the senate. Hadrian visited many provinces, which the people regarded as a great honor. He reviewed the soldiers, presented the cities with new public buildings, studied what the provinces needed and what they could produce, and in general tried to create enthusiasm for the empire.

Gladiators fought each other or wild animals in the Colosseum in Rome.

Nevertheless, some of the people in the provinces were not content to belong to the empire and tried to revolt and become independent. Every 15 or 20 years somewhere in the empire there was a revolt against the Romans. But the Romans always managed to win back the dissatisfied members. Sometimes, too, there were invasions from outside. The emperor Marcus Aurelius (A.D. 121–180) had to fight against a great invasion of Germanic tribes who needed land and wanted to come into the Roman territory and settle down there. Other invaders sometimes made quick raids to steal what they could and carry it away.

▶ LIFE IN THE EMPIRE

Many people lived a prosperous life as members of the Roman Empire. There was less war than there was before the Romans came, so that men did not lose their property in wars so often or get carried off into slavery.

In those times most people were farmers. There were no large factories and only now and then a small factory, where perhaps 20 men worked. Most things—shoes, for instance —were made in tiny shops where one or two

Roman soldiers in full battle array.

Wealthy Romans entertained their guests in a reception room called the *atrium*.

men worked and sold what they made to their customers.

Farming. Many farmers, of course, produced practically everything that they needed. They grew wheat or rye for making bread, and they produced poultry, vegetables, fruit, and milk. They had bees to provide honey for sweetening. They could preserve milk by making it into cheese, and grapes by making them into wine. Their sheep produced wool for clothes. Most farmers used wood for fuel, and many had deposits of clay that could be made into simple dishes. The skins of cows provided leather for harnesses, belts, and footwear.

Manufacturing. In spite of the fact that many small farmers produced all the simple things they needed, many beautiful things were manufactured in small shops or by trained slaves working in rich households. Long before the time of the Roman Empire, people had learned how to build large and handsome buildings and make statues of stone. They could weave beautiful fabrics. They made fine jewelry and ornaments of gold and silver.

A fine red pottery called Arretine ware was made in Italy and shipped all over the empire. Archeologists have found samples of it in India, which was outside the empire. Fine fabrics for clothes or rugs were woven in Asia Minor. Arabia sent incense to be burned on the altars of the gods. Spain produced gold, silver, and horses and dogs for hunting.

City Life. The people were encouraged to create small cities all over the provinces. The emperor Hadrian encouraged the establishment of schools where students would study the Latin language and read Roman books. City officials got full Roman citizenship, which was much desired and was not granted to everyone. The cities put up smaller public buildings like the large ones at Rome—a city hall, a forum, temples to the same gods that were worshiped in Rome, a theater, and a place for horse racing and general entertainments.

Every city had a list of official holidays, many of which had some connection with the emperor. His birthday and the day on which he became emperor were holidays, for example. Thus, the holidays and the celebrations seemed to come from the emperor. All these things made people all over the empire feel that they, too, were Romans and increased their loyalty to the empire.

▶ **GREEK INFLUENCE ON THE ROMANS**

Another important thing about the Roman Empire (in addition to the fact that it kept

GROWTH OF THE ROMAN EMPIRE

Roman Territory before 264 B.C.

added before death of Julius Caesar, 44 B.C.

Maximum extent, up to 275 A.D.

peace for 200 years) was that it helped to preserve the literature and science of Greece and pass them on to the modern Western world. Although the Greeks were not the first civilized people in the ancient world, their civilization was more advanced than any other. In addition to making important contributions of their own in many fields, they improved the knowledge of earlier peoples and organized what they knew much as we do today. The Greeks were not a great military people and might have been conquered by such people as the Germans or the Huns. If this had happened, all the civilization of the Greeks might well have disappeared, since the barbarians had little interest in it. It would then have taken hundreds of years longer for modern Western civilization to grow up.

But the Romans admired Greek civilization and tried to imitate it. They studied the poetry and plays and the history written by the Greeks and wrote similar works in their own language, Latin. The Latin language is the basis for the French, Spanish, Italian, Rumanian, and Portuguese languages of today. The Romans studied Greek ideas of government, and their lawyers learned to present arguments in court as the Greeks did. They learned mathematics and astronomy from the Greeks. Many Greeks came to Rome to teach the Romans or to work in skilled occupations, such as medicine and architecture.

The Romans themselves were great engineers and builders. They excelled in the building of roads, bridges, sewers, and aqueducts. Many of these still can be seen today. The Romans also were great statesmen and administrators. Their ideas and practices of government were very advanced. Perhaps Rome's greatest contribution to the modern world was in law. Roman law is the basis of the legal systems in many of the countries of Europe and Latin America today.

Thus, the Romans protected Greek civilization and added something of their own to it and passed on the combined Greco-Roman civilization to the peoples of the empire. They spread this civilization in the west—France, Spain, some of Germany, and England—where otherwise it might have been little known.

▶ **CHRISTIANITY IN THE ROMAN EMPIRE**

Christianity began during the Roman Empire. Jesus Christ was born in the reign of Caesar Augustus. During Christ's lifetime he attracted many followers. The Christian Church, which grew up after his death, was mostly in the territories of the empire.

The Romans punished people who were

IMPORTANT DATES IN ROMAN HISTORY

753 B.C.	According to tradition, Romulus and Remus founded Rome.
510	First year of the republic.
451–450	Twelve Tables of Roman law published.
264–241	First Punic War; it ended with Sicily as the first Roman province.
218–201	Second Punic War.
149	Third Punic War began.
44	Caesar assassinated (ides of March).
27	The empire began; Caesar Augustus (Octavian) recognized as first Roman emperor.
A.D.	
64	Great fire at Rome; persecution of the Christians.
70	Titus captured Jerusalem.
79	Vesuvius erupted, destroying Pompeii.
286	Diocletian divided the empire into two parts.
293	Diocletian further divided the empire into four districts.
313	Constantine's Edict of Milan granted religious toleration to the Christians.
330	Constantine moved the capital to Byzantium.
410	The Visigoths captured and sacked Rome.
455	Vandal tribes attacked Rome.
476	Odoacer deposed Romulus Augustulus, the last Roman emperor in the west.
1453	The Roman Empire in the east fell when the Turks captured Constantinople.

known to be Christians. This was partly because the Christians denied that the old gods existed. People were shocked by this and called Christians "atheists" (unbelievers). The Christians also refused to bow down before the statue of the emperor every year, although everyone else was glad to do it. The Christians believed that to bow before the emperor would be to treat him like a god, although others thought that it was only a sign of respect for the head of the empire. The Christians stayed apart in their own group and did not mix with other people. This, too, made the rest of the population dislike them.

Christianity struggled along for 300 years as an illegal organization. Sometimes the government persecuted the Christians and put many of them to death. Then for long periods of time they would let the Christians go their own way and not bother them. Finally the emperor Constantine the Great declared in the Edict of Milan in 313 that Christianity was a legal religion. He believed that the organization the Church had slowly built up could be useful to the government. From this time on, the Christians ceased to stand apart. They held places in the government and fought in the Army. More and more people now became Christians all over the empire. Christianity became the state religion of the Roman Empire around 380.

▶ **THE DECLINE OF THE EMPIRE**

The end of the Roman Empire in the west came very gradually. There was no "fall." Between 400 and 430, several large groups of people from the outside managed to force their way into the empire and settled down in France, Spain, and North Africa. If they were allowed to have land, they were willing to be subject to the Roman Government and fight for it. Little by little, however, they asserted their independence from the Romans. By about 500 all the western part of the empire—Italy, North Africa, France, and Spain—was ruled by Germanic kings who were independent of Rome. In 476 the Germanic king Odoacer (434?–493) deposed Romulus Augustulus (461–?), the last Roman emperor of the west.

These Germanic people admired the Romans, and many wanted to govern in the Roman way. They were less civilized people, however, and did not want to live in the more complicated Greco-Roman way. Not many of them wanted to read and write. They did not like to live in cities. They did not know how to manage the financial affairs of government except in a very simple way. The result was that for a while, during the so-called Middle Ages, the people in western Europe lived much more simply than the Romans did.

The emperor Diocletian (A.D. 245–313) had divided the empire into two parts in 286. Long after the western part of the empire "fell," the eastern part of the empire remained strong. Its center was the old city of Byzantium, renamed Constantinople by the emperor Constantine, and now called Istanbul. For almost 1,000 years this city was the chief city of the world and the capital of the Roman Empire in the east. At last this empire fell when the Turks captured Constantinople in the year 1453.

RICHARD M. HAYWOOD
New York University
Author, *Myth of Rome's Fall*

See also BYZANTINE EMPIRE; LATIN LANGUAGE AND LITERATURE; PUNIC WARS; ROMAN ART AND ARCHITECTURE; ROME.

ROMANESQUE ART AND ARCHITECTURE

One of the most important styles of art that developed during the Middle Ages was called Romanesque. This style began during the 11th century and lasted for more than 200 years. Although there were slight variations in each country, Romanesque art dominated Western Europe until it was replaced by the international Gothic style.

Prior to the Romanesque period, powerful rulers like Charlemagne and Otto the Great helped to lay the foundations for this new style. They ordered builders to design palaces and churches similar to ancient Roman temples. Although the new architecture did use some Roman elements in its design, the buildings were actually created from combinations of many styles. Barbarian, Byzantine, and Muslim forms were mixed with those of Roman and early Christian origin.

Romanesque painting flourished. It followed the traditions set by the spiritual art of the Byzantine empire. Realism was not stressed; the artists concentrated mainly on expressive color and rhythmic compositions in order to stir religious emotions within the viewer. Many murals were painted during this period, and the production of illuminated manuscripts increased.

In sculpture, for the first time since the days of the ancient Roman world, monumental work was created. Most of the work was religious—statues depicting scenes from the Bible, statues of saints, and statues of martyrs.

Both painting and sculpture in the Romanesque age were very decorative. Highly ornamental compositions were used, often incorporating strange entwining plant forms and grotesque imaginary animals.

Romanesque architecture is massive, low, and solid-looking. Round arches, thick walls, and small windows are typical of the buildings. Churches were built in the shape of a cross, using the basilica (a type of Roman building) as the basis for the design.

See also: ARCHITECTURE; CATHEDRALS; MIDDLE AGES, ART AND ARCHITECTURE OF THE; SCULPTURE.

ROMANIA. See RUMANIA.

ROMAN NUMERALS

If you had lived many centuries ago in ancient Rome, you would have written V to stand for the number five. The symbols V and 5 stand for the same thing—the idea of five. A symbol that stands for a number is called a **numeral**. The number symbols used by the Romans some 2,500 years ago are called **Roman numerals**.

As the Roman Empire spread, the use of Roman numerals spread. Roman numerals were used in Europe for almost 2,000 years. Today Roman numerals are rarely used, except on some clock and watch faces, on public buildings, for dates in motion pictures, preface pages in books, and so on. But centuries ago they were used by the Romans for almost all mathematical work.

The seven basic Roman numerals are:

I	1
V	5
X	10
L	50
C	100
D	500
M	1,000

All other numbers are represented by combinations of these numerals. The numbers are written from left to right and are usually formed by adding numerals together. Seventeen, for example, is

$$X + V + I + I = XVII$$
$$10 + 5 + 1 + 1 = 17$$

and 667 would be

$$D + C + L + X + V + I + I = DCLXVII$$
$$500 + 100 + 50 + 10 + 5 + 1 + 1 = 667$$

Roman numerals were formed by subtracting as well as by adding numbers. For example, instead of adding four ones to make four—IIII—the Romans usually subtracted one from five, writing IV. In general, the symbol for the smaller number—the number to be subtracted—was written to the left of the symbol for the larger number. Using this general rule, the Romans were able to simplify many numbers, writing IX instead of VIIII for nine, and CD instead of CCCC for four hundred.

The origin of the Roman symbols is not known exactly. There are two main theories, for example, about how V and X developed. Some scholars say that five was first shown by holding up one hand with the thumb held apart from the other four fingers. The hand was imitated in drawings and was later simplified to V. Two hands—two V's—were then joined to make X, representing ten.

Another theory is that the X came from crossing out a row of 10 lines: ▭━▨. Five could then be represented by half the X, or V.

At first the Romans had several symbols for 100, including ⊗, ⊖, and ⊕. Any one of these earlier signs may have been the origin of C. The use of C as a symbol for one hundred was probably strengthened by the fact that C is the first letter of *centum*, the Latin word for "hundred."

The symbol L for fifty first appeared in various forms, such as ↓ , ↓ , and ⊥ .

There were also many symbols for one thousand. Some of these were Φ , ⊕ , and ⊂|⊃ M may have come from these signs. M is also the first letter of *mille*, the Latin word for "thousand." This may have reinforced its use as a symbol for one thousand.

The symbol D for five hundred was written as either |⊃ or ⊂|. It might easily have come from half the earlier sign ⊂|⊃ for one thousand.

Roman numerals are easy to work with when you want to add or subtract numbers, but multiplication and division are very awkward to carry out. This is the main reason Roman numerals are not used very often today.

CARL B. BOYER
Brooklyn College

See also MATHEMATICS; NUMERALS AND NUMERATION SYSTEMS.

ROMANTIC AGE IN MUSIC

"Romantic" means "having to do with romance"—with fantasy, imagination. Until the 19th century a composer thought only of writing a beautiful piece of music. He often composed at the command of a court or to meet the demands of the church. In the 19th century, however, music began to express the composer's own personality. Musicians began reading more widely. What they read excited their musical imaginations in new ways.

Romantic Opera

The full tide of romanticism in music began in the 1820's. It was most noticeable first in opera. Tales of the Middle Ages (such as Walter Scott's novels), old German legends, and Shakespeare's plays were the fashion during the 1820's and 1830's. German composers such as Carl Maria von Weber (1786–1826), Ludwig Spohr (1784–1859), and Heinrich Marschner (1795–1861) wrote operas based on tales of goblins and evil spirits, knights and ladies, pages and jesters. Italian composers wrote operas based on Shakespearean subjects, such as *Otello,* by Gioacchino Rossini (1792–1868), and *I Capuleti ed i Montecchi* (The Capulets and the Montagues), by Vincenzo Bellini (1801–35); and on Scott's novels, such as *Lucia di Lammermoor,* by Gaetano Donizetti (1797–1848).

During the 1830's Giacomo Meyerbeer (1791–1864), a German living in France, wrote works that combined the atmosphere of the Middle Ages, wicked spirits, and history with grand stage spectacle.

From Parisian grand opera and German romantic opera developed the work of the greatest German opera composer of the 19th century, Richard Wagner (1813–83).

The Romantic Orchestra

In creating music for the scenes and incidents of romantic opera, composers had to invent new orchestral sounds. They tried new and bold harmonies and mixtures of instruments that they had not used in music for the concert hall or even in the older kinds of opera. After experimenting with music for the stage, they used some of the same effects in music for the concert hall. They began to write concert overtures, not meant to be played before an opera or play but suggested by a play or even a book. One of the earliest and best was the overture to Shakespeare's

Midsummer Night's Dream, written in 1826 by Felix Mendelssohn (1809–47).

Another famous concert overture of Mendelssohn's is called *Fingal's Cave.* Mendelssohn went to Scotland for a holiday, and there he got the idea for a sort of musical picture of gray, rough seas and low clouds. The same Scottish holiday also suggested his *Scotch* Symphony, the opening of which came into his head at Holyrood Palace, Edinburgh. A visit to Italy produced his *Italian* Symphony.

Hector Berlioz (1803–69), a Frenchman who was in Italy at the same time as Mendelssohn, also wrote an Italian symphony. It is called *Harold in Italy* (after the hero of a poem by Byron) and consists of a number of scenes. A melody played on the viola represents Childe Harold. Berlioz' *Fantastic* Symphony tells a truly fantastic story in a series of dream episodes. *Romeo and Juliet* brings in vocal soloists and a chorus. *The Damnation of Faust* is really an opera without scenery. Berlioz also wrote concert overtures, such as one to Shakespeare's *King Lear,* one to Walter Scott's novel *Waverley,* and a *Roman Carnival* Overture, which is a scene from one of Berlioz' operas arranged for orchestra.

During the 1850's the Hungarian composer Franz Liszt (1811–86) published a collection of concert overtures and other orchestral pieces, calling them "symphonic poems." Before long this name became very popular. Composers sometimes renamed their concert overtures symphonic poems and printed short programs, or explanations, of what the music was about as prefaces to the scores.

Don Juan, by the German composer Richard Strauss (1864–1949), was the earliest of a whole series of tone poems. Some of them (for instance, *Till Eulenspiegel's Merry Pranks* and *Don Quixote*) tell more or less connected stories.

The Russian composer Peter Ilyich Tchaikovsky (1840–93) wrote concert overtures and symphonic poems, one symphony (*Manfred*) with a definite program, two or three symphonies with secret programs that he told only to his friends, and symphonies with no programs at all.

Two of the greatest symphonists of the latter part of the 19th century, Johannes Brahms (1833–97) and Anton Bruckner (1824–96), would have nothing to do with program music. Neither would the Czech composer Antonin Dvořák (1841–1904) for his symphonies, though he wrote some story-telling symphonic poems.

Piano Music

Music that expressed a composer's more secret thoughts and feelings was usually written in the form of quite short pieces for the piano. Mendelssohn composed sets of what he called *Songs Without Words.* Some of the short piano pieces of his friend Robert Schumann (1810–56) are just that—songs with piano accompaniment, re-arranged for piano only.

Another great piano composer of the 1830's and 1840's was Frédéric Chopin (1810–49), a Pole who went to live in France. He also wrote songs without words, called nocturnes, but they were more like opera arias without words. Chopin and Liszt introduced quite new ways of writing for the piano in order to get the utmost beauty and variety of sound from it.

Nationalism

Chopin and Liszt both came from countries that were oppressed by powerful neighbors. They took a special interest in their own national music. Chopin wrote many pieces in the style of the aristocratic polonaise and the peasant mazurka (inspired by Polish tunes). Liszt composed big, brilliant rhapsodies and other works that introduced the songs and dances of the Hungarian gypsies.

This kind of romanticism flourished among peoples who felt that their national culture was being overlaid by the culture of Central Europe. In Russia quite a number of musicians, such as Mikhail Glinka (1804–57), Mily Balakirev (1837–1910), Alexander Borodin (1833–87), Modest Mussorgsky (1839–81), and Nikolay Rimsky-Korsakov (1844–1908), proclaimed themselves nationalists. In Bohemia the Czech composers Bedřich Smetana (1824–84) and, to a lesser extent, Antonin Dvořák did the same. Even Norway had a nationalist master in Edvard Grieg (1843–1907).

GERALD ABRAHAM
Author, *A Hundred Years of Music*
See also CLASSICAL AGE IN MUSIC.

The ruins of the Colosseum, built in the 1st century A.D. The Colosseum was used for spectacles such as gladiatorial contests.

The Spanish Steps lead up from the Piazza di Spagna to the Church of Trinità dei Monti.

The Palazzo della Civiltà is a modern government building in Rome.

ROME

Rome, the capital of Italy, is really three cities. There is the Rome of antiquity, the Rome of the popes, and modern Rome. The three Romes merge and overlap and contrast in a remarkable manner. It is possible in Rome to stand in almost any place and see evidence of the three Romes. A small square called the Piazza Minerva, for example, has at one corner the Pantheon, a temple with an enormous concrete dome. It was built by the inhabitants of Rome 27 years after the birth of Christ. In the center of the Piazza Minerva stands a charming statue of an elephant, sculpted in 1667. The name of the pope who ruled Rome at that time is engraved on the statue's base. As for modern Rome, the Piazza Minerva has a bus stop, a taxi stand, and a newspaper kiosk, and it is near a hotel favored by tourists, who also patronize souvenir shops on the same square.

Rome is called the Eternal City because it has survived wars, plagues, floods, earthquakes, and the ravages of time. Its often sunny climate and architectural beauty have attracted artists and poets for many centuries and have inspired such extravagant, if debatable, lines as those written by Henry Wadsworth Longfellow:

. . . There may be other cities
That please us for a while, but Rome alone
Completely satisfies. . . .

▶ THE ETERNAL CITY

Rome has a population of about 3,000,000 people. Even 18 centuries ago Rome is estimated to have had a population of over 1,000,000. At that time Rome was the center of the civilized Western world, and its large population was a reflection of its role. Parts of the walls that served as defenses for ancient Rome still survive and still encompass much of what is central Rome. However, Rome has spread far beyond its walls, and apartment houses extend into the countryside.

Many of Rome's cobbled streets are very narrow, dating from the days of chariots and carriages. Because automobile traffic has increased, there are often traffic jams. But wisely, laws have been made that provide for the preservation of Rome's old churches, palaces, and other monuments.

The construction of wider streets and underpasses often is impossible because it would mean destroying or altering an old wall or an antique temple. Even subway construction is limited by the underground network of catacombs, the burial places of long ago.

▶ SIGHTS OF ROME

The Colosseum is perhaps the most striking of the city's monuments. It took only 8 years to build, so skilled were the ancient Romans as engineers. This amphitheater, or stadium, completed in A.D. 80, held at least 45,000 spectators, the capacity of many a large football stadium even today. Here man fought man in gladiatorial contests. It still is possible to imagine from the remains of the building what this great structure looked like in the days of Rome's greatness.

Other famous Roman sights are the Roman forums. Their remaining marble columns and triumphal arches are reminders of the most important political and religious buildings of 20 and more centuries ago.

Elaborate fountains grace many of the city's *piazze* ("squares"), and there are no fewer than 450 churches. The largest and most splendid is St. Peter's Church in Vatican City.

Art treasures are housed in a number of galleries and museums, as well as in important churches. The principal gallery is in the Villa Borghese, formerly the private estate of a noble family.

The Tiber River flows through Rome. It is spanned by bridges built in different ages. The sturdiest bridge is the oldest. It is called the Ponte Milvio and was finished in the 2nd century B.C. Originally Rome was built on seven hills, but in the course of time several of the hills have disappeared.

▶ CAPITAL OF ITALY

Rome is the capital of Italy, and many Romans work in government offices. The two chambers of Parliament are housed in separate old palaces, a dozen blocks apart. Large buildings in various parts of the city contain government ministries and offices. There are also many embassies of countries that have diplomatic relations with Italy.

The president of Italy lives in the Quirinale Palace, atop one of the original seven hills of Rome. The history of the rust-colored Quir-

The ruins of the Roman Forum. Some of the buildings date from the 5th century B.C. The forum, begun as a marketplace, became the government center of ancient Rome.

St. Peter's Basilica rises over St. Peter's Square in Vatican City, the center of the Roman Catholic world.

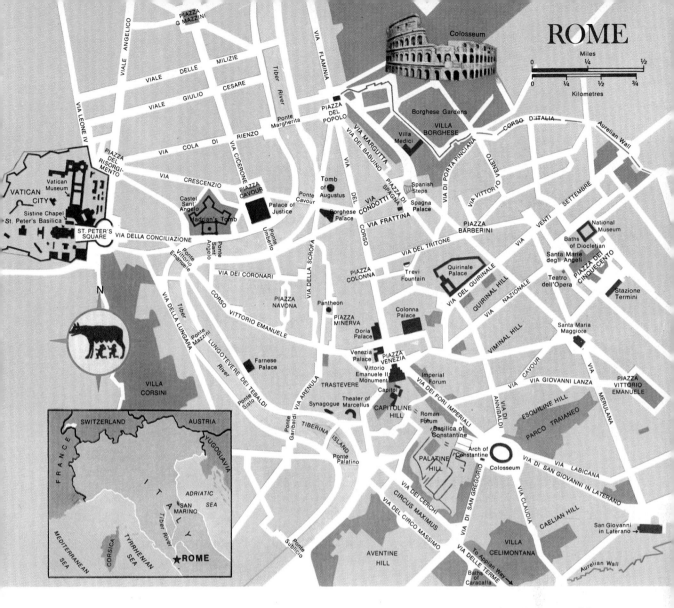

ROME

Miles
Kilometres

inale Palace reflects the varied history of the city. It was begun in 1574 as a summer residence of the popes. The Quirinale Palace later became the home of the Italian king, who replaced the pope as the ruler in Rome. It has been the residence of the president of the Italian Republic since 1947.

▶DAILY LIFE IN ROME

Rome is not one of Italy's main industrial cities, but many sizable factories operate on its outskirts. Food processing and the manufacture of textiles and drugs are some of the main industrial activities.

Tourism provides a major source of income. Almost 1,000,000 tourists arrive each year at Rome's big international airport, 20 miles from the city's center, or at its modernistic central railroad station. They also arrive by car on one of the many highways leading to Rome. There are hundreds of hotels and restaurants. The flood of sightseers provides a livelihood for Roman guides, souvenir sellers, and guidebook publishers.

The city's work schedule, like that of many Mediterranean lands, includes a midday siesta. At 1 P.M. all offices, department stores, shops, universities, schools, and even many churches close. Stores and public buildings usually reopen between 3 and 4 P.M. This gives the Romans time for a long lunch and perhaps a nap.

The Victor Emmanuel Monument on the Piazza Venezia was built as a memorial to the first king of united Italy.

Another characteristic feature of Roman life is the bar. A bar in Italy sells both ice cream and alcoholic beverages. It is the place to buy candy, sandwiches, and most important from a Roman's point of view, coffee. The Roman favors a bitter black coffee with a strong, pleasant aroma served in a small cup and called *espresso*. Almost all bars have outdoor tables, which provide a pleasant place for the animated conversation that Romans enjoy.

A frequent topic of conversation for young Roman men is the current fortunes of their favorite soccer team. Soccer is the city's favorite sport, followed closely by bicycle and automobile racing. These and other sports are practiced in Rome's splendid arenas. Many of these were built for the Olympic Games that took place in Rome in 1960.

▶ROME'S HISTORY

No one really knows when Rome began. Therefore, a legend substitutes for historical fact. According to the legendary story of the founding of Rome, the abandoned twin sons of a pagan god were discovered in the marshes by a she-wolf, who nursed the infants. These twins, Romulus and Remus, became the founders of the city. Likenesses of the twins and the wolf adorn many Roman emblems even today.

The traditional date for Rome's founding is 753 B.C. It is believed that Rome was begun as a simple marketplace or a fortified village at a spot where the territories of three ancient peoples—the Latins, the Sabines, and the Etruscans—met. Rome's geographical position in the center of the peninsula, near the sea, contributed to its growth in importance, as did the bold, adventurous character of its people.

First under the rule of kings and then, from 510 B.C., under a republic, Rome's armies steadily expanded the city's territory. By the time the republic had become an empire in 27 B.C., Rome ruled much of the known Western world. Rome's maximum expansion was achieved under the Emperor Trajan (A.D. 53?–117), who ruled from 98 to 117. In that period Rome governed not only the shores of the Mediterranean but also much of what is now Austria, the Balkans, Hungary, Great Britain, Spain, Portugal, France, Switzerland, and part of Asia Minor.

In the 5th century barbarian tribes from what is now Germany began invading Rome. Rome was sacked by people known as the Goths and the Vandals. In 476 Rome fell as capital of the western part of the empire. (More than a century earlier, an eastern capital had been established at Constantinople, now Istanbul, in Turkey.)

The glory of ancient Rome was gradually succeeded by the glory of the Rome of the popes. The Catholic Church and its leaders remained in Rome after its fall, and the pope emerged as ruler of Rome and of a territory twice the size of the state of Massachusetts.

In the 1800's a movement arose in Italy to unite the peninsula, which at that time still consisted of many separate nations. But the city of Rome and the area surrounding it resisted unification until 1870, 10 years after most of Italy had been united.

United Italy was governed by a king, and Rome was proclaimed the capital. After World War I, Benito Mussolini, leader of the authoritarian, warlike Fascist Party, rose to power. The building on the Piazza Venezia where he had his office, with a balcony from which he used to address large crowds, was opened as a museum in 1944. Mussolini ruled from 1922 until 1943. When the Italian Republic was proclaimed after World War II, Rome, which was little damaged in the war, continued as the capital of the country.

IRVING R. LEVINE
Author, *Main Street, Italy*
Reviewed by MARIANITA GARGOTTA
Librarian, Italian Cultural Institute

See also ITALY (Italian Art and Architecture); VATICAN CITY.

ROMEO AND JULIET

Shakespeare's play *Romeo and Juliet* is the most famous story of young love ever written. It tells the tragic story of two lovers who are kept apart and finally destroyed because their families hate each other, and it is written in such intense, ardent, glowing poetry that young people of every generation recognize themselves in it.

Romeo and Juliet first meet at a feast that is given by Juliet's father, Lord Capulet. Juliet falls in love with a stranger and then discovers that his name is Romeo and that he is the son of her father's enemy, Lord Montague. She cannot stop loving him, and later on that night she goes out on her balcony to dream of Romeo. She does not know that he has climbed over the orchard wall to be near her, and that he is standing below, hidden by the night and listening to her words.

JULIET. O Romeo, Romeo! wherefore art thou Romeo?
Deny thy father and refuse thy name;
Or, if thou wilt not, be but sworn my love,
And I'll no longer be a Capulet.
ROMEO (*aside*). Shall I hear more, or shall I speak at this?
JULIET. 'Tis but thy name that is my enemy:
Thou art thyself, though not a Montague.
What's Montague? It is nor hand, nor foot,
Nor arm, nor face, nor any other part
Belonging to a man. O, be some other name!
What's in a name? That which we call a rose
By any other name would smell as sweet:
So Romeo would, were he not Romeo called,
Retain that dear perfection which he owes
Without that title. Romeo, doff thy name,
And for thy name, which is no part of thee,
Take all myself.
ROMEO.   I take thee at thy word!
Call me but love, and I'll be new baptized:
Henceforth I never will be Romeo.
JULIET. What man art thou, that, thus be-screened in night,
So stumblest on my counsel?
ROMEO.   By a name
I know not how to tell thee who I am.
My name, dear saint, is hateful to myself,
Because it is an enemy to thee.
Had I it written, I would tear the word.
JULIET. My ears have yet not drunk a hundred words
Of thy tongue's uttering, yet I know the sound.
Art thou not Romeo, and a Montague?
ROMEO. Neither, fair maid, if either thee dislike.
JULIET. How camest thou hither, tell me, and wherefore?

The orchard walls are high and hard to climb,
And the place death, considering who thou art,
If any of my kinsmen find thee here.
ROMEO. With love's light wings did I o'er-perch these walls,
For stony limits cannot hold love out.
And what love can do, that dares love attempt:
Therefore thy kinsmen are no stop to me.

The famous balcony scene continues, and the two young lovers find that it is almost impossible to tear themselves away from each other.

JULIET. Good night, good night! Parting is such sweet sorrow
That I shall say good night till it be morrow!
ROMEO. Sleep dwell upon thine eyes, peace in thy breast!
Would I were sleep and peace, so sweet to rest!

Since they cannot live without each other, they plan to have a secret marriage, and at the risk of his life Romeo spends his wedding night in Juliet's room. When daylight comes, Juliet refuses to believe that their night together is over, and she tries to persuade her young husband that the bird they hear singing must be the nightingale. Romeo answers her sorrowfully.

It was the lark, the herald of the morn,
No nightingale. Look, love, what envious streaks
Do lace the severing clouds in yonder east.
Night's candles are burnt out, and jocund day
Stands tiptoe on the misty mountain tops.
I must be gone and live, or stay and die.

Again the lovers have to submit to being separated, and again they struggle to be near each other. In the end they die in each other's arms, never to be separated again. And the play ends when the Capulets and Montagues at last give up their ancient hatreds and join together in mourning the death of the two young people whom their enmity has slain.

It is a story set to music, the music of Shakespeare's poetry, and as such it has become immortal.

MARCHETTE CHUTE
Author, *An Introduction to Shakespeare*

ROOSEVELT, ELEANOR (1884–1962)

Anna Eleanor Roosevelt was known throughout the world as a crusader for human rights. The wife of one United States president, Franklin D. Roosevelt, and the niece of another, Theodore Roosevelt, she was born in New York City on October 11, 1884. Her parents died when she was young, and Eleanor went to live with her grandmother. She completed her schooling in England, and in 1905 she married her fifth cousin, Franklin Roosevelt. They had six children.

Eleanor had her first taste of politics when Franklin was elected a New York State senator in 1911. When he ran for the vice-presidency of the United States in 1920, she campaigned with him. After Franklin Roosevelt was stricken with polio in 1921, Eleanor increased her political activities to encourage her husband. She worked for the New York League of Women Voters and in 1924 became finance chairman of the women's division of the state Democratic committee.

During the 1920's she established the Val-Kill Furniture Shop in Hyde Park, New York, for unemployed workers. She taught at the Rivington Street Settlement House and began the Todhunter School for girls in New York City. When Franklin Roosevelt was elected governor of New York in 1928, she commuted from Albany to teach at the school.

Franklin Roosevelt became president in 1932, and Eleanor began her 12 years as First Lady. Because of her husband's infirmity she did much of the traveling for him. She spoke in the United States and abroad, promoting social welfare and human rights. She continued her activities on radio programs and in syndicated newspaper columns.

Franklin Roosevelt died in 1945. That same year Mrs. Roosevelt was appointed United States representative to the United Nations, a post she held until 1961. Between 1946 and 1951 she was chairman of the United Nations Commission on Human Rights.

She died in New York on November 7, 1962, and was buried at the Roosevelt home at Hyde Park, New York.

See also FIRST LADIES.

FRANKLIN D. ROOSEVELT (1882–1945)

32ND PRESIDENT OF THE UNITED STATES

ROOSEVELT, FRANKLIN DELANO. Franklin D. Roosevelt served longer than any other president of the United States. He held office from 1933 until his death in 1945 at the beginning of his fourth term. During his presidency he led the United States through two great crises—the Depression of the 1930's and World War II.

Roosevelt was a man of unusual charm and great optimism, which he was able to communicate to others. He had a broad smile and an easygoing way of nodding agreement to whatever proposals were made to him. But beneath his outward friendliness was an inner reserve and an iron will. He became one of the most beloved as well as one of the most hated of American presidents. His admirers emphasized the courage with which he met his illness—an attack of polio that left him permanently unable to walk—and the way in which, as president, he met the nation's problems. They praised him for insisting that the federal government must help the underprivileged and that the United States must share in the responsibility for preserving world peace. Roosevelt's opponents denounced him for increasing the role of the federal government in the economic life of the country and

for the heavy spending of his administration. His opponents also criticized his wartime leadership. They claimed that he unnecessarily involved the United States in World War II and that he was fooled by the Communists.

Yet friend and foe alike agreed that Roosevelt made a vital impact upon his times, and that his policies exerted great influence on the future.

▶EARLY YEARS

Roosevelt was born on a comfortable estate overlooking the Hudson River at Hyde Park, New York, on January 30, 1882. He had a pleasant, sheltered childhood. His father, James Roosevelt, then in his middle 50's, was a well-to-do investor and vice-president of a small railroad. His mother, Sara Delano Roosevelt, came from a wealthy family of New England origin. During his childhood Franklin was taught by a governess and was taken on frequent trips to Europe. Once his father took him to the White House to see President Grover Cleveland. Cleveland, saddened and worn by the burdens of office, said he hoped that young Franklin would never have the misfortune of becoming president.

WHEN FRANKLIN D. ROOSEVELT WAS PRESIDENT
New York held its first World's Fair in 1939. The blue eagle, symbol of the National Recovery Administration, was a familiar sight during the Depression of the 1930's. World War II (1939–45) raged during the second half of Roosevelt's administration. Roosevelt's birthplace was in Hyde Park, N.Y.

Left: Franklin Roosevelt as a young boy. Right: The Roosevelts in 1920. At rear (left to right): Franklin Roosevelt, Mrs. Sara Delano Roosevelt, Eleanor Roosevelt; at front: Elliott, Franklin, Jr., John, Anna, James.

At 14 Roosevelt entered Groton School in Massachusetts. From Groton he went to Harvard University. There he concerned himself more with social life and other activities than with his studies. He was especially proud of the fact that he was president (chief editor) of the Harvard *Crimson,* the student newspaper. He graduated in 1904 and went on to Columbia University Law School. Meanwhile, he had become engaged to his slim, attractive distant cousin, Eleanor Roosevelt. At the wedding in 1905 Eleanor's uncle, President Theodore Roosevelt (who was Franklin's fifth cousin), gave her in marriage.

Roosevelt was an indifferent law student and did not bother to complete work for his degree after passing his bar examination. Nor was he much interested in his work with a prominent Wall Street law firm.

▶HE ENTERS POLITICS

In 1910 the Democratic leaders in Dutchess County, New York, persuaded Roosevelt to run for the New York State Senate. The Senate contest seemed hopeless for a Democrat. Nevertheless Roosevelt conducted an energetic campaign, touring the Hudson River farming communities in a red Maxwell automobile. The Republicans were split that year, and he won his first election. Shortly before his 29th birthday he entered the New York Senate.

Roosevelt supported Woodrow Wilson for the presidential nomination, and when Wilson became president in 1913, Roosevelt was appointed assistant secretary of the Navy. He still seemed too handsome and too unpredictable in dashing from one place to another to be taken very seriously. Some people said that his initials "F. D." stood for "feather duster." Yet Roosevelt was especially successful as an administrator during World War I. He was also achieving a reputation as a rising young progressive. In 1920, at the age of 38, he won the Democratic nomination for vice-president, running with James M. Cox (1870–1957) of Ohio. But the Democrats were buried in the landslide victory of Warren Harding.

HIS ILLNESS

Biding his time, Roosevelt entered private business. Then, in the summer of 1921, while vacationing at Campobello Island in Canada, he was suddenly stricken with polio. Even after the worst had passed, he was still paralyzed from the waist down. Not yet 40, he seemed finished in politics. His mother wanted him to retire to Hyde Park. His wife, Eleanor, and his private secretary, Louis Howe, disagreed. They felt that his recovery would be aided if he kept his political interests. Eleanor, now the mother of five children (a sixth child had died in 1909), cast aside her acute shyness and learned to make appearances for her husband at political meetings. In spite of his illness, Roosevelt remained one of the dominant figures in the Democratic Party during the 1920's.

Above all, during these years Roosevelt turned his energies to recovering his health. He achieved the best results when he began swimming in the hot mineral waters at Warm Springs, a resort in Georgia. Roosevelt turned Warm Springs into a great national center for the treatment of polio. But he was still unable to walk without leg braces, a cane, and a strong arm upon which to lean.

GOVERNOR

In 1928 Governor Alfred E. Smith (1873–1944) of New York urged Roosevelt to run for governor of New York. Smith was then the Democratic candidate for president. Reluctantly, Roosevelt agreed; he had wanted to wait several years until he regained the use of his legs. Herbert Hoover defeated Smith for the presidency, but Roosevelt was elected governor by a narrow margin. His re-election in 1930 by a record majority made him the leading candidate for the Democratic presidential nomination in 1932.

During the 1932 election campaign the Depression overshadowed all other issues. In accepting the nomination, Roosevelt had promised the American people a "New Deal." A great majority of the voters were eager to try anything that might rescue them from their economic distress. They voted overwhelmingly for Roosevelt, who defeated Herbert Hoover by more than 7,000,000 votes.

Conditions became worse between Roose-velt's election on November 8, 1932, and his inauguration on March 4, 1933. (The Twentieth Amendment to the Constitution, changing the presidential inauguration date to January 20, did not go into effect until October, 1933.) Thousands of banks failed as depositors, fearful of losing their savings, withdrew their money. A quarter of the nation's wage earners were unemployed, and many of the rest lived in misery. Families on relief sometimes received no more than 75 cents a week for food. Farmers were in an equally desperate plight because of low prices on basic crops.

PRESIDENT

Amid these grim conditions Roosevelt took his oath of office as president. He brought promise of immediate action to combat the Depression. "The only thing we have to fear is fear itself," he said in his inaugural speech. The words were not new, but the way Roosevelt said them gave people new hope. As a first step he closed all banks in the United States to prevent further collapse. Then he called Congress into special session to pass emergency banking legislation. Within a few days most banks were reopened, and people who had withdrawn their money redeposited it. (The Federal Deposit Insurance Corporation was established soon after. It insured bank deposits and protected people from losing their savings.)

Thus far Roosevelt had done little more than restore public confidence. But the American people were so enthusiastic about him that Congress seemed his to command. During the first 100 days of his administration he presented to Congress a wide variety of legislation. This became the first New Deal program. These early measures contained one notable reform—the creation of the Tennessee Valley Authority (TVA). The TVA provided flood control, cheap electricity, and better use of the land for the entire poverty-stricken Tennessee River area.

Relief and Recovery

For the most part the early New Deal measures were meant to bring immediate relief to the needy and recovery to the economy. A federal agency was set up to provide the states with funds to feed the hungry.

President Roosevelt in 1939, delivering one of his "fireside chats" to the nation.

Legislation was passed to aid farmers and homeowners in danger of losing their property because they could not keep up mortgage payments. The Civilian Conservation Corps (CCC) was organized, providing jobs for unemployed young men in forest conservation and road construction work.

A series of recovery measures was enacted to raise farm and industrial prices, increase wages, and put people back to work. Many economists believed that low prices and wages (deflation) were at least partly responsible for the continuing Depression. At the President's urging, Congress took the United States off the gold standard and devaluated the dollar. This lowered its exchange value, allowing American products to be sold to better advantage abroad.

The AAA and NRA. At the heart of the recovery program of the early New Deal were the Agricultural Adjustment Administration (AAA) and the National Recovery Administration (NRA). Under the AAA, production of basic crops and livestock was limited in order to raise prices and thus increase farmers' incomes. Farmers were rewarded by benefit payments for reducing production.

The NRA was a more complicated plan. Created by the President under the terms of the National Industrial Recovery Act of 1933, it was meant to aid both business and labor. The NRA established codes of fair competition in major industries. Price cutting and various unfair business practices were prohibited in order to help manufacturers. In turn, businessmen were expected to pay at least minimum wages and to work their employees for no more than established maximum hours. Furthermore, under the terms of the Recovery Act, workers were given the right to bargain collectively; that is, to join unions of their choice, which would negotiate wages and working hours with the employers. These collective bargaining provisions were replaced in 1935 by the National Labor Relations Act (the Wagner Act). This law gave strong protection to unions and encouraged the growth of the labor movement.

None of Roosevelt's recovery measures worked quite satisfactorily, and the road to recovery was one of ups and downs. In 1935 the Supreme Court declared the NRA code system unconstitutional, and in 1936 they ruled against part of the AAA. Nevertheless, in 1935 and 1936 the economy was showing a marked improvement.

Other Measures. But although recovery seemed on the way, unemployment remained high. In the first winter of the New Deal, Roosevelt had tried a temporary work relief program for the unemployed—the Civil Works Administration (CWA). In 1935 he undertook a large-scale work program—the Works Progress Administration (WPA). Opponents of the New Deal criticized the government's heavy spending, which led to an increase in the national debt. And they denounced Roosevelt for interfering in the economy.

The opposition of these critics, many of whom were well-to-do, seemed to drive Roosevelt in the direction of greater reform. Early in his administration he had tried to give balance to his program so that it would benefit business and banks as well as the underprivileged. Now he regarded the conservative leaders as ungrateful.

Three Reforms. In the summer of 1935 Roosevelt pushed through Congress three important reform measures. The Public Utility Holding Company Act placed restrictions on gas and electric utilities. The Revenue Act of 1935 placed heavier tax burdens on those in the upper income brackets. (Roosevelt's opponents called it the "soak the rich" tax.) Most important of the three was the Social Security Act. This provided for unemployment insurance, pensions for the aged, and aid to widows and orphans.

His Second Term

By 1936 Roosevelt had clearly become the champion of the underprivileged. He was re-elected over the Republican candidate, Alfred M. Landon (1887–   ), by a margin so sweeping that he carried every state except Maine and Vermont.

The Supreme Court Crisis. Re-election by such a wide margin seemed to call for further reform. "I see one-third of a nation ill-housed, ill-clad, ill-nourished," Roosevelt declared in his second inaugural address. As a first step to aid the underprivileged, he wanted to end the Supreme Court's invalidation of New Deal measures. Roosevelt felt that these laws were constitutional but that the Supreme Court interpretation of them was sadly out of date. Therefore, in February, 1937, he asked Congress to authorize him to appoint as many as six new justices to the Court.

A great controversy swept Congress and the country. Many people denounced the proposal as being the way a dictator would seek power. Roosevelt's plan failed, but the gradual retirement of the older justices brought more liberal ones to the Supreme Court. Even while the debate was going on, the Court had modified its decisions. Thereafter it approved of most government regulation of the nation's economy.

Toward Recovery. By 1937 the economy had reached almost the prosperity levels of the 1920's, although unemployment continued to be high. When Roosevelt cut New Deal spending in an effort to balance the federal budget, a sharp recession followed. He returned to heavy spending, and the trend toward recovery resumed. Large sums were provided for the WPA and for a vast public works project —the Public Works Administration (PWA). Roosevelt also obtained from Congress the Fair Labor Standards Act of 1938. This set a national standard of minimum wages and maximum hours for workers and prohibited the shipping in interstate commerce (commerce between states) of goods made by child labor. It was the last important piece of New Deal reform legislation. Thereafter Roosevelt and the American people were concerned with events in Europe and Asia, where the aggressive policies of Hitler and Mussolini and the Japanese military leaders threatened to lead to war.

Life in the White House

Even under the great pressures of office Roosevelt found time to swim daily in the White House pool and to relax with his family and aides. The President's children and his many grandchildren often stayed at the White House, and during World War II, Prime Minister Winston Churchill was a frequent guest.

Roosevelt enjoyed entertaining informally. When King George VI and Queen Elizabeth of Great Britain paid a state visit to the United States in 1939, the President took them to Hyde Park for a picnic of frankfurters and baked beans.

The Approach of World War II

In his first inaugural address, in 1933, Roosevelt had pledged the United States to a "good neighbor" policy. Roosevelt had carried out this pledge in Latin America. Indeed, he tried to follow a policy of goodwill throughout the world. As the threat of war became more ominous during the mid-1930's, both the President and the American public wished to remain neutral. But at the same time, Roosevelt did not want to see the aggressors triumph. When Japan invaded northern China in 1937, he declared in a speech that war, like a dangerous disease, must be quarantined.

War finally broke out in Europe when Hitler invaded Poland in 1939. Roosevelt wished to help the democratic nations without involving the United States in war. But gradually, as the crisis deepened, he took greater risks of involvement. After the fall of France in 1940, Roosevelt, with the approval of Congress, rushed all possible weapons to Great

---

IMPORTANT DATES IN THE LIFE OF FRANKLIN D. ROOSEVELT

1882	Born at Hyde Park, New York, January 30.
1904	Graduated from Harvard University.
1905	Married Anna Eleanor Roosevelt.
1907	Admitted to the bar; went to work for a New York City law firm.
1911–1913	Member of New York State Senate.
1913–1920	Assistant secretary of the Navy.
1920	Unsuccessful candidate for vice-president.
1921	Stricken with polio.
1929–1933	Governor of New York.
1933	Inaugurated as 32nd president of the United States, March 4.
1937	Inaugurated for a second term, January 20.
1941	Inaugurated for a third term, January 20; Japanese attacked Pearl Harbor, December 7; war declared against Japan, December 8; war with Italy and Germany, December 11.
1945	Inaugurated for a fourth term, January 20; died at Warm Springs, Georgia, April 12.

Prime Minister Winston Churchill, Roosevelt, and Premier Joseph Stalin at the Yalta Conference in 1945.

Britain in order to help the British in the fight against Hitler.

His Third Term

In the election of 1940 Roosevelt ran against the Republican candidate, Wendell Willkie, who held similar views on aid to Great Britain. Isolationists, who wished the United States to keep out of European affairs, campaigned vigorously against Roosevelt. In spite of their opposition, he was elected to a third term.

Early in 1941, at the President's urging, Congress passed the Lend-Lease Act. This provided further aid to Great Britain and other nations fighting the Axis. Roosevelt was also trying to block Japanese advances into China and Southeast Asia. The Japanese felt they faced a choice of giving up their policy of expansion or fighting the United States. On December 7, 1941, Japanese planes attacked the American naval base at Pearl Harbor, Hawaii. The next day Congress declared war on Japan. On December 11, Germany and Italy declared war on the United States. The nation had been swept into a world conflict.

With the United States at war, Roosevelt temporarily set aside his plans for further New Deal reform. He now sought to increase American war production and to lead the country in a great alliance against the Axis

powers. As commander in chief of the armed forces he helped plan major offensives in Europe, leading to the Normandy invasion in 1944. At the same time, the Japanese were gradually pushed back in the Pacific.

His Plans For the Future. From the beginning Roosevelt was concerned with planning a better postwar world. Even before the United States entered the war, he had declared that the American aims were the Four Freedoms: freedom of speech, freedom of worship, freedom from want, and freedom from fear.

As the war progressed, Roosevelt became increasingly interested in planning for the future self-government and economic development of colonial areas. He also hoped that an international organization could be created to prevent future wars. This organization was to be the United Nations. Roosevelt felt that the keeping of peace would depend to a considerable extent upon goodwill between the United States and the Soviet Union. He thus tried to establish friendly relations with Soviet premier Joseph Stalin at the Teheran Conference in 1943 and at the Yalta Conference in 1945.

His Fourth Term

In 1944 Roosevelt was nominated for a fourth term, running against Thomas E. Dewey (1902–71). Roosevelt appeared thin, worn, and tired, but late in the campaign he seemed to gain renewed energy. Again he was re-elected. But his health, which had been declining since early in 1944, did not improve. After returning from the Yalta Conference, he went to Warm Springs to rest. There on April 12, 1945—less than a month before the war in Europe ended—he died of a cerebral hemorrhage. As the world mourned Roosevelt's death, Vice-President Harry S Truman took over the duties of office as the new president of the United States.

At the time of his death Roosevelt had been working on a speech. In it he wrote: "We have learned in the agony of war that great power involves great responsibility. . . . The only limit to our realization of tomorrow will be our doubts of today. Let us move forward with strong and active faith."

FRANK FREIDEL
Author, *Franklin D. Roosevelt*
See also ROOSEVELT, ELEANOR; WORLD WAR II.

THEODORE ROOSEVELT (1858–1919)

26TH PRESIDENT OF THE UNITED STATES

ROOSEVELT, THEODORE. Theodore Roosevelt was one of the most popular American presidents as well as one of the most important. With his zest for life and his love of controversy, he captured the public's imagination as no president since Andrew Jackson had done. His willingness to shoulder the burdens of world power and to struggle with the problems caused by the growth of industry made his administration one of the most significant.

Roosevelt was a strong nationalist and a dynamic leader. He greatly expanded the power of the presidency at the expense of Congress, the states, and big business. He made the United States the guardian of the Western Hemisphere, especially in the Caribbean. He increased regulation of business and encouraged the labor movement. He led a long, hard fight for the conservation of natural resources. And he broadly advanced the welfare of the people as a whole. At the same time he was a compelling preacher of good government and responsible citizenship.

Roosevelt was sworn in as president on September 14, 1901, following the assassination of President William McKinley. At 42 years of age he became the youngest president in American history. Fortunately, 15 years of public service in local, state, and federal posts made him one of the best prepared. His most valuable experience had been as governor of New York. There he had shown the striking capacity to lead that made his presidency so notable. He had also become painfully aware of the need for social and economic reform. In fact, it was largely because of his efforts to regulate business and run the government honestly that New York Republican bosses decided in 1900 that Roosevelt should be eased out of the state by being made vice-president.

▶ EARLY YEARS

No president led a more varied, interesting, or adventurous life than Theodore Roosevelt. He was a hunter, rancher, and explorer as well as a soldier, naturalist, and author. As a youth, however, he had to struggle against poor health. From his birth in New York City on October 27, 1858, until his late teens, he suffered from asthma and was generally weak and frail. Otherwise he had many advantages. His father, after whom he was named, came from an old New York Dutch family of moderate wealth and high social

WHEN THEODORE ROOSEVELT WAS PRESIDENT
The city of San Francisco was partly destroyed by an earthquake and fire in 1906. The first successful flights in a heavier-than-air craft were made by Orville and Wilbur Wright in 1903. A United States fleet was sent on a cruise around the world in 1907 to demonstrate American naval strength.
Roosevelt's birthplace was in New York City.

position. His mother, Martha Bulloch, belonged to a prominent family from Georgia. Both parents were kind and affectionate. His father, in particular, concerned himself actively with Theodore's development. He encouraged Theodore to build up his body by doing hard exercises and engaging in sports. He arranged for his son to be educated by excellent private tutors until it was time to enter college. And most important of all, he taught Theodore the difference between right and wrong and gave him an unusually strong sense of responsibility. When Theodore entered Harvard College in 1876, he was healthy in body and mind, except for a trace of snobbishness, which he later lost.

At Harvard, Roosevelt wrote a senior honors thesis and was elected to Phi Beta Kappa, the student honor society. He graduated 21st in a class of 158. He probably would have done even better, for his intelligence was high and his memory keen, but he spent much of his time in outside activities. He played tennis and boxed, read hundreds of books not related to his courses, and wrote the first two chapters of a quite good book, *The Naval War of 1812*. He also became so interested in politics and government that he decided not to become a professional naturalist as he had originally intended.

In 1880, a few months after graduation, Roosevelt married a charming young lady, Alice Hathaway Lee of Chestnut Hill, Massachusetts. After a short honeymoon he started to study law at Columbia University. He had little interest in legal details, however. In 1881, he gave up the study of law upon his election to the first of three terms in the New York State Assembly.

Roosevelt was only 23 years old when he took his seat in January, 1882. But his courageous support of good government soon earned him a state-wide reputation. He became the leader of a group of reform-minded Republicans and pushed through several bills strengthening the government of New York City. At the same time, he overcame a belief that government should not interfere in the economy and fought successfully for the regulation of tenement workshops.

Early in his third term, in 1884, Roosevelt's mother died. A few hours later his wife, who had given birth to a baby girl a short while

IMPORTANT DATES IN THE LIFE OF THEODORE ROOSEVELT	
1858	Born in New York City, October 27.
1880	Graduated from Harvard College; married Alice Hathaway Lee.
1882– 1884	Served in the New York State Assembly.
1886	Married Edith Carow, his first wife having died in 1884.
1889– 1895	Member of United States Civil Service Commission.
1895– 1897	President of New York City board of police commissioners.
1897– 1898	Assistant secretary of the Navy.
1898	Organized and then commanded the 1st United States Volunteer Cavalry Regiment ("Rough Riders") during Spanish-American War.
1899– 1901	Governor of New York.
1901	Inaugurated vice-president of the United States, March 4; sworn in as president upon the death of President William McKinley, September 14.
1901– 1909	26th president of the United States.
1909– 1910	Hunted in Africa.
1912	Organized the Progressive ("Bull Moose") Party; was defeated as its presidential candidate by Woodrow Wilson.
1913	Explored in South America.
1919	Died at Oyster Bay, Long Island, January 6.

before, also died. Though grief-stricken, Roosevelt carried on his duties until the end of the session. As he wrote to a close friend, "It was a grim and evil fate, but I have never believed it did any good to flinch or yield for any blow, nor does it lighten the blow to cease from working." That summer he retired temporarily from politics and went out to the Dakota Territory to raise cattle on his ranch on the Little Missouri River.

When Roosevelt first appeared in the West, veteran cowboys and hunters were amused by his thick glasses, eastern accent, and gentlemanly manners. But after he had knocked out a drunken stranger who threatened him with two pistols and had proved himself in a half dozen other incidents, he was accepted. Within a year he was regarded as one of the region's ablest young leaders. Besides running cattle, Roosevelt spent his time in the West writing a biography of Thomas Hart Benton (1782–1858), a Missouri senator of the pre-Civil War period. He also planned a four-volume history of the westward movement, later published under the title *The Winning of the West*.

▶ PUBLIC SERVICE

Roosevelt returned from the West in the fall of 1886 to suffer defeat in a race for mayor of New York. That same year he married a childhood sweetheart, Edith Carow, and settled in a great rambling house on Sagamore Hill, overlooking Oyster Bay, Long Island. Four sons and a daughter were born to them.

But Roosevelt's energy was too great and his ambition too driving for him to be satisfied with life as a sportsman and writer. Besides, he felt that men of independent means were obligated to serve the public. So in 1889 he accepted an appointment to the United States Civil Service Commission. Roosevelt at once gave the commission new life, and for 6 years he enforced the laws honestly and fearlessly. When he resigned in 1895 to accept the presidency of the New York City Police Board, the civil service system had become an important part of American government.

As New York police commissioner, Roosevelt prowled the streets after midnight, overhauled the promotion system, and modernized the force. In 1897 he resigned from the Police Board to become assistant secretary of the Navy.

▶ ROUGH RIDER AND GOVERNOR

Roosevelt's service in the Navy Department and in the war against Spain brought out his aggressive qualities. He believed at the time that power was necessary for a country to achieve greatness, and that war was a test of manliness. He also believed that civilized nations had a right to interfere in the affairs of less advanced nations in order to forward the march of civilization. He demanded that the United States build up its fleet, drive Spain from the Western Hemisphere, and acquire colonies of its own.

Soon after the Spanish-American War broke out in 1898, Roosevelt helped organize the First United States Volunteer Cavalry Regiment (the "Rough Riders"). He took command of the regiment in Cuba, and on July 1 he led an assault on a hill outside Santiago. For hours he braved withering gunfire from the heights as he rode up and down the line urging his men, who were on foot, to press the attack. His elbow was nicked, a soldier was killed at his feet, and he had several other narrow escapes. But he rallied his own and other troops, and the hill was captured.

As soon as Roosevelt returned to New York in the fall of 1898, Republican bosses nominated him for governor. They hoped that his war record and reputation as a reformer would cause the voters to overlook a series of recent scandals within the party. After being elected by a narrow margin, Roosevelt compelled the bosses to accept a

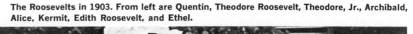

The Roosevelts in 1903. From left are Quentin, Theodore Roosevelt, Theodore, Jr., Archibald, Alice, Kermit, Edith Roosevelt, and Ethel.

Roosevelt (*center*) and his Rough Riders in Cuba in 1898.

number of reform measures. These included a tax on corporation franchises, regulation of sweatshops, a raise in schoolteachers' salaries, and a conservation program. This angered the businessmen who supported the bosses. So Republican leaders practically forced Roosevelt to accept the vice-presidential nomination in 1900, although he wanted a second term as governor. In the election McKinley and Roosevelt defeated the Democratic candidates, William Jennings Bryan and Adlai E. Stevenson (1835–1914).

Roosevelt was a vigorous public speaker. This picture was taken in 1902, during a speech in Concord, N.H.

Six months after their inauguration McKinley was dead and Roosevelt was the new president of the United States.

▶ PRESIDENT

The main drive of Roosevelt's administration was toward a balance of economic interests. He believed that he should represent all the people—farmers, laborers, and white-collar workers as well as businessmen. Roosevelt called his program the Square Deal. He began to put it into effect 5 months after he took office by starting antitrust proceedings against the Northern Securities Company, a giant holding company. Holding companies controlled other companies and were thus able to reduce competition. Then in the fall of 1902, Roosevelt helped settle a long coal strike on terms favorable to the workers. This marked the first time that a president who took action in a strike had failed to side with management.

Despite his popular fame as a "trustbuster," Roosevelt continued to believe that bigness was good economically. He felt that large corporations should be regulated rather than destroyed. In 1903 he pushed through Congress a bill to form a Bureau of Corporations. That same year he gave his support to the Elkins Bill to prohibit railroad rebates. This was a practice in which railroads returned part of their payment to favored customers.

Foreign Policy

Roosevelt's foreign policy was guided by the belief that the United States must police the Western Hemisphere and should accept the responsibilities of world power. He felt that the United States was morally bound to uplift the people of the Philippines, which the United States had acquired from Spain. He worked conscientiously to improve the economy of the Filipinos and prepare them for self-government. In 1902 he persuaded Germany to arbitrate a dispute with Venezuela. In 1903 he acquired the Canal Zone after Panama broke away from Colombia. The circumstances left a feeling of ill will in Colombia.

In 1905, at the request of the government of Santo Domingo (now the Dominican Republic), Roosevelt took over control of customs collections in that misgoverned country. He did not want to do so. But he feared that European powers might take control for nonpayment of debts if the United States did not act. He then announced in a public letter that the United States had a right to intervene in the internal affairs of Latin-American countries unable to keep order. This policy became known as the Roosevelt Corollary to the Monroe Doctrine.

Second Presidential Term

Roosevelt's flair for the dramatic combined with his solid achievements to assure him a term in his own right. In the election of 1904 he won a landslide victory over his conservative Democratic opponent, Judge Alton B. Parker (1852–1926) of New York. The most productive years of his presidency followed. In a masterful display of leadership, Roosevelt forced the conservative Republicans into line by threatening to lower the tariff—the tax on imports. The conservatives then gave their support to the Hepburn Act (1906) to regulate railroads, a meat inspection measure (1906), the Pure Food and Drug Act (1906), and employers' liability legislation (1906 and 1908).

Meanwhile, Roosevelt and his chief forester, Gifford Pinchot (1865–1946), pushed conservation forward. Their program was based on the theory that (1) natural resources belong to all the people, (2) scientific forestry would provide a constant supply of timber, and (3) river valleys should be developed as

This cartoon, entitled "Hands Off," illustrates Roosevelt's determination to enforce the Monroe Doctrine.

entire units. Roosevelt and Pinchot were bitterly opposed by small lumber companies, electric power corporations, and states' righters. But progress was made. The Reclamation Act of 1902 provided for a large irrigation project in the Southwest. Many big lumber companies were won over to scientific forestry. Over 50,500,000 hectares (125,000,000 acres) were added to the national forests, and the number of national parks doubled. Sixteen national monuments were created, and 51 wildlife refuges were established.

In foreign affairs Roosevelt's second term saw a retreat from his earlier imperialism. He tried mainly to protect the Philippines, support a balance of power in the Far East, and build up friendship with the Japanese. In 1905 he offered his good offices to end the Russo-Japanese War. His mediation proved successful and earned him the Nobel peace prize. On the other hand he served notice that he still carried a "big stick" by sending the American fleet on a world cruise in 1907.

As Roosevelt's term of office neared its end, Congress grew more and more resentful of his strong leadership and progressive policies. Again and again during his last 2 years Congress refused to do what he asked. Roosevelt's insight into the nation's problems continued to deepen, however. On January 31, 1908, he sent Congress the most radical message written by a president to that time. It called, among other things, for better conditions for workers and for the arrest of businessmen who broke the law.

In spite of his troubles with Congress, Roosevelt's great energy and straightforward speeches appealed more than ever to the man in the street. He could have been renominated easily had he chosen. But he decided instead to support the candidacy of one of his dearest friends, Secretary of War William Howard Taft. Soon after Taft was inaugurated in 1909, Roosevelt left for Africa to hunt big game and collect specimens for the Smithsonian Institution.

The Bull Moose Party

While Roosevelt was in Africa, progressivism was gaining new force in the United States. But instead of encouraging its growth as Roosevelt had done, President Taft tried to hold it back. This put him on the side of the Republican conservatives who had opposed Roosevelt's policies.

In 1910 Roosevelt returned to the United States. Although irritated at Taft's policies, he at first tried to avoid hurting his old friend. But it was not in Roosevelt's nature to keep silent. In a series of speeches in the Midwest he set forth his own views, which he called the New Nationalism.

The New Nationalism was an extension of the progressive program he had urged in the last years of his presidency. It called for steeply graduated income and inheritance taxes and a long list of other social and political reforms. Finally, in 1912, Roosevelt yielded to the pleas of progressive midwestern Republicans and challenged Taft for the presidential nomination. But the Republican Convention failed to nominate Roosevelt in spite of his two-to-one victory over Taft in the primary elections. Roosevelt then organized the Progressive, or Bull Moose, Party. ("I am as strong as a bull moose," he had once said.) The new party was supported by most of the country's social workers, intellectuals, and progressive-minded citizens.

Roosevelt's leadership of the progressive movement stirred the social conscience of middle-class America. Though Woodrow Wilson, the Democratic candidate, won the three-cornered contest with about 42 percent of the popular vote, Roosevelt ran far ahead of Taft. In a sense, too, Roosevelt was vindicated in defeat. For by 1916 Wilson had written a great deal of Roosevelt's New Nationalism into law.

South American Exploration

After his defeat in 1912 Roosevelt wrote his autobiography. It is a colorful and vigorously written book and still the most informative memoir ever written by a former president. During this period, too, Roosevelt gave a memorable speech as president of the American Historical Association. In it he pleaded with professional historians to make history as interesting as literature.

Then, in 1913, Roosevelt decided to indulge his love of adventure once more by exploring an unknown South American river, the River of Doubt. It was a harrowing experience. He almost died of an injury suffered in a heroic effort to save two capsized boats. He was then stricken with malaria. Realizing that he was a burden, Roosevelt begged his companions, who included his son Kermit, to go on without him. But they insisted on bringing him out of the jungle.

World War I

Upon the outbreak of World War I in 1914, Roosevelt at first refused to take sides. But after a few months, he decided that the interests of the United States and the world would best be served by Germany's defeat. Early in 1915 he became a leader of the movement to prepare the United States for possible entry into the war. When the United States declared war against Germany in 1917, Roosevelt asked Wilson for permission to raise a volunteer division. But Wilson refused, and Roosevelt devoted himself to spurring the war effort at home. On January 6, 1919, 18 months after his youngest son, Quentin, was killed in an air battle over France, Roosevelt died in his sleep at Sagamore Hill.

WILLIAM H. HARBAUGH
Author, *Power and Responsibility:
The Life and Times of Theodore Roosevelt*

See also PANAMA; PANAMA CANAL AND ZONE.

Strands of rope are twisted together into a cable.

ROPE

A rope is made up of fibers that are twisted together into many small yarns. The yarns are gathered together into strands (hanks) that usually are twisted into three- or four-strand ropes. Sometimes they are braided, or plaited. Rope fibers usually come from plants, but the fibers may be of almost any material that can be cut or combed into strips and twisted, such as nylon, wire, or leather.

"Rope" is a general term used to describe any kind of cordage or line. But to a ropemaker, a rope is at least 5 millimeters (³⁄₁₆ inch) thick. Large ropes generally are called cables. A rope large enough to moor a ship is called a hawser. When yarns are single or when two or three are twisted together, they are called twine.

Rope is usually classified by its circumference (the distance around it), but sometimes it is classified by its diameter. For example, a rope 8 millimeters (⁵⁄₁₆ inch) in diameter measures 25 millimeters (1 inch) around and is called a 25-millimeter rope. The circumference is about three times the diameter.

▶ HOW ARE FIBER ROPES MADE?

Ropemaking is almost entirely a process of twisting. When a bundle of fibers is twisted, the fibers pack together, and friction helps to hold them in place. But the twisting must be done just right. Too tight a twist makes the fibers cut each other. Too loose a twist gives a weak rope. Ropemaking is an art as well as a science.

Single fibers are twisted together to make a yarn; yarns are twisted together to form strands; strands are twisted together to make rope. Every time a unit of rope is put through one of these twisting operations, it is twisted in the direction opposite to the direction in which it was twisted before. This makes the rope hold together because each twist binds the other.

The basic steps in making rope are the same whether they are done slowly by hand or rapidly by huge, powerful machines:

(1) Fibers are separated and put in parallel formation on a combing machine. This machine puts them into the form of a continuous ribbon.

Philippine workers prepare abaca, the chief natural fiber used for ropes.

(2) The ribbon of fibers is spun out into a thin, round, twisted yarn.

(3) Groups of yarn are twisted into strands.

(4) The strands, tightly stretched, are passed through a tight, cone-shaped die in groups of three and twisted to make rope. This is the final step in the process of making most ropes.

(5) To make cables, groups of three-strand ropes are again twisted through a die.

(6) Cables are passed through dies and twisted under very severe tension to form hawsers.

▶**KINDS OF ROPE**

Some jobs need a soft twisted rope. Others need a hard twisted rope. The fiber chosen for a rope depends upon the job the rope is to do. The main rope fibers are abaca (Manila), sisal (agave), henequen, flax, cotton, leather, wire, and synthetics (nylon, polypropylene, and Dacron). Hemp used to be an important rope fiber, but it has been replaced by abaca. Hemp is a soft rope fiber made from the stalks of the hemp plant, which grows in most countries that have a warm, temperate climate.

Abaca. Abaca, often called Manila hemp, is the fiber most often used in ropes, but synthetics are slowly replacing it. Actually abaca is not hemp at all. Abaca fiber comes from the abaca plant, which was discovered in the Philippines. The plant is related to the banana plant. Abaca makes a much stronger and more durable rope than hemp does.

When abaca's value as a rope became known, it rapidly replaced hemp as the most important rope fiber.

Ropes made of abaca are durable, strong, flexible, and reasonable in price. They resist weather and rot.

Sisal and Henequen. The other important rope fibers are sisal and henequen. Sisal comes from Haiti, South America, and Africa. Henequen comes from Mexico. Both are fairly strong and hard plant fibers that come from the spiny leaves of similar semitropical plants. The fibers are shorter and a little weaker than abaca fibers and do not weather as well. Sisal and henequen baler twines tie well. They are used in the automatic knotters of the harvesting machines that form bales. Sisal ropes are also good utility ropes and are widely used by farmers.

Nylon. Nylon is a synthetic fiber that makes a very strong, lightweight, stretchable rope. Nylon ropes are very elastic—that is, they can stretch a long way under strain and then recover their size and shape. Their ability to absorb a violent jerk is important in the climbing ropes used by mountaineers, the lines used by waterskiers, fishing lines, and mooring lines.

Dacron and Polypropylene. Dacron and polypropylene are strong synthetic fibers that are also weatherproof. They are used when cost is not especially important. When hemp rope was used on early 19th-century sailing ships, it had to be repeatedly coated with pine tar to prevent rotting. Abaca rope must be oiled during manufacture. But Dacron or polypropylene rope has permanent rot protection because of the fiber itself.

Dacron or polypropylene rope is used whenever a strong, weatherproof rope without much stretch is needed.

Flax. High-grade flax fiber (linen) makes a beautiful, smooth rope that does not stretch, wears well, resists weather, and takes up very little room. It is used for signal ropes and pennant ropes on yachts.

Cotton. Cotton rope is fairly strong, wears exceptionally well, and wedges snugly into grooved pulleys. It is well suited for use as window sash cord and for small pulleys.

Leather, or Rawhide. For a rope that is moderately strong, very supple, long-wearing, and weatherproof, leather is used. In addition, leather can take a severe jerk. Leather, or rawhide, rope is made by hand from strips of untanned cowhide. The strips are braided carefully together so that they are perfectly even and free of kinks. Oil, lanolin, or wax is rubbed into them to make them supple and to preserve them. Rawhide was once used to

make the lariat, the cowboy's rope. Its use is now quite limited.

Wire. When tremendous strength and as little bulk as possible are needed in a rope, wire is used. Wire ropes are used for elevator cables, towlines used by tugboats, and guy lines that brace telephone poles and masts. They are also used for the suspension lines on bridges. Wire rope can be used even when there are rapid changes of load due to quick starts and stops or sudden, violent motions. Huge fiber hawsers could carry great loads and absorb the jerk, but they are too large to be handled practically.

Wire ropes come in all sizes—they may be very fine and supple or big enough for a load of 100 tons. Wire ropes are made by the same general methods used in making fiber ropes. They are smaller than fiber ropes of the same strength, and they wear longer. But larger wire ropes are very heavy. Some are too stiff and heavy for people to use easily and are used only on machines.

Reviewed by HAROLD M. WALL
Chairman of the Board
Wall Industries, Inc.

See also KNOTS.

ROPING

To the working cowboy, roping means throwing a rope so that a loop at the end of it encircles and catches cattle or horses. This form of roping is called catch-roping or lassoing. The word "lasso" comes from a Spanish word, *lazo,* meaning "slipknot" or "snare."

Since the early days of cattle ranching in the American West, catch-roping has been one of the cowboy's most useful skills on the ranch and on the range.

A newer form of roping is rope spinning. This is enjoyed as a sport or hobby both on and off the ranch. In rope spinning, the roper tosses a loop of rope into the air and quickly turns the loop so that it widens into a circle. The roper keeps this circle spinning while doing tricks and stunts.

The art of rope spinning developed in Mexico and was introduced in the United States in the late 1800's. Cowboys, who were already skilled in rope handling, began to practice

rope spinning in their spare time. Today boys and girls and adults in many areas enjoy rope spinning as a hobby.

If you have ever been to a rodeo, you have seen a demonstration of the third and most difficult kind of roping: trick and fancy roping and horse catching. Rodeo performers do a number of stunts with a spinning rope and then throw the rope to catch a horse or steer. The humorist Will Rogers (1879–1935) was one of the greatest trick and fancy ropers of all time.

▶**ROPING AS A HOBBY**

To enjoy roping as a hobby, you need only a rope and a small outdoor area in which to practice. You must start, though, with the right kind of rope. An old clothesline or string will not do.

In the early days of the West, ropes were made of horsehair. Later they were made of buffalo, buck, or elk hide. Today cowboys use an extra-quality hemp rope about $\frac{7}{16}$ inch thick and about 40 feet long as a catch-rope or lariat. (The term "lariat" comes from *la reata,* meaning "the rope" in Spanish.)

For spinning, the best rope is a braided cotton rope known as spot cord. The spinning rope is about 20 feet long. In trick and fancy roping, a four-strand maguey rope 35 to 50 feet long is used.

The ropes can be bought in a well-stocked hardware store or in a Western-goods store.

The three ropes are similar in construction. All three have a honda, or small loop or eye, at one end. ("Honda" means "sling" in Spanish.)

The length of rope from the honda to the end held in the hand is called the spoke or stem.

The first step in roping is learning to coil the rope neatly, so that it runs out smoothly when it is thrown. Before starting, loosen up a hemp or maguey rope by pulling it back and forth over a fence or post.

▶ THE FLAT LOOP

A rope may be spun in circles that are parallel to the ground (flat spins) or in circles that are at right angles to the ground (vertical spins).

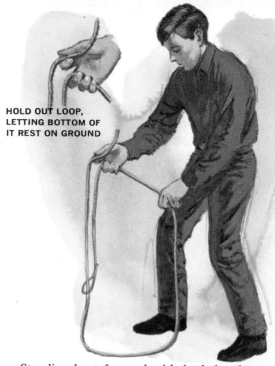

HOLD OUT LOOP, LETTING BOTTOM OF IT REST ON GROUND

Standing bent forward with both hands a little below waist level, hold the loop out a foot or two from your body. The bottom of the loop should rest on the ground, and the honda should clear the ground. The spoke should go straight up into the right hand from the honda. The spoke is held with the thumb and forefinger, and the loop is held with the other fingers of the right hand.

DOUBLE BACK END OF ROPE AND FASTEN WITH WIRE TO FORM HONDA

FORM LOOP BY PASSING END OF ROPE THROUGH HONDA

TOSS LOOP OUT TO LEFT AND AWAY FROM YOU

For beginners, the first spins to master are the flat spins. The basic flat spin is the flat loop. To do this spin, pass the end of the rope through the honda and form a loop, using about 10 feet of rope.

Now, with your right hand holding both the loop and spoke, toss the loop out to the left and away from you. Let go of the loop with your left hand as you toss.

MOVE RIGHT HAND IN COUNTERCLOCKWISE CIRCLE, LETTING GO OF LOOP

CONTINUE TO SPIN LOOP BY MAKING CIRCLES WITH RIGHT HAND

Immediately move your right hand in a counterclockwise circle parallel to the ground and about the size of the loop you want to spin. As you complete the circle, let go of the loop with your right hand. Holding only the spoke, raise your hand a little and continue to make circles in the air. As the loop spins, you can make smaller and smaller circles (the size of the loop remains the same), until you are spinning the loop with just a circular motion of the wrist. Hold the spoke end loosely, so that it can turn in your hand as you spin. This prevents the rope from kinking.

GENE AUTRY

ROSS, BETSY (1752–1836)

Schoolchildren all over the United States are familiar with the legend that the first Stars and Stripes flag was designed by a Philadelphia woman named Betsy Ross. The account of the part she played in creating the flag was first told by her grandson, William Canby, in 1870. But no one has been able to prove that the story is true.

Elizabeth (Betsy) Griscom was born in Philadelphia, Pennsylvania, on New Year's Day, 1752, the eighth child of Samuel and Rebecca Griscom, a devout Quaker couple. When she was a young woman, Betsy ran off and married a furniture upholsterer named John Ross. Ross was not a Quaker, and Betsy's parents objected to the marriage.

John Ross opened an upholstery shop on Arch Street in Philadelphia. He also served in the militia. One day while he was on guard duty, Ross was wounded by an explosion of gunpowder. Shortly afterward he died of his wounds, and Betsy was left to carry on her husband's business, to which she added flag-making.

According to Canby, General George Washington and two other men came to the Arch Street shop one day. They asked Betsy Ross to make a new flag for the 13 states. The three men brought with them a rough design (possibly by Francis Hopkinson), which she improved upon, changing the original six-pointed stars to five-pointed ones. However, there is little evidence to support Canby's claim, and it is not really known who made the first Stars and Stripes.

Soon after her husband's death Betsy Ross married Captain Joseph Ashburn. Two daughters were born to them. Ashburn was captured by the British. He died in prison, and in 1783 Betsy married John Claypool. This marriage produced five more daughters.

Betsy Ross died in Philadelphia on January 30, 1836. The Arch Street shop still stands, and thousands of people visit it every year.

Drawing of Christina by her brother Dante Gabriel.

ROSSETTI FAMILY

Dante Gabriel, Christina Georgina, Maria Francesca, and William Michael were the children of the Italian poet Gabriele Rossetti. He fled from Italy after the revolution of 1820 and became a professor of Italian at King's College, London.

Dante Gabriel, who was called Gabriel, was born in London on May 12, 1828. He began to write and draw when he was very young. His imagination was stirred by tales of adventure and terror. When he was 13, he left school and studied drawing.

By the age of 20, Gabriel was the leader of a group of young artists who admired the realistic style of Italian painting of the time before Raphael (1483–1520). They called themselves the Pre-Raphaelite Brotherhood. In 1850 they published *The Germ,* a magazine of art and poetry. In it appeared original poems by three Rossettis—Gabriel, Christina, and William.

In the 1850's and 1860's, Gabriel spent most of his time painting, but he also continued to write. The publication of a collection of his poems in 1870 established his reputation as a major Victorian poet. In his last years, he was mentally unstable and dependent on drugs. But he stood at the center of a new Pre-Raphaelite circle of writers who followed his poetic example. In 1881 he published *Ballads and Sonnets,* a fine volume of new and revised work. He died on April 9, 1882.

Gabriel's sister Christina was born on December 5, 1830. She was educated at home and began writing verses in early childhood. Her grandfather, Gaetano Polidori, owned a private press, and he printed her first book of poems in 1847. Christina's contributions to *The Germ* three years later showed a fine sense of form and a musical ear. In 1862 she published *Goblin Market and Other Poems,* with two illustrations by Gabriel. The title piece tells an exciting story in rollicking rhymes and colorful detail.

As a young woman, the beautiful Christina often modeled for the Pre-Raphaelite painters. In later life she suffered a long, painful illness. But she kept active as a poet and storyteller until her death on December 29, 1894. She is remembered as the author of charming nursery rhymes, love lyrics and sonnets, and hymns of great religious intensity.

''Who Has Seen the Wind?'' is one of Christina Rossetti's best-known poems for young readers.

Who has seen the wind?
  Neither I nor you:
But when the leaves hang trembling
  The wind is passing thro'.

Who has seen the wind?
  Neither you nor I:
But when the trees bow down their heads
  The wind is passing by.

Maria, born on February 17, 1827, was the most practical of the children. She helped in the home and had a gift for educational work. Her best book, *A Shadow of Dante* (1871), carries on the work of her scholarly father. Her lifelong interest in religious teaching appears in *Letters to My Bible-Class* (1872). Maria entered an Anglican convent in 1873 and died there on November 24, 1876.

William was born on September 25, 1829. From 1845 to 1894 he worked in a government office, and his salary was the chief support of the family. He was editor of *The Germ* in 1850, and for the rest of a long life he edited family diaries and journals, as well as collections of the works of Gabriel and Christina. His own poems are less important than his literary essays. He remained, until his death on February 5, 1919, the faithful recorder of Pre-Raphaelite life and art.

JEROME H. BUCKLEY
Harvard University

ROTHSCHILD FAMILY

Mayer Amschel Rothschild, the founder of the great banking house of Rothschild, was born in the ghetto, or Jewish section, of Frankfurt am Main, Germany, in 1743. The family took its name from the red shield (*rotes Schild* in German) that was painted above the door of an ancestral home. Mayer was given a Jewish education. Instead of becoming a rabbi, as his father had hoped, he became a dealer in old coins.

Mayer's business grew. He started a small banking establishment and was soon making business loans. When he was successful enough to support a wife, he married Gutele Schnapper. The couple had ten children, five girls and five boys.

One of Mayer's clients, Prince William of Hesse-Kassel, was so impressed by Mayer's keen business sense that he made Mayer his personal adviser. Mayer's business grew so large that he sent four of his sons to open offices abroad. Salomon went to Vienna, Na-than to London, Karl to Naples, and James to Paris. The fifth son, Amschel, stayed in Frankfurt. The offices flourished, and the Rothschild name was soon known in banking circles around the world.

Mayer's sons carried out their father's deathbed instructions to work harmoniously and keep the business together. Their banks made huge loans to businesses and governments. In 1822, Emperor Francis I of Austria made all five of them barons.

From these beginnings the house of Roth-schild continued to grow. The family produced doctors, writers, scientists, and philanthropists. Mayer's grandson Lionel took his seat as the first Jewish member of the British House of Commons in 1858. Lionel's son Nathan became a member of the House of Lords in 1885. Another grandson, Alphonse, served in the French Senate. The house of Rothschild, headquartered in London and Paris, is still a powerful force in international finance.

Reviewed by GERARD BRAUNTHAL
University of Massachusetts, Amherst

ROUSSEAU, JEAN JACQUES (1712–1778)

The philosopher, novelist, and essayist Jean Jacques Rousseau was born in Geneva, Switzerland, on June 28, 1712. His mother died about a week after his birth. His father, a watchmaker, was his first teacher.

When Jean Jacques was 10, his father was forced to leave Geneva after a duel. He moved to Nyon, leaving Jean Jacques in Geneva in the care of relatives. Young Rousseau attended a boarding school and was later apprenticed to an engraver. But he became restless, and in 1728 he ran away. In France he met Madame de Warens of Annecy, who befriended him. He spent long periods in her house, reading, writing verse, and composing music.

In 1741, Rousseau went to Paris. Through friends he obtained the position of secretary to the French ambassador in Venice. After a year and a half he returned to Paris.

His first fame came in 1750, when he won an essay contest with his *Discourse on the Arts and Sciences*. This was followed in 1754 by his *Discourse on the Origin and Foundations of Inequality* and in 1762 by *The Social Con-tract*. In these works, Rousseau stated that unjust laws and customs deprived people of their natural equality and freedom.

Rousseau also wrote a successful operetta, which was presented before the king and at the Paris Opéra. Further success came with a novel, *The New Héloïse* (1761), and a book on education, *Émile* (1762), which describes the growing up of a child. Rousseau believed that a child should remain in a "state of nature," learning from experience and example rather than from books. Rousseau's ideas were so revolutionary that the government ordered his arrest. He fled to Môtiers in the principality of Neuchâtel (now in Switzerland).

In 1765 a booklet attacking him so aroused the people of Môtiers that they stoned his house. Rousseau moved to England in 1766. He returned to France finally and spent his last years writing his autobiography, the *Confessions*. He died on July 2, 1778.

Reviewed by RAMON M. LEMOS
Author, *Rousseau's Political Philosophy:
An Exposition and Interpretation*

Rowing is an exciting sport and an excellent form of exercise.

ROWING

Rowing—moving a boat through water with oars—was an important means of transportation to early people. The ancient Greeks and Romans used galleys (huge boats) for transportation and warfare. These boats had oars arranged in tiers, one above the other. Some had as many as three tiers. They were rowed by slaves. The largest galleys had as many as 80 oarsmen.

Today rowing is popular as a pleasant exercise and as a means of transportation around small lakes and coves. With a little patience and practice almost anyone can learn to handle a small rowboat.

The oars fit into oarlocks on the sides of the boat. The rower sits between them facing the stern, or back. To row a straight course, you must pull equally on the two oars. To turn slightly, you must use more power and stroke on the side opposite the direction in which you wish to turn. For a sharper turn, you must row with one oar only. To row backward, you must reverse the stroke, pushing the oar handles away from yourself. A good rower rows smoothly and rhythmically and is careful not to splash water on passengers in the boat.

▶RACING BOATS

Modern racing boats are called shells. They are long, narrow boats made of a thin wooden or fiberglass skin over a frame. The rowers sit on sliding seats facing the stern. They tie their feet into shoes fixed into the boat.

Racing shells are of two types—sweeps and sculls.

In **sweep rowing,** each rower uses one oar, or sweep, 3.7 meters (12 feet) long. There are three basic sweep boats—pairs (with two rowers), fours (four rowers), and eights (eight rowers). Pairs and fours may be with or without coxswain. A coxswain is always used in eights. In crews without coxswain, one of the rowers steers the boat with a toeplate attached to the rudder lines.

In **sculling,** each rower uses two oars, or sculls, which are each 2.7 meters (9 feet) long. There are three basic sculling boats—single sculls (one rower), double sculls (two rowers), and quadruple sculls (four rowers). Scullers steer by varying the pressure on their oars.

▶THE COXSWAIN

In some races, a coxswain sits in the stern, facing forward, and steers with the tiller ropes. The coxswain also directs the timing of the oar strokes, which usually range from 28 to 45 strokes a minute. Since the coxswain does not row, he or she should be light in weight. The coxswain should also be keen, decisive, and able to inspire the crew.

▶ROWING RACES

Men's races are 2,000 meters (1.24 miles), and women's are 1,000 meters (0.62 miles). The course must be straight, wide enough for six crews, and of even depth. Crews begin rowing on the signal from the starter. The boats must stay in their lanes. But crews that

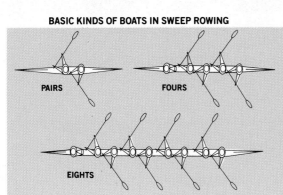

BASIC KINDS OF BOATS IN SWEEP ROWING

PAIRS FOURS

EIGHTS

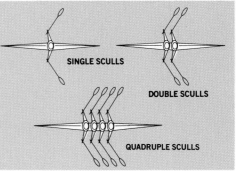

BASIC KINDS OF BOATS IN SCULLING

SINGLE SCULLS

DOUBLE SCULLS

QUADRUPLE SCULLS

stray out of their lanes are not penalized if they do not hinder other boats.

The race is followed by a referee in a motorboat. Judges at the finish line determine the order of finish and take times. The winning boat is the one whose bow (front) first crosses the finish line.

▶ ROWING ACTION

A single stroke of the oar takes two seconds or less. Rowers use their legs, backs, and arms to generate the power needed to propel the shell to speeds as great as 24 kilometers (15 miles) an hour. In addition to strength and endurance, the rowers must possess grace and co-ordination in order for the boat to move smoothly through the water.

There are three parts to the rowing stroke—catch, pull-through, and finish. At the beginning of the stroke, you move your seat to the front of the slide as you take the oar back. This brings your knees up in front of you. Then you dip the oar to the full depth of the blade and push with your legs. This sends the seat sliding back. You complete the stroke with a backward body-and-arm swing. At the finish, you bring the blade cleanly out of the water, moving your hands first quickly, then slowly, away from your body.

▶ RACING HISTORY

During the 16th century, the Thames River in England was one of the world's busiest inland waterways. Accidents became so common that King Henry VIII ruled that only licensed oarsmen could row on the river. More than 3,200 licenses were issued. These professionals took great pride in their skill. Soon races were held to decide who were the best oarsmen.

In 1715, Thomas Doggett, an Irish comedian, offered a silver badge and orange livery to the winner of a race from London Bridge to Chelsea. This 7.2-kilometer (4½-mile) race was first held in 1716. The prize is known as Doggett's Coat and Badge, and the race is still one of the most popular in the world.

English university students became interested in rowing early in the 1800's. Cambridge and Oxford met in the first intercollegiate rowing race on June 10, 1829. This race is held every year. The most famous of all rowing races is the annual Henley Royal Regatta at Henley-on-Thames. Rowers from all over the world now compete in this colorful regatta, which was first held in 1839.

In the United States, Harvard and Yale met in the first intercollegiate regatta on Lake Winnipesaukee, New Hampshire, in 1852. These universities have raced almost every year since. The Intercollegiate Rowing Association, founded in 1895, gave the sport its great popularity in the United States. Colleges from all over the country enter the association's annual regatta on Onondaga Lake, Syracuse, New York.

In 1858 several boat clubs around Philadelphia formed the "Schuylkill Navy." They made the first rules for amateur rowing in the United States. In 1872, the National Association of Amateur Oarsmen was organized. It changed its name to the United States Rowing Association in 1981. It is the governing body for rowing in the United States.

Rowing has been included in the Olympics since 1900. In that year, nine countries entered the rowing events. In recent Olympic Games, many more countries have competed in the rowing contests. Women's rowing made its first Olympic appearance in 1976.

ERIC E. STOLL
United States Rowing Association

See also BOATS AND BOATING; OLYMPIC GAMES.
RUANDA-URUNDI. See BURUNDI; RWANDA.

RUBBER

Rubber is one of the most widely used and important raw materials in the world. There are thousands of rubber products that make our daily lives safer, more comfortable, and more convenient. Rubber is useful because it has many valuable properties. It is waterproof. It does not conduct electricity. It holds air. Rubber is elastic, and it can grip a surface without slipping. And rubber helps keep out noise.

The scientific name for the white fluid of the rubber tree is **latex**. "Latex" is a Latin word meaning "liquid." Latex is something of a mystery to scientists who study trees. They have never been able to decide what its function is in the tree. Unlike sap, it does not seem to carry nourishment.

The latex is held in a network of tiny tubes under the bark of the tree. When the bark is cut, the white, milky juice oozes out. Tiny particles of rubber float in this liquid in much the same way that particles of butterfat sometimes float in milk.

At the moment it comes from the tree, latex contains about 30 to 35 percent pure rubber. The remainder is mostly water, with small amounts of other materials, such as resins, proteins, sugars, and minerals.

In addition to getting natural rubber from trees, people have learned to manufacture latex by combining chemicals in certain ways. This rubber is called synthetic rubber.

▶ HISTORY OF NATURAL RUBBER

When Europeans first went to the New World more than 400 years ago, they saw people in Central and South America playing a game with a bouncing ball. The Europeans learned that the ball had been made out of a white liquid that oozed from under the bark of certain trees. The American Indians had collected the liquid, allowed it to dry, and then boiled it in water. The liquid formed a soft mass that could be shaped into a ball. The explorers took pieces of the gummy material back to Europe as souvenirs or novelties. But Europeans did not pay much attention to this interesting material until nearly 200 years later.

In 1735 the French scientist Charles de La Condamine (1701–74) went to South America as a member of a scientific exploring group. As he traveled up the Amazon River, he asked about the strange tree that could produce balls that bounced. The natives told him that they called the tree *cau-uchu,* a word meaning "weeping wood." The drops of sticky fluid oozing out of the tree reminded them of tears. La Condamine named the fluid *caoutchouc* (kow-chook) after the native name for the tree. Forms of the French name still are used in many countries around the world. The English word "rubber" came from the discovery that the gummy material could erase, or rub out, pencil marks on paper.

La Condamine's voyage up the Amazon was both difficult and dangerous, but he man-

SOME OF RUBBER'S MANY USES

SHOE BOTTOMS

BALL

BALLOON

RUBBER DUCK

BICYCLE TIRE

RUBBER GLOVES

RUBBER–POWERED MODEL AIRPLANE

GARDEN HOSE

aged to return to the coast with samples of rubber. In a port of French Guiana he met another French scientist, François Fresneau (1703–70). Fresneau soon shared La Condamine's interest in the strange material, and the two men tried various experiments with pieces of rubber. But the scientists found the dried rubber was almost impossible to work with because it was too stiff. Shortly after liquid rubber comes from the tree it dries into a springy but very stiff lump. Fresneau decided to make a trip up a nearby river to look for the *cau-uchu* tree himself. He wanted to tap the tree and study the liquid rubber before it dried. Fresneau's trip was a success. To show how rubber could be used, he coated a pair of old boots with the liquid. Fresneau was the owner of one of the first pairs of waterproof boots.

When La Condamine and Fresneau returned to France, they published reports on rubber. Europeans were very interested in the commercial possibilities of rubber, but first some method had to be found to make the dried rubber soft and workable. Fresneau tried soaking the rubber in turpentine. The turpentine turned the rubber into a liquid that could then be brushed over shoes and other pieces of clothing to make them waterproof. Other scientists and some manufacturers experimented further on rubber with different solvents.

Solid rubber had a limited commercial value. Thomas Hancock (1786–1865), an Englishman, cut strips of rubber from large balls shipped from South America. He covered the strips with cloth and sold them as elastic bands to hold clothing in place. The floor of Hancock's workshop was littered with scraps of rubber left from the cuttings. He could not roll them into a ball because the scraps lost their adhesiveness after they were exposed to air. The scraps had to be swept up and thrown away. There seemed to be no way to use the leftover rubber.

In 1820 Hancock designed a machine to chew the rubber scraps into tiny bits. He planned to stick the bits together before the adhesive quality disappeared. He called his machine a masticator. The masticator was made of two rollers, one fitting inside the other. The rollers were studded with teeth to grind the rubber into little bits. But Hancock found that the machine pressed the rubber scraps into a large ball. The ball gave Hancock a large amount of solid rubber, which he could cut into different shapes. The masticator also made the rubber softer by kneading it. The invention of the masticator marked the beginning of rubber manufacturing as we know it today.

Three years later Charles Macintosh (1766–1843) introduced a new process to waterproof cloth with rubber. Macintosh first dissolved the rubber in a solution of coal-tar naphtha, which was a better solvent than turpentine. The liquid was brushed over two pieces of fabric, and the rubber-coated pieces were laid back to back and squeezed together. Rain and sleet could not penetrate this inner layer of rubber.

Although the rubberized coats were practical and could be marketed successfully, many rubber products were useless because they stiffened in the winter and became soft and sticky in the summer. Sometimes they became so soft that they lost their shape entirely. In spite of this, quite a few companies in the United States started producing a variety of rubber goods. These companies were soon in financial trouble because people did not want to buy products that could not keep their shape.

A young inventor, Charles Goodyear, became interested in the changeable nature of rubber and decided to try to find a way to make rubber long-lasting. By combining rubber with different chemicals, he did make it better in some ways. But year after year the hot days of summer proved that the problem had not been solved.

In 1838 Goodyear heard that Nathaniel M. Hayward (1808–65) had discovered a way to make rubber less sticky by mixing it with sulfur. Goodyear hired Hayward to continue experimenting with rubber. He also bought the rights to Hayward's patent. One day Goodyear accidentally dropped some of the rubber-and-sulfur mixture on a hot stove. Instead of melting, the rubber turned into a leatherlike strip that did not become sticky or brittle as the temperature changed. From this accident Goodyear was able to work out the heat processing method which he called vulcanization, after Vulcan, the Roman god of fire. The discovery of vulcanization was the

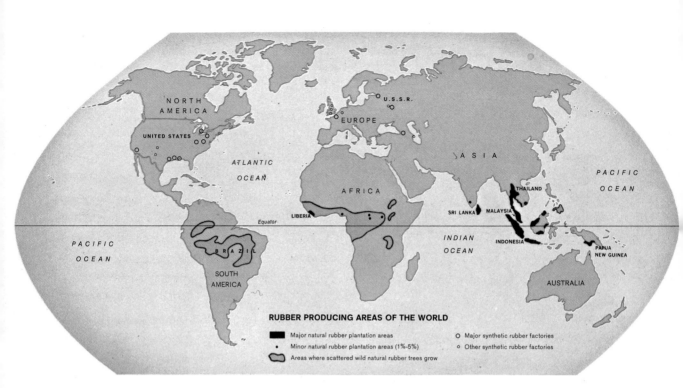

RUBBER PRODUCING AREAS OF THE WORLD

■ Major natural rubber plantation areas   ○ Major synthetic rubber factories
• Minor natural rubber plantation areas (1%-5%)   ○ Other synthetic rubber factories
◌ Areas where scattered wild natural rubber trees grow

turning point in the rubber industry. With vulcanized rubber, manufacturers were able to make reliable products, and the rubber industry began to grow rapidly.

Rubber solved many problems in the developing industrial age. Leaks in a steam engine could be quickly and effectively sealed with elastic, airtight rubber. Wires carrying electricity were made safer by insulating them with rubber. Air brakes for trains were connected by hoses of fabric and rubber, strong enough to stand heavy pressure and yet flexible enough to carry the braking system from car to car.

▶ THE SEARCH FOR A NEW SOURCE OF RUBBER

The demand for rubber increased steadily during the last half of the 19th century. Many new uses were found and many new factories were begun. With the start of automobile manufacturing, rubber became even more important. Practically the only sources of natural rubber were the jungles of South and Central American countries, mainly Brazil, where rubber trees grew wild.

But collecting rubber from the dense jungles of the Amazon was difficult and expensive. Growers began to look elsewhere for a supply of rubber. In 1861 the Dutch started a rubber plantation in Java, using native trees. Rubber could be gathered more easily and economically from trees planted in orderly rows on a plantation than from trees scattered here and there in the jungles.

The next major attempt to domesticate a wild rubber tree was made by the British in their colonies in Southeast Asia. They chose the *Hevea brasiliensis,* a wild rubber tree native to Brazil.

In 1876, Sir Henry Wickman took 70,000 seeds from the Hevea trees of Brazil. He planted them in greenhouses of the Royal Botanical Gardens near London. The seeds were buried in deep, rich soil, and the greenhouses were kept hot and moist like tropical jungles of Brazil. About 2,500 of the 70,000 seeds grew. As the seedlings gained strength, they were taken to what is now Sri Lanka and Malaysia for replanting. The climate and soil conditions of Sri Lanka and Malaysia were very similar to those of Brazil. But the jungle was not so dense, and workers for the plantations were available. Rubber became an important plantation crop throughout southeastern Asia.

The best area for growing rubber covers

about 1,100 kilometers (700 miles) on each side of the equator. Today most of the world's supply of natural rubber comes from Malaysia, Sri Lanka, Indonesia, and other countries of Southeast Asia. There also are important plantations in Liberia, Ghana, Nigeria, the Philippines, Brazil, and Guatemala.

As the demand for rubber continues to grow, people are looking for new sources of this material. Renewed interest is being shown in a wild bush called guayule (wy-oo-lee), which grows in desert areas of Mexico and southwestern United States. This bush produces rubber. It was used during World War II, when natural rubber supplies in the United States were scarce. After the war the rapid growth of the synthetic rubber industry ended interest in guayule. But now research work is again under way to see whether this plant can be successfully cultivated and processed into quality rubber products.

▶A RUBBER PLANTATION

The Hevea trees grown on plantations today have come a long way from the seedlings originally planted in Malaysia. The trees have been improved by careful breeding. They produce a bigger yield and are more resistant to disease.

Rubber trees are improved by plant selection and bud grafting. In plant selection, seeds of the best-producing trees are planted, and seeds of poor producers are destroyed.

Bud grafting begins when a seedling is about a year old. A small flap is slit in the bark of the trees near the ground. A bud cut from a high-yielding tree is slipped under the flap and taped in place. The grafted bud becomes a part of the seedling tree. When the bud has sent out a new shoot, the trunk of the seedling is cut off, and the new shoot becomes the main trunk of a new tree.

On plantations, the Hevea tree grows to a height of about 20 meters (65 feet). It has smooth, light-colored bark and shiny, dark leaves. Latex is first taken from the tree when it is 6 to 7 years old. The average rubber tree reaches its period of highest yield about its fourteenth year. After 20 to 30 years the amount of rubber a tree yields becomes less and less. The Hevea tree must then be replaced.

About 250 trees are grown on a hectare

Rubber trees on a plantation in Malaysia.

(2½ acres) of land. On a high-yielding plantation, a hectare of trees may yield as much as 2,250 kilograms (5,000 pounds) of dry rubber in a year.

On a large plantation, there are millions of rubber trees. The job of collecting and processing latex for shipment involves many steps.

▶COLLECTING LATEX

The first step is to tap the tree. The tappers, as the workers are called, start out at daybreak because latex flows most freely in the coolness of the morning. Using a sharp knife with a curved blade, the tapper cuts a narrow groove in the tree bark about 1.5 meters (5 feet) above the ground. The groove slants down and goes about halfway around the tree. The tapper sticks a V-shaped metal spout in the lower end of the cut and hangs a small cup under the spout.

Once the groove has been cut in the tree, the latex begins to ooze out. Drop by drop it is caught by the spout and flows into the cup. The tapper goes on to the next tree and does the same thing again. In one day the worker

A woman taps a rubber tree by cutting a groove in the trunk of the tree.

A cup catches the milky latex as it oozes from the cut in the tree.

taps about 500 trees. When all these trees are tapped, the tapper makes a second round. At each tree there is about a cupful of latex.

Slung across the tapper's shoulders is a wooden bar from which hang two large pails. The tapper empties each cup of latex into these pails. When the last cup has been emptied, the tapper carries the full pails to the collecting station. By this time the tapper has been working for five or six hours.

On some plantations the trees are tapped every other day. On other plantations, trees are tapped every day for 15 days and then go untapped for 15 days.

When returning to a tree to tap it again, the tapper slices off another thin shaving of bark, slightly below the first groove. This reopens the latex veins. The tapper must be very careful not to cut beyond the bark into the wood itself. Too deep a cut could seriously damage the tree.

Each day's tapping, or slicing of the bark, brings the groove closer to the ground. When the ground is reached on one side of the tree, the tapper begins the process on the other side.

When the second side has been tapped to the ground, enough time has passed for the bark on the other side of the tree to renew itself. It is once again ready for tapping.

▶ PROCESSING THE RUBBER

An important part of operating a rubber plantation is processing the latex so that it can be shipped to manufacturing centers. The latex from the tappers' pails is emptied into tank trucks. The trucks carry the latex to the factory, where the latex can be processed either in liquid form (concentrated latex) or in solid form (crepe, smoked sheet, or block rubber).

If the latex is to remain in liquid form, it is run through centrifuges similar to the separators used on a dairy farm. This removes most of the water. To protect the latex from bacteria and to keep it from coagulating, a preservative such as ammonia is added at various stages from the collection cup through final processing. Liquid latex is shipped all over the world in tanker vessels and drums. Products such as rubber gloves, tubing, balloons, and toys are made by dipping a mold into liquid latex. Some latex is extruded (forced, or pressed) through tiny tubes and coagulated (thickened, or clotted) to make rubber thread. Other important products include adhesives, foam rubber for automobile weather stripping, and cushion backing for carpets.

If processed into a solid form, the latex is first coagulated into a solid mass, with the appearance and consistency of Jell-O. This mass is called coagulum. If crepe or smoked sheet is to be made, the coagulum is passed between rollers that squeeze out most of the water. The remaining water is removed by drying.

In making crepe, the rollers roughen and crinkle the sheets of coagulum. This gives them ridges, like thick crepe paper. The sheets are then hung up to dry in the sun or in a heated room. This type of rubber is used to make crepe-rubber soles for shoes and for many other products, including adhesives and white sidewalls for tires.

To make smoked sheet, the coagulum is passed through rollers that give the sheets a ribbed appearance. The sheets are hung in a hot smokehouse for several days to dry. The smoke colors the rubber and helps to preserve it. When dry, the rubber is pressed into bales weighing 102 kilograms (224 pounds) for shipment. It is used principally in tires.

To make block rubber, the coagulum is formed into small particles like crumbs (in fact, they are known by that name) and then dried. The dried crumb is then pressed into small bales that weigh about 34 kilograms (75 pounds).

▶ SYNTHETIC RUBBER

In 1826, Michael Faraday, the famous English scientist, discovered that rubber is a hydrocarbon—that is, a combination of the elements hydrogen and carbon. This was the beginning of the formal study of the chemistry of rubber.

In 1860 another English scientist, Charles Grenville Williams, found that rubber was composed of a basic material that he called **isoprene**. Each molecule of isoprene was found to contain five atoms of carbon and eight atoms of hydrogen. Chemists write this in a formula as C_5H_8.

Later, chemists learned that rubber is a

Above: A worker examines sheet rubber and sorts it for packaging. Below: These sheets of crepe rubber have been hung on racks to dry.

giant molecule formed by joining together many isoprene molecules. They join together like the links of a chain. When the isoprene molecules link together, they no longer behave as separate molecules. They form a material with entirely different properties. This new material is called a **polymer**, from the Greek *poly* ("many") and *meros* ("part").

Early attempts to produce rubbery materials by synthetically linking together isoprene molecules were not very successful. The resulting rubber was of poor quality and costly to produce. But when supplies of natural rubber from the Far East were cut off from the United States during World War II, chemists made an all-out effort to find ways to make synthetic rubber. A commercially successful process was quickly developed. But this would not have been possible without the knowledge gained over the previous 100 years by chemists studying natural rubber and other polymers.

Today in the United States and Canada, synthetic rubber accounts for about 75 percent of all rubber used. In the world as a whole, it accounts for more than 65 percent of all rubber used.

Some products, such as gaskets, washers, and wire coating, can be made entirely of synthetic rubber. Other products, such as tires used for trucks, airplanes, and earth-moving equipment, are best made almost entirely from natural rubber. Many other products, such as automobile tires, are made of a combination of natural and synthetic rubbers.

There are many different kinds of synthetic rubber. The type produced in the largest quantity is a general purpose rubber called **styrene-butadiene rubber**, or SBR. This rubber is durable and comparatively inexpensive. It is easy to process and is compatible with other tire rubbers. Its two main ingredients are buta-diene and styrene. Butadiene is a gas made from petroleum. Styrene is a liquid made from petroleum or coal.

The original process for making SBR was developed during World War II. It starts as butadiene and styrene are pumped into a large reactor or tank containing a soapy mixture. The soapy solution makes it easier for the rubber particles to form. A catalyst (a chemical that speeds up the reaction) is added. As the mixture in the reactor is stirred, it gradually changes to a milky white liquid. This is synthetic latex. It is very similar in appearance to the natural latex that comes from the rubber tree. When the synthetic latex has developed to a proper state, a chemical is added to stop the reaction. The latex then is pumped into a tank together with acids and brine (salt water). The mixture is stirred to coagulate it. The coagulated pieces of synthetic rubber look like gray crumbs. After being washed to remove any extra chemicals, the synthetic rubber is dried and pressed into bales.

The reactors were at first kept at 50°C (122°F). Some are still kept at this temperature, but scientists discovered that, in general, rubber made at lower temperatures has better wearing qualities. SBR produced at lower temperatures is used in tire treads and other products in which long wear is particularly important.

Basic synthetic rubber can be varied by adding other ingredients or by combining the ingredients in different ways. Many different kinds of synthetic rubber tailored for special uses can be made in this way.

A number of special-purpose synthetic rubbers that can withstand chemicals and harsh conditions have been developed. They are resistant to gasoline, oil, sunlight, ozone, and high temperatures, which can be very harmful to natural rubber and SBR. **Neoprene**, for instance, is a rubber made from acetylene gas and hydrogen chloride. It is used for gasoline hose and to cover electrical wires that come in contact with oil or are exposed to sunlight.

Butyl rubber is made from the gas isobutylene and a small amount of the liquid isoprene. Both ingredients are obtained during petroleum refining. Butyl is much better than any other rubber for holding air. It is used for automobile inner tubes and as a lining for tubeless tires.

Synthetic rubber looks like this when it is being dried.

Nitrile rubber is made of butadiene and acrylonitrile. It is exceptionally resistant to oil and is used for seals, gaskets, fuel hose, and other products that must resist oil.

Specialty rubbers that can withstand very high or extremely low temperatures also have been developed. These include **silicone, fluorocarbon**, and **phosphazene**. These rubbers often are expensive and difficult to produce. But they are vital for parts used in such products as jet engines and pollution-control devices.

The production of **polyurethane rubber** involves a different concept of making the giant molecule needed to get rubberlike properties. An intermediate molecular weight liquid, called a prepolymer, is formed first. Then a chemical is added that rapidly joins the prepolymer molecules together to form the high molecular weight rubber. This technique is especially useful for making soft foam rubber for cushions and mattresses and very large molded rubber items such as automobile body parts.

Most rubbers must be vulcanized, or cured, but some synthetic rubbers have recently been developed that do not require vulcanization. They are called **thermoplastic elastomers**. They flow into a mold at high temperature and retain their shape and elasticity without vulcanization.

▶ MAKING RUBBER PRODUCTS

In manufacturing rubber products, natural rubber and synthetic rubber are treated in much the same way. The bales are cut into small pieces for easier handling. Various ingredients are added to the rubber to give it qualities such as strength and elasticity. Pigments may be added to color the rubber.

Carbon black (a soft, powdery form of carbon) is one of the most important ingredients added to rubber. It makes the rubber tougher and more resistant to abrasion (harsh rubbing). Another important addition is sulfur. Under heat, sulfur combines with the rubber and other chemicals and pigments and causes the vulcanization to take place. Without the proper amount of sulfur, rubber products would be over-cured or under-cured and therefore of inferior quality.

When all the necessary chemicals have been added to the rubber, it is emptied into a Banbury mixer. This operates like a giant dough mixer. After it is thoroughly mixed, the batch goes to a mill, where it is rolled into a sheet about 6 millimeters (¼ inch) thick.

Rubber is made into a finished product by **calendering**, **extrusion**, or **molding**.

A calender is a machine with a series of huge rollers. Its main use is to press rubber into fabric for tires. Another use is to press rubber into a sheet.

Extrusion is the most widely used method of forming rubber products. The soft rubber is pushed out through holes in a metal shaping device called a die. The shaped rubber is squeezed from the die much as toothpaste or shaving cream is squeezed from a tube. Examples of extruded products are inner tubes, tire treads, and rubber strips used as seals around automobile windshields and doors.

In molding, the rubber is placed in a metal form and heated until it has taken on the shape of the mold. Many small products, such as handlebar grips, foot pedals, and mats, are made in this way. Any product made of rubber must be vulcanized, or cured, so that it will keep its molded shape.

Throughout the world, rubber is used mostly for making tires. In the United States and Canada, 64 percent of all the rubber used goes into tires and other rubber parts needed by the transportation industry.

The possibilities for new products and new uses of rubber are limitless. Scientists in the rubber industry are continually developing new kinds of rubber and new uses for it.

▶ RECYCLING RUBBER

Researchers have been trying to develop practical methods of disposing of the millions of worn tires scrapped each year. Some of these tires are ground up, and the rubber is reclaimed for use in new rubber products. Some are used as artificial reefs on ocean bottoms, to provide havens for fish. Still others are ground up and used in asphalt for paving.

Another method of disposing of the tires is to use them as a source of energy. By burning them in specially-designed, pollution-free incinerators, old tires could become a valuable energy resource. But this method is extremely costly. (A synthetic rubber fuel containing an oxygen-rich chemical is used in rockets.)

RICHARD A. RILEY
Firestone Tire & Rubber Company

RUBBINGS

Have you ever put a piece of paper on top of a coin and then rubbed a pencil over it until the pattern of the coin appeared? That is a very simple form of rubbing. Rubbing is an easy way to reproduce many designs and textures—even very complicated ones.

You can rub all kinds of things, from small coins to large wall carvings, manhole and sewer covers, and even stained-glass windows. In the United States old gravestones are often good subjects. The stones in New England graveyards are especially popular because of their interesting designs. In Britain the floors of churches are often set with brass plaques, some of which date back to medieval times. Many plaques mark the graves of important people. People enjoy doing rubbings of these plaques, with their designs of knights and ladies or religious subjects.

Rubbing is an exciting way to learn about history and architecture. It may help you to notice things in your town that you never noticed before. It is also a way to preserve, on paper, images of things that may one day be destroyed or worn away. Frame your rubbings and hang them on your walls, or use them as patterns for needlepoint, block printing, and other crafts.

There are two basic rubbing techniques.

The wax method is used for rubbing flat surfaces or surfaces with designs carved into them. The graphite method is used on surfaces with raised designs.

▶ THE WAX METHOD

To do a rubbing with this method, first decide what you want to rub and get all your materials together. You will need a sheet of paper large enough to cover your subject. The paper should be fairly strong but not too thick. Brown wrapping paper, newsprint, and rice paper are all good. You will also need masking tape, scissors, a natural-bristle brush, and a crayon. Special rubbing wax is available in some art-supply stores. It is less likely to smear than crayons.

Go over your subject with the brush so that it is cleaned of dirt. (Never use a metal-bristle brush, as the bristles may damage the object.) Cut your paper to a size that will completely cover the design you want to rub. Then tape it down securely at the edges. Next, rub the colored wax or crayon lightly over the entire surface of the paper to block in the design. Feel around on the paper with your fingers to make sure you have covered all parts of the design. When you can see the whole design, decide where you want to darken the rubbing. If you press harder with the wax, the rubbing will become darker, and more details will show up.

To do a rubbing by the wax method, first get all your materials together. Use a natural-bristle brush to clean dust and dirt from the object you plan to rub.

The paper you use should be strong but not too thick. Cut the paper to a size that will completely cover the design, and then tape it down securely at the edges.

Continue rubbing until you think you have all the details you want. To see if you have missed any, you can peek beneath the paper by lifting one section of tape. But make sure that the rest of the tape is tightly attached. Never lift the paper all the way off—it will be impossible to put it back exactly the way it was. When your rubbing is finished, gently remove the tape by peeling it toward the edges of the paper.

For a different effect, try metallic or white wax on black paper. Fabric may be used instead of paper, but you will need special fabric-dying crayons.

▶ THE GRAPHITE METHOD

In this method, rubbing is done with a paste of mineral oil and graphite. (Graphite is the soft, black carbon that is used in pencils.) Working with graphite is messy. You should wear old clothes and use utensils that can be thrown away. Cover your work area with newspapers or a plastic drop cloth.

You can buy mineral oil at a drugstore and powdered graphite at an art-supply or a hardware store. Find an old but clean can and a mixing stick. Put some graphite in the can and slowly stir in mineral oil until the mixture is thick and pasty, like canned shoe polish. If the mixture gets too thin, add more graphite. Store the mixture in a covered plastic bowl to keep it from drying out.

Rub crayon or colored wax over the entire surface to block in the design. Then darken the rubbing and bring up details by going over it with the crayon again.

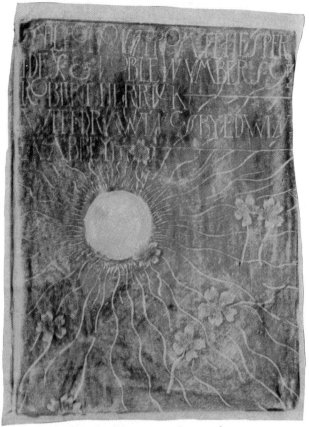

The finished rubbing. Different colors of wax and crayon have been used to highlight the design.

You will also need scissors, masking tape, a natural-bristle brush, two small pieces of cloth, a spray bottle filled with water, and paper. The paper must be strong when it is wet, like the paper used in tea bags. Paper made with hemp or some other fiber is good.

To begin, brush the object clean, and tape the paper loosely but securely over it. Use the spray bottle to dampen the paper, but do not soak it. The idea is to soften the paper so that it will mold to the design underneath. Now wrap one of the small cloths around your finger, and dip it into the graphite mixture. Wipe most of the mixture off onto the second cloth. This will remove large clumps of graphite that might smear and spoil your rubbing. With the first cloth, apply the graphite to the dampened paper, blocking in the design lightly. Darken areas of the rubbing by going over them again in the same way. When the rubbing is completed, gently remove the tape by pulling it toward the edge of the paper.

CECILY BARTH FIRESTEIN
Author, *Rubbing Craft*

RUBENS, PETER PAUL (1577–1640)

The Flemish painter Peter Paul Rubens was one of the greatest artists of northern Europe. He was also an honored scholar and a respected diplomat.

Rubens was born on June 28, 1577, in Siegen, Germany. After his father died, his mother returned with her family to her native Antwerp in Flanders (now part of Belgium). Rubens was apprenticed at the age of 14 to an artist in the city. From 1600 until 1608, he lived in Italy as court painter to the Duke of Mantua. There he fell under the influence of such Italian masters as Titian, Michelangelo, and Caravaggio.

On his return to Antwerp in 1608, Rubens was appointed court painter to the Spanish governor of Flanders. In 1609, he married Isabella Brant.

Rubens was in great demand by the leading rulers of Europe. He decorated churches and palaces and painted countless portraits, landscapes, and events in classical mythology. He had to employ many assistants to complete his numerous commissions. Rubens was known above all for the brilliant color of his works. Even today we admire the robust, pink-cheeked beauty of the women he painted.

After his wife died in 1626, Rubens entered the diplomatic service. He went on several missions to Holland and England. On his return to Antwerp in 1630, Rubens mar-

Hélène Fourment and Her Children, by Peter Paul Rubens.

ried the young and beautiful Hélène Fourment—the subject of many of his later and gentler paintings. He died in Antwerp on May 30, 1640, at the height of his popularity.

Reviewed by ARIANE RUSKIN BATTERBERRY
Author, *The Pantheon Story of Art for
Young People*

RUGBY

Rugby is an outgrowth of a kicking game that was originally called football. Rugby rules allow players to advance the ball by either kicking or carrying it. Lateral—but no forward—passing is permitted. A player carrying the ball may be tackled, as in American and Canadian football.

In 1823, William Webb Ellis, a student at the Rugby School, England, picked up the ball during a soccer game and ran with it. Students at other schools heard of Ellis' mistake and developed a new game that allowed players to carry the ball. This new game was called "the Rugby game."

Some athletes preferred the old rules. In 1863, they formed the London Football Association and called their game Association Football. Later it was called soccer.

Rugby players discovered that their rules varied. In 1871, representatives from 20 teams met in London and formed the Rugby Union. They made game rules that have changed little since.

There are 15 players on a team. Eight are forwards and seven are backs. The forwards usually are the biggest and strongest players. Their main job is to control the ball with their feet and dribble it forward. Or, in a formal scrummage, they attempt to pass the ball back to their own halfback.

A player fights his way out of a dangerous position in front of his own goalposts.

The Scrummage

A formal scrum, or scrummage, is called by the referee after a minor rule infraction. It is a little like a scrimmage in American football. The forward players of both teams line up opposite each other, parallel to the goal lines. They are usually in a 3-2-3 or 3-4-1 formation. All are bent down from the waist. The front rows of each team are in shoulder-to-shoulder contact. Their teammates are braced together behind them. When the ball is tossed into the scrum, between the front rows of each team, the players surge forward. Their object is to gain possession of the ball, either by pushing the other team away from it or by feeding it back with their feet through the scrum to a halfback. No one may touch the ball with his hands until it is clear of the scrum.

Scoring

There are two basic ways to score. One,

called a **try**, is like a touchdown in American football and counts 4 points. To score a try, a player must carry the ball into the other team's in-goal area and touch it to the ground before being tackled. If the player does not touch the ball to the ground, no try is scored. After a try, the scoring team attempts a **conversion**. This is a placekick or a dropkick from a spot directly opposite the point where the ball was grounded. The ball, when kicked, must pass between the uprights and over the crossbar of the goalposts, as in American football. A successful conversion adds 2 points to the try, for a total of 6.

All other kicked goals count 3 points. A player on the attack may drop-kick a goal. Goals also may be made on penalty kicks and awarded after rules violations.

A fair catch is made when a player catches the ball directly from an opponent's kick while in a stationary position. The player may then call for a scrummage or take a free kick. The

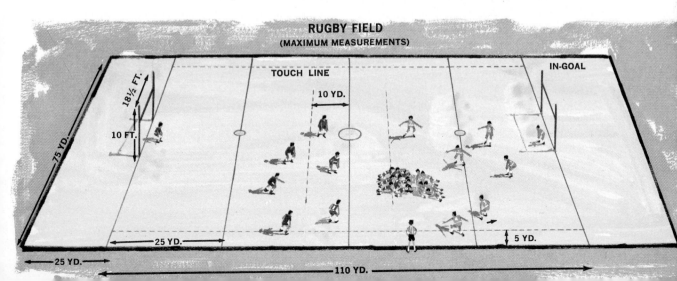

RUGBY FIELD
(MAXIMUM MEASUREMENTS)

free kick may be simply a downfield punt, or it may be a dropkick or placekick. It may not be kicked for points.

Equipment

The rugby ball is oval. It is leather and is inflated with a rubber bladder. The ball is rounder at the ends and thicker in the middle than the American football.

The players wear light uniforms—shorts and jerseys—and cleated leather shoes. Hard protective equipment, which could injure another player, is illegal.

The Game

A rugby match consists of two 40-minute halves. Time out is permitted in case of serious injury. But the injured player must resume play or leave the field within 1 minute. No substitutions are allowed.

The game is started by a kickoff from midfield, somewhat as in American football. A kickoff is also used to continue play after scores and at the start of the second half.

Play is interrupted only for violations and out-of-bounds. When the ball crosses a touch line, it is said to be "in touch," which means out-of-bounds. It is returned to play by a **line-out** where it crossed the touch line. In a line-out the forwards of both teams form two rows at right angles to the touch line. The ball is thrown in by a member of the team that did not send the ball into touch. It must go at least 5 meters (5½ yards) before it is considered in play.

Players must stay behind the ball when a teammate of theirs is controlling it. If they are ahead of the ball, they are offside and may not participate in the play until they return to onside position.

Rugby is a game of continuous action. A player who is tackled must release the ball immediately.

Speed, stamina, and quick thinking are the assets of a good rugby, or "rugger," player. There is little individual stardom. The best players are those who work best for the team.

ROBERT L. ("DINK") TEMPLETON
Member, 1920 United States
Olympic Rugby Team

Reviewed by NEIL SORBIE
Executive Director
Ontario Rugby Union

RUGS AND CARPETS

Rugs and carpets are heavy fabrics used to cover floors. The first rugs were made long before recorded history. People probably began weaving rugs by hand from animal hair and wool to protect themselves from the damp floors of their primitive homes. By the time of the early Babylonians and Egyptians, rug weaving was an established craft.

For many centuries only a very rich person could afford a rug. The rugs had to be woven by hand, and hours of skilled labor went into each rug. Today rugs and carpets are made on machines that rapidly turn out a wide variety of **floor coverings**. As a result, rugs and carpets can be sold at a price that most people can afford.

Carpets have been prized through the ages for many reasons. They are decorative and are comfortable underfoot. They help seal out cold drafts and cut down noise. Carpets also provide safety. People cannot slip on a carpet as they can on a polished floor. If a person does fall, the soft carpet acts as a cushion.

Many rugs are considered valuable works of art because of their beautiful colors, textures, and patterns. In some countries they are hung on the walls. Nomadic tribes of the Middle East use rugs as beds, as tent flaps, and as saddles for their camels and horses.

▶HISTORY OF RUGS AND CARPETS

Amazingly enough, the basic steps of weaving have not changed much since primitive people first wove carpets. Vertical strands of yarn, called the **warp**, are first strung on a rectangular frame called a **loom**. Other strands of yarn, called the **weft**, are passed under one warp thread and over the next across the loom. This weaving method creates a simple rug or carpet fabric known as a **flat fabric**.

Threading the weft yarn over and under warp yarn by hand is very time-consuming. Early weavers wound the weft yarn on a piece of wood, which they passed over and under the warp threads. The piece of wood is known as the **shuttle** and is shaped like a toy boat. Another early invention was the **weave shed**. The weave shed is created by raising alternate sets of warp yarns so that the shuttle can be quickly passed across the loom.

As early as 2000 B.C. rug makers had learned how to work in another layer of yarns, called the **pile**. Pile adds thickness and durability to a carpet. In rugs woven on a hand-loom, the pile is made by taking several strands of yarn and knotting them around one or two warp threads. The strands of yarn are cut, and the weft yarn is inserted and pulled tightly against the pile knots to hold them in place. The protruding ends of the knots are called **tufts**. The number of knots and the length of the tufts determine the quality of the rug.

Rugs were made by these painstaking methods for thousands of years. Throughout the Middle East and in India, whole villages made their living by the slow, laborious creation of luxurious rugs. The yarn for the rugs was dyed in beautiful colors and woven into elaborate patterns. Each pile knot was tied by hand, and the value of the rug was judged by the number of knots. Some rugs contained more than 60 knots per square centimeter (400 knots per square inch).

Crusaders returning from the religious wars brought rugs and other rich possessions of the East into medieval Europe. The rugs added welcome color and warmth to the cold stone floors and walls of European castles. Because these rugs came from the East, they were called Oriental rugs.

European artisans developed a rug-weaving style, too. They wove patterned rugs for the few nobles who were rich enough to afford these intricately designed floor coverings. By the 16th century, Europe's center of weaving was the city of Brussels.

Many of the weavers were Protestants. As the 16th century progressed, these weavers were forced to flee from Brussels because of their religious beliefs. Many weavers settled in France until the French Government also tried to stamp out Protestantism. Some of the weavers finally found a safe refuge in England, where they helped establish a highly skilled carpet-weaving trade.

But France remained a very important center of weaving, too. Under the direction of Louis XIV's finance minister, Jean Baptiste Colbert (1619–83), expert weavers were gathered together in state-operated workshops. For the next 300 years beautiful rugs and tapestries were woven at the Gobelins workshop in Paris and in the towns of Aubus-

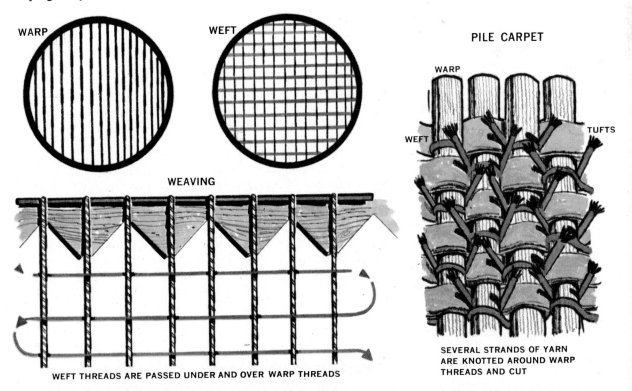

WARP

WEFT

PILE CARPET

WARP

WEFT

TUFTS

WEAVING

WEFT THREADS ARE PASSED UNDER AND OVER WARP THREADS

SEVERAL STRANDS OF YARN ARE KNOTTED AROUND WARP THREADS AND CUT

son and Beauvais. Each workshop developed its own style of weaving.

These rugs were woven on huge looms known as **draw looms**. For each part of the pattern, different sets of warp threads had to be raised. An assistant known as a drawboy studied a chart of the pattern and then pulled the master cords that raised the proper warp yarns. Not only was this a difficult and lengthy process, but the drawboy could easily ruin the pattern by pulling the wrong cord. The mistake in the design would not be seen until the pattern began to take shape.

During the 18th century various artisans worked on a mechanism that would set the pattern threads automatically. Eventually a system was developed that worked somewhat like a player piano. The master cords were attached to needles that moved across a card. The card had the pattern outlined in tiny holes. When a needle reached a pattern hole, it dropped in and held the right warp yarn ready for the drawboy.

In 1801, a French weaver, J. M. Jacquard (1752–1834), invented an automatic mechanism for pulling the pattern cords. Jacquard's device combined many of the features of the card-and-needle system. But Jacquard's cord-selecting system could be worked directly from the loom. The Jacquard loom used for weaving patterns today is based on the French weaver's invention.

The Development of Power Looms

England was the center of mass-produced carpets from about the middle of the 18th century through the middle of the 19th. Towns such as Wilton, Kidderminster, and Axminster turned out rugs in such quantities that the names of the towns were given to the different weaving techniques developed there. But even though carpetmaking was a growing industry, the looms were still powered by hand.

The great revolution in carpetmaking occurred in the United States when Erastus Brigham Bigelow (1814–79) invented the first power loom for carpets in 1839. Power looms did away with hours of painstaking work by hand. The industry rapidly became mechanized, and the United States took the lead in carpet production. Each year more than 840,000,000 square meters (1,000,000,000

What is the difference between a rug and a carpet?

The words "rug" and "carpet" are generally used to describe a covering for the floor. But in recent years the word "carpet" has come to mean fabric that covers the whole floor in a room and is fastened to the floor, as in wall-to-wall carpeting. The term "rug" generally refers to a fabric that is not fastened to the floor and does not cover the entire floor. Rugs come in precut shapes and sizes. Rugs can be rectangular, circular, oval, or free-form. Carpeting comes in huge rolls. The amount a customer wants is cut from the roll and trimmed to fit a specific room.

---

square yards) of carpet are manufactured in mills in the United States.

▶ MANUFACTURE OF CARPETS AND RUGS TODAY

There are three basic methods used to manufacture carpets and rugs. They are weaving, tufting, and knitting.

Weaving

Most woven carpets have pile on the face. Warp and weft yarns, usually made of jute or cotton, form the structural foundation for the pile yarns. (Jute is a fiber used in making burlap.) The warp and weft yarns are called **backing yarns**, since they are on the back of the carpet and thus are hidden from sight when the carpet is laid on the floor.

Velvet Loom. The velvet loom is the least complex of the specialized weaving equipment used for making carpets. The loom is very similar to Bigelow's original power loom. The pile yarns are lifted over **wires**, which are strips of steel mechanically inserted in the loom. The wires form the pile yarns into loops. Some of these wires may have sharp knives at their ends. The knives cut the pile yarns into what is known as **plush**, or **cut-pile**, fabric. Velvet carpets are usually solid colored, but the texture of the yarn may vary.

Looms for Pattern Carpets. Carpets with a pattern in them may be made on either Wilton or Axminster looms. These looms are named after the towns where the carpets were first made.

Wilton carpets are woven on velvet power looms that have been adapted to the Jacquard system. A series of cards punched with holes automatically regulates the feeding of two to five different-colored yarns to form the pattern in the carpet. In Wilton carpets the pile is very thick and is often made in different heights, which gives the appearance of a carved design in the rug.

The **Axminster** loom is used for carpets with complex designs in many colors. The Axminster loom does mechanically what a weaver making an Oriental carpet does by hand. Each tuft of yarn for the pile is inserted separately into the carpet by the loom. Carpets from these looms have floral, geometric, scroll, leaf, and many other intricate patterns. Some of these designs may contain as many as 100 different-colored yarns.

Tufting

Tufting is a high-speed method of carpet manufacturing that originated in the United States in the 1920's. Today's machines are like huge sewing machines and use hundreds of fast-moving needles to punch the pile yarns through the backing fabric. The pile yarns are anchored to the backing by coating liquid latex on the carpet back.

The tufting process was at first used mainly for manufacturing solid-color or **tweed** carpeting. Tweed carpets are made from two or more different-colored yarns. Now carpets of many different colors and textures can be made with the tufting process. Detailed patterns, also, can be created in tufted carpets by inserting colored yarns in the carpet with a hand-tufting machine. This process is known as **overtufting**.

Tufted carpets can be produced at lower

Rugs of different countries and periods show a wide variety of design. (1) 19th-century hooked rug from Vermont. (2) Chinese rug of the K'ang-hsi period (1662-1722). (3) 16th-century Persian rug. (4) 15th-century Spanish rug. (5) Contemporary Danish rug. (6) Modern American carpet with sculptured pile.

cost than woven carpets because they can be made more quickly and fewer people are needed to work the machinery. The tufting industry has grown so rapidly that it now accounts for more than 95 percent of the total amount of carpet made in the United States. Tufting also has increased in Canada, the United Kingdom, and West Germany.

Knitting

The knitting of carpets was developed commercially in the United States in 1951. Three sets of needles loop together the backing yarn, stitching yarn, and pile yarn in much the same way that hand knitting is done. Hundreds of fast-moving knitting needles are used on specialized machinery that can turn carpet at a fairly fast rate. Carpets are knitted in solid colors or tweed blends. Different textures are made by varying the pile height and combining cut and uncut yarns.

Handmade Rugs

Although the power loom has replaced the handloom for mass-produced rugs and carpets, the ancient craft of hand weaving still continues. Among the most beautiful are the Oriental rugs made in Iran, India, Egypt and other Arab countries, the southern part of the Soviet Union, and China.

An important characteristic of handwoven rugs is the wealth of pattern and color they contain. Since each tuft of yarn is added by hand, weavers can use as many colors as they wish to make a design.

Two other methods are also used in handmade rugs—hooking and braiding. For a hooked rug, a piece of sheet or heavier material is used as a backing fabric. Then a hook is used to pull pieces of colored fabric or yarn through the backing. For a braided rug, long pieces of fabric are braided into long cords. The cords are then coiled into spirals or ovals and sewn together to make the rug.

▶ MATERIALS USED IN RUGS AND CARPETS

Wool has long been the most important natural fiber used in carpets and rugs. In some countries, linen has been a rug material. And the Chinese even made expensive and delicate rugs out of silk. Cotton was once popular for making inexpensive rugs.

The wool used in carpets is very different from the soft, fine wool used for clothes. Carpet wool must be strong, springy, and coarse. Wool for rugs and carpets comes from sheep raised in countries where the climate is severe and the countryside rugged. Major producers of carpet wools include New Zealand, Argentina, India, Pakistan, Iraq, Syria, Scotland, and Ireland.

The wools are first scoured and washed to remove grease, dirt, and other impurities. Different kinds of wool are blended together so that the special characteristics of each are used to their best advantage. It is not uncommon for the pile yarns in a carpet to be made from wools grown in as many as five different countries.

In the United States, most carpets and rugs have face yarns made from synthetic fibers. These made their appearance in the late 1940's. Their use has grown until today they represent nearly 99 percent of the fibers used for face yarns. Nylon, polyester, acrylic, and polypropylene fibers are the main synthetics used. Each has definite characteristics. Special properties—such as resistance to soil, static electricity, and fire—can also be built into them.

Both natural and synthetic fibers are colored with dyes that resist fading. For handmade Oriental rugs the dyes are taken from herbs such as turmeric and shrubs such as sumac and henna. Many dye formulas have become the closely guarded secrets of families, tribes, or villages.

After dyeing, the fibers are combed into straight rows. Modern carpet factories use a carding machine. Hand weavers use an instrument much like a haircomb. The combed fibers are then spun into yarn. Spinning is done by tightly twisting the loose fibers into strong yarns on special machinery.

Sometimes the fibers are first spun into yarn and then dyed. Manufacturers of tufted carpets often prefer to dye the carpet after it is completed. This is called piece dyeing. In addition, some manufacturers have perfected a method of printing a pattern of varied colors on a finished carpet.

RICHARD NED HOPPER
Carpet and Rug Institute

See also TAPESTRY.

RULES OF ORDER. See PARLIAMENTARY PROCEDURE.

RUMANIA

Rumania is on the Balkan Peninsula, in southeastern Europe. It was first settled more than 2,000 years ago by an ancient people called Dacians. Since then the size of Rumania has changed many times as a result of repeated invasions, foreign occupations, and wars. From the late 1300's until the mid-1800's, the country consisted of two principalities—Moldavia and Walachia. In 1859 these two principalities were united under the name Rumania. In addition to Moldavia and Walachia, Rumania today includes the regions of Banat, Transylvania, Bukovina, and Dobruja.

▶ THE PEOPLE

Most of the Rumanian people are descendants of the Roman colonists who overthrew the ancient Dacians. There are small Hungarian and German minorities.

The language of Rumania is a Romance language like French, Italian, Spanish, and Portuguese. The Slavic languages spoken by Yugoslavs, Bulgarians, and Russians have contributed many words. But Rumanian grammar is based almost completely on Latin.

Education

Before World War II, French influence was very strong in Rumania. This was reflected in the school system. As in France, some young people attended *lycées* (high schools). Graduation from a *lycée* and the passing of an examination were required for entrance to a university. But very few young Rumanians attended *lycées*.

Since the Communist government revised the educational system in 1948, the number of young people receiving high school education has increased. Many technical or vocational schools have been established. But the importance of the *lycée* in preparing students for university training has continued. Rumania has a number of universities. The majority of the students receive scholarships.

Religion

After 1945 the Communist government insisted on controlling the clergy of Rumania's

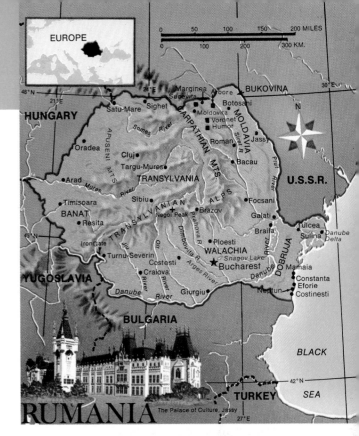

The Palace of Culture, Jassy

churches as closely as possible. The government pays the salaries of the clergy and provides funds for upkeep of the churches. The Eastern Catholic Church was abolished by the government in 1948. Its property was transferred to the Orthodox Church. As a result, most people belong to the Rumanian Orthodox Church. The Hungarian and German minorities are mainly Protestant.

▶ THE LAND

The Banat region is located in the southwestern corner of the country, bordering Yugoslavia and Hungary. This small region is mainly a flat, fertile plain.

Transylvania occupies an elevated plateau surrounded by mountains in the center of the country. The cool climate of Transylvania and its mineral and forest resources make it one of the richest areas in the country.

Bukovina, to the northeast of Transylvania, has forests and mountains in its northern section. It slopes down to a lowland in the south. Moldavia, in the northeast, contains high mountains and fertile plains.

The plains region of Walachia, bordering the Danube River, covers a large part of southern Rumania. Dobruja, on the Black

Sea coast, consists chiefly of marshy plains and hilly lowlands. The Danube River plain, or delta, is in this region. The delta is formed where the Danube turns northward at the Bulgarian border and divides into three arms. The Danube delta is a refuge for unusual birds, such as the white pelican.

Rivers

The Danube River is Rumania's most important waterway. Along part of its course, the Danube marks the boundaries between Rumania, Yugoslavia, and Bulgaria. Some of the most fertile soils in Europe are in the valley of the Danube.

Except for its northern tributary, the Prut, the Danube is the only navigable river in Rumania. Other tributaries of the Danube are the Mures, the Jiu, the Olt, the Somes, and the Siret.

There are a few natural harbors along the Black Sea coast. But most of the shoreline consists of crumbling cliffs and salty marshlands.

The Carpathian Mountains and the Transylvanian Alps (the southwestern extension of the Carpathian chain) stretch across central Rumania in the shape of a jagged triangle. Negoi Peak, in the Fagaras Mountains of the Transylvanian Alps, is the highest mountain in Rumania.

The mountain village of Cuneni in Transylvania.

Climate

Rumania is a land of great extremes of climate—very hot summers and windy, bitterly cold winters. The average January temperature in Bucharest, the capital, is about –13°C (9°F). In July it is about 23°C (73°F). Rainfall is moderate, and most of the rains come in May. During the months of July and August there are often periods of severe drought.

Natural Resources

Along with its fertile soil and forests, Rumania has a number of other valuable natural resources. The nation's once-vast petroleum reserves are declining, but exploration is being made for deposits off the coast in the Black Sea. There are also large known reserves of natural gas. Other mineral resources include coal, iron ore, salt, copper, manganese, uranium, lead, bauxite (aluminum ore), and gold. Deposits of these minerals are scattered throughout the mountainous regions of the country.

FACTS AND FIGURES

SOCIALIST REPUBLIC OF RUMANIA is the official name of the country.

CAPITAL: Bucharest.

LOCATION: Southeastern Europe. **Latitude**—43° 37′ N to 48° 16′ N. **Longitude**—20° 15′ E to 29° 42′ E.

PHYSICAL FEATURES: Area—237,500 km² (91,700 sq mi). **Highest point**—Negoi Peak, 2,548 m (8,361 ft). **Chief rivers**—Danube, Mures, Somes, Olt, Siret, Jiu, Prut. **Chief mountain ranges**—Carpathian Mountains, Transylvanian Alps, Apuseni Mountains, Banat Mountains.

POPULATION: 22,000,000 (estimate).

LANGUAGE: Rumanian.

GOVERNMENT: Communist republic. **Head of state**—president of the State Council. **Head of government**—premier. **International co-operation**—United Nations, Council for Mutual Economic Assistance (COMECON), Warsaw Pact.

NATIONAL ANTHEM: *Te Slavim Rominie* ("We Praise Thee, Fatherland Rumania").

ECONOMY: Agricultural products—corn, wheat, oats, barley, rye, vegetables, grapes, flax, hemp, sugar beets, livestock. **Industries and products**—petroleum refining, petrochemicals, fertilizers, iron and steel products, heavy machinery, locomotives, tractors, electrical equipment, clothing, shoes, food, textiles, lumber, furniture. **Chief minerals**—petroleum, natural gas, coal, iron ore, salt, copper, manganese, uranium, lead, bauxite, gold. **Chief exports**—tractors, machinery, furniture, electrical equipment, petrochemicals. **Chief imports**—electrical equipment, machinery, vehicles. **Monetary unit**—leu.

THE ECONOMY

Since World War II, emphasis has been placed on developing Rumania's mineral resources and heavy industry. But agriculture still plays an important part in the country's economy, and it employs a considerable percentage of the work force.

Corn and wheat are Rumania's big crops, and the country ranks as one of the world's leading corn-producing nations. Other crops include vegetables, oats, barley, rye, fruits, flax, and hemp. Sheep and cattle are the most important livestock. Pigs are also raised, chiefly in the Banat region.

When the Communist government came to power, the land was taken from the big landowners. Part of it was divided among poor farm workers. But the major part (about 90 percent) was taken over by the state. There are state farms, which are owned by the government, and collective farms, or agricultural co-operatives, in which the farmers pool their land and equipment. The collective farms also are controlled by the state.

Oil refining and the manufacture of petrochemicals and chemical fertilizers have become important industries. But Rumania now imports oil for use in the petrochemical industry. Other industries include the manufacture of steel; heavy machinery for use in the mining, chemical, and construction industries; tractors and other agricultural machinery; locomotives; iron and steel products; and electrical products. Food processing and the manufacture of textiles, clothing, and shoes are also of major importance to the economy of Rumania.

The mining of iron and coal and the extraction of petroleum and natural gas are leading industries. Rumania's forests provide timber for a growing lumber industry, and furniture has become a leading export. An increase in the generation of electrical power has made further industrialization possible.

CITIES

Bucharest is the capital and largest city in Rumania. With a population of over 1,500,000, it is the commercial, industrial, and cultural center of the country. Before World War II, Bucharest was known as the Paris of the Balkins—a city of glittering palaces, hotels, cafés, and theaters. It remains a

The Iron Gate, a narrow gorge on the Danube River, is the site of a Rumanian hydroelectric plant.

lovely city today, but the luxury for which it was noted is past.

Cluj is the second largest city in Rumania. It is the capital of Transylvania, which was part of Hungary until the region became part of Rumania after World War I. More than 50 percent of the people of Cluj are of Hungarian descent. Cluj is a major industrial and cultural center. Because of its location in the foothills of the Apuseni Mountains, it is a popular winter sports resort. The fruits and wines from the countryside around the city are among the best in Rumania.

Constanta, on the Black Sea, is Rumania's chief seaport. It is also the commercial center of the Dobruja region and the country's leading seaside resort. Eforie and Mamaia, small towns near Constanta, are also popular seaside resorts.

Jassy, the leading city in Moldavia, is an old cultural center. It is famous for its university, Rumania's oldest, and for its academies of art, music, and drama.

GOVERNMENT

Rumania is controlled by the Rumanian Communist Party. The State Council is the country's highest executive body, and the president of the State Council is the head of state. The premier heads the government. The Grand National Assembly is the legisla-

A government housing project in Bucharest.

tive body of the government. The Assembly is a one-house legislature whose members serve 4-year terms.

The Assembly, however, meets only twice a year. In between these brief sessions the legislative power is in the hands of the State Council. The Grand National Assembly chooses the State Council, which has executive power and administers government policy.

▶HISTORY

In the 2nd century, Roman legions under the Emperor Trajan (52–117) conquered and settled in the region called Dacia, northeast of the Danube River. The language and customs of Rome took root, and Dacia became one of the most prosperous provinces of the Roman Empire. Toward the end of the 3rd century, when the Roman Empire began to break up, Dacia was overrun by barbarian invaders—Goths, Huns, and Slavs. Beginning in the 9th century the Magyars began swarming eastward across the Carpathian Mountains and conquered Transylvania. This territory was then fought over by the Hungarians and the Rumanians.

Until the 19th century the country that is now Rumania consisted of two provinces, or principalities. These were Walachia and Moldavia (including the region of Bessarabia). By the end of the 16th century the Turks ruled both principalities, and by the 18th century Turkish influence had grown so strong that the Turks started sending trusted Greek merchants, called Phanariotes, to take care of the business matters of the principalities. While the Phanariotes grew rich, the people of the principalities were left in poverty.

The Turks began battling the Russians for power in the Balkans during the 19th century. In 1858 Walachia and Moldavia won some degree of independence from Turkey. Alexandru Ioan Cuza (1820–73), a leading boyar (landowner), was elected prince of Moldavia and Walachia. Cuza united the two provinces under the name of Rumania in 1859. During his reign Cuza made it easier for the peasants to own land.

In 1866 Cuza was forced to abdicate and the Rumanian Government chose a German prince to rule. He was Charles of Hohenzollern-Sigmaringen (1839–1914), who became King Carol I. Complete freedom from Turkish control was formally won at the end of the Russo-Turkish war, 1877–78. But the Rumanian Government was not strong. Bessarabia had been ceded to Russia in exchange for the much less desirable territory of Dobruja. Carol I played an important role in transforming the newly independent Rumania into a strong nation. Industries were established and railroads were built. Most of the power, however, still remained in the hands of the great landowners. In 1907 the peasants revolted. The government brutally slaughtered thousands who took part in the revolt.

In World War I, Rumania joined the Allies (France, Great Britain, Italy, Russia, and the United States) against the Central Powers (Germany, Austria-Hungary, and Turkey). When the Allies won in 1918, Rumania received Transylvania from Austria-Hungary and Bessarabia from Russia. The nation was twice its former size, and its population had doubled.

But the new territories were not a complete blessing. The state found it difficult to govern so many non-Rumanian minorities. In addition, by 1930 Rumania was affected by the worldwide Depression. King Carol II

Square of the Republic, in Bucharest, was formerly the Square of the Royal Palace.

(1893–1953) was crowned in 1930, but his reign was marked by continuous intrigues and misunderstandings between himself and the two leading political parties. An organization called the Iron Guard grew up. The Iron Guard had strong sympathies with Nazi Germany and Fascist Italy. The years leading up to World War II were marred by violence and disorder. In 1940 the Soviet Union, with Germany's agreement, occupied Bessarabia and northern Bukovina. Rumania lost northern Transylvania to Hungary and part of South Dobruja to Bulgaria. King Carol II was forced to abdicate in favor of his young son, Michael (1921–   ). In the meantime Rumania had become a German ally, and the

Mamaia, a popular beach resort on the Black Sea, attracts vacationers from all over Rumania.

real ruler of the state was General Ion Antonescu (1882–1946).

In June, 1941, Rumania entered the war as an ally of Germany and attacked the Soviet Union. In August, 1944, the Soviet armies advanced toward Jassy. King Michael switched Rumania to the side of the Allies, and he declared war against Nazi Germany. But the Soviet Union occupied and seized control of Rumania.

The first government established after World War II included some members of the Communist Party. The Communists refused to co-operate with the other political parties. Backed by the Soviet Army, the Communists overwhelmed all opposition in the 1946 elections. Prominent anti-Communists were sentenced to prison, and Michael was forced to abdicate in 1947. In 1952, Gheorghe Gheorghiu-Dej, head of the Communist Party in Rumania, became chief of state. He held that position until his death in 1965. His successor as party leader was Nicolae Ceaușescu. In 1967, Ceaușescu became president of the State Council and thus chief of state. In 1974, he was elected president of the republic.

Under Ceaușescu, Rumania has often acted independently of other Communist-bloc countries in its domestic affairs and its foreign relations. But it remains an ally of the Soviet Union, and the Communist Party controls the economic and political life of the country. Rumania faces economic problems because of poor harvests, declining oil production, and inefficient management. The standard of living is lower than in most European countries.

JAMES CHACE
Managing Editor, *Foreign Affairs*

RUSSELL, BERTRAND (1872–1970)

In 1918, Bertrand Russell wrote, ''I want to stand at the rim of the world and peer into the darkness beyond, and see a little more than others have seen. . . . I want to bring back into the world of men some little bit of new wisdom.''

Bertrand Arthur William Russell was born on May 18, 1872, in Trelleck, Wales. Before he was 4, both his parents died, and he and his elder brother went to live with their grandparents. When his brother died in 1931, Bertrand inherited the title 3rd Earl Russell.

Bertrand was tutored at home until he entered Trinity College, Cambridge, in 1890. He had been a shy, silent boy, but at Cambridge he became a great talker. He questioned everything. After three years of mathematics he decided that what he was being taught was full of errors. He sold his mathematics books and turned to philosophy.

In 1894, he married Alys Pearsall Smith, the first of his four wives. His first book, *German Social Democracy* (1896), was written after a trip to Germany. In *The Principles of Mathematics* (1903) he outlined a theory connecting mathematics and logic. He demonstrated this theory in *Principia Mathematica* (1910–13), a three-volume work written with Alfred North Whitehead. Besides writing books and philosophical articles, Russell found time for politics and social problems. He also lectured at Cambridge and Harvard.

In 1918, Russell was jailed for criticizing the United States Army in a newspaper article. He spent his time in prison writing *Introduction to Mathematical Philosophy* (1919). After visiting the Soviet Union and China, he wrote *The Practice and Theory of Bolshevism* (1920) and *The Problem of China* (1922). *A History of Western Philosophy* (1945) was based on lectures he gave in the United States.

Russell's beliefs are stated in *Human Knowledge: Its Scope and Limits* (1948). In 1950, he received the Nobel prize for literature. In later years he led demonstrations against the nuclear bomb. *The Autobiography of Bertrand Russell* was published in three volumes in 1967–69. Russell died on February 2, 1970, in his native Wales.

Reviewed by HOWARD OZMON
Author, *Twelve Great Philosophers*

RUSSIA. See UNION OF SOVIET SOCIALIST REPUBLICS.
RUSSIAN ART AND ARCHITECTURE. See UNION OF SOVIET SOCIALIST REPUBLICS.
RUSSIAN LANGUAGE AND LITERATURE. See UNION OF SOVIET SOCIALIST REPUBLICS.
RUSSIAN MUSIC. See UNION OF SOVIET SOCIALIST REPUBLICS.

RUTH, GEORGE HERMAN (BABE) (1895–1948)

In the long history of baseball, no one stands near him. He is big and alone, like a giant. He is known wherever baseball is played as the Babe.

Just a glance at the things he did tells why he looms so large. Ruth held more than 50 records. Known as the Sultan of Swat, he hit 714 home runs. From 1919 to 1931, except for two years, he led the American League in home runs. In 1927 he hit 60. His career batting average of .342 is one of the highest.

George Herman Ruth was born in Baltimore, Maryland, on February 6, 1895. When he was 7, his father placed him in St. Mary's Industrial School in Baltimore. There Ruth learned to play baseball. And there he developed his lifelong love for children.

The Babe started his professional career with the Baltimore Orioles of the International League in 1914. He was soon sold to the Boston Red Sox. Ruth was a pitcher then, and one of the best. The record book shows 94 wins and 46 losses. In 1920 he was sold to the New York Yankees. There he became an outfielder and started slugging his way into the hearts of millions of fans. Ruth stayed with the Yankees until the end of the 1934 season. He finished his playing career with the Boston Braves. He had become a legend. In 1936 he was one of the five original players named to the Baseball Hall of Fame.

The Babe—big, colorful, ever ready with a handshake for any child—died of cancer in New York City on August 16, 1948.

Reviewed by MONTE IRVIN
Member, Baseball Hall of Fame

See also BASEBALL.

RUTHERFORD, ERNEST, LORD (1871–1937)

Ernest Rutherford was a British scientist whose work led to our knowledge of the atom's structure and of nuclear energy. He was born in New Zealand—near Nelson, on August 30, 1871—and received his education through college in New Zealand.

By 1893, Rutherford had begun research in physics—the study of matter and energy. In 1895, he won a scholarship to Cambridge University, England. At its Cavendish Laboratory, under the great physicist J. J. Thomson, he began to study X rays, which had just been discovered. He also studied radiation from the element uranium.

In 1898, Rutherford became a professor at McGill University in Montreal, Canada. He continued research in radioactivity. This is a process in which certain atoms give off "bullets" of energy called beta rays and gamma rays. As a result of this process, one element may change to another—for example, uranium changes to a form of lead. Rutherford discovered that a radioactive element also gives off another "bullet," which he called alpha particles.

In 1900, Rutherford was married in New Zealand and then returned with his wife to McGill. That same year he was joined in his research by the English scientist Frederick Soddy. In 1902, Rutherford and Soddy published a new theory. It stated that radioactivity results from the breakdown of atoms of an element.

Rutherford returned to England in 1907 as a professor at the University of Manchester. In 1908, he received the Nobel prize in chemistry for his work in radioactivity. This work led to the theory on which we base our present idea of the structure of the atom. It stated that an atom is composed of a small but heavy nucleus surrounded by one or more electrons.

In 1919, Rutherford announced that he had bombarded nitrogen atoms with alpha particles to produce oxygen and hydrogen atoms. This was the first time a scientist had succeeded in changing one element into another.

Rutherford became head of the Cavendish Laboratory in 1919. There, many who later became great scientists studied under him. He was made a peer (1st Baron Rutherford of Nelson) in 1931. He died in Cambridge on October 19, 1937.

JOHN S. BOWMAN
Author and Science Editor

See also ATOMS; NUCLEAR ENERGY; RADIOACTIVE ELEMENTS.

Rwanda is a small, hilly country in east central Africa just south of the equator. It is one of the most densely populated countries in Africa and has the highest population density of any African nation south of the Sahara desert.

▶ THE PEOPLE

Rwanda's population is chiefly made up of three ethnic groups—the Hutu (also called Bahutu), the Tutsi (or Batutsi), and the Twa (or Batwa). The majority of the Rwandese are Hutu, a Bantu people living in most countries of central and southern Africa. The Hutu are farmers, growing bananas, cassava, sorghum, and millet. They supplement their diet with products from their herds of goats, sheep, and cattle. The Hutu do little hunting, but they do fish on Lake Kivu. They live in beehive-shaped thatched houses. The Hutu houses usually stand separately on the hills rather than being grouped into villages.

The handsome and well-built Tutsi are fewer in number than the Hutu, but they ruled the country for centuries. Some Tutsi are more than 210 centimeters (7 feet) tall. It is believed that their ancestors came to Rwanda from Ethiopia about the 16th century. They learned to use the Bantu language of the Hutu. The Hutu wanted cattle, which were considered a sign of wealth, and the Tutsi needed workers for their land. So in return for cattle the Hutu were obliged to give their land to the Tutsi and to work for them. The Hutu thus became the serfs of the Tutsi.

The Twa, numbering only several thousand, are a Pygmylike people. Many still carry on their old way of life, hunting animals and gathering fruits and nuts in the mountains of the Virunga (or Mfumbiro) region. They live apart from the other Rwandese and have very little contact with the outside world. Others live a more settled life on the plains near Lake Kivu. They make pottery and work in metal.

Christian missionaries have worked in Rwanda for many years, and today about half the people of the country are Christians. The rest of the people follow traditional religions such as animism.

For many years all schools in Rwanda were run by the Christian missions. Today there are both public schools and mission schools, and education is free for all children from 7 to 16 years of age. But there are not enough schools and teachers. Many children do not attend primary school, and only a few attend secondary school. The National University, which is located in Butare, was opened in 1963.

▶ THE LAND

Most of Rwanda is covered by mountains and plateaus. The average elevation of the country is more than 1,800 meters (6,000 feet). The highest peak, Mount Karisimbi, rises to 4,505 meters (14,780 feet). It lies in the Virunga mountains in the northern part of the country.

Lake Kivu is situated on the western border of Rwanda. North and south of the lake there are active volcanoes. Rwanda was once covered with forests. But as a result of the extensive cutting of trees, the mountains are now nearly bare. Several rivers flow through the country, including the Kagera in the east, the Nyawarongo in the center, and the Akanyaru and Ruzizi in the south.

The climate of most of Rwanda is pleasantly cool, especially in the central plateau. It is hotter in the southeast, and temperatures sometimes fall below freezing in the northern

---

FACTS AND FIGURES

REPUBLIC OF RWANDA is the official name of the country.

CAPITAL: Kigali.

LOCATION: East central Africa. **Latitude**—1° 03′ S to 2° 49′ S. **Longitude**—28° 51′ E to 30° 54′ E.

AREA: 26,338 km² (10,169 sq mi).

POPULATION: 4,500,000 (estimate).

LANGUAGE: Kinyarwanda, French (both official).

GOVERNMENT: Republic (under military rule). **Head of government**—president. **International cooperation**—United Nations, Organization of African Unity (OAU).

NATIONAL ANTHEM: *Rwanda Rwacu* ("Our Rwanda").

ECONOMY: Agricultural products—coffee, cotton, tea, tobacco, cattle, bananas, cassava, sorghum, millet, pyrethrum. **Industries and products**—furniture, clothing, soap, bricks. **Chief minerals**—tin, gold. **Chief exports**—coffee, tin, cotton, pyrethrum. **Chief imports**—fuel, vehicles, cloth, iron, machinery. **Monetary unit**—Rwanda franc.

and western mountains. Average annual rainfall ranges from 1,000 millimeters (40 inches) in the northeast to 1,500 millimeters (60 inches) in the southwest.

THE ECONOMY

Most of Rwanda's people are farmers, growing only enough food for their own use. Food crops include bananas, cassava, sorghum, and millet. Coffee grown on large plantations is the nation's chief export. Other important commercial crops are cotton, tea, and pyrethrum. Cattle, goats, and sheep are raised.

Rwanda has little industry. Furniture, soap, bricks, and shoes are made for use within the country. Some tin and gold are mined for export. But poor transportation makes mining difficult. Some Rwandese work in the copper mines of neighboring Zaïre.

There are no railroads in Rwanda. Because of rapids, none of the rivers can be used for transport. But steamboats run on Lake Kivu.

CITIES

Rwanda has no real cities—only a few towns. The largest is Kigali, the capital, which is located in the center of the country. Other major towns are Butare and Cyangugu.

HISTORY AND GOVERNMENT

The first European to reach Rwanda was the British explorer John Speke, who arrived in 1858. He was followed by the German explorer G. A. von Gotzen, who sighted Lake Kivu in 1894. When the Europeans arrived, the country was ruled by the powerful Tutsi, who were led by a *mwami,* or king. In 1897 a treaty between the mwami and Germany made the country a German protectorate. When Germany was defeated in World War I, the League of Nations gave Rwanda to Belgium to govern as part of the Ruanda-Urundi mandate. After the United Nations was founded, Belgium continued to govern the region as a trust territory.

In 1959 the Hutu revolted against the Tutsi. After considerable bloodshed, they drove the *mwami* and many of his followers out of the country. In 1961 the majority of the people voted to establish a republic. The country was separated from Urundi (now Burundi) and became the independent Republic of Rwanda in 1962.

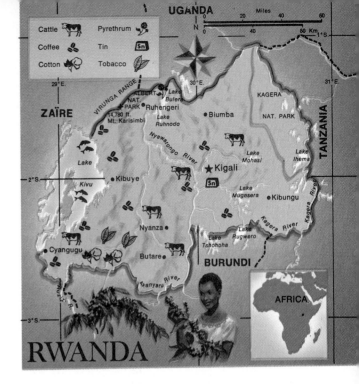

RWANDA

Under its original constitution, Rwanda's government consisted of an elected president and a legislature, the National Assembly. The country's first president was Gregoire Kayibanda. He was overthrown by the military in 1973, and General Juvénal Habyalimana became president. The National Assembly was suspended. In 1978 a new constitution was approved. This was announced as the first step toward new legislative elections.

ROBERT O. COLLINS
Williams College

An outdoor market near Lake Kivu.

RYE

Rye is a hardy cereal grass closely related to wheat. It is hardier than wheat and is often grown where wheat would fail because of low soil fertility. Rye is widely cultivated as a food grain, especially in central and northern Europe. It is the chief ingredient of the "black bread" common there.

Rye seems to have first appeared about the 1st century B.C. It grew as a weed in the wheat fields of the kingdoms around the Black Sea. Rye seeds were often accidentally mixed in with the wheat seeds saved for the next year's planting. Where the soil or the climate was not good, the rye grew better than the wheat. Each year there was more rye and less wheat in the grain that was harvested. After a time the rye crowded out the wheat entirely. For hundreds of years the people who worked in the rye fields believed that wheat turned into rye after several seasons of planting.

The culture of rye spread from the lands around the Black Sea through the northern areas of Europe and Asia. During the Middle Ages the sour, gummy black bread made from whole rye kernels was one of the main foods of the peasants. It was not until the 18th century that wheat production increased, as a result of better agricultural practices. In England and western Europe black bread was eaten only by the very poor. But in central Europe and the Soviet Union rye ranked with wheat as a bread cereal.

▶ CULTIVATION

Most rye is sown in the fall, although a little is planted in the spring. Rye usually grows about 1.5 meters (5 feet) tall. The grain is harvested by combines. In poor soil, rye yields about 750 kilograms per hectare (12 bushels per acre). But if rye is properly cared for, the yield may be twice as high. It is difficult to grow a pure variety of rye because the pollen from the flowers of one rye plant can fertilize only the flowers on another rye plant.

Ergot, leaf and stem rust, stalk and head smut, and some root rots are common enemies of rye. But except for ergot these diseases do little serious damage. Ergot is a fungus that makes the young rye kernels become very hard and turn a purplish-black color.

Infected kernels are poisonous to both humans and livestock. One of the best ways of controlling ergot is to rotate rye with crops that are immune to the fungus.

The largest producers of rye are the Soviet Union and Poland. World production totals about 28,000,000 metric tons. This is a small figure in comparison to that for wheat, which totals more than 415,000,000 metric tons.

▶ USES OF RYE

In making rye flour, rye is milled very much like wheat. But it is not so carefully graded or purified. Rye is first cleaned and then ground between rollers into pieces called middlings. These are sifted to remove the bran, which is the outside covering of the kernel. The rye bran sticks very closely to the seed and is almost impossible to remove completely. The highest grades of rye flour are produced by special rolls that crush the middlings into powder. Dark rye flour with a strong rye flavor is made from middlings that still carry bits of bran. Pumpernickel bread is baked from a coarse, unsifted rye flour.

Rye flour is inferior to wheat flour in baking quality because rye cannot form the elastic gluten that helps bread rise. Since rye does not have all of the proteins that make up gluten, the dough is sticky and claylike. In the United States and Canada rye bread is made from mixtures of rye flour and an equal or even greater amount of wheat flour. The gluten in the wheat dough makes the rye bread lighter. Usually a sourdough (dough left over from an earlier mixing) is used instead of yeast as leavening for rye bread.

A large percentage of the yearly crop is made into mash for whiskey. The rye is crushed into a meal and soaked in a specially prepared liquid until it ferments.

Generally, animals do not like rye as much as they do wheat and other cereals. Lambs sometimes fatten on rye. But it is fed to most animals in limited amounts because they have difficulty digesting it. Since rye can be grown under difficult conditions, it makes good emergency pasture. Tough, fibrous rye straw makes excellent bedding for animals.

C. HAMILTON KENNEY
Canada Department of Agriculture
See also GRAIN AND GRAIN PRODUCTS; WHEAT.

Q, 17th letter of the English alphabet **Q** 1
See also Alphabet
Qabus ibn Said, sultan of Oman **O** 116d

Qaddafi (guht-DAH-fee), **Muammar el-** (1942–   ), Libyan leader, b. Misurata, east of Tripoli. As a young officer, he led the military coup that overthrew King Idris I in 1969. He became head of the armed forces and the Revolutionary Command Council and, in 1977, the president of Libya. Although he now holds no official title, Qaddafi remains the most powerful figure in the country. An ardent Arab nationalist, he is a supporter of the Palestinian independence movement. **L** 205

Qamaran Island *see* Kamaran Island
Qand (GOND), Arabic word for sugar **C** 98
Qatar (KA-tar), emirate, Arabia **Q** 2–3
  flag **F** 240
  Organization of Petroleum Exporting Countries
    O 211
  Qatar, peninsula, Arabia **Q** 2

Quackery, practices of one who pretends to have medical skills. "Quack" is a shortened form of "quacksalver" (from Dutch *kwaksalve*), meaning one who quacks, or boasts, of his salves and their healing qualities.

Quadrants, navigation instruments **N** 64
Quadrilaterals (qua-dri-LAT-er-als), geometric forms
    G 126
Quadrille, dance **D** 27
Quadros (QUA-drush), **Jânio,** president of Brazil **B** 384
Quadruple (qua-DRU-ple) **Alliance** (Grand Alliance),
    1815 **I** 324
  formed at Congress of Vienna against Napoleon I
    I 324
Quad stereo **T** 20, 21
Quagga (QUAG-ga), zebra **H** 244
Quahog (QUAW-hog), shellfish **R** 215, 217
Quai d'Orsay (kay d'or-SAY), Paris **P** 70

Quail, several species of small game birds. Quail found in Europe, Africa, and Asia are about 18 cm (7 in) long, while American quail, such as the bobwhite, are somewhat larger. Quail live on the ground, eat insects and seeds, and travel in flocks called coveys. Picture **B** 233
  birds of the fields **B** 220

Quakers **Q** 4–4a
  American colonies **A** 191–92
  continuing Reformation in England **R** 135
  Penn, William **P** 127
  Philadelphia **P** 182–83
  prisons, reform of **P** 468
  Underground Railroad **U** 11, 12
Quaking aspen, tree, picture **T** 278
Quality control, testing system
  automobiles **A** 548
Quanah, Indian chief *see* Parker, Quanah
Quantitative analysis, in chemistry **C** 218

Quantrill, William Clarke (1837–65), American Confederate leader, b. Canal Dover, Ohio. He was a school-teacher and a gambler before the Civil War began in 1861, when he became leader of a guerrilla unit (known as Quan-

trill's Raiders). He helped capture Independence, Mo. (1862), and received a captaincy in the Confederate Army. He was killed near Taylorsville, Ky.

Quantum theory, in physics
  Bohr's work basis of **B** 300
  light **L** 272–74
  radiation **R** 45
Quarantine
  astronauts returning from the moon **S** 340
  disease, prevention of **D** 221
  duties of Public Health Service officers **P** 504
  flag **F** 246
Quark, subatomic particle **C** 216; **N** 369

Quarles, Benjamin (1904–   ), American historian, b. Boston, Mass. He was dean of instruction at Dillard University, New Orleans, La. from 1946 to 1953, and head of the history department at Morgan State College, Baltimore, Md. from 1953 to 1968. Among his books are *The Negro in the American Revolution, Lincoln and the Negro,* and *Blacks on John Brown.*

Quarrying **Q** 4b–5
  Barre, Vermont **V** 318–19; picture **V** 314
Quarterbacks, in football **F** 362–63
Quarter horses **H** 232, 244; picture **H** 239
Quartering Act, 1765 **R** 195
Quart, measure of volume **W** 111, 115
  different quarts pictured **W** 113
Quartet, musical form **M** 534, 537
Quartz **Q** 6–7
  abrasive for grinding and polishing **G** 387–88
  crystals **C** 541
  gemstones **G** 75
  gold found in **G** 248
  quartz-crystal controlled clocks **T** 193
Quartz-iodine lamps **L** 286
Quartzite, metamorphic rock **R** 269–70; picture
    R 269
Quasars, star-like radio sources **Q** 7–8; **A** 476a
  radio universe **U** 201, 203
Quasimodo (qua-si-MO-do), **Salvatore,** Italian poet
    I 480; picture **I** 481
Quasimodo (Hunchback of Notre Dame), picture **F** 112
Quasi-stellar radio sources *see* Quasars
Quatrain, four lines of verse **P** 353
Quebec (que-BEC), **Battle of,** 1759 **F** 461–62
Quebec, Canada **Q** 9–16
  Allied Conference, 1943 **W** 297
  Anticosti Island **I** 426
  Champlain, Samuel de **C** 69, 186a
  founding of and early history as part of New France
    C 69–70
  Montreal **M** 443–45
  Quebec Act of 1774 and British Canada **C** 71
  Revolutionary War, American **C** 71; **R** 201
  separatist movement **C** 75
Quebec Act of 1774 **C** 71
Quebec City, capital of Quebec, Canada **C** 65; **Q** 11,
    12, 13, 16–17; picture **F** 461
  Saint Lawrence River, history of **S** 16
  Winter Carnival, picture **C** 121
Quebracho (kay-BRA-cho), tree **A** 393

Quechua (KECH-wa), Indians of South America
  Bolivia   **B** 302
  Peru   **P** 160
Quechua, language of the Incas   **I** 207;   **P** 160

Queen, Ellery, pseudonym of **Frederic Dannay** (1905–82) and **Manfred B. Lee** (1905–71), American writers, both b. Brooklyn, N.Y. Dannay and Lee (cousins) began their collaboration with *The Roman Hat Mystery* (1929), their winning entry in a writing contest. Their pen name was also the name of their hero, who became world famous through movies, radio, television, novels, and collections of short stories. Their last novel was *A Fine and Private Place* (1971). Dannay and Lee co-edited *Ellery Queen's Mystery Magazine* from 1941 until Lee's death, when Dannay took over as sole editor.

Queen Anne's lace, flowers, picture   **W** 168
Queen Anne style, in art and architecture   **E** 240
  furniture design   **F** 507
Queen Anne's War, 1702–13   **F** 459
Queen ants   **A** 323, 326; picture   **A** 328
Queen bees   **B** 117–18, 121–24
Queen Charlotte Islands, British Columbia, Canada
  B 402
Queen Elizabeth, ocean liner   **O** 21
Queen Elizabeth 2, ocean liner   **O** 18, 21, 23
Queen Mary, ocean liner   **O** 21
Queen of the May   **M** 182
Queens, borough of New York City   **N** 228
Queen's Birthday, holiday   **H** 150

Queensberry rules, rules of boxing drawn up by the Scotsman John Sholto Douglas, Marquis of Queensberry (1844–1900). A sportsman, he sponsored the rules, drafted by John G. Chambers in 1867, that govern to-day's boxing. By 1889 the rules were standardized and in use in both England and the United States.   **B** 353

Queensland, Australia   **A** 511
Queen's Plate, Canadian horse race   **H** 232
Queenstown, New Zealand, picture   **N** 238
Queensware, pottery   **P** 418
Queequeg, character in *Moby Dick*   **M** 217–18

Queirós (kay-ROSH), **Pedro Fernandes de** (1560?–1614), Portuguese navigator. He sailed (1595) on an expedition to the Pacific as second in command to Alvaro de Mendaña de Neyra (1541–95), discoverer of the Marquesas and Solomon islands, and upon the death of his commander continued the expedition and discovered the New Hebrides (now Vanuatu) and the Tuamotu Islands.
  Solomon Islands   **S** 252b

Quemoy (ke-MOY), island group, off China's mainland
  C 273;   **T** 12
Quenching, of metals   **M** 233

Quercia (QUAIR-cha), **Jacopo della** (1378?–1438), Italian sculptor, b. Siena. Son of a goldsmith and sculptor, he is probably most famous for his Gaia fountain in Siena and the scenes from Genesis and the life of Christ on the doorway of Bologna's church of San Petronio. Quercia's work reflects a change from Gothic to Renaissance style and is said to have influenced Michelangelo.
  Renaissance sculpture   **S** 99

Question and Answer, sculpture by David Smith, picture
  M 397
Question marks, punctuation   **P** 531

Questionnaires
  opinion surveys   **O** 159

Quetzal, large Central American bird. It is found in rain forests from southern Mexico to Costa Rica. The male quetzal is brilliant green with a bright crimson abdomen. Long feathers above the tail sometimes reach a length of 60 cm (2 ft). Females are less brilliantly colored.
  Guatemala's national symbol   **G** 391

Quetzalcoatl (ket-zol-co-OT-el), Aztec god. Some legends claim that Quetzalcoatl actually existed and was a ruler of the ancient Toltec civilization of Mexico. The Toltecs worshiped him as the god of science and the arts and as the discoverer of maize. The name Quetzalcoatl means "feathered serpent" in the Nahuatl language, and a feathered serpent is the symbol of Mexico.
  Cortes and the Spanish conquest of Mexico   **C** 508;
    M 247
  Toltec Indian culture and mythology   **I** 198;
    M 561–62

Quevedo (kay-VAY-do), **Francisco de,** Spanish poet
  S 369
Quezon (KAE-zone), **Manuel,** Philippine statesman
  Q 18
  Philippines, history of   **P** 190
Quezon City, Philippines   **P** 189
Quick breads   **B** 386
Quicksand   **Q** 18–19
Quicksilver *see* Mercury
Quiet Don, The, novel by Sholokhov   **N** 348
Quiet One, The, documentary motion picture   **M** 476
Quileute (quil-e-UTE), Indians of North America
  myths of   **M** 559–60
Quill pens   **P** 146
  steps in the history of writing   **C** 431
Quills, of animals
  porcupine   **R** 280
  protective devices   **M** 67

Quince, fruit of a tree belonging to the rose family. A small, spicy, acid, hard-fleshed fruit, quince is used for making marmalade, jelly, and preserves. The quince tree is native to Central Asia but can be grown in any temperate climate. The tree may grow to a height of 4 to 5 m (12 to 16 ft). It grows best in rich, well-drained soils. Picture   **G** 36

Quincy, Josiah (1772–1864), American statesman, b. Braintree (now Quincy), Mass. He was a Massachusetts state senator (1804–05) and a United States congressman (1805–13), vacating the latter position because he opposed the War of 1812. He returned to the state senate (1813–20) and later was mayor of Boston (1823–28), president of Harvard (1829–45), and author of *Memoir of the Life of John Quincy Adams.*

Quinidine (QUIN-i-dene), drug   **D** 326
Quinine (QUINE-ine), drug made from cinchona bark
  D 213
  plants, medicinal   **P** 311–13
  sources of drugs   **D** 323
Quinterna, musical instrument, picture   **S** 438

Quintero (keen-TER-o), **José** (1924–   ), American theatrical director, b. Panama City, Panama. He trained at Chicago's Goodman Theater and achieved fame as a director of off-Broadway revivals of such plays as Tennessee Williams' *Summer and Smoke* and Eugene O'Neill's

The Iceman Cometh. He also directed Broadway productions of O'Neill's *Long Day's Journey into Night* and *A Moon for the Misbegotten.*

Quintet, in music **M** 534
Quintilian (quin-TIL-ian), **Marcus Fabius,** Roman rhetorician **O** 181
   Silver Age of Latin literature **L** 80

Quintuplets (from Latin *quintuplex,* "quint-" meaning "fifth" and "-plex" meaning "fold"), five children born at one birth. The word "quintuplets" became widely known in modern times with the birth of Canada's Dionne quintuplets in 1934.

Quipus, knotted strings, record keeping of Inca Indians **I** 207; picture **C** 451
Quirinale (QUIR-in-al) **Palace,** Rome, Italy **R** 313, 315

Quirino (ki-RI-no), **Elpidio** (1890–1956), Philippine statesman, b. Luzon, Vigon province. Entering politics in 1913, he was a member of the Philippine Senate (1925–35, 1941–45), secretary of finance (1934–36), secretary of the interior (1936–38), and secretary of foreign affairs (1946–48). He worked actively for Philippine independence and served as president (1948–53).
   Philippines, history of **P** 190

Quiroga, Horacio, Uruguayan writer **L** 72

Quirós (ke-ROCE), **Cesáreo Bernaldo de** (1879–1968), Argentine painter, b. Gualeguay. He studied at Buenos Aires' Academia Nacional de Bellas Artes and specialized in paintings that depict gauchos and their life on the pampas (treeless plains of Argentina).

Quisling, Vidkun, Norwegian Nazi **W** 288
   underground movement working for Hitler **U** 10
Quito (KI-to), capital of Ecuador **E** 57; pictures **E** 52 **L** 57
   San Francisco Monastery **L** 64
Quiver, case for carrying arrows **A** 367
Quixote, Don *see* Don Quixote
Quiz shows, on television **T** 70d
Qumran, community on northwest shore of Dead Sea **D** 48, 49
Qumran texts *see* Dead Sea Scrolls
Quoits
   deck tennis **D** 58

Quonset hut, prefabricated shelter built of corrugated metal, which forms a semicircular arching roof over a base of steel trusses. The huts' name comes from Quonset Point, R.I., where they were first used during World War II for army personnel and for storage.
   Rhode Island's products **R** 213

Quorum, number of the entire body of an organization that must be present in order to conduct business legally. In England "quorum" originally referred to certain justices of the peace who were required to be present at court sessions.
   parliamentary procedure, rules of **P** 79

Quota Act, 1921, limiting immigration **I** 100
Quotas, trade barriers **I** 328
Quotation marks, punctuation **P** 532
Quotations **Q** 19–20
   excerpts from Lincoln's writings **L** 294

famous quotes from Shakespeare's plays **S** 133–37
   selections from *Poor Richard's Almanack* **F** 452
   some ironical observations of Mark Twain **H** 281
   use exact words in formal speech **S** 376
   See also Epigram; Proverbs, traditional sayings; sayings by the first word of the quotation
Quotient (QUO-shent), in division **A** 400–01

Quo vadis? (quo VA-dis), Latin for "Where are you going?" *Quo Vadis?* is also the name of a popular historical novel written (1896) by a Pole, Henryk Sienkiewicz, and filmed several times.
   first motion picture spectacle **M** 484

Quraish, Arab tribe
   Mohammed's tribe in Mecca **M** 404, 405
Qu'ran *see* Koran
Qurnat al-Sawda, mountain, Lebanon **L** 121

R, 18th letter of the English alphabet **R** 21
   See also Alphabet
Ra *see* Re, Egyptian god
Rabat (ra-BOT), capital of Morocco **M** 461
   Muslims in prayer, picture **I** 416
Rabbinical (rab-BIN-ic-al) **literature, Hebrew** **H** 101–02
Rabbinic Hebrew language **H** 100–01
Rabbis (RAB-byes), Jewish religious leaders **J** 120
   Talmudists **T** 15
Rabbits **R** 22–24
   Australia overrun with **A** 506–07
   Beatrix Potter's *The Tale of Peter Rabbit* **C** 242
   man changes distribution of life **L** 238
   March Hare in "Alice in Wonderland" **A** 164
   New Zealand pest **N** 240
   pets **P** 179–80
   tracks, picture **A** 271
   tularemia **I** 287
   What is the difference between a rabbit and a hare? **R** 23
   White Rabbit and March Hare in "Alice in Wonderland" **A** 164
   why some small animals hibernate, picture **H** 124
Rabbit's foot, charm **S** 473
Rabe, David, American playwright **A** 215
Rabelais (ra-BLAY), **François,** French poet **F** 436–37

Rabi (RA-bi), **Isidor Isaac** (1898–), American physicist, b. Rymanow, Austria-Hungary (now Poland). He was awarded the 1944 Nobel prize in physics for his method of determining the magnetic properties of atomic nuclei. He assisted in the development of radar and of the atomic bomb. He taught (1929–67) in the physics department of Columbia University.

Rabi *see* Rambi, Pacific island
Rabies, virus disease **I** 286–87
   achievement in the history of medicine **M** 208
   foxes spread infection **D** 249
   Pasteur, Louis **P** 97
   vampire bats as carriers **B** 94

Rabin (rah-BEEN), **Yitzhak** (1922–), Israeli military and political leader, b. Jerusalem. Rabin was Israel's first native-born prime minister, holding that office and leadership of the Labour Party from 1974 to 1977. He began his military career at the age of 19, when he joined Haganah, the Jewish underground army in Palestine. A

Rabin, Yitzhak (continued)
hero of the 1967 Arab-Israeli war, he was Israel's ambassador to the United States from 1968 to 1973.

Rabinovich, Solomon J. *see* Aleykhem, Sholem
Rabun (RAY-bun) **Gap,** Georgia **G** 132
Raccoon dog **D** 250
Raccoons **R** 25–26
   animal tests **A** 285; picture **A** 286
   furs **F** 519
   tracks, picture **A** 272
Race, Day of the (El Día de la Raza), Latin American
    holiday **H** 150
Race, trough for water **W** 61
Race music *see* Rhythm and blues music
Races, human **R** 29–32
   Africa **A** 55
   Asia **A** 459
   Australian aborigines, Australoids **A** 6a, 500
   civil rights conflicts **C** 315–16
   distribution of genes in population **G** 87
   Eskimos (Inuit) **E** 284–91
   Europe, classification of people in **E** 316–17
   language families **L** 38–39
   Latin America **L** 48–49; **S** 282
   North America **N** 295
   prehistoric people **P** 442–46

Rachel (ra-SHEL) (stage name of Élisa Félix) (1820–58), French actress, b. Mumpf, Switzerland. A street singer in her youth, she studied drama in Paris and achieved her first success (1838) as Camille in *Horace* by Corneille. She subsequently appeared in London, Berlin, St. Petersburg, and the United States. Noted for her parts in plays by Racine and Corneille, she received greatest acclaim in title roles of *Phèdre,* by Racine, and *Adrienne Lecouvreur,* by Eugène Scribe and Gabriel Legouvé.

Rachel (RAY-chel), in Old Testament (Genesis 29–35), daughter of Laban and wife of Jacob. When fleeing from Laban with Jacob, she took household gods and hid them. She bore Jacob two sons, Joseph and Benjamin.

Rachmaninoff (rock-MA-ni-nof), **Sergey Vassilievitch** (1873–1943), Russian pianist, composer, and conductor, b. Onega, near Novgorod. He conducted opera at Bolshoi Theater (1904–06), made first American tour in 1909 and 1910, and conducted Philharmonic Society in Moscow (1911–13). He left Russia permanently in 1917. His compositions, influenced by Tchaikovsky and other 19th-century Russian composers, include four piano concertos, three symphonies and other orchestral works, three operas, *Rhapsody on a Theme of Paganini,* many piano pieces, choral works, and songs.
   Russian music **U** 63, 64

Racine (ra-CENE), **Jean Baptiste,** French dramatist
   R 32
   French literature, place in **F** 438
   Greek unities of time, place, action **D** 296
Racine, Wisconsin **W** 204
Racing **R** 33
   air races and long-distance flights **A** 570
   automobile racing **A** 538–40
   chariot racing **W** 157
   horse racing **H** 231–34
   iceboating **I** 29–30
   karting **K** 196
   model car **A** 536–37
   motorcycles **M** 488d
   Olympic Games **O** 103–116c

   pigeons bred for racing **B** 247
   powerboat racing **B** 264
   regattas **R** 338–39
   roller-skating **R** 284
   rowing races **R** 338–39
   sailing **S** 13
   skiing **S** 184d–187
   Soap Box Derby **S** 215
   speed skating **I** 50–53
   swimming **S** 493
   track events **T** 237–39
Racing homers, pigeons **B** 247; **O** 180
Racing shells, boats **R** 338

Racism, the belief that one race, by heredity, is superior to other races. Most scientists believe that differences in intelligence and personality are caused not by inherited physical traits but by the surroundings in which people grow up. Racism leads to prejudice and discrimination against certain groups. It has occurred in many parts of the world and in many periods of history, but it has been strongest in the 19th and 20th centuries in western European countries and the areas colonized by those countries. Racism sometimes becomes part of government policy. In South Africa, for example, *apartheid,* the segregation of blacks from whites, is practiced by law.

Rack-and-pinion, devices used for cog railroads **R** 78
Racket sports **R** 34–34c

Rackham, Arthur (1867–1939), English artist and illustrator, b. London. He contributed artwork to periodicals, including *Punch,* but was best known for his illustrations of children's books, including Grimm's *Fairy Tales,* Andersen's *Fairy Tales, Gulliver's Travels,* and *Peter Pan.*
   "Rumpelstiltskin" **I** 93

Racquetball, sport **R** 34b
Radar (RAY-dar) **R** 34d–37
   astronomy *see* Radar astronomy
   changes in fishing industry **F** 217
   electric waves **L** 269
   electronic "frog's eye" **F** 478
   magnetrons (electron tubes) **E** 148
   North American defense bases **C** 82
   ocean liners **O** 24
   primitive radar of electric fishes **F** 202
   signals equal to speed of light **L** 265
   tornado detection **H** 299; picture **H** 298
   UFO reports traced to freak weather conditions
    F 287
   unit being checked by engineers, picture **E** 205
   United States Navy electronics and weapons
    U 193
   See also AWACS
Radar astronomy (a-STRON-omy) **R** 73–74
   astronomy, history of **A** 476b–477
   new kinds of astronomical observation **E** 30
   telescopes **R** 73
Radcliffe, Ann Ward, English novelist **E** 260
Radcliffe College, women's college of Harvard
   founded by Elizabeth Cary Agassiz **A** 80

Radhakrishnan (ra-da-KRISH-non), **Sir Sarvepalli** (1888–1975), Indian philosopher and statesman, b. Madras. He was professor of Eastern religions and ethics, Oxford University (1936–52), and chancellor of Delhi University (1953–62). A member of the International Committee of Intellectual Cooperation, League of Nations (1931–39), he also headed the Indian delegation to

UNESCO (1946–52) and served as Indian ambassador to the Soviet Union (1949–52). He was vice-president (1952–62) and president (1962–67) of India.

Radial engines, of airplanes   A 557
Radial symmetry, of body plan, diagram   B 269
Radial tires   T 197, 198; picture   T 196
Radiant energy   E 199
   discoveries of radiant energy   P 236–37
Radiant heaters   E 117
Radiation, in physics   R 40–45
   aging hastened by   A 85
   astronomers get information from radiation from space   A 476a–476c
   atmosphere a shield against sun's radiation   A 482
   belts see Radiation belts
   cancer   C 90–91, 92–93, 95
   cosmic rays   C 511
   Curies' experiments   C 553
   earth and its sun   E 24–25
   Geiger counter   G 67–68
   heat energy   H 95, 97
   how radiation begins, picture   L 46a
   infrared light waves   L 268
   International Geophysical Year findings   I 312
   irradiation of food   F 349
   lasers   L 46a–46d
   light   L 46a, 260–74
   measured by satellites for weather scientists   W 87
   moon without protection from   M 450
   orbiting observatories, findings   O 14
   quantum theory   L 272–74
   radioactive elements   R 67–68
   radio and radar astronomy   R 69–76
   research on radiation from space using balloons   B 33
   solar energy   S 235–36
   space exploration and travel, dangers from   S 342
   studies by physicists   P 236–37
   X rays   X 339–41
Radiation belts   R 46–49
   cosmic rays   C 512
   earth's magnetic field   E 27
   International Geophysical Year findings   I 313–14
   ions and ionization   I 352–53
   space exploration and travel, dangers from   S 342
Radiation fog   F 289
Radiators, cooling systems of engines   I 307
   use in heating systems   H 98–99
Radical Republicans, Reconstruction Period   R 117–20
Radio   R 50–61
   advertising   A 27, 28–29, 32;   S 203
   amateur see Radio, amateur
   American pop music   R 262b
   atmospheric waves   A 481
   communication advanced by   C 439
   country and western music   C 524b
   electronic communication, history of   E 142b–142c
   electron tubes   T 252
   fadeout   I 317
   first commercial radio station, picture   E 147
   How does a microphone work?   R 55
   journalism's use of   J 144
   Marconi's invention of wireless telegraphy   M 98
   model car racing   A 537
   navigation, uses of   N 67–68
   piezoelectric crystals of quartz   Q 6
   propaganda   P 481
   radiation frequency   R 42
   remote-control model airplanes   A 105–06

   rock music   R 262a, 262b
   satellites transmit radio signals   S 41
   signals amplified by triodes (electron tubes)   E 148
   space exploration, communication during   S 340a, 341
   transistors and integrated circuits   T 253–54
   walkie-talkies   R 50
   What is static?   R 50
   Why can you hear radio stations from farther away at night?   R 50
   See also Loran; Radar; Radar astronomy; Shoran; Sonar; communication section of country, province, and state articles
Radio, amateur   R 62–63
   electronic communication, uses of   E 142c
Radio, short-wave   R 58;   T 59
   See also Radio, amateur
Radioactive dating   R 64–66
   age of the earth   E 21
   archeological dating   A 361–62
   for ice age dating   I 22–23
   timetables in geology   G 119
Radioactive decay   M 454;   N 358–60;   R 68
Radioactive elements   R 67–68
   astatine, a halogen made by atomic reaction   I 349
   atoms   A 488–89
   cancer   C 92–93
   chemistry, history of   C 216
   dating   R 64–66
   elements, some facts about   E 158, 159
   environmental problems of disposal   E 272b, 272g
   fallout   F 35–36
   Geiger counters register radiations from   G 67–68
   pouring of, picture   D 221
   Rutherford, Ernest, Lord   R 361
   uranium   U 230–31
Radioactive fallout see Fallout
Radioactive isotopes (I-so-topes)   N 357
   cancer treatment   C 91, 95
Radioactive radiation   R 45
Radioactive wastes   E 202c, 203;   N 370
Radioactivity   N 358–60
   cancer   C 92–93
   changes in atomic nuclei   M 178
   Curies' experiments   C 553
   dust particles   D 347
   earth's formation   E 18
   food contamination from fallout   F 355
   ions detect   I 353
   light rays   L 269
   ore deposits, detection of   M 316
   radioactive dating   A 361–62;   R 64–66
   radioactive elements   R 67–68
   Rutherford, Ernest, Lord   R 361
   science, history of   S 76
   See also Radioactive elements
Radio astronomy   R 69–76;   A 476b;   E 30
   observatories   O 10–11
   quasars and pulsars   Q 7–8
   radio telescopes   T 64
   radio universe   U 200–01
   science, history of   S 76
Radio broadcasting   R 53–58
Radio broadcasting stations   R 50–52
Radiocarbon dating   R 65–66
Radio Corporation of America (RCA)   P 197
   electronic music improvements   E 142g, 142h
Radio detection and ranging see Radar

Radio Free Europe/Radio Liberty (RFE/RL), a private organization that broadcasts uncensored news and other programs to the Soviet Union and eastern Europe. Radio Free Europe/Radio Liberty was formed in 1976 by a merger of two separate networks—Radio Free Europe, founded in 1950, and Radio Liberty, founded in 1951.

Radio frequency bands R 58
Radio galaxies U 201, 203
Radioisotopes see Radioactive isotopes
Radiology, branch of medicine that uses X rays X 339
Radio paging E 142c
Radio programs R 59–61
Radio range stations, airway checkpoints A 561
Radio receivers R 51
Radiosondes (RAY-dio-sonds), instruments to observe weather in upper atmosphere W 84–85
Radio stars, space bodies R 75, 76
exploration by radio in astronomy A 476b; Q 7–8
Radio telegraphy T 54
Radiotelephones R 50; picture E 142a
new means of communication C 439
radio telephony T 59
telephone, descendants of, in electronic communication E 142a–142b
Radio telescopes A 476b; E 30; R 69–72; picture I 314
electric waves L 269–70
Jansky's experiments T 64
Milky Way galaxy, study of U 200–01
moon M 451
quasars and pulsars Q 7–8
radio waves of the sun, studies of S 467
Radio transmitters R 53
Radio waves R 44, 54
ice thickness measured by radio waves I 10
masers L 46c
Milky Way galaxy, study of U 200–01
quasars and pulsars Q 7–8
television T 66–67, 68
transistors and integrated circuits T 253–54
travel through a vacuum V 264
Radishchev, Aleksandr, Russian author U 59
Radishes V 292
roots we eat P 307; pictures P 291, 306
Radisson (ra-di-SON), **Pierre,** French explorer O 127
Hudson's Bay Company, fur traders F 520
Saint Lawrence River S 16
Radium (RAY-dium), element E 155, 164
atomic structure unstable A 488
Curies' discovery C 553; U 230
metals, ores, location, properties, uses M 227
radioactive decay of radium N 358–59
Radius, of a circle G 127
Radome (RAY-dome), for satellites
located near Andover, Maine M 33
Radon (RAY-don), element E 155, 164; N 109
Raduga 4, Soviet communications satellite C 440
Radula (RAD-ul-a), tongue of snail O 278

Raeburn, Sir Henry (known as the Scottish Reynolds) (1756–1823), Scottish portrait painter, b. Stockbridge, near Edinburgh. Persuaded by Sir Joshua Reynolds to study art in Rome, he returned to Edinburgh in 1787. He painted portraits of leading men of his day, including Sir Walter Scott, James Boswell, and David Hume.

Royal Academy, Age of E 238

Raffaello, S.S., ocean liner O 22
Raffles, fictional character created by Hornung M 554

Raffles, Sir Thomas Stamford (1781–1826), English colonial administrator, b. at sea near Jamaica. He became assistant to first governor at Malaysian settlement of Penang (1805) and served as lieutenant governor of Java (1811–16) and of Bencoolen, Sumatra (1818–23). He influenced Britain to purchase Singapore from the Netherlands (1819). He compiled historical knowledge of Malaysia and Indonesia in his *History of Java*.

Malaysia and Singapore, history of M 54; S 184a

Raft of the Medusa, painting by Géricault F 427
Rafts, watercraft T 257
Amazon River, picture A 179
ancient ships S 155
water transportation I 337
Rag chewing, the conversation of amateur radio operators R 62
Rag dolls D 266
Raggedy Ann makeup, picture P 340
Raglan sleeve C 352
Ragtime, music rhythm J 57
introduced into musical comedy M 542
Ragweed, plant, picture W 105
hayfever, cause of D 190

Rahman (RAH-mon), **Abdul** (1903–73), Malaysian statesman, b. Alor Star, Kedah. Elected to Federal Legislative Council (1955), he led delegation (1955) to discuss Malayan independence from Great Britain. He was minister of external affairs (1957–63), and was instrumental in the formation of the Federation of Malaysia. He served as prime minister of Malaysia (1963–70).

Malaysia, history of M 55

Rail fences P 255
Railroad lantern, picture L 283
Railroads R 77–90
Africa A 64–65
Andes mountain region A 253
Asia A 466
broader gauge used as defense by Russians U 40
canal traffic affected by C 84–85
Casey Jones, story of T 74
communication advanced by C 436
diesel locomotive and train, picture D 168
first "road of rails" L 329
first U.S. transcontinental A 204
flanged wheels W 158
folk songs and stories F 317; T 74
growth affected United States interstate commerce I 331–32
highest standard-gauge in the world P 164
How did 4 feet 8½ inches come to be picked for the width of track? R 86
locomotives L 327–32
Midnight Special, The, folk song F 319
model railroads R 91–92
monorails, Aerotrains, turbotrains T 267
narrow-gauge, in operation A 138; C 410
postal service P 405, 407
rails, expansion and contraction of, picture H 94
Rocky Mountain routes R 274
South Carolina, early transportation in S 301–02
transportation, history of T 263
tunnels T 314
United States U 110
viaduct in Switzerland, picture E 328
Westinghouse's air brake W 125
yard at Winnipeg, picture M 77

See also Transportation section of country, province, and state articles
Railroads, model R 91–92
Railroad terminals R 83
Railroad ties W 226
Railroad Unemployment Insurance Act, 1938 L 14
Rails, Midway, extinct birds B 231

Railway brotherhoods, five trade unions that represent railroad workers in negotiations with railroad companies. The unions are those of engineers, conductors and brakemen, firemen and enginemen, trainmen, and switchmen.

Railway Labor Act, act passed (1926) to insure quick settlement of disputes between railroad companies and employees. The law provided for a board of mediation and an arbitration board and outlined procedures in case of emergency. An amendment (1934) set up the more effective National Railroad Adjustment Board at Chicago.

Railways *see* Railroads
Rain and rainfall R 93–95
    acid rain A 110, 111
    Africa A 50, 62
    Asia A 451–52
    cave formation by erosion C 153–54
    climate, effect on C 343–48
    clouds, nimbo-stratus, bring rain C 360; picture C 361
    cloud "seeding" W 67, 91–92
    control of W 91–94
    deserts D 124
    dust particles and liquid droplets D 348
    equatorial climate in the rain forests E 272h
    floods and flood control F 254, 256
    forest growth F 371
    hurricanes and tornadoes H 292–99
    hydrologic, or water cycles W 52
    mountains influence rainfall M 497
    rain forest averages R 99
    North America, average precipitation in, map N 302
    prairies P 430
    rainmaking W 91–94
    South America S 279
    trade winds' influence T 246
    tree rings, record of T 286–87
    water supply W 67
    weather elements W 76, 80
    What is the shape of a falling raindrop? R 93
    world water resources W 257
    See also Clouds; climate section of country, province, and state articles
Rainbow R 98
    a natural prism of color, picture D 138
    effect of atmosphere A 482
    over Victoria Falls, pictures A 47, R 247
    radiation passing through rain R 44
    See also Iris, Greek goddess
Rainbow Bridge National Monument, Utah U 250
Rainbow (42nd) Division, United States Army
    MacArthur, Douglas M 2
Rainbow trout, fish, picture F 210
Raindrops, how shaped R 93

Rainey, Joseph Hayne (1832–87), American politician, b. Georgetown, S.C. He was a member of the executive committee of the newly formed Republican Party of South Carolina (1867) and was elected a delegate to the state constitutional convention (1868) and a state senator (1869–70). He became the first black member of the U.S. House of Representatives (1870–79).

Rainfall *see* Rain and rainfall
Rain forest R 99–100; pictures A 47, L 235
    birds of B 225
    Brazil's Amazon Basin B 380
    climate, types of C 345
    jungles compared to J 154
    layers of habitation L 254
    Olympic National Park, Washington W 22; picture W 19
    Puerto Rico, picture N 283
    South America S 280
    tropics T 294
    Zaïre Z 366b
    See also Jungles

Rainier III (ren-YAY) (Louis Henri Maxence Bertrand Rainier de Grimaldi) (1923–), prince of Monaco, b. Monaco. A descendant of the Genoese Grimaldi dynasty that ruled Monaco (968–1731), he became prince of Monaco in 1949. He served in the French Army (1944–45) and founded the Monaco Red Cross (1948). In 1956 he married American actress Grace Kelly.
    Monaco, history of M 407

Rainier (rain-IER), **Mount,** Washington W 12, 14; pictures C 343, W 23
    grindstone clouds look like UFO's, picture F 285
    Seattle, picture S 112

Rain-in-the-Face (named when his war paint streaked in the rain) (1835?–1905), American Sioux Indian chief, b. near forks of Cheyenne River, N.Dak. He fought at battle of Little Bighorn (1876) and fled to Canada with Sitting Bull. He surrendered to American soldiers (1880).

Rainmaking W 91–94
    climate control C 348
Rain shadows, dry areas on leeward sides of mountains M 497
Rainy Lake, Minnesota-Ontario M 325

Raisin, iron- and sugar-rich dried fruit made from grapes of the European *vinifera* variety. Fully ripe grapes are dried in the sun or by artificial heat. Raisin grapes have been grown from ancient times, mainly in Greece, Spain, and the Near East. In the 20th century, raisin-grape production in California and Australia has become important. The major varieties of raisin grapes are Muscat, and Thompson or Sultana seedless.
    raisin grapes G 297
    Why are dried grapes called raisins? D 317

Raj Path, avenue in New Delhi D 103; picture D 101

Rajputs (ROJ-poots), Hindu people, divided into over 30 clans, residing chiefly in the northwestern Indian state of Rajputana. They claim to be offspring of the ancient warrior caste of the Kshatriyas. Rajputs were at the height of their power as the ruling caste from their historical appearance in the 7th century until the 12th century. Today they are the ruling group of Rajasthan and are traditionally of the military profession.
    Rajput school of miniature painting O 215

Rákosi, Mátyrás, Hungarian political leader H 288
Raksha Bandhan (rok-SHA bont-ON) **Day,** India H 158

Rale (RAHL) (or Rasle), **Sebastian** (1654?–1724), French Jesuit missionary, b. Pontarlier. After joining the American missions, he spent two years among Illinois tribes. Assigned (1693) to serve among the Abnaki Indians, he established a mission at Norridgewock, present-day Maine. He was distrusted by the British for fomenting Indian hostility against English colonists and died in an English attack on Norridgewock (1724). He compiled a dictionary of the Abnaki language, published in 1833.

Raleigh (RALL-e), capital of North Carolina **N** 318; picture **N** 319
Raleigh, Sir Walter, English soldier, courtier, and poet **R** 101
  American colonies **A** 180–81, 182
  planted first potato in Ireland **I** 390
  poetry of **E** 251
Rallentando, musical term **M** 534
Ram, constellation *see* Aries
Rama, hero-god of Hinduism **H** 132
Rama I, king of Thailand **B** 43
Ramadan (ram-a-DON), month of religious fasting for Muslims **R** 155
  Koran **K** 295
  observance of the holy month in Morocco **M** 458–59

Raman (RA-mon), **Sir Chandrasekhara Venkata** (1888–1970), Indian physicist, b. Trichinopoly. He was awarded the 1930 Nobel prize in physics for discovering the Raman effect, observed when light is scattered by the molecules of a substance through which it is passed. Some of the light rays lose energy and change in wavelength. By studying this effect, scientists have greatly increased their knowledge of the molecular structure of gases, liquids, and solids.

Ramanuja, Indian philosopher **O** 220e
Ramayana (ra-MA-ya-na), Hindu epic poem **H** 132; picture from **O** 220d
  Hindu theater **T** 163
  Indian literature **O** 220d
Ramazzini (ra-ma-TZI-ni), **Bernardino,** Italian doctor **O** 16
Rambert, Marie, English ballet director **B** 28–28a

Rambi (ROM-bi) (or Rabi), volcanic island in South Pacific, in the northern district of Fiji Islands. It has a tropical climate and fertile land. Originally owned by Lever Brothers, it was purchased and resettled by the people of Banaba (Kiribati). **K** 266

Rameau (ra-MO), **Jean-Philippe** (1683–1764), French composer and musical theorist, b. Dijon. Following the success of his opera-ballet *Les Indes galantes* and his masterpiece, the opera *Castor et Pollux,* he became the leading composer of operas in France and was named composer of the king's chamber music. He wrote church music and several suites for harpsichord.
  ballet-opera **D** 36; **O** 132
  French music **F** 445
  innovator in handling the orchestra **O** 184

Rameses *see* Ramses
Ramgoolam, Sir Seewoosagur, prime minister of Mauritius **M** 181
Ramie, kind of nettle *see* Nettle
Ramjet engines **J** 89; diagram **J** 90
  types of engines **E** 211
Rampant, position of lion in heraldry, picture **H** 117

Ramparts, The, peaks in the Rocky Mountains, picture **J** 55
Rams, male sheep **S** 145
Ramsay, Allan, Scottish painter **E** 238
Ramsay, Sir William, British chemist **N** 110
Ramses II (RAM-sese), king of Ancient Egypt **E** 91
  Abu-Simbel temple **E** 100; picture **E** 101
  statues moved from Aswan High Dam site **D** 21
Ramses III, king of ancient Egypt **E** 100

Ramsey, Alexander (1815–1903), American politician, b. near Harrisburg, Pa. He was a member of Congress (1843–47), governor of the territory of Minnesota (1849–53), mayor of Saint Paul (1855), governor of the state of Minnesota (1859–63), U.S. senator (1863–75), and secretary of war (1879–81).
  Minnesota, history of **M** 335, 337

Ram's horn, Hebrew shofar **B** 429
Rana family, of Nepal **N** 113–14
Ra Nahesi (ra na-HAY-si), Egyptian pharaoh **N** 89
Ranch life **R** 102–06
  Australia's sheep industry **A** 498
  desert ranchers **D** 128
  New Mexico **N** 187
  outback of Australia **A** 499
  prairies, land use of **P** 431; picture **P** 433
  roping **R** 333–35
  Uruguay **U** 237; picture **U** 236
  Venezuelan llanero **V** 296
  See also Cattle; Livestock
Ranch mink, fur **F** 513–14
Ranch-style homes **H** 183; picture **H** 168

Rand, Ayn (1905–82), American novelist, b. St. Petersburg (now Leningrad), U.S.S.R. Rand aroused much controversy with novels based on a philosophy called Objectivism. This philosophy includes the ideas that people should act on the basis of "rational self-interest" and that self-fulfillment is a moral responsibility. Her novels include *The Fountainhead* (1943) and *Atlas Shrugged* (1957). In the book *For the New Intellectual* (1961), she brought together the main philosophical ideas from her novels.

Rand, South Africa, gold deposit site **G** 253
Randall, James Ryder, American songwriter **N** 25
Randall's Island, New York City **N** 228

Randolph, A. Philip (Asa Philip Randolph) (1889–1979), American labor leader and civil rights activist, b. Crescent City, Fla. A respected leader in the black labor movement, he organized the Brotherhood of Sleeping Car Porters (1925). In spearheading a drive to insure equal job opportunities for blacks in defense industries, he planned a massive march on Washington, D.C. (1941). To prevent this march, President Franklin D. Roosevelt established the Fair Employment Practice Committee. Randolph was also influential in persuading President Harry Truman to ban segregation in the armed forces (1948). He became a vice-president of the AFL-CIO in 1957. In 1963 he was an active participant in the civil rights march on Washington, D.C. Picture **N** 100

Randolph, Martha Jefferson, acting first lady in Jefferson's administration **F** 165–66
  known as Patsy, picture **J** 67

Randolph family, prominent Virginia family whose members held important posts in the Virginia and U.S. governments. They were descended from **William** (1651–1711), who came to Virginia from England (1673?) and became a leading Virginia planter. **Peyton** (1721–75), grandson of William, served in the House of Burgesses of Virginia and as president of the Continental Congress (1774–75). **John** (1773–1833), great-grandson of William, served as leader in the U.S. House of Representatives and Senate. He was a leading supporter of Thomas Jefferson's policies until 1805. **Edmund** (1753–1813), nephew of Peyton, proposed the Virginia Plan at the Constitutional Convention (1787). He served as Virginia's first attorney general (1789–94).

Edmund Randolph's Virginia Plan **U** 146

Random sampling, in statistics **S** 418
Rangefinders, optical instruments **O** 170–71
cameras **P** 203, 204

Rangeland, open land that is used for grazing. Rangeland is any area of the world where animals *range,* or roam, to feed on grasses, shrubs, or other low-growing plants. In some places, as in the western United States, sections of rangeland may be seeded to provide pastures for horses or cattle. Rangeland is used by people for recreational activities, such as backpacking, hiking, camping, fishing, and bird watching.

ranch life **R** 102–06

Ranger, name of series of U.S. moon probes. Rangers VII through IX, launched in 1964 and 1965, took close-up photographs of the moon's surface, and Ranger IX also sent back live television images. The first six Ranger probes failed to complete their missions. Part of the Apollo manned space program, these probes were designed to gather information about landing conditions on the moon. **S** 348

Rangers, loosely organized body of armed men, usually mounted, who are employed by some constituted authority to defend or protect an area. They helped defend the American frontier against Indians.

Rangoon (ran-GOON), capital of Burma **B** 458–59
Shwe Dagon Pagoda, picture **B** 454
Rangoon, University of, Burma, picture **B** 458

Rankin, Jeannette (1880–1973), American legislator and suffragist, b. near Missoula, Mont. A participant in women's suffrage movements, she was the first woman elected to Congress and served in the House of Representatives (1917–19, 1941–43). She voted against U.S. entry into World War I and was the only member of Congress to oppose war declaration against Japan (1941). **M** 441

Rankin, Louise Spiker (1897–1951), American author of children's books, b. Baltimore, Md. Her travels through Europe, India, and Burma gave her the background for many of her books, including *Daughters of the Mountain* and *Gentling of Jonathan.*

Ransom, John Crowe, American poet and critic **A** 210; **T** 88
Ransom, payment for freedom from captivity **P** 263
making warfare pay in the Middle Ages **K** 273

Ransome, Arthur (1884–1967), English author, b. Leeds, Yorkshire. Though best known as a children's author, he also wrote miscellaneous adult books, including several literary critiques *(Edgar Allan Poe)* and travel books *(Six*

Weeks in Russia). His children's stories include *Swallows and Amazons, Swallowdale,* and *Winter Holiday.*

Rape of the Lock, The, by Pope **E** 258
Raphael (ra-pha-EL), Italian painter **R** 106
Italian art in Florence and Rome **I** 469
Madonna della Sedia, painting, picture **R** 106
Renaissance art **R** 162, 167, 169
Saint George and the Dragon, painting **I** 471
School of Athens, The, detail **P** 332
School of Athens, The, painting **R** 168
style of his paintings of the Madonna and Child **P** 21
Rapid City, South Dakota **S** 324
Rapid eye movement, indication that a person is dreaming **D** 306
Rapids, parts of a river where water rushes over and through rocks
Colorado River, picture **G** 291
Rapp (ROPP), **George,** German religious leader **I** 143
Rappel (rap-PEL), descent of a mountain by means of a rope **M** 491
Rapture of the deep (nitrogen narcosis), illness that attacks deep-sea divers **D** 82
preventing narcosis **U** 15–16
Rapunzel (ra-PUNZ-el), fairy tale by Grimm brothers **G** 378–80
Rare-earth elements **E** 158–59
magnets **M** 29
Rare gases *see* Noble gases
Raritan River and Bay, New Jersey **N** 166–67
radar map compared with map of the area **R** 36
Rarotonga, capital of the Cook Islands **P** 6
Ras al Khaima, state, United Arab Emirates **U** 64a
Rashtrapati Bhavan (RUSH-tra-pa-ti BA-van), president's residence in Delhi, India **D** 103
Rask (ROSK), **Rasmus,** Danish language scholar **L** 39

Raskin, Ellen (1928–   ), American author and illustrator of children's books, b. Milwaukee, Wis. Raskin's book *The Westing Game* won the Newbery medal in 1979. She also wrote and illustrated *Nothing Ever Happens on My Block* (1966) and *A & THE, or, William T.C. Baumgarten Comes to Town* (1970). Among other works she has illustrated is *A Child's Christmas in Wales* (1959) by Dylan Thomas.

Rasle, Sebastian *see* Rale, Sebastian

Rasmussen (RAS-muss-en), **Knud Johan Victor** (1879–1933), Danish explorer and ethnologist, b. Jacobshavn, Greenland. He led numerous expeditions (from 1902) in Greenland to research his theory that Eskimo and North American Indians can be traced to a common Asian ancestry. He founded the Thule, Greenland, settlement (1910), which became a base for further explorations. He was responsible for discovering and preserving Eskimo folklore. Among his books translated into English are *Greenland by the Polar Sea, Myths and Legends from Greenland,* and *Across Arctic America.*

Raspberries **G** 298, 301; picture **G** 299

Rasputin (ra-SPU-tin), **Grigori Efimovich** (1872?–1916), Russian holy man, b. Tobolsk province, Siberia. An unlearned peasant who dedicated himself to mysticism (about 1904) and proclaimed himself a holy man. Because he apparently cured the sick crown prince with prayers and mystic rites, he gained complete power over

Rasputin, Grigori Efimovich (continued)
Czarina Alexandra and Czar Nicholas II. An advocate of autocracy, he used his hypnotic power over the Czar and Czarina to rid the court of all liberal ministers, replacing them with his sympathizers. During World War I his control became corrupt, and he was finally assassinated.

Rasses, small civet cats **G** 93
Rastafarianism see Reggae
Ratels (RA-tels) (honey badgers) **O** 246
Ratification, of treaties **T** 271
Ratings, grades of skills in U.S. Navy **U** 190
Ratio, in mathematics **M** 155
    probability **P** 471
Rational numbers, quotients of two integers **N** 385
    new numbers in history of mathematics **M** 155

Rationing, equal distribution or economical use of a supply, especially during times of disaster, such as war or famine. In the United States during World War II individual allotment of goods including canned foods, meats, gasoline, and fuel oil was controlled by issuance of ration coupons.

Ratites, group of flightless birds **O** 236á–236c
Rat kangaroos **A** 506; **K** 170; picture **K** 168
Ratline (clove) **hitch,** knot **K** 292
Ratoons, pineapples **P** 249
Rats, rodents **R** 277–78
    aging experiment, picture **A** 85
    animal maze tests **A** 284
    bubonic plague **I** 287; picture **I** 286
    disease prevention and rat control **D** 221
    experiment with living space **L** 253
    household pests **H** 264
    how rats are classified **K** 252
    learning experiments, picture **L** 102
    pack rats **R** 279
    tracks, picture **A** 271
Rattan palm, tree **J** 154
Rattigan, Terence, English dramatist **E** 268
Rattlesnake flags **F** 247; picture **F** 229
Rattlesnakes **S** 209; pictures **S** 210
    animals harmful to people **I** 284, 285
    sensory system of **B** 366
    timber rattlesnake, picture **I** 282
Rauschenberg, Robert, American artist **M** 397; **P** 31
Rauscher viruses, picture **C** 93
Rauwolfia (ra-WOLF-ia), plant **P** 313; picture **P** 312

Ravalli, Antonio (1811–84), Italian missionary, b. Ferrara. He went to Canada (1844) and soon began working among the Indians in what is now Montana. He moved to northern Idaho and was accepted as a leader by the Indians. As white settlers came west, he became priest and physician to Indians and miners.
    Idaho, history of **I** 68

Ravel (ra-VEL), **Maurice Joseph** (1875–1937), French composer, b. Ciboure, Basses-Pyrénées. His music was controversial and for many years considered too advanced for contemporary tastes. His greatest success was the orchestral work *Boléro* (originally a ballet). Other well-known works include ballets *Daphnis et Chloé* and *La Valse;* an opera, *L'Heure espagnole;* two piano concertos; *Rhapsodie espagnole;* many songs, including the cycle *Shéhérazade;* piano pieces, including *Pavane for a Dead Princess.* Picture **F** 448
    chamber music, new **C** 186
    French music **F** 447; **O** 138
    L'Heure espagnole, opera **O** 145

Raven, constellation see Corvus
Ravenna (ra-VEN-na), Italy
    Byzantine art of **B** 484
    Sant' Apollinare in Classe church, picture **A** 370
Ravens, birds **P** 86
    ravens, of Odin, Norse god **N** 278
    Sam Houston's Indian name **H** 271
    symbol of England's royal family **H** 115
Rawalpindi, Pakistan
    bazaar, picture **P** 39
Rawhide
    lariats **R** 333
Rawlings, Flight Lieutenant Jerry J., Ghanaian political leader **G** 198
Rawlings, Marjorie Kinnan, American novelist **A** 212–13
    illustration by N. C. Wyeth for *The Yearling* **C** 248d
Raw materials
    forests **F** 371–74
    life, food chains in **L** 239, 242
    mines and mining **M** 314–20
    primary products in international trade **I** 327
    wood **W** 222–28
    See also agricultural products by name, as Corn
Raw silk **S** 179
Ray, John, English naturalist **B** 191
Ray, Man, American artist **M** 393
    Gift, The (Le Cadeau), dada sculpture, picture **M** 394
Ray, Satyajit, Indian motion picture director **M** 488
Rayburn, Samuel T., American statesman **T** 135
    helpful to Johnson's early political career **J** 128
Rayleigh (RAY-le), **Lord,** British chemist **N** 110
Rayon, synthetic fiber **N** 424, 428
Rays, fishes **S** 140–43
Rays, in geometry **G** 124
Rays, on the moon **M** 450
Rays, cosmic see Cosmic rays
Raza, El Día de la (Day of the Race), Latin American holiday **H** 150
Razorback hogs **H** 211; picture **H** 210
RBI see Runs batted in
RCA see Radio Corporation of America
RDX, explosive **E** 394

Re (RAY) (or Ra), in ancient Egyptian religion, chief deity and sun god. Re was often compounded with other gods, and from 2000 to 1800 B.C. his name was joined with that of Amon, who later reigned supreme. According to legend, Re created himself from nothingness and then created air, moisture, and eventually mankind. He was considered first king of Egypt, and all succeeding kings took his name. He was symbolized by hawk, scarab, or serpent.

Reaction, force in direction opposite to action **M** 471
    jet propulsion **J** 88
    reaction engines **E** 209, 211
Reaction, in psychology
    response to environment **K** 255–56
Reaction engines **E** 209, 211
Reactions, chemical **C** 196–97, 201
    catalysis **C** 199
Reaction turbines **E** 210

Reade, Charles (1814–84), English author, b. Oxfordshire. He began his career as a dramatist with the production in 1851 of the comedy *The Ladies' Battle.* He is chiefly remembered for his novels, including his best-known, *The Cloister and the Hearth,* depicting early Renaissance life, and novels exposing social injustice, such as *It Is Never Too Late to Mend* and *Hard Cash.*

Reader's Digest, The, magazine **M** 15
Readers' Guide to Periodical Literature R 130
  indexes to magazines **I** 115
Reading R 107–11
  book reports and book reviews **B** 314–17
  language arts reading program **L** 36
  library reading clubs **L** 171–72
  media center encourages reading for enjoyment
    L 176
  new and old readers, pictures **E** 77
  nonsense rhymes need to be seen **N** 272
  phonics in teaching reading **P** 193–95
  vocabulary, how to increase **V** 372
  See also Children's literature
Reading (RED-ing), Pennsylvania **P** 142
Reading readiness R 107–08
Ready-made clothing C 353
Reagan, Nancy Davis, wife of Ronald Reagan **F** 180b;
    R 112b; picture **R** 112c
Reagan, Ronald Wilson, 40th president of the United
    States **R** 112–112c

Reaganomics, a popular term for the economic policies of U.S. president Ronald Reagan. In general, these policies are based on the idea that a healthy economy will be achieved through free enterprise. They include lowering taxes and lessening government regulation of business. Such policies are intended to give producers of goods and services (the "supply side" of the economy) free rein to expand. Other administrations have favored policies intended to increase the demand for goods and services—the "demand side" of the economy.

Real estate R 112d–113
  disposed of by a will **W** 174
  noise pollution **N** 270
Real images, light pictures **L** 263
  lenses **L** 144
Realism, in art
  Dutch and Flemish art **D** 350–51, 352
  French painting **F** 426
  modern art **M** 386–87
Realism, in literature
  American literature **A** 206
  children's literature **C** 240–44
  drama **D** 297
  German literature **G** 178–79
  Italian 20th-century literature **I** 481
  Russian literature **U** 60
  Spanish literature **S** 370
Realistic stories
  list of, for children **C** 248b–248d
Real numbers, include rational and irrational numbers
    N 385–86
Real property *see* Real estate
Realtors R 112d, 113
Reaney, James, Canadian poet and playwright **C** 64
Reaper, harvesting machine **M** 186
  farm machinery **F** 60
Re-apportionment, of government representatives
    S 415
Reason for the Pelican, The, poem by John Ciardi
    N 274
Reasoning *see* Thinking

Réaumur (ray-o-MUR), **René Antoine Ferchault de** (1683–1757), French scientist, b. La Rochelle. His greatest contribution to science is a six-volume work on insect anatomy and behavior. He was first to collect and isolate stomach juices, by recovering sponges swallowed by birds. He showed that food is digested by these juices. He devised a thermometer scale, named for him, that separates boiling and freezing points of water by 80 degrees.
  wood pulp as a source of paper suggested by study of
    wasp behavior **C** 432; **P** 56–57

Rebec (RE-bec), Arabic musical instrument **V** 342
Rebecca, novel by Daphne du Maurier **M** 556

Rebekah (or Rebecca), in the Old Testament (Genesis 24–27), daughter of Bethuel, son of Abraham's brother Nahor. She was escorted from Abraham's birthplace to Negeb to marry Isaac. She bore Isaac two sons, Esau and Jacob, and lived with him in Gerar and Beersheba. She helped Jacob, her favorite son, take Esau's place and receive Isaac's blessing. She was buried next to Sarah, her mother-in-law, in the Cave of Machpelah.
  how a proper wife was found for Isaac **I** 413

Rebellion of 1837, Canada, led by Louis Joseph
    Papineau **C** 73
Rebellious Stripes, flag **F** 247
Rebuses (RE-bus-es) **W** 236–37
  button collection displayed **B** 480; picture **B** 478
Rebuttal, in a debate **D** 55
Recall *see* Impeachment; Initiative, referendum, and
    recall, legislative processes

Récamier (ray-ca-mi-AY), **Madame** (Jeanne Françoise Julie Adélaïde Bernard Récamier) (1777–1849), French society leader, b. Lyons. The wife of Parisian banker Jacques Récamier, she was known as a beautiful and charming hostess who entertained noted people of her day. Her friends included author Madame de Staël and statesman-writer Chateaubriand. Her memoirs were published as *Souvenirs et correspondances* ("Memories and Letters").

Recapitulation, in music **M** 534, 539, 540
Receptors, specialized nerve cells **B** 365
  body's senses **B** 283
  parts of insects that receive sensation **I** 266
Recessions *see* Depressions and recessions
Recessive traits, in genetics **G** 80–81
Recharge wells, wells that pump water into the ground
    W 122
Recife (ray-CI-fay), capital of Pernambuco, Brazil
    B 383
Recipes (RES-ip-ese) **R** 114–16
  barbecue sauce **O** 247
  Halloween party food and drink **H** 17
  shish kebab **O** 248
Reciprocal (re-CIP-ro-cal) **Trade Agreement Act,** 1934
    I 329
  tariff in international trade **T** 25
Reciprocating engines I 303
Reciprocity (re-ci-PROS-ity) **Treaty,** 1854 **C** 73
Recitals (re-CY-tals), of art songs **V** 376
Recitatives (res-i-ta-TEVES), sung dialogues or speech-
    songs **M** 537; **O** 131
  musical term, invented during baroque period
    B 63
Reclamation Act, 1902 **R** 329
  land under irrigation in Nebraska **N** 87

Reclining Figure, sculpture by Henry Moore, picture **E** 242

Recoil mechanism, of artillery **G** 425

Recombinant DNA *see* Gene splicing

Reconstruction Act, 1867, United States **R** 120

administration of Andrew Johnson **J** 125

Reconstruction Finance Corporation H 224

Reconstruction Period, in United States **R** 117–20

black history **N** 96

Hayes' election compromise **H** 79–80

Johnson, Andrew **J** 125

Lincoln's plan for **L** 297

Record collecting R 124–25

basic collection of jazz records **J** 62

Recorder, musical instrument **R** 121–22

in concert, picture **I** 482

types of musical instruments **M** 547, 549

Recorders, tape *see* Tape recorders

Record hops, dances **R** 262b

Recordings, phonograph *see* Records, phonograph

Record player *see* Phonograph

Records, phonograph P 196–97

country and western music **C** 525

electronic music, outstanding compositions **E** 142h

hi-fi and stereo recording **H** 125–26, 127

jazz, outstanding recordings **J** 62

record collecting and basic record library **R** 123–25

rock music **R** 262b

talking books for the blind **B** 252–53

Recreation

family amusement in colonial America **C** 392

camping **C** 40–47

mountains, importance of for recreation **M** 498

national recreation areas **N** 52

parks and playgrounds **P** 76–78

parties **P** 87–89

pioneer life **P** 258

rivers **R** 240

snowmobiles **S** 215

television **T** 65–71

United States **U** 101–02

vacations and travel **V** 258–59

See also Games; Hobbies; Indoor activities; Play; Sports

Rectal thermometers M 208f; **N** 414

Rectangles, geometric forms **G** 126

Rectifiers, electric **E** 146

Rectilinear movement, of snakes **S** 211

Recycling, and re-use, of waste materials **C** 486; **S** 31

aluminum **A** 177

environmental problems of solid-waste pollution **E** 272g

metal cans sorted at a center, picture **C** 483

rubber tires **R** 347

Red, Red Rose, A, poem by Robert Burns **B** 460

Red and the Black, The, novel by Stendhal **N** 348

Red ant, picture **A** 323

Red Badge of Courage, The, book by Stephen Crane **A** 206

Redbed Plains, Oklahoma **O** 82

Red-bellied woodpeckers, birds, picture **B** 239

Red blood cells *see* Red corpuscles

Redbud tree, picture **G** 45

state tree of Oklahoma, picture **O** 81

Red cabbage

as an acid-base indicator **C** 217

Red cedar, tree, picture **T** 278

Red China *see* China, People's Republic of

Red Cloud (1822–1909), American Indian chief, b. near Platte River, Nebr. As chief of Oglala Teton Sioux, he opposed U.S. government construction of road from Fort Laramie, Wyo., to gold regions in Montana. After leading Sioux and Cheyenne Indians in Fetterman massacre (1866) and Wagon Box fight (1867), he signed peace treaty (1868) in which the government agreed to abandon construction of the road.

Red clover, plant

Vermont, state flower of, picture **V** 307

Redcoats, nickname for British soldiers **R** 196

French and Indian War **F** 460

Red corpuscles, in the blood **B** 256; picture **D** 191

anemia **D** 199

circulatory system of human body **B** 275–77

medical laboratory tests **M** 201

use in medicine **M** 211

Red Crescent, symbol of Muslim Red Cross Societies **R** 126

flag **F** 226

Red Cross R 126–27

Barton, Clara, founder of American branch **B** 68

flag **F** 226

Red Cross Youth R 127

Red Deer Valley, Alberta, Canada **A** 146a

Red desert soils S 233

found in African deserts **A** 52

Redding, Jay Saunders (1906–   ), American educator and author, b. Wilmington, Del. For many years he was a professor of literature in various Southern colleges and universities. In 1963 he received his D.Litt. from Brown University. He has won many awards for his books and for his contribution to interracial understanding. His writings include *To Make a Poet Black* (1939), *They Came in Chains* (1950), *On Being Negro in America* (1951), and *The Lonesome Road* (1958).

Red Eagle, Creek Indian leader **A** 112

Redeye, missile **M** 348

Red-eyed vireos, birds, picture **B** 239

Red-figure pottery, ancient Greece **P** 414

Red Flag Act, 1865 **A** 542

Red foxes D 248–49; **F** 396b

Redgrave, Vanessa, British actress **M** 488c

Red Guards, militant Communist Chinese youth organization. It was formed to support, with violence if necessary, the Cultural Revolution. This is the name given Communist Party Chairman Mao Tse-tung's campaign to impose a more austere form of Communism on China. **C** 272

Red Jacket (Sagoyewatha) (1758–1830), American Indian chief, b. Seneca County, N.Y. He was chief of Seneca Indians and was noted particularly for his oratory upholding Indian traditions. He received his popular name from his custom of wearing a red jacket given to him by a British officer. He resisted introduction of white institutions, particularly Christianity. In War of 1812 he lent support to the United States.

Red Jungle Fowl, ancestor of chickens **P** 420

Red kangaroos K 170; picture **K** 168

Red-letter days, memorable or important days. The term arose from the custom of indicating holy days in red on church calendars.

Red light rooms, in zoos   Z 379
Red Lion, running and chasing game   G 21
Red Lion and Sun, symbol of the Red Cross of Iran
R 126
flag   F 226
Redman, Don, American jazz composer   J 59
Red maple, tree
Rhode Island, state tree of, picture   R 213
Red Mill, The, operetta by Victor Herbert   O 158
Red oak, tree
New Jersey, state tree of, picture   N 164
Redonda, uninhabited island, Antigua and Barbuda
A 316b
Red on yellow, kill a fellow, saying about snakes
S 209
Red Paint Indians, original inhabitants of Maine   M 46
Red pepper   S 382
Red (Norway) pine, tree
Minnesota, state tree of, picture   M 323
Red planet, Mars   M 105
planets of our solar system   P 273
Red raspberries, picture   G 299
Red River, of southern United States   O 83;   T 125
Louisiana   L 351
Red River, southeast Asia   R 245;   V 333, 334a
Red River carts, two-wheeled carts of pioneers   N 329
early transportation in Minnesota   M 322
Red River colony, Canada, founded by Lord Selkirk
C 72, 73
Manitoba, settlements in   M 76, 82
Red River of the North
Manitoba   M 76
Minnesota   M 325
system in North Dakota   N 325
Red Rock River, considered as first portion of the
Missouri   M 383
Red Rover, running and chasing game   G 20
Red Sea   O 48
continental drift   E 20;   G 116
Red shift, change in galaxy spectrum   U 201–03
Doppler effect, law in physics   L 268
Redshirts, guerrilla band led by Italy's Garibaldi   G 57
Red Shoes, The, story by Hans Christian Andersen
A 248
Red snow
algae   A 156
red dust   R 95
Red spiders, mites   P 286
Red Spot, Jupiter   P 275
Red Square, Moscow   M 466; picture   U 27
Redstarts, birds, picture   B 240
Redstone Arsenal, Huntsville, Alabama   A 113, 124
Red Studio, The, painting by Matisse   M 389

Red tape, rigid conformity to formal rules of a large organization, hindering or preventing action or decision-
making. The term originates from English 17th- and
18th-century procedure of binding documents and official papers with red tape and was popularized in the writings of Thomas Carlyle against official inertia.

Red tides, marine organisms   A 157
Reduction, of metals   M 226
direct reduction of iron ore   I 406
Red wines   W 188
Red-winged blackbird, pictures   B 216, 240
Red wolves   W 210
dog family   D 245–46
Redwood, tree   T 274
California forests   C 19

giants of nature   G 200, 202–03
leaves, needlelike, pictures   L 119
plants, odd and interesting   P 316
uses of the wood and its grain, picture   W 224
why called sequoias   S 124
Redwood National Park, California   C 24
Reed, Walter, American doctor   R 128
proved theory of insects as disease carriers   D 215
results of Spanish-American War   S 376
Reed boats, water craft   S 155
Bolivia, picture   B 304
Reed instruments   M 547, 549;   W 182–83
Reed organ   O 208
Reefs, coral   C 503–04
Pacific islands   P 2
underwater life, picture   O 40
Reelfoot Lake, Tennessee   T 77, 84
Reels, for fishing   F 206, 209; pictures   F 207
Re-entry, of spacecraft   S 340j
Reeve, Tapping, American lawyer and educator   C 478
Referee (ref-er-EE), in sports
basketball   B 83
boxing   B 351–52
football   F 362
soccer   S 218a
Reference books   R 129–31
atlases   M 93
Book Review Digest   B 317
dictionaries   D 164–65
encyclopedias   E 193–97
how arranged in libraries   L 185
indexes and indexing   I 114–15
magazine lists   M 15
quotations   Q 19
research methods   R 183
use in a library research project   L 187
word origins, source books   W 241
See also Textbooks
Referendum *see* Initiative, referendum, and recall,
legislative processes
Referent (re-FER-ent), in semantics, what a word stands
for   S 117
Refining, of fats and oils   O 78
Refining, of metals   M 228–29
aluminum   A 176–77
gold   G 249
Refining, of petroleum   G 63;   P 174; picture   P 175
Reflecting telescopes   T 61, 62
lenses   L 147
Reflection, in physics
light   L 260, 262–63
reflective insulation   I 291
Reflection of the Big Dipper, painting by Jackson
Pollock, picture   P 387
Reflectors, in photography   P 210; picture   P 209
Reflectors, of radio telescopes   R 72
Reflex action (reflexes), in psychology   P 496
sense of touch and reflex action   B 287
spinal cord functions   B 368
Reflex finders, in cameras   P 203
Reforestation   F 372–73
Asia   A 463
Reformation (ref-or-MAY-tion)   R 132–35
Calvin, John   C 30
Christianity, history of   C 285–87
Christmas outlawed in England by Puritans   C 291
education in national languages promoted   E 67–68
Erasmus' views on the Reformation   E 274
Germany's early religious divisions   G 159–60

Reformation (continued)
    Luther, Martin, leader of Protestant movement
      L 378
    monument to Farel, Calvin, Beza, and Knox,
      pictures **C** 287
    Protestantism **P** 482–83
    reforms for Roman Catholic Church **R** 293–94
    Switzerland **S** 496, 502
Reformatories, prisons that attempted to reform
    inmates **P** 469–70
Reform Bill, 1832, England **E** 227
Reform Judaism (JU-da-ism) **J** 118, 119, 120
Reform schools, for juvenile offenders **P** 470
Refracting telescopes **T** 61–62
    lenses **L** 147
Refraction, of light **L** 263–64
    lenses **L** 142–43
    optical instruments **O** 166
    prisms reveal spectra of light **L** 266
Refractive index, of light **O** 173–74
    brilliancy of gemstones **G** 69
Refractometer (re-frac-TOM-et-er), optical instrument
    O 173–74; picture **O** 169
Refractories, ceramics that can hold up under high
    temperatures **C** 180
Refractors, optical instruments **O** 169
Refrain, in music **M** 534
Refreshments, for parties **P** 89
Refrigerants, substances that do the cooling in
    refrigerators **R** 136–37
    food preservation and processing **F** 347
Refrigeration **R** 136–38
    air conditioning **A** 103
    Bacon's experiment **B** 7
    cool storage of food **F** 346–47
    food poisoning **S** 31
    foods, preservation from spoilage **F** 355
Refrigerators
    electric appliances **E** 119
    food spoilage **F** 354–55
    frozen foods **F** 346
    liquid gases **L** 308
    nitrogen gas used as refrigerant **G** 60
    refrigerator cars, of railroads **R** 82
    trucks **T** 296
Refugee-Escapee Act, 1957 **I** 101
Refugee in America, poem by Langston Hughes **H** 274
Refugee Relief Act, 1952 **I** 101
Refugees
    aliens in the United States **A** 166
    exodus from East to West Germany **G** 164
    Hong Kong **H** 205
    Jews after World War II **J** 111
    Korean War victims, picture **K** 305
    Palestinian Arab refugees **J** 136, 139; **L** 121, 123
    poverty, victims of **P** 424a
    stateless persons **P** 94
Refuse (REF-use) **and refuse disposal** *see* Solid-waste
    disposal
Regattas (re-GA-tas)
    rowing races **R** 338–39

Regelation, refreezing of ice that has melted under pressure. When ice is compressed, it becomes liquid and re-
freezes at a temperature lower than the normal freezing
point of water. Regelation takes place within a snowball
when it is packed tightly. Regelation is involved in the
movement of glaciers.

Regency, period in a country's history when the monarch
is too young, too ill, or otherwise unable to rule and

someone else, called a regent (from the Latin word for
"ruler"), rules in his place. The term "Regency" now
most often refers to the years 1811–20 in England, when
the Prince of Wales (later King George IV) was regent for
his father, King George III. It is also used to describe the
period's styles of architecture, furniture, and dress.
    furniture, picture **F** 506
    London of Regency period **L** 336

Regenerated fibers **F** 108; **N** 424, 427–28
Regeneration, in biology
    crustacea replace lost appendages **S** 171
    experiments with amphibians **F** 478
    hydra **J** 73
    starfishes **S** 403
Regent diamond, picture **D** 156
Regent's Park, London, England **P** 77
Regent Street, London, England **L** 336

Reggae, a popular music and dance style that originated
in Jamaica. The music combines features of soul and
rock. The songs deal mainly with economic and social
injustices. Reggae was made popular outside the Caribbean by the musician **Bob Marley** (1945–81). Reggae is
linked to **Rastafarianism,** a Jamaican religious movement. Rastafarians believe in the divinity of the former
Ethiopian emperor Haile Selassie (who was known originally as Ras Tafari). They think of themselves as exiled
blacks who will eventually return to Ethiopia as their reward.

Regiment, army troop unit **U** 172
Regin (RAIG-in), dwarf in Norse mythology **N** 280–81
Regina (re-GINE-a), capital of Saskatchewan, Canada
    S 38g; picture **S** 38b
    cities of Canada **C** 67

Regina medal, juvenile literary award founded (1959) by
the Catholic Library Association. It is presented annually
to an author, illustrator, or editor, regardless of religion
or nationality, whose career has been devoted to the advancement of children's literature.

Regional geography **G** 108
Regional libraries **L** 174
Regional literature, American **A** 204–05
    fiction **F** 109–10
    local-color short stories **S** 167
    novels **N** 349
Registan, I., Russian poet **N** 19
Registered mail **P** 409
Registered nurses **N** 412
Registration of aliens **A** 166

Registration of voters, official enrollment of persons
qualified to vote. Generally the voter presents his qualifications to the proper officials before an election, and
these registration lists serve as check lists at the polls. In
periodic registration the process is repeated before each
election. In permanent registration, lists are made up at
longer intervals and kept up to date.
    elections **E** 112–115

Regs, gravel plains **S** 8
Regulus (REG-u-lus), star **C** 492
Regurgitation, of animals
    owls **O** 269
Rehabilitation, after illness **H** 248–49
    medicine, tools and techniques of **M** 208d

Rehabilitation of the handicapped see Handicapped, rehabilitation of the

Rehavia, residential community, Jerusalem **J** 82

Rehearsals (re-HER-sals), of plays **P** 336, 339; pictures **T** 157

Rehnquist, William Hubbs (1924–), American jurist, b. Milwaukee, Wisc.; educated Stanford University. He practiced law in Arizona before becoming an assistant U.S. attorney general in 1969. President Nixon appointed him to the Supreme Court in 1972.

Rehoboam (re-o-BO-am), in Old Testament, son of Solomon and Naamah; king of Judah (933?–917 B.C.). His high taxes and forced-labor policy led to the division of the nation into two kingdoms—Israel and Judah.

Reich (RIKE), German word for empire
    First Reich, founded by Charlemagne **G** 159
    Second Reich, of Germany **G** 160–61
    Third Reich, of Germany **G** 162–63

Reichenbach (RIKE-en-bock) **Falls,** Switzerland **W** 56, 57

Reichstadt, Duke of see Napoleon II

Reichstag (RIKE-stoc), national German parliament of elected representatives. Established under the German Empire (1871), it was recreated by the Weimar Constitution (1919), which strengthened it with executive power to check actions of chancellor and president, although the president could replace the Reichstag with an emergency cabinet in time of conflict. It surrendered its power by voting for the "enabling act" (1933), which granted legislative power to Chancellor Adolf Hitler and his cabinet.

Reichstag fire, 1933 **N** 70
    Hitler comes to power **W** 285

Reid (REED), **Samuel,** American naval officer **F** 248

Reign (RAIN) **of Terror,** in the French Revolution **F** 416, 467–68
    events in Paris **P** 73

Reilly, Charles, English architect and teacher **E** 241

Reincarnation (re-in-car-NATION), rebirth of the soul in a new body **D** 53; **R** 146
    Hinduism **H** 131

Reindeer (RAIN-deer) **D** 83; picture **H** 215
    cave drawing, picture **D** 303
    hoofed mammals **H** 214
    Lapland **L** 45
    milk **F** 333
    Siberia **A** 451

Reindeer moss **F** 95

Reiner (RY-ner), **Fritz** (1888–1963), American conductor, b. Budapest, Hungary. He was music director at Royal Opera House, Dresden, Germany (1914–21). He came to United States (1922) to become music director of the Cincinnati Symphony Orchestra (1922–31) and was director of opera and orchestra departments and conducting teacher at Curtis Institute of Music, Philadelphia (1931–41). He served as conductor of the Pittsburgh Symphony Orchestra (1938–48), the Metropolitan Opera in New York (1948–53), and the Chicago Symphony Orchestra (1953–63).

Reinforced (re-in-FORCED) **concrete** **B** 434; **C** 168; picture **C** 167
    architectural possibilities **A** 385, 386a, 386b
    building material **B** 431

    homes of **H** 175
    use in Latin America **L** 67

Reinforcement, stimuli procedure in learning **L** 100

Reinhardt, Django, Belgian jazz musician **J** 60

Reinhardt (RINE-hart), **Max** (Max Goldmann) (1873–1943), Austrian theatrical producer, b. Baden, near Vienna. He was director at Deutsches Theater, Berlin (1894–1903, 1905–20, 1924–32). Among his renowned productions in Europe were *The Miracle, Everyman,* and *Oedipus Rex.* He came to the United States (1933), at the rise of the Nazis. His stage and screen productions were famous.
    drama, history of **D** 298

Reinisch, Rica, East German swimmer **O** 116b; picture **O** 116c

Reintegration, correctional program **P** 470

Reisen, Abraham, Yiddish author **Y** 351

Rejection of organ transplants see Transplants of body organs

Relative humidity **G** 101; **W** 75–76, 80–81
    wet-and-dry-bulb readings, table **W** 81

Relative pronouns **P** 91

Relatives, in grammar **G** 289

Relatives, maternal and paternal, in the family
    presidents, U.S., related to other presidents **P** 450

Relativity (rel-a-TIV-ity), a theory in physics **R** 139–44
    Einstein's life, and how he worked out his theories **E** 104–06
    Einstein's new theory of gravitation **G** 325
    science, history of **S** 76

Relay races, track events **T** 238
    games **G** 18–20
    passing the baton, picture **T** 239
    team racing **R** 33
    world records **T** 238

Relief, in sculpture **S** 90
    ancient art **A** 233, 238–40, 242–43
    Egypt, ancient **E** 96, 99, 101–02
    Ghiberti's doors **I** 467–68; picture **R** 165
    Romanesque carving **M** 297

Relief, public see Welfare, public

Relief maps **M** 90

Relief printing **G** 302; **L** 315

Religion, primitive **R** 145

Religions **R** 145–52
    anthropological studies **A** 304
    art, the meanings of **A** 438
    art as a record **A** 438f
    Asia **A** 460, 468
    Buddha's teachings **B** 423
    Christianity **C** 279–89
    civil rights conflicts **C** 315–16
    colonial America **C** 393–94, 395
    Confucius' teachings **C** 460
    death, beliefs about **D** 53
    divorce **D** 236
    Eskimo religion **E** 288
    Europe **E** 317–18
    fire worship in primitive religions **F** 144
    folk art **F** 292–93
    folk music **F** 324
    food customs **F** 335
    funeral customs **F** 492–95
    Hinduism **H** 130–32
    Indians of North America **I** 171
    Islam **I** 414–16
    Judaism **J** 114–20
    Middle East **M** 305

Religions (continued)
  Mormons **M** 457
  mythology **M** 557–64
  Orthodox Eastern Churches **O** 228–30
  pioneer life **P** 259
  prayer **P** 434–35
  primitive rites based on search for food **F** 332
  Protestantism **P** 482–86
  Roman Catholic Church **R** 287–302
  voodoo **H** 9
  wedding customs **W** 100–03
  women, role of **W** 211
  Zoroastrianism **Z** 380
  See also facts and figures and people sections of
    continent and country articles
Religious art
  African art **A** 72; pictures **A** 74
  Angelico, Fra **A** 259
  Byzantine **B** 483–90
  Caravaggio **C** 105
  Chagall, Marc **C** 184
  Dutch and Flemish painting **D** 349–58
  illuminated manuscripts **I** 87–88
  Islamic art and architecture **I** 417–22
  Italian **I** 463, 468–70, 472
  Latin America **L** 64
  Middle Ages **M** 296–97
  Raphael **R** 106
  Renaissance **R** 162, 166
  Spanish art and architecture **S** 361–62
Religious drama
  liturgical dramas for modern audiences **F** 444
  Middle English literature **E** 249–50
  miracle, morality, and mystery plays **D** 295
Religious education **E** 69
  parochial schools **E** 75
Religious freedom *see* Freedom of religion
Religious holidays **R** 153–55
  Christmas **C** 290–94
  December celebrates Christmas and Hanukkah
    D 56
  Easter **E** 41–42
  fasts of the Orthodox Eastern Churches **O** 229–30
  Hanukkah **H** 35
  holy days for Roman Catholics **R** 290
  Japanese **J** 31
  New Year celebrations around the world **N** 208–09
  origin of the trade fair **F** 10
  Passover **P** 93–94
  Purim **P** 540
  toys **T** 233
Religious liberty *see* Freedom of religion
Religious music
  American Indian **I** 160–61
  ancient Hebrew **A** 246
  Christmas carols **C** 122
  Germany **G** 182
  hymns **H** 309–13
  Negro spirituals **N** 105–07
  Renaissance music **R** 172, 173–74
  Spain **S** 372
  See also Church music
Religious orders
  founding of Dominicans and Franciscans **R** 292
  Jesuits **R** 294
  Loyola, founder of Jesuits **L** 369
  See also Monks and monasticism; Nuns
REM *see* Rapid eye movement
Remainder, in subtraction **A** 399
Remagen (RAY-mog-en), Germany

battle for the Rhine bridge, 1945 **W** 306
Remarque (rem-ARK), **Erich Maria,** German-born
  American novelist **G** 180
Rembrandt, Dutch painter **R** 155–56
  Abraham's Sacrifice, etching **D** 358
  Aristotle Contemplating the Bust of Homer, painting
    G 354
  art of the artist **A** 438f
  Blindness of Tobit, The, etching **G** 304
  Dutch and Flemish art **D** 357–58
  etching technique **G** 305–06
  Faust in His Study, Watching a Magic Disc, painting
    F 73
  Gilder Herman Doomer, The, painting **A** 438c
  importance to baroque period **B** 61–62
  importance to history of painting **P** 24
  Night Watch, The, painting, detail **R** 156
  Polish Rider, The, painting **P** 25
  Six's Bridge, etching **B** 61
  Syndics of the Cloth Guild, The, painting **D** 359
  View near Rampoortje, Amsterdam, drawing **D** 302
  Windmill, The, etching **E** 294
Remedial (re-ME-di-al) **reading** **R** 111
Remembering, in psychology **P** 493
  learning **L** 105
Remember the Alamo, rallying cry of the Mexican War
  H 271; **T** 122
Remember the Maine, Spanish-American War cry
  S 374
Remembrance Day, Canada **H** 152
Remembrance of Things Past, novel by Marcel Proust
  F 442; **N** 348
Remington, Frederic, American artist **U** 121–22
  Fight for the Waterhole, painting **U** 119
  museum, Ogdensburg, New York **N** 219
  paintings at Amon Carter Museum of Western Art,
    Forth Worth, Texas **T** 131
Remizov, Aleksei, Russian author **U** 61
Remoras, fishes **F** 203–04
  curious ways animals move about **A** 266
Remote controlled mechanical systems
  hydraulic machines **H** 301–02
  model airplanes **A** 105–06
  model racing cars **A** 537
Remote releases, in photography **P** 207
Remus *see* Romulus and Remus
Renaissance (ren-ais-SONCE) **R** 157–62
  cities, history of **C** 308c
  dance and pantomime **D** 24–25
  drama **D** 295–96
  education **E** 67–68
  exploration during **E** 375
  historical writings **H** 135
  Italian literature **I** 476–79
  Italy **I** 455–56
  Leonardo da Vinci **L** 152–54
  libraries **L** 196–97
  medicine **M** 205–06
  rebirth of science **S** 66
  Reformation a part of the changing world **R** 132
  Roman Catholic Church **R** 293–94
  upholstery began to be used **U** 226
Renaissance architecture **R** 163–71
  building during the Renaissance **R** 161–62
  cathedrals **C** 132–33
  England **A** 382–83
  Foundling Hospital, in Florence, Italy **A** 438e–438f;
    picture **R** 165
  France **A** 381–82
  Giotto's bell tower, Florence **G** 211

homes **H** 179–80
Italy **A** 380–81, picture **A** 384
Michelangelo **M** 257
Renaissance art **R** 163–71
art, the meanings of **A** 438
Bellini family **B** 136
Botticelli, Sandro **B** 340b
decorative arts **D** 73–75
Donatello **D** 285
Dürer influenced by **D** 345
France **F** 421–22; picture **A** 438a
furniture design **F** 505–06
German painting and sculpture **G** 169
Giotto di Bondone **G** 211
golden age of **R** 161–62
humanism in **A** 438e–438f
Italian art and architecture **I** 464–65
Italian painting **P** 20–21, 23; picture **A** 438a
jewelry making developed **J** 94
Michelangelo **M** 255–57
Raphael **R** 106
sculpture **S** 98–99
tapestries **T** 22–23
Titian **T** 199
Renaissance Center, Detroit, Michigan **D** 151
Renaissance man **R** 162
Renaissance music **R** 172–74
choral music **C** 277
Dutch and Flemish music **D** 364
French music **F** 444–45
Italian music **I** 483
Renal dialysis treatment, medicine **M** 211
Rendering, extracting oils and fats from animal tissues
O 78
Rendezvous (RON-dae-voo), system of fur trading
F 523
Rendezvous and docking, in space flights **S** 344, 345
Rennet, (rennin), enzyme used for curdling milk **D** 13
cheesemaking **F** 334
Reno, Jesse, American inventor **E** 175
Reno, Jesse Lee, American general **W** 139
Reno, Marcus, American army officer **I** 214
Reno, Nevada **N** 134
Renoir (ren-WA), **Jean,** French film director **M** 485
Renoir, Pierre Auguste, French painter **R** 174
Girl with a Watering Can, painting, picture **N** 39
Mother and Child, drawing, picture **D** 304
On the Terrace, painting, picture **F** 429
postimpressionism in French painting **F** 431
Two Sisters, painting, picture **R** 174
use of impressionist techniques **P** 29
Re-odorization, chemicals disguise odors **D** 117
Reorganization Act, 1933 **N** 50
Reparations, payment for damages caused by war
Versailles Treaty, 1919 **W** 281, 282–83
Repartee, humorous speedy dialogue **H** 278
Repeating rifles, guns **G** 422
Repertory theaters **T** 159
Repletes, liquid-storing ants **A** 327
Reporters and reporting **N** 201–02
interviewing Truman, picture **T** 302
Pulitzer prizes in journalism **P** 524
Reports **R** 175–76
bibliography **B** 170
how to use the library for finding material
L 182–88
how to write a report on an experiment **E** 351
opinion surveys **O** 160
oral book reports **B** 315
outlines **O** 249–51
proofreading **P** 479
research methods **R** 183
scientific reports use taxonomy **T** 28–29
See also Compositions
Repoussé (rep-oo-SAY), technique of raising designs by
hammering on reverse side **D** 68
Representative government
beginnings in America **A** 185, 188
democracy **D** 104–05
parliaments **P** 81–82
problems of local governments **M** 508
state governments **S** 415
Representatives, United States House of
see United States House of Representatives

Reprieve (from French *reprendre,* meaning "to take
back"), in criminal law, the postponement or suspension
of the execution of a sentence. It is declared by the court
or the pardoning power.

Reproduction **R** 176–80; **L** 211
algae **A** 155
animals: communication and social organization
A 278
baby **B** 2
bacteria **B** 10
breeding and migration **H** 188–91
earthworms **W** 311
eggs and embryos **E** 88–90a
ferns **F** 93–94
fishes **F** 195–96, 200–01
flowers and seeds **F** 276–83
fungi **F** 497
genetic engineering **G** 88–91
genetics and heredity **G** 77–88
grasses **G** 316–17
human **R** 179–80
insect control **I** 258
jellyfishes and other coelenterates **J** 73
mammals **M** 70–71
mosses **F** 94–95
process characteristic of all living things **K** 254–55
spores **F** 497
turtles **T** 334a
vegetative reproduction **P** 300
viruses **V** 364–65, 369
Reptiles **R** 180–81
aging process **A** 83–84
ancestors of birds **B** 206, 207
crocodiles and alligators **C** 533–35
desert animals **D** 124
dinosaurs **D** 172–81
fossils **F** 383, 387
giants of nature **G** 200
heart, two-chambered **M** 72
largest animals in this class **A** 263
life, adaptation to surroundings **L** 214–15
lizards and chameleons **L** 318–21
prehistoric animals, development of **P** 437, 438
reproduction **R** 179
snakes **S** 204–14
turtles **T** 331–334a
Reptiles, Age of **M** 63
Republic, dialogue by Plato **G** 353–54
Republican Party, United States **P** 380–81
formation in Wisconsin **W** 207
Lincoln, Abraham, first elected president
L 295
Roosevelt, Theodore, and the Bull Moose Party
R 330

Republican Party (continued)
  symbols   **C** 126;   **P** 382
  Willkie, Wendell   **W** 173
Republic House, in Ghana, picture   **G** 194
Republics, governments of elected representatives
      D 104
  government of the United States   **U** 135
Requiem (RE-qui-em), poem by Robert Louis Stevenson
      S 424
Requiem mass, a musical form   **M** 537
Resaca de la Palma (ray-SA-ca day la POL-ma), **Battle
  of,** 1846   **M** 238
  Taylor and the Mexican War   **T** 35
Research   R 182–83
  authorship of books   **B** 329–30
  encyclopedia a valuable tool   **E** 197
  indexes, how to use   **I** 114–15
  library research project   **L** 186–88
  recording information sources   **R** 131
  reference books   **R** 129–31
  reports   **R** 175–76
  research libraries   **L** 176–77
  textbooks   **T** 138–39
  tracing a family tree   **G** 76b–76d
Research, scientific   S 80–82
  a four-step process   **R** 139–40
  balloons and ballooning   **B** 33
  basic and applied   **C** 195;   **R** 182–83
  chemical industry   **C** 194, 195
  cosmic rays, how observed   **C** 512
  Edison's "invention factory"   **E** 60
  experiments in weather control   **W** 94–95
  explaining biological clocks   **L** 249–50
  foundations   **F** 390
  International Geophysical Year   **I** 310–20
  libraries   **L** 177
  methods of the sociologist   **S** 228
  New Jersey, concentration in   **N** 169, 171
  opinion surveys   **O** 159–60
  Paracelsus, beginnings of scientific method
      C 208–209
  polar regions   **P** 363–64
  public health   **P** 504
  satellites, use of   **S** 42
  science, history of   **S** 60–77
  Smithsonian Institution, Washington, D.C.   **S** 202
  solar energy   **S** 239
  underwater exploration   **U** 13–24
  veterinarians and medical research   **V** 324
Research libraries   L 190
Research Triangle, of North Carolina   **N** 307, 311, 313
Reserpine (re-SER-pin), drug   **D** 323
  plants, medicinal   **P** 313
  sedatives and tranquilizers   **D** 326
Reservations, Indian see Indian reservations
Reserves, of the United States armed forces
  Air Force Reserves and Air National Guard   **U** 162,
      165
  Army reserve components   **U** 175
  draft exemptions and regulations   **D** 289
  Marine Corps Reserve   **U** 180, 182
  Naval Reserves   **U** 191
  See also National Guard
Reserve system, in baseball   **B** 75
Reservoirs (RES-erv-wars)
  aqueducts   **A** 344
  artificial lakes   **L** 25
  dams   **D** 16, 18, 19
  flood control   **F** 257
  water supply   **W** 66, 67

Residence, legal   E 113
Resident aliens   A 166
Resident doctors, in hospitals   **H** 250
Residential property   R 112d, 113
Residual (re-SID-ual) **powers,** in government   **U** 139
Resins   R 184–85
  paints and pigments   **P** 32
  plastics   **P** 325, 327
  synthetic adhesives   **G** 243
  turpentine   **T** 330
Resistance, in biology
  insect control   **I** 257
Resistance, in electricity see Electric resistance
Resistance arms, of levers   **W** 248
Resistance movements, against the Nazis in World War
  II   **F** 419
Resistance welding   W 118
Resistance wire, in electric appliances   **E** 117
Resist method, of printing textiles   **D** 372
Resistors, in electronics
  semiconductors   **E** 148
Resnais (ren-AY), **Alain,** French director   **M** 488a
Resolution, Captain Cook's ship   **C** 494b
Resolution, in music   **M** 534
Resolving power, of a microscope   **M** 283
Resonance (RES-on-ance), in physics
  sound   **S** 262
  tides   **T** 184
Resource geography   G 108
Resources, natural see Natural resources

Respighi (ray-SPI-ghi), **Ottorino** (1879–1936), Italian
composer, pianist, and conductor, b. Bologna. He studied with Rimsky-Korsakov and Max Bruch. He is best
known for his symphonic poems, which combine lyric
melody with rich harmony. Among his other works are 10
operas, including *Re Enzo* and *Semirama.*   **I** 486

Respiration, act of breathing   **B** 278;   **M** 208e–208f
  artificial respiration   **F** 158, 160
  oxygen and oxidation   **O** 271
  plants   **P** 294
  vocal organs   **V** 375
  See also Breathing
Respiratory (RES-pir-a-tory) **system,** of the body,
      diagram   **D** 203
  air pollution   **A** 109, 110
  breathing system of fishes   **F** 186–87
  breath of life   **B** 277–78
  of insects   **I** 271–72
Responses, in psychology
  characteristic of living things   **K** 255–56
  reactions to stimuli   **L** 98
Responsible government, retains the vote of confidence
      of the legislative body   **P** 82
  Canadian system   **C** 77
  concentration of responsibility (British system)
      G 277
  prime minister responsible to parliament   **P** 456
Rest, in music   **M** 534
Restaurants   R 186–87
  See also Hotels; Motels; Ocean liners
Restigouche River, New Brunswick, Canada   **N** 138a
Restitution, correctional program   **P** 470
Reston, Virginia, picture   **U** 234
Restoration period, in English history   **E** 223–24
  drama   **E** 256–57
  upsurge in dramatic entertainment   **D** 297
Restraining Act, 1775   **R** 197
Restriction enzymes, of bacteria   **G** 89–90

Rests, in music **M** 530
Resumption Act, 1875 **H** 81
Resurrection, of Jesus Christ **J** 86
Resurrection, The, fresco by Piero della Francesca
    E 41
Resurrection City see Poor People's March
Resuscitation see Artificial respiration
Retables (RE-tables), altar screens **L** 63
    decorative arts **D** 75
    Spanish art **S** 363
Retailing, selling goods to a consumer **R** 188–89
    consumer education and reliable dealers **C** 494a
Retail stores R 188–89
    advertising **A** 30
    co-operatives **C** 499–500
    installment buying **I** 288–89
    marketing for the home **M** 100–03
    outlet for industrial products **I** 248
    selling **S** 116–17
    See also Department stores; Mail order;
      Supermarkets
Retail trade T 243
Retaliation, law of L 88
Retardation, mental R 189–91
    development of the intelligence test **T** 117
    See also Mental illness
Reticulum, second section of the stomach of a
    ruminant **H** 209
Retina (RET-in-a), of the eye **B** 284
    lenses of the eye and vision **L** 149
    seen with an ophthalmoscope, picture **M** 208g
    sensory system within the brain **B** 365
Retired Senior Volunteer Program A 7
Retirement O 97–101
    social security **S** 221–22
Retirement villages O 99–100
Retorts, special containers used in chemistry
    pressure cookers **F** 346
Retrievers, dog breed **D** 259; pictures **D** 253
Retrograde (RET-ro-grade) **motion,** of planets **A** 471
Retrorockets, to reduce speed of satellites **S** 41
    deceleration of spacecraft **S** 340h; picture
      S 340b
Retting, of fibers **F** 106
Return, income-tax statement **I** 111

Reuben (RU-ben), in Old Testament (Genesis), eldest son
of Jacob and Leah. He intervened in the plotted murder
of Joseph by his brothers. He was also the ancestral patriarch of one of the 12 tribes of Israel that possessed
the land of Trans-Jordan (now Jordan).

Réunion (rai-u-ni-ON), French overseas department of
volcanic origin, part of Mascarene Islands group in Indian Ocean. Its capital is Saint-Denis. Chief export is
sugar, trade being mainly with France. Its status
changed from that of a colony to that of an overseas
department in 1946. It is governed by a French-ap-
pointed prefect and an elected council. Its area is 2,512
km² (970 sq mi), and its population is 477,000.

Reuters (ROI-ters) **Limited,** common name for Reuter
Agency, an agency that gathers and transmits news. It
was founded by Paul Julius von Reuter as a simple telegraph line between Aachen, Germany, and Verviers, Belgium (1849). Headquarters were moved to London in
1851, and coverage has become practically worldwide.
    news services **N** 201

Reuther (REU-ther), **Walter P.,** American labor leader
    L 6; **W** 139; picture **L** 7
    labor conference, picture **L** 13
Reveille (REV-ell-e), military bugle call **B** 429
Revelation, book of Bible, New Testament **B** 162

Revels, Hiram Rhoades (1822–1901), American senator
and clergyman, b. Fayetteville, N.C. The first black congressman, he was chosen to succeed Jefferson Davis as
United States senator from Mississippi (1870). He had
been ordained as African Methodist minister (1845). He
established a school for freed slaves in St. Louis (1863).

Reventazón (ray-ven-ta-SONE) **River,** Costa Rica **C** 517
Revenue (REV-en-ue), income from taxation **T** 26–27
Revenue Act, 1862 **I** 110
Revenue Act, 1969 **I** 111
Revenue Cutter Service and **Revenue Marine,** early
    names of the United States Coast Guard **U** 175

Revenue sharing, a process by which the U.S. federal
government gives money to state and local governments
for their own use. The State and Local Assistance Act of
1972 authorized giving $30,212,500,000 to state and lo-
cal governments over a period of five years. Two thirds
of this amount went to local governments; one third, to
state governments. States were free to spend the money
as they wished. Spending by local governments was restricted to the general areas of public safety, environmental protection, public transportation, health and recreation, social services, financial administration, and
libraries. In 1976 Congress extended the revenue sharing program for five more years. In 1981, under President Ronald Reagan, the way in which money was distributed was changed. Funds that had gone directly to
localities were given instead to the states. The purpose
of these "block grants" was to give the states a greater
say in how the money would be spent.

Reverberation (re-ver-ber-A-tion), of sound **S** 260
Reverberatory (re-VER-ber-a-tory) **furnaces M** 228
Revere, Paul, American patriot **R** 192–93
    antique silver, picture **A** 321
    buried in Boston, Massachusetts **B** 339
    Johnny Tremain accompanies Mr. Revere on the
      Boston Tea Party **R** 209–10
    portrait by Copley **U** 118
    Revolutionary War begins **R** 198
Reverse, now hearts, card game **C** 112
Reverse transcriptase, protein in Rous virus **V** 369
Reversing Falls, New Brunswick, Canada **C** 52;
    N 138f
Revisionists (Social Democrats) **S** 220
Revivalist, art movement **E** 241
Revival of learning see Renaissance
Revivals, of religious feeling **C** 289; **H** 313
Revolutionary Tribunal, in French Revolution **F** 467
Revolutionary War, 1775–81 **R** 194–209
    Adams', Samuel, role in organizing **A** 16–17
    Allen, Ethan, and Green Mountain Boys **A** 167
    Arnold, Benedict **A** 436
    Attucks, Crispus, first American to die **N** 92;
      R 196
    blacks who fought in it **N** 92
    Breed's Hill **M** 146
    Burke's speech on conciliation **E** 259
    Canada's role in **C** 71, 79
    "Concord Hymn, The," poem by Emerson **E** 190
    Continental Marines **U** 177
    Declaration of Independence **D** 59–65

Revolutionary War (continued)
famous spies   **S** 388
first American historical society, outgrowth of
   H 136
flags carried   **F** 247; pictures   **F** 229
Franklin's activities   **F** 455
French aid   **F** 416
Hale, Nathan   **H** 12
Henry, Patrick   **H** 113–14
Independence Hall, a shrine of   **I** 113
Indian allies of the British   **I** 212
Jones, John Paul, naval hero   **J** 134–35
Lafayette, Marquis de   **L** 22–23
Liberty Bell symbol of   **L** 169
Marion, Francis   **M** 99
Paine, Thomas   **P** 13
Pennsylvania   **P** 145
Purple Heart medal established   **M** 198
Revere, Paul   **R** 192–93
Salomon, Haym, helped finance the army   **S** 19
seizure of weapons in New Hampshire, one of first
   events   **N** 163
songs of   **N** 23
underground movements   **U** 10
Washington, George, commander in chief
   W 39–40
What was Guilford Courthouse?   **N** 316
Who was Molly Pitcher?   **R** 205
See also French and Indian War
Revolution of 1910, Mexico   **M** 250
Revolutions
Communism   **C** 443, 445, 446
in Latin America   **L** 59, 61
Marx, Karl   **M** 114
underground movements   **U** 10
See also French Revolution; Revolutionary War;
   Russian Revolution and Civil War
Revolvers, guns   **G** 421–22
Revue, form of musical comedy   **M** 542
Rewrite staff, on newspapers   **N** 202

Rey (RAY), **Hans Augusto** (1898–1977), American author
and illustrator of children's books, b. Hamburg, Germany. After working 12 years for an import firm in Brazil, he returned to Europe (1936) and began his writing
career. He fled Paris (1940) shortly before the Nazi invasion and went to the United States. His "Curious
George" stories were especially popular.

Reyes, Neftali *see* Neruda, Pablo

Reye's (RYES) **syndrome,** a rare illness occurring in children and sometimes in young adults. The syndrome usually develops three to seven days after the start of a viral
illness, such as influenza or chicken pox. The symptoms
are projectile (forceful) vomiting and unusual behavior,
such as confusion, irritability, aggressiveness, or leth-
argy. Reye's syndrome can lead to convulsions, coma,
and even death. But most victims recover fully if the illness is diagnosed early and treated in a hospital. Aspirin
should not be given to a patient thought to have Reye's
syndrome, since a link between aspirin and the illness is
suspected. The syndrome was first described in 1963 by
Dr. R. Douglas Reye, an Australian pathologist.

Reykjavik (RAIK-ya-veek), capital of Iceland   **I** 43;
   picture   **I** 45
Reynard (RAY-nard) **the Fox stories**
allegorical figure   **F** 436

influence on fable writers   **F** 4
Reynaud, Paul, French premier   **W** 289

Reynolds (REN-olds), **Quentin James** (1902–65), American journalist and author, b. New York, N.Y. He began as
a sports writer for the New York *Evening World* and
World Telegram and joined (1932) the International
News Service. He was an associate editor for *Collier's*
(1933–45) and a war correspondent during World War II.
His books for children include *The F.B.I. Story* and *Winston Churchill.* In a famous lawsuit he successfully
charged Westbrook Pegler with libel and in 1954 received the largest amount ($175,001) ever awarded until
that time for damages.

Reynolds, Sir Joshua, English portrait painter   **R** 210
English art   **E** 238;   **P** 24
Georgiana Seymour, painting   **E** 239
views on color   **D** 143
Reza Khan Pahlavi, shah of Iran   **I** 377
Reza Pahlavi, Mohammed, *see* Mohammed Reza Pahlavi
RFD *see* Rural Free Delivery

Rhadamanthus (rhad-a-MAN-thus), in Greek mythology,
brother of King Minos of Crete and son of Zeus and Eu-
ropa. He was chosen for his integrity and justice to be
judge of the dead in the underworld, along with Aeacus
and Minos.

Rhaetian Alps, Switzerland, picture   **S** 495
Rhapsody, musical form   **M** 535, 537
Rhapsody in Blue, by George Gershwin   **G** 190
Rhazes, Arab physician
medical encyclopedias by Arab scientists   **S** 64
Rhea (RHE-a), Greek goddess   **G** 356
Rheas, flightless birds   **O** 236a–236c
giant birds of the dry tropics   **B** 226;   **G** 204

Rhee, Syngman (1875–1965), Korean statesman, b.
Whanghai province. A supporter of Korean independence, he was head of provisional government at Shanghai (1919–41). During World War II he served as head of
Korean Commission in Washington, D.C., returning to
Korea after fall of Japan (1945) and becoming chairman
of National Assembly (1948). He was president of Republic of Korea (South Korea) from 1948 to 1960.
Korea, history of   **K** 304

Rheims (RHEEMS) **Cathedral,** France, pictures   **C** 131,
   G 264
Gothic architecture, window tracery of   **G** 268–69
statues, pictures   **G** 270
Rheims-Douai (RHEEMS-doo-AI) **Version,** of the Bible
   B 153
Rheingold (RHINE-golt), **Das,** opera by Wagner
   O 151–52
Rhenium (RHE-nium), element   **E** 155, 164
Rhesus (RHE-sus) **monkeys**   **M** 420
Rh factor in blood named for   **B** 258
Rhetoric (RHET-or-ic), study of speaking and writing
   O 180
schools in ancient Athens and Rome   **E** 64, 65
Rhetors, early Greek teachers of oratory   **O** 180
Rheumatic (rheu-MAT-ic) **fever**   **D** 204
heart damaged by   **H** 86b–86c
Rheumatoid arthritis (RHEU-ma-toid ar-THRY-tis), type
of arthritis   **D** 192
Rh factor, blood group   **B** 258
possible cause of mental retardation   **R** 190
transfusion, blood   **T** 251

Rhine, Joseph Banks, American psychologist **E** 397–98
Rhine River, Europe **R** 245; picture **R** 244
    major river in Europe **E** 326
    source in Switzerland **S** 499
    system in Germany **G** 153–54, 156
Rhinestones, jewelry cut from rock crystal **G** 75
Rhinoceroses (rhy-NOS-er-os-es) **R** 211; pictures
    H 207, **L** 218
    extinct woolly rhinoceros, picture **E** 340
    horn, a variety of mammal hair, picture **M** 64
    odd-toed hoofed mammals **H** 208
Rhizomes (RY-zomes), underground stems **G** 41
    banana rootstock **B** 37
    garden selection **G** 29
    growing new plants without seeds **P** 300
Rhode Island R 212–27
    American colonies **A** 188–89
    colonial life in America **C** 385–99
    founded by Roger Williams **W** 172
Rhode Island, Battle of R 227
Rhode Island, University of R 218
Rhode Island Red, chicken **P** 420; **R** 217; pictures
    P 421, **R** 219
    Rhode Island, state bird of, picture **R** 213
Rhodes, Cecil, British statesman in South Africa
    R 228
    Kimberley diamond mines, interest in **M** 320
    Kipling's friendship with **K** 261
    plotted to bring Boers under British rule **S** 273
    Zambia, history of **Z** 368
    Zimbabwe, history of **Z** 368d
Rhodes, island in the Aegean Sea **I** 430
    Colossus of Rhodes **W** 216; picture **W** 215
Rhodesia (rho-DE-sia) *see* Zimbabwe (Rhodesia)
Rhodesia and Nyasaland, Federation of M 49; **Z** 368,
    368d

Rhodesian Ridgeback, a large, muscular dog originally
bred in South Africa to hunt lions. It is also known as the
African lion hound. Along its back is a band of hair that
grows forward against the direction of the rest of its
coat. This produces the distinctive ridge that gave the
breed its name. The short coat ranges in color from
wheat to reddish wheat. The Rhodesian Ridgeback
stands up to 69 cm (27 in) at the shoulder and weighs up
to 34 kg (75 lb). **D** 261; picture **D** 260

Rhodes scholarships R 228
Rhodium, element **E** 155, 164
Rhododendrons (rho-do-DEN-drons), shrubs, picture
    G 37
    Washington, state flower of, picture **W** 13
    West Virginia, state flower of, picture **W** 127
Rhodolite, garnet gemstone **G** 71, 75
Rhombus, geometric form **G** 126
Rhone River, Europe **R** 245
    source in Switzerland **S** 499
Rhubarb, plant **P** 307, 321; picture **P** 306
    supposed medicinal powers **F** 335
Rhyme P 352–53
    nonsense rhymes **N** 272–74
    rhyming terms in slang **S** 194
Rhymed couplets, verse form **A** 203
Rhyolite, lava **V** 379, 380
Rhythm, in design **D** 134
    folk art **F** 291
Rhythm, in music **M** 534
    African **A** 78
    ancient music **A** 246
    dance music **D** 36

    electronic music, rhythmic precision in **E** 142g
    folk music **F** 328
    jazz **J** 57, 61, 62
    modern music **M** 399
    Oriental music **O** 221
    rock music **R** 262c
Rhythm, in poetry **P** 349
    Beowulf **B** 141
Rhythm, in plant and animal life **L** 243–50
Rhythm and blues music R 262a, 262b
Rialto (ri-AL-to) **Bridge,** Venice, Italy **B** 396

Ribault (ri-BO), **Jan** (Jean Ribaut) (1520?–65), French naval officer, b. Dieppe. He was directed by Admiral Gas-
pard de Coligny to establish a French colony in the New
World to provide asylum for Huguenots. He landed in
Florida and set up a colony (the present Port Royal) on
the South Carolina coast (1562) but abandoned it that
same year. After returning (1565) with reinforcements
and supplies for the Fort Caroline colony, set up by Lau-
donnière, he was killed by the Spanish and the colony
was wiped out.
    Florida, history of **F** 273

Ribbed vaults, in architecture **G** 265

Ribbentrop, Joachim von (1893–1946), German diplomat, b. Wesel. As ambassador at large (1935) for the
Nazi government, he negotiated the Anglo-German Naval
Agreement. He was appointed ambassador to Great Britain (1936) and from there negotiated the German-Japa-
nese anti-Comintern pact. In 1938 he returned to Germany to become minister of foreign affairs, a post he
held until the end of World War II. His most famous diplomatic achievement was the Russo-German nonaggres-
sion pact (1939). He was hanged as a war criminal.

Ribbing, in knitting **K** 280
Ribbon Fall, California **W** 56b, 57
Ribbon grasses, water plants **P** 320
    gift wrapping **G** 206, 208
Ribbon lightning, picture **T** 172
Ribbons, of typewriters **T** 348
Ribera (ri-VAER-a), **José,** Spanish painter **B** 60
    Tenebrist style in Spain **S** 362

Ribicoff, Abraham A. (1910–), American public official
and legislator, b. New Britain, Conn. Ribicoff, a Democrat, was serving his second term as governor (1955–61)
of Connecticut when he was appointed secretary of
health, education, and welfare in the administration of
President John F. Kennedy. He resigned the cabinet post
in 1962 and was elected to the U.S. Senate, where he
remained until his retirement in 1981. Earlier, he had
served in the Connecticut House of Representatives, as
well as in the U.S. House of Representatives.

Riboflavin (ry-bo-FLAY-vin), vitamin B_2 **V** 370d
    body chemistry **B** 294
Ribonucleic acid *see* RNA
Ribonucleotides (ry-bo-NU-cle-o-tides), nucleic acid
    chains **B** 291, 295–96
Ribose (RY-bose), body sugar **B** 291
Ribosomes (RY-bo-somes), in cells **C** 162
    how genes work **G** 84
Ribs, of the human body **B** 270
Rib vaulting, in architecture **A** 378; diagram
    A 379
Ricci (RI-chi), **Matteo,** Italian priest and missionary
    C 271

Rice **R** 229–30
  Arkansas, land use in **A** 424, 425
  beriberi caused by diet of polished rice **V** 370a, 370c–370d
  cereal grasses **G** 317
  Ceylon, paddies in, picture **C** 178
  fields, pictures **B** 44a, **C** 261, **G** 280, **I** 220
  food you eat depends on where you live **F** 332, 339
  grain and grain products **G** 282, 287
  harvesting in Liberia, picture **L** 166
  Indian rice, or wild rice **M** 329; **R** 230
  Japanese rice farming **J** 37; picture **J** 24
  Korea, paddies in, pictures **K** 296, 301
  Luzon, the Philippines, pictures **A** 446, **S** 330
  paddies in Sri Lanka, picture **S** 392b
  Philippine miracle rice **F** 343
  plowing, picture **A** 99
  seeds, pictures **G** 238
  Southeast Asia's main crop **S** 332–33
  Taiwan, picture **T** 12
  terraced fields in the Philippines, picture **P** 187
  transplanting, picture **I** 129
  Vietnam, chief crop in **V** 334a
  wedding customs, use in **W** 100–01
  wild rice, or Indian rice **M** 329; **R** 230
  world distribution **W** 264
Rice, Elmer, American playwright **A** 215

Rice, Grantland (1880–1954), American sports journalist, b. Murfreesboro, Tenn. In 1930 he originated a syndicated daily column, "The Sportlight." He did the narration for many motion pictures. In 1943 he won an Academy Award for a one-reel movie.

Rice University, Houston, Texas **T** 131
Richard I (Richard the Lion-Hearted), king of England **F** 443
  led Third Crusade **C** 540

Richard II (1367–1400), king of England (1377–99), b. Bordeaux, France. He succeeded his grandfather Edward III as king in 1377, but until 1389 the government was controlled mainly by his uncle the Duke of Lancaster (John of Gaunt). Lancaster's son, Henry Bolingbroke, became Richard's rival and was banished by Richard, who took over his Lancastrian estates (1389–99). Richard was finally defeated and captured by Bolingbroke (later King Henry IV), deposed by Parliament, and probably murdered in prison.

Richard III ("the Crouchback") (1452–85), king of England (1483–85), b. Fotheringhay. He was made duke of Gloucester (1461) and became protector of Edward V at death of Edward IV (1483). The murder of Edward V and his brother Richard, Duke of York, followed Richard's usurpation of throne (1483). He quelled revolt under Duke of Buckingham (1483). Increased opposition to his rule resulted in his death at the hands of Henry Tudor, Earl of Richmond, who succeeded to the throne. **E** 220
  boy prisoners in the tower **P** 470

Richard (ree-SHAR), **Maurice** (Joseph Henri Maurice Richard) (1921–), Canadian ice hockey player, b. Montreal, Quebec. Richard, nicknamed the Rocket, was one of the greatest scorers in National Hockey League history. As right wing for the Montreal Canadiens, he scored 544 goals in 18 seasons (1942–60). He was the first NHL player to score 50 goals in one season (1944–45). Ri-

chard was inducted into the Hockey Hall of Fame in 1961.

Richard II, play by Shakespeare **S** 136
Richard III, play by Shakespeare **S** 136
Richard Roe *see* John Doe and Richard Roe

Richards, Laura Elizabeth (1850–1943), American author, b. Boston, Mass. Daughter of Samuel Gridley Howe and Julia Ward Howe, she is best known for her books for children, which include *Captain January, Tirra Lirra,* and the "Hildegarde" books. She also wrote an autobiography *Stepping Westward,* and biographies of Abigail Adams, Joan of Arc, Samuel Gridley Howe, and (with her sister Maud Howe Elliott) Julia Ward Howe, the last of which received the Pulitzer prize for biography (1917).
  "Eletelephony," nonsense verse **N** 274

Richards Deep, trench in Pacific Ocean **M** 499
Richardson, Henry Handel, Australian novelist **A** 501
Richardson, Henry Hobson, American architect **L** 361; **U** 124
Richardson, Robert Clinton, American baseball player **S** 309
Richardson, Samuel, English novelist **E** 260
  emotionalism of his novels **N** 346
Richard the Lion-Hearted *see* Richard I
Richelieu (RI-shel-lu), **Cardinal,** French statesman **R** 231
  builder of the Bourbon monarchy in France **F** 416
  Palais-Richelieu now the Palais-Royal in Paris **P** 73
Richibucto, New Brunswick, Canada, picture **N** 138c

Richler, Mordecai (1931–), Canadian author, b. Montreal. Richler's novels reflect his upbringing in a Jewish area of Montreal. His novel *The Apprenticeship of Duddy Kravitz* (1959) tells of a Jewish youth whose early values become lost when he enters the business world. Some of Richler's novels, such as *The Acrobats* (1954), tell of Canadians who, like the author, have chosen to live in Europe. Richler's other works include *Cocksure* (1968), *St. Urbain's Horseman* (1971), and *Joshua Then and Now* (1980). **C** 64

Richmond, capital of Virginia **V** 357; picture **V** 356
  Civil War **C** 323, 326
  Confederate capital **C** 321

Richter (RICK-ter), **Conrad Michael** (1890–1968), American author, b. Pine Grove, Pa. His novels are noted for portrayal of American frontier life. His works include The Sea of Grass, a trilogy comprised of *The Trees, The Fields,* and *The Town,* which was awarded the Pulitzer prize for fiction (1951), and *The Waters of Kronos,* which received the National Book award (1961).

Richter (RICK-tair), **Svyatoslav Teofilovitch** (1915–), Soviet pianist, b. Zhitomir, Ukraine. He is famous for his vast repertoire, skillfully and imaginatively interpreted. He studied at Moscow Conservatory (1937–47) and introduced the 6th, 7th, and 9th piano sonatas by Prokofiev, with whom he was closely associated. He toured Europe and the United States (1960–61, 1965) and was awarded Stalin prize.

Richter scale, for measuring the magnitude of an earthquake **E** 38

Rickenbacker (RICK-en-back-er), **Eddie** (Edward Vernon Rickenbacker) (1890–1973), American aviator and airline executive, b. Columbus, Ohio. He won the Medal of Honor as commander of the 94th Aero Pursuit Squadron in World War I and was special representative for the secretary of war during World War II. As an airline executive he became (1938) president, general manager, and director of Eastern Air Lines, Inc. He wrote *Fighting the Flying Circus* and *Seven Came Through*.

United States Air Force, history of **U** 159

Rickets, a deforming disease that attacks children. It is caused by lack of vitamin D and sunlight. This lack affects proper hardening of the bones and results in deformity. A similar disease in adults is called osteomalacia. The origin of the word "rickets" is unknown, but it may derive from Anglo-Saxon word *wrick,* "to twist."

nutritional disease **D** 216
vitamin D **V** 371

Ricketts, John, English circus producer **C** 300
Rickettsias (rick-ETT-si-as), micro-organisms
M 281–82

Rickover, Hyman G. (1900–), American naval officer, b. Makov, Russia (now Makow, Poland). A graduate of the U.S. Naval Academy at Annapolis in 1922, Rickover directed the U.S. Navy project that developed the first atomic-powered submarine, S.S.N. *Nautilus* (1953). He then took charge of the nuclear-propulsion division of the Bureau of Ships and was made chief of the naval-reactors branch of the U.S. Energy Research and Development Administration. He is the author of several books, including *American Education: A National Failure* and *Eminent Americans—Namesakes of the Polaris Submarine Fleet*. In 1965 he won the Enrico Fermi award for his contribution to atomic science. Rickover was retired from the Navy in 1982. At the time of his retirement, he called for the elimination of nuclear weapons.

Ricotta, Italian cheese **D** 13
Riddles **J** 132–33
African literature **A** 76b
folklore, a section of **F** 304
word games **W** 236–37
Rideau Canal, Ontario, Canada **O** 236f–237
Rideau Hall, residence of the governor-general of
Canada **O** 237
Ride up high, O uncle, tag game **G** 17

Ridge, Major (1771?–1839), American Indian, b. probably Hiwassee County, Tenn. As Cherokee Indian leader with rank of major, he supported Americans in Creek War (1814). Without tribal authority he ceded Cherokee lands east of Mississippi to United States, thus forcing the tribe to move westward. He was killed in revenge for causing westward migration. His son, **John Ridge** (1803–39), was also a tribal leader.

Ridges, oceanic **G** 114–15, 116; **O** 29–30

Ridgway, Matthew Bunker (1895–), American army officer, b. Fort Monroe, Va. Noted for commanding the 82nd Airborne Division, which participated in large-scale operations in Italy, Sicily, and Normandy during World War II, Ridgway was U.S. Army representative to the United Nations Military Staff Committee (1946–48). He succeeded Douglas MacArthur (1951) as supreme commander of Allied forces in Pacific, and he was supreme commander of NATO forces in Europe (1952–53) and army chief of staff (1953–55). He retired in 1955.

Riding *see* Horseback riding
Riding Mountain National Park, Manitoba, Canada
M 81
Riebeeck (RE-bake), **Jan van,** Dutch founder of Cape
Town, South Africa **C** 101; **S** 271

Riel (ri-EL), **Louis** (1844–85), Canadian rebel leader, b. St. Boniface, Manitoba. He led the Métis in resisting (1870, 1885) incorporation of Northwest Territory into Dominion of Canada. Riel established provincial government (1869, 1885) but was captured (1885), tried, and executed for treason.

Canada, history of **C** 73, 74; **M** 4; **S** 38h

Riemenschneider, Tilman, German sculptor
Saint Sebastian, picture **G** 165
Riffle shuffle, for playing cards **C** 107
Rifle marksmanship **R** 231–33
Oakley, Annie **O** 2
Rifles, guns **G** 415, 422, 423; pictures **G** 416, 418,
422, 423
antique rifle, picture **D** 66
hunting **H** 291
rifle marksmanship **R** 231–33
Rifling, of guns **G** 415, 420
Rif, mountains, Morocco **M** 460
Rift Valley, Africa *see* Great Rift Valley
Riga, capital of Latvia (Latvian Soviet Socialist
Republic) **U** 44
Riga, Gulf of, an arm of the Baltic Sea **O** 45
Rigel (RY-ghel), star **C** 491
brightest stars **S** 407
Riggin, Aileen, American swimmer **O** 109
Rigging, lines and ropes used to work sails
full-rigged ship, picture-diagram **S** 11, 159
sailboats **S** 10
Riggs, Lynn, American playwright **O** 94
Right, political term, origin of **P** 379
Right angles, in geometry **G** 124; diagram **G** 125
Right Bank, of the Seine, Paris **P** 73
Right of deposit, in Spanish territories **T** 108
Right of way
boats **B** 262
Rights, civil *see* Civil liberties and civil rights
Rights of Man and of the Citizen, Declaration of the *see*
Declaration of the Rights of Man and of the
Citizen
Right to vote *see* Suffrage
Right to work *see* Open and closed shop
Right triangle, diagram **G** 125
Right whales **W** 149; picture **W** 148

Right wing, persons and groups who hold to conservative political doctrine, often advocating compliance with strong governmental authority. The term is derived from certain European legislatures, where conservatives sat to the right, the moderates in the center, and radicals to the left of the presiding officer. It is often applied inaccurately to both moderate conservatives, who resist certain political or economic changes, and to extreme rightists, who would forcibly establish conservative government.

Rigoletto (rig-o-LETT-o), opera by Giuseppe Verdi
O 151
Rig Veda, Hindu religious text **H** 132; **O** 220d

Riis (REES), **Jacob August** (1849–1914), Danish-American journalist and author, b. Ribe, Denmark. He went to United States in 1870 and became a police reporter for the New York *Tribune* (1877–88) and the New York *Evening Sun* (1888–99). A well-known reformist lecturer and writer, he was author of *How the Other Half Lives,* (1890) and *The Children of the Poor* (1892). **C** 308d

Riiser-Larsen (RE-ser-LAR-sen), **Hjalmar** (1890–1965), Norwegian naval officer and polar explorer, b. Oslo. He accompanied the Amundsen-Ellsworth North Pole expedition (1925) and Amundsen-Ellsworth-Nobile transpolar flight (1926). He commanded a Norwegian relief party in search of Nobile's expedition (1928) and two Norwegian expeditions to Antarctica (1929–30, 1930–31). During World War II he was appointed commander in chief of the joint Norwegian Air Forces (1944–46).

Rijksmuseum (RAKES-muse-e-um), Amsterdam, picture **M** 515
    carillon **B** 138
Riker's Island, New York City **N** 228
Rila Monastery, Bulgaria, picture **B** 441
Riley, James Whitcomb, American poet **I** 149
Rilke, Rainer Maria, Austrian poet **G** 181
Rilles, twisting, valleylike clefts
    Mars **P** 273
    moon **M** 450; picture **M** 452

Rillieux, Norbert (1806–94), American engineer, b. New Orleans, La. Born a slave, he was educated in France. After returning to Louisiana, he developed a process that cut the production cost and raised the quality of sugar. Although one of the most prominent men in the state, he left Louisiana when, as a black, he was required to carry a pass. In Europe he continued to make inventive contributions to the sugar industry and also worked at deciphering hieroglyphics.

Rimbaud (ran-BO), **Arthur,** French poet **F** 440
Rimsky-Korsakov (RIM-ski-KOR-sa-kof), **Nikolay,**
    Russian composer **U** 63
    influence on Stravinsky **S** 437
    opera **I** 136
    teacher of Prokofiev **P** 477

Rinehart, Mary Roberts (1876–1958), American novelist and mystery story writer, b. Pittsburgh, Pa. Her works include *The Circular Staircase, The Man in Lower Ten*, and numerous stories about Tish. **P** 143
    mystery and suspense stories **M** 554

Ring des Nibelungen (NI-be-lung-en), **Der,** music
    dramas by Richard Wagner **O** 151
Ringed seals, animals **W** 8
Ringer, game of marbles **M** 95

Ringling Brothers, seven brothers, five of whom formed Ringling Brothers Classic and Comic Concert Company. They organized a circus (1884) that by 1900 was one of the major ones in the United States. They then enlarged by absorbing Forepaugh-Sells (1906) and Barnum and Bailey (1907) circuses.

Ring-necked pheasant
    South Dakota, state bird of, picture **S** 313
Ring-necked snake, picture **S** 205
Ring of Fire (Circle of Fire), volcanoes along the Pacific
    Ocean **M** 499

Ring of the Fisherman, famous religious ring
    J 99
Ring of the Nibelung, in Norse mythology **N** 281
Ringroads, or beltways, around cities
    Baltimore and Washington, D.C. **M** 123
Rings, jewelry **J** 98, 99
Rings, use in gymnastics **G** 432; pictures **G** 430, 431
Rings of Jupiter **P** 275; **S** 349
Rings of Saturn **P** 276–77; **S** 349
Rings of Uranus **P** 277
Ringstrasse, circular boulevard in Vienna **V** 332a
Ringtails, animals related to raccoons **R** 26
Ringtaw, English game of marbles **M** 95
Ringworm, skin infection **D** 206
Rio de Janeiro (RI-o day jan-AIR-o), Brazil **R** 234–35;
    B 382–83; pictures **B** 379, **C** 308e
    central east section of Brazil **B** 378
    slums, picture **L** 58
    soccer game on beach, picture **B** 376
Río de la Plata, South America *see* Plata, Río de la
Rio Grande (GRAND), river between United States and
    Mexico **R** 245; picture **R** 233
    rises in Colorado **C** 403
    Texas **T** 124
Río Muni, province of Equatorial Guinea **E** 273–74
Río Piedras (pi-A-dras), Puerto Rico, pictures **P** 519,
    521
Riots
    ghetto riots of the 1960's **N** 104a–104b

Riparian (ri-PARE-ian) **rights** (from Latin *ripa,* meaning "bank"), rights of people who own land on the banks of rivers and streams concerning their use of the water and ownership of the soil beneath the stream.

Ripieno, musical term **M** 534

Ripley, Elizabeth Blake (1906–69), American author and illustrator of children's books, b. New Haven, Conn. She wrote a number of biographies of artists, including Leonardo da Vinci, Michelangelo, Rembrandt, and Picasso. She illustrated *Riddle Me This, This Little Boy Went to Kindergarten,* and other books.

Ripley, Robert Le Roy (1893–1949), American cartoonist and author, b. Santa Rosa, Calif. His "Believe It or Not" cartoon series ran in newspapers all over the world and was also published in book form. Ripley appeared on radio and TV and in motion pictures in shows based on his collection of incredible events.

Riposte, counterattack in fencing **F** 86
Riprap, stones used to cover the face of a dam **D** 16,
    18
Ripsaws, tools **T** 212
Ripton, Vermont
    memorial to Robert Frost **F** 480
Rip Van Winkle, story by Washington Irving **S** 166;
    excerpt **I** 411–12
Risorgimento (ri-sor-gi-MENT-o), Italian literary
    movement **I** 479
Ritardando, musical term **M** 534

Ritchie, Roland Almon (1910–), Canadian judge, b. Halifax, Nova Scotia. A member of the bar since 1934, he was appointed to the Supreme Court in 1959. He is a member of the board of governors of the University of Kings College.

Rite of Spring, The, ballet, by Igor Stravinsky   **M** 400;
    S 437;   **U** 64
Rites and ceremonies
    American Indian dances, pictures   **I** 161
    ancient Greek drama   **D** 294
    ceremonials of Judaism   **J** 116–20
    funeral customs   **F** 492–95
    knights and knighthood   **K** 272–77
    marriage rites   **W** 101–03
    Muslim law   **I** 414–15
    sacramentals of the Roman Catholic Church
        R 301
    tea ceremony of Japan   **J** 37
    See also Religious holidays; religions by name;
        people section of country articles
Ritscher, Alfred, German explorer   **P** 368
Rittenhouse, William, American clergyman, built first
        paper mill in America   **C** 432;   **P** 56
Ritter, Johann Wilhelm, German scientist   **P** 236

Ritter, Joseph Elmer, Cardinal (1892–1967), American
Roman Catholic clergyman, b. New Albany, Ind. He was
made a cardinal (1961) after serving as bishop
(1934–44) and archbishop (1944–46) of Indianapolis
and archbishop of St. Louis, Mo. (1946–67).

Ritter, Karl (1779–1859), German geographer, b. Qued-
linburg. A founder of modern scientific geography, he
explained how geography affects history and studied human ecology.
    modern geography, beginnings of   **G** 99

Ritter, Tex, American actor and singer   **C** 524b
Rivals, play by Richard Brinsley Sheridan
    scene with Mrs. Malaprop, picture   **E** 257
Rivas (RI-vos), **Duke of,** Spanish writer   **S** 369
Rivera (ri-BAY-ra), **Diego,** Mexican painter   **L** 67
    Flower Festival, Feast of Santa Anita   **L** 65
Rivera, José Eustasio, Colombian writer   **L** 72

Rivera y Orbaneja (ri-BAY-ra e or-ba-NAY-ha), **Miguel
Primo de** (Marqués de Estella) (1870–1930), Spanish
general and dictator, b. Cádiz. During Spanish-American
War he served in Cuba and the Philippines (1898), and
he later served in Morocco (1909–13). In 1923 he seized
power as dictator of Spain. He relinquished some of the
power to the king in 1925 but was forced to retire in
1930.

River blindness (onchocerciasis), disease   **B** 252
Riverfront Stadium, Cincinnati, Ohio   **O** 71; picture
    O 72
River of No Return, nickname for Salmon River, Idaho
    I 54
Rivers   **R** 235–47
    Amazon River   **A** 178–79
    Atlantic Ocean drainage area   **A** 478
    Canada's drainage basins   **C** 51–52
    channels deepened to control floods   **F** 256
    conservation and pollution problems   **C** 483
    dams   **D** 16–21
    erosion caused by   **E** 282, 283
    Ganges River, India   **G** 25
    harbors and ports   **H** 35–37
    how lake basins are formed   **L** 25
    Mississippi   **M** 364–65
    Missouri River   **M** 383
    Nile River   **N** 260–61
    systems in Africa   **A** 49–50
    systems in Asia   **A** 448

    systems in Europe   **E** 309
    systems of North America   **N** 288
    systems of South America   **S** 277–78
    tidal bores   **T** 185
    waterfalls   **W** 56b
    waterpower   **W** 61–63
    See also land section of country, province, and state
        articles; names of rivers
Riverside Church, New York City
    largest carillon in world   **B** 138
Riverside Geyser (GUYS-er), Yellowstone Park,
    Wyoming, picture   **G** 193
Riverview Gardens, Missouri
    elementary school, picture   **S** 56
Rivets, fasteners   **N** 3
Riviera (riv-i-AER-a), Mediterranean coastal region of
    Italy and France
    Monaco   **M** 406
Riyadh (ri-YODH), capital of Saudi Arabia   **S** 48

Rizal (ree-ZAHL), **José** (1861–96), Philippine national
hero who helped inspire rebellion against Spain, b. Ca-
lamba. The son of Filipino landowners, Rizal studied
medicine in Spain. There he began to write essays and
poems encouraging Filipinos to take pride in their heritage. His novel *Noli me tangere (The Social Cancer)*
called for reforms in Spanish rule, and it was banned.
Under pressure from the Spanish, Rizal lived abroad. He
became a historian and an artist, as well as a physician
and a writer. His second novel, *El Filibusterismo (The
Subversive),* was also banned by the Spanish. Rizal returned to the Philippines in 1892 and was exiled to the
island of Mindanao. He refused to join a revolutionary
group. But when revolution broke out in 1896, he was
arrested and shot for inciting revolt.   **P** 189

Rjukanfoss, falls, Norway   **W** 57
R.N. *see* Registered nurses
RNA (ribonucleic acid)   **G** 84; diagrams   **B** 292,   **G** 85
    cell nucleus   **C** 161
    chemical makeup of viruses   **V** 363, 369, 370
    function in body chemistry   **B** 291, 296
Roaches, insects   **H** 262
Roadbeds, under tracks of railroads   **R** 78–79
Road camps, places of short-term imprisonment
    P 468
Road Not Taken, The, poem by Robert Frost   **F** 480
Roadrunners (chaparral birds)
    New Mexico, state bird of, picture   **N** 180
Roads and highways   **R** 248–51
    Alaska Highway   **A** 138;   **C** 61
    automobile design affected by   **A** 545
    Brazil, picture   **B** 377
    bridges   **B** 395–401
    buses and bus travel   **B** 465–66
    construction, picture   **E** 391
    driver education   **D** 318–21
    early travel and trade   **T** 258–59
    explosives used in construction   **E** 396
    expressway in Chicago, picture   **U** 111
    Going-to-the-Sun Road, in Glacier National Park
        M 436
    interstate highways, map   **U** 100
    Khyber Pass, Asia, picture   **A** 467
    log roads in Siberia, picture   **S** 173
    longest overwater highway, Lake Pontchartrain,
        Louisiana   **L** 33
    Los Angeles freeways, picture   **L** 345
    maps, use of symbols   **M** 88, 90; picture   **M** 91
    national parkways   **N** 52

Roads and highways (continued)
overland trails **O** 251–67
paints for highways **P** 34
Pan American Highway **P** 50
Pennsylvania Turnpike, picture **P** 136
plank roads in Louisiana **L** 357
road-building equipment **B** 448
road signs, picture **D** 319
Roman *see* Roman roads
stabilization by salt **S** 21
Stockholm, Sweden, picture **E** 328
superhighways in Venezuela, picture **L** 58
traffic control **T** 247–48
Trans-Amazon Highway **B** 382
Trans-Canada Highway **C** 61
trucks and trucking **T** 295–96
tunnels **T** 313–18
U.S. interstate commerce **I** 331
See also transportation section of country, province,
and state articles
Roanoke (RO-an-oke), Virginia **V** 357
Roanoke Island, North Carolina **N** 306
American colonial settlement **A** 181
Roaring 20's (the Jazz Age), United States
Coolidge's administration **C** 496–97
Roark, Helen Wills *see* Wills, Helen
Roasting, of ores **M** 228
Robber crabs, crustaceans **S** 169
Robbery, crime
crime rates **C** 532c
Robbia, della, family *see* Della Robbia, Luca; Della
Robbia family

Robbins, Jerome (1918–   ), American choreographer
and director, b. New York, N.Y. In 1944 he became
known for his ballet *Fancy Free*. The ballet was later expanded into the Broadway musical *On the Town*. Robbins was both director and choreographer of *West Side
Story* (1957) and *Fiddler on the Roof* (1964). In 1962 he
received an Academy Award for his choreography in the
film version of *West Side Story*. He was associate artistic
director of the New York City Ballet from 1949 to 1963.
In 1969 he returned to the company as ballet master.
His ballets include *Dances at a Gathering* (1969) and
Chansons Madecasses (1975). **B** 29; **D** 34; **M** 543

Robbins, Marty, American singer **C** 525
Robe, The, motion picture **M** 487

Robert I (Robert Bruce) (1274–1329), king of Scotland
(1306–29), b. probably Turnberry. He was crowned king
of Scotland (1306) but was defeated by the English army
at Methven (1306) and forced to hide on an island off the
Irish coast. It was there that he is supposed to have been
inspired to return to Scotland (1307) by a spider's per-
sistence in spinning a web. He eventually defeated the
English, and gained Scotland's independence (1328).
Scotland, history of **S** 88

Robert, Nicholas Louis, French paper manufacturer
P 57

Roberto, Holden Alvaro (Joseph Robert Haldane Gil-
more) (1927–   ), Angolan nationalist leader, b. San Sal-
vador. He organized the Union of the Peoples of Angola
(UPA) (1954), which supported northern Angola guerrilla
revolts against Portuguese rule (beginning in 1961). He
was president of the National Front for the Liberation of
Angola (FNLA) and premier of the Revolutionary Government of Angola in Exile. Following Angolan indepen-

dence in 1975, rivalry among liberation groups led to
civil war, and Roberto's group was defeated.

Roberts, Elizabeth Madox (1886–1941), American novelist and poet, b. Perrysville, Ky. She began her career as a
poet, winning several prizes, and then published her first
novel, *The Time of Man*. She wrote of the mountain folk
and "poor whites" of Kentucky. Other novels are *My
Heart and My Flesh* and *The Great Meadow*.
"Firefly," poem and its interpretation **P** 351–52

Roberts, Joseph Jenkins (1809–76), Liberian statesman,
b. Petersburg, Va. He went to Liberia in 1829 and later
became an assistant to the American colonial governor,
Thomas Buchanan. He was the first black governor of
Liberia (1842–47) and its first president when it became
a republic (1847). He served as president of Liberia
(1847–55, 1871–76) and as the first president of the
College of Liberia (now called University of Liberia)
(1856–76).
Liberia, history of **L** 167

Roberts, Kenneth, American novelist **A** 213
Roberts, Tom, Australian painter **A** 501
Robertson, Alice Mary, American educator and social
worker **O** 93

Robertson, James (1742–1814), American pioneer, b.
Brunswick County, Va. He led a group of settlers to the
site of present-day Nashville, where he served as presiding officer of the court, negotiated treaties with the Indians, and was a trustee of Davidson Academy (later the
University of Nashville) and a delegate to the North Carolina assembly (1785, 1787) and the Tennessee senate
(1798). In his last years he was Indian agent to the
Chickasaw.

Robertson, Oscar (1938–   ), American basketball
player, b. Charlotte, Tenn. He is among the all-time leading scorers in National Basketball Association (NBA) history. A guard who was supremely adept at ball-handling,
he also set the NBA career record of 9,887 assists—
passes to teammates that lead to field goals. Robertson
was an all-American at the University of Cincinnati. He
joined the Cincinnati Royals in 1960 and was named
NBA Rookie of the Year. In 1970 he was traded to the
Milwaukee Bucks. He retired in 1974. Robertson, who
was nicknamed the Big O, was elected to the Basketball
Hall of Fame in 1979. **T** 88

Robert's Rules of Order, for parliamentary procedure
P 79
Robert Bruce *see* Robert I

Roberval (ro-bair-VOL), **Jean François de la Rocque, Sieur
de** (1500?–60?), French colonizer, b. Carcassonne. He
was appointed by King Francis I viceroy and lieutenant
general of New France and leader of first French coloniz-
ing expedition (1541). He reached Newfoundland in
1542 and led an unsuccessful expedition in search of
fabled Saguenay wealth. He returned with survivors to
France in 1543.
Cartier, Jacques, and Roberval **C** 124d

Robeson, Paul (1898–1976), American concert baritone
and actor, b. Princeton, N.J. He won acclaim for English
and American performances in Eugene O'Neill's *Emperor Jones* and Shakespeare's *Othello*. He made numerous concert tours through United States, Europe, and
Soviet Union. His film appearances included roles in

Showboat, Emperor Jones, and *Jericho.* His deep concern over U.S. racial prejudice against blacks led him to uphold Communism. He is the author of the autobiographical *Here I Stand.*

Black Renaissance **N** 100, 107

Robespierre (robes-pi-AIR), **Maximilien,** French revolutionary leader **F** 466, 467, 468

Robidou (ro-bi-DO), **Antoine** (1794–1860), American trader and trapper, b. St. Louis, Mo. He was one of the first traders to reach (1822) Taos, N.Mex., and he founded (1832) a major fur-trading post, Fort Uinta (also called Fort Robidou), in northeastern Utah. His brother **Joseph Robidou** (1783–1868) established (1826) a trading post on the site of present-day St. Joseph, Mo. Three other brothers also became well known as traders and trappers on the Western frontier.

Robie House, designed by Frank Lloyd Wright *see* Frederick C. Robie House
Robin Goodfellow, character in English folklore **M** 308
Robin Hood, book by Orville Prescott, excerpt **R** 252–53
Robin Hood, legendary English hero and outlaw **R** 251–53
　duels in literature **D** 341
　king of the May **M** 182
　legends, types of **L** 129
Robins, birds **B** 219, 223; picture **B** 240
　Connecticut, state bird of, picture **C** 466
　feeding signals **A** 276; picture **A** 277
　Michigan, state bird of, picture **M** 259
　observing robins as a science activity **E** 355
　tracks, picture **A** 272
　Wisconsin, state bird of, picture **W** 193

Robinson, Bill (Bojangles) (1878–1949), American tap dancer, b. Richmond, Va. He danced in nightclubs and in musical comedies (1906–30) and motion pictures, such as *Rebecca of Sunnybrook Farm* and *The Little Colonel* with Shirley Temple. He invented many steps, including his widely imitated stair tap—dancing up a flight of stairs. Picture **M** 475
　Black Renaissance **N** 100

Robinson, Charles A. (1900–), American author and educator, b. Princeton, N.J. Formerly professor of classics at Brown University, he took part in the excavation of ancient Greek cities and was a member of the Commission for Excavation of the Athenian Agora. Among his books for young people are *The First Book of Ancient Bible Lands, The First Book of Ancient Egypt,* and *The First Book of Ancient Rome.*

Robinson, Edwin Arlington, American poet **A** 208
　"Dark Hills, The," poem **P** 355
Robinson, Frank, American athlete **B** 77
Robinson, Jackie (Jack Roosevelt Robinson), American baseball player **R** 254; **B** 77
　years of change for blacks **N** 102

Robinson, James H. (1907–72), American religious leader, b. Knoxville, Tenn. He founded Operation Crossroads Africa (1957), a private summer work program that starts schools, community centers, clinics, and libraries in Africa. A graduate of the Union Theological Seminary in New York City, he established the Church of the Master in Harlem. He is the author of *Road Without Turning* (1950).

Robinson, John (1576?–1625), English minister, b. Lincolnshire. As pastor of the Separatist Church in Leiden, the Netherlands, he encouraged his followers to migrate to America and helped organize the expedition that, after sailing to England (1620), went to America in the *Mayflower.* Robinson intended to follow the expedition but died in Leiden.

Robinson, Joseph Taylor, American statesman **A** 431

Robinson, Sugar Ray (Walker Smith, Jr.) (1920–), American boxer, b. Detroit, Mich. He is regarded by many as one of the best fighters in boxing history. He held the middleweight crown five times during the years 1951–60 and was welterweight champion from 1946 to 1951. In his 25-year professional career, Robinson fought 202 bouts. He seldom lost, and he knocked out 109 of his opponents. Robinson took the nickname "Sugar" after a sportswriter had described his boxing style as "sweet as sugar." After he retired (1965), he became an actor, and he established the Sugar Ray Youth Foundation. In 1967, he was elected to the Boxing Hall of Fame. **B** 354

Robinson Crusoe, by Defoe **E** 259–60
　books for children **C** 238
　fiction, development of **F** 111
　novel in down-to-earth style **N** 346
　setting, an island off Chile **C** 250
Robinson Crusoe Islands *see* Juan Fernández Islands

Robot (RO-bot), an automatic machine that can carry out tasks generally performed by human beings. The term was introduced by the Czech writer Karel Capek in the play *R.U.R.* (Rossum's Universal Robots). **A** 533–34

Rob Roy (from Gaelic for "Red Robert," derived from his hair color) (Robert MacGregor or Campbell) (1671–1734), Scottish outlaw. He opposed the rich but gave to the poor. He is subject of Scott's novel *Rob Roy.*

Robson, Mount, British Columbia, Canada **J** 55
Robusta, a type of coffee **I** 491
Robusti, Jacopo *see* Tintoretto

Roc, in Arabian folklore, a monstrous bird so large it could carry elephants. It transported Sinbad the Sailor to the Valley of Diamonds in the *Arabian Nights.* The roc is possibly related to other giant birds of Turkish, Egyptian, and Babylonian mythology.

Rochambeau (ro-shom-BO), **Jean Baptiste Donatien de Vimeur, comte de,** French military commander **R** 208
　aided Washington in Revolutionary War **W** 40
　Rhode Island, history of **R** 227
Rochdale, England
　co-operative movement, basic principles of **C** 499
Rochester, Minnesota **M** 334
Rochester, New York **N** 223
Rock and roll music *see* Rock music
Rock climbing *see* Mountain climbing
Rock collecting **R** 273
Rock crystal, crystalline quartz **Q** 7
　gemstones **G** 75
Rock doves (pigeons), birds **B** 219
Rock dusting, in coal mining **C** 367
Rockefeller, John D., American industrialist **R** 254
　founded Standard Oil Company in Cleveland **C** 338

Rockefeller, Nelson Aldrich (1908–79), American public official, b. Bar Harbor, Me. He was the third of the six children of John D. Rockefeller, Jr., and Abby Green Aldrich Rockefeller. After graduating from Dartmouth College, he held appointive positions in the administrations of Presidents Roosevelt, Truman, and Eisenhower and then won election to four successive terms as governor of New York. He was vice-president of the United States from 1974 to 1977.

  as vice-president, picture **V** 331
  New York **N** 224

Rockefeller Center, New York City **N** 231
  Christmas tree **C** 291
  outdoor dining, picture **N** 233
Rockefeller Foundation **F** 390
Rockefeller Museum *see* Archaeological Museum

Rockefeller University (formerly Rockefeller Institute for Medical Research), graduate university (since 1954), that promotes medical research through research grants, laboratory study, and clinical observation. It was founded (1901) by John D. Rockefeller. Its headquarters are in New York, N.Y.

Rocker, tool used in print making **G** 307
Rocket, early locomotive **L** 330; picture **L** 331
Rocket engines **E** 211
  jet propulsion **J** 89–90
  supersonic planes, use in **S** 471–72
Rocket planes
  space exploration of the future **S** 343, 348
Rockets **R** 255–62
  buzz bombs of World War II **W** 300
  Cape Kennedy, picture **F** 266
  engines **E** 211
  fuels **F** 490
  G-force produced by acceleration **G** 324–25
  Goddard, Robert Hutchings, inventions of
    G 244–46; **I** 338
  hailstorms, use in taming **W** 95
  Huntsville, Ala., space center **A** 113, 124
  hydrogen fuel **G** 61
  IGY studies, picture **I** 314
  ion-drive **I** 351
  jet propulsion **J** 89–90
  liquid gases **L** 308
  missiles **M** 343–49
  model kits of rockets **A** 106
  Oberth, Hermann, pioneer in rocketry **O** 6–7
  oxygen gas used for liquid fuel **G** 60
  replacing cannons for many uses **G** 426
  satellite, launching of **S** 40–41
  spacecraft, launching of **S** 339, 340d
  synthetic rubber fuel **R** 347
  Tsiolkovsky, Konstantin, pioneer rocket scientist
    T 306–07
Rock Falls Colonel, champion English setter dog
    D 261
Rockfish, picture **F** 192
Rockford, Illinois **I** 83
Rock gardens, pictures **G** 35
Rock Hill, South Carolina **S** 308
Rocking Chair II, sculpture by Henry Moore
    D 137
Rock music **R** 262a–262d
  Beatles, The **B** 108
  country rock **C** 525
  dancing **D** 28, 37
  electronic amplification of sound **E** 142h

Rock music festivals **R** 262d
Rockne, Knute, American football coach **F** 364
Rock of Ages, hymn, words and music **H** 310
Rock of Gibraltar *see* Gibraltar
Rockport, Massachusetts, picture **M** 140
Rocks **R** 263–69
  Can changes in temperature break up rocks?
    S 230
  coal **C** 362–68
  contain fossils **F** 378, 380
  Do growing plants break up rocks? **S** 231
  earth's mantle **E** 19
  geological and geophysical studies **G** 115–16
  geologists at work **G** 119–20
  geology, history of **G** 117–18
  ice ages **I** 18
  Idaho's City of Rocks **I** 64–65
  Kansas' "Rock City," unusual geological area
    K 187
  mines and mining **M** 314–20
  moon (lunar) rocks **M** 449, 453, 454; **S** 340a,
    340i
  quarrying **Q** 4b–5
  radioactive dating **R** 64
  rock collecting **R** 273
  stone **S** 433
  See also Sedimentary rocks; Stone
Rock salt **S** 20
  mine in Colombia **C** 382–83

Rockwell, Norman (1894–1978), American illustrator, b. New York, N.Y. During World War I he painted military portraits for Navy and patriotic pictures for national magazines. He is best known (since 1916) as cover and story illustrator for *Saturday Evening Post* magazine. His works include *The Four Freedoms.*
  most famous of American illustrators **I** 95

Rock wool, insulation fibers **I** 290–91
Rocky Landscape, painting by Cézanne **M** 389
Rocky Mountain bighorns *see* Bighorns, or Rocky
    Mountain sheep
Rocky Mountain Fur Company **F** 523
Rocky Mountain National Park, Colorado **C** 402, 410
Rocky Mountains, North America **R** 274
  Canada **C** 51, 55
  Colorado **C** 400–03
  Denver, trade center **D** 116
  Glacier National Park **G** 221–22
  gold discoveries **G** 251, 253
  Idaho **I** 56
  Jasper National Park **J** 54–55
  Lewis and Clark Expedition **L** 162–63
  Mackenzie, Sir Alexander, early explorer **M** 4a
  Montana **M** 429–30
  mountains and mountain building **M** 499
  North American Cordillera **N** 282, 284
  Pikes Peak, picture **C** 402
  United States **U** 91
  upslope fog **F** 289
  Utah **U** 243
  westward movement **W** 146
  Wyoming **W** 325
Rocky Mountain sheep (Bighorns) **H** 221; **S** 145;
    picture **H** 220
Rocky Mountain spotted fever **I** 283; **S** 388
  wood tick, carrier, picture **S** 387
Rocky Mountain Trench, North America **C** 51
Rococo (ro-CO-co), style of decorative art **D** 75, 77
  compared to baroque **B** 62

Fragonard, Jean Honoré **F** 402
France **F** 425
   furniture design **F** 508; pictures **F** 509
   German music of the period **G** 183
   Germany **G** 169–70
   Italian art and architecture **I** 473
   painting **P** 24
   sculpture **S** 101
Rodentia, order of mammals **M** 62; **R** 275
Rodents **R** 275–80
   beavers **B** 112–14
   disease carriers **I** 287
   gerbils **G** 408
   guinea pigs **G** 407
   hamsters **G** 407–08
   mammals, orders of **M** 62, 69
   pets **P** 179–80
   rabbits a separate order **R** 22
   teeth for different diets **M** 65–66
   See also Hares; Rabbits
Rodeos **R** 281–82
   Arizona, picture **A** 413
   roping demonstrations **R** 333–35
Rodgers, Jimmie, American singer **C** 524b
Rodgers, Mary, American writer **C** 243
Rodgers, Richard, American composer **M** 542, 543
   dance music **D** 37
Rodin (ro-DAN), **Auguste,** French sculptor **R** 283
   Burghers of Calais, sculpture **S** 103
   French art of the 20th century **F** 426, 431
   modern art **M** 387–88
   Monument to Balzac, picture **M** 387
   place in the history of sculpture **S** 102–03
   The Thinker, statue **F** 426
Rod mills, in steel production **I** 400, 401, 406
Rodney, Caesar, American statesman **D** 98
Rodnina, Irina, Russian figure skater **O** 115, 116c
Rod puppets (stick puppets) **P** 535; picture **P** 534
Rodrigues, island dependency of Mauritius **M** 181
Rodríguez de Francia, José Gaspar *see* Francia, José
   Gaspar Rodríguez de
Rods, of retina of the eye **B** 284–85
   birds **B** 204
Rods, for fishing **F** 206, 209; pictures **F** 207
Roe, Richard *see* John Doe and Richard Roe

Roebling (ROE-bling), **John Augustus** (1806–69), American engineer, b. Mühlhausen, Germany. A pioneer in suspension bridges, he performed the "impossible" engineering feat of building (1851–55) a suspension bridge over Niagara Falls, using wire-rope cable he had developed. His most famous bridge is the Brooklyn Bridge, which was finished (1883) by his son, **Washington Augustus Roebling** (1837–1926), when Roebling died in an accident soon after the bridge was begun.
   modern suspension bridges **B** 398, 399

Roemer (RUR-mer), **Olaf,** Danish astronomer **L** 264
Roentgen (RENT-gun), **Wilhelm Conrad,** German
   scientist **X** 339
   cancer research **C** 92–93
   discovery of new range of radiation of light **L** 269
   studies by physicists of radiant energy **P** 237;
      picture **P** 236
   supplied medicine with a new tool **M** 208
Roentgen rays *see* X rays
Rogers, Bruce, American book designer **B** 326

Rogers, Joel Augustus (1883–1966), American writer, b. Jamaica. His research on black culture has produced

many books, including *From Superman to Man, The World's Great Men of Color,* and *Africa's Gift to America.* For a number of years he wrote a column on black history for the Pittsburgh *Courier.*

Rogers, Richard, English architect **A** 387
Rogers, Will, American actor and humorist **O** 94
   trick and fancy roping **R** 333
   Will Rogers Memorial **O** 89; picture **O** 91

Rogers, William Pierce (1913–   ), American lawyer and government official, b. Norfolk, N.Y. He served as U.S. attorney general (1958–61) under President Eisenhower. Later, he served on the U.N. South-West Africa ad hoc committee and was a member of the U.S. presidential commission on law enforcement and administration. From 1969 to 1973, he served as secretary of state under President Nixon.

Rogers' Rangers, military group in British-American army during 18th-century French and Indian War in America. Led by Major Robert Rogers (1731–95), they were known for their boldness and courage in warfare. Memorable daring encounters include "battle on snowshoes" (1758) at what is now Rogers' Rock, Lake George, N.Y.

Rogerus, first known French architect of Gothic style
   G 266
Roget's Thesaurus (ro-JAY's the-SAUR-us), book of
   synonyms and antonyms **S** 504
Roggeveen, Jakob, Dutch explorer of Easter Island
   I 430
Rogue elephants **E** 167
Rogue novels *see* Picaresque novels
Rogue River, Oregon **O** 194, 195
Rogunsky Dam, Union of Soviet Socialist Republics
   D 20
Rohde, Ruth Bryan, American diplomat **N** 85
Rohe, Ludwig Miës van der *see* Miës van der Rohe,
   Ludwig

Rojankovsky (ro-jon-KOF-ski), **Feodor** (1891–1970), American illustrator of children's books, b. Mitava, Russia. He left Russia after the Revolution and worked in Poland (1920–25) as an art director of a fashion magazine and publishing house. He spent 14 years in Paris and then went to the United States (1941). Works he illustrated include *Great Big Animal Book, Rojankovsky's Mother Goose,* and *Little Golden Mother Goose.* He won the Caldecott medal in 1956 for *Frog Went A-Courting.*

Rojas (RO-hos), **Fernando de,** Spanish writer **S** 368
Rojas Pinilla, Gustavo, Colombian president **C** 384
Roland, hero of epic poem **C** 189; **L** 129
   early French literature **F** 435

Roland (ro-LON) **de La Platière, Madame** (Jeanne Manon Phlipon) (1754–93), French revolutionist, b. Paris. She was the wife of Jean Marie Roland de La Platière, one of the leaders of the Girondists. Her salon in Paris was party headquarters (1791–93). When the Girondists were overthrown by the Jacobins (1793), she was arrested. On her way to the guillotine she cried out to the statue of Liberty in the Place de la Révolution, "O Liberty! What crimes are committed in thy name!" Her *Mémoires,* written in prison, were published in 1795.

Roland and Oliver, legend **L** 130–33
Roldos Aguilera, Jaime, Ecuadorian president **E** 58

Rolfe, John (1585–1622), English colonist, husband of Pocahontas, b. Norfolk. He went (1609) to Virginia, where he contributed greatly to the colony by introducing a new method of curing tobacco, which became a profitable export crop. His marriage (1614) to the Indian Pocahontas, daughter of Chief Powhatan, forged a peaceful union with the Indians. He was the colony's recorder and secretary (1614–19) and a member of the Council of State (1621–22).

new type of tobacco as a cash crop introduced at Jamestown, Va. **J** 21; **T** 200; **V** 358–59

Rolland (roll-ON), **Romain**, French novelist **F** 442
Rolled gold plate **G** 248
Rolled oats **G** 285
Roller Derby, sport **R** 284
Roller disco, dance **R** 284
Roller gin, cotton cleaning machine **C** 521
Roller hockey **R** 284
Rollers, construction machines **B** 447–48
Roller-skating **R** 284–85
Rolling, of metals **M** 231
Rolling mills, for steel shaping **I** 399–402

Rolling Stones, The, an English rock music group. Mick Jagger is the leader of the group, which includes Keith Richard, Charlie Watts, Bill Wyman, and Ron Wood. "Satisfaction" and "Get Off of My Cloud" are among their best-known songs. The Rolling Stones' 1969 United States tour was the subject of the film *Gimme Shelter.* Their 1981 United States tour was the most profitable and publicized in the history of rock music. **R** 262d

Rollo, duke of Normandy **V** 339
Roll of Thunder, Hear My Cry, book by Mildred Taylor **C** 243
Jerry Pinkney illustration **C** 243
Rölvaag (ROLE-vog), **Ole Edvart,** Norwegian-born American author and educator **M** 335
American literature, place in **A** 207
Roly poly, running and chasing game **G** 21
Romains (ro-MAN), **Jules,** French novelist **F** 442
Roman, typeface design **T** 345
Roman architecture **R** 285–86
achievements in engineering and masonry **A** 375–77
aqueducts **A** 344; picture **A** 231
Arch of Constantine, picture **A** 231
building construction methods **B** 435
cement and concrete, use of **C** 167
influence on later architecture **A** 384
Roman art **R** 285–86
art as a record **A** 438b
cameo portrait, picture **A** 230
coins, picture **A** 232
decorative arts **D** 71–72
furniture design **F** 505
Metropolitan Museum of Art collection **M** 237
painting **P** 17
sculpture **S** 95
Roman baths **B** 91
Roman Britain *see* Britain
Roman calendar **C** 12
Julius Caesar corrected the ancient calendar **C** 6
Roman Catholic Church **R** 287–302
Apocrypha **B** 156–57, 159
art, the meanings of **A** 438
art as a record **A** 438e
Bombay, picture **R** 149
Brazil has largest Catholic population **B** 375

choral music **C** 276, 277
Christianity, history of **C** 279–89
divorce **D** 236
Douay Bible **B** 153
duelists refused burial by **D** 340
ecumenical movement **P** 486
England, history of **E** 219–24, 228
Evangelists, feast days of the, **E** 335
forms of address for the clergy **A** 21
Germany's early religious divisions **G** 159–60
Henry VIII, break with the Church **E** 220, **H** 109
Holy Roman Empire, emperors and popes **H** 162–64
hymns **H** 309, 310, 311, 313
Inquisition **I** 256
Ireland **I** 385
Italy **I** 448, 454–55
Kennedy, first Catholic U.S. president **K** 204
Latin, the official language **L** 76
Latin America **C** 289; **L** 50–51
Loyola, founder of Jesuits **L** 369
Luther excommunicated from **L** 378
marriage rites **W** 101
meaning of the term **R** 298
North America **C** 288–89
parochial schools **E** 75
Philippines, a Christian majority **P** 185
Quebec, Canada **C** 69; **Q** 10a
Reformation **C** 285–87
religious holidays **R** 153–55
Vatican City **V** 280–82
What are holy days? **R** 290
What are sacramentals? **R** 301
Why is it called the Roman Catholic Church? **R** 298
women, role of **W** 213
See also names of saints, popes, and Christian leaders
Romance languages, derived from the Latin of the Romans **L** 40
Europe **E** 317
French **F** 433–35
in comparative linguistic studies **L** 303
Italian **I** 474
Rumanian **R** 355
Spanish **S** 365–66
Romances, story poems, songs, and novels
Arthur, King, legends of **A** 442–45
ballad cycles **B** 22
early novels **N** 345
medieval tales of chivalry in German literature **G** 174
nineteenth-century American literature **A** 206
"Song of Roland" **C** 189; **F** 435
Roman Curia, administrative body of the Church **R** 293
Roman Empire, 27 B.C.–A.D. 476 **R** 303–08
Austria, history of **A** 524
Britain, conquest of **E** 215–16
Caesar, Julius, lays foundation for **C** 5
cities, history of **C** 308a
citizenship **C** 311
clothing symbolic of class **C** 351
Constantine the Great, emperor **C** 489
Eastern *see* Byzantine Empire
feudalism follows decline of Roman Empire **F** 99–103
Holy Roman Empire, how named **H** 161, 164
imperialism **I** 109
legal system protected citizens **C** 314
loss of power in western Europe **M** 289

Mark Antony and events leading to the Empire
M 100
Nero N 114
persecution of Christians R 288 .
road builders R 248
Spain, province of S 351
Titus destroys Jerusalem J 106
Why were the Roman emperors called Caesars?
C 6
See also Rome, ancient
Romanesque (ro-man-ESK) **art and architecture** R 309
architecture, history of A 377–78
cathedrals C 131–32
France F 421
Germany G 166
Gothic architecture based on G 264
Italian churches I 460
Middle Ages, art and architecture of the M 296–97
sculpture S 96, 98
Roman Forum, ruins, picture R 314
Roman law L 87, 88
ancient civilizations, contributions of A 232
civil liberties, historical origins of C 314
Roman numerals R 309–10
abacus used instead of A 2
numerals and numeration systems N 391
Romanovs (RO-ma-nofs), Russian ruling family M 467;
U 48
Roman Question R 296, 298
Roman Republic R 303
Roman roads A 231
Britain E 215
history of transportation T 259
Romans, best engineers in ancient world E 208
Romans, book of Bible, New Testament B 161
Romansch (ro-MANCH) **language** S 495
Romantic age, in music R 310–11
Wagner's music dramas D 297
See also Classical age in music
Romanticism, in art
Delacroix, Eugène D 85
France F 425–26; P 29
Germany G 171
modern art M 386–87
sculpture S 102
Romanticism, in literature
Balzac, Honoré de F 441
English literature E 260–61
French literature F 439–41
German literature G 177
historical writing H 137
in drama D 297
Spanish literature S 369
Romanticism, in music R 310–11
German composers G 186
opera O 134
operetta O 156–58
sonatas M 539–40
symphony M 541

Romanticism, movement arising in 18th-century Europe that influenced literature, philosophy, art, and music. Characterized by stress on expression of emotion, it is often said to be in direct contradiction to the rationality and order of classicism. In art, 19th-century romantic painters used dramatic color, form, light, and shadow to arouse the imagination, and stimulate a feeling.

Romanus, pope R 296
Romany (ROM-any) (Gypsy) **language** G 434

Romberg, Sigmund, Hungarian-born American
composer O 157
Student Prince, The, operetta O 158
Rome, ancient A 230–32
Acta Diurna ("acts of the day"), early newspapers
J 142
alphabet A 171, 173; C 431
aqueducts A 344
architecture *see* Roman architecture
armor A 433
art *see* Roman art
beauty culture B 110–11
bookmaking B 319
breadmaking industry B 388b
bridge building B 395
burning of (A.D. 64) C 280
Caesar, Gaius Julius C 5–6
Caesar's calendar C 12
canal builders C 84
cement and concrete discovered C 167
census C 169
central heating system H 98
ceremonial dancing D 23
Cicero supports the republic C 298
cities, history of C 308a
citizenship C 311
clothing symbolic of class C 351
concrete, discovery of B 393–94
cork, uses of C 505
cosmetics, use of C 510
drama patterned after Greek plays D 295
education E 64–65
Empire, Roman R 303–08
engineering feats E 208
fire in primitive religions F 144
founding and history of the city R 316
fountains F 394–95
glassmaking G 229
government P 378
highways leading to and from Rome T 259
homes H 178
hospitals, early beginnings M 204
jewelry J 94
knives and spoons K 286
Latin language L 76–77
Latin literature L 77–80
lead water pipes, use of L 94
legal system protected citizens C 314
libraries L 194–95
Livy's history L 317
locks and keys L 322–23
Mark Antony M 100
Merino sheep breeding C 145–46
mining M 320
minting of coins M 338
mythology G 356–66
New Year's gifts N 208
Olympic Games deteriorated O 105
parades P 61
physical education P 224–25
plan of early cities U 232
postal system C 435
public health measures M 204
Punic Wars P 533
roads E 208; R 248; T 259
Roman Empire R 303–08
Roman numerals R 309–10
ships and shipbuilding S 155, 158
slavery S 196
standards and flags F 225

Rome, ancient (continued)
  stylus, use of **C** 432
  tools **T** 211
  water clock **W** 45
  See also Roman Empire
Rome, capital of Italy **R** 312–17; picture **C** 308e
  architecture of Italian Renaissance **I** 465, 467
  cities of Italy **I** 449–50
  fountains **F** 395
  Little Sports Palace, picture **A** 386b
  Olympic Games, 1960 **O** 112
  painting **P** 21
  political banners, picture **C** 445
  Renaissance art and architecture **R** 167
  San Carlo alle Quattro Fontane church, picture **A** 383
  Tiber River, picture **R** 247
  Trevi Fountain, picture **F** 395
  Vatican City **V** 280–82
Rome, Georgia **G** 135
Rome, Treaty of, 1957, Common Market agreement **E** 334; **I** 329
Rome-Berlin Axis **F** 64
  World War II **W** 286
Romenenko, Yuri V., Soviet cosmonaut **S** 345
Romeo and Juliet, ballet, picture **B** 23
Romeo and Juliet, play by William Shakespeare **R** 317–18; **S** 132
  balcony scene, excerpts **R** 317–18
  outline of the plot **S** 137

Rommel, Erwin (1891–1944), German general, b. Heidenheim. A master tactician in tank warfare during World War II, he won distinction (and the nickname "the Desert Fox") as commander of the Afrika Korps. He later (1944) commanded the Army Group in France during the Allied invasion of Normandy.
  World War II **W** 290, 291, 303

Romney, George, English painter **E** 238

Romney, George Wilcken (1907–), American politician, b. Chihuahua, Mexico. After serving as a Mormon missionary in Britain, he entered the business world, rising to the position of president of American Motors Corporation. Elected governor of Michigan (1962, 1966), he was named (1969) secretary of housing and urban development. In 1972 he resigned, and the following year he became chairman of the National Center for Voluntary Action.

Romney, West Virginia **W** 140

Romulo (ROM-u-lo), **Carlos Pena** (1901–), Filipino statesman, b. Manila. He won a Pulitzer prize in 1941 for a series of articles on conditions in Asia, and served as press aide to General MacArthur during World War II. He was a member of the Quezon (1943) and Osmeña (1944) cabinets. In 1945 he became head of the Philippine U.N. delegation, and in 1949 he was elected president of the U.N. General Assembly. He was ambassador to the United States from 1952 to 1953 and from 1955 to 1961. From 1962 to 1968 he was president of the University of the Philippines. He was named secretary of foreign affairs in 1969.

Romulus and Remus, in Roman legend, founders of the city of Rome. Twin sons of Mars and vestal virgin Rhea Silvia, and grandsons of Numitor, King of Alba. When Numitor was deposed by Amulius, the twins were ordered to be abandoned to die. Suckled by a wolf and taught by shepherds, they later killed Amulius and returned Numitor to the throne. They founded Rome, and Romulus allegedly became the first king (753–716 B.C.) after killing Remus. According to legend, Romulus was carried off to heaven in the midst of a storm and thereafter was worshipped as Quirinus. **I** 454

Romulus Augustulus, Roman emperor **R** 308
Ronchamp, France
  chapel of Notre Dame du Haut designed by Le Corbusier, picture **A** 386a
Rondo, musical form **M** 535
  classical age in music **C** 332
Ronne, Finn, American explorer **P** 368
Ronsard (ron-SAR), **Pierre de,** French poet **F** 436
Roof bolting, of coal mines **C** 367
Roof of the World, Himalaya Mountains
  Tibet **T** 175
Roofs, of buildings **B** 434; **H** 169–70
  mansard roof **F** 421–22
Rook, in chess, picture **C** 221
Rookeries, breeding grounds of birds or animals
  penguins **P** 120
Roosa, Stuart A., American astronaut **S** 345
Roosevelt (ROSE-ev-elt), **Anna Eleanor,** wife of Franklin D. Roosevelt **F** 178–79; **R** 320
  crusader for human rights **R** 318
  See also Roosevelt Memorial Foundation
Roosevelt, Edith Kermit Carow, wife of Theodore Roosevelt **F** 175–76; **R** 327; picture **F** 177
Roosevelt, Eleanor *see* Roosevelt, Anna Eleanor
Roosevelt, Franklin Delano, 32nd president of the United States **R** 319–24
  banking legislation **B** 49
  conservation projects in government **C** 486
  Franklin D. Roosevelt National Historic Site, Hyde Park, New York **N** 220
  Johnson, Lyndon B., and Roosevelt, picture **J** 129
  letter to his mother **L** 156b
  modifies capitalism **C** 104
  New Deal program **D** 122
  presidential leadership **P** 451
  quotation from First Inaugural Address **Q** 20
  Roosevelt Campobello International Park **M** 43; **N** 138f
  Supreme Court **S** 476
  Teheran Conference, 1943, picture **W** 298

Roosevelt, Kermit (1889–1943), American soldier, explorer, businessman, and writer, b. Oyster Bay, N.Y. A son of Theodore Roosevelt, he accompanied him on a hunting trip to Africa (1909–10) and explored regions in Brazil (1914). He served in both the British and U.S. armies during World Wars I and II and was president of the Roosevelt Steamship Co. and vice-president of U.S. Lines Co. Among his books are *War in the Garden of Eden* and *The Happy Hunting Grounds.*

Roosevelt, Nicholas J. (1767–1854), American inventor and engineer, b. New York, N.Y. In 1798 he built an experimental steamboat, the *Polacca,* which traveled at 5 km (3 mi) per hour. He and Robert Fulton first used steamboats on Western rivers in 1809 and built the steamboat *New Orleans.* In 1811 the *New Orleans* ran from Pittsburgh to New Orleans in 14 days. Roosevelt was granted a patent in 1814 for his invention of vertical paddle wheels.

Roosevelt, Theodore, 26th president of the United
States **R** 325–30
as vice-president, picture **V** 329
creates career Foreign Service **F** 370
football rules to make game safer **F** 356
interest in conservation **C** 485
Kipling's correspondence with **K** 261
ranching in North Dakota **N** 322–23
Rough Riders in Spanish-American War **S** 375
Sagamore Hill National Historic Site, Oyster Bay,
New York **N** 220–21
Taft, feuding with **T** 8–9
Theodore Roosevelt National Park, North Dakota
N 49, 333
"the Trust Buster" **C** 104

Roosevelt, Theodore, Jr. (1887–1944), American government administrator, soldier, and author, b. Oyster Bay,
N.Y. The son of Theodore Roosevelt, 26th president of
the United States, he was elected to the New York State
legislature (1919, 1921) and served as assistant secretary of the Navy (1921–24), governor of Puerto Rico
(1929–32), and governor-general of the Philippine Islands (1932–33). His works include *Average Americans,
All in the Family,* and *Colonial Policies of the United
States.* An officer in both world wars, he died at the front
in France during World War II.

Roosevelt families
Franklin D. Roosevelt family, picture **R** 320
Theodore Roosevelt family, picture **R** 327
Roosevelt Island, New York City **N** 228
Roosevelt Lake, Washington **D** 19

Roosevelt, Eleanor, Memorial Foundation, organization
established to carry on ideals of Eleanor Roosevelt
(1884–1962). Founded in 1963 by congressional charter,
the organization has headquarters in New York, N.Y. Its
first head was UN ambassador Adlai E. Stevenson. Its
concern is for human rights and the support of the
United Nations as a force for peace. It aids underprivileged children.

Roosevelt River, Brazil (ancient name, River of Doubt)
R 330
Roosters, male chickens **P** 423
Root, in music **M** 534

Root, Elihu (1845–1937), American statesman and lawyer, b. Clinton, N.Y. While U.S. secretary of war
(1899–1904) he directed administration of Cuba and
Philippine Islands and reorganized the army. As secretary of state (1905–09) he restored good relations with
Latin-American countries. He served as senator from
New York (1909–15). He was prominent in settling the
North Atlantic Fishery dispute (1910) and was a member
of the commission that planned the Permanent Court of
International Justice (1920). He received a Nobel peace
prize (1912).

Root, George F., American composer **N** 25
Rootabaga (root-a-BAY-ga) **Stories,** by Carl Sandburg
S 26; excerpt **S** 26a
Root crops **P** 307
potatoes **P** 411–12; **V** 292, 293
Rooters, plowlike machines **B** 447
Root hairs, of trees **T** 280
Root knots, galls caused by round worms **P** 286
Roots, book by Alex Haley **G** 76a
Roots, of plants **P** 290; pictures **P** 291

poisonous **P** 322
"root-bound" house plants **H** 267–68
roots we eat **P** 307; picture **P** 306
trees **T** 279–80
weeds **W** 104
Roots, of words **W** 239
Roots, television program **N** 105
Rootstocks, seedlings
orange trees **O** 178
Rope **R** 331–33
games with rope and string, pictures **A** 304
knots **K** 289–92
Rope spinning **R** 333–35
Rope tricks **T** 288–89
Roping **R** 333–35
rodeo events **R** 281–82
Roquefort (ROKE-fort), cheese **C** 192–93
action of molds **F** 498
blue cheese, a dairy product **D** 13
Roraima, Mount, Guyana **G** 428
Rorquals (fin whales) **W** 149

Rorschach (ROR-shock), **Hermann** (1884–1922), Swiss
psychiatrist and neurologist, b. Zurich. He devised the
ink-blot test known by his name. The test is widely used
in the diagnosis of psychopathologic conditions. In it the
subject describes what he sees in 10 ink blots of differ-
ing forms and colors. The test is based on the hypothesis
that a person's interpretations of what he sees project
aspects of his personality and emotions.

Rosario (ro-SAR-yo), Argentina **A** 394
Rosary, prayer of Roman Catholic Church **R** 302

Rosas (RO-sos), **Juan Manuel de** (1793–1877), Argentine
dictator, b. Buenos Aires. Though governor only of Buenos Aires (1829–32, 1835–52), he maintained dictatorial
rule over other allied provinces. When his war against
Montevideo (1842–51) was finally brought to defeat by
Brazil, he fled to England (1852–77). **A** 395

Rosbaud, Hans (1895–1962), Austrian conductor, b.
Graz. He was director of the municipal music school of
Mainz (1923–30) and of the Munich Konzertverein
(1945–48). As music director of the Baden-Baden radio
orchestra (1948–62), he toured widely and introduced
the works of many contemporary composers.

Rösch, G. A., German scientist
studies of bees **B** 119

Rose, Pete (Peter Edward Rose) (1942–   ), American
baseball player, b. Cincinnati, Ohio. Rose began his major league career in 1963, playing second base for the
Cincinnati Reds. He was named the National League's
Rookie of the Year. He became a regular outfielder in
1968. He got the 3,000th hit of his professional career
during the 1978 season. In the same season he tied a
National League record by hitting safely in 44 consecu-
tive games. In 1979 Rose joined the Philadelphia Phillies
of the National League as a first baseman. In 1981, he
became the National League lifetime leader in hits. Picture **B** 76

Rose Bowl, Pasadena, California, New Year's Day
football game **F** 365
Rose-breasted grosbeaks, birds, picture **B** 240

Rosecrans, William Starke (1819–98), American soldier,
b. Kingston, Ohio. He served as a general in the Union

Rosecrans, William Starke (continued)
Army during the Civil War and was considered a great strategist. After resigning from the Army (1867), he served as U.S. minister to Mexico (1868–69), representative to Congress from California (1881–85), and register of the treasury (1885–93).

Civil War, United States, campaigns of **C** 326

Rose Festival, Portland, Oregon **P** 398
Rose garden, picture **G** 31
Rosemary, herb **S** 382; picture **S** 381

Rosenberg, Anna Marie (1902–   ), American public and industrial consultant, b. Budapest, Hungary. She served with the National Recovery Administration (1934–39) and was regional director of the Social Security Board (1936–43) and of the War Manpower Commission (1942–45). She held the office of assistant secretary of defense (1950–53), highest military post ever attained by a woman. She was assigned by President Roosevelt (1944) and President Truman (1945) to study problems of rehabilitating U.S. soldiers. She was a recipient of the Medal of Freedom (1945).

Rosenberg, Julius (1918–53) and **Ethel** (1915–53), American man and wife convicted of espionage, b. New York, N.Y. Found guilty of delivering (1944–46) secret atomic bomb information to Soviet agents, they were sentenced to death (1951). They were convicted on the testimony of David Greenglass, brother of Ethel employed at a New Mexico atomic research center, who received a 15-year sentence for treason. Their execution (1953) resulted in controversy over the nature of the trial and use of death sentence for espionage in peacetime.

Rosenfeld, Morris, Yiddish author **Y** 351
Rosenkavalier (RO-sen-ka-va-lier), **Der,** opera by Richard Strauss **O** 153

Rosenquist, James (1933–   ), American artist, b. North Dakota. He studied at the Art Students League in New York and early in his career was employed by The General Outdoor Advertising Company as a billboard painter. Considered a super-realist by many, his paintings are in both the realistic and abstract styles.

Rosenwald, Julius, American merchant and philanthropist **I** 85

Rosenwald, Julius, Fund, foundation established (1917) by Julius Rosenwald (1862–1932), American merchant and philanthropist. Originally, its purpose was to build rural schools for underprivileged children, but it was later expanded to include support for projects that would improve opportunities and living conditions for disadvantaged groups, particularly blacks. It gave assistance to hospitals and health agencies, black schools and colleges, and poorly equipped school libraries. The fund aided many promising students, artists, writers, and musicians. It was discontinued in 1948.

Rosenwald, Lessing J., American merchant and art collector **N** 40

Rose of Lima (LEE-ma), **Saint** (1586–1617), Peruvian Dominican ascetic, b. Lima. She entered the Third Order of St. Dominic (1606) and lived an extremely austere life. Canonized in 1671, she was the first saint born in the New World.

Rose-quartz, gemstone **G** 75; **Q** 7; picture **R** 265
Roses, City of, Portland, Oregon **P** 398
Roses, flowers **G** 46, 51; pictures **G** 27, 31, 49
Bulgaria, center of rose-growing industry **B** 441
New York, state flower of, picture **N** 210
parts of a flower, diagram **P** 295
rose designs in furniture, pictures **F** 505, 507
wild rose, state flower of Iowa, North Dakota, pictures **I** 357, **N** 323
Roses, Wars of the, 1455–85 **E** 219–20
Rosetta Stone, first clue to understanding Egyptian hieroglyphics **W** 318; picture **W** 319
displayed in the British Museum **M** 514
Rosette nebula, picture **S** 411

Rose water, fragrant solution prepared with the scented parts of the rose. It is used as a perfume and, infrequently, in cooking.

Rosé (rose-AY) **wines** **W** 188
Rosewood, tree
uses of the wood and its grain, pictures **W** 224
Rosh Hashanah (rosh a-SHO-nah), religious holiday **R** 154
facts about Judaism **J** 120

Rosicrucianism (rosi-CRU-cian-ism), mystical religious philosophy probably established in the early 14th century by Christian Rosenkreutz, who imparted knowledge acquired during his travels in Middle East and Spain to three companions, thus founding the original Society of the Rose and Cross. The cult spread throughout Europe, Britain, and the United States in the 17th century. It emphasizes development of the latent human capacity to achieve understanding of the spiritual realm, which permeates nature.

Rosin, resin of certain pine trees **R** 184
by-product from the extraction of turpentine **T** 330
flux in soldering and brazing **S** 249
Ross, Betsy, American maker of first stars and stripes flag **R** 335
flag of 1777 **F** 244; picture **F** 229
Ross, Diana, American singer and actress, picture **R** 262d
Ross, Edmund Gibson, American statesman **K** 189

Ross, George (1730–79), American jurist, b. New Castle, Del. He was elected to the provincial assembly (1768), serving seven years, and to the Continental Congress (1774–77), where he signed the Declaration of Independence. He was commissioned a judge of the admiralty court of Pennsylvania (1779).

Ross, Sir James Clark (1800–62), English polar explorer, b. London. He was a member of Arctic expeditions under Sir William Edward Parry (1819–27). He joined an Arctic expedition (1829–33) under his uncle Sir John Ross and determined the position of the north magnetic pole (1831). He led an Antarctic exploratory voyage (1839–43) that discovered Victoria Land and commanded an Arctic relief expedition in search of Sir John Franklin (1848–49). He was author of *A Voyage of Discovery in the Southern and Antarctic Regions.* Ross Sea, Ross Island, and Ross Ice Shelf in Antarctica are named for him.

Ross, John (Cherokee name, Cooweescoowe) (1790–1866), Cherokee chief, b. near Lookout Mountain,

Tenn. He served in the War of 1812 under Andrew Jackson. He was president of the national council of Cherokees (1819–26) and chief of eastern Cherokees (1828–39). After an attempt to prevent removal of Cherokees from Georgia, he led movement to present-day Oklahoma (1838–39). He was chief of the united Cherokee nation (1839–66).

Ross, Sir John (1777–1856), Scottish Arctic explorer, b. Inch, Wigtonshire. He led expeditions in search of the Northwest Passage (1818, 1829–33) and explored Boothia peninsula, Gulf of Boothia, and King William Land. He was a consul in Stockholm (1839–46) and headed an expedition in search of Sir John Franklin (1850). He was author of *A Voyage of Discovery* and *Narrative of a Second Voyage in Search of a Northwest Passage*.
>   Northwest Passage   **N** 338

Ross, Malcolm, American military balloonist   **B** 32
Ross, Nellie Tayloe, American political figure
>   **W** 336

Ross, William P., American newspaper editor   **O** 88
Rossetti (ro-SET-ti), **Christina,** English poet   **R** 336
>   place in English literature   **E** 263
>   "Who Has Seen the Wind?," poem   **R** 336

Rossetti, Dante Gabriel, English painter and poet
>   **R** 336
>   drawing of Christina Rossetti, picture   **R** 336
>   engraving for Tennyson's *Poems,* picture   **E** 263
>   Pre-Raphaelite Brotherhood   **E** 241

Rossetti, Gabriele, Italian poet   **R** 336
Rossetti, Maria, English writer   **R** 336
Rossetti, William, English art critic and essayist
>   **R** 336

Rossini (ro-SI-ni), **Gioacchino Antonio** (1792–1868), Italian composer, b. Pesaro. He was a master of Italian comic opera. Lyric charm and clear texture characterize his nearly 40 works, of which *The Barber of Seville* remains most popular. Other operas include *Tancredi, Otello, La Cenerentola,* and *The Lady of the Lake.* He composed his last opera, *William Tell,* at the age of 37.
>   *Barber of Seville, The,* opera   **O** 140
>   *Cenerentola, La,* opera   **O** 143
>   Italian opera   **I** 485;   **O** 135

Rossiter, Thomas, American artist
>   *Signing the Constitution,* painting, picture   **F** 391
Rosso, Giovanni Battista, Italian artist   **R** 171
Ross Sea   **O** 48
Ross Shelf, Antarctica   **I** 12

Rostand (ros-TON), **Edmond** (1868–1918), French poet and playwright, b. Marseilles. The youngest member ever elected to the French Academy (1901), he is best known for his romantic drama *Cyrano de Bergerac.* Other works include *La Princesse Lointaine, L'Aiglon,* and *Chantecler.* Several of his plays were written for Sarah Bernhardt.
>   drama, history of   **D** 298

Roswell, New Mexico   **N** 193
>   Goddard's experimental rocket station   **G** 246
Rotary drilling, for petroleum   **P** 172
Rotary engines   **I** 303
Rotary-hoe cultivators   **F** 59

Rotary (RO-tary) **International,** service organization of business and professional people with clubs located in

151 countries. The first club was founded in 1905, and the National Association of Rotary Clubs was formed in 1912. The international association was established in 1922. Originally, meetings were held in rotation at the homes of members, and from this system the club derived its name. Headquarters are in Evanston, Ill. Publications are *The Rotarian* and *Revista Rotaria.*

Rotary presses, for printing   **P** 462
>   newspapers' use of   **N** 203, 204
Rotary tillers, picture   **I** 362
Rotation of crops   **A** 93
>   insect control   **I** 258
>   vegetable gardening   **V** 288
ROTC, Reserve Officers' Training Corps   **U** 162, 190
Rotenone (RO-ten-ohn), insecticide   **I** 257
Roth, Philip, American writer   **A** 214
Rotherhithe, etching by Whistler   **E** 294
Rothko, Mark, American artist   **M** 397
Rothschild, Lionel, English financier and statesman
>   **J** 110
Rothschild, Mayer Amschel, German financier   **B** 48;
>   **R** 337
Rothschild family   **R** 337
>   banking enterprises   **B** 48–49
Rotifers (RO-ti-fers) (wheelworms), class of invertebrate
>   animals   **P** 281
>   nervous system, diagram   **B** 363
Rotisseries (ro-TISS-eries), electric   **E** 120
Rotogravure (ro-to-gra-VURE), printing   **P** 460
Rotogravure vinyls, plastics   **V** 341
Rotonda, villa designed by Palladio   **I** 467; picture
>   **I** 464
Rotors, electromagnets of motors   **E** 136–37; picture
>   **E** 141
Rotors, rotating air foils
>   autogiros and helicopters   **H** 104–05, 106
Rotterdam, ocean liner   **O** 22
Rotterdam, Netherlands   **N** 118; picture   **N** 120
>   harbor, picture   **H** 36
>   leading port of Europe   **E** 326
Rotunda of University of Virginia, picture   **A** 384
Rouault (roo-O), **Georges,** French painter   **F** 431;
>   **M** 388
>   *Old King, The,* painting   **F** 430
Rouge (ROOGE), cosmetic   **B** 110;   **C** 509
Rouge, polishing powder   **O** 174
Rouget de Lisle (roo-JAY d'LEEL), **Claude Joseph,**
>   French officer and composer   **N** 17–18
Roughing mills, in steel production   **I** 399–400
Roughnecks, workers who handle oil drilling equipment
>   **P** 172
Rough Riders, United States Volunteer Cavalry, led by
>   Theodore Roosevelt   **R** 327; picture   **R** 328
>   Spanish-American War   **S** 375
>   term used by Antoine de Vallambrosa   **N** 335
Roumania *see* Rumania
Round, musical form   **M** 538
>   African music   **A** 78

Roundheads, Puritans or Parliamentarians, especially the soldiers under Cromwell, during the English Civil War period (1642–49). The term was used by the Cavaliers, or Royalists, who wore long hair, in derogatory reference to the Puritans, who wore short hair.
>   Cromwell and the Roundheads   **C** 536

Round Table, of King Arthur   **A** 442, 444
Roundups, of cattle   **C** 146
>   ranch life   **R** 105

Roundworms (nematode worms) **W** 312
   plant enemies **P** 286; picture **P** 287
Rous, Peyton, American physician **C** 93
Rous sarcoma (rouse sar-CO-ma) **virus V** 369

Rousseau (roo-SO), **Henri** (Le Douanier, or "custom-house officer") (1844–1910), French primitive painter, b. Laval. After retiring (1885) from service as a customs official, for which he received his nickname, he concentrated on painting. He exhibited at the Salon des Indé-pendants (1886–98, 1901–10). His work, often depicting dreams and exotic landscapes, includes *Sleeping Gypsy.*

Rousseau, Jean Jacques, Swiss-born French philosopher
   and writer **R** 337
   education theories **E** 68
   French Revolution **F** 463
   novels **N** 348
   Voltaire and Rousseau **F** 439
Rouvroy, Claude Henri de *see* Saint-Simon, Claude
   Henri de Rouvroy, comte de
Rover Scouts B 360

Rowan (RO-wan), **Andrew Summers** (1857–1943), American army officer, b. Gap Mills, Va. (now W. Va.). Following the outbreak of Spanish-American War, he entered Cuba to inquire about the state of Cuban forces. After meeting with General Calixto García Iñiguez (1898), he returned to the United States with important information from Garcia. His feat was heralded in an essay by Elbert Hubbard inaccurately titled "A Message to Garcia." Rowan served in Mindanao, Philippines (1905–07), and wrote *The Island of Cuba* and *How I Carried the Message to Garcia.*

Rowan, Carl Thomas (1925–   ), American diplomat and writer, b. Ravenscroft, Tenn. He worked as a copyreader and staff reporter on the Minneapolis *Tribune* (1948–61). After serving in the State Department as deputy assistant secretary of state for public affairs (1961–63), he assumed the post of United States ambassador to Finland (1963–64). He served as director of the United States Information Agency (1964–65), becoming the first black to hold a National Security Council post. He was a columnist for the Chicago *Daily News* (1965–78) before joining the Chicago *Sun-Times* as a columnist. He is also a television commentator. **N** 102

Rowan, William, Canadian zoologist **H** 191
Row-crop tractors F 55, 57
Rowing R 338–39
   Olympic events **O** 108

Rowland, Henry Augustus (1848–1901), American physicist, b. Honesdale, Pa. He was the first professor of physics at Johns Hopkins University (1876–1901). His greatest achievement was the invention of the concave diffraction grating—a series of lines scratched on a concave mirror, which then produces a spectrum when it reflects light. Concave gratings are more precise and less costly and cover a wider range of light than the earlier, flat gratings.

Rowlands, Gena, American actress **M** 488c
Rowlandson, Thomas, English cartoonist **C** 125
   famous illustrator and caricaturist **I** 91
   Sports of a Country Fair, an illustration **I** 90
Rowson, Susanna Haswell, English-born American
   novelist **A** 198

Roxas y Acuña (RO-hos e a-COON-ya), **Manuel** (1892–1948), Philippine statesman, b. Capiz. He was a member of the house of representatives (1922–34) and national assembly (1935–38), secretary of finance (1938–41), and president of the Philippines (1946–48).
   Philippines, history of **P** 190

Royal Academy of Arts (Royal Academy), British association of 40 artists elected as royal academicians, and approximately 30 associates. Founded in London in 1768 by George III, it promotes the arts of painting, sculpture, and architecture by exhibiting the works of contemporary artists and providing art instruction. The Academy also provides financial aid for needy artists.
   English art, age of the Royal Academy **E** 238
   National Gallery **N** 36

Royal Academy of Music, Paris, France **D** 36
Royal and Ancient Golf Club (R.A.G.C.), Saint Andrews,
   Scotland **G** 256
Royal Ballet B 28a
Royal Caledonian Curling Club of Scotland
   C 555
Royal Canadian Academy of Arts N 41
Royal Canadian Air Force C 82
Royal Canadian Mint M 338
Royal Canadian Mounted Police P 374, 375, 377;
   picture **C** 78
   law enforcement in Canada **C** 78
Royal Canadian Mounted Police Museum and Barracks,
   Regina, Saskatchewan **S** 38f
Royal Canadian Navy C 80–82
Royal Danish Ballet B 28a–28b
Royal Gorge, of the Arkansas River, picture **C** 412
Royal Greenwich Observatory *see* Greenwich
   Observatory, Royal
Royal Institution of Great Britain T 166
Royal jelly, food of bees **B** 122
Royal Montreal Golf Club, Canada **G** 261
Royal Ontario Museum, Toronto, Canada, picture
   M 520
Royal Shakespeare Theatre, Stratford-on-Avon, England
   T 159
Royal Society of London S 70
   based on principles of Francis Bacon's scientific
   method **S** 67–68
   Boyle, Robert **B** 354
Royalty, payment to an author or composer **P** 514
   check on royalties if you charge admission to your
   play **P** 335
   copyright **T** 245
Royal Winnipeg Ballet, Canada **B** 28b

Rozier (roze-YAY), **Jean François Pilâtre de** (1754–85), French physician and balloonist, b. Metz. He made the first aerial ascent (1783), in a balloon designed by the Montgolfier brothers. With Marquis d'Arlandes, he crossed Paris in first free-balloon flight (1783). He developed and piloted a balloon utilizing hydrogen and hot-air sacs, but he was killed when the hydrogen caught fire and exploded.
   balloons and ballooning, history of **B** 30

R. R. Bowker Company L 192
RSVP *see* Retired Senior Volunteer Program
R.S.V.P., invitation requiring reply **L** 159
   parties, etiquette of giving **P** 88
Rua Cana Falls, Angola **W** 57
Ruanda-Urundi *see* Burundi; Rwanda

Rubàiyat (RU-by-ot) **of Omar Khayyàm** (O-mar ky-OM), The **E** 263; **I** 374

Rub'al Khali (roob-ol KA-li), desert region of Saudi Arabia **S** 46; **U** 64a; picture **A** 446

Rubato (ru-BA-to), musical term **M** 534; **O** 189

Rubber **R** 340–47
  dolls made of **D** 267
  first rubber balls **B** 20
  Goodyear's vulcanization process **G** 263
  leading industry **I** 246–47
  rubber-powered airplane models **A** 105
  silicones **S** 177
  synthesized by chemists **C** 195
  tires **T** 196–98

Rubber tiles, floor covering **V** 341
Rubber trees **R** 340, 342–44
Rubbing alcohol **A** 147
Rubbings, reproductions of designs and textures **R** 348–348a; **D** 136
Rubbish, solid waste **S** 31
Rube Goldberg, complicated device or scheme *see* Goldberg, Rube
Rubella (ru-BELL-a), German measles **D** 194–95
Rubens, Peter Paul, Flemish painter **R** 348b; **D** 352
  Adoration of the Magi, painting **D** 356
  baroque painting **P** 24
  etchings of his paintings **G** 305
  gallery in the Louvre, picture **L** 367
  Hélène Fourment and Her Children, painting **R** 348b
  Marie de Medicis, Queen of France, Landing in Marseilles, painting **P** 25
  northern baroque art **B** 60
  Peasant Dance, painting **B** 58
Rubeola, disease **D** 194

Rubicon (RU-bic-on), small river in northern Italy that flows into the Adriatic Sea and in ancient Roman times formed the boundary separating Italy and Cisalpine Gaul. It is historically famous as the river Julius Caesar and his army crossed in 49 B.C., precipitating civil war.
  Caesar's career **C** 6

Rubidium (ru-BID-ium), element **E** 155, 164
Rubidium-87, radioactive element **R** 65
Rubies, gemstones **G** 69
  lasers **L** 46b
  superstitions about **G** 71

Rubik's Cube, a cube-shaped puzzle made up of 26 connected sections, or boxes. A mechanism in the center of the cube allows sections of the cube to be rotated independently. Each of the 6 faces of the cube has 9 squares. When the cube is in its original state, each of the faces has its own color. But when the sections are rotated, or scrambled, different-colored squares appear on each face. The puzzle involves scrambling the sections and then returning the cube to its original state, with all squares on each face having the same color. The record time for solving the puzzle is less than half a minute. The cube was invented by Ernö Rubik, a Hungarian professor of architecture.

Rubinstein, Anton Grigorievich (1829–94), Russian composer and pianist, b. Vykhvatinetz. He won wide acclaim as a pianist throughout Europe and the United States. In Russia he became imperial concert director (1858), and he founded St. Petersburg Conservatory of Music

(1862), serving as its director (1862–67, 1887–91). His compositions include *Ocean Symphony,* the opera *The Demon,* piano concertos, and solo pieces.
  Russian music **U** 63

Rubinstein, Artur (1886–1982), American pianist, b. Lodz, Poland. A widely acclaimed virtuoso, he made concert tours in numerous countries throughout Europe and South America and in the United States. He was best known for his interpretation of Chopin and Spanish composers, such as Albéniz and Granados. His own compositions include piano pieces and chamber music.

Rublev, Andrei, Russian artist **U** 54
  Archangel Michael, icon **U** 55
Rudbeckias (rud-BECK-ias), flowers, picture **G** 28
Rudders, steering devices
  airplane **A** 556–57
  ships **I** 337
Rudolf, Lake, eastern Africa **L** 33
Rudolf of Habsburg, ruler of Austria **A** 524

Rudolph, Wilma (1940–   ), American track star, b. St. Bethlehem, Tenn. In the 1960 Olympics she won three gold medals—for the 100- and 200-meter dashes and as anchor on the women's 400-meter team. Associated Press chose her Female Athlete of the Year (1960). **O** 112

Rudolphine tables in astronomy, work of Tycho Brahe **B** 361
Ruffed grouse, bird **B** 208
  Pennsylvania, state bird of, picture **P** 129
Rufisque (ru-FEESK), Senegal **S** 120

Rugambwa (ru-GAM-bwa) (means "high renown"), **Laurian, Cardinal** (1912–   ), Tanzanian ecclesiastic, b. Bukongo, Kiyanja. He was ordained a Catholic priest in 1943. He studied in Rome (1948–51) and was appointed bishop of Rutabo (1953). Chosen cardinal by Pope John XXIII (1960), he became the first black to hold that office.

Rugby **R** 348b–50
  See also Football
Rugs and carpets **R** 350–54
  Chinese carpet; picture **D** 66
  Islamic art **I** 422
  Kashmir, picture **K** 199
  Persian rugs of Iran, picture **I** 373
  Samarkand, picture **U** 36
  What is the difference between a rug and a carpet? **R** 352
Ruhr district, of West Germany **G** 155, 156, 157
Ruidoso, New Mexico
  Sierra Blanca ski area, picture **N** 191
Ruins *see* Archeology

Ruisdael (ROIS-dol) (or Ruysdael), **Jacob van** (1628?–82), Dutch landscape painter and etcher, b. Haarlem. After moving to Amsterdam (1657), he traveled through Holland and Germany. He is best known for his landscapes, especially forest and mountain scenes.
  Dutch landscape painting **D** 357

Ruiz, José Martínez *see* Martínez Ruiz, José
Ruiz (ru-EETH), **Juan,** Spanish poet **S** 367
Ruiz (RU-ees) **Cortines, Adolfo,** Mexican president **M** 251

Rukavishnikov, Nikolai N., Soviet cosmonaut
S 345
Rule, Britannia, patriotic song, words by James
Thomson **E** 258; **N** 27
Rule of Saint Benedict **C** 283, 284
Rulers, measuring tools **T** 215–16
geometry, use in **G** 130
woodworking tools for measuring **W** 230
Rules Committee, United States Congress
U 141–42
Rules of order *see* Parliamentary procedure
Rules of the road
boats and boating **B** 261–62
sailing **S** 13–14
Rum, a distilled beverage **W** 159
Rum, Romanism and Rebellion, election campaign
catch-words **C** 341
Rumania **R** 355–60
Balkan wars **B** 19
flag **F** 238
national anthem **N** 22
World War I **W** 275
Rumanian Orthodox Church **R** 355
Rumba, dance **D** 27–28
Rumen, first chamber of the stomach of a ruminant
H 209
Rumford, Count *see* Thompson, Benjamin
Ruminants (RU-min-ants), order of cud-chewing
mammals **H** 209, 217, 221
cattle and other livestock **C** 147
Rummy, card game **C** 112–13
canasta **C** 113–14
gin rummy **C** 115
Rumpelstiltskin, folk tale in *Grimm's Fairy Tales*
Rackham illustration **I** 93
Rump Parliament, England **E** 223
Runabouts, small powerboats **B** 260
Runaway, The, poem by Robert Frost **P** 355

Runes, characters of the alphabet used in ancient Scan-
dinavian and Teutonic cultures probably after about A.D.
200. The oldest alphabet comprised 24 signs, whose
simple lines were suited for carving or etching on wood,
bone, metal, or stone.

Runge, Philipp Otto, German artist **G** 171
Running
animals: locomotion **A** 292–94
mammals, speed of **M** 63
Running, sport **T** 237–39
Bannister, Roger, mile-run champion **B** 51
jogging and running **J** 120b–121
world records **T** 238
Running and chasing games **G** 20–22
Running stitches, in sewing **S** 128b
Runnymede, meadow near London
Magna Carta, signing at **M** 22
Runs batted in (RBI), in baseball **B** 75
Runways, of an airport **A** 563–64; picture **A** 565

Runyon, Damon (Alfred Damon Runyon) (1880–1946),
American journalist and writer, b. Manhattan, Kans. A
Hearst war correspondent in Mexico (1912, 1916) and in
Europe (1917, 1918), he was a columnist from 1918 for
King Features and International News Service. In his
short stories about New York underworld, as *Guys and
Dolls,* he made use of current slang. **A** 208; **K** 190

Rupert's Land, Canada **M** 82
fur trade in Canada **C** 72

Rupp, Adolph F. (1901–77), American basketball coach,
b. Halstead, Kans. As coach at the University of Kentucky from 1930 to 1972, Rupp won 879 games, more
than any other coach in college basketball history. His
teams won four national championships (1948, 1949,
1951, 1958), and he was co-coach of the U.S. Olympic
basketball team that won the gold medal in 1948. Rupp,
who was nicknamed the Baron, coached numerous All-
Americans, and many of his players became professional
stars. He was elected to the Basketball Hall of Fame in
1968.

Rural Free Delivery (RFD), of mail **P** 409
Rural life *see* Farm life
Rural poverty **P** 424–424b
Rurik, Russian ruler **M** 466

Rush, Benjamin (1745–1813), American physician and
politician, b. Byberry, Pa. Active in state and federal government, he became a member of the Continental Congress (1776) and was a signer of the Declaration of Independence. He was a physician at Pennsylvania
Hospital (1783–1813) and treasurer of U.S. Mint
(1797–1813). He wrote on medicine and on social reform.

Rush-Bagot Agreement, 1817 **C** 81
Rushes, of motion picture scenes **M** 482
Rushlights **L** 279–80; picture **L** 282
lights before candles **C** 96

Rusk, Dean (1909–   ), American statesman, b. Cherokee County, Ga. He worked for the State Department
(1946–52) in various capacities, particularly in the field
of foreign relations. From 1952 to 1960 he was president
of the Rockefeller Foundation. He served as U.S. secretary of state (1961–69), receiving the Medal of Freedom
in 1969. In 1970, he became a professor of international
law at the University of Georgia.

Ruskin, John, English critic and author **E** 262
criticism of Whistler's painting **W** 160
Russell, Bertrand, English philosopher and writer
R 360

Russell, Bill (William Felton Russell) (1934–   ), American basketball player, b. Monroe, La. Russell played on
the victorious U.S. Olympic basketball team in 1956. He
joined the Boston Celtics of the National Basketball Association (NBA) in 1956, leading them to a record number of championships. Russell was known especially for
his defensive play and his rebounding. He won the
NBA's Most Valuable Player award 5 times (1958,
1961–63, and 1965). Russell, 208 cm (6 ft 10 in) tall,
was appointed the Celtics' coach in 1966, the first black
to direct a major professional sports team. He resigned
in 1969 to become a television sportscaster but later returned to coach professionally. In 1975 he was elected to
the Basketball Hall of Fame.

Russell, Charles Marion, American artist **M** 441
C. M. Russell Gallery, Great Falls, Montana **M** 437
Russell, George William (pseudonym: AE), Irish poet
E 266
Russell, Henry N., American astronomer **A** 476

Russell, Lillian (Helen Louise Leonard) (1861–1922),
American comic-opera singer, b. Clinton, Iowa. Im-
mensely popular and renowned for her great beauty, she
had leads in such Broadway successes as *The Great Mo-*

gul, Patience, and *The Sorcerer.* In 1899 she became part of the Weber and Fields company.

Russell Cave National Monument, Alabama **A** 121
Russia, now Union of Soviet Socialist Republics
    ballet **B** 26–28
    costumes, traditional, pictures **C** 349; **D** 264
    fairs and expositions **F** 11
    flag (until 1917) **F** 227
    history to 1917 **U** 47–50
    Napoleon's invasion **N** 11–12
    origin of name "Russia" **F** 134; **S** 486
    Peter the Great **P** 168
    Vikings **V** 339
    World War I **W** 271–72, 279
    See also Union of Soviet Socialist Republics
Russian America, early name for Alaska **A** 143
Russian architecture U 52–54
Russian art U 52, 54–58
    Hermitage Museum **H** 119–20
Russian baths B 91
Russian Blue cats C 142; picture **C** 143
Russian language U 27, 28, 58
Russian literature U 58–62
    contributions to art of the novel **N** 347–48
    fairy tales **F** 22
    realistic drama **D** 298
    See also names of Russian authors
Russian music B 22; **U** 63–64
    opera **O** 136
    See also names of Russian composers
Russian Orthodox Church in America O 230
Russian Revolution and **Civil War,** 1917–1921 **U** 50
    Communism **C** 443
    Lenin made Moscow the capital again **M** 467
    underground movements **U** 10
    World War I **W** 279
Russian Soviet Federal Socialist Republic U 43
    languages **U** 27
    Siberia **S** 173
    western half in Soviet Europe **E** 307
Russian thistle, weed, picture **W** 105
Russo-Finnish War, 1939 **W** 288
Russo-German Pact, 1939 **W** 287

Russo-Japanese War (1904–05), conflict between Russia and Japan arising from Russian possession of Port Arthur (1898), expansion into Manchuria, and subsequent threat to Japanese dominance in Korea. Japanese forces captured Port Arthur and Mukden and totally defeated the Russian Baltic Fleet in Tsushima Strait (1905). The treaty, concluded at Portsmouth, N.H., acknowledged Japanese supremacy in Korea and provided for simultaneous withdrawal of Russian and Japanese troops from Manchuria. Among the agreements were Japanese acquisition of the following: leased territory in Manchuria; railway between Chanchun and Port Arthur; mines along the railway; southern half of Sakhalin Island; fishery rights along Maritime Province of Siberia. The war established Japan as a major power and contributed to Russian internal disorder (1905).

Russo-Turkish War, 1877–78
    Bulgaria **B** 444

Russwurm, John Brown (1799–1851), journalist and educator, b. Port Antonio, Jamaica, B.W.I. He was co-founder of an early black newspaper in the United States (1827). Seeking freedom for slaves, he moved to Liberia (1829) where he was active in education, newspaper publishing, and government.
    black educators **N** 93, 94

Rust
    phlogiston, theory of **C** 210
    rusting, slow combustion **F** 137
    slow oxidation **O** 270
    See also Corrosion

Rustin, Bayard (BY-urd) (1910–), American civil rights leader and lecturer, b. West Chester, Pa. One of the chief strategists in the black civil rights movement, he helped to form the Congress of Racial Equality (CORE) in the 1940's and the Southern Christian Leadership Conference (SCLC) in the 1950's. In 1947 Rustin participated in the first freedom ride into the South to test antidiscrimination rulings. A noted advocate of nonviolent protest , he was one of the chief organizers of the civil rights march on Washington, D.C. in 1963. Since 1964 he has headed the A. Philip Randolph Institute in New York City. He is the author of *Down the Line.*

Rusts, fungi **F** 498
    diseases of oats **O** 4
Rutgers—the State University, New Brunswick, New Jersey **N** 172–73
Ruth, Babe (George Herman Ruth), American baseball player **R** 361
    home run king of baseball **B** 78, 80; picture **B** 81
    signature reproduced **A** 527
    with Harding, picture **H** 40
Ruth, book of Bible, Old Testament **B** 156
Ruth, Old Testament heroine **J** 106
Ruthenium, element **E** 155, 164
Rutherford, Daniel, Scottish chemist **C** 210
Rutherford, Ernest, 1st Baron Rutherford of Nelson, New Zealand-born British physicist **R** 361; picture **C** 215
    modern physicists **P** 237; picture **P** 232
    nuclear energy **N** 353
    radio, early history of **R** 52
    science, history of **S** 76
    work on atomic structure **C** 216
Rutherfordium, radioactive element **E** 155, 164; **R** 68
Rutilated quartz Q 7
Rutland, Vermont **V** 318

Rutledge, Ann (1816–1835), daughter of an innkeeper in New Salem, Ill. Abraham Lincoln lived in her father's inn before going to Springfield and was said to have been engaged to her. She died of malarial fever. Many poems and stories have been written about her and her possible connection with Lincoln.
    Lincoln's early life in Illinois **I** 81; **L** 293

Rutledge, Edward, American official **S** 308
Rutledge, John, American jurist **S** 308
Ruwenzori (ru-wen-ZO-ri) **Mountains,** central Africa **U** 5; **Z** 366b
    plantain farm near the mountains, picture **U** 7
Ruysch (ROIS), **Johannes,** Dutch mapmaker **M** 93
Ruysdael, Jacob van *see* Ruisdael, Jacob van
Rwanda R 362–63
    flag **F** 236
    independence from Belgium **B** 131
    See also Burundi
Ryder, Albert Pinkham, American painter **U** 121
    Toilers of the Sea, painting **U** 119

Rye **R** 364
    cereal grasses **G** 318
    grain and grain products **G** 282, 285
    seeds and ear, pictures **G** 283
    Triticale, species hybrid of wheat and rye **G** 287
Rye-an' injun, colonial American bread **C** 390
Ryerson, Adolphus Egerton, Canadian educator **O** 127
Rymer, Thomas, English critic and writer
    O 236d–236e
Rymill, John, English explorer **P** 368

Ryoanji Temple, Kyoto, Japan **K** 311
Ryukyu Islands, Pacific Ocean **P** 8
    Okinawa, in World War II **W** 305, 308
Ryumin, Valery, Soviet cosmonaut **S** 345

Ryun, Jim (James Ronald Ryun) (1947–), American track athlete, b. Wichita, Kan. The first high school athlete to run a mile in less than 4 minutes (1964), he competed at the 1968 and 1972 Olympics. He turned professional in 1973 and retired from track in 1976.

PHOTO CREDITS

The following list credits, by page, the sources of photos used in THE NEW BOOK OF KNOWL-EDGE. Credits are listed photo by photo—left to right, top to bottom. Wherever appropriate, the name of the photographer has been listed with the source, the two being separated by a dash. When two or more photos by different photographers appear on one page, their credits are separated by semicolons.

Q-R